PENGUIN BOOKS

THE SECRET STATE

'A detailed and disturbing account of how our masters proposed
to protect us from the dangers of communism and nuclear war'
BBC History Magazine

'This book would have been inconceivable even twenty years ago.
Its theme is such that historians would have had to wait a hundred
years before any kind of documentary access was possible . . . no
one had pursued the study of the nature of British institutions and
how they actually worked with such persistence as Peter Hennessy
. . . with the intensity and insight, and above all the ability to
engage the confidence of the retired permanent under-secretaries
and their equivalents in politics, which he commanded. This book
is filled with the joy of the hunt'
Donald Cameron Watt, *Political Quarterly*

'A mind-boggling tale' *Glasgow Herald*

'One of the many qualities of Professor Hennessy's fascinating new
history of Whitehall and the Cold War is that it never underestimates
the depth of fear that existed among those in the know . . . charts that
neatly tot up the likely number of British deaths in an atomic war still
retain the capacity to shock' Craig Brown, *Mail on Sunday*

'Fascinating . . . There is no guide to the oddities and quirks of
Whitehall more sure-footed than Professor Hennessy'
Anthony Howard, *New Statesman*

'Hennessy shows that those responsible were not in the grip of the
paranoid fantasies often assumed to be the hallmark of the cold
warrior . . . few can match him when it comes to recreating the cast
of mind and the thought patterns of the old establishment'
Lawrence Freedman, *Evening Standard*

'A valuable guide to our knowledge of Cold-War intelligence'
John Crossland, *Sunday Times*

BY THE SAME AUTHOR

States of Emergency
(with Keith Jeffery)

Sources Close to the Prime Minister
(with Michael Cockerell and David Walker)

What the Papers Never Said

Cabinet

Ruling Performance (edited with Anthony Seldon)

Whitehall

Never Again: Britain 1945–1951

The Hidden Wiring: Unearthing the British Constitution

*Muddling Through: Power, Politics and the
Quality of Government in Postwar Britain*

The Prime Minister: The Office and Its Holders Since 1945

The Secret State: Whitehall and the Cold War

Having It So Good: Britain in the Fifties

*The New Protective State: Government,
Intelligence and Terrorism* (editor)

Cabinets and the Bomb

PETER HENNESSY

The Secret State

PREPARING FOR THE WORST
1945–2010

Second edition

PENGUIN BOOKS

PENGUIN BOOKS

Published by the Penguin Group
Penguin Books Ltd, 80 Strand, London WC2R ORL, England
Penguin Group (USA), Inc., 375 Hudson Street, New York, New York 10014, USA
Penguin Group (Canada), 90 Eglinton Avenue East, Suite 700, Toronto, Ontario, Canada M4P 2Y3
(a division of Pearson Penguin Canada Inc.)
Penguin Ireland, 25 St Stephen's Green, Dublin 2, Ireland (a division of Penguin Books Ltd)
Penguin Group (Australia), 250 Camberwell Road, Camberwell, Victoria 3124, Australia
(a division of Pearson Australia Group Pty Ltd)
Penguin Books India Pvt Ltd, 11 Community Centre, Panchsheel Park, New Delhi – 110 017, India
Penguin Group (NZ), 67 Apollo Drive, Rosedale, North Shore 0632, New Zealand
(a division of Pearson New Zealand Ltd)
Penguin Books (South Africa) (Pty) Ltd, 24 Sturdee Avenue, Rosebank,
Johannesburg 2196, South Africa

Penguin Books Ltd, Registered Offices: 80 Strand, London WC2R ORL, England

www.penguin.com

First published by Allen Lane 2002
Revised and updated edition published in Penguin Books 2003
Published with further updates and revisions 2010

1

Copyright © Peter Hennessy, 2002, 2003, 2010

The moral right of the author has been asserted

Set Sabon Lt Std 9.25/12.5 pt
Typeset by Palimpsest Book Production Limited, Falkirk, Stirlingshire

Printed in Great Britain by Clays Ltd, St Ives plc

A CIP catalogue record for this book is available from the British Library

978-0-141-04469-9

www.greenpenguin.co.uk

IN MEMORY OF SIR MICHAEL QUINLAN
1930–2009

'BIG Q'

FRIEND, MENTOR AND DEFENCE
INTELLECTUAL PAR EXCELLENCE

We need to remember that security provision is in the insurance business – it has to be, in a sense, pessimistic, calibrated to what we fear might happen, not to what we would like to happen or even what we think most likely to happen.

Sir Michael Quinlan, former Permanent Secretary to the Ministry of Defence, speaking at, 'The Global Non-Proliferation Context of the UK's Trident Renewal Debate', United Nations Association/David Davies Institute, Cathays Park, Cardiff, 2 December 2006

Contents

List of Illustrations   xi

Prologue to the New Edition:
  The Cold Rules for National Safety   xiii
Introduction: From Total War to Absolute War?   xxvii
Prelude: 'The Queen Must Be Told'   xxxiii

1   'Secrets and Mysteries': The Intelligence Picture   1
2   The Importance of Being Nuclear:
    The Bomb and the Fear of Escalation   46
3   Defending the Realm: Vetting, Filing and Smashing   81
4   'Beyond the Imagination':
    The Spectre of Ever-Greater Annihilation   153
5   'Breakdown': Preparing for the Worst   179
6   Endgames: The Transition to World War III   217
7   'London Might Be Silenced': The Last Redoubt   258
8   The Human Button: Deciders and Deliverers   310
9   The Safety of the Realm since 2001   360
10   Towards a National Security Strategy   390
    Epilogue: Living on the Dark Side   403

Notes   416
Index   467

List of Illustrations

Every effort has been made to contact all copyright holders. The publishers will be glad to make good in future editions any errors or omissions brought to their attention. Photographic acknowledgements are given in parentheses.

1. Sir John Winnifrith (Topham Picturepoint)
2. Ministry of Information poster (Public Record Office Image Library [Ref. INF 13/203])
3. Sir William Strath (Camera Press)
4. Civil Defence poster (The National Archives Image Library [Ref. INF 13/281])
5. Air Chief Marshal Sir Kenneth Cross (Topham Picturepoint)
6. Air Vice-Marshal Bobby Robson (Courtesy Air Vice-Marshal R. Robson)
7. Vulcan crews scramble (Popperfoto)
8. Sir Michael Cary (Topham Picturepoint)
9. The Cary memorandum (The National Archives Image Library [Ref. CAB 21/4840])
10. Gervase Cowell (Topham Picturepoint)
11. First draft of the 1965 drill for the transition to war (The National Archives Image Library [Ref. CAB 21/5655])
12. TURNSTILE: telephone exchange (Cecily Crombie)
13. TURNSTILE: The World War III War Cabinet bunker entrance (Cecily Crombie)
14. Peter Hudson, the author and David Young in the Prime Minister's Map Room in TURNSTILE (Cecily Crombie)

15. The author in the Prime Minister's Room in TURNSTILE (Cecily Crombie)
16. TURNSTILE teacups (Cecily Crombie)
17. TURNSTILE canteen (Cecily Crombie)
18. Alert board for World War III (Jason Orton)
19. 'ATOM' sign (Jason Orton)
20. The last flying Vulcan (Courtesy of Ian Finch)
21. Sir Michael Quinlan in Hungary, 1992 (courtesy of Lady Quinlan)
22. Sir Frank Cooper (Topham/Press Association)
23. The Northwood Bunker: Task Force 345 (Richard Knight)
24. Lieutenant-Commander Peter Noblett and Lieutenant-Commander Mitch Puxley (Richard Knight)
25. Commander Richard Lindsey and fellow officers decode the firing instruction aboard HMS Vanguard (Richard Knight)
26. HMS *Victorious* about to dive (Professor Paul Cornish)
27. HMS *Victorious* fires its Trident missile (Royal Navy)

Prologue to the New Edition:
The Cold Rules for National Safety

It was not the pomps or profits of governing Africa which moved the ruling élite, but the cold rules for national safety handed on from Pitt, Palmerston and Disraeli.
> Ronald Robinson and John Gallagher, *Africa and the Victorians: The Official Mind of Imperialism*, 1961[1]

Intelligence is the last assurance of our national sovereignty.
> Sir Richard Dearlove, former chief of the Secret Intelligence Service, MI6, 2009[2]

We don't do own-side intelligence. A JIC paper on derivatives would not have been a winner.
> Sir Richard Mottram, former chairman of the Joint Intelligence Committee, 2009[3]

During the Cold War, because the opposition was so rooted in a secret state, we needed a bit of a secret state ourselves . . . We were there to do things nobody else was allowed to do – receive stolen goods; arrange defections; envelopes full of money. The Sovbloc may have been a historical wrong-turning, but it jolly well mattered at the time.
> Former senior Secret Intelligence Service officer, 2009[4]

The state, General de Gaulle liked to remark, is the 'coldest of cold monsters.'[5] And in open societies, like Britain's, its intelligence and security capabilities especially comprise its chilliest parts, however much the 'cold rules for national safety' are redefined generation-upon-generation.

Since British intelligence and security came of age in the Second World War and remained a sustained and substantial national instrument during the four decades of Cold War that followed there have developed three unspoken deals between the UK secret state in its various configurations and the politicians and public it serves.

Firstly, that the covert capabilities of the state should be confined to penetrating those elements of external and domestic threats which are beyond the reach unaided of the usual institutions for national protection such as the police, the armed forces or Revenue and Customs. Secondly, that those threats should be as effectively countered as possible either through counter-espionage, civil defence and what is called today resilience planning and investment. Thirdly, that encroachments upon the liberties of the Queen's subjects in pursuit of deals one and two should be as limited as possible in both extent and duration.

The danger of 'mission creep' is powerfully undermining of the three deals because it risks a loss of confidence in the overall secret apparatus of the state. The triple deal, which itself represents one of the 'cold rules for national safety', is tacit rather than explicit in the UK and has been under considerable strain since 11 September 2001, given the extension of the state's legal and technical reach as part of its counter-terrorism strategies. Such tensions were present, too, during the country's responses to the Cold War throughout the various phases of the long East–West confrontation when, until its very last days, much of the secret state operated without the benefit of statute, external regulation or oversight.

This book is about the activities, the geography and the anthropology of the UK secret state during the forty-plus years of East–West confrontation during the Cold War and the early years of what may prove to be at least a forty-year struggle against jihadi-related terrorism. The two parts of the UK response are clearly linked, as the book will show. The senior generation in Whitehall who constructed a new protective state at considerable speed in the UK after 11 September 2001 came to their formation in the Cold War years. Several of them had been involved, too, in what was a forty-year struggle against Northern Ireland-generated terrorism, principally, but not solely, stemming from the activities of the Provisional IRA. Their early twenty-first-century remaking of the 'cold rules for national safety' was conditioned, in part, by these shared experiences – though all involved recognized the limits the singular ingredients of post 9/11 threats placed on parallels and lessons. Nevertheless, the question of where the lines are, or should be, drawn around the secret state, applies today as it did during the Cold War.

The chief architect of the early twenty-first-century riposte to the post 9/11 threat, now known as CONTEST 1 (CONTEST standing for Counter Terrorism Strategy), was Sir David Omand during his spell as Security and Intelligence Coordinator in the Cabinet Office, 2002–5. He had accumulated a long experience of Cold War policy and operations first at GCHQ and then the Ministry of Defence from the early 1970s, becoming director of the Government Communications Headquarters (the signals and electronic intelligence agency based in Cheltenham) 1996–7 before serving as Permanent Secretary at the Home Office 1998–2001.

He illuminates the 'change of paradigm with the end of the Cold War' by drawing a contrast between the Whitehall he joined in 1970 and the Whitehall from which he retired in 2005:

'THE SECRET STATE' OF THE COLD WAR

- Thinking the unthinkable with nuclear deterrence.
- Civil defence, but with plans kept secret from the public.
- The secret, unavowed status of intelligence agencies.
- International mistrust and intelligence competition (except for US, UK, Australia, Canada and New Zealand).

'THE PROTECTING STATE' OF MODERN COUNTER-TERRORISM

- The public sees what is being done in their name.
- Intelligence agencies are avowed and regulated.
- Widespread international co-operation in policing and intelligence.
- Community engagement in emergency planning.[6]

The most obvious continuity between the two states is a high and understandable level of operational secrecy about human and technical means of gathering intelligence, of surveillance and of blunting attacks on the UK home base and its interests abroad.

There are other, less obvious ones. For example, in the days immediately following 9/11, the then Cabinet Secretary, Sir Richard Wilson, exhumed the old Cold War nuclear retaliation files from the early 1960s (of which more later) when Harold Macmillan as Prime Minister picked two 'nuclear deputies' from amongst his Cabinet authorized to take the decision if he were out of reach or killed by a 'bolt-from-the-blue' attack. The system lapsed after the demise of the Cold War. Tony Blair reinstated it in 2001 and it was maintained by his successor. There are also three ministerial deputies (not necessarily the same ones) for taking a decision to shoot down a hijacked airliner whose hijackers intend to fly it into 9/11-type targets.[7]

Perhaps the most crucial continuity of all is what intelligence can and cannot provide. For all the developments in electronic surveillance and so-called 'data mining' since the Berlin Wall came down, there remain serious limits to what UK national intelligence capabilities can produce for their customers in Whitehall, the armed forces and the police. Such limitations are not readily appreciated in the aftermath of an attack when the label 'intelligence failure' is usually instantly draped across the newspaper headlines. Such accusations can be justified as with President Obama's strictures about the failure of US intelligence to prevent the 'Christmas Day Bomber' from boarding the North-West Airlines flight bound for Detroit in December 2009. But, I suspect, this instinctive reaction is also partly due to the erroneous impression in what were then Fleet Street newsrooms from the emergence in the mid-1970s of the formidable World War II code-breaking triumphs of Bletchley Park (the 'Ultra' secret, in the shorthand) that British boffinry had the Axis tyrants wired-up-for-sound twenty-four hours a day. Of course, they did not. Codes changed and the capacity to break was lost again. Some were never broken – and the listening stations could only pick up messages sent by wireless, not those transmitted across the land-lines of 'Fortress Europe'.

Combating jihadi-inspired international and domestic terrorism adds its own sheaf of difficulties. When the Soviet Union and its satellites were the chief target of the UK's intelligence attack and counter-intelligence effort, Whitehall had states – and highly bureaucratic and hierarchical ones at that – as the object for penetration and surveillance. Similarly, the Provisional IRA, though not a state (even within a state), had a hierarchy of command against which to operate. Al-Qaeda has none of these. It is a state-of-mind rather than a state, presenting a shifting, fluid yet tough target.[8]

Both the purposes and limitations of intelligence and counter-intelligence were captured to considerable effect in the first years of the new century by a pair of insiders. One was a former customer for intelligence, Sir Michael Quinlan; the second an anonymous provider, Peter Freeman, a long-standing GCHQ analyst. In 1993, having retired from the Ministry of Defence in 1992, Quinlan was asked by the then Prime Minister, John Major, to review the need for secret intelligence in the post-Cold War world and to examine the systems for tasking and financing it. He reported in the spring of 1994. In 2004, the *Review of Intelligence on Weapons of Mass Destruction*, the report prepared by the former Cabinet Secretary, Lord Butler, and a team of privy counsellors, contained a chapter on 'The Nature and Use of Intelligence' drafted by Peter Freeman, which Eliza Manningham-Buller, former Director-General of the Security Service, MI5, described as 'one of the best descriptions of intelligence I know.'[9]

Only a part of the Quinlan Report has been declassified under freedom-of-information provisions.[10] But Sir Michael delivered a summary of its thrust and philosophy in September 1999 during a conference at St Antony's College, Oxford, whose papers were published the following year.[11] Quinlan was writing in what now appears to be that strange limbo world between the collapse of the Soviet Union and the attacks on the Twin Towers – that heady decade of 1991–2001. His inquiry, too, was conducted against the backdrop of a Treasury drive to find a substantial intelligence 'peace dividend', which included an absurd idea pushed by the Treasury that intelligence operations should be undertaken only if a Whitehall customer asked for them and was prepared to pay for them.[12] (It was absurd because it wholly failed to appreciate the serendipitous character of much intelligence gathering, the indispensability of a long-term accrual of assets both human and technical and the degree to which an attack on an intelligence target cannot be sliced up into mini-operations to meet an immediate but possibly transient need.)

Quinlan advanced three reasons for the sustenance of the country's covert intelligence capabilities in the early post-Cold War world:

1: . . . the countries in relation to which the West . . . is most likely to have to contemplate difficult external-policy decisions against the wishes of others will more often than not be precisely those whose character makes sure and timely information hardest to come by openly, especially in time of crisis.

2: . . . the West increasingly recognises a need to deal with formidable non-state actors, often operating globally or at least across some borders, in fields – notably terrorism, narcotics, illegal armaments trade and financial wrong-doing – where the attempted concealment of information is at the centre of the business.

3: . . . secret intelligence may have special value in support of international treaties and other agreements, as in arms control, trade bargains or sanctions regimes.[13]

The Major government accepted the Quinlan justifications and to this day Sir Michael is credited by the Whitehall intelligence community with having saved them from even deeper cuts in the late 1990s.[14]

In two respects his mid-nineties thinking anticipated some of the factors shaping Peter Freeman's analysis in 2004. Firstly, given the controversies on which the Butler Report concentrated about the publication of Iraq-related intelligence dossiers and Tony Blair's use of the intelligence product on the road to war in the Gulf, one Quinlan sentence, as spoken at St Antony's, stands out:

However splendid the covert intelligence we collect, it has in practice to operate through various gears or filters, which, if they are not up to the job, may gravely dilute or even destroy eventual value.[15]

His other naturally unanticipated link with Butler's later concerns has to do with the classic distinction made in the intelligence world between secrets which can be covertly acquired (order of battle of a potential enemy's forces; the capabilities of his weapons) and mysteries (whether or not he intends to use them; against whom; and when). Or as Quinlan himself put it, 'even the most successful covert intelligence capability cannot find out what is not available to be known'.

The distinction between secrets and mysteries is, I think, well established in intelligence discourse; but I am not sure that publics and Parliaments always grasp the difference between finding out existing but concealed facts and divining the likely course of future events amid the caprices and uncertainties of world affairs. It is foolish to expect, or to claim, too much in the latter respect.[16]

The classic late-twentieth-century example of this is Western intelligence on Mikhail Gorbachev's Soviet Union in the late 1980s. Even if the UK's Secret Intelligence Service had been running a top flight 'mole' at the highest level inside the Kremlin in regular receipt of Mr Gorbachev's confidences, MI6 could not have had early warning of the demise of the Soviet Union, because the Soviet leader himself (a) had no inkling of this eventuality; and (b) certainly did not intend it to be the outcome.

Even when hard intelligence is acquired which stands up to all the scepticism and the testing of the old (and now, post-Iraq, restored) Requirements Section of SIS (MI6's in-house 'oh, come off it' capability), it is dangerous to confer too much predictive power upon it. As the social anthropologist of institutional life Professor Mary Douglas put it: 'Certainty is only possible because doubt is blocked institutionally. Most individual decisions about risk are taken under pressure from institutions . . . We know that certainty cannot be squeezed out of facts.'[17] This is especially so in the intelligence world. The crucial and continuous test of intelligence is the question 'What load will it bear?'

Peter Freeman probed uncertainty, too, as part of his 'Nature and Use of Intelligence' chapter in the Butler Report, claiming 'Intelligence merely provides techniques for improving the basis of knowledge. As with other techniques, it can be a dangerous tool if its limitations are not recognised by those who seek to use it' in the preamble to his section on 'The Limitations of Intelligence', which is now regarded in Whitehall as a primer for new customers for the intelligence product, including ministers.[18]

Freeman began by describing the gold standard for the triple, linked processes of 'validation, analysis, assessment' which

are designed to transform the raw material of intelligence so that it can be assimilated in the same way as other information provided to decision-makers at all levels of government. Validation should remove information which is unreliable (including reporting which has been deliberately inserted to mislead). Analysis should assemble fragmentary intelligence into coherent meaningful accounts. Assessment should put intelligence into a sensible real-world context and identify how it can affect policy-making.

Then came the caveats: 'But there are limitations, some inherent and some practical on the scope of intelligence, which have to be recognised by its ultimate recipients if it is to be used wisely.'[19] He singled out 'incompleteness' as the 'most important limitation on intelligence':

Much ingenuity and effort is spent on making secret information difficult to acquire and hard to analyse. Although the intelligence process may overcome such barriers, intelligence seldom acquires the full story. In fact, it is often, when first acquired, sporadic and patchy, and even after analysis may still be at best inferential.

And here, without quite saying so, Freeman swung into the central critique of the Blair government's use of intelligence in the run-up to the Iraq War of 2003:

The very way that intelligence is presented can contribute to this misconception. The necessary protective security procedures with which intelligence is handled can reinforce a mystique of omniscience. Intelligence is not only – like many sources, incomplete, it can be incomplete in undetectable ways. There is always pressure, at the assessment stage, if not before, to create an internally consistent and intellectually satisfying picture. When intelligence becomes the dominant, or even the only, source of government information, it can become very difficult for the assessment process to establish a context and to recognise that there may be gaps in that picture.[20]

Which brought Freeman to his version of the secrets and mysteries conundrum:

A hidden limitation of intelligence is its inability to transform a mystery into a secret . . . mysteries are essentially unknowable: What a leader *truly* believes, or what his reaction would be in certain circumstances, cannot be known, but can only be judged. JIC [Joint Intelligence Committee] judgements have to cover both secrets and mysteries. Judgement must still be informed by the best available information, which often means a contribution from intelligence. But it cannot import certainty.[21]

This takes us back to Mary Douglas – the institutional pressure for certainty. Freeman concluded by stressing the indispensability of

ensuring that the ultimate users of intelligence, the decision-makers at all levels, properly understand its strengths and limitations and have the opportunity to acquire experience in handling it. It is not easy to do this while preserving the security of sensitive sources and methods. But unless intelligence is properly handled at this final stage, all preceding effort and expenditure is wasted.[22]

I would add another permanent and binding criterion to the Quinlan/Freeman requirements. It was one frequently stressed in conversation by Professor Sir Harry Hinsley, Bletchley hand, official historian of British intelligence during the Second World War and my mentor at St John's College, Cambridge in the late 1960s. For Harry the prime virtue of British intelligence tradition, as refined during World War II, was that it always rigorously kept separate those who painted the intelligence picture and those who decided what or what not to do on the basis of it. The duty of the producers was to speak reality unto authority, never to varnish it to suit the existing views of the customers, ministers in particular. This secret-state version of the wider crown service tradition of speaking truth unto power was, in Harry Hinsley's view, what gave British intelligence its competitive edge over rival systems. He made this point with particular force to a group of senior businessmen at Templeton College, Oxford, on the 'Stimulus 2000' course run by Sir Douglas Hague, Norman Strauss and myself in March 1991. In fact, the Hinsley precept is a fourth deal of the UK system, this one being an unwritten pact between insiders – ministers and the British intelligence community.

But how best to school new political masters into this tradition or indoctrinate them into the traditional deal between producers and customers? It is exceedingly hard – impossible, in fact – to do this for rookie prime ministers or ministers who have no prior intelligence experience from an earlier incarnation. Now that all the intelligence agencies are avowed and non-partisan creatures of statute, premiers-in-waiting can and do have private prior conversations with their chiefs or directors.[23] Yet even when, once in office, they have acquired some experience in one area of intelligence and security it does not necessarily transfer to another. For example, pre 9/11, Tony Blair and several of his colleagues were very well primed on Northern Ireland-related terrorism. There was more human and technical surveillance at work in the province than probably anywhere else in the democratic world. (Contrast that with the meagreness and unreliability of SIS's human sources in Iraq pre-invasion.)[24] But though the JIC Assessments Staff had produced six papers on Osama bin Laden pre-9/11, the primary focus of their most important ministerial readers fell upon such briefings only after the atrocity had occurred.[25] There are human and understandable reasons for this: there are limits to the width and sustainability of concentration and every hugely busy Prime Minister especially has to ration his or her attention. In the early days of his presidency, at the height of the Cold War and the rolling Berlin crisis of 1958–62, Jack Kennedy told Richard Rovere: 'The intelligence cables are all fire alarms,'[26] by which he meant genuine causes for concern not just routine drills – a judgement British heads of government would recognize. ('A warning is a different thing from it happening, isn't it?' as the former Conservative Prime Minister, Alec Home, once put it to me.[27])

At crisis moments, during the Cold War, as now, the 'fire alarm' reports surge. This was certainly true of the Security Service, MI5, after the London bombings of 7 July 2005.[28] But there has been a significant shift in the overall intelligence picture since the collapse of the Soviet Union, for in the post-9/11 world the secrets and mysteries problem has reversed. In the Cold War, certainly once the first US spy satellites were aloft after August 1960,[29] Western intelligence was generally and continuously well primed on the 'secrets' of what military kit the Soviet Union and its allies had and where.[30] The mystery remained not the *capabilities* of the Warsaw Pact countries but the *intentions* of the leadership in the Kremlin. This is why all the transition-to-war exercise scenarios *began* with a change to a bunch of real hardliners (and adventurous ones, to boot) in Moscow and *finished* with a nuclear exchange, as we shall see later.

In the early twenty-first century, there was no mystery at all about the *intentions* of Al-Qaeda, its associates and its imitators. They wished to wreak as much havoc, the more spectacular and indiscriminate the better, as they possibly could, as often as they could. The immediately compelling problem was where the terrorist was, in which back street or which hotel room and what was the nature and destructive power of his explosive device, that is, his capacity. The institutional arrangements for vigilance have changed, too. In the Cold War both sides watched each other constantly, using signals and electronic intelligence especially,[31] like a pair of hi-tech hawks. But the normal duty-officer watch system converted into a twenty-four-hour intelligence alert only on receipt of warnings and observations listed on two JIC 'Watch Lists' – the Red List, dealing with actions the Soviet bloc would take rapidly in the last days of peace if planning an attack on the West from pretty well a standing start; the Amber List, reflecting a slower and considerably more detectable build-up to war.[32] Now the Joint Terrorism Analysis Centre (JTAC) and the Intelligence Operations Centre (IOC, also known as 'Phoenix') are permanently at twenty-four-hour readiness in the Thames-side headquarters of the Security Service, bringing together not just MI5 officers but those of SIS, GCHQ, the armed forces and the police.[33] These contrasts and others – including the physical consequences and aftermaths of attacks – will be described and discussed in this expanded version of my original *The Secret State* (first published in 2002 and updated in 2003).

The core of the book remains its original Cold War sections, although refreshed in several places thanks to new documents and new studies that have appeared since 2003. I have separated out the transition-to-war exercises into a free-standing chapter 'Endgames' (Chapter 6). It also contains a new chapter on the 'Last Redoubts' of the Cold War (Chapter 7), especially the Corsham bunker intended to house the World War III War Cabinet in the 1960s, about which we know much more thanks to a spate of Cabinet Office declassifications. There is a fresh examination, too, of the human side of national nuclear capability, those men and women – Prime Ministers, alternative nuclear decision-takers, military and Civil Service advisers, the men of the RAF V-force and of the Royal Navy Polaris and Trident squadrons who have, so far, comprised 'The Human Button'. This is based on a BBC Radio 4 programme with that title, first broadcast on 2 December 2008, made by Richard Knight and myself and Chapter 8 very much reflects our combined effort. (In fact, the book concentrates a good deal on the first and last lines of UK defence – intelligence collection and analysis and, as you read this, the Trident submarine somewhere in the North Atlantic on what is known as the Royal Navy's Continuous At Sea Patrol.)

If Sir Richard Dearlove is right and British intelligence *is* 'the last assurance of our national sovereignty', perhaps, at some point, the country will have to examine it in the way it has the concept of an independent nuclear deterrent since the V-bombers gave way to Polaris submarines carrying US-made missiles topped with UK warheads. When the Joint Intelligence Committee meets on Wednesday afternoons, between 50 and 80 per cent of the product discussed stems from US sources of one kind or another, according to private estimates I have heard. Its intelligence and nuclear sharing aspects are far and away the most important elements in the US–UK 'special relationship' (the balance of intelligence trade about four to one in the UK's favour in the early twenty-first century). In the absence of sharing arrangements, Britain would no longer enjoy global intelligence reach, leaving only the US and Russia in that position. As for nuclear weapons, without Anglo-American collaboration over the past forty-plus years it would have cost the country three times as much to maintain a deterrent comparable to France's. Indeed, now, without sustained co-operation under the 1958 Mutual Defence Agreement, the UK would swiftly cease to be a nuclear-weapons power.

Chapter 9 concentrates on 'The Safety of the Realm Since 2001'. The book is rounded off by an attempt in Chapter 10 to describe a national security strategy which embraces not just the themes and anxieties caught by the old secret state and the new protective state, but those threats to the country which at the moment escape its net, such as volatile financial instruments and other aspects of 'own-side intelligence', as Richard Mottram put it, that feature neither at the Wednesday afternoon meetings of the Joint Intelligence Committee in the Cabinet Office nor at the Home Secretary's Security Meeting in the Home Office on Thursday mornings.

In preparing this expanded *Secret State* I have incurred substantial debts from academic colleagues (my current and former research students especially); the participants in *The Human Button* and my outstanding producer, Richard Knight; records staff in the Cabinet Office and at the National Archives in particular; and from friends, serving and retired, in the secret world.

The book is dedicated to a remarkable and special guardian of the nation's security, Sir Michael Quinlan. Michael was *the* Whitehall defence intellectual of the post-war years. He brought to the grimmest aspects of the state not just a formidable set of grey cells but a genuine humanity and, when possible, lightness of touch. For example, cricket somehow often seemed to insert itself into Michael's version of the defence of the realm. It was he who pointed out to me that our moment of greatest peril in the Cold War was, in a sense, not October 1962 and the Cuban missile crisis but June 1963 and the Lord's Test, England versus West Indies. The last over saw a lowering sky, a very fast Wes Hall bowling to David Allen of Gloucestershire with Kent's Colin Cowdrey, nursing a broken arm, at the other end. The result was still truly open. A West Indies win. An England win. A draw or a tie. All were possible. It took longer than four minutes to complete that over, said Michael, and all the screens of the RAF's operations room in Whitehall were switched from the Ballistic Missile Early Warning system at RAF Fylingdales on the North Yorkshire Moors to the Lord's Test. The Russians could have had us cost-free!

In his days as Permanent Secretary at the Ministry of Defence in the late 1980s and early 1990s, Michael was on the distribution list for the SIS's weekly summary of its ten most important reports. To make sure he read it, the SIS officer who drafted it, another cricket-lover, would always write a cricket question at the end. Not once did Michael Quinlan fail to answer it and get it right.[34] A great man.

Introduction:
From Total War to Absolute War?

Many of you may know the striking comment penned by
Wilkie Collins in 1870, at the time of the Franco-Prussian
war: 'I begin to believe in only one civilising influence – the
discovery one of these days of a destructive agent so terrible
that War shall mean annihilation *and men's fears will force*
them to keep the peace.' My own view is that the reality of
that in the nuclear age was deeply recognised and internalised
by ultimate political decision-takers almost throughout the
Cold War. But the logic of preventing war did nevertheless
require that terrible 'What if?' questions be truly faced . . .

Sir Michael Quinlan, former Permanent Secretary,
Ministry of Defence, 2002[1]

Neither the saint nor the revolutionary can save us; only the
synthesis of the two. Whether we are capable of achieving it
I don't know. But if the answer is in the negative, there seems
to be no reasonable hope of preventing the destruction of
European civilization, either by total war's successor Absolute
War, or by Byzantine conquest – within the next few decades.

Arthur Koestler, *The Yogi and the Commissar*,
October 1944[2]

That neither absolute war nor the equivalent of Byzantine conquest
happened – at least during the following five or more decades since he
wrote – would have struck Koestler and many of his internationally
attuned contemporaries as near miraculous. Of course, when he penned

those words the number of people in the United Kingdom who knew how far the intensely secret combined US, UK and Canadian atomic weapon programme had progressed was limited to a tiny circle around Winston Churchill[3] – though Stalin knew, thanks to the extraordinarily rich supply of human intelligence from his agents inside the Manhattan Project (the US codename for the bomb programme),[4] whose later discovery, as we shall see, did much to stimulate the construction of a vetting system that was to become an integral part of the British Cold War state.

It is simple to the point of being seriously misleading to suppose that the creation of a nuclear weapons capability on both sides of what became the Cold War divide within four years of the dropping of the atomic bombs in Hiroshima and Nagasaki in August 1945 offers an all-embracing explanation of why the nuclear taboo has not been broken since those devastating blows were visited upon Japan, powerful factor though it was, as Sir Michael Quinlan has made plain. But whatever the cause, the result has been that my own generation, born in the early post-war years, have enjoyed a kind of 'armistice with history' of the sort attributed by George Steiner to the European *bourgeoisie* roughly 'from the time of Waterloo to that of the massacres on the western front in 1915–16'.[5]

The Cold War had plenty of casualties, physical and psychological, but not only did the unimaginable body counts of Mutually Assured Destruction fail to materialize, no external enemy has launched an armed assault across Europe's boundaries (the Balkans apart) since 1945 either. Nor, since the passing of national military service in the early 1960s, has a young British male been required by being conscripted to die or risk death in the uniform of sovereign and country. The twentieth century as a whole is littered with the corpses of British dead – but not my half of it.

Because what President Kennedy later described to Harold Macmillan as 'the conventions of the international stalemate'[6] were not ruptured to the point where one or both superpowers released nuclear weapons (though Kennedy considered Nikita Khrushchev had broken the conventions by placing missiles on Cuba in 1962), the history of the Cold War can be reflected upon in the kind of tranquillity which may too easily lead to a failure to appreciate the degree of peril generated and the scale of impact involved within the state, society and economy of even a second-rank participant such as the United Kingdom. Yet in British terms what might be called the short post-war – the first twenty or so years after VJ Day – were to an extraordinary degree shaped by the failure of the main Potsdam powers (the USA, the USSR and the UK) to reach a European accommodation in 1945 amid the ruins of Hitler's push for supremacy. It is the Cold War which gives the UK of the late forties, the fifties and the sixties one of its most special flavours and distinguishes it from what came after, even though formally the Cold War had another two decades to run.

The book which needs to be written about it is huge, probably multi-volumed, and some way off. More is required by way of declassification of the official British archives before it can be fully attempted [there has been a considerable flow of declassifications since 2003, so the day of a truly substantial survey is much closer now than it was when this Introduction was written]. The process of review and release set in train by the Major government under the so-called 'Waldegrave Initiative' in 1992[7] does mean, however, that a first stab can be made at an anatomy of the Cold War state which British insiders built alongside the existing one, from roughly 1947 onwards. Describing this construction site, the impulses and thinking behind it, is the purpose of this book.

Apart from the new material (much of it of intense sensitivity when created) which has reached the National Archives/Public Record Office in successive tranches over the past fifteen years, this book has enjoyed two other stimuli. The first has been the pleasure of going through swathes of the primary material with the first and second cohorts taking my 'Secret State' undergraduate special subject at Queen Mary, University of London. Their companionship and insights combined to provide a necessary though not a sufficient condition for my writing on this subject. For it was the invitation from Penguin Books and the University of London's Institute of Historical Research to deliver the Penguin Lectures in the autumn of 2001 which caused me to pick up my pen. The theme of those four lectures is also that of this book.

It should be seen very much as work in progress – not mine alone but that of a vigorous platoon of academic colleagues from the Study Group on Intelligence, and from former insiders such as Sir Percy Cradock[8] and Sir Michael Quinlan[9] who are writing or have already written to such great effect. I have not sought either in the compass of the Penguin Lectures or within this book to replicate, for example, Professor Richard Aldrich on the US–UK intelligence relationship or active Cold War operations such as those mounted for counter-propaganda or deception purposes by the Information Research Department of the Foreign Office or the Ministry of Defence's Directorate of Forward Plans.[10] Nor have I sought to tackle the history of the Joint Intelligence Committee on the scale of Sir Percy Cradock,[11] or to wrap my mind around the theocratics of nuclear deterrence like Sir Michael Quinlan,[12] or intelligence philosophy in the manner of another former insider, the historian and philosopher of intelligence Michael Herman.[13]

I entertain the fond hope that it will be one of my students who will, in the fullness of time, direct his or her mind to the great work of synthesis on Cold War Britain. And it is with those who attended the first two runs of 'Secret State' Monday afternoon seminars in the Mile End Road that my gratitude must begin. Matthew Grant, Samina Malik, Justine Rainbow, Alban Webb, Helen Welch, Rezia Choudhury, Jo Lang, Dean Jeffreys, Daniel Sherman, Ian Trembling, Robert Walker, Robert Worthington and Joseph Wright took it as an undergraduate course. Matt Lyus, Roderick Jones and Jon Davis attended as research students. David Frank, Matthew Laban and Catherine Haddon sat in while pursuing their MA in Contemporary British History. The groups saw things in the papers that would have remained lost on me. From the first week to the end (when we relived, as it were, the actual Whitehall transition-to-war exercise of autumn 1968), the sessions were events I looked forward to, not least when former Cold War operators came to pool their insights now that a good portion of their old archives had been (legitimately) sprung. Thanks must go to Matt Lyus, without whose word-processing prodigies the Penguin Lectures and this volume would have missed their deadlines, and to my daughter Polly for unearthing some special gems at the Public Record Office.

In preparing the 2010 extended edition of *The Secret State* I have acquired still more debts. I am hugely thankful to Alan Glennie and

Nick Weekes in the Cabinet Office and David Chinn at the National Archives for helping me navigate my way through the streams of Cold War-related files declassified since 2002–3. I am enormously indebted to my friend and library builder, Joe Few, for converting my scribbles and lines into the organograms of the post-9/11 'new protective state'. Stuart Proffitt and the team at Penguin have done me proud as always and I am very grateful to my copy-editor, Trevor Horwood, for agreeing to look after me once more. My daughter, Cecily Crombie, took some marvellous new pictures of the Corsham bunker, TURNSTILE, when we visited it with Peter Hudson, David Young and Richard Knight, my BBC producer for the Radio 4 *The Human Button* documentary in 2008. Rich made all the difference to the making and shaping of that programme and was the ideal travelling companion as we struggled in and out of the last flying Vulcan bomber and clambered down the ladders of the Royal Navy's Trident submarine HMS *Vanguard*.

Finally, I should like to acknowledge the help given to me by a range of people of my generation and older during the 2002 and subsequent literary festivals at Cheltenham, Hay, Dartington and Edinburgh, who have added through their recollection of the Cold War years to both my detailed and general sense of that extraordinary epoch in our country's experience. My college room-mate Bob Salem, long resident in Brazil, was back in Britain during the spring of 2002 when the first edition of *The Secret State* was published. I told him I was surprised by both the pace and quantity of sales. Bob reckoned it might be partly because we had not cared to ponder what might await us in too much detail back in the 1950s and 1960s. 'Perhaps it's a kind a retrospective panic buying,' he said.[14] An intriguing thought.

The last word on this, to illustrate the Salem theory, should perhaps go to another friend, Giles Dolphin, who was at school with me in Stroud in mid-Gloucestershire from 1959 to 1965. Giles waited until 2002 to tell me of the nightmare he had in the autumn of 1962 just after Cuba. In his dream, Giles said, the missile crisis had continued and worsened to the point of war and beyond. We were just outside the gym at Marling School with a group of friends when suddenly, over Selsey Hill to our south, there was a huge vivid flash. I turned to Giles with the words, 'Fuck! There goes Bristol!'[15] (where my sister, Maureen, was living). The Dolphin dream adds a whole new dimension to the notion of 'Forty Years On!'

In the days spanning the fortieth anniversary of the Cuban missile crisis, I wrote the Epilogue for the first paperback edition of the book, comparing the UK's Cold War processes with the management of the protracted emergency which followed upon the events of 11 September 2001. As I finished, the Prime Minister, Tony Blair, made my point for me when he told the Lord Mayor's Banquet in the City of London on Remembrance Day, 11 November 2002, that 'extremism, personified either in terrorist groups or rogue states, is now preoccupying decision-makers in the way that the struggle between liberal democracy and communism had dominated the thinking of Western leaders during the Cold War'.[16] Four days after the Prime Minister spoke, I read a fifty-two-year-old file at the Public Record Office which powerfully underscored *his* point. In a report drawn up during the anxious early months of the Korean War in September 1950, a highly sensitive White-hall group, operating under the harmless and deliberately misleading title of the Imports Research Committee, examined the possibility of a clandestine atomic attack on the United Kingdom launched by the Soviet Union. They examined the contingency of 'the detonation of an atomic bomb in a "suicide" [civil] aircraft flying low over a key point'.[17] The IRC concluded, 'it is possible and there doesn't seem to be any answer to it. The crew of the aircraft in order to detonate the bomb at the right time would have to know what their cargo was and would therefore be a suicide squad. Short of firing on every strange civil aircraft that appears over our shores we know of no way of preventing an aircraft that sets out on such a mission from succeeding.'[18] Few files I have read in the course of preparing this book have had such a dreadful contemporary resonance.

Peter Hennessy
Walthamstow and Mile End

Prelude: 'The Queen Must Be Told'

We agreed that there is a requirement for the Queen to be
informed, wherever she may be . . . of decisions to implement
the various stages and procedures for a transition to war.
Commander J. R. Stephens to Denys Laskey,
Cabinet Office, 5 March 1965[1]

Historically speaking, scraps of paper have had something of a bad
press since Neville Chamberlain landed at Heston Aerodrome on 30
September 1938 fresh from Munich and told the waiting newsmen,
'This morning I had another talk with the German Chancellor, Herr
Hitler, and here is the paper which bears his name upon it as well as
mine . . .'[2] But for those who both devil and revel in archives, their
discovery can bring moments of pure elation and illumination. The file
coded CAB 21/5655 containing the internal exchange quoted above
between Commander Stephens, the keeper of the Government War
Book in the mid-1960s, and his boss, the head of the Cabinet Office's
Overseas, and Defence Secretariat, contained a classic of this kind when,
with one of my students, I called at the Historical and Records Section
of the Cabinet Office in Marsham Street, Westminster, one Friday afternoon in the spring of 2001 to inspect it.

I had long been keen to read the GWB, as it is known – the central
War Book which pulls together all the individual department versions
of itself and lays plans for a World War III supreme command built
around the Prime Minister and a small War Cabinet. In correspondence
with the head of the Historical and Records Section, Mrs Tessa Stirling,
I had sought access to it and its supporting documentation.

On 26 January 2001 Mrs Stirling (whose staff had worked tirelessly at re-reviewing Cold War material under the 'Waldegrave Initiative' for several years) replied in a moderately encouraging letter but warned me not to be too expectant. 'As to CAB 21/5655,' she wrote,

I have asked my Archives Section to remove the sensitive information so that it can be released in redacted form. From our discussions some while back, you will realise that the file is likely to be extensively sanitised and the result may not be of great interest. The material that is likely to be released deals mainly with matters associated with the maintenance of the Government War Book (GWB) and its circulation rather than a copy of the GWB itself. But as you pointed out to me, every little helps.

The GWB itself is in CAB 134 [the class containing Cabinet committee minutes and papers] and is presently retained under Section 3 (4) of the Public Records Act. This too is under review but I have to say that I think it is unlikely that the review will result in the release of the GWB once it has been completed.[3]

The supporting file, CAB 21/5655, in 'redacted' form as Mrs Stirling had indicated, was quickly made available. And, as my students needed it for their 'Secret State' course, we were kindly allowed to view it at the Cabinet Office before its dispatch to the Public Record Office. At first glance, it was as routine as we had expected, consisting chiefly of correspondence between the Cabinet Office's War Book-keepers – Mrs Beryl Grimble (of whom more in Chapter 6) and a succession of military officers for whom she worked – plus Mrs Grimble's correspondence on questions of updating and classification of the Government War Book (with the General Post Office, for example, about the timing of the erection of protective blocks outside telephone exchanges during a transition to war).[4]

Suddenly the file came to life, when the war planners realized the following spring that, though no fewer than ninety-six copies of the GWB were in circulation,[5] Buckingham Palace did not have one. The Queen did not fully know either the drill that, should the stage of a nuclear exchange be reached, would leave her kingdom largely a smoking and irradiated ruin or the plans for carrying on her government in its aftermath. 'It's very strange, isn't it,' Sir Derek Mitchell, the Prime Minister's

Principal Private Secretary in 1965, who was involved in putting this right, commented when I talked to him thirty-six years later about the Queen and the potential end of the world.[6] Indeed it was – nearly seventeen years after the Berlin airlift (which gave an immense stimulus to contingency planning for a third world war) and over two years after the Cuban missile crisis, the Palace was, unusually, very largely in the dark about an important area of state.

The files suggest that it was a new arrival in the top military seat of the Cabinet Office Secretariat, Commander J. R. Stephens, RN, who noticed the omission (perhaps as part of reading his way into the job). For the first trace of 'the Queen must be told' question is a minute from W. I. McIndoe, Private Secretary to the Cabinet Secretary, Sir Burke Trend, to Commander Stephens, dated 22 February 1965, recalling:

You asked me a few days ago whether I knew who was responsible for informing the Palace of decisions to implement the various stages and procedures for a transition to war.

I have spoken to Mr Mitchell who tells me that No.10 have no War Book of their own and are not aware of any obligation to inform the Palace.

You may therefore wish to consider whether our War Book ought to contain some instruction to the effect that we (or some other Department) must inform the Palace of the various steps which are to be taken.[7]

After a dash of toing and froing between Stephens and the head of the Cabinet Office's Overseas and Defence Secretariat, Denys Laskey,[8] it was agreed that the Queen should be told of the drills and that the Cabinet Office, rather than No.10, would be responsible for this.[9]

Stephens finished by reminding Laskey, 'You invited me to suggest a list of decisions which should be communicated to The Queen. I attach such a list at Annex.' The annex to this memo of 5 March 1965, however, has been retained under Section 3 (4) of the Public Records Act 1958 – plainly still deemed too sensitive for release.[10] Four days later McIndoe in Trend's office wrote to Mitchell in Harold Wilson's following up a telephone conversation 'about our discovery that there appear to be no War Book arrangements for informing the Queen, wherever she may be, of the major decisions taken during the transition to war'.[11]

McIndoe, briefed by the war planners, thought

It should not be necessary to inform Her Majesty of the mass of detailed measures, and we suggest that the decisions which ought to be communicated to Her might be those at Annex. You may wish to suggest additions or deletions. Since the meaning and scope of some of those decisions will not be known to the Queen, a brief guide would need to be provided to her Private Secretary.[12]

No sign of the annex here, either.

But there is a god of the archives and he was with us that day in the Cabinet Office reading room. For tucked away in the file and easily overlooked was a scrap of rough paper upon which Stephens had drafted in longhand the decisions to be 'communicated to the Queen'. As can be seen from the photographic section, he has written it out in three sections, in Biro with amendments in pencil. From the Ministry of Defence's 1963 War Book,[13] which was declassified in full some three months before our eyes fell upon CAB 21/5655,* it is possible to decode most of it, 'it' being a neat summary of the very Government War Book which is still too delicate for outsiders to read. As Derek Mitchell said when it was described to him (neither he nor Bill McIndoe[14] had any recollection of the episode): 'People had a great gift for summarizing.'[15]

It began with the NATO sequence:

NATO

1. Simple Alert. [The 'preparatory measures which will place assigned forces in a state of combat readiness and should bring forces earmarked for assignment to minimum attainable readiness for war'.[16]]

2. Reinforced Alert. [The 'measures necessary to place NATO forces in the best possible position to meet an attack'.[17]]

3. Military Vigilance (ORANGE). ['State Orange . . . comprises the military measures when information received indicates a possible enemy attack within one or more hours'.[18]]

4. Counter Surprise (SCARLET). ['State Scarlet . . . comprises the military

---

* The 1962 Government War Book, volumes one and two, is expected to reach the National Archives at some point during 2010 where it will be retrievable in CAB 175/13.

measures when information received indicates an enemy attack within a few minutes'.[19]]

5. Assumption of operation command by NATO Major Commanders.

USA/RUSSIA

1. Any important information concerning transition to war of these countries.

UK

1. MACMORRIS. ['. . . a warning state during which Departments are merely required to have available a responsible officer and a WTN [Whitehall Tele-printer Network] operator who can be contacted by telephone out of work hours'.[20]]

2. FLUELLIN. [This should be 'FLUELLEN, which would be instituted, for example, on the declaration of a NATO Simple Alert, when Departments are required to establish immediately and maintain on a 24-hour basis a Depart-mental Control Point'.[21]]

The creators of codewords have shown a pleasing literary touch here. For Captains Fluellen and Macmorris provide the stage Welshman and Irishman respectively in Shakespeare's *King Henry the Fifth*.[22] Along with Corporal Nym, Lieutenant Bardolph and Ancient Pistol, this pair, as Professor Sir Michael Howard has noted, constitute the first instance of professional soldiers, rather than gentlemanly knights, making their appearance in military literature.[23]

3. Mobilisation. [Cabinet decision to order a partial or general mobilisation; proclamations to be issued; Parliament to be informed, if sitting, and messages from Parliament to be conveyed to the Queen; if Parliament is not sitting, 'the Queen to make a Declaration in Council in respect of each Service to be mobilised. . .'[24]

Here, originally, Stephens had placed at 5 the 'Setting Up of Regional Govt'. In pencil, however, he has moved it down to rest with the 'Disper-sal of Central Govt' or, in his redrafted version, the 'manning of TURNSTILE', the central government bunker under the Cotswolds between Bath and Corsham.

So, his revised sequence from 'Mobilisation' onwards reads like this (the numbers are now out of kilter so I have not used them).

Assignment of forces to NATO.

Repatriation to UK of dependants overseas.

Dispersal of 'priority classes' [women, children and the elderly] of population within UK.

Originally, alongside 'Dispersal of Central Govt' Stephens had placed 'Reinforcement of BAOR [British Army of the Rhine]'. 'Manning of TURNSTILE' becomes his revised number 9. Pencilled-in as the last stage of the transition to war is number 10, 'Operation VISITATION', which looks like the early to mid-1960s codename for nuclear retaliation.[25] 'That would be a logical deduction to make,' as one old nuclear hand put it.[26] It has a truly Old Testament ring to it. So Stephens's summary of the sequence to World War III – Koestler's Absolute War – starts with Shakespeare and ends with the Bible.

My guess about Operation VISITATION turned out to be wrong when in 2007 the relevant file reached the National Archives. It was the codename for the plan to whisk the Prime Minister, the Foreign Secretary and twenty-three others in their inner group of official and military advisers, away from Whitehall to Corsham at the last minute once it was plain that their last-ditch efforts at preventive diplomacy had failed and war was imminent. VISITATION involved RAF helicopters based at Little Rissington in Gloucestershire flying to RAF Northolt in the north-west suburbs of London to refuel before carrying on to Horse Guards Parade ready for the prime ministerial party to come out of the back gate of the No. 10 garden and climb aboard.[27]

Stephens's scrap of paper is, in its way, a remarkable historical artefact. Not only does it give its reader the essence of a very substantial item of evidence he or she could not yet actually consult; (until the 1970 Government War Book was declassified in 2009 as we shall see in Chapter 6) it reflects a huge piece of government apparatus constructed piece by piece since the late 1940s, when the intelligence world, senior officials and military, and certain ministers came to appreciate the magnitude of the Soviet 'threat' – that, in Eric Hobsbawm's phrase, 'the strength of the Cold War and its justification was that the potential aggressor to American ideals and interests was a real and formidable superpower'.[28] From the earliest days of the Cold War, it was plain to British war planners that, with or without a home-grown nuclear capability, the United Kingdom, as the USA's number one ally in Europe and, from 1948, a forward base for its soon-to-be-atomic bombers, would be a prime target for Soviet bloc assault in the opening phase of a global war and that, in the meantime, the Russian intelligence service would expend every effort to penetrate the country's state, military and intelligence machinery. Stephens's draft encapsulated the interlocking measures pieced together to protect as far as was deemed feasible the Queen's (and her father's) realm from the possible attentions of Stalin and his successors. There is no evidence that Her Majesty or her Private Office, on receipt of Stephens's summary, asked for a short historical explanation of how her Cold War machine came to be as it was by the spring of 1965. But, if such a volume *had* been requested, it *might* have looked like this . . .

I

'Secrets and Mysteries': The Intelligence Picture

The long-term aim of the Russian leaders is to build up the Soviet Union into a position of strength and greatness fully commensurate with her vast size and resources. They are convinced of the greatness of Russia's future under the Soviet system. We believe it to be their firm conviction that, within the next fifty years or perhaps a hundred years (unlike Hitler they are not pressed for time), the Soviet Union will inevitably become the most powerful, the richest and the best ordered country in the world.

'Russia's Strategic Interests and Intentions', Joint Intelligence Committee report, 1 March 1946[1]

The policy of the Soviet Union can only be understood if it is realized that she is not merely, like Nazi Germany, a totalitarian dictatorship engaged in power politics, but a unique and abnormal member of international society inspired by a dynamic ideology with a strong international appeal.

'Soviet Interests, Intentions and Capabilities . . .', Joint Intelligence Committee report, 6 August 1947[2]

Neither side would allow themselves to believe the other side was as frightened as they were.

Senior British intelligence officer looking back on the Cold War, 2001[3]

As the twentieth anniversary of the fall of the Berlin Wall approached, a British intelligence veteran, who, suitably disguised, had crossed it both ways several times during his service, mused about the old days when the Queen's most secret servants were up against the KGB. This former officer was not in the habit of belittling his opponents or exaggerating their undoubted weaknesses. Quite the reverse. They gave him the most stretching time of his career. 'The dreamtime', he called it (in the way the Australian Aborigines talk of their ancestral provenance[4]).

Another officer of the same vintage reckoned that

not until late in the Cold War did we achieve consistent success against the Russians. They were always difficult to work against. The East Europeans were much easier. At the time, Penkovsky was something of a one-off. Gordievsky came later and was very important. His high point was the 1980s, by which time we were doing really well. But this was against the backdrop of Soviet decline when the West was taking a decisive strategic advantage – something we were slow to realize at the time.[5]

The former officer who recalled 'the dreamtime' had not the slightest doubt that 'we were the decent ones' any more than one of his chiefs, Sir Colin McColl, had the slightest hesitation in telling Gordon Corera, the BBC's security correspondent, that recruiting agents behind the Iron Curtain was nothing more than asking them 'to betray something that needs betraying', when he spoke on the BBC Radio 4 programme *MI6: A Century in the Shadows* in July 2009.[6]

During the forty-year Cold War, the intelligence was was the surrogate for hot war. It was unceasing at both the human and the technical level. As Gordon Barrass, who was chief of the Cabinet Office Assessments Staff with a seat on the Joint Intelligence Committee as the Cold War ended, put it: 'Historians have had difficulty assessing the contribution intelligence makes to the conduct of hot wars. In the Cold War, however, intelligence unquestionably had a powerful impact, because each side had time to check whether its judgements were well founded and to make the necessary adjustments to its policies and forces.'[7] The Cold War, in the intelligence sense, was a professionals' contest.

In general terms, too, the Cold War was a specialist's confrontation, not a people's conflict, though it aroused fear on a wide scale, not just among rival sets of war planners and decision-makers. Shortly before the Chinese entered the Korean War, for example, a Gallup poll indicated that 14 per cent of those surveyed in the UK thought 'that the fighting in Korea will lead to the Third World War' with 29 per cent returning a 'don't know'.[8] But even though 749 British troops lost their lives during that three-year conflict,[9] and the last national serviceman was not called up until 1960[10] (the final batch being released by the end of 1963[11]), it was not the widespread, shared and shaping experience of the kind encountered by previous generations of conscripts. As Denis Healey, a veteran of World War II and a considerable player in the cold one, has put it:

The last two world wars were unique in our history, not least for the cultural shock they inflicted on the whole of our society. Each of them took millions of young men and women away from their families and friends at the most sensitive stage in their lives. It put them into uniform to serve under strict discipline with total strangers in closed communities. It sent them abroad to kill other young men and women hundreds or thousands of miles away – in cities, fields, and mountains, in deserts and jungles.[12]

In one way, the Cold War reversed the process observed by Clausewitz early in the nineteenth century whereby wars ceased to be the concerns of professional armies to become conflicts of peoples. Michael Howard characterized the post-1945 world as one in which: 'war is now seen as being a matter for governments and not for peoples; an affair of mutual destruction inflicted at remote distances by technological specialists operating according to the arcane calculations of strategic analysts. Popular participation is considered neither necessary nor desirable'[13] – though, had the Cold War tipped into World War III, civilian casualties would have mounted on a scarcely imaginable scale. But for these reasons, the Cold War neither socialized large numbers of people into its disciplines, its rationales and its complexities nor did it, in modern argot, give them a sense of ownership or outcome (apart from the natural relief when, without a nuclear or a direct conventional exchange, the Berlin Wall fell in 1989 and Mikhail Gorbachev kept the Red Army in its eastern European barracks rather than turning its tanks on the rebellious citizens of its soon-to-be-separated satellites). The conduct and the management of the Cold War was largely an insiders' affair. This was especially so in its intelligence and counter-intelligence aspects. As one former British operator behind the Iron Curtain put it: 'the hot end of the Cold War was espionage'.[14] Michael Herman, himself a former secretary of Whitehall's Joint Intelligence Committee,[15] expressed the same idea forcefully in the last days of the confrontation when he said: 'The Cold War was in a special sense an intelligence conflict . . . Never before in peacetime have the relationships of competing power blocks been so influenced by intelligence assessments. Never before have the collection of intelligence and its denial to the adversary been such central features of an international rivalry.'[16]

To an extraordinary and hugely disproportionate extent, the world sees this clash of the secret worlds through supposedly British eyes – it has been claimed 'that half the world's population has seen a [James] Bond film . . .'.[17] Certainly, the Whitehall setting of the intelligence Cold War was accurately characterized by the ghastly Roddy Martindale in John le Carré's *Tinker, Tailor, Soldier, Spy* as 'Little reading rooms at the Admiralty, little committees popping up with funny names . . .'.[18] And if, like George Smiley in his hunt for 'Gerald the mole', you 'go forwards, go backwards'[19] through the now declassified files, it is possible to reconstruct most of the considerable Cold War apparatus which was pieced together in the fourteen years between the Berlin airlift[20] and the Cuban missile crisis.[21]

Not every piece of this infrastructure was part of the British intelligence community but all of it, to some degree, was suffused by the product of the agencies which carried out collection and counter-intelligence as tasked by and filtered through what one of its former chairmen has characterized as the 'high table' of British intelligence[22] – the Joint Intelligence Committee.

The JIC stood (and still stands) at the apex of the British intelligence process, bringing together and analysing intelligence material which flows to it from covert and overt sources: the human intelligence procured by the Secret Intelligence Service (MI6), the signals and electronic intelligence gathered by the Government Communications Headquarters (GCHQ), the counter-espionage intelligence obtained by the Security Service (MI5) as well as material from relatively more open sources gleaned by the armed services' intelligence branches (merged after 1964 into the Defence Intelligence Staff), the Diplomatic

Service and the defence attachés stationed within embassies. The JIC's staff undertake an all-source analysis (until 1957, the JIC was part of the Chiefs of Staff organization; since then it has been a Cabinet committee and part of the Cabinet Office). From 1951 until 2008 it produced a weekly survey of intelligence known as the Red Book from its cover (for its demise see page 381). At its table sit the heads of the secret agencies plus Whitehall representatives, and it reaches agreed views, by consensus, which are circulated to an inner group of ministers and departmental customers.[23]

As Sir Michael Palliser, a former head of the Diplomatic Service said of the post-war years: 'The Cold War is a thread that has run through verything in that period.'[24] And to a very large extent, the Whitehall tapestry of that war, from beginning to end through all its mutations, was painted and continually rewoven by the JIC. In a strange way – given that it was a war that involved neither declaration nor surrender – the JIC has been a concealed surrogate for such missing moments.

The end moment, in JIC terms at any rate, is easier to date than the start-line. It is late August 1991, and the coup against Gorbachev, led by, among others, Vladimir Khryuchkov, the head of the KGB, has just failed. One intelligence insider recalls the formidable and especially influential chairman of the JIC, Sir Percy Cradock, producing champagne for his fellow professionals and toasting the intelligence community as a whole on the ending of the Cold War with the words: 'We *didn't* have a war. We *did* win.'[25] Sir Percy himself, true to form, describes the occasion a trifle less dramatically in his book *In Pursuit of British Interests*:

The Joint Intelligence Committee is an austere body. It rarely rejoices and it lives too close to the dark side of political activity, the plots, revolutions, defections and betrayals, to find much ground for surprise, let alone celebration in the events it analyses. But the proscription of the Soviet Communist Party, which had been the prime object of its study for so many years, was memorable even against that bleak background. After our meeting of 29 August I asked the Committee to join me for a glass of champagne. We drank to the demise of the Party and added a toast to the plotters of 19 August who, in the best Marxist fashion, had given a push to history.[26]

The realization of the magnitude, peril and likely duration of the Cold War – the non-champagne moment, it might be called – is far harder to date.

Scholars such as Professor Richard Aldrich have described the debates in World War II Whitehall about the degree of threat the Soviet Union might pose in the post-war period. The Chiefs of Staff, led by Sir Alan Brooke, the Chief of the Imperial General Staff, were pessimistic compared to some in the Foreign Office, for example.[27] For instance, during the summer of 1944, in the privacy of his diary, Brooke opined that 'Germany is no longer the dominating power of Europe, Russia is. Unfortunately, Russia is not entirely European. She has, however, vast resources and cannot fail to become the main threat in fifteen years from now.'[28] By early 1946, as we have seen, the JIC's assessment of both the magnitude and the imminence of the Soviet threat made Brooke's notion that it would emerge as this by the late 1950s look positively Pollyanna-ish.

It is important to trace the mutations of the JIC's threat assessments as it was largely (but not wholly) on these that ministers, civil servants, diplomats and the military based their anxieties about what Stalin and his successors *could*, as opposed to *might*, do. Intentions, of course, remained far harder to divine than capabilities – the distinction, again, between the 'secrets' that intelligence could, with effort, skill and no little luck, hope to uncover and the 'mysteries' which, in the near continuous absence of human agents close to the epicentre of the Soviet power structure, were to remain a closed book to the UK's secret world. As Michael Herman put it when reviewing the grand sweep of Western intelligence during the Cold War: 'On a medical analogy, the West by the 1980s had become well informed about Soviet anatomy and physiology; but the windows to the antagonist's mind remained largely opaque.'[29]

But before describing the picture painted by Whitehall's all-source intelligence analysts for their customers from the monarch down (traditionally the no. 1 copy of the 'Weekly Summary of Current Intelligence' goes to Buckingham Palace[30]), it is useful to reconstruct the mixture of images which went into the making of the big picture of the possible threat from the Soviet Union and its allies.

Nearly ten years after the end of the Cold War, the Cabinet Office declassified a particularly fascinating file containing the JIC's warning indicators for 1962 – the 'Red List' ('those preparations which the Soviet Union would consider essential to make before launching a surprise attack on the West') and the 'Amber List' ('the more important of the additional preparations for war which the Soviet Union might make if achieving strategic surprise was not considered possible'),[31] together formally titled 'Indications of Sino-Soviet Bloc Preparations for Early War'. These were circulated in 1962, an especially fraught year when the Cuban missile crisis took Western intelligence unawares some seven months after the lists were distributed.[32]

The document did not deal with the 'warning which we would hope to obtain from the general political situation'.[33] Instead the JIC broke down its adversaries' possible preparations for war into three:

(a) Those indicating long-term military preparations for war.
(b) Those indicating that the whole nation is being prepared for war.
(c) Those indicating the bringing of operational units and facilities, and also civil defence, to immediate readiness for war.[34]

The JIC indicators paper concentrated on category (c), breaking it down still further into the Red and Amber lists.

A very senior intelligence figure, a veteran of the Cold War whose service included spells behind the Soviet bloc lines, going through the declassified lists many years later said they aroused two thoughts in particular:

It's frightfully difficult now to put yourself in the context of 1962–1963. There was a very real feeling of threat. I remember just a few years earlier saying to my wife, 'If it happens, where should we take our children – Chile or New Zealand?' It was a well-justified worry. We'd had Berlin and Hungary and Cuba was to come. So this document must be seen in that context or it's unreal – Dr Strangelove.[35]

The 'Red List' of 1962 contained seventeen indicators which the JIC simply itemized without placing a priority on them. They were these:

1. Unusual flight activity or the lack of flight activity in the Long-Range Air Force which indicates a departure from normal peacetime operations.

2. The bringing to an increased state of readiness of Soviet strategic missile units wherever they may be, including the movement of the missiles themselves into forward areas; the identification, outside fleet areas, of numbers of missile firing submarines, or, in time of tension, the absence of such submarines from local communication networks.

3. Unusually high state of readiness of all components of the Soviet air defence system, wherever located.

4. Sudden or unexplained redeployment and dispersal of Soviet ground forces, particularly in peripheral areas.

5. Sudden dispersal of naval ships from fleet bases.

6. Increased deployment of Soviet submarines in sea areas of interest to the Western Powers.

7. Dispersal of vital components of Soviet Government headquarters.

8. Redeployment of Soviet air force servicing units to, and build-up of aviation fuel stocks at or near, airfields in East Germany and the Satellites.

9. Issue of nuclear weapons to airfields where they are not normally stored, and issue of nuclear warheads to missile launching sites.

10. Provision of operational servicing facilities at suitable airfields in China to act as forward bases for Soviet medium and heavy bombers and the deployment of Soviet all-weather fighter units to protect these bases.

11. Arrival of Soviet army specialist units in forward areas (especially missile, medical and interrogation units) and military personnel wearing rocket insignia.

12. Redeployment or reinforcement of Soviet army units with a nuclear capability in forward areas.

13. Unusual deployment of missile guidance radar in the Soviet field armies.

14. Unusual signals activity, particularly if this suggests:

(a) Increased central control of various components of Soviet strategic offensive.

(b) Increased state of readiness throughout the armed forces. This could take the form of either an abnormally high, or an abnormally low, level of activity.

(c) Disguise of preparatory measures.

(d) A widespread and radical change of signal data.

15. Priority for Soviet military traffic, reduction of civil traffic on East German

and Satellite railways, unusual concentrations of rolling stock, and the appearance of movement control staff.

16. Sharp increase in air transport flights between guided missile production factories, storage centres and known missile launch complexes.

17. Intensified security measures in the Soviet Union and Satellites.[36]

The 'Amber List' spelt out forty-seven:

(ADDITIONAL SOVIET PREPARATIONS WHICH MIGHT BE MADE AND BLOC PREPARATIONS FOR HOSTILITIES)

ARMED FORCES

Common to All

1. Bringing units up to wartime strength and readiness through:
    (a) Recall of reserve personnel.
    (b) Postponement of demobililsation of trained soldiers.
    (c) Cancellation of leave, confinement of troops at barracks, increase of security patrols in vital areas.
    (d) Reassignment to full military duty of those units employed on civil projects.

2. Redesignation of military districts or formations as fronts and/or their reinforcement by high-ranking officers.

3. Readying of combat headquarters of ground and air units and the setting up of Joint-Services or Operations Headquarters.

4. Increases in the number of high-ranking officers in Soviet and Chinese missions in *bloc* countries.

5. Extension of military hospital accommodation at the expense of civil establishments and the formation of emergency stockpiles of medical equipment and drugs.

6. Abnormal censorship of forces mail.

7. Accelerated build-up of missile units.

8. Change in pattern of activities at missile test ranges.

Ground Forces

9. Unusual reinforcing of the striking forces or the movement and concentration of troops to form a striking force.

10. Sudden or unexplained redeployment and dispersal of ground forces.

11. Assembly of airborne units in the vicinity of airfields on which transport planes are, or could be, concentrated.

12. The positioning of bridging equipment ready for use.

13. Building of bridges serving secondary routes.

14. Preparations for unusually large-scale exercises involving Soviet Ground Forces being deployed into Satellite countries.

Air Forces

15. Unusually high state of readiness of *bloc* air defences.

16. Bringing into use inactive landing strips and airfields.

17. Dispersal and concealment of military aircraft.

18. Increase in the strength of air units on active airfields and reinforcement of air armies on the periphery of the *bloc*.

19. Unusual activity suggesting an assembly of military and/or civil air transport aircraft and airborne forces.

20. Interference with civil and military flight in the Berlin air corridor and with civil flight over *bloc*-controlled territory.

21. Extension of military control of civil air movement and disruption of *bloc* civil air schedules. The withdrawal of civil transport aircraft for military use.

22. Occupation by Chinese ground staff of North Vietnamese airfields.

23. Movement of bomber and fighter aircraft to airfields within striking distance of pro-Western countries.

24. Increase in aircraft delivery form Soviet Union to China.

25. Increase in POL [petrol, oil and lubricant] supplies to China, North Korea and North Vietnam.

Navy

26. Increased movement of small ships and submarines through the Soviet canal systems.

27. Reinforcement of naval air units; redeployment of Soviet naval units from their normal operating areas, particularly movements of submarines through the Sound or the Belts (Baltic) and from the Straits (Bosphorous).

28. Redeployment of submarine depot ships and support groups from the normal bases.

29. Significant changes in normal commercial maritime traffic. Recall of

merchant ships or abnormal decrease of the number of those ships on the high seas.

30. Abnormal concentration in harbours of merchant ships or fishing vessels, adaptable for amphibious and supply operations.

31. Damaging of fixed Western anti-submarine detection systems, *e.g.*, by cutting associated cables.

32. Deployment of Chinese North and Eastern fleet units to southern ports.

33. Abnormal concentration of junks and landing craft in southern Chinese ports.

34. The movement of Chinese naval staff officers into North Vietnamese ports.

Logistics

35. Establishment of dumps in forward areas and increase of stocks, or sudden increases in military stockpiling near frontiers, communication centres, ports and airfields.

36. Change in supplies and distribution to East Germany. Change from long-haul replenishment by rail to local issues from depots and supply points and to increased use of road transport, including the requisitioning of road transport, for military supply in the USSR and the Satellites.

37. Priority for Satellite military traffic, with consequent loss of traffic for civil purposes, and the appearance of movement control staff.

38. Assembly of rolling stock of all types for Satellite forces and particularly of specialised rolling stock in main supply areas and in distribution centres.

39. Increase in the number of hospital trains in service and preparation for service.

40. Unusual movement of special trains for transporting ballistic missiles and/or fuels.

CIVIL DEFENCE

41. Bringing to a state of readiness civil defence measures on a large scale such as initiation of black-out measures and announcement of evacuation.

42. Dispersal of government and administrative headquarters.

SIGNALS

43. Transmission of jamming signals directed against radio communications, radar and missile guidance systems.

44. Setting up of new communication links applicable to specific military operations.

45. The interruption of Western communications by the deliberate cutting of submarine cables.

SECURITY

46. Increased activity of security organisations.

47. Bans on visits to and scheduled flights over sensitive areas, and the forced evacuation of local inhabitants from those areas, when the latter are likely to include ballistic missile launching sites.[37]

As a former senior intelligence operator put it, the 'key to all of the indicators is to (a) notice any change, and (b) to assess its significance. Any change is bad news.'[38]

For historians, the wider significance of this list is how revealing it is of the range of activities carried out by the collectors of British and allied Cold War intelligence. It is dominated by signals intelligence (the interception of military traffic especially) and electronic surveillance (the tracking of Soviet and Warsaw Pact radar). Human intelligence, though a relatively small component, is there, too, such as the number 11 on the 'Red List' – the 'Arrival of Soviet army specialist units in forward areas . . . and military personnel wearing rocket insignia.'[39] (The United States by 1962 was putting its early Corona satellites over Soviet territory, but they could not deliver cap-badge imagery. Agents observing in the field could.) Similarly on the 'Amber List', the railway sections implied informants in the marshalling yards and, perhaps, number 6, 'Abnormal censorship of forces mail',[40] would best be detected by an agent of Western intelligence serving inside the Red Army.

It is also quite plain from the Red and Amber lists how important was the constant surveillance by Western intelligence of the Soviet bloc's periphery. Michael Herman, later characterized this as having a touch about it of

a multinational Great Game, played out not only along the German border, but also in Berlin around the rest of the Soviet periphery – the Baltic, North Norway and the Barents Sea, the Black Sea, the Sea of Okhotsk and elsewhere:

tough men rolling for weeks on station in small ships; patient monitors on quiet islands; aircraft of many nations flying every day, packed with technical equipment; and much else.[41]

Herman goes on to observe that: 'Much of the timely intelligence produced by the West was, strictly speaking, totally useless; its twenty-four-hour surveillance was a precaution, for warning of an attack that never came.'[42]

Certainly, throughout the bulk of the Cold War, the JIC's 'Weekly Summary of Current Intelligence' began with the words: 'There are no indications of Soviet Military aggression.'[43] Yet, as Herman recognizes, reassurance of this kind *was* hugely – I would say centrally – important: 'American Presidents never believed that they were about to be Pearl Harbored. Western confidence in intelligence warning provided some stability in Cold War management.'[44]

Back in the formative years, however, in the days long before satellites, or U2 or even RAF Canberra overflights of Soviet territory, the JIC's preoccupation was with capabilities and indicators. Intentions it would dearly have loved to gauge but the late 1940s assessments were commendably candid about their shortcomings here. In that crucial twenty-five-page assessment of 'Russia's Strategic Interests and Assumptions' of 1 March 1946, the diplomats, civil servants, military and intelligence chiefs on the JIC were quite frank with their customers about 'our difficulties in obtaining intelligence on Russian intentions. Decisions are taken by a small group of men, the strictest security precautions are observed and far less than in Western Democracies are the opinions of the masses taken into account.'[45]

JIC (46) 1 (o) was the first major analysis of the Soviet Union's strategic interests and intentions the committee had produced since December 1944,[46] and it was especially notable as it reflected a sustained surge of pessimism on the part of the analysts from the final months of World War II. Such growing anxiety was reflected, famously, by Winston Churchill during his last weeks in No. 10 when, in Brooke's words, he

gave a long and very gloomy review of the situation in Europe. The Russians were further West in Europe than they had ever been except once. They were all powerful in Europe. At any time that it took their fancy they could march across the rest of Europe and drive us back into our island. They had 2 to 1 land superiority over our forces and the Americans were returning home.[47]

A very great deal turned on those mid-to-late 1940s JIC assessments, not just in terms of ministerial perceptions and anxieties about that vast military machine to the east of the Elbe, but in the rationale, perhaps even the imperative, they provided for the sustenance of a sizable military and intelligence capacity on the part of the UK into the increasingly uneasy peace. As Michael Howard put it , the post-war Chiefs of Staff (to whom, as we have seen, until 1957 the JIC reported before the committee was removed from their orbit into the Cabinet Office, partly to increase the product's flow to senior ministers)[48] continued fighting their own private turf wars, but '[t]his did not matter so long as they had plenty of men and money to dispose of, which, thanks to the Cold War, they had.'[49] Defence spending as a proportion of Gross National Product stood at 7.1 per cent in 1948, and peaked at 9.8 per cent in 1952 thanks to the Korean War-inspired rearmament programme. As late as 1963 it still stood just above 6 per cent and only nudged below 5 per cent in 1969 thanks to the Wilson governments' near perpetual series of defence reviews.[50] And, as the post-war and the Cold War deepened in tandem, successive generations of ministers and officials on the inner intelligence loops came to appreciate, in Sir Burke Trend's words, that: 'After the Second World War, it became apparent that we should henceforth have to make our way in the world by influence rather than by power and that political intelligence would henceforth be at least as important as military intelligence, if not more so.'[51]

What was it in those assessments which led to so high a proportion of the UK's national wealth being deployed for so long on politico-military purposes? The opening sections of the 1 March 1946 analysis of 'Russia's Strategic Interests and Intentions' is especially intriguing as it sets out the collection famine which its compilers had to overcome as best they could, before going on to outline the reasons for its descent into pessimism compared to the last big examination of the same theme in December 1944. 'Any study of Russia's strategic interests and intentions,' the JIC warned its inner circle of readers, must be speculative, as we have little evidence to show what view Russia herself takes of her strategic interests, or what policy she intends to pursue. We have practically no direct intelligence, of a detailed factual or substantial nature, on conditions in the different parts of the Soviet Union, and none at all on the intentions, immediate or ultimate, of the Russian leaders . . . Our present appreciation is based, therefore, on the limited evidence which we have, on deductions made from such indications of policy as Russia has given, and on reasonable conjecture concerning the Soviet appreciation of their own situation.[52]

Reprising its portrait of the likely post-war condition and stance of the Soviet Union drawn in the last weeks of 1944, the JIC recalled the stress it had placed on the primacy Stalin and the 'inner circle controlling the Communist Party of the Soviet Union' would place on the 'greatest possible measure of security' with every precaution taken to prevent a future invasion of Soviet territory. To this end: 'She [Russia] would wish to improve her strategic frontiers and to draw the states along her borders, particularly those in Europe, into her strategic system.' Another primary impulse would be the securing of 'a prolonged period of peace in which to restore devastated areas, to develop her industry and agriculture, and to raise the standard of living'.[53]

The JIC had not been overly optimistic, as the Allied armies converged on Germany, that their co-operation would continue once that great concentrator of collective minds – Adolf Hitler – had received his deserts, but it did believe that Russia

would at least experiment with collaboration with Great Britain and America in the interests of world security. But if she came to believe that we were not sincerely collaborating, she would probably push her military frontiers forward into the border states in Europe, try by political intrigue to stir up trouble in Greece, the Middle East and India, and exploit her interest over the Communist parties in the countries concerned to stimulate opposition to anti-Russian policy.[54]

Despite what Bradley Smith has called the 'record of four years of East–West intelligence co-operation' from Hitler's invasion of the Soviet Union in 1941 to the end of the Japanese War in August 1945, which he describes as 'the most extensive and successful such effort carried out by reluctant allies in the history of modern warfare',[55] the JIC concluded in December 1944, when these intelligence exchanges were still flowing, that:

While Russia would not follow an aggressive policy of territorial expansion, her suspicion of Great Britain and America would continue to cause difficulty, as would also her tactlessness in the handling of international relations. Her relations with us would depend very largely on the ability of each side to convince the other of the sincerity of its desire for collaboration.[56]

The thrust of that late-1944 assessment was that the chances of a post-Axis world of great powers cohabiting and collaborating in wary tolerance of each other were seriously limited but not altogether impossible.

The intelligence community, however, did not wait long to resume operations as usual against Soviet targets. As Bradley Smith has shown, while '[i]t must now be recognized that although the West avoided making serious intelligence attacks on the USSR during World War II, within days of its conclusion, British intelligence was working on Soviet military codes and ciphers.'[57] What persuaded British intelligence during the course of 1945 that the faint hopes for a co-operative, united-nations post-war world had been dashed? The JIC adduced four influences which had hardened the mind-set of Stalin's inner group:

(a) The speed of the Western Allies' advance, after crossing the Rhine in March 1945 must have given rise to Russian fears that their allies would beat them in the race to Berlin, would then refuse to withdraw into their allotted Zones and so would rob the Soviet Union of many of the spoils of victory.

(b) The use of the atomic bomb disclosed a weapon which seemed to constitute a new threat to that security for which they have been striving ever since 1917 and which, in late 1944, they seemed, at last, to be on the point of attaining.

(c) The attitude both of the Americans and ourselves towards Russia seemed to them to harden after the end of hostilities. Both in South-East Europe and in the Far East, the United States Government seemed to them to be pursuing a policy designed to restrict Russia's aspirations. His Majesty's Government appeared to be pursuing a similar policy in South-East Europe, Turkey and Persia.

(d) On the other hand they must now appreciate that both the British Commonwealth and the United States are incomparably weaker than they were in the summer of 1945. Great Britain is faced with great man-power and financial problems leading to rapid demobilisation, while the United States has let her military forces disintegrate, and since the death of President Roosevelt has an executive which lacks decision.

In an intriguing afterthought to this disquisition on what it thought the Soviet leadership had in mind, the JIC, in a sentence surprising to post-Cold War eyes, saw Stalin as a force for relative moderation in the Politburo:

When Stalin has himself intervened in the past in negotiations between Russia and Great Britain and the United States, the result has usually been to make Russian tactics more flexible and accommodating: we cannot tell whether this will continue now that the war is over, but in the event of Stalin's death it is reasonable to assume that the absence of this modifying influence would be felt.[58]

Was the JIC failing to appreciate reality in both Washington and Moscow in the late winter of 1945–6? It is surprising that President Truman could have been regarded as indecisive as late as that. As for Stalin, the former KGB officer-turned-analyst Oleg Tsarev has painted a picture of him as an avid reader of 'intelligence in its raw form',[59] including documents purloined by his human agents in the UK such as Kim Philby, Guy Burgess and John Cairncross which went to him, dangerously, without the 'evaluation and assessment, which would have involved political judgements his aides were too afraid to make', meaning 'that such materials lacked depth and background'.[60]

According to Tsarev, Stalin convinced himself that some of the thinking in the JIC assessments in the early post-war period reinforced his view that the British Empire and the United States were preparing for hostilities against the Soviet Union. Tsarev placed particular emphasis on Russian translations of documents prepared by the UK Chiefs'

Planning Staff in June 1945 on imperial defence which reached Stalin's desk thanks to Philby.[61] Similarly, late 1940s Western intelligence assessments suggesting the Soviet Union would not be militarily or industrially ready to fight a global war until 1955–7 appear, according to Tsarev, to have been interpreted in the Kremlin as identifying the period in which the US and the UK would 'unleash' war against the Soviet Union.[62]

If this was so, it involved a profound misreading of Chiefs of Staff and JIC material, illustrating how dangerously distorting can be the effects of unprocessed and unassessed intelligence documents, even though they were provided by what was probably as well-placed and rich a seam of human intelligence as one great power has ever enjoyed for use against another. Documents such as JIC (46) 1 (0) bear careful scrutiny for themselves. But read with Stalin's delusions in mind, the fear and sense of vulnerability in the West in 1945–6 were replicated in Stalin's office, and based partly on the very same material which led Attlee's ministers and the British military eventually to conclude that the Cold War was going to be a global, dangerous and prolonged affair. The JIC March 1946 assessment expressed its judgement that:

In considering what action she can take, short of a major war, to attain her immediate aims, Russia will no doubt give full weight to the fact that Great Britain and the United States are both war weary, faced with immense internal problems and rapidly demobilising their forces. By comparison, Russia's own forces and industry are still on a war basis. No further demobilisation has been announced, and Russian divisions are being rapidly re-equipped with the latest material.[63]

Not much sign here of an Anglo-American preventive-war-in-the-making.

Could handwritten copies of the vast KGB archive which MI6 spirited out of the Soviet Union, along with its archivist, Vasili Mitrokhin, in 1992 provide part of the explanation for Stalin's determination to convert in his own mind British anxiety into Anglo-American bellicosity? It is one of the greatest paradoxes of intelligence history that the so-called 'Magnificent Five' (Philby, Anthony Blunt, Burgess, Donald Maclean and John Cairncross) came under deep suspicion during World

War II. As Professor Christopher Andrew, Mitrokhin's collaborator in organizing the archive for publication, has explained:

The problem for the professionally suspicious minds in the [Moscow] Centre was that it all seemed too good to be true. Taking their cue from the master conspiracy theorist in the Kremlin [Stalin], they eventually concluded that what appeared to be the best intelligence ever obtained from Britain by any intelligence service was at root a British plot. The Five, later acknowledged as the ablest group of agents in KGB history, were discredited in the eyes of the Centre leadership by their failure to produce evidence of a massive, non-existent British conspiracy against the Soviet Union. Of the reality of that conspiracy, Stalin, and therefore his chief intelligence advisers, had no doubt.[64]

The Mitrokhin material, therefore, suggests Whitehall's all-source intelligence analysts were wrongly attributing to Stalin and his intelligence assessors the kind of rationality and detachment to which the JIC itself aspired.

The short executive summary of JIC (46) 1 (o), designed to meet the needs of busy readers without the time to absorb the full, 127-paragraph report, itself alone dispels any fantasies about either the West itching for war or the Soviet Union trembling on the brink of a westward and irresistible march to the English Channel. It acknowledged that while the long-term aim of the Soviet leaders was to let time and the superiority of their system win for them 'an ultimate position of predominance in the world', the short-term preoccupation of the USSR will be to surround itself with 'a "belt" of satellite states with governments subservient to their policy', behind which Russia would rebuild 'her military and industrial strength to make up fully for her war losses and relative backwardness in the latest technical developments'. Should she perceive the West as seeking to compromise her position inside the protective 'belt', Russia

will retaliate by using all weapons, short of major war, to frustrate these attempts. She will make full use of propaganda, of diplomatic pressure and of the Communist parties abroad both to this end and to weaken foreign countries.

Measures short of war would also be used in an attempt to bring within her 'belt' contiguous areas such as Turkey and Persia which 'she considers it strategically necessary to dominate'. Russia will avoid, however, areas where she would encounter 'firm combined resistance from the United States and Great Britain together'. 'Elsewhere she will adopt a policy of opportunism to extend her influence wherever possible without provoking a major war, leaving the onus of challenge to the rest of the world. In pursuing this policy she will use, in the ways she thinks most effective, Communist parties in other countries and certain international organisations . . .'[65]

So, in the eyes of the JIC, by late winter 1945–6, the Soviet Union had moved firmly and irrevocably beyond being an awkward partner in world affairs to a formidable adversary within its own satellite belt, with troublesome branch offices in many more countries in the form of indigenous Communist Parties – the whole apparatus operating a twin-track approach to eventual global predominance based on immediate reconstruction and security priorities that would eventually give way to wider ambitions as the sinews of military, political and economic superiority waxed ever stronger. The JIC summed up this Soviet approach as being 'aggressive by all means short of war'.

Would war come, however? The British intelligence community answered the question in two parts:

1: The ingredients of a capacity to wage a sustained global war. Oil output will not reach pre-war levels, [it was thought], until 1950. It was 'unlikely' that the USSR will possess 'significant quantities of atomic weapons before about 1955–60 . . .' By 1952, Russia will have made up wartime losses in manpower. By about 1955–60 the development of Russian industry will have made her self-sufficient in time of war.[66]

2: As to intentions, the Soviet Union may pursue defensive policies, but 'the tactics will be offensive, and the danger always exists that Russian leaders may misjudge how far they can go without provoking war with America or ourselves'.[67]

Herein lay many of the particles which went into the making of the JIC's Cold War state of mind: an intense concentration on what became the Soviet bloc's capacity to wage war, alongside a persistent under-estimation of the speed with which they would make their leaps in military technology; and a recognition of the inherent caution of the regime, alongside a sustained appreciation of the danger of war-through-miscalculation. The pattern of analysis, anticipation and anxiety was set. Here was a formidable, totalitarian adversary which differed from the tyranny from which Europe and the world had been delivered so recently in the durability and reach of its threat.

This latter aspect was the subject of a special JIC assessment in the summer of 1946 with a quite considerable input from MI6 (which is evident in its pages) and the codebreakers (which is not). One seasoned MI6 Cold War-hand took particular pride in his service's sustained ability to rub the noses of successive generations of ministers in the sheer nastiness of life in the Soviet bloc: 'The main contribution of MI6, the HUMINT [human intelligence] service at the level of our government,' he said,

was really quite humdrum. We reminded them on a weekly, sometimes a daily basis of the reality of the Soviet and other regimes. They had no chance to have illusions about what life was like behind the Iron Curtain . . . and there were constant reminders of what Soviet espionage was about.[68]

The 23 September 1946 JIC report, 'The Spread of Communism Throughout the World and the Extent of Its Direction from Moscow', very much carries this flavour.

It is difficult to know how much SIGINT (signals intelligence) influenced JIC (46) 70 (0). The defection of the Soviet GRU (military intelligence) cypher clerk Igor Gouzenko in Ottawa in September 1945, with 'more than a hundred classified documents under his shirt', had exposed a major spy ring in North America.[69] The first breakthroughs into the so-called VENONA traffic, a cache which would rise to nearly 3,000 intercepted Soviet intelligence communications from New York to Moscow between 1940 and 1948,[70] were probably not made by US codebreakers until just after 'The Spread of Communism' document had circulated in Whitehall.[71] By 1950–51, a substantial penetration of the diplomatic and nuclear capacities of both the United States and the United Kingdom had been exposed, albeit to a very limited number of intelligence and counter-intelligence experts within the VENONA loop and, most probably, to Clement Attlee and a small circle of his ministers.[72]

The September 1946 JIC assessment concluded starkly 'that Communism is a serious menace to the interests of the British Commonwealth both outside British territory, and to a lesser extent inside it, and we are of the opinion that it is essential that some immediate counter-action should be taken against this danger'.[73] It was unusual for a JIC paper to make a specific recommendation, but it was heeded, as we shall see in Chapter 3, when Attlee set up first his Cabinet Committee on Subversive Activities in June 1947[74] and a pair of official committees on Communism (Home) and Communism (Overseas) two years later.[75]

The JIC at this stage treated international communism as if it were one and indivisible. The dissolution of the old Communist International, the Comintern, in May 1943,

appears to have had no effect on the cohesion and discipline of the Communist movement. Minor tactical differences exist between some of the national Parties, but on essential issues (and particularly on those in which the Soviet Union has declared its line) the Communist movement acts as a single whole.[76]

The British analysts, in a curious way, mingled intense dislike with considerable respect for this new adversary:

The appeal of Communism is based on an all-embracing idealogy [sic], to which Communists adhere with religious fervour, and on the promise of a better world free from exploitation and war. The Communist Parties are led by nuclei of able, experienced and devoted men, capable of directing mass movements, and firm in the belief that they are assisting in an inexorable historical process.

Since the Russian Revolution, the Communist movement has been dominated by the prestige and influence of the Russian Communists. The Soviet Union is by far the most powerful element in the Communist movement, and its defence, therefore, is an essential point in all Communist policy.[77]

This was converted directly into an internal threat directed, as it were, from the same source as controlled the Red Army.

Communist Parties accept willingly and loyally the obligations involved in the Soviet Union. In general they lend themselves readily to use as instruments of Soviet policy, if necessary at the expense of their own 'bourgeois' Governments . . . The membership of the Communist Parties provides a ready field of recruitment for agents and informants prepared to serve the Soviet Union, and officials of Soviet Missions have made considerable use of Communist Party members for espionage and subversive political activities.[78]

The fact that until the suppression of the Hungarian uprising by Khrushchev's tanks in the autumn of 1956, the Communist Party of Great Britain sustained a capacity to retain the loyalty of some of the most gifted and charming men and women of high intelligence (and a few thereafter), along with its influence within certain trade unions, gave the CPGB the capacity politically to punch far above its numerical weight, as the British intelligence community plainly appreciated.

Though but a small proportion of the membership could ever be described as agents of the Soviet Union in the intelligence sense, it would be intriguing to know if MI5 was aware of the pitch employed by Harry Pollitt, General Secretary of the CPGB, who would instruct young communist undergraduates at Cambridge University during the last years of World War II to forget about selling the *Daily Worker* on street corners or the pursuit of lesser jobs out of a sense of solidarity with the proletariat. The Party required them to get Firsts and to secure high positions in the state.[79] The British Security Service may well have been apprised of the Pollitt line as it is quite plain that it had substantial sections of the Party wired up for sound throughout the Cold War (as we shall see in Chapter 3 on the assessment and handling of the internal 'threat'). As late as the start of the twenty-first century, a decade after the 1991 Congress voted to dissolve the CPGB after seventy-one years of political life and to reconstitute itself as the Democratic Left,[80] more than one MI5 officer could be heard to claim that (a) the British Security Service 'had been virtually running the CPGB at the end', and (b) to bemoan how much the pensions of its former agents within the CPGB were absorbing from current budgets.[81]

Place the big 'Russia's Strategic Interests and Intentions' assessment of March 1946 alongside 'The Spread of Communism . . .' paper of September that year and you can see the firming up of the classic British intelligence analysis of this extraordinary threat. Events in eastern Europe in 1947 and the Berlin crisis of 1948 set this picture hard for nearly ten years and, in some ways, until the Soviet superpower 'died in the saddle' in 1989–91.

The August 1947 JIC assessment of 'Soviet Interests, Intentions and Capabilities' still stressed the 'preoccupation with security' of the Russian leadership and that it was

unlikely . . . before 1955–60 [that] the Soviet Union will be capable of supporting her armed forces entirely from natural resources and industrial potential under her own control, in any major war, except one of very short duration. Nevertheless, if Russia wished to go to war, economic considerations would not in themselves be enough to prevent her from doing so, in the event of her feeling confident of rapid victory.[82]

And here one found *the* spectre haunting early post-war western Europe in the '175 divisions' Stalin was thought to have at his command. 'The very scanty evidence at our disposal,' the JIC told its customers just a month after the Soviet Foreign Minister, Vyacheslav Molotov, led the Russian and satellite delegations out of the Marshall Plan discussions in Paris, marking the start of the 'high Cold War'[83] and a protracted period of peril and confrontation,

indicates that in the event of mobilisation, this total of 175 divisions could be approximately doubled in 30 days, although the proportion of new armoured and mechanised formations is likely to be low owing to limitations of tank production and specialists . . . A vast programme of re-organisation and re-equipment is in progress throughout the Soviet Army with the object of bringing a large proportion of its divisions up to Western standards . . .[84]

Half a mile from the secret world of the JIC, in Transport House, a young Denis Healey, then in charge of Labour's International Department, concluded that: 'All that the Red Army needed in order to reach the North Sea was boots.'[85]

The JIC agreed, though without the aid of such graphic images to chill the bones of its readers:

The Soviet land forces, with their close support aircraft, are sufficiently strong at the present time, to achieve rapid and far-reaching successes against any likely combination of opposing land forces. The strategic air situation, however, remains adverse to the Soviet Union, in that she has no satisfactory answer either to atomic weapons or to opposing strategic bomber forces. She cannot thus count, as yet, upon a reasonable degree of immunity for her centres of population and industry from serious air attack. Her future readiness to embark upon a major war is likely, therefore, to be conditioned by considerations of her own air power in relation to that of probable opponents.[86]

The nuclear factor was central throughout the Cold War.* Likely and, later, actual Soviet nuclear capabilities were a continual 'Priority I' target for British intelligence from the later 1940s on[87] and represented a considerable failure in forecasting terms, as we shall see in a moment when we examine the JIC's record as Whitehall's primary early-warning mechanism.

But first, another element of the big JIC assessment of the summer of 1947 needs to be highlighted. Though in the late 1940s the JIC had no knowledge of Stalin's devouring of purloined Whitehall documents and fitting them into his mental picture of aggressive and menacing Western powers, its analysts were aware of the honoured place of the British democratic socialist tradition in the Soviet leader's demonology, predicting that:

. . . the Soviet Government will continue their present flow of propaganda designed to set world opinion against imperialist and capitalist governments in general, and against His Majesty's and the United States Government in particular. It should be emphasised that Soviet propagandists continue to represent this country as imperialist and capitalist, despite its Labour Government. In fact the Soviet leaders are especially hostile to 'reformist socialism' which they regard as a dangerous competitor for working-class support in many countries.[88]

---

* We shall examine the importance of being nuclear to Labour and Conservative governments alike from Mr Attlee onwards in Chapter 2.

No trace here of any of the nonsense which later affected a small part of the British intelligence community who believed that Labour was soft on communism and that Harold Wilson was a long-term communist agent.[89]

A pronounced feature of the JIC's large surveys of Soviet intentions and capabilities were their area-by-area, often country-by-country, examination of Soviet influence and the likely location of potential hot spots. How well did Whitehall's chief window on the Cold War world perform as a predictor of trouble in the early years of the great confrontation? The short answer is, not very. As Alex Craig, the first scholar to attempt a performance assessment of the early Cold War JIC, has written of the committee:

Most importantly, it failed to predict either the Berlin Blockade or the outbreak of the Korean War. [Scholars] have emphasised the extent of JIC culpability for the failure to predict the Soviet atomic test [in August 1949].[90] However, what has not been fully recognised by historians is that these were essentially failures in intelligence *collection* rather than analysis. They resulted from the inevitable post-war famine of good intelligence from deep inside a secretive Soviet Union, rather than from JIC mistakes. The JIC never attempted to conceal from policy-makers gaps in their knowledge and reports frequently contained caveats to indicate their limited information about particular subjects, especially about the Russian atomic and biological weapons programme.[91]

The familiar secrets/mysteries dilemma is at work here as well as a sheer shortage of hard facts.

Berlin was and remained a particular problem. There was nothing secret about the centrality of Germany to the Cold War. In its August 1947 grand-sweep appraisal, the JIC showed itself well aware in macro terms of what a united *and* communist Germany would mean to the Soviet Union and the East–West balance. On a micro level, British analysts knew that 'the Russians have been training ex-German officers and NCOs with a view to their filling important posts in the future administration of Germany, both in their own Zone and eventually in the Western Zones'.[92]

But whether and when the Russians would move against the isolated

Western sectors in Berlin, 100 miles inside the Soviet Zone, was very difficult to divine. The fusing of the full-scale Western Zones and the issue of a new currency for their use, in the teeth of Russian opposition in June 1948, was a certainty in terms of tension-raising. But a military move to sever the road, rail and canal ties could be – and was – effected from a standing start. No revealing build-up of troops was necessary.

As General Sir Brian Robertson, the Military Governor and Commander-in-Chief of the British Armed Forces in Germany, acknowledged at a Chiefs of Staff Committee meeting in the first weeks of the Berlin crisis, 'our intelligence of Russian military movements in the Eastern Zone of Germany was reasonably good', adding that he 'could see no sign of any preparations that might indicate that Russia was preparing for war'.[93] This was before special British air reconnaissance operations were mounted to increase surveillance around Berlin from September 1948.[94] Alex Craig is right to describe the Berlin blockade as one of those crises where the JIC was able to exert 'a calming influence on policy-makers'[95] by stressing the unlikelihood of its being the foreplay to World War III.

The Berlin experience gave a considerable stimulus to civil defence and war planning in London and to a sharpening up of the early-warning indicators and processes. At the weekly JIC meetings 'a regular item entitled "Russian Preparedness for War" was added to the agenda', with personal copies sent to the Foreign Secretary, Ernest Bevin.[96] As we have seen, virtually throughout the 1950s this was the first line of its weekly 'Red Book', which replaced this particular agenda item. Even during the second Berlin crisis in the late 1950s, by which time the indicator process was highly developed and Berlin contingency planning immensely elaborate, the Chiefs' joint planners needed to remind their masters that 'The opportunities for physical obstruction are so great that the Soviets/GDR [German Democratic Republic] do not need to use force, and may not do so.'[97]

The failure to predict the invasion of South Korea by communist forces from the North in the middle of the night on 25 June 1950 cannot be so easily explained away. In this instance, however, it was largely an American failure. The secret 1948 UK/USA Agreement had divided up the world between the two countries for eavesdropping purposes. The Korean peninsula was an American target. Christopher Andrew, reflecting on the chaotic procedures which operated in this branch of US intelligence until the National Security Agency was created in November 1952 (and in which immense resources were invested chiefly in response to the inquest into the failure of June 1950[98]), has written that 'largely as a result of the lack of co-ordination, North Korea did not become a priority SIGINT target until after it had attacked the South'.[99] As Richard Aldrich has pointed out, the North Koreans were good at signals security. The Russians had trained them well. Very little of value was there for the eavesdropping, though in terms of what little there was, Western intelligence was 'not well disposed to intercept it'.[100]

Top-flight SIGINT, however, was not the only way to gauge a military build-up, and this one was huge with some 90,000 troops involved.[101] The CIA station in Seoul had a few agents in the North who reported 'on increased troop movements and armoured build-ups. This had not led to a direct prediction of the invasion. But it had allowed the CIA to circulate warnings on 20 June about North Korean mobilisation to members of President Truman's Cabinet . . .'[102]

Tom Dibble has shown how dependent British intelligence remained on the United States' product throughout the Korean War for its raw material on the conflict.[103] But its assessments of the significance of the shock of Korea were very much its own. In the weeks following the invasion, as South Korean, American, British and other United Nations forces struggled to retain a toehold on the peninsula, the JIC, 'in the light of recent developments', prepared a report for pooling at US/UK/Canada meetings on 'The Likelihood of War with the Soviet Union and the Date by which the Soviet Leaders might be Prepared to Risk It'.[104] The tone is still generally one of reassurance but a distinctly anxious note is audible too:

We do not know whether the Soviet Leaders believe that, provided the Soviet Union is strong enough to deter capitalist aggression, world Communism under Soviet hegemony can in the long run be achieved without the Soviet Union becoming involved in a major war with the non-Communist world, but it is reasonable to conclude that they wish to achieve their aims this way.

The shock of 25 June 1950 along the 38th Parallel which divided the two Koreas is reflected directly in the JIC's picture presented to Whitehall and to the UK's foremost intelligence allies:

The Soviet Leaders will, however, continue to press their plans for the extension of Communist influence by political, economic and ideological warfare, and by subversion and civil war.

In a further reference to the Korean case, the JIC warned about the possibility, despite the UN's resistance to the North Korean advance, that the Soviet leadership might once again and elsewhere be tempted 'to press home the advantage of local military superiority even at the risk, which they may underestimate, of provoking armed Western counter-action, always provided that the Soviet armed forces are not directly engaged and that military operations can be localised'.[105]

It was during this particularly raw and risky phase of the East–West conflict (what might be called the perilously high Cold War between the outbreak of the Korean War in June 1950 and the death of Stalin in March 1953) that the more thoughtful members of the British intelligence community became especially anxious about their American counterparts in exactly this area – the possible overreaction to Soviet provocation. Richard Aldrich has discovered that while the Whitehall analysts tried to make sense of what Korea meant in the summer of 1950, one of the figures around the JIC table went so far as to warn those on the inner loop a year later of the threat the *United States* posed to world peace.

Vice-Admiral Eric Longley-Cook, Director of Naval Intelligence, felt moved in his last weeks of service to prepare a 'Where are we going?' think piece which eventually found its way to Mr Attlee and, on the demise of the Labour government in October 1951, to Mr Churchill. His memo reflected the consistent JIC view (despite that surge of concern the previous summer) that the Russians would not pursue their objectives through 'a general military offensive ("Total War")' but through 'economic and psychological' pressure directed against the non-communist world. From his 'conversations with many responsible and influential Americans who are obviously convinced that war with Russia is inevitable', Longley-Cook had reached the alarming conclusion that they had fixed a date for such a war in their minds 'for mid or late 1952', that it was 'doubtful whether, in a year's time, the US will be able to control the Frankenstein monster which they are creating' and that there was 'a definite danger of the USA becoming involved in a preventive war against Russia, however firmly their NATO allies object'.

What is especially interesting about Longley-Cook's summer 1951 reflections is the degree to which he highlights the differences between British and American intelligence assessments of the Soviet threat. He had been alarmed during the combined US/UK intelligence conference in Washington in October 1950 by the degree to which the American equivalent of the JIC produced assessments that 'tend to fit in with the prejudged conclusion that a shooting war with the Soviet Union at some time is inevitable . . . Although the Americans were eventually persuaded to endorse a combined appreciation of the Soviet threat, based on reason and factual intelligence, they were quick to alter it to fit their own preconceived ideas as soon as the London team had returned to this country.'

Longely-Cook's paper, clearly reflecting the big JIC threat assessments of the late 1940s (he actually cites JIC (48) 9 (0) of July 1948), concentrates on why the London analysts interpreted the same evidence so differently from their Washington opposite numbers. Certainly the Soviet leaders had decided 'to retain their war machine at great strength even after the defeat of Germany and Japan'.

As a constant threat, the Soviet war machine plays an important part, but, in considering the size of the Soviet Army, it should be remembered that Russia has always required a very large standing army for the garrisoning of her very long frontiers. It is not primarily intended for offensive purposes, and it should not be allowed to drive the Western powers into attempting an exact balance of military power.

Longley-Cook saw the Americans as interpreting the Soviet war machine as a direct threat to the USA and thought that their policy was 'based on false reasoning, and on intelligence which it shaped to fit a preconceived idea', and 'a nearly successful attempt at a further Communist advance in the Far East (Korea) brought about the decision of the

United States to rearm on a scale never before known in peace time'.

British intelligence, by contrast, knew that war could come through miscalculation and/or either side misinterpreting the other's intentions. But this was unlikely, meaning that the 'struggle between the Western Democracies and the Soviet Block is going to be a very long-term affair' that could not be solved by 'Total War'. This was why, since the big July 1948 assessment of the Soviet leadership's intentions, 'We have invariably stated our opinion that their long term aim is to achieve world domination by all means short of war. But we have at the same time advised that they might be frightened into using their immense army if they felt their last chance of survival had come in the face of the rapid build up of US forces and/or German rearmament on a very big scale.'[106]

At the heart of Longley-Cook's warning was not just the purposes of the immense Red Army but the atomic dilemma too. In the days following the invasion of South Korea, he and his colleagues had based their continuing assumption that Stalin's people would not risk a major war on the premise that,

[s]o long as they estimate that the United States have a commanding superiority in atomic weapons and that their air defences are unable to prevent the incalculable damage which the highly centralised Soviet system might expect to suffer from atomic warfare, it is not likely that the Soviet Leaders would wish to become involved in a world war.[107]

A year later, Longley-Cook's reading of the American mind saw many as arguing that '"we have the bomb; let us use it now while the balance is in our favour. Since war with Russia is inevitable, let's get it over with now"'[108] (a truly alarming counterpoint to Stalin's misreading of the UK documents purloined for him by Philby and the others).

Intriguingly, Churchill himself was prone to take this view in his gloomier moments. In the summer of 1954 he prepared a fascinating note on the thoughts he wished to present to Cabinet as part of his case for going all out to bring the Soviet Union and the United States together at a summit meeting. He was greatly worried by 'the argument which must be present in many American minds', which he simulated thus:

We alone have for the next two or perhaps three years sure and overwhelming superiority in attack, and a substantive measure of immunity in defence. Merely to dawdle means potential equality of ruin. Ought we not for the immediate safety of our own and the American people and the incidental rescue of the Free World to bring matters to a head by a 'show-down' leading up to an ultimatum accompanied by an Alert?[109]

Such thoughts continued to plague Churchill in retirement. That accomplished diarist James Lees-Milne penned a particularly vivid entry in September 1957 on a drinks party at Lord Beaverbrook's villa in the South of France, where the Churchills were staying when the shadow of the bomb briefly eclipsed the sunshine:

Sir Winston sitting slumped in an armchair in the middle of the room to whom we talked in turns. A [Alvide, Lee-Milne's wife] told him how much she was impressed by Neville Shute's book *On the Beach* [110] [about the last survivors of a global nuclear war set in the future – 1961 – in the last days of their lives in and around Melbourne, Australia], which he too had read. He said he was sending it to Khrushchev. She asked would he not also send it to Eisenhower? Sir W.'s retort: 'It would be a waste of money. He is so muddle-headed now' . . . He said to Montague Browne [his Private Secretary]: 'I think the earth will soon be destroyed . . . And if I were the Almighty I would not recreate it in case they destroyed him too next time.'[111]

Whether the old warrior did or did not send a copy of *On the Beach* to the Kremlin for the attention of Mr Khrushchev is not known.[112]

The bomb suffused *all* Cold War thinking for the duration of the conflict. Nothing, apart from warnings of imminent attack, surpassed the nuclear-weapons question in terms of Cold War intelligence priorities, and the intelligence world carried special scars on matters nuclear. Its failure to predict how soon the Soviet Union would cross the nuclear weapons threshold was probably the greatest single failing of Western intelligence in the early Cold War period and explains the preventive-war psychosis which so exercised Longley-Cook and Churchill. For so much rested on Western nuclear superiority that any misreading of Soviet capabilities was bound to fuel the belief that such an advantage would be very short lived.

From the outset, in the big mid-to-late-1940s assessments of the Soviet threat, the United States' monopoly of atomic weapons was seen as trumping Stalin's huge conventional-weapons superiority. The JIC's March 1946 paper did not entirely discount the possibility that the Soviet leadership might seek to secure its objectives 'by bluff', but it would estimate carefully the margin of risk involved:

Russia must also realise that America would be unlikely to stand aloof from a major war and that it might, therefore, be one of long duration. She is likely to be deterred by the existence of the atomic bomb.[113]

Central to every subsequent analysis of the big strategic picture, until the Soviet atomic test of August 1949 shook the Russia-watchers rigid, was the assessment of when the Soviet Union would bust America's monopoly.

The March 1946 assessment 'tentatively estimated that the USSR will not have atomic weapons before the early 1950s, and even if new sources of raw materials which are at present necessary be found, that the numbers of atomic weapons possessed by the USSR will not be significant until about 1955–60'.[114] The JIC, however, disagreed with 'American economic experts' who reckoned Russia's post-war economic plans meant that insufficient resources would be available for the development of atomic energy and the creation of a bomb plant: 'In our view . . . it would be dangerous to assume that the Soviet Union cannot develop the economic resources necessary for the building up of atomic bomb production plant and at the same time carry through their planned programme of reconstruction and development.'[115] The JIC was right. On Stalin's behalf, his ghastly secret policeman Lavrenti Beria ensured, from the end of August 1945, that the bomb programme had overwhelming priority, tripling the science budget and building what became in 1948 Arzamas-16, a secret nuclear-weapons city some 250 miles east of Moscow near Sarov.[116]

By the time of its August 1947 *tour d'horizon*, the JIC reckoned that two factors were 'probably' hampering the Soviets' nuclear effort: the 'difficult industrial techniques' required and a 'serious shortage of uranium' which was likely to continue until methods were found of extracting the necessary material from low-grade ores or high-grade ore was discovered within the territory Russia controlled. The latest estimate was that by January 1952, 'the Soviet Union's stock of bombs is unlikely to exceed 5 though it may possibly reach 25'.[117]

The summer assessment of 1948, just under a year before the first Soviet atomic test in Kazakhstan, saw the JIC reprising for its customers the industrial/uranium refinement problems and concluded:

Existing estimates of the date when the Russians began their programme and of their ability to overcome the technological difficulties involved suggest that they may possibly produce their first atomic bomb by January 1951 and that their stockpile of bombs in January 1953 may be of the order of 6 to 22.

Here a touch of Western technological hubris distorted the estimate still further: 'These figures, however, are the maximum possible based on the assumption that the Russian effort will progress as rapidly as the American and British projects have done. Allowances for the probably slower progress of the Russian effort will almost certainly retard the first bomb by some three years',[118] i.e. until early 1954.

So, when debris from the 29 August test at Semipalatinsk-21 was picked up after attaching itself to the filters of a US Air Force B-29 on a weather mission over the North Pacific on 3 September 1949, what Lorna Arnold has described as the 'rude shock',[119] in both London and Washington intelligence circles, was genuine and profound, as it was to the world generally when President Truman broke the news on 23 September. Why had Igor Kurchatov's research team and Soviet industrial capacity been so underestimated? For several years an explanation – alarming and consoling in equal measure – was available. From early March 1950, when the British physicist Klaus Fuchs, who had worked on the Manhattan Project during World War II and the British nuclear programme thereafter, was revealed as a spy, the explanation seemed as obvious as Chapman Pincher in the *Daily Express* made it appear:

In 90 minutes at the Old Bailey yesterday, a riddle was solved: How did Russia make the atomic bomb so quickly? Dr Klaus Emil Julius Fuchs, confidant and leading member of Britain's atom team, who began a 14-year jail sentence last night, gave them the know-how.[120]

In subsequent years, when the scale of Stalin's human intelligence on the American and British bomb programme became apparent (all-in-all a 'spectacular' element in a huge Soviet effort directed at scientific and technical intelligence[121] which on the bomb alone left thousands of pages of reports awaiting evaluation in Moscow as World War II ended[122]), Pincher's conclusion was fortified. When interrogated by MI5, Fuchs reckoned what he had passed to his GRU controller, Ursula Beurton,[123] had accelerated Stalin's bomb 'by one year at least'.[124]

Such a cornucopia of information must have helped enormously, not least by preventing Kurchatov's laboratories from pursuing scientific and technological culs-de-sac. With the ending of the Cold War, a row erupted between the veterans of the 1940s Soviet intelligence and atomic communities – a debate which has been monitored by the official historian of the British H-Bomb, Lorna Arnold. Writing in 2001, Arnold described this as a 'war of words' because

[s]ome of the scientists thought that self-justifying members of the secret services were spreading 'myths and legends', exaggerating the part played by the intelligence community. On the other hand it was argued that the scientists wanted to minimise the intelligence contribution because it seemed to detract from the brilliance and originality of their own achievements . . .[125]

It may be, as Arnold suggests, that because the source of intelligence knowledge was kept so tight, scientists outside the loop had not appreciated that some of the most valuable insights promulgated by those within it had been shaped by material purloined by Stalin's atomic friends in the West.

Either way, to create the atomic device which went up in the Kazakhstan steppe in 1949 was a huge scientific and industrial achievement. It does seem from recent scholarship that British intelligence was right to see the uranium-processing question as a key factor of the programme's timing. Fuchs himself, as scholars discovered when the transcript of his scientific interrogation in January 1950 were declassified in 2001, expressed himself 'extremely surprised that the Russian explosion had taken place so soon as he had been convinced that the information he had given could not have been applied so quickly and that the Russians would not have the engineering, design and construction facilities that would be needed to build large production plants in such a short time'.[126] It is plain from the inquest carried out by Eric Welsh, the naval intelligence commander who ran the UK's atomic intelligence capacity, that the lack of hard information from human or technical sources meant that Whitehall had made 'a very poor stab of it in the field of Atomic Energy Intelligence. Long distance detection techniques supply History *not* News. Nothing is as stale as yesterday's newspaper. What the JIC want and what the JIC demand is preknowledge of what are the enemies' intentions for tomorrow.'[127]

To be fair to the JIC pre-August 1949, not only did it have scanty information on the Soviet bomb programme from any source, but the immense scale of the KGB and GRU's penetration of the American and British projects had still to be fully appreciated. It took a while for technological hubris to dissipate and the appreciation to harden that a second- to third-world domestic consumer society can co-exist with a first-world military economy.

The view of the potential enemy had set hard by the early 1950s, and with it the belief of British intelligence that direct military conflict – World War III – was highly unlikely, in large part because of the unarguably catastrophic consequences all round of a nuclear exchange (especially once both sides had become fully fledged *thermo*nuclear adversaries). Much effort was expended, however, on how war might come by inadvertence or miscalculation. Intriguingly, the early-1950s JIC, during the period of what I have termed the high Cold War, thought that those in Washington whose instincts told them World War III had to be fought before the adversary became even more intimidating had their counterparts in Moscow.

In a February 1951 appraisal for its readers on the 'Likelihood of Total War with the Soviet Union up to the End of 1954', the committee declared:

. . . we cannot exclude the possibility that the Soviet leaders may consider the immense scale of American rearmament [stimulated by the surge of anxiety following the Korean War] and the rearmament of Western Germany to be a direct threat to the security of the Soviet Union and may decide that their best course is to start a total war before Western rearmament becomes effective. Such a war might be 'preventive' in the strict sense, that is, intended to forestall a Western attack which they genuinely believed to be inevitable; or, alternatively, it might be undertaken because they feared that once Western rearmament became effective, further Communist expansion would be impossible; or for a combination of both reasons.[128]

The JIC saw a malign fusion of timing on the part of the pre-emptive schools of thought within the two superpowers: 'The period of greatest danger appears to be about the end of 1952 when American and West German rearmament cannot yet have become fully effective and by which time the Soviet Union will have in part made good some of its major deficiencies and will have accumulated a stock of atomic bombs.'[129] Despite this nightmare possibility of war for fear of war, the JIC, true to form, reassured its customers that: 'Provided the Western Powers can combine resolution with restraint' – i.e. sensible if illusion-free containment – 'there should be no total war during the next four years.'[130]

It took the huge step change in destructive power from atomic weapons to hydrogen bombs, which by the end of 1954 both superpowers had completed[131] (and the British had decided to take as soon as possible, as we shall see in Chapter 2), effectively to remove from the minds of British intelligence the possibility of deliberate, pre-emptive strikes. In mid-1955 the JIC reckoned that the Soviets' nuclear stockpile was already sufficient 'to cause very major damage to the UK' and to parts of the USA; that the fabled 175 divisions were now well trained, well equipped, well led and in a condition of high morale; that the Soviet navy was now comparable in size to NATO's, though still lacking aircraft carriers. Nevertheless, '[t]he probability is that the present [post-Stalin] Soviet leaders have realised the full implications of nuclear war and have come to the conclusion that general war at present would involve mutual annihilation.'[132]

The JIC had been tasked in 1954 to produce an estimate of the likely H-bomb assault on the UK in such a general war and, strongly influenced by its report on this theme of January 1955, Whitehall's home defence planners rethought fundamentally previous calculations of the prospects for national survival.* And for all the ghastly reassurance the prospect

---

* As we shall see in Chapter 4.

of mutual annihilation might provide (not least by banishing what had been seen as that late-1952 possibility of resolving the Cold War through pre-emptive strike), the possibility of mistakes and misperceptions continued to haunt the JIC assessments, including that of September 1955:

It is unlikely that the Soviet leaders think that the Western Powers will launch a premeditated attack on the Soviet Union. They may think, however, that there is a danger of war breaking out as a result of miscalculation . . .[133]

Just over a year later, the twin crises of Suez and Hungary suggested that a combination of destabilizing events and the rise in global tension that ensued might tip the balance of possibility towards global war.

The JIC expressed this with stark clarity in a special assessment amid the ruins of the Hungarian uprising and the Suez affair. In mid-December 1956, it informed its customers that:

The present world tension comes from civil disturbances and/or war in two areas. The events leading up to the warfare in the two areas were unrelated but the trouble came to a head more or less simultaneously; this has had the effect of heightening the tension and hardening relations between the West and the Soviet Bloc. Events in the satellites and the Middle East have given rise to instability in both areas, which will certainly last for several months and which could last much longer. While this instability exists the incidence of events causing international friction is likely to be greater than it was before last October, and the possibilities of one side taking action, the effects of which might be other than they had expected, will be greater.[134]

Hungary had demonstrated

the view we have always held that the Soviet leaders would go to almost any lengths to retain their hold on the Satellites . . . Any action by the West to assist a Satellite to free itself from Soviet domination would be likely to result in violent Soviet reaction, and, through a confused series of events, including threats and counter threats made under mounting nervous pressure, could lead up to a global war.

So, according to JIC doctrine, there would be a grave risk in any notion of a liberation crusade if future Hungarys erupted. 'Unless the political situation changes in some completely unexpected fashion (such as through the emergence of more aggressive Soviet leaders)', NATO and the doctrine of containment, whereby 'the West maintains its strength and cohesion and continues to act with restraint', should together hold the peace. The JIC continued to believe in the aftermath of the accumulated traumas of October–November 1956 in the Middle East and Mitteleuropa 'that the Soviet leaders do not want war, but . . . the chances of global war arising through a chain of circumstances and miscalculations have somewhat increased'.[135]

When we examine the simulations and scenarios which underpinned the actual, Whitehall, transition-to-war exercise (INVALUABLE),* we will see that it was just such a shift to a hard-line leadership in Moscow that triggered the events which culminated in the simulation of the path to World War III. By coincidence, though long-planned, INVALUABLE was exercised in the aftermath of the next Hungary – the Soviet suppression of the 'Prague Spring' in August 1968.

What of the moment when nervous pressure mounted to greater heights than at any previous or subsequent stage in the Cold War – the Cuban missile crisis of October 1962? Alban Webb's researches have shown how as early as 1957, the JIC envisaged the possibility of a Cuban-style crisis. The committee's forecasters thought the Soviet Union might 'be prepared in extreme cases to send "volunteer" formations' to a sympathetic country outside the bloc and the Russians 'might well feel their policies and prestige would suffer a serious blow if they failed to respond to a request for help . . . by making nuclear weapons available to . . . [a] . . . non-Communist Power'.[136] As Webb noted, the JIC lost sight of the possibility of Russia overreaching in this fashion, leading to escalation, confrontation and possible global war, and did not return to it even after Castro's seizure of power in Cuba in 1959. The focus of the JIC's collective eyes tended to be absorbed by the regular hot spots.

By the early weeks of 1962, when the JIC took a forward look at 'The Likelihood of War with the Soviet Union up to 1966', British intelligence was case-hardened by its constant fixations with the chance of war erupting over Berlin (which had only recently begun to emerge, though not yet

* See Chapter 6.

fully, from the protracted crisis of 1958–61, when Khrushchev presented the Western powers with a series of deadlines for a conference to resolve all difficulties associated with that city's four-power occupation) and through a possibility of toxic combinations in the Middle East. Despite the recent perils of the Berlin confrontation (armed American and Russian tanks facing each other, feet apart, at Checkpoint Charlie being the image, second only to the Berlin Wall itself, which is scored most deeply into the historical memory[137]), the JIC continued to believe the stakes were vastly too high for either side to contemplate deliberate and major war.

The immense latent power of each other's nuclear arsenals, and their state of readiness, had, by this stage, added new levels to old anxieties. It was the danger of 'accident and miscalculation' which now represented the great preoccupation of British intelligence. In that short hiatus between the Berlin and Cuban crises, the JIC concluded:

Even when there is no particular political tension each side now has a proportion of its nuclear strike forces constantly at immediate alert. There must always be a risk, however remote, that by pure mechanical or electrical accident one of the missiles might be launched; or that through misunderstanding one might be launched by human agency without this being the intention of the Government concerned; or that one side might interpret the evidence of its early warning devices to mean that an attack had been launched by the other when in fact this was not so. We believe that the Soviet leaders are as aware as the West of the possibility of such accidents and take equally elaborate precautions to prevent them.[138]

Setting aside the notion of war-by-accident, the JIC, on the assumption 'that the Soviet leaders act rationally', saw the possibility of war-through-miscalculation erupting due to the lighting of three fuses: if

(a) the Soviet Union or the West in some critical or tense situation were to make a false appreciation of what was considered by the other side to be intolerable; or
(b) the Soviet Union or the West were to believe wrongly that the other had weakened in its determination to use nuclear weapons if pressed too far; or
(c) either side were to fail accurately to foresee the consequences of the policies being pursued by a third party with which it was associated.[139]

Elements of each of these were bound up in the Cuban crisis seven months later, from the moment when US reconnaissance U2 flights suggested that new missile sites under construction in Cuba could be for something bigger and nastier than air-defence weapons.[140]

Interestingly enough, the JIC had included Cuba as an example in its explanatory paragraph on third-party triggers of a war-through-miscalculation. Crises involving third countries created

a particular risk that one side might fail accurately to recognise that the situation was becoming one which the other side would consider intolerable. The chances of such dangerous situations arising in future will be increased if recent Soviet expressions of support for 'national liberation wars' mean a greater willingness to intervene in such disputes. By this term Soviet leaders apparently mean risings against Western colonial powers (e.g., Algeria) or rebellion against 'reactionary' pro-Western regimes (e.g., Castro's revolt). They have described such hostilities as 'just' and 'inevitable' and have said that it is the duty of the Soviet Union to support them, though they have not made clear the nature and extent of this support.[141]

The committee concluded that if 'general nuclear war arose through miscalculation it would probably be preceded by a period of limited hostilities, however short'.[142]

As the Cuban crisis moved into its acute phase on 22 October 1962, when sixteen medium-range ballistic missile sites 'appeared to be operational' to US intelligence,[143] the intolerability of Khrushchev's move on Castro's terrain became obvious to the United States. In the words of a JIC assessment of 26 October, it was apparent that, if nuclear warheads were fitted to them, 'the overall Soviet initial launch capability against the US will have increased significantly to the end of 1962'.[144] Dr Len Scott has emphasized how the routine flight off Alaska of a CIA reconnaissance U2 on 27 October 1962 went wrong when the plane drifted into Siberian airspace, causing Soviet MiGs to be scrambled to shoot it down and US F-102s sent up to protect it. Mercifully the F-102s reached the spy plane first and escorted it back safely. If they had not, with the level of tension prevailing, who knows what would have happened if the Soviets had treated this as the last reconnaissance flight before a pre-emptive American strike against Russia.[145]

As the JIC compiled its private inquest into Cuba[146] and the war planners began their post-Cuba review of 'War Book' and readiness procedures,* government ministers admitted in Parliament that 'we were very near the edge'[147] during the crisis that almost came out of nowhere. As an old man, Macmillan suffered recurrent nightmares of Cuba having gone wrong.[148]

British intelligence, however, true to form, was a soother rather than an inflamer of ministerial and military minds during the Cuban missile crisis. One of the days of greatest tension, Saturday 27 October 1962 when Macmillan authorized the V-bombers to be placed on Alert Condition 3 (i.e. fifteen minutes' readiness at the end of their Lincolnshire runways),[149] the JIC produced an assessment of 'Possible Soviet Responses to a US Decision to Bomb or Invade Cuba' calculated to defuse any notions that East and West were on an irreversible march to and over the brink. The report could well have reinforced Macmillan's desire to avoid provocative moves such as ordering the V-bombers to their dispersed airfields or any other overt preparations for war.[150]

The picture the JIC presented was of a Russian leader, Khrushchev, behaving in a 'relatively moderate' fashion over the five days since President Kennedy had gone on television to announce the presence of Soviet missile sites on Cuba and to tell the world that this shift in the balance of power could not be tolerated by the United States. The turning back of their missile-carrying freighters had already amounted to 'a considerable climbdown and to a loss of face' on the Russians' part. It could well be that the Soviet Union's placing of a new offensive capability on Cuba in the first place might have been prompted by its leadership's awareness 'of an overall strategic inferiority vis-à-vis the US'.[151] The JIC did not see Khrushchev's response to a US attack on Cuba as the much planned for snuffing out of the Western position in Berlin 'in view of the clear warning from the US that this would bring about a full confrontation. Indeed, central to Soviet thinking in deciding upon their reply will be their fear of doing anything that might escalate into general nuclear war.'[152]

According to the JIC, the Russians' 'most likely' armed response to

---

* Which we will examine in Chapter 4.

a US move against Cuba 'will be a tit-for-tat as nearly parallel as possible to the US action. It seems unlikely, therefore, that they will attack directly either US territory or the territory of the NATO powers. The closest parallel would appear to be a US base in some third country or an attack on some major US naval vessel.'[153] Here, as at so many other moments post-1945, one sees the antithesis of any crude portrayals of British intelligence as being the captive of inflamed Cold Warriors. The files, taken together, do justify the overall conclusion of their earliest appraiser, Dr Alex Craig, that: 'There was . . . no attempt to demonise the Soviet Union in JIC analysis.'[154] Though well aware of their failure to *predict* many of the great Cold War episodes except, at best, in terms of general possibility, Craig nonetheless was right to emphasize 'the broad success of JIC threat assessment' during the early and middle Cold War years as the top deck of British intelligence was neither 'alarmist' nor did it 'underestimate the scale of the Soviet threat'.[155]

Much of the inflamed view of British intelligence as a force for reaction comes from the notion of the character and political thinking of some secret service figures such as George Kennedy Young, who reached the number two position in MI6,[156] or Peter Wright, still the most notorious counter-intelligence officer MI5 has ever produced.[157] There is something in this unnerving portrait. A very accomplished Whitehall figure, with long association with the secret world, has said of some parts of the 1950s and 1960s Secret Intelligence Service, 'they were very right wing' (he had in mind a section called Special Political Action which tried to influence the press).[158]

Imagery is a problem for any treatment of the Queen's secret servants. Quite apart from our own rich and widely read spy literature and the reach and grip of the Bond films on the global imagination, other intelligence professionals have a certain idea of the British secret services. I have heard a senior figure in the secret world of an allied country declare, once the senior intelligence operators of East and West began to pool experience in the early 1990s, that MI6 was the service the Russians regarded as their toughest and worthiest opponent.[159] Ten years after the end of the Cold War, the head of a secret service in a former Soviet bloc country talked to me of his huge admiration for 'the British intelligence services, with their great traditions, which have been on the winning side in the *three* wars of the twentieth century'.[160] A former chief of SIS once explained what a huge asset such impressions remained. Such is the image of the service around the world that when one of his officers, after a long and careful cultivation of a potential agent, finally revealed himself or herself and made the pass, the object of their attention would often 'virtually stand-to-attention, such was the honour'.[161]

There is one former member of his service who, I think, I would place alongside the best of the JIC's analysts in terms of balance and restraint. He was the MI6 officer, operating undercover in the Moscow Embassy in the autumn of 1962, responsible for running the most important human agent the West possessed throughout the early Cold War, Colonel Oleg Penkovsky. Veterans of those days still describe Penkovsky in terms of pure gold and stress that 'we had him at the crucial time'[162] of hyper-anxiety about nuclear weapons and the possibility of war as a bolt-from-the-blue. Penkovsky had been arrested by the Soviet authorities on 22 October 1962 at the moment the world became aware of the possible linkage between Cuba and Armageddon. The KGB did not immediately announce his capture. But various things convinced his MI6 controller that something was amiss and ignored messages which would usually have summoned him to a crash meeting with Penkovsky.

On 2 November 1962, nearly a week after the Cuban missile crisis had eased (but when British V-bombers still stood on Alert Condition 3[163]), a prearranged set of noises came down the MI6 officer's telephone which Penkovsky was to use if and when a Soviet nuclear attack on the West was imminent (three blows of breath, repeated in another call one minute later). Shortly before he died, I asked Gervase Cowell, the SIS man who took the call, what he did on hearing those sounds. Certain that Penkovsky was captive and had had information extracted from him about call-signs, rendezvous and so on, Cowell decided to do nothing (the delphic Mr Cowell did not elaborate upon how he reached this conclusion). He alerted neither his ambassador, Sir Frank Roberts, nor his chief in London, Sir Dick White.[164] Mr Cowell, a small, humorous, unassuming man, delivered himself of this recollection without personal grandeur or historical drama. He is, however, the only man I have ever met who has found himself in such a precarious and classically Cold War position. For the bomb made error so terrible and potentially terminal virtually from the beginning to end of the East–West confrontation. It was the nuclear question, and what it might mean to the UK as either the receiver or deliverer of the ultimate weapon, that placed an awesome, mushroom-shaped shadow over the Cabinet Room from Attlee's time onwards.

2

The Importance of Being Nuclear:
The Bomb and the Fear of Escalation

We must do it. It's the price we pay to sit at the top table.
Winston Churchill, 1954, on being told what it would take
for the UK to manufacture its own hydrogen bomb[1]

*Over port and brandy Harold [Macmillan] held forth. The
great thing for a country was to be rich as we were in the
nineteenth century, he mused; and why should we not give
up spending millions on atom bombs, why should we not
give up Singapore, sell the colonies, sell the West Indies too
to America, and just sit back and be rich?*
Harold Macmillan, as recorded by Cynthia Gladwyn after
dinner in the British Embassy in Paris, December 1956,
shortly before becoming Prime Minister[2]

*Because with the submarine [Polaris] system the deterrent
remains constantly at sea, a blunting attack against the fleet
is not feasible. Nor would attack against communications
frustrate retaliation . . . there is very much to be said for a
system which is quietly unobtrusive, secure in a relaxed way
and ultimate in its bulldog-like determination to retaliate
if the homeland is attacked. The submarine system seems
in every way compatible with the British character. Let us
have it.*
Joint Inter-Services Group for the Study of All Out War,
'U.K. EYES ONLY', 'A New Strategic Deterrent for the
UK', June 1960[3]

The Committee has been told that Polaris or Polaris-type missiles do not have Union Jacks or Stars and Stripes on them.

Lord Rothschild, minority opinion appended to the Kings
Norton Report, July 1968[4]

Singapore has gone, the colonies and the West Indies, too, long disposed of, if not sold. Yet as the twentieth century turned into the twenty-first, there was still a highly sophisticated nuclear submarine, huge, silent and undetectable, being driven at a fast walking pace in a thoroughly British way by a Royal Navy crew somewhere between Scotland and Murmansk armed with a sheaf of Trident missiles, not one of which, if fired, could be distinguished by Russian (or anybody else's) radars from their US Navy counterparts. Continuing secrecy still prevents a precise costing of the British nuclear weapons programme from the moment Attlee's Cabinet committee, GEN 163, authorized the manu-facture of the first UK bomb in January 1947, to now. But, by the late 1980s, it had probably absorbed between £40 and £50 billion all told.[5] As I write, it is government policy to go for a so-called 'Trident upgrade' to keep a British deterrent in being until the 2050s. The nuclear impulse plainly remains part of what the anthropologist Clifford Geertz might have called the 'deep play'[6] of successive British governments. No UK administration would now seek to acquire a nuclear weapons capabil-ity if the UK did not possess one, but, so far, it has never seemed quite the right moment to dispose of it, even though in the mid- to late 1960s, there was a group of ministers for whom abandonment was at least a possibility, as we shall shortly see.

I have written elsewhere on the inner group/machinery of govern-ment aspects of the handling of nuclear weapons policy from Attlee to Blair.[7] For the purposes of this study, I shall concentrate on the reasons given at various stages in the years between 1947 and 1968 for the importance of becoming, and remaining, nuclear. In the UK context, this was, and still is, significant in several senses. A nation is changed both when it decides to make a nuclear bomb and at the point it has acquired a serious capability to deliver usable weapons in strength (roughly speaking 1947 and 1957 in the British case). Secondly, and more widely, the Cold War, like no conflict before or since, was soaked in the nuclear factor in a manner that everyone, expert or inexpert, could understand. If it had come to it, and the nuclear taboo which had held since the atomic bomb fell on Nagasaki on 9 August 1945 was broken, the world, or at least what was left of it if East and West had unleashed their arsenals against each other, would have been transformed for ever. Thirdly, the question arose in 1947 (and still does) of the utility to the UK of retaining an individual nuclear weapons capability usable, as a last resort, outside the NATO alliance (which came into being just over two years after Attlee and his Cabinet committee had decided to make an atomic bomb). And finally, the capacity to retaliate against a Soviet bloc attack with nuclear weapons became the political, psychological and, above all, financial reason for *not* creating a serious civil defence system in Britain. This imperative held good from the anxious weeks following the start of the Berlin airlift in the summer of 1948 (as we shall see in Chapter 4) to early October 1989 when Mikhail Gorbachev told the East German leader Erich Honecker that Soviet troops based in the GDR would *not* be available for internal repression (the rupture of the Wall following on 9 November).[8]

In 1945 the new Labour Prime Minister, Clement Attlee, knew full well that the bombs dropped on Hiroshima and Nagasaki, to whose research and construction the British had made a considerable contribution,[9] had changed the world. By the end of August 1945 he had put his thoughts on paper: 'It is difficult for people to adjust their minds to an entirely new situation . . .', he wrote. 'Even the modern conception of war to which in my lifetime we have become accustomed is now completely out of date . . . it would appear that the provision of bomb-proof basements in factories and offices and the retention of ARP [Air Raid Precautions] and Fire Services is just futile waste . . . The answer to an atomic bomb on London is an atomic bomb on another great city.'[10] Brian Cathcart has traced how what was for Attlee in the first weeks of his premiership the imperative of a 'new World Order', to prevent war by controlling through international means this dreadful new invention, gradually succumbed to reality as did his inner group of ministers on GEN 75, the Cabinet Committee on Atomic Energy, to whose members he distributed his August 1945 paper. By the time his GEN 163 group met in January 1947 for the first and only time, it was evident to Attlee that Britain must go it alone and manufacture its own atomic weapon in a vexing world replete with continuing British global responsibilities and with the United States unwilling to sustain the wartime nuclear collaboration.[11]

The Chiefs of Staff, wishing, in Sir Michael Howard's phrase, to have 'every club in the bag',[12] including atomic weapons (and never starry-eyed about the possibility of international control of the weapon), were working in the last months of 1945, in the words of the 18 December meeting of GEN 75, on 'a report on our requirements for atomic bombs and the possibility of making consequential reductions in other forms of armament production'. At the same meeting the Cabinet committee approved the construction of a first pile to produce plutonium – indispensable to the making of a Nagasaki-type weapon.[13] Though GEN 75 heard on this occasion (and later) some ministers' concerns about the 'heavy demands' that the construction of two possible piles would make 'upon the capacity of the chemical engineering and heavy electrical industries, both of whom were of great importance to the revival of our export trade',[14] there is what might be called an atomic bias detectable in GEN 75's deliberations from this point on.

Within less than a year, the passage of the McMahon Act by the US Congress in August 1946 prohibiting collaboration with *any* other country (even the Manhattan Project partners – Britain and Canada), meant that if the UK did go ahead with its bomb, it would be a more costly and difficult business because American industrial know-how (rather than the science of the bomb, which was in the heads of the returning UK team that had worked alongside the Americans at Los Alamos), would be denied the British weaponeers. Added to this would be the cost of developing the jet bombers needed to deliver the British weapon. The RAF was already planning what became the V-force in the autumn of 1946 with its specification for an aircraft capable of carrying a single 'special bomb' of 10,000 pounds weight 'to a target 2000 nautical miles from a base which may be anywhere in the world'.[15]

There may have been a bias towards procuring the biggest conceivable 'club in the bag' to place at the disposal of a future British Prime

Minister, but the leading economic ministers on GEN 75 – Hugh Dalton, Chancellor of the Exchequer, and Sir Stafford Cripps, President of the Board of Trade – put up a fight against acquiring it in the autumn of 1946, smoking out as they did so Ernest Bevin, the hugely powerful Foreign Secretary, who was compelled to give his unvarnished reasons for wanting a British bomb at all costs.

Dalton and Cripps took their stand when GEN 75 was informed that the Ministry of Supply (the bomb-making department) needed £30–40 million over four or five years to build a gaseous diffusion plant for the production of uranium 235. According to Sir Michael Perrin (present at GEN 75 for the Ministry of Supply alongside his boss, Lord Portal, the former wartime Chief of the Air Staff, now the Ministry's Controller of Production of Atomic Energy), Dalton and Cripps were doing well until Bevin waddled late into the Cabinet Room, explaining he had eaten a heavy lunch and had fallen asleep.[16]

The sparse minutes of GEN 75 capture the Dalton/Cripps line:

In discussion it was urged that we must consider seriously whether we could afford to divert from civilian consumption and the restoration of our balance of payments the economic resources required for a project on this scale. Unless present trends were reversed we might find ourselves faced with an extremely serious economic and financial situation in two to three years' time.[17]

Sir Dennis Rickett's note of Bevin's rejoinder certainly does not do justice to the Foreign Secretary's virtuoso, British bulldog performance. 'On the other hand,' the minutes record,

it was argued that we could not afford to be left behind in a field which was of such revolutionary importance from an industrial, no less than from a military point of view. Our prestige in the world, as well as our chances of securing American co-operation [i.e. by restoring the collaboration severed by the McMahon Act] would both suffer if we did not exploit to the full a discovery in which we had played a leading part at the outset.[18]

According to Perrin, Bevin's intervention countering the Dalton/Cripps argument was less grammatical but much more potent. 'No, Prime Minister, that won't do at all. We've *got* to have this,' he declared. 'I don't mind for myself, but I don't want any other Foreign Secretary of this country to be talked at, or to, by the Secretary of State in the United States as I just have in my discussions with Mr Byrnes. We've got to have this thing over here, whatever it costs. We've got to have the bloody Union Jack on top of it.'[19] Bevin prevailed and, two generations on, there is still a White Ensign (to be precise) metaphorically on top of it.

On the last day of 1946, Portal circulated a minute arguing that 'a decision is required about the development of Atomic weapons in this country. The Service Departments are beginning to move in the matter . . .'[20] Attlee agreed and during the first days of 1947 convened another special 'Atomic Energy' Cabinet committee for the purpose. GEN 163 consisted of Attlee and five other ministers but *not* Dalton and Cripps, the GEN 75 awkward squad.[21] The nuclear quintet were Bevin, Herbert Morrison (Lord President), A. V. Alexander (Minister of Defence), Lord Addison (Dominions Secretary) and John Wilmot (Minister of Supply). When GEN 163 met at No. 10 on the afternoon of 8 January 1947, Bevin once more pursued his American-related concerns. The minutes do not record anyone specifically mentioning Russia or the Soviet threat, though Stalin *is* there by implication in Bevin's reference to 'other countries':

THE FOREIGN SECRETARY said that in his view it was important that we should press on with the study of all aspects of atomic energy. We could not afford to acquiesce in an American monopoly of this new development. Other countries also might well develop atomic weapons. Unless therefore an effective international system could be developed under which the production and use of the weapon would be prohibited, we must develop it ourselves.[22]

Attlee is not minuted as having given his views to GEN 163. But recalling the decision in later life, he took a decidedly Bevin-like line. 'We had to hold up our position *vis-à-vis* the Americans. We couldn't allow ourselves wholly to be in their hands, and their position wasn't awfully clear always,' he explained to his former press secretary, Francis Williams. 'At that time we had to bear in mind that there was always the possibility of their withdrawing and becoming isolationist once again. The manufacture of a British atom bomb was therefore at that stage essential to our defence.'[23] From the moment of atomic creation, the doctrine of unripe time fused powerfully with the importance of being nuclear. It would do so again. As Attlee told Williams, 'we had to face the world as it was'.[24]

The nastiness of the world and the unreliability of the Americans were what drove Churchill, too, in the late spring and early summer of 1954 when he had to contemplate choreographing his ministerial colleagues through the very considerable leap from atomic to hydrogen bombs. He did so in the knowledge that the most recent US test ('Bravo' in the Pacific in May 1954[25]) produced, as the Chiefs of Staff informed his nuclear-loop of ministers, an explosion 'approximately 1,500 times more powerful' than the atomic bomb. To this the Chiefs appended a warning that 'There is no theoretical limit to the destructive power which can be achieved with the latest techniques.'[26]

The awesomeness of that particular piece of analysis made 1954 the pivotal year for all the nuclear-related aspects of the secret state. It forced interlocking reappraisals right across the policy spectrum, from the nature and scope of the UK nuclear weapons programme and its place within defence strategy as a whole, through civil defence and the wider 'home defence' concept in which it was couched, to the durability of the post-nuclear attack British state itself. And it was unsurprisingly Sir Norman Brook, that guarantor of joined-up secret government in the UK of the high Cold War, who saw this and on 12 March 1954 summoned a super-sensitive meeting of the permanent, inner guardians of the bomb-touched realm in his room at the Cabinet Office to ponder the implications.[27]

Brook's group consisted of Edwin Plowden from the nascent Atomic Energy Authority; two scientists, Sir John Cockcroft from Harwell and Sir William Penney from Aldermaston; plus a trio of crown servants from the Ministry of Defence led by one of its deputy secretaries, Sir Richard Powell. Brook opened by saying that this was a preliminary gathering ahead of a meeting a week later at which the Chiefs of Staff would be briefed on 'the latest available information concerning the development of the hydrogen bomb' by both the United States and the Soviet Union. Brook 'believed that the development of this bomb had now reached a stage which required us to re-assess first, our foreign policy and general strategy and, thereafter, the "size and shape" of the Armed Forces, our civil defence policy and our atomic weapons programme'.[28] He asked Penney, recently returned from the United States, to brief the meeting on the latest American and Russian technology.

Penney's presentation is the reason the minutes of Brook's gathering took so long to appear at the Public Record Office, as did the Chiefs of Staff paper which I quoted above,[29] which was circulated on 1 June after the Chiefs and their planners had absorbed the new material and pondered its implications. Penney took Brook's group through the steps the USA and the Soviet Union had taken, and were taking, to thermo-nuclear status. In 1952 the Americans 'had exploded a 14 megaton bomb' (the 'Mike' device) at Eniwetok in the Pacific. In August 1953 the Russians had tested a 1-megaton bomb.

Penney explained the difference between them:

There were two forms of hydrogen bomb – a 'hybrid' bomb and a 'true' hydrogen bomb. The 'hybrid' bomb was something like the earlier atomic bomb but 'boosted' with lithium deuteride. The Russians had developed a 'hybrid' bomb . . . in 1953. The 'true' hydrogen bomb was a new departure: it involved a series of chain-reactions which at the last stage produced very fast neutrons; and in theory there was no limit to the size of explosion which could be produced by a bomb of this type. Moreover, it used uranium or thorium, not plutonium, as the main explosive element; and was highly economical in its use of fissionable material. Its cost was therefore relatively low (about £1.5 to £2 millions a bomb).[30]

The Russians, Penney added, 'were likely to develop the "true" hydrogen bomb before long' and it would be possible to detect when they had from the magnitude of the explosion.[31] (The Soviets reached this point in November 1955, dropping 'Joe 19' from a Tupolev bomber over the Semipalatinsk test site in Kazakhstan, which yielded 1.6 mega-tons[32] and was deemed a 'true' H-bomb by Western analysts[33].)

Penney, who had a great gift for explaining the highly technical and the complicated to a lay listener,[34] painted two vivid word-pictures for Brook's group on the effect of a 'true' and a 'hybrid' bomb on the area they could see from the Cabinet Secretary's window that March morn-ing. First a 5-megaton 'true':

A bomb dropped on London and bursting on impact would produce a crater ¾ mile across and 150ft deep, and a fire-ball of 2¼ miles diameter. The blast from it would crush the Admiralty Citadel [a stone-clad World War II signals centre across Horse Guards Parade next to the Mall – which is still there] at a distance of 1 mile. Suburban houses would be wrecked at a distance of 3 miles from the explosion, and they would lose their roofs and be badly blasted at a distance of 7 miles. All habitations would catch fire over a circle of 2 miles radius from the burst.[35]

Next, the impact of a 'hybrid' of 1 megaton (i.e. the most lethal yet devised by the Russians):

It would produce a crater 1,000-yds across and 150-ft deep; the Admiralty Citadel would be wrecked at a distance of 1,200 yds from the point of burst, houses would be wrecked at 2 miles, and bad blast would be experienced at 4 miles.[36]

Brook's meeting felt that: 'Whatever progress the Russians might make from now on in developing the hydrogen bomb, we should be justified in advising ministers now that the Russians had already developed the material for an attack on this country, the intensity of which far exceeded our previous assumptions and the plans which we had based on them.'[37]

All this had a profound effect on Churchill. He made the easement of the Cold War, and the pursuit of a summit meeting to engineer this before thermonuclear destruction engulfed the world, the centrepiece of his last years in No. 10. He would regale ministers with 'Gibbonesque' (Harold Macmillan's description) soliloquies about 'the most terrible and destructive engine of mass warfare yet known to mankind'.[38] For him, a *British* H-bomb was crucial to his and his successors' capacity to shift the two superpowers towards a safer world.

At some point before Brook's meeting with the scientists and officials, Churchill had his session with Edwin Plowden, which Lord Plowden recalled many years later for the BBC radio documentary *A Bloody Union Jack on Top of It*. 'I got a minute from the Prime Minister, from Churchill,' Plowden told me,

saying to let him know what it would cost, what effort would be necessary to develop and manufacture hydrogen bombs. And under the direction of Bill Penney and the collaboration of Hinton [the third of the 'atomic knights', as Penney, Cockcroft and he were known in Whitehall; Hinton ran the factories making fissile material for the weapons] and Cockcroft, I was given the answer to his question, and I went to see Churchill in his room in the House of Commons after lunch, and when I'd explained what the effort necessary would be he paused for a time, and nodded his head, and said in that well-known voice of his, 'We must do it. It's the price we pay to sit at the top table.' And having said that, he got up and tied a little black ribbon round his eyes, and lay down on his bed in his room, and went to sleep.[39]

Brook concluded the meeting, in his characteristically tidy and action-orientated way, with an explanation that:

He had already suggested to the Prime Minister that it was necessary to re-assess, in the light of the new information about the hydrogen bomb, the following points:

(i) The likelihood of war.
(ii) The form which war was most likely to take if it came.
(iii) The changes which would need to be made in the pattern of our defence arrangements, active and passive, in order to adjust them to meet the most likely contingency.
(iv) The extent to which we should ensure [insure?] against the possibility that war might take some other form than that which now seemed most likely.[40]

Brook had also briefed Churchill that the existing atomic weapons programme had to be reassessed. The Cabinet Secretary urged that the various studies should be parcelled out to the Chiefs and the relevant departments, and that a small ministerial committee should oversee the whole swathe of activity.[41]

Churchill followed his advice and involved the full Cabinet to an unusual degree in the later stages in July 1954. Before this, the shadow of the H-bomb darkened two Cabinet committees. First, GEN 464, which met in mid-April to approve moves to acquire the raw material needed for a British H-bomb ahead of the actual decision to make one (there was a sense of urgency here as the Americans were buying up great quantities of thorium[42]). Churchill told the five colleagues he placed on GEN 464 (Anthony Eden, Foreign Secretary; R. A. Butler, Chancellor of the Exchequer; Lord Alexander, Minister of Defence; Lord Swinton, Commonwealth Secretary; and Lord Salisbury, Lord President) 'that he would like to invite the Cabinet at an early date to decide in principle that hydrogen bombs should be made in the United Kingdom', and the meeting agreed this.[43]

Churchill took the thermonuclear question through another stage between GEN 464 and the full Cabinet which only recently have scholars been able to reconstruct. For several years I thought it was the regular, standing Defence Committee of the Cabinet which had taken the interim decision to go ahead on 16 June 1954.[44] If I had read the Cabinet minutes for 7 July 1954 more carefully, I would have realized that the ministerial group cited as having done this was a different configuration – the Defence *Policy* Committee (my emphasis).[45]*

DPC was essentially a fusion of Churchill's GEN 464 inner group with the Home Secretary, the junior service ministers and the Chiefs of Staff added and brought together to consider defence spending in the round (the H-bomb in particular) and to consider the substantial new study from the Chiefs and their briefers on 'United Kingdom Defence Policy'.[46] DPC confronted a dilemma. Churchill wanted both spending cuts *and* a new H-bomb (the final results of this protracted exercise were published nearly three years later in the famous Sandys Defence White Paper which so alarmed many of those who went on to form the Campaign for Nuclear Disarmament).†

Churchill concluded the DPC meeting of 20 May 1954 with a hugely interesting *tour de force* which blended a whole variety of other elements with the economy theme – including the 'top table' requirement and the anxiety about the Eisenhower administration's possible inclination for a pre-emptive war. Brook allowed himself to draft a minute which did not muffle Churchillian cadence or curtail his grand sweep:

THE PRIME MINISTER, summing up the discussion, said that the difficulties of choice which lay before the Committee had been put boldly

---

* My student, Alban Webb, brought this to my attention in early 2001 when, at last, the minutes of the DPC were declassified.
† As we shall see in the next chapter.

forward. The problem was to decide what practical steps could be taken to effect the saving of £200 million a year, with the least risk of weakening our influence in the world, or endangering our security. Influence depended on possession of force. If the United States were tempted to undertake a fore-stalling war, we could not hope to remain neutral. Even if we could, such a war would in any event determine our fate. We must avoid any action which would weaken our power to influence United States policy. We must avoid anything which might be represented as a sweeping act of disarmament. If, however, we were able to show that in a few years' time we should be possessed of great offensive power, and that we should be ready to take our part in a world struggle, he thought it would not be impossible to reconcile reductions in defence expenditure with the maintenance of our influence in world councils.[47]

Here was the bloody-Union-Jack-on-top-of-it syndrome with a vengeance. The bomb as the salvation for a great power seriously on the slide in terms of its finances and its armed forces relative to the superpowers; go thermonuclear and thereby both save money *and* increase your relative clout in the world. The atomic knights had shown it was within budget at £1.5 to £2 million per bomb. The Chiefs of Staff's memorandum for the DPC ministers a couple of weeks later pushed this notion even more forcefully than had Churchill by combining the indispensability of nuclear deterrence with the irreplaceable presence of British experience at the top table – '. . . we must maintain and strengthen our position as a world power so that Her Majesty's Government can exercise a powerful influence in the counsels of the world'. And, in a section on 'deductions' to be drawn from the new thermonuclear world which must have brought a glow to Churchill as he read on, the Chiefs (Admiral of the Fleet Sir Rhoderick McGrigor; Field Marshal Sir John Harding; and Air Chief Marshal Sir William Dickson) declared:

(a) Short of sacrificing our vital interests or principles, we must do everything possible to prevent global war which would inevitably entail the exposure of the United Kingdom to a devastating nuclear bombardment.
(b) The ability to wage war with the most up-to-date nuclear weapons will be the measure of military power in the future.

(c) Our scientific skill and technological capacity to produce the hydrogen weapon puts within our grasp the ability *to be on terms* [emphasis added] with the United States and Russia.[48]

This document is one of the most significant to be produced by the Chiefs in the mid-1950s as Churchill allowed it to be circulated to the full Cabinet as a Cabinet Paper on 23 July 1954[49] (though one piece of information was deemed too sensitive to be divulged to them all – the number of H-bombs the UK was forecast to be likely to have by 1959 (10) and 1960 (20) 'if production were started now'[50]).

The Chiefs did not spare their ministerial readers on what would await the UK if deterrence failed. If H-bombs, each one 1,000 times more powerful than the A-bomb, were dropped on ten UK cities, 'the death roll would be . . . 12 millions'. However good the developments in our defence in coming years, complete protection against these weapons was impossible. And the fear of escalation was present from the moment Churchill and his ministers pondered the thermonuclear world.

Each member of the Cabinet was invited by the Chiefs of Staff to peer into the abyss:

We have given much thought to the highly speculative question whether, if global warfare should break out, there might initially be mutually acceptable restrictions on the use of nuclear weapons. We have come to the conclusion that, if war came in the next few years, the United States would insist on the immediate use of the full armoury of nuclear weapons with the object of dealing the Russians a quick knock-out blow. We must therefore plan on the assumption that, if war becomes global, nuclear bombardment will become general.[51]

The Chiefs, however, drawing avowedly on the resources of the Joint Intelligence Committee, were able to calm ministers' anxieties about the 'likelihood of war', but it was going to be a long haul:

(a) Russia is most unlikely to provoke war deliberately during the next few years, when the United States will be comparatively immune from Russian attack.

(b) The danger the United States might succumb to the temptation of precipitating a 'forestalling' war can not be disregarded. In view of the vulnerability of the United Kingdom we must use all our influence to prevent this.

(c) Careful judgement and restraint on the part of the Allies on a united basis will be needed to avoid the outbreak of a global war through accident or miscalculation resulting from an incident which precipitated or extended a local war . . .

(e) Even when the Russians are able to attack North America effectively, the ability of the United States to deliver a crippling attack on Russia will remain a powerful deterrent to the Soviet Government.

(f) It is most probable that the present state of 'cold war' will continue for a long time with periods of greater or lesser tension.[52]

For the 16 June meeting of DPC, the Chiefs appended an annex on 'Hydrogen Bomb Research and Production in the United Kingdom' based on a report from the Working Party on the Operational Use of Atomic Weapons.[53] Such was its sensitivity and detail on the number of weapons envisaged that it did not go to the full Cabinet with the main document.

Given the Chiefs' paper, Churchill's grand strategic sweep at the earlier meeting and the nuclear temptation (the H-Bomb as squarer of circles), it is not surprising that the Defence Policy Committee on 16 June 1954 '[a]uthorised the Lord President [the Marquess of Salisbury] and the Minister of Supply [Duncan Sandys] to initiate a programme for the production of hydrogen bombs . . .'.[54]

The full Cabinet proved more troublesome, partly because some of its members (Harry Crookshank, the Leader of the House of Commons, in particular[55]) felt that Churchill was bouncing them into a decision because 'they had had no notice that this question was to be raised', as Crookshank put it,[56] and by Churchill's introducing the item on the Cabinet agenda for 7 July 1954 with the information 'that the Defence Policy Committee had approved, on 16th June, a proposal that our atomic weapons programme should be so adjusted as to allow for the production of hydrogen bombs in this country'.[57]

Churchill had to bring the H-bomb back to Cabinet twice. On 8 July there was a substantial debate. Opting out of the nuclear race was raised (the minutes do not say by whom: 'Some of our other defence preparations were already based on the assumption that we should not engage in a major war except as an ally of the United States: could we not continue to rely on the United States to match Russia in thermo-nuclear weapons?'[58]).

Even a pre-echo of the Campaign for Nuclear Disarmament could be heard: 'Was it morally right that we should manufacture weapons with this vast destructive power? There was no doubt that a decision to make hydrogen bombs would offend the conscience of substantial numbers of people in this country. Evidence of this was to be found in the resolutions recently passed by the Methodist Conference in London.' It would be fascinating to know which of Churchill's ministers spoke for Methody.*[59]

The 'reply' and the passage which follows it, though not attributed to Churchill, sound like him. There was 'no difference in kind between atomic and thermonuclear weapons'.[60] As soon as the anxious Cabinet member received the Chiefs' paper on 22 July he or she (there was only one lady present, Florence Horsburgh, the Minister of Education) would have had his or her appreciation of the vastness of the difference under-scored. If there was a 'moral principle' involved, the Cabinet was told, 'it had already been breached by the decision of the Labour Govern-ment to make the atomic bomb'.[61]

The great power/mature-influence-at-the-top-table argument was deployed here (almost certainly by the Prime Minister himself) to quell all doubts:

No country could claim to be a leading military power unless it possessed the most up-to-date weapons; and the fact must be faced that, unless we possessed thermonuclear weapons, we should lose our influence and standing in world affairs. Strength in thermonuclear weapons would henceforth provide the most powerful deterrent to a potential aggressor; and it was our duty to make our contribution towards the building up of this deterrent influence.[62]

Churchill's anxiety about the United States, currently backing Chiang Kai Shek's Formosa in its stand-off with mainland China over

* When the Cabinet Secretary's 1954 Notebook was declassified we discovered it was Churchill himself.

the islands of Quemoy and Matsu (he would later warn Eisenhower that 'a war to keep the coastal islands for Chiang would not be defensible here'[63]), surfaced at this stage of the meeting:

It was at least possible that the development of the hydrogen bomb would have the effect of reducing the risk of major war. At present some people thought the greatest risk was that the United States might plunge the world into war, either through a misjudged intervention in Asia or in order to forestall an attack by Russia. Our best chance of preventing this was to maintain our influence with the United States Government; and they would certainly feel more respect for our views if we continued to play an effective part in building up the strength necessary to deter aggression than if we left it entirely to them to match and counter Russia's strength in thermonuclear weapons.[64]

On 16 July Churchill told the Queen that the Cabinet 'are considering whether it would be right and advantageous for this country to produce the hydrogen bomb . . . There is very little doubt in my mind what it [the decision] will be.'[65] And decide to go ahead the Cabinet finally did on 26 July 1954.[66]

Listening and learning throughout the H-bomb Cabinets was Harold Macmillan. As Minister of Housing and Local Government, he did not sit on GEN 464 or the DPC. Only when he became Churchill's Minister of Defence in October 1954 did he move inside the inner nuclear circle and it fell to him to announce in the 1955 Defence White Paper the following February that Britain was making an H-bomb.[67]

Lorna Arnold has shown how the 'months following the White Paper of February 1955 were an anxious time for the Aldermaston theoreticians as they groped for solutions' on how to make a British H-bomb.[68] There was a great deal of research and development still to do. By the time British designs were put to the test (the May 1957 'Grapple' shot on Christmas Island being a 'hybrid'; the November 1957 'Grapple X' was a 'true'[69]), Macmillan was in No. 10 Downing Street and pursuing what Edwin Plowden called the 'great prize'[70] of restored nuclear collaboration with the United States. This, thanks to the November 1957 test (Edwin Teller later told his British opposite numbers that it was obvious that the laws of physics operated on both sides of the Atlantic[71]), was achieved in the autumn of 1958 with the 'Agreement for Co-operation on the Uses of Atomic Energy for Mutual Defence Purposes' concluded between the Eisenhower administration and Her Majesty's government.[72]

With the V-bombers coming on stream in significant numbers during 1957, Macmillan can be seen as the first fully nuclear-armed British Prime Minister, especially after the first British H-bombs, the Yellow Suns Mark II, were allocated to the bombers in 1961[73] (though, technically, the distinction could go to Churchill from November 1953 when the first 'Blue Danube' atomic bomb was delivered to RAF Wittering[74]). But Macmillan also saw the substantial unravelling of several of the arguments for going thermonuclear he had heard around Churchill's Cabinet Table that July morning in 1954.

Before such awkward new realities had to be faced, however, Macmillan set down *his* reasons in 1957–8 for sustaining an 'independent nuclear capability' for the UK:

(a) To retain our special relation with the United States and, through it, our influence in world affairs, and, especially, our right to have a voice in the final issue of peace and war.

(b) To make a definite, though limited, contribution to the total nuclear strength of the West – while recognising that the United States must continue to play the major part in maintaining the balance of nuclear power.

(c) To enable us, by threatening to use our independent nuclear power, to secure United States co-operation in a situation in which their interests were less immediately threatened than our own.

(d) To make sure that, in a nuclear war, sufficient attention is given to certain Soviet targets which are of greater importance to us than to the United States.[75]

This quartet of justifications was very much in line with the mood of 1954 within Churchill's nuclear councils. For all his musings around the Gladwyns' table in Paris in late 1956, Macmillan was determined that he and the UK should be a serious, if second-rank, nuclear player in the world (though there is no wishful thinking here, as there was in the summer of 1954, about the H-bomb putting Britain back, in the Chiefs' words, 'on terms' with the two superpowers).

But in the mid-1950s technology and money were moving power-fully against Britain's notions of its nuclear place in the world, which the restoration of US/UK collaboration on warhead know-how from the autumn of 1958 only partly mitigated. Peter Nailor, a nuclear policy civil servant before becoming an academic, has spoken graphically of the gap which opened up between the United States, the Soviet Union and the UK at the very time – 1954 – when the Chiefs' vintage thought Britain's technological skills would be narrowing it. Immediately behind the 'step change' of the thermonuclear weapon,

you got quite unexpectedly fast technical breakthroughs in reliable solid-fuel rocket motors, the development of miniaturized components, both for warheads and for guidance and instrumental systems. And the pace of change was accelerating to an extent where a country like Britain was being forced to make technical choices with bewildering rapidity. The V-bomber/free-fall [bomb] combination was a jolly good combination, but it was already becom-ing obsolescent almost before squadron service capability had been reached, and the question, the specific question for British defence planners, was: what came next? Could we, in fact, find something that would enhance and prolong the service life of the V-bombers, or would we have to make the switch straight away to something like land- or sea-based missiles? That was an option which . . . as late as 1954–5 nobody thought would be an immediate problem. By 1957–8 it was already knocking on the door.[76]

The first attempts to resolve the dilemma failed very publicly and absorbed a great deal of time, energy and, senior ministers feared, substantial political capital from the Macmillan governments, especially after the UK's attempt to construct its own land-based ballistic missile, Blue Streak, had to be abandoned in 1960 on grounds of both cost and vulnerability (it was liquid- rather than solid-fuelled and so took dangerously long to prepare for launch).

The huge investment in the Valiants, Victors and Vulcans of the RAF's V-force, then arriving from the factories at airfields in Lincoln-shire, on Cyprus and in Singapore, meant that the next solution had to be a system which would prolong the operational life of those aircraft in increasingly difficult circumstances given improvements in Soviet air defence. It forced a huge step-change in British thinking. Macmillan and his Cabinet had to accept a serious loss of independence in asking the Americans for the Skybolt stand-off missile (then in the process of development for the US Air Force) to be capped by a British-made warhead and fitted to the V-bombers.[77]

Philip de Zulueta, Macmillan's Private Secretary for foreign and defence matters, captured for me the difficulties and dilemmas involved when Macmillan and his team visited President Eisenhower at his Camp David retreat in 1960 to seek American help in the increasingly stretching task of keeping a Union Jack on top of it (even if much of the 'it' had to be US-provided):

It was not at all agreeable to have to do that, but there was really no alternative, and he fortunately managed to succeed in doing it. Curiously enough, when he was asking for Skybolt at the Camp David meeting, the Americans in the background were talking about Polaris. I remember Eisenhower's naval aide, who was a charming man, had got a model of the Polaris there. Of course, he was the Navy lobby, and was trying to persuade one to go ahead with Polaris. I discussed it with Sir Norman Brook, and he said, 'For goodness' sake, let's hope they don't raise that question; we must have an airborne missile, because we want to use our bombers.'[78]

Deep in Whitehall, as we have seen, the doomsday planners of JIGSAW, the Joint Inter-Service Group for the Study of All-Out War, were preoccupied with the need for an invulnerable, second-strike system as represented by Polaris which would avoid the need to cobble together interim solutions to keep the V-force as the H-bomb's national carrier.

But only when Skybolt failed to perform on its test ranges in 1962 ('It was an absolute pile of junk,' Kennedy's Defense Secretary, Robert McNamara, would tell me with great force many years later[79]) was Macmillan confronted with the need to go under water. The Americans' abandonment of Skybolt came as a terrible shock to Macmillan as, in the words of Alec Home, his Foreign Secretary: 'We'd set a lot of store by its success . . . and it was widely known that the government set a lot of store by it . . .'[80] When Macmillan, Home, Defence Secretary Peter Thorneycroft and Commonwealth Secretary Duncan Sandys set off in December 1962 for a meeting at Nassau with Kennedy hoping to salvage a serious British nuclear capacity from the wreckage, they were convinced, as Home told me later, that their personal political stakes were of the highest. Had the Nassau negotiation failed and the British team returned empty handed, 'we would have been in a very, very nasty position politically. I think that the government would probably have been beaten. It might well have been a case for an election, I would have thought.'[81]

Macmillan did pull it off against the advice of several in the Kennedy administration.[82] But it was the triumph of a nuclear mendicant rather than a serious, independent contributor to the West's combined nuclear profile. The illusions of that Churchillian summer of 1954 were cruelly exposed. Such moments are highly public events in the life of the secret state. But particularly interesting are the rationales used by the key players to convince themselves, and others, in private of the need for staying a nuclear player despite the dependence on another power.

With Kennedy at Nassau, Macmillan had pulled out all his histrionic and historical stops. As de Zulueta recalled:

He made a most moving and emotional speech, about the great losses and the great struggles for freedom and so on, and Britain was a resolute and a determined ally, who was going to stand firm, and that it was very unreasonable for the United States not to assist her to do so . . . And it was very well done indeed and very effective, and there wasn't a dry eye in the house.

Sir Philip was (and remained) well aware of Macmillan's underlying purpose – 'that we should have enough nuclear power to prevent some foolish decisions being made to our detriment on the other side of the Atlantic . . .' in de Zulueta's own words.[83] Here lay the thread linking Bevin, wheezing into GEN 75 in the autumn of 1946, with Churchill in his H-bomb summer of 1954 to Macmillan doing his 'veteran of the Somme'[84] impression at Nassau. Nassau took place within weeks of the Cuban missile crisis, during which Macmillan had pointed out to Kennedy that if Khrushchev retaliated against the US blockade of Cuba with a Warsaw Pact equivalent against Berlin, 'as envisaged in the various contingency plans', this 'will lead us either to an escalation to world war or to the holding of a conference'.[85] Macmillan's preference for conference over catastrophe had also been evident during the Berlin crisis of 1958–61, given his private conviction (as he expressed it to Norman Brook at a particularly acute phase of Berlin-related tension in July 1961) that 'any real war *must* escalate into nuclear war . . .'[86]

In the weeks between Cuba and Nassau, the JIC had prepared a bespoke paper on the theme of 'Escalation', which had been shared with the Americans.[87] The JIC defined escalation as 'the process by which any hostilities, once started, might expand in scope and intensity, with or without the consent of Governments'. Its analysts did not accept Macmillan's apocalyptic teleology, but they came close to it. Their general conclusion was, 'In any hostilities between the Soviet Union and the West, escalation to global war could only be avoided if at some stage in the process a cease-fire were agreed. When this might happen must depend primarily on the importance attributed by each side to the issues at stake and each side's appreciation of the other's determination.'[88]

But the JIC was well aware of the short timescales involved in securing a cease-fire *and* the difficulty of either side backing down:

Once any hostilities had started agreement on a cease-fire would involve one side or the other accepting a tactical defeat or both sides a stalemate on what must be a highly important issue. The chances of such an agreement would be better if the attacking side realised that it had miscalculated the importance to the other side of the interests involved or the will and ability of the other side to resist.[89]

The JIC's analysts brought some solace to their readers in the jumpy weeks following Cuba. The other side were just as anxious on this matter as the West:

The Soviet leaders have consistently affirmed in public their realisation of the grave risk of escalation in limited hostilities with the West. Indeed, at times they have even implied that the process would be virtually uncontrollable. One of the arguments on which they base this view is that nations having two such fundamentally opposed social systems could consider compromise intolerable when once [*sic*] hostilities had been joined.[90]

Without, of course, saying so (or perhaps even knowing it to be so, given the small number of people who would have seen Macmillan's deeply pessimistic scribbles on Norman Brook's minutes), the JIC saw similar views prevailing in the Kremlin to those bothering the anxious old gentleman in Admiralty House (No. 10 was being rebuilt). Macmillan had confided to his diary (which nobody, not even Norman Brook, knew he was keeping) his own version of the JIC's reasoning. At a particularly fraught moment in the rolling Berlin crisis he foresaw a possible 'drift to disaster . . . a terrible diplomatic defeat or (out of sheer incompetence) a nuclear war'.[91]

The JIC, however, in November 1962, with East and West just back from the Cuba brink, saw such mutual anxiety as the best hope: 'It is now the fear of global war arising through a process of escalation which constitutes the deterrent to limited aggression, rather than the fear of immediate, massive retaliation.'[92] The JIC's top customers in Whitehall that Cuba autumn may not have been so sanguine as their intelligence advisers, however. Over lunch with Iverach McDonald of *The Times* before 'the ripples of the Cuba crisis had begun to die away', the Foreign Secretary, Lord Home, warned the assembled party (which included Walter Lippmann over from America) 'against too much cheerfulness now that the [Soviet Union's] gamble had failed. "The chief frightening thing about it all," he said, "is that Khrushchev could have miscalculated so badly. It could mean that he could blunder into war another time."'[93]

In such a mood did Home and Macmillan set off for Nassau. Any deal struck had to satisfy what the British team saw as the UK's need – to produce a weapons system capable of destroying something approaching the 'forty largest cities' in the USSR, which the JIC, based on the 'breakdown' studies made by JIGSAW, deemed 'quite unacceptable to the Russians'.[94] Macmillan also had to secure a clause in any agreement made with Kennedy whereby a British nuclear force, however dependent on the USA for its missiles, could be withdrawn from its NATO assignments and joint targeting if 'supreme national interests' were at stake. And it was this independence-of-action angle which concerned the Cabinet when it met, with Macmillan still in negotiation in Nassau, to discuss the telegrams he had sent Rab Butler, the Deputy Prime Minister, to be put before the meeting on 21 December 1962.

Butler told the Cabinet that the latest draft of the agreement included a new provision that our strategic nuclear forces would be used for 'the international defence of the Western Alliance in all circumstances except where Her Majesty's Government may decide that the supreme national interests are at stake.' The Prime Minister had particularly directed attention [in his telegram] to those words, which had the effect of giving us the sole right of decision on the use of our strategic nuclear forces, and had asked whether the Cabinet endorsed the view, which he shared with the Foreign Secretary, the Commonwealth Secretary [Sandys] and the Minister of Defence [Peter Thorneycroft], that these words could be publicly defended as maintaining an independent United Kingdom contribution to the nuclear deterrent.

Though anxious to have it clearly worded, the Cabinet went along with Macmillan's line as it 'safeguarded the essential principle of an independent United Kingdom contribution to the Western strategic nuclear deterrent', recognizing 'the value to this country of an arrangement by which we should eventually have within our own control a virtually indestructible second-strike deterrent weapon of proven capability, and with prospects of a long life . . .'[95]

Intriguingly, neither at this Cabinet meeting nor at the one on 3 January 1963 at which Macmillan gave a lengthy exposition of the Nassau negotiation, did any minister seek to discuss what kind of contingencies might qualify for the 'supreme national interests' clause to be invoked. It took a leak from a conversation Kennedy had 'on board his yacht' with the French Ambassador to the US, Herve Alphand, on 29 December for what the President had in mind to emerge. The Head of Chancery at the British Embassy in Paris was a given a sight 'in strict confidence' on 2 January 1963 of Alphand's telegram reporting what Kennedy said. Philip de Zulueta passed the British Ambassador's telegram, containing the leak, to Macmillan on the day the Cabinet met to hear his report on Nassau with the words: 'Prime Minister. This is an important telegram.'

This it was for several reasons (not least because Kennedy was offering a Polaris deal to France, which did not prevent President de Gaulle within days wrecking the Macmillan government's application to join the EEC on the grounds that the UK lived in a dependency culture with the USA on defence and other matters). Kennedy was making available a similar arrangement on 'supreme national interests' to France too. And what he said on this to Alphand included the kind of detail the British Cabinet neither sought nor was given when Macmillan delivered his account. 'The President,' the Paris Embassy's summary of the Alphand telegram reported,

confirmed that the right of Britain or France unilaterally to decide to use their Polaris forces in the event that their supreme national interests were at stake should be assured without equivocation. Thus the crews of their submarines would be composed entirely of British and French nationals and the submarines would be capable of acting independently without recourse to 'foreign [i.e. US] radio-electronic systems' . . . The President then cited Suez or Kuwait [the threatened Iraqi invasion of 1961] as examples of how the 'supreme interests' formula might be invoked. If some action on the part of the British or the French, not directly affecting the United States, led to the Russians threatening either country with missiles, they would be in a position to decide to use their own Polaris missiles against say Moscow or Kiev.

British or French acceptance of the Polaris system would in no way limit their right to develop other nuclear systems which would not, therefore, come within the Nassau Agreement; but they would find it extremely costly to develop and maintain two effective long-term nuclear systems.[96]

This latter paragraph must have resonated quite powerfully with Macmillan as he had spent a broody Boxing Day worrying about whether the Nassau Agreement would hold – and, if it did not, whether (as he put it in a top-secret minute to Thorneycroft and Home), 'if we were driven into a corner, we could either as a bluff or as a reality, make a Polaris missile perhaps of a simpler kind, ourselves from our own designs; how long would it take, etc.?'[97]

Macmillan followed this up with a select, inner-group meeting of ministers – Home, Thorneycroft, Ted Heath (Home's no. 2 at the Foreign Office) – and officials in Admiralty House on 31 December 1962. Sir Pierson Dixon, the British Ambassador to France, was over from Paris and Macmillan suggested that the French might be told

that we did not foresee that we should have to use [the 'supreme national interests'] right in any except the most grave circumstances. If, for example,

Indonesia threatened North Borneo we would not necessarily wish to pose a direct threat to President Soekarno, but if as a result of our adopting conventional methods of defending North Borneo the Russians threatened us direct as they had done in somewhat vague terms at the time of Suez,[98] then we might withdraw our Polaris force from the joint [NATO] forces to counter the threat from Khrushchev.[99]

The New Year's Eve meeting heard a revealing exchange between Heath and Thorneycroft. The 'Skybolt episode,' said Heath,

had brought before the public in a very clear manner the extent of our dependence on the United States. The same difficulty would be felt to apply to Polaris and until we actually had the missiles in our possession we would be at the mercy of the United States Government. For example, if there were some strong disagreement on important policy issues they might threaten to cancel the contract.

Thorneycroft chipped in to say 'that we would not be able to afford starting from scratch to develop a reinsurance system of [sic] posing the deterrent.'[100] Indeed, when he received the costings and timings of home-made alternatives to Polaris, in mid-January, in response to Macmillan's Boxing Day request, this was very apparent.[101]

Macmillan was at his consummate best before the full Cabinet on 3 January 1963. Not a trace of those private doubts about the deal – or of Nassau's vulnerabilities – was allowed to tarnish his *tour d'horizon*. How did he now define the importance of being nuclear? The old Churchillian tunes of 1954 plainly could not be reprised. But Bevin-style, there still had to be a Union Jack on it. Macmillan recognized, as Heath had, the degree of exposure made evident by the cancellation of Skybolt: 'Some sections of public opinion in the United Kingdom were disposed to take the view that this decision was intended to compel us finally to surrender any independent strategic nuclear capability. This was one indication of the current strains in the Western Alliance.' Here he alluded to his 'veteran of the two world wars' soliloquy at Nassau: 'The present United States Administration included hardly any of the men who had been associated with this country in the Second World War; and many of President Kennedy's advisers were inclined to indulge an inflated conception of the material power at the disposal of their Government.'[102]

Nonetheless, he and the Cabinet were 'bound to consider . . . whether it was right for this country to seek to continue to make an independent contribution to the Western strategic nuclear deterrent'. Here he engaged upon a fascinating mix of the old and the new – the UK was a pioneer in work on the bomb; the world was a nasty place; the need now was for interdependence rather than independence; and there was a whiff of his own version of the indispensability of UK wisdom and restraint at the top tables, the need, as he had put it nearly twenty years earlier in Algiers, to play the British Greeks to the American Romans.[103]

'The nuclear weapon,' Macmillan reminded his Cabinet,

had been invented originally by British scientists [this was something of an exaggeration; UK-based scientists had shown that such a weapon was practicable – getting there was a very different matter and depended hugely on US brains, dollars and industry] and we had made considerable progress, both before and after the amendment of the McMahon Act [in 1958], in its development. But the gradual introduction of Soviet defence systems posed new problems; and the elaboration of modern systems of guidance and delivery implied that the development of an effective deterrent would become progressively more sophisticated and expensive. There was, therefore, little attraction in a policy of complete independence in this respect.[104]

The use of the word 'attraction' is interesting. No hint here that going it alone was no longer a runner – that it was now a stark choice between buying a missile off the shelf from the United States or waiting for the effectiveness of the British nuclear force to decay as the V-bomber/free-fall H-bomb combination edged into deeper obsolescence.

'Nevertheless,' the Prime Minister insisted, 'there were several compelling reasons for seeking to preserve a measure of independence as regards control over our nuclear deterrent.'[105] So what did the Macmillan rationale (as packaged for his Cabinet) consist of in January 1963?

1: . . . the Western Alliance would cease to be a free association if the whole of its advanced scientific and technical capacity in this respect were vested in one member.

2: . . . we ought to ensure that we should always be able to react appropriately to a Soviet nuclear threat to this country, even if the United States for whatever reason, were disinclined to support us.

3: . . . a Soviet nuclear threat to which there was no United Kingdom counter-threat would render all our conventional forces ineffectual.

4: . . . if this country abandoned the attempt to maintain an independent nuclear deterrent, it would be unable to exercise any effective influence in the attempts, which would eventually have to be made, to achieve some international agreement to limit nuclear armaments.

The 'supreme national interests' clause, he explained, 'represented a realistic compromise, in present circumstances, between independence and interdependence'.[106]

The Cabinet concurred. But the Labour Opposition did not. Between the Cabinet backing the Nassau 'compromise' (and, in Michael Quinlan's words, 'a Mark I level of cover', an off-the-shelf insurance policy as opposed to the much more expensive and difficult Mark II level of insurance an all-British nuclear capacity would have represented[107]) and the House of Commons debating the Nassau Agreement, Hugh Gaitskell had died and had been replaced as Leader of the Labour Party by Harold Wilson. Macmillan's party – as opposed to Civil Service – advisers were concerned that Wilson's 'election to the party leadership . . . owed much to the support of the unilateralist wing [of the Labour Party], and this may influence his position as time goes on'.[108]

In fact, as the briefing attached to this warning penned for Macmillan's eyes showed, Wilson in the Nassau debate in the Commons on 31 January 1963 had taken a line similar to that voiced by Ted Heath in the privacy of Admiralty House on New Year's Eve a month earlier. 'We on this side of the House,' Wilson told the Commons,

have not been arguing either for Polaris or for Skybolt. We support neither . . . The Government have presented their case in terms of an answer to the question of whether the missile we should have from the Americans should be Skybolt or Polaris . . . Our criticism is not of the answer, but that the question is wrong. How can one pretend to have an independent deterrent when one is dependent on another nation – a reluctant one at that – to supply one with the means of delivery?[109]

Wilson sustained this argument right up to election day in October 1964. Labour's manifesto said of Polaris: 'it will not be independent and it will not be British and it will not deter'. An unequivocal pledge to abandon it was avoided, however. The manifesto committed a new Labour government to 'the renegotiation of the Nassau Agreement',[110] no more.

An impression was given, however, that Labour would begin the process of removing the Union Jack from the bomb. The letter of 22 April 1963 from the director of the Conservative Research Department, Michael Fraser, which Macmillan read (his initials are on it), told John Wyndham and his boss, in the context of Wilson and the nuclear question:

Perhaps the most revealing statement of his personal views was that made during an American television interview on April 8 this year. According to accounts in the Press, which have not been contradicted, he was asked repeatedly if the policy of renunciation of the nuclear deterrent would not commit Britain to the status of a second-class military power. Wilson is reported first to have denied it but then to have added: 'If being a first-rate military power means being a nuclear power, that is right.'[111]

However, Alec Home, who replaced Macmillan as Prime Minister six months later, never reckoned Wilson would abandon the bomb.

When interviewed for *A Bloody Union Jack on Top of It*, Home told me that he

had always found, in dealing with Harold Wilson on security matters [presumably on a private, privy councillor basis[112]] that he was reliable in terms of the national interest. And so in spite of the manifesto, in spite of what he said during the election campaign, I didn't think he'd be able to bring himself to cancel it [Polaris] when he understood the facts. There are quite a lot of facts the Leader of the Opposition does not have. When he got into government I thought he would carry on the programme, so it didn't worry me unduly.[113]

Nearly seven years later, I discovered one of the reasons Alec Home had been so confident about this. When his No. 10 files for 1964 were declassified in January 1995, I came across a note from Thorneycroft of a privy counsellor-basis meeting with the shadow Defence Secretary,

Denis Healey, on 3 February 1964 in which Healey had talked through the feasibility of pooling a British Polaris fleet with the Americans inside a NATO Atlantic force.[114] This, as we shall see in a moment, was the line Wilson pursued once inside No. 10. But why did he persist in public right up to election day on 15 October 1964 in creating the impression that Polaris would be cancelled? In private, he told Dick Neustadt (who prepared an autopsy on Britain and Skybolt cancellation for President Kennedy[115]) that he had little to lose by taking this line as he could not compete with Douglas-Home for the 'jingo vote'.[116]

Less than a month after taking office, Wilson, in a tiny Cabinet committee, MISC 16, consisting of himself, Patrick Gordon Walker (the Foreign Secretary) and Healey (the Defence Secretary), decided on 11 November 1964 (Armistice Day, intriguingly enough) that the construction of the Polaris fleet should continue; that when completed it should be assigned to a proposed Atlantic Nuclear Force (ANF); but its control technology 'would not mean that we could not regain independent control of our nuclear forces should, for example, the NATO Alliance dissolve'.[117] Wilson and his inner group wanted to run the idea of an ANF to thwart the creation of an American-backed multilateral force (MLF), which would involve a mixed-manned, nuclear-capable NATO surface fleet.

To increase the chances of this idea flying in Washington, MISC 16 was prepared to throw in, as it were, some V-bombers. The very paragraph in the minutes which incorporates this also gives away Wilson's *lack* of desire to remove for ever from a nuclear button the finger of a British Prime Minister:

The nuclear forces which we might offer to commit in accordance with these proposals would be part of the V-bomber force (the remainder being retained under United Kingdom control solely for us in a conventional role outside the NATO area) together with three POLARIS submarines. The three submarines would represent the minimum force which would be acceptable to us in the event of the dissolution of the NATO Alliance.[118]

Alec Home was right. Wilson could not bring himself to do it. The pull of the nuclear was too strong. He sold this line to a larger Cabinet committee, MISC 17, and the full Cabinet before Christmas 1964.[119]

Early in the new year, the Cabinet's Defence and Overseas Policy Committee decided to go for four Polaris boats.[120]

Much of it was classic Wilson smoke-and-mirrors. Denis Healey exposed one element of this in his memoirs, recalling that when he told Wilson and Gordon Walker 'it would still be possible to convert them [the UK Polaris boats] into hunter-killer submarines at no additional cost . . . they asked me not to let other members of the Cabinet know; Wilson wanted to justify continuing the Polaris programme on the grounds that it was "past the point of no return". I did not demur.'[121] The Cabinet minutes for 26 November record Wilson as saying, in the context of the proposed ANF,

we would commit irrevocably, so long as NATO existed, our V-bomber force assigned to Europe and such Polaris submarines as we might construct. The precise number of these submarines would be for further consideration; but it was relevant to a decision that the construction of some of them was already sufficiently advanced to make it unrealistic to cancel the orders. On the other hand the number to be retained would be smaller than the number [five] which the previous Government had envisaged and would be such as to make it clear that we no longer contemplated the maintenance of an independent nuclear force.[122]

But we – or rather he – did.

In January 1967, with all talk of an ANF or an MLF long past, Wilson's new Ministerial Committee on Nuclear Policy, PN (which had first met the previous September[123]), authorized Healey

to inform the authorities of the North Atlantic Treaty Organisation of our intention to assign the POLARIS submarines to NATO in terms which would retain ultimate United Kingdom control . . . As a result, SACEUR [NATO's Supreme Allied Commander Europe] has been given a firm assurance that, in accordance with the Nassau Agreement, our POLARIS missiles will be assigned to him as soon as the first submarine becomes operational i.e. in 1968.[124]

The moment my student Matthew Grant brought Healey's minute of 3 August 1967 into my seminar room during the spring of 2001 (having just discovered it at the PRO), it confirmed that Wilson's finger had never been prised from the release codes. The assignment of Polaris to NATO, Healey made plain, would not change this:

Ultimate United Kingdom control of the POLARIS force will not be affected, since control of the firing chain will remain in UK hands; in particular, no submarine commander will be authorised to fire the POLARIS weapons without the Prime Minister's specific authority.[125]

So much for the 1964 manifesto and all the flimflam in Cabinet and Cabinet committee that autumn. Alec Home had read his rival perfectly.

When I asked Denis Healey nearly a quarter of a century later why he and Wilson and Gordon Walker had decided the way they did in November 1964, he replied with a mixture of pragmatism and the doctrine of unripe time:

The basic reason was that the deal which Macmillan had got out of Kennedy was a very good one. It was a very cheap system for the capability it offered. We'd already got one boat nearly complete and another was on the stocks. So the saving from cancellation would have been minimal. And, given the uncertainties – the Cuban missile crisis was only a year or two behind us, the memory of Hungary was still in our minds, Khrushchev had been deposed the day before the British poll, the Chinese had just exploded their bomb the same day – we felt, on the whole, it was wise to continue with it.[126]

Wilson's equivalent rationale had a resonant echo of 1954 reasoning.

MISC 16 had 'borne in mind' that the acquisition of Polaris 'would, after the end of service of the V-bomber Force, be our only means of access to United States technology in the field of nuclear missiles'.[127] Over twenty years later, a frail Lord Wilson of Rievaulx deployed this argument, plus a dash of Churchill-like views on the need to watch the Americans, to justify his apparent volte-face in 1964:

I never believed we had a really independent deterrent. On the other hand, I didn't want to be in the position of having to subordinate ourselves to the Americans when they, at a certain point, would say, 'We're going to use it,' or something of that kind – though, in fact, I doubt anyone expected it ever to be used. It wasn't that we wanted to get into a nuclear club or anything of that kind. We wanted to learn a lot about the nuclear thing, and so on. We might need to restrain the Americans, if we learnt about new things that could happen of a devastating character.[128]

Wilson's reasoning should in no way be treated as casual, the 'we-might-as-well-keep-it' attitude of a new administration faced with a vexing international scene. For, as Matthew Grant has shown, even in the teeth of a prolonged sterling crisis in 1967–8, with Wilson declaring at a meeting of PN on 5 December 1967 that 'no particular element of the defence programme could be regarded as sacrosanct',[129] he kept open the possibility of the eventual improvement of Polaris (in what during the 1970s became the 'Chevaline' programme for coping with the anti-ballistic missile screen around Moscow[130]). At that very meeting of his nuclear policy committee in the days following the devaluation of sterling, Wilson avoided reaching a decision either for or against upgrading the weapon or for or against abandoning 'the whole of our nuclear capability as quickly as possible' to save money as the Treasury and the Department of Economic Affairs and their respective ministers (including the new Chancellor, Roy Jenkins) were urging.[131]

With all these factors in mind, there were two things, on reflection, I wished I had put to Wilson that morning in 1985 in his flat just across the road from Westminster Cathedral. The first was the argument I had heard privately four years earlier for going for the very latest version of the Trident missile as a replacement for Polaris:

The key to this is for us to possess a small amount of the latest American kit. If it comes to it, the Russian radar won't be able to tell if the Trident missile which emerges from the sea off Norway has a Stars and Stripes or the White Ensign on it. All they'll know is that it's a Trident and that it's coming at them ... This is one of the ways we keep the United States locked into the defence of Europe.[132]

As we have seen, Victor Rothschild reported a similar line of argument as having been given to the Kings Norton Committee (on the future of the Atomic Weapons Research Establishment at Aldermaston) in his minority report, which Wilson would have read when it went to PN in 1968.

The second regret is that I did not put to him the question with which A. J. P. Taylor roused the foundation meeting of the Campaign

which A. J. P. Taylor roused the foundation meeting of the Campaign for Nuclear Disarmament in the Central Hall, Westminster, on 17 February 1958.[133] After describing the catastrophic consequences of the H-bomb, Taylor cried: 'Knowing all this, who would press the button? Let him stand up.'[134] Would Wilson have *ever* authorized a nuclear release? I should have asked him as I have asked other (though not all) premiers since (see Chapter 8).

With the release of still more Cabinet and Cabinet committee papers after the paperback edition of *The Secret State* was published in 2003, I chaired a workshop on 'Cabinets and the Bomb', which included former ministers, senior officials and Whitehall scientists, staged by the British Academy and the Mile End Group on 27 March 2007, out of which, with the help of the National Archives, came a documentary reader (also called *Cabinets and the Bomb*). I shall not reprise its contents here, but after casting ourselves back over three decades, it became plain that for all the wealth of papers on political-cum-strategic justifications or financial considerations, reason and the arithmetic of cost-benefit analysis had not been the weathermakers in these most secret of ministerial discussions. In the end, as Michael Quinlan observed during a 2004 seminar at the National Archives (an accompaniment to 'The Secret State' exhibition at Kew), each generation of ministers, of both major parties, has produced for itself 'a set of rationales to clothe that gut decision'[135] – the decision that either this is the time for the UK to become a nuclear weapons power *or* that this is not the time to cease to be one.

The spoor of Michael Quinlan's thinking on 'rationales' and 'gut decisions' was very evident when the 'Future of the United Kingdom Nuclear Deterrent', an immensely secret 1978 study commissioned by Prime Minister Jim Callaghan, was released at the National Archives in 2010. The document is known in Whitehall as the Duff–Mason Report. The politico-military sections were drafted by a group under the chairmanship of Sir Antony Duff, a senior Foreign Office diplomat; the technical appraisals by a team under Sir Ronald Mason, Chief Scientific Adviser at the Ministry of Defence. Quinlan, as Deputy Secretary Policy and Programmes in the MOD, was highly influential in both.

Under the heading 'Political Status and Influence', the late-seventies paradox of Britain and the bomb was made apparent – we would not seek to become a nuclear weapons state if we were not one already; but ceasing to be one would be a decision freighted with significance. The key paragraph rings of Quinlan (and, indeed, reflects a view he expressed to me on more than one occasion):

The essential point to be made about the effect on our status is that this cannot be judged in the abstract. While it might be argued that if we were now contemplating becoming a nuclear power this would add little to our status, it cannot be assumed that abandonment of our capability would have a similarly limited effect. We were the first state to perceive the implications of atomic power, and the third state to become an effective nuclear power. If we were to turn our back on this history and abandon our role as NWS [nuclear weapons state], this would be regarded internationally as a momentous step in British history.

The report buttresses this argument by recognizing the UK's diminishing clout in economic and industrial terms: 'Finally, our status as a nuclear power is important for our relationship to other medium powers, since we have lagged behind them in other indicators of prestige. This stands to be especially significant in relation to West Germany (which we must assume will never become a NWS) and to France (which is certain to remain one).'[136]

The reference to France is intriguing. It is a country that seems to have avoided the regular cycles of national anguishing about the bomb that the British undergo when a nuclear decision looms. As Sir Kevin Tebbit, another former Ministry of Defence Permanent Secretary, and participant in the March 2007 British Academy/Mile End Group seminar, later observed, Britain has 'always been a reluctant nuclear power', but, for those whose job it has been to authorize, sustain or operate the UK nuclear deterrent, 'they are the ultimate backbone – this is what the people who do the nuclear provide. Governments know there is a point beyond which they cannot be intimidated.'[137]

This, in the end, is why, when the choice was put to them as an either/or, successive UK governments during the Cold War put the money into deterrence rather than civil defence (as we shall see in Chapter 5). The importance of being nuclear was also to do with what the American scholar-analyst-diplomat Joe Nye described as 'the crystal ball effect' of nuclear weapons.[138] Before 1945, no great power could foresee the endgame of a war. Once the thermonuclear stage had been reached, no crystal ball was required to foresee the outcome if the conflict reached its ultimate extreme. The last resort was all too knowable. As one SIS Cold War veteran expressed it even more graphically, 'The Cold War was a strategic threat on steroids thanks to nuclear weapons.'[139]

3

Defending the Realm:
Vetting, Filing and Smashing

The tendency has persisted for Civil Servants and others in comparable positions to come to notice only from secret sources which, from their nature, are not necessarily able to provide a comprehensive picture of the situation at any given moment. The consequent difficulty of determining the extent of Communist penetration of the Civil Service is intensified by the fact that not infrequently people so employed may push their discretion to the point of avoiding any formal commitment to the Party.

MI5 report on 'The Communist Party. Its Strengths and Activities', 1 April 1948[1]

The [Moscow] Centre calculated that since their recruitment in 1934–5, Philby, Burgess and Maclean had supplied more than 20,000 pages of 'valuable' classified documents and agent reports.

Christopher Andrew and Vasili Mitrokhin, *The Mitrokhin Archive*, 1999[2]

The Security Service has for many years made a study of subversive bodies and their adherents, both open and covert, and has built up detailed records amounting in the case of the Communist Party and its fellow travellers to some 250,000 files.

Report of the Committee on Positive Vetting, 27 October 1950[3]

> *Organised sabotage before war is most unlikely because the*
> *Soviet leaders will be unwilling to give away their plans to*
> *Communists in the United Kingdom. No organised sabotage*
> *will take place after the outbreak of war because, as at*
> *present planned, the whole known organisation of the Brit-*
> *ish Communist Party will have been smashed. Even if a secret*
> *and unknown party organisation were in existence at the*
> *time, and we consider this unlikely, it would not devote itself*
> *to the task of organising sabotage.*
>
> Joint Intelligence Committee Report on the 'Likely Scale
> and Nature of an Attack on the United Kingdom in a
> Global War up to 1960', 10 May 1956[4]

If World War III had come, no chances would have been taken. Special
Branch, using the detailed picture pieced together by MI5, would – as
the 1956 JIC document makes plain – have destroyed the known
Communist Party apparatus in the United Kingdom, rounding up, no
doubt, those deemed most dangerous among the membership. It is very
easy to make mock of the point where the secret state would have
transformed itself into the take-no-chances state. And the transition-
to-war gaming fully built in the 'enemy within'[5] angle to its simulations,
as we shall see in a moment, as it did the activities of the Campaign
for Nuclear Disarmament and the more militant student activists of
the late 1960s.

To those potentially and actually on the receiving end of the secret
state's sifting and screening (the 'smashing', mercifully, never materialized), the notions on which MI5 based its work and justified it to
ministers could appear overdone to the point of being ludicrous. Looking back on the years since 1945 as the century turned, the historian
Eric Hobsbawm said:

After 1956, my activism was transformed into something different and more
detached. From that time, it was clear to me that the dream was over. The
general secretary of the Communist Party of Great Britain, of which I remained
a member almost up to the date of its dissolution [November 1991[6]], used
to say in difficult moments that he could have done with a direct telephone

line to Moscow. He thought the party was an army of messenger boys, while those who worked in the intellectual professions realised that we had to try to think things through on our own.[7]

Professor Hobsbawm later identified the man and the moment. 'It was Johnny Gollan in 1956,' he wrote. (Gollan had just succeeded Harry Pollitt.) 'Whether he meant it, or was just being ironic, I don't know. Certainly he had got the job suddenly (Harry's retina gave out suddenly) and was not completely at home in the job.'[8]

MI5 definitely wanted to know who the Party's 'messenger boys' were – and, beyond them, those who might be regarded as fellow travellers within the Party's unofficial penumbra. By the autumn of 1950 there were a quarter of a million files on these two categories combined, an awesome number (assuming that this reflected a tally of one person, one file). The Security Service's own estimate of CPGB membership at that time was 43,500.[9] At first glance it appears that over 200,000 people on top of this were deemed to be real or possible sympathizers. If so, around one in 200 of the UK's mid-twentieth-century population were treated as being communists or having communist-leaning beliefs. But after the first edition of this book appeared, a friend of mine who had served in the secret world cautioned me about converting that quarter-of-a-million figure into people. 'Perhaps there really were 250,000 files on suspicious persons of communist sympathies,' he explained privately. 'It's possible if they had a file for everyone who ever attended a Party meeting – but it sounds rather a lot and it's equally possible that among them were files on people who helped (you have to keep their names and addresses somewhere safe) on facilities such as OCPs [operational clandestine premises, more usually known as 'safe houses'], on subjects such as CPGB relations with Moscow, trades unions, the churches . . . on technical operations, on advice given to ministers, on intelligence produced . . . or on correspondence with . . . SIS, the police or foreign liaison services.' The quarter-of-a-million figure might also reflect the fact that by the late 1940s, MI5 had several files on the same person, particularly if they had been founder members of the CPGB in the early 1920s, as became apparent when personal files began to reach the National Archives.

However comprised, this was the product of a huge enterprise over the thirty or more years after 1917 since when, in the words of the internal history of the Security Service compiled in the last phase of World War II, 'it has been recognised that the fact that the Communist Party seized power in Russia in October of that year posed a problem for MI5'.[10] John Curry, the MI5 officer charged with writing its own secret history, reflected honestly the internal view that the Security Service had never cracked the enemy within:

Since the establishment of the Comintern or Third (Communist) International in March 1919 in Moscow and of the [British] Communist Party as a section of the Comintern in August 1920, the nature of this problem has varied even more widely. It is safe to say that the machinery in MI5 – or the Security Service – has never been adequate to cope with this problem in the sense of formulating a comprehensive appreciation of developments as they occurred, and that during the greater part of the time the material for an adequate understanding of it has been lacking.[11]

Curry, who had himself headed the new MI5 F section when it was created in April 1941 to deal with internal subversion of government departments and the armed forces by communists or fascists (these were the last days of the Nazi–Soviet Pact), and espionage by Soviet and Comintern agents, was graphic about the problems he and his colleagues faced after the German invasion of Russia in June 1941, with the Soviet Union now a member of the anti-Axis alliance:

The evidence available to the section soon made it clear that in spite of the Communist Party's support of the war effort its long-term policy was unchanged and the long-term policy of the section had to be adapted accordingly. It was not always easy to put this view before Government Departments which were profiting from the cessation of Communist obstruction and were in receipt of offers of positive help. It fell to members of the section to convince their opposite numbers in Government Departments that their views were soundly based on knowledge and experience. They felt that they had to make it clear that their views were 'not merely the reactionary outpourings of people who had stuck to one job so long that their opinions had become ossified'.[12]

The watchers of MI5 pressed on as hard as they could. For example, in a passage worthy of John le Carré's fictional Connie Sachs, the great expert on KGB figures operating within the UK in *Tinker, Tailor, Soldier, Spy*,[13] Curry writes of F.2.b (the sub-group of F Branch responsible for watching former operators of the now disbanded Comintern from whom Whitehall seemed to have averted its collective gaze): 'The only palliative to this situation was that F.2.b was in the hands of Miss Bagot whose expert knowledge of the whole subject enabled her to find and make available a large variety of detailed information based on records of the past.'[14] The truly formidable Miss Bagot, a classics graduate from Oxford, joined the Security Service in 1931 and was 'the Service's leading expert in Soviet Communism and its allies, gradually acquiring an encyclopaedic knowledge which impressed even J. Edgar Hoover [Director of the US Federal Bureau of Investigation]'.[15]

F Branch learned a great deal about Communist methods for penetrating the wartime Civil Service and armed forces when David Springhall, the national organizer of the British Communist Party, was arrested in June 1943 and convicted the following month of offences against the Official Secrets Act for obtaining information from a young woman in the signals branch of the Air Ministry and from Captain Desmond Uren, an officer in the Special Operations Executive, for onward transmission to Moscow.[16]

As a result of the apprehension of Springhall and Uren, F Branch circulated a memo, which reached Churchill, listing fifty-seven members of the CP 'known to be engaged in the Services or in Government Departments or in the aircraft or munitions industries of some secrecy'.[17] MI5 admitted that these people had acquired sensitive posts partly because of loopholes in the vetting system and because of 'the absence of a general policy in different Government Departments towards the problem created by the existence of the Communist Party'.[18] F Branch felt it got nowhere and its anxieties increased when evidence procured by 'secret means' indicated that the CP was engaged upon 'a series of instructional classes . . . held in various parts of the country to train new candidates for positions of trust'.[19]

Two figures, who later forsook the affiliations of their youth and rose to prominent positions in public life, have spoken to me about what in modern management jargon might be called the 'succession planning' in which the wartime CPGB engaged. One recalled how the Party indicated which branches of the armed forces those with officer potential should seek to join: 'Tank regiments were among them.'[20] And we have already encountered Harry Pollitt coming to Cambridge in the last phase of the war and telling the Party's undergraduates to get the kind of degrees that could carry them high in the public service.[21]

Both the Party and MI5 were utterly serious and the Security Service finished the war in a state of high anxiety, partly through its inability to infuse other departments with a sense of urgency and partly because of the shadow of Springhall: inquiries into his activities had 'led to the disclosure of the fact that he was in touch with an organised group of Communists among the professional and intellectual classes'.[22]

Despite the eventual accumulation of a quarter of a million files, MI5 was chiefly interested in that inner core of first-class minds in high positions within the state. Party membership had stood at 17,500 at the outbreak of the war in September 1939, fallen to some 14,000 in the period of Nazi–Soviet co-operation and surged to 56,000 at its peak in 1942 ('in part', as British intelligence recognized, 'due to an enthusiasm for the Red Army's resistance'[23]). But the rank-and-file were not regarded as the problem even when the Cold War was well under way. There is a symmetry between Curry's 1944–5 analysis (when Whitehall generally was not minded to listen) and that of the big, early Cold War MI5 assessment of the penetration threat compiled in the first months of 1948 (when it was).

For Curry,

[though] the Communist Party remained a very small affair and failed to make any effective appeal, or to obtain any important increase in influence or membership, the situation created by the fact that so many of its members secured important positions gave it a potential importance far greater than that warranted by its numbers. The alliance with the Soviet Government and the common purpose in the war were obstacles in the way of a more drastic policy for excluding Communists from positions of trust.[24]

The Security Service analysts of 1947–8 were even more precise in their categorization of Stalin's Brits, of whom, they believed, there were just over 45,000 by this stage, split into the regular Party membership of 43,500, 2,000 members of the Young Communist League, and 'the secret members of the Party, who, contrary to estimates frequently given in the Press, cannot number more than a few score at the most'.[25] They saw the Party membership as

[falling] into two distinct sections. By far the larger of these sections, consisting of the full-time executives and the working class members, is mainly concerned with domestic policy; wages, housing, education, taxation, unemployment, health, pensions and so on. It is not well informed about or profoundly interested in foreign affairs and it accepts the central policy on Spain, Palestine or Greece without demur.[26]

MI5 here seems to have fallen into a crude class analysis of its own as well as exhibiting an enormous condescension towards the rank-and-file of a Party which was both unusually internationally minded and exceptionally energetic in pursuing its own notions of political education. Be that as it may, it was this larger section which led MI5 to conclude that: 'The most striking feature about the British Communist Party is that it is, first and foremost, a political party like other political parties. In so far as it partakes also of the character of a subversive or conspiratorial organisation, it does so to a secondary degree.'[27]

It was the brains of the CP, carried in the heads of its professional classes, against which the realm of George VI had to be defended:

The smaller section, the intellectuals of the Party, comprising University students and graduates, civil servants and members of the professions, is on the other hand primarily concerned with international issues and this is the interest which it has in common with the amorphous body of 'communist sympathisers', who are less sympathetic to the British Communist Party than to the ideological conception of international communism. If there were any subversive activity on behalf of a foreign power carried out in peacetime, we would expect it to be carried out by individuals of the intellectual group acting on their own initiative. The working class group is unlikely to be the source of peace-time espionage.[28]

The 'if' is significant. Even as late as the spring of 1948 there is a tentative air about this MI5 assessment. The VENONA traffic, the

1940s Soviet Military Intelligence Signals, was in the process of being broken, but British counter-intelligence, for all Curry's anxieties in 1944–5 and the JIC's depiction in 1946 of the communist movement having 'an appeal of its own which cannot be disregarded without seriously under-rating its strength and resilience',[29] was nowhere near appreciating just how successful Stalin's recruiters had been in the British universities, Cambridge in particular, a decade earlier.

The counter-penetration defences the Attlee government set about constructing between 1947 and 1951, including GEN 183, the Cabinet Committee on Subversive Activities,[30] might well have failed to deter or catch the 'Magnificent Five' even had they been in place by 1930, but the Soviet Union's greatest ever human intelligence bonanza was long in the bag. Had the MI5 assessors, and their ministerial and Whitehall customers, known about Philby, Burgess, Maclean, Blunt and Cairncross as World War turned into Cold War, their anxieties would have multiplied several fold – not least because Kim Philby, as head of SIS's Section IX (the special group formed to study Soviet and Communist activity)[31] from the end of 1944 to 1947, was almost certainly one of the chief framers of the JIC study on 'The Spread of Communism Throughout the World and the Extent of Its Direction from Moscow' of September 1946.[32] No doubt Philby directed that very document to Moscow himself.

The secret defenders of the realm may have been unaware of Philby and co.'s betrayals, but other spies and events *had* pushed counter-espionage high up the Whitehall and intelligence agenda even before the first of the VENONA intercepts had been decoded in the United States during the last months of 1946. The factor which propelled the issue upwards was the defection of Igor Gouzenko, a cypher clerk in the Soviet Embassy in Ottawa, in September 1945. Not only did Gouzenko expose a serious GRU spy ring in Canada, he also supplied the Canadian – and through them, the British and American – authorities with 'fragmentary intelligence' on KGB operations.[33]

The Gouzenko revelations were the trigger for Attlee's establishing of GEN 183, his Cabinet Committee on Subversive Activities, in the spring of 1947. Why the delay? MI5, as we have seen and as the first paper prepared for GEN 183 made plain, had long been 'satisfied that

the Communist organisation, which has foreign support, and is subservient to a foreign power, at present constitutes the principal danger
[as opposed to 'the Fascist organisations, or at the other extreme, the
Revolutionary Communist Party']'.[34] But it was the 'mass of concrete
evidence on this subject' contained in the account compiled by the
investigatory Royal Commission set up in Canada in the wake of
Gouzenko's defection and which had recently reported that led to such
'disquiet' in London, 'particularly in the light that it throws on the
methods used so successfully by the Russians to recruit as agents, and
to obtain information from, persons employed in the service of the
Canadian Government'.[35]

British counter-intelligence, despite the best efforts of MI5's F Branch
and the comprehensive bugging of the CPGB's headquarters in Covent
Garden,[36] had still much to learn about the methods of Soviet intelligence in open societies. The Gouzenko experience, too, reinforced the
MI5 view that overt, rank-and-file communists were not the problem:

It seems to be the general policy of the Communist Party not only in Canada,
but elsewhere, to discourage selected sympathisers from joining the Party
openly. One purpose no doubt is to allay suspicion, but a further object may
be to produce a psychological atmosphere of conspiracy which would be
favourable to the demands made on the individuals selected for use in this
way.[37]

The Canadian lesson was read over directly to other Western societies and in their advice to ministers, the working party could not 'escape
the conclusion that what was done in Canada might be attempted with
comparable if not equal success in any other democratic country including our own'.[38]

In sweet innocence of the shoals of documents that had flowed, and
were still flowing, from the 'Magnificent Five' to their Soviet controllers
usually but a few miles from MI5 headquarters, the working party
advised Mr Attlee and the small group of ministers within his counter-
subversion circle that

It is not possible to say with any authority whether or not an organisation
of the size of that exposed in Canada exists here at the present time, but it is

significant that over the last twenty years a number of cases of Communist and Russian-inspired espionage against this country have come to light.[39]

Ministers were give a summary of these in a special annex with particular emphasis on the Springhall case as it had 'a number of points of similarity with the Canadian case'.

A more recent episode preoccupied the early post-war intelligence community as it both linked the UK to Canada *and* furnished real evidence that the same thing was going on here in the area of number one anxiety – atomic research. The British physicist Alan Nunn May, who had worked at the Chalk River establishment in Ontario (Canada's contribution to the Manhattan Project, the US codename for the bomb programme), had been exposed by the Gouzenko defection in the bundle of documents and signals he carried out with him. Now back at King's College, he had been arrested in London in March 1946.[40] What alarmed the threat-assessors in London was the fact that

On May's arrival in Canada the Soviet Military Attaché there was instructed to approach him and was given a password. This indicates that May had already been contacted, probably in England. Elaborate arrangements for a further meeting with 'our man in London' – probably a member of the staff of the Soviet Military Attaché – were made in a series of telegrams between Ottawa and Moscow, though this meeting was never kept, presumably owing to the fact that the Russian informant [Gouzenko] came over to the Canadian authorities before May's return to this country.[41]

MI5's belief that 'secret sources' were the 'only' way to uncover spies in the public service, as it put it a year later,[42] rested, no doubt, on the Gouzenko experience and what was by the spring of 1948, thanks to the VENONA attack on the signals traffic between the Moscow Centre and its American residences, a considerable and growing body of evidence 'of massive espionage in the wartime United States'.[43] Basing itself on its own and Gouzenko-supplied experience, the GEN 183 working party warned ministers of the swathe of information the KGB and GRU would be seeking to purloin from the UK:

First and foremost come military secrets, including scientific developments such as atomic research, radar, etc. and industrial intelligence bearing upon our war potential. But this does not by any means exhaust the vulnerable field: information may be sought about Government policy or intentions in almost any field, either by the Russian Government or by the Communist Party at home, and the leakage of economic or purely industrial information may be no less serious.[44]

Counter-measures needed, therefore, to cover a wide terrain.

Here the vulnerability to penetration was plain. MI5's 'vetting' procedure was rudimentary. It relied mainly on MI5's own records, which, 'while extensive, cannot be said to be exhaustive' – a revealing comment on that huge file mountain. For some reason, MI5 had not extended its gaze to the Young Communist League so had nothing on any CP-inclined youthful recruits to the clerical or executive classes of the Civil Service. It admitted, too, that clearance was virtually valueless: 'A "clean bill" only means that the individual concerned has not come to notice; it is no *proof* of his trustworthiness. This limitation is of importance, since it means that some "undercover" members of the Party, and those who are instructed not to join it (potentially the most dangerous category), may not come under notice at all.'[45] A plaintive echo of Curry's wartime cry was heard at this point. MI5 could only advise government departments on who not to employ and the 'field over which enquiries are made' about an individual also depended on their department rather than the Security Service.

The Canadian Royal Commission Report had persuaded the GEN 183 group that 'existing arrangements must be considerably tightened up'. There were difficulties, however, the first being the question of civil and personal liberty. Should membership of the CPGB, open or covert, of itself be 'a bar to employment in the Public Service on *secret work*, or whether other facts beyond mere membership must be advanced, e.g. friendship with fellow-Communists suspected of contact with the Russian services in this country'. Attlee's security advisers came down in favour of a hard line as it was impossible to separate those British communists who would spy for Russia from those who would not until the damage had been done.

In effect, the GEN 183 team constructed a revised definition of loyalty

to what was already by the spring of 1947 becoming a new notion of
the state shaped by the Cold War – a definition devised by its most secret
element, the security and intelligence community. 'We appreciate,' they
told Attlee and his ministers,

the objections to the adoption, in times of peace, of a procedure under which
candidates for or members of the Public Service might be penalised simply
because they are – as they have a legal right to be – members of the Communist Party. On the other hand, the first duty of every Civil Servant is to give
his individual allegiance to the State, and the State has a right – indeed the
duty – to protect itself by ensuring that its interests are not endangered by
the employment of persons who may not accept this view of their obligations.
The ideology of the Communist involves, at the least, a divided loyalty, which
might in certain contingencies become active disloyalty: the Canadian case
has amply demonstrated the reality of this danger.[46]

It may be that the framers of the first paper to go to the Cabinet
Committee on Subversive Activities were aware that several Labour
ministers would have known and liked, and have very likely worked
with, members of the Communist Party of Great Britain quite recently
during the Grand Alliance years between June 1941 and August 1945.
Demonizing decent people might have been counter-productive.

Whether sensitive to this possibility or not, they penned a section
which appeared to take account of it:

This is not to say that all Communists would be prepared, even after long
exposure to Communist indoctrination, to betray their country by consenting
to work for Russian espionage agents; but there is no way of separating the
sheep from the goats, at least until the damage has been done or suspicion is
aroused, and even if a Communist Party member conceives himself to be
entirely loyal to this country, he may not be averse from furthering what he
regards as the constitutional aims of the Party by supplying information which
may be of use in their political manoeuvres. Such an individual may easily
become an unconscious espionage agent by supplying information which he
thinks will be used for political purposes only, but which is being passed to
the Russian agents by intermediaries.[47]

The conclusion, therefore, was the absolutist one 'that the only safe course is to decide that a member of the Communist Party is not to be employed on work where he may have access to secret information'.[48]

Within three weeks of the report being circulated, ministers had accepted it. Under the chairmanship of the Minister of Defence, A. V. Alexander, a mixed committee of ministers and officials including the Foreign Secretary Ernest Bevin, the Home Secretary James Chuter Ede and the Minister of Labour George Isaacs with the Director-General of MI5, Sir Percy Sillitoe, and the head of the Civil Service, Sir Edward Bridges, met on 16 June 1947. There was swift 'general agreement' on this core recommendation from the working party 'and the discussion turned mainly' on the areas to which the no-communists rule should apply and how the new arrangements should be presented to the Civil Service unions.[49] The formal conclusion of the first meeting of GEN 183 placed fascists within the ban, too. The committee

Agreed that members of all subversive organisations of the Right or Left should continue to be subject to security scrutiny and should not be employed on work involving access to secret information, and that, in particular, Communists should not be employed in the public service on such work.[50]

Built in at the start – and maintained throughout the Cold War and since – was a 'no martyrs' policy, whereby officials already in post 'in respect of whom adverse advice had been received from the Security Service' should be redeployed where possible in other branches of the public service which did not involve 'contact with secret matters'.[51] Only in cases where this was not possible would they be sacked.[52]

So here, in the realms of vetting, like the British intelligence community's perception of the wider Soviet threat, the mould was set by the summer of 1947. The enemy within and the enemy without had been assessed and integrated. But, as with the JIC's sweeps of the world, the internal security picture was not static. For the 'tightening up' which the GEN 183 working party sought was refined several times in the 1940s, 1950s and 1960s and never seemed foolproof to the defenders of the realm – as it could not be, given the openness of British society and the weight of the GRU and KGB operations against the UK which the Mitrokhin Archive has substantiated in great detail.

The first efforts at raising the level of defence now appear truly feeble. The GEN 183 working party identified certain departments and areas of Civil Service work which, by their very nature, generated material whose disclosure 'would be definitely prejudicial to the normal national interest' – the Cabinet, Foreign Office and Home Office were included as was the Ministry of Supply as the home of atomic research and general weapons work. The private offices of ministers and senior civil servants would be no-go areas for communists. No one aged under twenty-one was to be employed on secret work as MI5 had not investigated the YCL. What is mystifying about the GEN 183 report, which ministers accepted, with the resultant measures being announced in the House of Commons by Mr Attlee on 15 March 1948,[53] is that the *existing* procedures for vetting would be applied more widely and integrated with the new ban on communists and fascists. Despite MI5's candour about the inadequacy of the contents of its files, there was no suggestion that steps should be taken to improve the quality of the information apart from the stricture that: 'Departments should continue to exercise care even as regards staff who have been cleared by the Security Service.'[54]

When MI5 produced its next big survey of the communist problem in the public service in the spring of 1948, the working party felt able to reassure itself and its ministerial customers (this time on GEN 226, Attlee's Cabinet Committee on European Policy – a strange body to be considering such matters)

that Communism in the Civil Service does not at present constitute any serious threat to the loyalty of the Service as a whole. The problem in relation to the Civil Service is, therefore, entirely one of security in its narrow sense i.e. of ensuring that individual civil servants are not given access to secret information. This risk has been dealt with and there is, therefore, nothing more we need to say.[55]

What makes this so surprising is that the MI5 paper on which it was based, on the face of it, gave no grounds for such complacency. As we have seen, the Security Service stated in this assessment that usually it was only 'secret sources' which threw up the names of Stalin's UK civil servants and, in a paragraph devoted specifically to the senior ranks, Sillitoe's people declared:

The number of known cases of people in the Administrative Grade of the Civil Service who are members of the Communist Party, or who can be regarded as virtually committed to it, does not exceed a score. None is of higher rank than Assistant Secretary and a number are unestablished. They form, however, a valuable reservoir of expert knowledge on which the Party can draw as required and as individuals they present security problems of real difficulty.[56]

Within two years, such complacency (however caveat-laden) was brutally exposed and a proper look at vetting was commissioned by Clement Attlee.

It has long been realized that the arrest of Klaus Fuchs, '[t]he most important of the British atom spies,'[57] in January 1950 administered a profound shock to the guardians of British national security. Painstaking work on the VENONA intercepts had the year before revealed that the wartime atomic spy codenamed 'Charles' at Los Alamos in New Mexico had been Fuchs.[58] Only when the VENONA secret was fully divulged by the declassifications in Washington and London in the mid-1990s was it appreciated just how important the flow of its decrypts had been for those charged with gauging the degree of Soviet intelligence penetration of the Western allies. Though the documentation surrounding GEN 183, GEN 226 and the Committee on Positive Vetting (PV) naturally does not allude directly to the VENONA material, it can be deduced that it was a powerful factor driving Attlee's decision in 1950 to commission yet another review.

The question was, did the secret state need a step-change in its defences from what became known as 'negative vetting' (the checks on the files which continued as the basis of security screening even after the 1947 review and the 1948 announcement of the restrictions on employment of communists and fascists in the public service) to a more intrusive and focused system of investigation known as 'positive vetting'? After a meeting of GEN 183 which he chaired on 5 April 1950, Attlee appointed a Committee on Positive Vetting 'to consider the possibility of listing a limited number of posts in regard to which positive vetting could be undertaken and to assess the risks and advantages of embarking upon any such system of positive enquiry'.[59]

The PV Committee was chaired by John Winnifrith, the senior Treasury official who almost certainly invented the phrase 'positive vetting' and who did much of the Civil Service personnel work for Sir Edward Bridges, and two MI5 men, Roger Hollis and Graham Mitchell (both suspected later of having been Soviet agents themselves and accused of trying to delay and thwart the attack on the VENONA intercepts[60]). Continuity with the 1947 and 1948 working parties was provided in the person of S. J. (Joseph) Baker, the senior Home Office official who had signed off both the earlier reports.

Winnifrith and his colleagues deliberated at a time of considerable hysteria in the United States. The House Committee on Un-American Activities had been in full swing for several years. Loyalty oaths were being imposed on public servants. And in February 1950, Senator Joe McCarthy made his famous speech in Wheeling, West Virginia, claiming to have in his possession a list of 205 known communists in the US State Department.[61] And the United States was very much in Attlee's and Bevin's minds; for great efforts were underway to reconstitute the World War II collaboration between the Manhattan Project partners broken by the 1946 McMahon Act and only very partially restored by the 1948 'Modus Vivendi' between the US and UK governments (which allowed, for example, continued intelligence pooling on Soviet atomic activities).[62] The exposure of Fuchs had intensified American concerns about British security arrangements, especially on matters nuclear. The PV Committee inquiry was fuelled by the need to find a way of reassuring the United States without imitating its excesses – hence the emphasis on the risks as well as the advantages of more vigorous procedures, not least because the UK had, so far, avoided any naming and shaming of suspected security risks. Attlee, like Churchill after him, regularly rebuffed requests from the Conservative backbencher Sir Waldron Smithers to set up a House of Commons Select Committee on Un-British Activities.[63]

The question Winnifrith and his team posed to themselves was: 'Is there an inner circle of special secret posts and can such a category be confined within reasonable limits?'[64] They seem to have excluded the secret agencies from their reach from the outset, presumably because it was assumed that extra, special screening measures were already applied to them. MI5, through its Director-General, had been insisting for some time, as Sillitoe told GEN 183 in June 1947, 'that it was important that the number of names submitted to the Security Service should be kept to an absolute minimum if the process of vetting was to work efficiently and smoothly, and from his point of view any arrangement which, by narrowing the definition of "secret work", reduced the area over which vetting would have to be applied'.[65]

Hollis and Mitchell succeeded in ensuring that the MI5 line suffused the work of the Winnifrith Committee, which produced a 'formula for defining such posts':

Posts to be included on the special list must make the holder privy to the whole of a vital secret process, equipment, policy or broad strategic plan, or to the whole of an important section of that process, equipment, policy or plan, where disclosure would be of crucial value to an enemy or potential enemy strategically or politically.[66]

Driven by this desire to avoid cost and the overloading of MI5, the committee convinced itself that the senior military could be excluded from any new vetting procedure as 'the need for special enquiries in the case of such officers is less, because in general more is known of the private background of serving officers than civil servants so that any undesirable associations are more likely to be known to their personnel branches'.[67] Added to this touching faith in the 'good chap' theory of crown service was the view that 'subordinate staff' should, with a few exceptions, remain outside the inner PV circle 'regardless of the admitted security risk involved', as their inclusion would be 'unmanageable'. The Treasury was to be brought in to ensure that departmental lists of sensitive posts did not get out of hand. By these means, the total of vettees 'would not contain more than 1000 posts' across the whole public service.[68]

What of the enhanced procedures to which the secret thousand would be subjected? The committee began with existing British practice before turning to the latest US methods:

Under present procedure the names of officers to be employed in connection with work the nature of which is vital to the security of the State (a category which is loosely defined and covers in present practice a very wide area of the Civil Service) are submitted by Departments to the Security Authorities. The Security Service has for many years made a study of subversive bodies and their adherents, both open and covert, and has built up detailed records amounting in the case of the Communist Party and its fellow travellers to some 250,000 files. Names submitted by Departments are checked against these records of persons of doubtful associations. In certain cases this some-times is supplemented by a further check of the Central Criminal Records at New Scotland Yard. These procedures do not, unless the man concerned is on the list of known suspects, reveal any facts about his wife, let alone his other relations, friends or associates.[69]

In the main, Whitehall departments did no more than 'rely completely on the check provided by the Security Service . . . without making any conscious effort to determine whether the candidate has the required degree of trustworthiness'. The Foreign Office *did* go further with staff to be posted behind the Iron Curtain, undertaking 'a very careful check based on an examination of their personal file'.

The America of J. Edgar Hoover's Federal Bureau of Investigation and the Washington of loyalty oaths is given short shrift in a single paragraph:

We understand that the FBI system is extremely elaborate. Before any person is appointed to any Government post in which he would have access to clas-sified information, his name is checked over FBI records and he has to fill in a detailed and lengthy form listing his ancestry and the whole of his previous career, education etc. He is then subject to intensive overt police enquiries based on this form. We consider that any such procedure would be repugnant to British thinking.[70]

So with the UK status quo inadequate and the American way intol-erable, what was the middle course devised by the Winnifrith Committee?

Driven powerfully by the need to clear any individual with 'access to cosmic documents' ('cosmic' being the special nuclear classification) they came up with a five-point plan to protect the secret state generally and its atomic segment in particular:

1: Existing screening methods should in the case of posts on the proposed vital list be supplemented by positive enquiries, the Department in all cases making a conscious effort to confirm the officer's reliability before appointing him to a post on the vital list.

2: Positive enquiries should normally take the simple form of a careful study of his records . . . combined with enquiries within or without the Department.

3: Personal records of officers likely to be appointed to vital posts should be maintained more fully than at present.

4: Where the study of an officer's record supplemented by departmental enquiry discloses that the Department knows nothing whatever about him, further enquiries should be made through the Security Authorities.

5: Where an officer has been appointed to a vital post, the Department should maintain as full a record as practicable of his background and associates. They should from time to time review his case and ensure, so far as possible, that nothing has occurred since his appointment to cast doubt on the initial presumption as to reliability.[71]

Herein lay a significant move, but a reluctant one. Winnifrith and his team loaded it with caveats, some of which had a touching, Ealing-comedy air to them.

They were terribly concerned that word would get out that a civil servant was being vetted and suspicion would be aroused about 'men of blameless life and unblemished reputation' within their own departments and the neighbourhoods where they lived. Chief constables should be involved to make sure that inquiries were undertaken by experienced police officers. Such policemen would need to ask questions of the civil servants' associates, tradesmen and 'domestic servants'. However discreet the policework, word might get out.

Perhaps most significant of all was the combination of reluctance *and* scepticism about the value of positive vetting which overlay the Winnifrith Report. At least two of the committee's members – Hollis and Mitchell – would by mid-1950 have begun to appreciate the magnitude of the 1930s and 1940s penetrations, thanks to the VENONA decrypts, and the failure of MI5's efforts to break into them (which would probably have continued if GRU cypher security had not briefly turned sloppy with the reuse of one-time encoding pads in the late

World War II and early post-war years that gave the VENONA code-breakers their chance).[72]

Compared to the rich counter-intelligence VENONA revealed, positive vetting was, and would always be, nowhere. And, without, of course, mentioning signals intelligence, the Winnifrith Report said:

We do not suggest that this procedure will yield substantial results by way of disclosure of unreliable civil servants. It is reasonable to assume that the small total percentage (about 1%) of unreliables in the community at large is reflected in the Civil Service, though the percentage may be higher in the Scientific Civil Service. Moreover, the great majority of unreliable persons will already be known to the Security Authorities and their presence disclosed by current methods. Hence the chances of detecting the occasional individual who may have escaped the notice of the Security Authorities are very slight.

In line with earlier analyses of the internal threat, Winnifrith knew full well it was a small number of carefully camouflaged Soviet agents-in-place that comprised the real threat to security and whose existence would only be detected if they made a mistake themselves or they were exposed by a defector or a SIGINT breakthrough.

The additional enquiries which we propose will, moreover, be open enquiries which will only produce the open information likely to be known to a man's neighbours and acquaintances. Whilst, therefore, these enquiries may reveal open association with Communists, they will fail to detect the really danger-ous crypto-Communist. The latter's true nature will not be revealed by his accomplices and is unlikely to be known to his ordinary acquaintances. The detection of such persons can only be secured by the scientifically planned study of Communist activities which it is the task of the Security Authorities to carry out.[73]

Nonetheless, the report, prepared for a meeting of the Cabinet Committee on Subversive Activities (with Attlee in the chair on this occasion), reached the firm conclusion that

The case for positive enquiries, which we recommend, is that it is the duty of the public service to take all reasonable steps to check the reliability of persons holding vital posts, that they would bring home to Departments their duty to consider security when making such appointments and that the detection of even a very small number of unreliable persons in such posts would counter-balance any disadvantages in the system.[74]

In the chill climate following the arrest of Fuchs, with the Korean War in an acute phase, Attlee and his colleagues had no difficulty in accepting the Winnifrith proposals when GEN 183 met on 13 November 1950. Manny Shinwell, the Minister of Defence, said exactly this once Winnifrith had finished his presentation of the report: 'In present circumstances the country could not afford to take the risk of neglecting any practicable measure for increasing security.'[75] There was no dissent around the table, though the junior minister from the Air Ministry, Aidan Crawley, warned that American experience showed that FBI methods could impair scientific vitality. Attlee, a great believer in discretion and the self-disciplining concept of public service and personal duty, added a very British tone to this extension of the reach of the secret state that afternoon in the Prime Minister's Room at the House of Commons. For him,

the chief point arising from the report was the need to change the attitude of Departments to one of conscious endeavour to confirm the reliability of holders of key posts, and to ensure that all in positions of responsibility become security-minded. It followed that Departments should not too easily accept the results of routine enquiry when deciding on the fitness of an individual to hold a key post, and should be prepared to go further if necessary. This was not likely to apply to most regular civil servants: the difficulties would be greatest in Departments of recent growth employing staff who had not absorbed the traditions of the public service. Special enquiries through the Security Service and the local police should, however, be quite exceptional and should be undertaken only with the approval of the Minister concerned.[76]

This was Attlee the public school headmaster, as Patrick O'Donovan characterized him a year or so later[77] – decency blended with a touch of naivety about the goodness of others.

For positive vetting took on a life on its own and became far from 'quite exceptional'. Two middle-ranking ministers present at GEN 183 that day, John Strachey, the former Marxist now Secretary of State for

War, and Arthur Henderson, Secretary of State for Air, thought the list of PV posts in their departments 'were not full enough'.[78] How right they proved. PVing, as it became known in Whitehall, spread mightily. When Christopher Andrew's official history of MI5, *The Defence of the Realm*, was published to mark the agency's centenary in 2009, it became apparent just how swiftly the Security Service was swamped by the growing demands of the still-infant positive vetting system as, under US pressure following the defection of Burgess and Maclean and the earlier conviction for atomic espionage of Klaus Fuchs, the numbers to be PV'd shot up from 1,000 to 11,000.[79]

Figures are hard to come by both for the full reach of positive vetting and for those transferred or dismissed on the basis of its inquiries. But, in the early 1980s, I managed to acquire privately a set of figures for the Home Civil Service and published them in *The Economist*, where I then worked. Since the adoption of the first 'purge procedure' in 1948, twenty-five British officials had been dismissed for security reasons, twenty-five resigned, eighty-eight people were transferred to non-sensitive work and thirty-three officials were later reinstated. None were named. In the United States, by contrast, security purges had led to the sacking of 9,500 federal civil servants. A further 15,000 resigned while under investigation for suspected communist affiliations. All were named.[80] At much the same time as I acquired the figures for UK purgees, the Security Commission, under the Law Lord, Lord Diplock, published in a 1982 report the fact that positive vetting now drew 68,000 posts inside its net.[81] Quite apart from the naivety of the original aspiration to confine the reach of PV to an inner one thousand, successive developments and refinements of the system (often in reaction to specific security failures) exerted a multiplier effect. My student Daniel Sherman has mapped the road from GEN 183 to the world Lord Diplock and his fellow Security Commissioners observed[82] some thirty years after it fell to Winston Churchill on 8 January 1952 to announce the implementation of a positive vetting scheme for state servants engaged in exceptionally secret work.[83]

As Sherman noted, the British state exhibited something of a 'split personality', showing political hostility towards communism and at the same time 'maintaining Whitehall's delicate balancing act of safeguarding freedom of expression and the maximum possible civil liberties, while doggedly vetting . . . to try and achieve the best security possible'.[84]

In December 1953, the Chiefs of Staff Committee decided that positive vetting would be applied to those members of the armed forces who were granted 'constant and regular access to top secret defence information'.[85] Just over a year later, the procedure was extended to 'senior staff of firms handling top secret Government contracts'.[86]

Instead of the police, the Ministry of Supply, which contained the largest number of posts to be vetted from the start, became responsible for running a team of investigating officers to carry out the inquiries across Whitehall. The Ministry of Defence took over responsibility for this on the demise of the Ministry of Supply.

From 1955, following inquests into the defection to the Soviet Union of Guy Burgess and Donald Maclean in 1951, what today would be called the sexual preferences of those within the reach of PVing were added to the scope of inquiry on the grounds that certain activities could, if concealed or illegal, leave an official liable to blackmail by a hostile intelligence service.[87] A glance at Air Ministry files for the early 1960s, shows just how unexceptional positive vetting had now become in what was then the department for the nuclear deterrent. An internal notice to divisional heads explained that

A special procedure, known as positive vetting (PV) is used to determine the reliability of civilian staff who are to be employed on particularly secret work. This procedure is to be applied to any member of the staff who is required to have

(a) regular and constant access to top secret defence information; or
(b) any access to top secret atomic or cosmic information.[88]

The 'Security Questionnaire' attached to the file covers standard curriculum vitae matters plus relatives living abroad, foreign travel, offences against the law and fascist or communist affiliations, sympathizers or associates ('the word "Communists" embraces Trotskyists for the purposes of this form' adds a nice, definitional touch). The vettee is warned that 'enquiries which will be made will not necessarily be confined to the former or present employers and character referees named in your answers . . .'[89]

Serious vetting of a different kind was extended to senior officials of Civil Service trade unions who were involved in pay and conditions negotiations on behalf of public servants within the secret state following the Radcliffe Report of 1962, which examined the implications of, among others, the case of John Vassall, the homosexual Admiralty clerk who had been blackmailed into spying for Russia.[90] As a result the government decided not to allow some very senior trade unionists to negotiate on behalf of their members in the Cabinet Office, the Ministry of Defence, the Service Departments, the Foreign Office and the Atomic Energy Authority.[91] The vetting of senior politicians has never been admitted. But throughout the Cold War years it was the practice of the head of MI5 on a change of government to leave a dossier containing things the new Prime Minister needed to know when first back from the Palace before making his or her ministerial appointments.[92] A small number of journalists, too, had inquiries made about them if their reporting took them some way into the workings of the secret state.[93]

Was PVing worth it? A former Special Branch policeman, now an investigating officer, asked me this in the late 1980s after I had helped him renew a senior civil servant's clearance. He plainly thought the effort and expense was very much open to question. I was not so sure for two reasons: one, pure Winnifrith, was that such steps were necessary if even a few genuine security risks were either deterred from trying to move into sensitive posts or discovered if they did so, and, secondly, the process of PVing, including the completion of the questionnaire, made those concerned directly and personally aware that they were shifting into the inner circle of the state where security really mattered. This was particularly important, I thought, as Section 2 of the 1911 Official Secrets Act (not repealed until 1989) was so crudely and widely drawn as to be discredited and 'signing' it – as new civil servants were required to do – was largely meaningless.

What of the wider 'communist problem'? Apart from deeply concealed agents-in-place, the main concern from the late 1940s on was with the influence the CPGB wielded among the senior officers of trade unions, which was out of all proportion to overall numbers (30,000 out of 8.7 million UK trade unionists, MI5 reckoned in 1948[94]), the personal qualities of some communist union leaders such as Arthur Horner of the Mineworkers,[95] and the 'central discipline and co-ordination' the Party brought to the trade unionists within its ranks.[96] In 1955 MI5 briefed the Prime Minister (Eden being alarmed by the current level of industrial unrest) that, as Cabinet Secretary Sir Norman Brook's summary put it, the CPGB believed that 'the advocacy of strike action would more often hinder than help it in its primary objective of penetrating and eventually controlling the trade union movement . . . while its members account for less than one in 500 of the national trade union membership, the Party now controls the Executive Committees of three trade unions; and thirteen General Secretaries and at least one in eight of all full-time officials are Communists'.[97]

Reading the files, including those dealing with the internal threat posed by the CPGB and the Party's dealings with Moscow which reached the JIC, it is striking to see the detail with which inner-party matters are displayed. One gets the unmistakable impression that MI5 had the insides of 16 King Street (the Party's headquarters in Covent Garden) very well covered in terms of both human agents and technical surveillance.[98] When the CPGB, in severe financial difficulties, sold 16 King Street to Lloyds Bank for over £1 million in 1980, 'a hidden microphone was found embedded in the wall'.[99] It is plain from Curry's internal history that MI5 was monitoring throughout World War II 'a steady flow of secret information about weapons and about operations to Party Headquarters' provided by the 'Forces Organisation' of the CP, some of the most important of which Curry listed.[100] And the huge haul of KGB archive material copied by its archivist Vasili Mitrokhin, and removed (along with Mitrokhin and his family) to the UK by MI6 in 1992,[101] demonstrated the unsurprising fact that Soviet intelligence knew King Street was bugged, thanks to Anthony Blunt's presence in MI5. Blunt told his controller, Boris Krotenschield (whom he shared with Philby), that James Klugmann, a leading British communist intellectual who later wrote two volumes of the Party's official history,[102] had boasted within the walls of 16 King Street of passing to Yugoslav communists classified information gleaned in the course of his work in the Yugoslav Section of the Special Operations Executive in Cairo.[103] King Street's telephones were tapped continually.[104]

Christopher Andrew's authorized history of MI5 revealed that by '1952 the Security Service reported that a comparison of its existing files on the CPGB with the latest sample of current Party membership records it had purloined indicated that it had identified approximately 90 per cent of the 35,000 CPGB members. The missing 10 per cent were thought to be mostly young or new members "who have not yet come to notice and who are so far of minor security significance".'[105]

Though Christopher Andrew could not identify her, MI5 was about to succeed in placing an agent inside the CPGB in a position that was positively plated with red gold. Julia Pirie became personal assistant to the Party's General Secretary, John Gollan, and stayed there for two decades. As her obituary in the *Daily Telegraph* put it: 'Julia Pirie would pass over her regular reports and photocopied documents to her MI5 handlers during cricket matches at the Oval cricket ground, a procedure that left her with a lifelong love of the game.'[106]

Her *Telegraph* obituarist also speculated that it was 'highly likely' that Miss Pirie was instrumental in enabling the Security Service 'to obtain the entire secret membership of the Party . . . [members who] were told to keep their membership secret so that they could be used by the KGB or Soviet military intelligence (the GRU) in operations in Britain'.[107]

If war had come, MI5 and Special Branch, in organization-smashing mode, would have known quite well who and where most overt Party members were and very likely the covert ones too. The detailed contingency plans for the round-up are not yet declassified. But we do know from fragments of the Defence Transition Committee archive that by early 1949, plans were in place to reopen, if necessary, internment camps on the Isle of Man which had been used to house so-called 'enemy aliens' during World War II.[108]*

Since the first editions of *The Secret State* were published, an MI5 file has been declassified which reveals just how sizeable and elaborate

---

* The 1948 Government War Book indicated that in the run-up to global war MI5 would '[s]end to the Home Office lists of persons in respect of whom Detention Orders might be required', some of which might be placed upon 'prominent trade unionists'.

the World War III internment plans became in the early and mid-1950s. The planning was jointly conducted by the Security Service and the Home Office. Operation HILLARY involved a substantial round-up and detention of possible subversives and saboteurs who might become active during a transition to war.

It embraced 3,000 people in all: 1,000 were British subjects (including about 200 women); 2,000 were aliens (of whom 500 were women). The UK males earmarked for detention who lived in England south of a line from the Severn to the Wash would be kept initially on Epsom racecourse in Surrey; northerners would be taken to a holiday camp in Rhyl, North Wales. Southern-based aliens would go to Ascot racecourse in Berkshire; northern aliens to Rhyl. The women would be sent either to Holloway Gaol in north London or to an unspecified prison in the north of England. Once processed, they would all be sent, if circumstances allowed, to various holiday camps on the Isle of Man.[109] Neither the MI5 files available at the National Archives nor Christopher Andrew's official history of MI5 tells us who was on those early 1950s lists and which members of the Communist Party of Great Britain were deemed subversive and which were not.

In a strange way, both MI5 and the CPGB knew where they stood with each other. Their tussle had been continuous, as Curry indicated,[110] since 31 July 1920 when 160 'revolutionary socialists with new hope in their hearts' strode into the Cannon Street Hotel near St Paul's Cathedral in the City of London to set about founding a Communist Party of Great Britain with Lenin's encouragement.[111] From the very earliest years Party people knew they were under surveillance, some of which went ludicrously awry. In 1924 the speaker at a CP meeting opened a trapdoor beneath the stage 'to discover two men taking short-hand notes. The police were called and they arrested the men, only discovering later that they had arrested fellow policemen.'[112]

By 1957, however, both Party and Security Service had to face a new phenomenon which left both, initially, somewhat surprised and baffled. This was the sudden surge to prominence of a revived peace movement in the run-up to what became the foundation of the Campaign for Nuclear Disarmament. For historians of peace movements, however, the bigger retrospective surprise is that a serious anti-nuclear weapons movement did not form earlier. Attlee's Defence Minister, A. V. Alexander, had announced in the House of Commons on 12 May 1948, in reply to a planted parliamentary question, that 'all types of modern weapon, including atomic weapons, are being developed',[113] and the press and the political nation had hardly taken any notice.[114] A month before, there had been a meeting on atomic weapons at Caxton Hall in Westminster addressed by such peace-movement stalwarts as Vera Brittain and Ritchie Calder,[115] but it took another nine years before a coalescence of radical and pacifist groups came together with a degree of force and verve that enabled them to catch and ride a mood which left both the Labour Party and the CPGB somewhat baffled.

It is intriguing to compare the histories of CND Mark I (1958–64 as distinct from its 1980s revival) written in the early 1960s by Christopher Driver, a sympathetic observer, for a public audience[116] and the much shorter MI5 one prepared for a very select audience of one – Prime Minister Harold Macmillan.[117] In the spring of 1963 Macmillan held a meeting on 'Security', partly prompted by the so-called 'Spies for Peace'. During the Easter 1963 CND Aldermaston March (Aldermaston being the site of the government's Atomic Weapons Research Establishment) the direct-action offshoot of CND, the Committee of 100, began distributing a pamphlet of six sheets of duplicated foolscap as the march passed through the Berkshire woods on its way to Reading.[118]

The timing and location were perfect. The pamphlet's authors, the 'Spies for Peace', knew that one of the government's new underground regional seats of government (which we will examine more fully in Chapter 4), RSG-6, lay nearby close to the village of Warren Row. The flimsy document carried a dramatic title, 'Danger! Official Secret: RSG-6', and it went on to inform its avid readers 'about a small group of people who have accepted thermo-nuclear war as a probability, and are consciously and carefully planning for it . . . They are based in fourteen secret headquarters, each ruled by a Regional Commissioner with absolute power over millions of people.'[119]

This disclosure represented a substantial breach of official secrecy. The 'Spies for Peace', who have never been identified, but who 'emerged' from the London Committee of 100 over the winter of 1962–3,[120] had actually managed to break into the Warren Row installation in February

1963 and left after photographing several classified files and removing a suitcase full of material.[121] As a result, on Easter Saturday 1963 hundreds of marchers left the main column to demonstrate outside Warren Row '[m]uch to the annoyance of the CND leadership.'[122]

Within a few days, Macmillan held his 'Security' meeting (the minutes of which have not been declassified) and asked for information on 'the development of the Nuclear Disarmament Movement'. Within a day, Sir Charles Cunningham, Permanent Secretary to the Home Office, forwarded to No. 10 'a memorandum which has been prepared summarising the information available to us'.[123] It is plainly an MI5 brief as it deals with the degree to which CND had been penetrated by communists.[124]

The MI5 paper opened with a very succinct history of the faltering, early, pre-CND days. The nuclear disarmament movement

grew from small beginnings in the early and middle 1950s. Two small demonstrations, one at Aldermaston, took place in 1952 [organized as a one-off by Hugh Brock, then editor of *Peace News*[125]]. In 1954, the year of the American Pacific test with its effects on the crew of the Japanese fishing smack 'Lucky Dragon', Canon Collins [of St Paul's Cathedral], Fenner Brockway, MP and Dr Donald Soper [leading Methodist minister] tried to mount an anti H-bomb campaign.[126]

The huge US thermonuclear explosion at Bikini Atoll on 1 March 1954 (at 15 megatons the 'Bravo' shot was the largest the Americans ever mounted[127]) covered the Japanese fishermen, their ship eighty-five miles away and outside the exclusion zone, with fall-out. They returned to Japan with nearly the whole crew ill 'with classic symptoms of radiation sickness'.[128] The Japanese government protested. The outside world, for the first time, began to appreciate fully what these weapons could do and debate was widespread, including in the House of Commons on 5 April 1954, which led to the foundation of the Hydrogen Bomb National Campaign two days later,[129] to which the short MI5 history of CND and its precursors referred.[130]

It still surprises me that this pressure group resonated so feebly. As Christopher Driver wrote less than ten years after Soper, Collins and Brockway made their initial attempt to mobilize opinion: 'The Hydrogen

Bomb National Campaign is little remembered and it is an index of its obscurity that a year or two later, when anti-nuclear agitation sprang up spontaneously in various parts of the country, most people felt that they were starting something fresh . . .'[131]

There were a few mid-1950s sputterings which the MI5 analyst felt worth summarizing:

In 1956, the year when the British Government announced its intention to test a thermo-nuclear bomb at Christmas Island, a National Council for the Abolition of Nuclear Weapons Tests was set up with Peggy Duff as Organiser and Secretary and Lord Russell as one of its sponsors. Small independent demonstrations occurred from time to time; for instance, shortly before the Christmas Island test in May 1957, a procession of women in black sashes marched from Hyde Park to Trafalgar Square.[132]

But what were the factors which led to the welling up of spontaneous anti-nuclear agitation in 1957? The Driver and MI5 analyses overlap to a considerable degree. For the Security Service, 'an organised Nuclear Disarmament Movement can perhaps be said to have begun with the formation of the Direct Action Committee in November 1957 and the Campaign for Nuclear Disarmament in February 1958'.[133]

MI5's dating of the origins of the DAC is a little awry. The Emergency Committee for Direct Action against Nuclear War, as it was first called, was created in April 1957 to help get Harold and Sheila Steele to the Pacific, where they wished to mount a floating protest against the Christmas Island test (in the event, they arrived too late to protest against the May explosion). MI5 was up against an unusually eclectic group in the DAC, as Driver neatly illustrated: 'Its sponsors included several Quakers (Horace Alexander, Ruth Fry, Laurence Hansman), an Earl (Russell), a Goon (Spike Milligan), and an Anarchist biologist (Alex Comfort).'[134] The 23 November 1957 meeting, which the Security Service analysts rightly saw as significant to the wider history of the revived peace movement, was held 'to welcome Harold Steele, who had returned from Japan, and to discuss further projects'.[135]

It was at this meeting, too, that the possibility of an Aldermaston march emerged. It was proposed by Hugh Brock, a veteran pacifist who had been imprisoned during World War II as a conscientious objector.

It had been suggested to him by Laurence Brown in May 1957 as they watched the procession in the pouring rain of 2,000 women in black sashes from Hyde Park to Trafalgar Square organized by the National Committee for the Abolition of Nuclear Weapons Tests,[136] the demonstration MI5 had thought worthy of inclusion in its paper for the Prime Minister.[137] The DAC recruited Pat Arrowsmith, a social worker and a NCANWT activist, who put off finding a new job to organize the first Aldermaston march instead[138] – an event central to CND's image which, along with other aspects of the campaign, changed the face of protest and pressure in post-war Britain and paved the way for Greenpeace and a host of single-issue organizations whose vitality and, in some cases, membership figures came to eclipse those of the mainstream political parties.[139]

MI5's dating system was a little astray too, on the foundation of CND. The key meeting took place on the evening of 15 January 1958 in Canon Collins's study at 2 Amen Court in the shadow of St Paul's Cathedral. The intention to proceed was announced at a press conference on 30 January and the inaugural meeting took place in Central Hall, Westminster, on 17 February (clearly the founding moment MI5 had in mind). The packed, 5,000-strong gathering was roused to passion by the political and diplomatic historian A. J. P. Taylor in particular, as we have seen.[140] The cause of unilateral British nuclear disarmament took flight.

It took many by surprise. What, retrospectively, did MI5 believe gave it lift-off? 'The factors,' it told Macmillan over five years later,

that prompted their formation at this time were increasing anxiety about testing; the public discovery that American planes carrying H-bombs were patrolling over Britain; inferences drawn from the Defence White Paper that nuclear forces would be used to reply even to conventionally armed enemy attack; the Anglo-American agreement on missile bases in Britain; and increasing publicity for the view that Britain could offer no realistic defence to nuclear attack.[141]

Driver's analysis is remarkably similar to MI5's, though he (unlike the Security Service, which may have felt constrained in addressing its Downing Street customer), filled in the wider picture of post-Suez and

Hungary disillusionment, 'which at one stroke turned the most sensitive minds of [this] ... generation [of the intellectual left] equally away from Communist leanings and from all forms of political bipartisanship ...'.[142]

Both MI5 and Driver placed great emphasis on the contribution of Macmillan's first Minister of Defence, Duncan Sandys, to the mix of causes which led towards the road to Aldermaston (the first march over Easter 1958 went from Trafalgar Square to the Atomic Weapons Research Establishment; subsequent ones went in the reverse direction). The 1957 White Paper containing the results of the Sandys defence review, with its promise both to reduce spending and to abolish conscription thanks to a central reliance on nuclear deterrence with the H-bomb-equipped V-force on the horizon, spared the Queen's subjects very little:

It must be frankly recognised that there is at present no means of providing adequate protection for the people of this country against the consequences of an attack with nuclear weapons. Though in the event of war, the fighter aircraft of the RAF would unquestionably take a heavy toll of enemy bombers, a proportion would inevitably get through. Even if it were only a dozen, they could with megaton [i.e. hydrogen] bombs inflict widespread devastation.[143]

The argument of the Macmillan government, as expressed in the Sandys White Paper, was that in the absence of international agreement, 'the only existing safeguard against major aggression is the power to threaten retaliation with nuclear weapons'.[144] Sandys went on to declare that:

While Britain cannot by comparison [with the United States] make more than a modest contribution, there is a wide measure of agreement that she must possess an appreciable element of nuclear deterrent power of her own. British atomic bombs are already in steady production and the RAF holds a substantial number of them. A British megaton weapon has now been developed. This will shortly be tested and thereafter a stock will be manufactured.[145]

It was Sandys's claim that there was 'a wide measure of agreement' on Britain as a nuclear deterrent nation that CND set out to disprove.

The Labour Party declined to make itself the vehicle for this during the famous debate at its Brighton Conference in October 1957 when the shadow Foreign Secretary, Aneurin Bevan, horrified many of his Bevanite followers by denouncing unilateralism as an 'emotional spasm' and deriding the notion that a British Foreign Secretary should have to stride 'naked into the international conference chamber'.[146] Though unilateral nuclear disarmament never did prevail as the numerically dominant strand of thought in the UK (the opinion polls suggest it peaked in April 1960, when 33 per cent indicated a belief that Britain should '[g]ive up nuclear weapons entirely'[147]), it exerted a huge appeal across a spectrum of opinion in the late 1950s before, briefly, capturing the Labour Party (though not the Labour leadership) at the 1960 Scarborough Conference.[148]

A future chief of the Secret Intelligence Service, David Spedding, went on the 1959 Aldermaston march and wrote it up as part of an anti-nuclear article in his school magazine at Sherborne, 'which caused some merriment when it was resuscitated by his MI6 colleagues many years later'.[149] A young grammar-school boy who within a few years would be one of MoD's nuclear retaliation planners was a keen CND member in its early days (a fact which gave his positive vetters pause – but they passed him. For his identity see p. 405).[150] Among the right-wingers there was a reaction too. Some, true to form, tried to convert future nuclear anxiety into present laughter. Noël Coward, on a flight to California to meet (among others) Marlene Dietrich in the summer of 1957, read Neville Shute's *On the Beach* on the plane. It is, he wrote,

a grisly description of a group of people left alive in Australia when the rest of the world has been annihilated by H-bombs. They are waiting for the spreading radioactivity to spread to them and wipe them out which, eventually, it does. It's written with his usual fluency and is a good idea, but all the characters are so sickeningly decent and 'ordinary' and such good sorts that personally I longed for the slowly approaching 'fall-out' to get a move on.[151]

Even P. G. Wodehouse managed to weave CND into his extraordinary world with 'Bingo Bans the Bomb' when Bingo Little finds himself pulled to the pavement in Trafalgar Square by a beautiful young spriguette of the aristocracy, Mabel Murgatroyd, his subsequent arrest and a photograph of it in the *Mirror* newspaper causing him no end of bother with 'Mrs Bingo'.[152]

One set of imaginations, however, which the anti-nuclear movement did not capture in 1957–8 were those possessed by Moscow's 'messenger boys' in King Street, but a few hundred yards from Trafalgar Square. Unlike several of those who quit the CPGB in horror at Hungary, to create the early 'New Left', who found in CND 'the cause and the comradeship'[153] they had lost by leaving the Party, the Gollan-led CP 'hesitated before lending its support to CND'.[154] Francis Beckett sees this as a crucial moment in the long decline of the British Communist Party, 'allowing its enemies on the left to claim that it had betrayed the one movement which offered hope for the world. Its instinctive radicalism had deserted it. Its leaders did not seem to understand that 1956 had broken the Party's near monopoly on the left.'[155]

In Driver's words:

Despite extensive early coverage by the *Daily Worker* the Communist Party as such did not begin to support CND systematically till 1959, and at the 1957 Labour Party Conference Communist-controlled [trades union] votes were actually cast against the unilateralist motion. By 1960 the position was reversed, and Communist activity in unions on behalf of unilateralism, though probably not decisive in terms of votes, did give plausibility to Mr Gaitskell's [the Labour Party Leader's] outburst at Scarborough against 'pacifists, unilateralists and fellow-travellers'.[156]

Driver noted that during the Scarborough conference, 'Communists were unusually conspicuous among the CND claque. But the more popular CND's own brand of protest became, the less point there was in the Communist Party crying up what it had failed to control.'[157]

The rather shambolic structure – or lack of structure – on which CND rested made the standard CPGB skills at taking over trade union branches inoperable.[158] And MI5 reported this accurately to Harold Macmillan:

Since 1959 the Communist Party have participated in the Aldermaston marches and other demonstrations organised by the C.N.D, Direct Action Committee and the Committee of 100. This is not from the belief in the unilateralist cause but because the Communists see in these movements a chance to embarrass the Government and weaken the NATO alliance. At the same time there is little evidence that the Communists have succeeded in penetrating the movements to any great extent.[159]

In a strange way, Macmillan and CND deserved each other. The critic and writer Anthony Hartley was among the first to notice the symmetry between the veteran of the Somme and the young veterans of the Aldermaston marches. Writing of CND in 1963, he pointed out that there existed a 'gulf between undirected idealism and political possibility which has been opened by the decline of Great Britain's world power'. Looking back twenty years later, A. J. P. Taylor agreed that 'we made one great mistake which ultimately doomed CND to futility. We thought that Great Britain was still a great power whose example would affect the rest of the world. Ironically we were the last Imperialists.'[160] In other words, the ministers round the Cabinet table in 1954 and 1962–3, so keen (with Churchill) to go thermonuclear as a way of keeping a place at the 'top table' and (with Macmillan) to purchase Polaris for an updated version of the same impulse, shared with CND a belief in Britain as a big player in the world's game and a powerful shaper of the behaviour of others.

Such speculations were not for MI5's analysts, however. They may not have seen Reds under every CND banner, but the real question for them was what kind of a threat did a non-CP-penetrated CND represent? And here they were particularly concerned with the direct activists on the DAC and, later, the Committee of 100. Indeed, these were the trigger for Macmillan's request for his spring 1963 briefing. This element of CND, the image of the aged and distinguished Bertrand Russell sitting down outside the MOD in Whitehall and demonstrators being carted, very roughly in some cases, away and placed in police Black Marias after the Committee of 100's sit-down in Trafalgar Square on 17 September 1961,[161] is the one that chiefly remains in the popular memory – partly because it was imitated endlessly by the student protest movement, powerfully driven from 1965 by the escalation of the Vietnam War, into which much of CND-style activist politics mutated.

As Driver put it: 'From 1957 until 1961 (when it was merged into the Committee of 100) the DAC was the heart and soul, or the thorn

in the flesh – according to taste – of CND.'[162] MI5 stressed the importance of direct action developments in 1960–61:

The Committee of 100 was launched in October 1960, under the leadership
of Lord [Bertrand] Russell and Rev. Michael Scott as a breakaway from CND.
The Committee felt that more directness and urgency were needed to change
national policy; they planned to do it by organising acts of civil disobedience
involving at least 2000 people at a time. The Direct Action Committee soon
became absorbed into the Committee of 100.[163]

MI5 listed for Macmillan the 'progressively more numerous and
stubborn encounters with the police and the courts' in which the
Committee of 100 engaged during 1961, culminating 'in Trafalgar
Square in September 1961 where crowds, including sightseers, at one
time reached 8,000; 1,297 arrests were made'.[164]

CND had a penchant for taking on nuclear-related defence installations from its early days when the DAC lobbied workers building a
missile site at North Pickenham near Swaffham in Norfolk in December 1958, enraging sections of those they sought to influence by sitting
down in a cement mixer.[165] It was the Committee of 100's spreading
of this practice which concerned the authorities and, later, in the weeks
following the Cuban missile crisis, attracted the attention of the Joint
Intelligence Committee.

In fact, two direct action veterans, arrested after National Disobedience Day, 9 December 1961, when three air bases (Wethersfield,
Ruislip and Brize Norton) were among the demonstrators' targets, have
entered British intelligence folklore. MI5 reckoned the subsequent
imprisonment of Michael Randle, Pat Pottle and four other members
of the Committee of 100 'and the failure of the "National Civil Disobedience Day" demonstrations marked the beginning of a decline in
the Committee of 100's influence'.[166] Pottle and Randle, however, MI5
would hear of again nearly thirty years later, for their names came up
in the memoirs of George Blake, the MI6 officer who spied for the
KGB and was sentenced to forty-two years for it in 1961.

In the spring of 1962 Blake found himself a member of the same
musical appreciation class in Wormwood Scrubs as Pottle and Randle,
who were serving eighteen months for conspiring to incite others to

commit a breach of Section 1 of the 1911 Official Secrets Act in and around RAF Wethersfield in Essex, on which US Air Force planes were parked.[167] As Blake explained much later:

From the very beginning there was a good rapport between us. We all three considered ourselves political prisoners, had all three been sentenced under the Official Secrets Act . . . It is true, that they in no way approved of what I had done – they condemned spying in general – and made no secret of this. But they thought the sentence I had been given vicious and inhuman . . . and had a great deal of sympathy for me.[168]

They were able to demonstrate this four years later when they helped shelter Blake after his escape from Wormwood Scrubs and later helped smuggle him out of the country to where he presented himself to surprised East German border guards.[169]

In 1963 MI5 reckoned that with Pottle and Randle and others at its heart in prison, 'increasing disagreement among the leaders, increasing debts and decreasing support by the public', the Committee of 100 was on the slide throughout 1962:

Plans to promote ideas of nuclear disarmament and disobedience tactics in the armed forces and in industry met with little success. The Committee aimed at getting a minimum of 7,000 pledges of support for a demonstration outside the Air Ministry in September 1962, but only 1,000 supporters turned up.[170]

Within weeks the Cuban missile crisis had come from nowhere and concentrated minds – including those of British intelligence – on CND's big theme quite like no other crisis before or since.

As MI5 reminded Macmillan six months later:

During the Cuban Crisis in October 1962, the CND and the Committee of 100 took part in a number of demonstrations which were largely spontaneous and fairly well supported. After the crisis, public support, which some of the leaders hoped would increase, appears to have dwindled; and in recent months, partly no doubt because of the weather [the 1962–3 winter was the worst since 1947], there has been little public activity until this Easter's Aldermaston march.[171]

Nonetheless, Cuba (as we will see in Chapter 4) concentrated the minds of Whitehall's nuclear and home defence contingency planners and the JIC, too, which commissioned a report on 'Anti-Nuclear Demonstrations at RAF Airfields in a Period of Tension'. And here elements within CND and the CPGB were treated as separate contributors to an identical problem. The report noted that since 'the Wethersfield demonstration support for the Committee of 100 has continuously declined, partly as a result of intrigues and partly because its more idealistic followers are shocked at the way it is been exploited for political purposes'.[172]

Consistent with its long-standing theme that CP membership does not itself indicate disloyalty, the JIC offered some reassurance (on this front, at least) to the Prime Minister and its other regular readers about a possible future transition to war:

If hostilities are imminent, natural loyalties will come into play and only a minority [of CND and Committee of 100 people] will be prepared to take active steps to impede the operation of the bases. A similar state of affairs will obtain in the Communist Party, which will lose much rank and file support. Those who continue to accept the party's discipline, however, can be expected to be particularly militant, stimulated not only by a desire to help Russia but by a belief that, when it comes to a real crisis, provided everything has to be done to undermine their position, the imperialists will give in without a fight. It is reasonable to conclude, therefore, that while the number of nuclear disarmers and Communists will be considerably reduced in a period of tension, there will be a militant rump which will try to be as obstructive as possible.[173]*

From Cuba on, Whitehall's intelligence and war-planning circles do appear to have shifted permanently from the late 1940s CPGB-driven notion of present internal danger, to a wider one which by the late 1960s had incorporated assessments of the problems the more militant

---

* During the September 1962 simulation of the transition to war by GEN 772, the FELSTEAD committee, a figure was given for the 'British subjects and aliens likely to be dangerous to the State'. The committee recommended that 'About 100 persons, three-quarters of them in London . . . be so detained' – a very considerable reduction from the early 1950s Operation HILLARY.

end of the student movement, as well as some nuclear disarmers, might impose during a transition to war.

Sixties historian Arthur Marwick cautions against too blithe a fusion of first-wave CND and mid-to-late sixties youth movements but sees some connection. Noting that after the 1963 Aldermaston march, enthusiasm for CND 'greatly waned', Marwick (perhaps wrongly) says the campaign 'was not really a part of youth subculture' (as a grammar-school boy, though a non-CND one, it struck me as very much a part of what then passed as a 'youth subculture' in Stroud in Gloucestershire). But Marwick does see CND as providing 'a link between the New Left revival of the mid-1950s, and the radical student movements of the middle and later sixties; it also provided a symbol, the upturned "Y" ,[174] and a badge, which many young protesters sported for the rest of the decade, even if not directly associated with CND'.[175]

In the aftermath of the Grovesnor Square demonstration of 17 March 1968, when 25,000 (mainly young) people took part in an anti-Vietnam War protest outside the US Embassy organized by the Vietnam Solidarity Campaign, the student demo factor was firmly built into transition-to-war planning. At and after Grovesnor Square, nearly 250 people were charged with offences; 45 demonstrators and 117 police officers received medical treatment after scenes which 'were the most violent yet seen on British television'.[176] MI5 carried out a new subversion threat assessment over the summer of 1968, which fed that autumn into a study for the Chiefs of Staff on the 'Security of the United Kingdom Base in the Pre-Attack Phase of General War',[177] which included protest movements as well as the CPGB and the smaller Trotskyist parties.

The MI5 report has not been declassified,[178] but its gist can be derived from the document compiled for the Chiefs by their Defence Policy Staff. Its overall conclusion, in the words of the DPS summary, was 'that it is doubtful whether the subversive threat as currently seen would be beyond the normal capacity of the police, though there could be interference with movement on a scale large enough to have a signif-icant cumulative effect on a complex timetable' for moving military 'reinforcements to the Continent in a period of tension'.[179]

The MI5 report concentrated 'on activity involving the Communist

Party of Great Britain and known Trotskyist or anarchist groups . . . since the SS [Security Service] regards as remote the likelihood that other protest movements or the like could reach the point of posing a significant subversive threat without members of these groups taking an active part in organising them, if only on a "bandwagon" basis'. MI5, however, appears to have been a touch uneasy about its generally reassuring assessment. This report, their policy staff told the Chiefs, 'relates to the position as it is known today. It is impossible in this field to make long-term forecasts with any confidence, though the SS [Security Service] is disposed to think that in general movements of a Trotskyist or anarchist [k]ind will tend to grow in strength. The SS has it in mind to review the assessment annually.'[180]

But what of the people the guardians of national security had been most concerned about since the very first report had been presented to GEN 183 over twenty years before – the sleepers, the concealed communist agents described as the 'dormant agents' by the JIC in its scenarios for the FALLEX/INVALUABLE transition-to-war exercise in 1968 (of which more in Chapter 6)? In 1968, they continued to regard their threat as saboteurs (rather than providers of information) as limited. In the Defence Policy Staff's report to the Chiefs that autumn, the MI5 view is recorded like this:

The SS concludes . . . that the USSR probably still has some capability for sabotage in the United Kingdom, though the likelihood of its being used in a period of tension is questionable; and that there is no evidence that any other organisations have sabotage plans on a substantial scale, though the possibility of isolated acts by individuals cannot be ruled out.[181]

The defence planners evidently thought MI5 a tad complacent here and let their bosses, the Chiefs of Staff, know this:

We deduce that while the currently assessed threat of interference which existing police capability could not contain is low, it is not so plainly negligible that it can be dismissed out of hand. It is important to note against the background of the difficulties of long-term prediction in this field, that a new or increased threat could develop faster than a counter-capability could be built from scratch to offset it.[182]

The military turned out to be nearer the mark than MI5, as became apparent three years later when Oleg Lyalin, a Soviet sabotage expert working under diplomatic cover in London, came over to British intelligence.

We know from the Mitrokhin Archive that in 1967, a year before the MI5 assessment, Yuri Andropov, on taking over the KGB, revitalized its sabotage capacity in the form of a new Department V.[183] Lyalin, 'an expert in hand-to-hand combat as well as a highly proficient marksman and parachutist',[184] was not on the list of intelligence officers operating out of the Soviet Embassy and Trade Delegation in London with which MI5, via the Foreign Secretary Michael Stewart, provided the Prime Minister Harold Wilson in September 1968.[185] When MI5 recruited him as a defector-in-place in the spring of 1971 (the following September he came in person[186]), Lyalin produced an alarming list of contingencies for which Andropov's saboteurs were planning in a transition to war. It was partly due to Lyalin's information that Edward Heath, Wilson's successor in No. 10, and Stewart's successor at the FCO Sir Alec Douglas-Home authorized the dramatic expulsion of 105 KGB and GRU officers operating undercover in the UK in 1971.[187]

George Walden, the FCO official who had much to do with devising the expulsion and coined its title – 'Operation FOOT (my none-too-clever code-name for giving the KGB the boot)'[188] – has a vividly written portrait of Lyalin in his memoir, *Lucky George*:

Lyalin was a good example of the problem we faced. He did legitimate work as an importer of clothes, travelling widely in the North of England and buying nothing more security-sensitive than knitware and woollen socks. In his spare moments he made sabotage plans for use in time of war, including maps for landing sites for Soviet submarines. His efforts, which I saw, appeared a little fantastical (park the sub, come up the beach, and turn right at the Bill and Duck), but he was the sort of person who, given the choice, you would prefer not to have running around.[189]

But Andrew and Mitrokhin's account suggests the planning went much further than this, from destroying the V-bombers on their airbases in Lincolnshire and blowing up the Ballistic Missile Early Warning system on Fylingdales Moor in Yorkshire to flooding the London

Underground and infiltrating KGB agents as messengers or delivery men into Whitehall's corridors, where they would scatter poison capsules designed to kill those who trod on them.[190] There were some small caches of explosives secreted in the British countryside which British counter-intelligence uncovered thanks to Lyalin's information.[191]

It is impossible to know how much of this really *was* fantasy – fairy-story possibilities spun to impress line managers in the KGB, the GRU and their customers in the Kremlin. Yet, at every stage of the British vetters', filers' and smashers' efforts to penetrate and thwart the 'enemy within', either in the form of KGB and GRU officers or that of the Queen's subjects they ran as agents, one gets the feeling that John Curry experienced when compiling his secret internal history of MI5 in the last stages of World War II – that the UK's security apparatus had never quite reached the level of adequacy needed to cope with the problem. The only way Curry or the anonymous senior Whitehall official on the nuclear side quoted at the end of Chapter 2 could have known whether it was or not (assuming they had lived) was if deterrence had failed and a real, deadly and ghastly transition to nuclear war really had occurred.

But in the late sixties and early seventies the secret state had much more to worry about than Curry's MI5 generation or the briefers of GEN 183 in 1947 who could simply concentrate on the CPGB as they did 'not consider that the Fascist organisations, or at the other extreme, the [Trotskyite] Revolutionary Communist Party, present any serious danger at the present time. The Fascist groups are disrupted and in-effective. They have no recognized leader, and what is more important, neither they nor the Revolutionary Communist Party look for instruction to any foreign power.'[192]

Since the first editions of *The Secret State* were published, the Joint Intelligence Committee archives have yielded a fascinating 1971 assessment, plainly prepared for them by MI5, on those groups – right as well as left – that might have sought to disrupt a UK transition to war. And the increase in the *width* of anxiety since the 1947 assessment for GEN 183 is astonishing – so great, in fact, that the Security Service broke its list of 'Subversive Organisations in the United Kingdom' down into five categories embracing no fewer than twenty-six parties, groups or movements as well as a smattering of 'front' organizations (as we shall see in a moment). The general categories were:

1: Orthodox Communist Organisations.
2: Trotskyist, Anarchist and Extreme Left Organisations.
3: Fascist Organisations.
4: Nationalist Organisations.
5: Racialist Organisations.[193]

The purpose of the JIC study was to examine 'The Security of the United Kingdom Base in a Situation Leading to a Threat of General War' and what were designated the subversive organizations were examined in this context. The questions posed, as the paper makes plain, 'are somewhat outside the normal purview of the JIC' and left the Assessment Staff a touch squishy about it: 'For example they require us to make assumptions about the moral judgements which will be made by important segments of British public opinion and about the way the British Government of the day will react to domestic as well as foreign problems.'

To aid their analysis, the JIC's officials examined four hypotheticals under two headings – external and internal:

a.1. Where there is a direct Russian threat to the United Kingdom as part of a threat to NATO and

a.2. Where there is a threat of United Kingdom involvement in a military confrontation between the United States and Russia arising from a situation outside Europe, which, however, escalates into a NATO–Warsaw Pact confrontation.

b.1. Where there is a general public awareness in the United Kingdom of threats under a.1. and a.2. . . . and the public (excepting certain extremist groups . . .) generally supports the Government's policy and handling of the situation; and

b.2. Where a large part of the (not necessarily extremist) public is, for one reason or another, opposed to the Government's actions under a.1. or a.2. . . .

Before treating their readers to a more intimate picture of the UK's subversive organizations, the JIC's analysts entered a number of qualifications:

... Where the majority of the public saw an impending Soviet attack on the United Kingdom as part of an act of aggression, the falling off of support for anti-Government activity within left wing subversive groups might be extensive. This could apply particularly to the CPGB. To use the present strengths and attitudes of these organisations as a yardstick for measuring the subversive threat in such a situation could therefore be misleading.

... There are no indications that any of the subversive organisations in Britain listed in the Annex to this paper [of which more details shortly] have contingency plans for sabotage, sedition or civil disobedience to meet the situation arising during a period of tension in which nuclear war involving the United Kingdom is imminent. Though the broad attitude of left wing subversive organisations in this country towards these issues can be forecast in general terms from their past postures and current policies, the precise manner of their reactions in the near-war situation under consideration cannot be assessed in advance. However, it is likely that the left wing subversive organisations would effectively be in agreement over the need to compel the Government to disassociate itself and withdraw the country from the impending conflict.

... The left wing subversive organisations are numerically small – under 40,000 – and apart from acts of sabotage their potential for disruptive activities likely to impede the transition of the armed forces to a state of war-readiness would depend on their ability to exploit the prevailing emotional climate ...

... Given a climate of opinion generally favourable to themselves in the face of visible and continuing Government preparations for a war which appeared imminent, the subversive groups of the left would probably try to promote political strikes, particularly in key engineering and servicing industries, to conduct violent demonstrations against Government at obvious centres of Government power and to obstruct the war effort by means of mass sit-downs at military and RAF establishments and at important road and rail centres. If these measures failed to deter Government some of the Trotskyist groups and perhaps certain Anarchists and other isolated individuals might contemplate acts of sabotage against civil and military establishments which were thought to be concerned with the preparations for war.[194]

The CPGB, with nearly 30,000 of the combined memberships of 40,000 calculated by the JIC's briefers, still took pride of place in any detailed analysis. But Whitehall knew full well this was not the Communist Party of the early post-war years. Hungary 1956* and Czechoslovakia 1968 had taken their toll. And 'in recent years', the CPGB's activity 'has been turned to increasing its appeal as a legitimate and respectable political party, mainly through its wide participation in electoral politics and, more effectively, through exploiting its strength in the trade unions'. However,

It can still be taken for granted that the bulk of the Party under its current leadership would oppose an Anglo-Soviet war whatever the circumstances, but there will still be wide variations in the nature of this opposition depending on the way in which the crisis had arisen.

If the threat of war arose demonstrably from aggressive Russian action, it is probable that the CPGB leadership and the majority of Party members would confine their opposition to pacifist non-involvement, though a diehard pro-Moscow faction, perhaps as high as 30 per cent of the membership, would be still likely to support the Soviet cause.

If a 'substantial element' of public opinion was against the British government's policy, the

Party's most effective contribution would probably be through the exercise of its strength in the transport industry to disrupt military movements. Its influence both locally and nationally in the Transport and General Workers Union . . . is sufficient to present a threat of stoppages at major ports. The Party's influence in the railway unions varies but local stoppages in the London and Manchester areas and Scotland could be expected. The Party might also try to bring about a refusal by seamen to man ships carrying war material.[195]

---

* In May 1957, Norman Brook circulated an MI5 report to the Cabinet covering the CPGB's 'Special (25th) National Congress' held over Easter 1957 amid the fall-out from Hungary and Khrushchev's 1956 speech to the Soviet's 20th Party Congress in Moscow during which he had denounced Stalin. The MI5 report concluded that the CPGB's 'revised "The British Road to Socialism" is designed to be more acceptable to all shades of left-wing opinion in the country, and the adoption of the report on Inner Party Democracy may involve minor changes to the Party's rules. Otherwise, the mixture remains as before, with significantly fewer people to mix it'. (TNA, PRO, CA 130/28, GEN 593/1, 'British Communist Party', 10 May 1957).

These possibilities were built into Whitehall's transition-to-war exercises, as we shall see when we reconstruct the 1968 exercise INVALUABLE in Chapter 6.

The Trotskyists and Anarchists, the paper reckoned, amounted in number to no more than an equivalent of one-sixth of the CPGB membership. They were fragmented and usually fractious – 'a good deal of their energies is devoted to mutual recrimination and argument over tactics. This, however, might be less pronounced when an issue such as peace or war was at stake' and experience since 1967 had shown that the International Socialists and the International Marxist Group had the ability 'to attract the support of students and as a result to bring on to the streets numbers of young people greatly in excess of the membership of these groups'. One or two individuals might attempt sabotage in a transition to war, though 'There is no evidence of any collective intention to [do] this . . .'

The sixties growth in student numbers worried the planners a bit – as did 'the "politicising" of the National Union of Students, to which most of [the approximately] 400,000 students belong':

The majority of its members have hitherto regarded the main function of their union to be the promotion of student welfare. Increasing left wing representation on the national executive, however (8 of whom the CPGB currently considers amenable to its policies) has led to its greater involvement in purely political matters with a corresponding increase in the influence of the CPGB and Trotskyist groups on what is done in the name of the union. Despite this the national executive is constitutionally unable to exercise direct or even close control over the activities of the members of the constituent student unions though in near-war contingencies its appeal and advice to the membership at large must be expected to have considerable influence.[196]

The recrudescence of the 'Troubles' in Northern Ireland in the late 1960s led to various republican and loyalist groups being included in the trawl. The far right fascist groups are there because of the likelihood of their using violence against left-wing demonstrators in a period of near war, adding 'to the tasks of a hard pressed Police Force'.

The JIC was quite relaxed at the *lack* of penetration by any of these groups within the regular armed forces or the reserves. But it was worried about the possible activities of the Russian and allied Warsaw Pact intelligence services, though

Any assessment of what . . . [they] . . . might do in a period of prolonged tension must be highly speculative. Their techniques include a. the use of forged documents, b. spreading false rumours and c. incitement to mob violence. Operations under at least the first 2 headings could be put into effect without difficulty by the existing apparatus here.

Such operations would be intended to reinforce the activities of subversive organisations and contribute to the sapping of public morale with the object of bringing about pressure on the Government to acquiesce in a settlement favourable to the Warsaw Pact countries. Were there an issue in the crisis on which a substantial part of the public opposed the Government, the Russians and their allies would have the capacity to use sophisticated disinformation techniques directed to increasing and hardening the opposition.

There is reason to believe that the Russians have prepared sabotage plans for the United Kingdom and the possibility that they might implement these before or at the same time as operations in Europe begin cannot be entirely ruled out . . . There would be, however, an element of risk to the Russians of premature detection of their operational plans.[197]

The annex to the JIC paper, 'Subversive Organisations in the United Kingdom', is a rare and fascinating snapshot of what MI5 believed it was facing in the early 1970s:

THE COMMUNIST PARTY OF GREAT BRITAIN (C.P.G.B.)

Political Attitude
This is the orthodox, original Communist Party, founded in 1920 as the British Section of the Comintern. Although traditionally aligned with Moscow, the bulk of the Party, including the current leadership, is no longer uncritically subservient to Soviet policy. An important minority, however, perhaps 30 per cent, forms a pro-Moscow faction within the Party.

<u>Headquarters</u>
16 King Street, London, W.C.2.

<u>Regional Organisation</u>
19 Districts, subdivided into local and factory Branches. Greatest concentration in industrial areas, especially in Scotland (approximately 7,000 members), London (5,000) and Merseyside (3,500).

<u>Membership</u>
Approximately 29,500.

<u>Activity Patterns</u>
The Party today advocates the achievement of a Socialist State through parliamentary means supplemented by the gradual capture of control of the Labour Movement in industry. The Party is opposed to illegal and violent activity in the present situation in the United Kingdom.

THE YOUNG COMMUNIST LEAGUE (Y. C. L.)

<u>Political Attitude</u>
The Y.C.L. is the official youth organisation of the C.P.G.B. and largely reflects its political ains and alignment, as well as its current factions.

<u>Headquarters</u>
16 King Street, London W.C.2.

<u>Regional Organisation</u>
19 Districts, subdivided into local Branches. Greatest concentration in London (nearly 1,000 members), Scotland and the industrial North of England and the Midlands.

<u>Membership</u>
Approximately 3,000.

<u>Activity Patterns</u>
The Y.C.L. supports the C.P.G.B.'s activities, but is prepared to cooperate more fully in the campaigns of other more militant left-wing groups.

COMMUNIST FRONT ORGANISATIONS

A number of organisations in the 'peace' and 'friendship' fields are sufficiently under Communist inspiration and control to be regarded as fronts for the C.P.G.B. They have mostly, however, declined in activity, militancy and membership in recent years and at present cannot be considered an effectual subversive force. The Party, however, might succeed in reviving them as vehicles for a civil disobedience campaign in the situation under review, especially contingency (b). The following is a list of the organisations concerned:

a 'Peace organisations

British Peace Committee

Campaign for Nuclear Disarmament (not under Communist control but subject to some degree of Communist influence)

British Campaign for Peace in Vietnam

Ex-Service Movement for Peace (a very small, but hard-line pro-Moscow organisation).

b 'Friendship' organisations

British Soviet Friendship Society

Scotland–U.S.S.R. Friendship Society

Society for Cultural Relations with the U.S.S.R.

British Hungarian Friendship Society

British–China Friendship Association

Society for Friendship with Bulgaria

British Czechoslovak Friendship League

British G.D.R. Information Exchange

British Romanian Friendship Association.

SOCIALIST LABOUR LEAGUE (S.L.L.)

Political Attitude
A classical Trotskyist party devoted to the overthrow of the capitalist system in accordance with the Transitional Programme prescribed by Trotsky. It believes that international capitalism is facing unprecedented crises which will precipitate a revolutionary situation which S.L.L. must be prepared to exploit.

Headquarters
180–168 Clapham High Street, London, S.W.2.

Regional Organisation and Concentrations
It is organised into branches, the principal strength is in London, the North Midlands, the North-East and the North-West. Control from its London headquarters is strong and precise. Its leading members have shown great mobility in moving to places where the situation is favourable to the S.L.L. development.

Membership – Strength and Composition
About 2,300 including its youth section the Young Socialists. The S.L.L. proper may have between 500 and 1,000 members most of whom are workmen employed in engineering factories. It is particularly strong in the motor industry and it has attempted to extend its influence to the docks. There is little influence exerted on universities as no separate student policy has been developed by the League.

Activity Patterns
Its international connections are tenuous although there is some co-operation between the Alliance Jeunesse pour Socialisme in France and the Young Socialists. S.L.L. policy is currently devoted to developing itself as an organisation capable of supporting and encouraging militants in industry and the promotion of unofficial strikes. It has established the All Trades Union Alliance which claims the attention of a large number of militant shop-stewards, many of whom are not members of S.L.L. Its activity is almost entirely devoted to industrial work.

<u>Other Remarks</u>
It possesses the only daily Trotskyist newspaper. This contains good industrial coverage, but S.L.L.'s influence is restricted because it is unwilling
to co-operate with any other political group, a fact which restricts both
its size and its potential for disruption.

SOCIALIST LABOUR LEAGUE YOUNG SOCIALISTS

<u>Political Attitude</u>
Nominally the same as S.L.L. (Trotskyist); however the bulk of this
membership is very young (under 17) and much of its political material
is immature.

<u>Headquarters</u>
Same as S.L.L.

<u>Regional Organisation and Concentrations</u>
Follows closely to S.L.L.'s distribution

<u>Membership – Strength and Composition</u>
Membership may be about 1,500 recruited almost entirely from working
class youths with about 50 university students. There is a rapid turnover
of membership.

<u>Activity Patterns</u>
Its activities are mainly social and few demands are made on Young
Socialists members. Few of them graduate into S.L.L. Their principal
function is to distribute propaganda and to collect funds for S.L.L.

<u>Other Remarks</u>
Young Socialists was established by S.L.L. after it had gained control of
the Labour Party Young Socialists in pursuance of its former policy of
infiltration of the Labour Party.

INTERNATIONAL MARXIST GROUP (I.M.G.)

Political Attitude
A revolutionary socialist party in the tradition of Marx, Lenin and Trotsky as part of an international movement for the overthrow of capitalism.

Headquarters
182 Pentonville Road, London, N.1.

Regional Organisations and Concentrations
Principal strength is in London but the membership is fairly strong in the Midlands. It is making a strong drive to recruit students and youth through the activities of its youth section the Spartacus League (q.v.).

Membership – Strength and Composition
About 300, a third of whom are in the London area. Its activities are conducted through Spartacus League branches and through social groups which centre on the distributors of the Red Mole, its fortnightly journal; these groups are called Red Circles. Its appeal is mainly to young militant Trotskyists. I.M.G. is trying to increase its influence, at present small, amongst the working class.

Activity Patterns
The I.M.G. is the British Section of the United Secretariat of the Fourth International of the Trotskyist Headquarters based in Brussels. It supports all forms of protest against 'Imperialism' and 'repression' of the working class. It has organised national demonstrations against the war in Vietnam, apartheid, the supply of arms to South Africa, and, lately, against the Industrial Relations Bill of the present Government.

Other Remarks
A small but militant group which attracts young people and students calling for 'action'. It believes that this class of person has the capacity to act as a detonator for the Marxist revolution. Its influence may increase, but its internal organisation is probably insufficient to support any activity on a larger scale than at present achieved.

SPARTACUS LEAGUE (S.L.)

<u>Political Attitude</u>
Militant revolutionary Trotskyist Youth group of the International Marxist Group (I.M.G.) (q.v.).

<u>Headquarters</u>
182 Pentonville Road, London, N.1.

<u>Regional Organisations and Concentrations</u>
Recruitment is taking place throughout the U.K. with a concentrated effort being made at universities and technical high schools.

<u>Membership – Strength and Composition</u>
About 250, mostly students.

<u>Activity Patterns</u>
Members of the Spartacus League try to take the lead under I.M.G. direction in student demonstrations based upon topical issues like 'anti-apartheid', 'racialism', arms to South Africa and the campaign against firms and banks with investments in South Africa.

<u>Other Remarks</u>
None.

INTERNATIONAL SOCIALISM GROUP (I.S.)

<u>Political Attitude</u>
I.S. is essentially a broad left group which believes in the overthrow of capitalism, the establishment of workers' control in industry, the support of national liberation movements abroad and opposition to racialism. It opposes the capitalist system of the West but also detects similar evils in the Soviet system and its attitude can be gauged from its slogan 'Neither Washington nor Moscow but International Socialism'. It claims to be a revolutionary Socialist organisation.

Headquarters
6 Cotton Gardens, London, E.2.

Regional Organisations and Concentrations
It has over ninety branches spread throughout the country, but it is most active in the London area and in the Midlands.

Membership – Strength and Composition
Its membership is about 1,000, of which more than one third are students or on the staff of universities. It is currently trying to recruit workers, but its fundamental attitudes are so involved that only its most intellectual members achieve any position of influence within it. Branches have a great deal of autonomy and much of its strength derives from energetic individuals rather than good organisation.

Activity Patterns
I.S. has no strong international links, but has some relations with Lutte Ouvriere, the French Trotskyist group which is moving closer to the United Secretariat of the Fourth International (see I.M.G.). I.S. is developing itself into a broad left movement party and has developed contacts with C.P.G.B. and others to the right of its position as sources of strength. It has attempted to achieve greater influence in industry and to lose the characteristic of a militant, student based group which specialised in demonstrations on behalf of students and Irish matters which it had earned during the period 1967–69.

Other Remarks
Its organisation is weak and it could probably be disrupted by the interference of other Trotskyist groups should this serve their purpose.

REVOLUTIONARY SOCIALIST LEAGUE (R.S.L.)

Political Attitude
Calls for the establishment of a united international movement of workers, students and peasants in the tradition of Lenin and Trotsky. It calls for the overthrow of the capitalist system by the exploitation of the class struggle.

Headquarters
197 Kings Cross Road, London, W.C.1.

Regional Organisation and Concentrations
There is concentration of power in London and the South but other groups exist in Bristol, Hull, Manchester, Liverpool, Tyneside and the West Midlands. These groups are very small and of little influence.

Membership – Strength and Composition
Membership is about 100–150. Apart from the old leaders of the R.S.L. most of its members are young and there is probably a fairly rapid turn-over of membership.

Activity Patterns
R.S.L. encourages a deep entry into the Labour Party and the Labour Party Young Socialists. It hopes to be able to secure support from more moderate members of the Labour movement to build up a revolutionary party. Similar activity is undertaken in trade union movements.

Other Remarks
This party is probably on the decline and although a vogue for broad left movements may enliven it temporarily it has suffered because of its 'entryist' policies during the currency of the Labour government when party discipline was sufficient to contain it. In practice its present influence is mainly through intellectual tracts put out under the name 'Militant' from Sussex University. A weakened or divided Labour Party might encourage its growth.

ANARCHIST FEDERATION OF BRITAIN

Political Attitude
Against all private ownership and in favour of complete social equality. Against all governments and laws.

Headquarters
No headquarters. Anarchists are kept in touch with each other by publications emanating from Freedom Press, 84b Whitechapel High Street, London, E.1.

<u>Regional organisation and concentrations</u>
There are regional groups throughout the British Isles but there is no organisation.

<u>Membership – strength and composition</u>
There is no membership. There is no means of assessing the total number of anarchists since the word embraces people with widely differing opinions. The number of groups listed in 'Freedom', the anarchist weekly, varies between fifty and a hundred. These may claim about a thousand supporters but since they have little unity among themselves the figure is not significant.

<u>Activity patterns</u>
Some anarchist support is always available for any campaign directed against authority, e.g. for strikes. Some individual anarchists are prepared to carry out acts of violence.

<u>Other remarks</u>
None

SYNDICALIST WORKERS FEDERATION (S.W.F.)

<u>Political attitude</u>
An Anarchistic group, advocating common ownership and workers' control of the land, industry and all means of production and distribution.

<u>Headquarters</u>
259 Hillcross Avenue,
Morden, Surrey.

<u>Regional organisation and concentrations</u>
None

<u>Membership – strength and composition</u>
The S.W.F. has been dormant for several years and membership dwindled to three or four. It was revived in 1970 under a provisional committee. The S.W.F. is a section of the International Working Men's Association.

Activity patterns
The S.W.F. advocates direct action and solidarity to bring about victory against class domination.

SOLIDARITY

Political attitude
Solidarity is an anarchist offshoot of the Trotskyist movement. Its aim is 'to develop the mass revolutionary consciousness necessary if society is to be totally transformed'.

Headquarters
None. The movement consists of local autonomous groups.

Regional organisations and concentrations
In October, 1970, local groups existed in London, Manchester and Scotland.

Membership – strength and composition
There is no formal membership. It is believed to have about two hundred supporters. These include university graduates and manual workers.

Activity patterns
Publication of 'Solidarity' pamphlets on topical issues, both social and industrial, with a view to hastening revolution.

Other remarks
None.

THE 'NEW LEFT' GROUP

Political Attitude
This group comprises some 30 intellectuals who produce the 'New Left Review'. While it cannot itself be described as an organisation in the sense that it has a party-type structure, it will, through its publications give support to organisations aiming to overthrow the capitalist system

and it believes that minority groups, such as the coloured population, students and national liberation groups in underdeveloped countries, are leaders in the struggle against capitalism and imperialism. It advocates the Castroist type of government but does not unequivocally say that this is the most suitable in a European context.

Headquarters
The New Left Review is published from 36 Waldorf Street, London, W. 1.

Regional Organisation and Concentrations
There is no membership: its influence is purely through its publications. Its leading members have engaged in activity on behalf of student organisations such as the Revolutionary Socialist Students Federation, which are currently on the decline but the influence secured through the agency of such organisations remains, and the New Left influence is strong in universities. In London, Oxford, Cambridge, Birmingham and the North-East New Left influence has been prominant [sic] in left wing circles. However, lacking organisation, it has not taken the initiative in any particular activity; this usually comes from Trotskyist and Communist groups but with New Left advice and support.

Activity Patterns
The publication of material supporting Castroism and the struggle of national liberation groups, the advocacy of Marxism through intellectual argument and support for activity against the present academic system have engaged the New Left's energy. Its contribution to the Vietnam Solidarity Committee campaign was probably very great and it seems likely that it would use its influence to secure student support for anti-war and anti-American demonstrations in periods of international tension.

Other Remarks
It is impossible to assess the influence of the New Left since it deals in ideas rather than membership and organisation. These ideas have, however, gained wide currency in intellectual circles and to this extent its influence must be taken seriously. However, it is impotent outside academic circles.

THE 'UNDERGROUND' PRESS

<u>Political Attitude</u>
This is not an organisation but a group of periodicals catering for what is vaguely described as the underground subculture. It is represented by periodicals like International Times, Friends, Oz etc. which are published regularly to meet the tastes of a largely youthful readership mostly under 30. The consistent theme is a mixture of revolutionary politics, sex, drugs and pop music with emphasis upon repression and violence and protest in society. Political articles from America are frequently reprinted. The emphasis is upon the need for individual freedom which is frequently menaced by Governments which engage in war. It is difficult to be clear about the effect of these periodicals upon young people but their capacity for influence should not be underestimated at a time of international tension leading up to the outbreak of hostilities.

<u>Headquarters</u>
Most periodicals are printed and published in London.

<u>Regional organisations and concentrations</u>
The periodicals circulate throughout the U.K. and particularly in London and University cities. Total readership is difficult to guess but Friends prints about 25,000 copies per issue and Oz 50,000.

<u>Membership – Strength and Composition</u>
Not applicable

<u>Activity Patterns</u>
Not applicable

<u>Other Remarks</u>
None

COMMUNIST PARTY OF BRITAIN
MARXIST-LENINIST (CPBML)

<u>Political Attitude</u>
The best known of the pro-Chinese Communist groups led by a prominent
trade unionist Reg BIRCH who is on the national executive of the Amalgamated Engineering and Foundry Workers' Union. At the end of 1970
a delegation from the C.P.B.M.L. visited China as guests of the central
committee of the Chinese Communist Party. The C.P.B.M.L. also has links
with Albania.

<u>Headquarters</u>
155 Fortess Road, London, N.W.5.

<u>Regional organisation and concentration</u>
Branches, sometimes of only one or two members, in many of the provin-
cial towns throughout the U.K.

<u>Membership – strength and composition</u>
Approximately 200 spread over a wide cross section of society from
ordinary admirers of China, former communists, trade unionists and
intellectuals.

<u>Activity Patterns</u>
Consistent support for the foreign policy and activities of the Chinese
Communist Party.

<u>Other Remarks</u>
Probably the largest of the pro-Chinese Communist groups in the U.K.

COMMUNIST FEDERATION OF BRITAIN
MARXIST-LENINIST (CFBML)

<u>Political Attitude</u>
A small pro-Chinese Communist group.

Headquarters
65 Sisters Avenue, London, S.W.11.

Regional Organisation and concentrations
There is a close association between the London office and local groups
operating under different names in the provinces at Bristol, Coventry,
Glasgow, Grimsby, Liverpool, Manchester and Yeovil.

Membership – strength and composition
Uncertain but probably not more than 100 all told.

Activity patterns
Hostile to the Soviet Union and to the activities of the C.P.G.B. and
Trotskyist groups and organisations in the U.K.

Other remarks
None.

THE REVOLUTIONARY MARXIST-LENINIST LEAGUE (R.M.L.L.)

Political attitude
Pro-Chinese Communist group and the spearhead of the Britain–Vietnam
Solidarity front. The leader of the R.M.L.L. Abhimanyu MANCHANDA,
an Indian journalist, also leads the organisation known as Friends of
China and is chairman of the 'Solidarity Front of Arab and Palestine
Liberation'.

Headquarters
58 Lisburn Road, London, N.W.3.

Regional organisation and concentration
None

Membership – strength and composition
Very small, possibly no more than a dozen but, for a special event such
as a demonstration or an emotional issue he can muster additional
support of up to, say, one hundred.

Activity patterns
The R.M.L.L. has been in the forefront of militant demonstrations. With anarchists it was responsible for a large part of the militant confrontation with the police in Grosvenor Square in October, 1968 and it has sponsored and supported many militant demonstrations since that time.

Other remarks
None.

ENGLISH COMMUNIST MOVEMENT, MARXIST-LENINIST @ ENGLISH STUDENT MOVEMENT AND VERY MANY OTHER NAMES

Political attitude
The members of this movement are fanatical Maoists. They advocate mass revolutionary struggle.

Headquarters
In Canada.

Regional organisations and concentrations
Local groups are based on Chinese propaganda bookshops. There is one at 569 Old Kent Road, London, S.E.1. and another at 8 Coombe Terrace, Lewes Road, Brighton, Sussex.

Membership – strength and composition
About fifty in England. They are all young.

Activity patterns
Their private meetings consist of readings and incantations of the thoughts of Mao Tse-Tung. Their public appearances are on occasions when they are likely to have large audiences for their shouting of Chinese slogans. They are disposed to acts of violence against authority.

Other remarks
None.

NATIONAL FRONT

Political Attitude
Despite its efforts to appear a respectable political party it has very strong Fascist tendencies and adopts racialist policies. It opposes Britain's entry into the Common Market. An amalgam of several extreme right wing groups which has included the League of Empire Loyalists.

Headquarters
92 Fleet Street, London, E.C.4.

Regional Organisation
The bulk of the membership comes from within the Greater London area but there is a shallow, fluctuating structure in the provinces. The National Front is run by John O'BRIEN, a moderate Fascist, who acts as Chairman of a Leadership Committee in London. It comprises seven very active Fascists.

Membership – Strength and Composition
Membership figures for the National Front which is by far the largest and most active of the extreme right wing groups are thought to be in the region of 4,000. This includes members of the old League of Empire Loyalists, which was merged with the National Front in 1967, but which may now be breaking away from it. 'Spearhead', organ of the Front, is published once a month.

Activity Patterns
Its racialist and anti-Common Market attitudes may be expected to lead the National Front to intervene at the public meetings of those organisations where policies run counter to these attitudes, such as anti-apartheid, anti-racialist movements. It may, through its propaganda, stimulate public backlash to this kind of issue.

Other Remarks
None.

UNION MOVEMENT @ NATIONAL
PARTY OF EUROPE

Political attitude
An ageing Fascist organisation.

Headquarters
76a Rochester Row, London, S.W.1.

Regional Organisation
The movement is centred in London. Regional organisation, if it exists, is insignificant. The leader of Union Movement is Sir Oswald MOSLEY, but as he lives in France and rarely visits this country the day to day running of the Movement is in the hands of Jeffrey HAMM and a Directory of five men, including HAMM, and Robert ROW, who is editor of 'Action', organ of Union Movement.

Membership – Strength and Composition
In December, 1969 the membership of Union Movement was between 200 and 250, the majority of whom are middle aged admirers of MOSLEY. Its recruitment performance is negligible.

Activity Pattern
Kerb-side public meetings take place in the East of London from time to time. There appears to be no activity outside London.

Other remarks
The organisation is short of money, and is drawing on a reserve of £3,000 left to Union Movement by a member.

BRITISH MOVEMENT

Political attitude
A small, extreme Fascist organisation.

Headquarters
42 Tudor Avenue, Broad Lane, Coventry (Home of Colin JORDAN, National Secretary of the British Movement).

Regional Organisations and Concentrations
National Executive Council, which consists of 7 members. Largely active in the Midlands, particularly in Birmingham, but there are members on Merseyside, in Scotland and in Plymouth.

Membership – Strength and Composition
The total membership is not known but it is thought to be small. There are approximately 30 members in the London area. The British Movement attracts the thug element. Activities are publicised by a Monthly Bulletin issued to members and associates by Colin JORDAN.

Activity Patterns
Meetings are held irregularly, chiefly in Birmingham, and members are known to travel from Merseyside to attend these.

Other remarks
None.

NATIONAL PATRIOTIC FRONT (NPF)

Political Attitude
The aims of the NPF are to provide Welsh Nationalists with an opportunity to protect Wales against anglicisation and achieve independence. Its founders advocate the use of force as a means of achieving publicity.

Headquarters
Cwmbran, Gwent.

Regional Organisations and Concentrations
None

Membership – Strength and Composition
Estimated not exceeding 30.

<u>Activity Patterns</u>
None in the recent past. It would appear that their intention is to form
a non-violent organisation as a front. Behind this there would be a trained
body of saboteurs recruited from those members with experience in the
use of explosives.

<u>Other Remarks</u>
Historically the N.P.F. dates from 1967 when a group of militant members
of the Free Wales Army expressed dissatisfaction with that organisation
and caused a split amongst its supporters. In its present form the Patriotic
Front cannot be said to amount to anything more than a rallying point
for a hard core of extremists and camp-followers. At present they are
devoid of any effective organisation and leadership.

IRISH REPUBLICAN ARMY (PROVISIONAL ARMY COUNCIL) (MILITARY/SINN FEIN (POLITICAL) – BRADY FACTION

<u>Political Attitude</u>
Principal aim is the reunification of all Ireland in a Catholic Irish Republic through military means.

<u>Headquarters</u>
Dublin.

<u>Regional Organisation and Concentrations</u>
Although based in Southern Ireland strongly represented in Co. Donegal
and border counties. Its main concentrations are in the Catholic areas of
Belfast other than the Lower Falls area.

<u>Membership – Strength and Composition</u>
Not accurately known. Estimated at between 1,200 and 1,500 either
trained or under training to bear arms or engage in acts of sabotage.
Organised in small military-type units under command of local brigade
groups. These are supported by unknown numbers of BRADY group
controlled Republican Clubs.

Activity Patterns

Very active in militarily opposing security forces in Belfast. Recently very active in training recruits from the North in Southern Ireland. Responsible for numerous sabotage acts against Government installations and public utilities in Northern Ireland.

Other Remarks

As part of the I.R.A. this faction is proscribed in Northern Ireland. It publishes a monthly newspaper 'An Phoblacht' and is in opposition to the Marxist theory of the GOULDING group I.R.A. Prior to January 1970 was part of the I.R.A. Sinn Fein (see I.R.A./Sinn Fein GOULDING group).

IRISH REPUBLICAN ARMY (MILITARY)/SINN FEIN (POLITICAL) – GOULDING FACTION

Political Attitude

Marxist orientated Socialist, Republican, aimed at securing the unification of North and South Ireland by political means reinforced by military activity.

Headquarters

Dublin.

Regional Organisation and Concentrations

Groups throughout Southern Ireland. Main concentrations in Northern Ireland are in the Lower Falls Area of Belfast and parts of Londonderry.

Membership – Strength and Composition

Not accurately known. Estimated at between 600 and 700 active members capable of bearing arms. A greater number, members of various Republican Clubs throughout Northern Ireland, are in support.

Activity Patterns

Very active politically in the field of civil rights and militarily in opposition to British security forces for the past two years. High degree of success in penetration of the Northern Ireland Civil Rights Association.

Other Remarks

The I.R.A. is a proscribed organisation in Northern Ireland and its monthly newspaper 'The United Irishman' is banned. In January 1970 the I.R.A. split into two factions (see I.R.A./Sinn Fein BRADY faction).

ULSTER VOLUNTEER FORCE

Political Attitude

Violently anti-Republican. Its main intention is to preserve the political status quo in Ulster by the use of violence if necessary.

Headquarters

Not known.

Regional Organisations and Concentrations

Not known.

Membership – Strength and Composition

Not known.

Activity Patterns

A large proportion of bomb explosions which occurred in Ulster in 1970 were claimed by a group calling itself 'U.V.F.'. Bombings were frequently carried out under the guise of I.R.A. outrages in order to provoke a Protestant reaction and to heighten the tension between the communities.

Other Remarks

It is doubtful whether the U.V.F. has any genuine corporate existence and the name, which historically is an emotive one in Ulster, provides cover for a number of small and virtually autonomous groups, largely criminal in character.

SAOR EIRE

Political Attitude
A splinter group of the I.R.A. Dedicated to the reunification of Ireland by force. Little evidence of political ideology to date.

Headquarters
Not known

Regional Organisation and Concentrations
Not known.

Membership – Strength and Composition
Not known but believed not to exceed 30.

Activity Patterns
It acts in a secure and clandestine manner and conducts frequent bank robberies. The use to which it puts the product of the robberies is not known but believed possibly that some of it finds its way into the BRADY group I.R.A. coffers.

Other Remarks
None.

COMMUNIST PARTY OF IRELAND

Political attitude
Its principal political target is the bringing together of the forces of the Left to form a united front. At the same time it is engaged in association with the Republican Movement to organise a campaign for a Bill of Rights.

Headquarters
Dublin – with the Headquarters of the Northern Area Committee in Belfast.

Regional Organisation and Concentrations
Earlier in the year the two sections of the Communist Party in Ireland
joined together and called themselves the Communist Party of Ireland.
The Northern Ireland element now forms a part of the C.P.I. with its
Northern Ireland Headquarters in Belfast.

Membership – Strength and Composition
Overall strength in Ireland does not exceed 300, 200 of whom are in the
South and the balance in Northern Ireland.

Activity Patterns
The C.P.I. has influence disproportionate to its size. It has done little in
its own name as it realises how much more effective is a policy of penetration. It wields considerable influence in partnership with Republicans
through its penetration of the Civil Rights Movement, the Trades Union
Movement and the Tenants and Housing Associations.

Other Remarks
None.

PEOPLES DEMOCRACY

Political Attitude
Trotskyist/Anarchist influenced body originally developed within Queens
University, Belfast at the time of the height of the Civil Rights Movement
campaign in 1968. Since disassociated with Northern Ireland Civil Rights
Association and now seeks to establish itself as a political body aimed
at achieving a thirty-two County Socialist Worker and Farmers Republic
of Ireland.

Headquarters
Belfast.

Regional Organisation and Concentrations
A Central Committee of nine members together with one delegate from
each branch with more than ten members (number of branches not known).

<u>Membership – Strength and Composition</u>
Approximately 230 most of whom live outside Belfast.

<u>Activity Patterns</u>
The P.D. tends to emerge only at times when the situation demands a protest.

<u>Other Remarks</u>
Publishes a weekly paper called 'Free Citizen' and a theoretical journal 'Northern Star'.

THE BLACK PANTHER MOVEMENT

<u>Political Attitude</u>
The Black Panther Movement (B.P.M.) is the most active of a small number of American-type Black Power organisations in the U.K. It is Marxist-Leninist orientated and committed, at least in theory, to the overthrow of the existing social and politican [*sic*] system 'by any means'.

<u>Headquarters</u>
<u>Regional Organisation and Concentrations</u>
It is based on London where it has a Central Corps and three Branches. Its influence outside the London area would seem to be marginal at present.

<u>Membership – strength and composition</u>
The B.P.M. appears to be organised by about 30 activists but there are probably between 5 and 10 times that number of followers who can be called out for demonstrations or special meetings. The members are principally West Indian but include a number of Africans.

<u>Activity patterns</u>
In recent months a tendency towards violence has been discernible on the part of the members, which has taken the form of scuffles with Police at demonstrations and on other occasions. This violence may be attributed in part to the influence of the U.S. Black Panther Party. However it probably also reflects a heightening of racial tension during the last few months in the London area.

There has recently been a marked increase in contact between the B.P.M. and the International Marxist Group (I.M.G. q.v.). The I.M.G. appears to have recognised that the B.P.M. constitutes a useful instrument with which to embarrass the forces of law and order. Towards this end the I.M.G. has arranged a Speaking Tour of British universities by leading members of the B.P.M.; it has organised pickets of courts where B.P.M. members are being prosecuted; and it has established a Black Defence Committee designed to mount a campaign against the alleged persecution of the black community by Police in Britain.

Other remarks

None.

22 March 1971[198]

The problem with several of the groups listed, as a senior MI5 officer explained nearly forty years later, is the *intention* of such bodies. Did they *intend* to subvert the UK's parliamentary system of government? Or should they be investigated because 'they might be in a position to do substantial damage to the state in certain circumstances', as in the kind of transition to war envisaged in the 1971 JIC assessment?[199] The inclusion of one group in the 'subversive' sweep strikes me as extremely odd – the members of the New Left Group, clustered round the *New Left Review*, many of whom had left the CPGB at the time of Hungary. For some reason, the document lumps them with Agitprop as the kind of organization that might increase militancy.

As we have seen, such an assessment was quite a rarity in Whitehall. Much more common, continuous even, was another Cold War 'what if?' activity – what would happen if that 'strategic threat on steroids' materialized in the shape of a thermonuclear war?

1. Sir John Winnifrith: designed the 1950 plan
to keep Stalin's Brits out of the Secret State.

2. Whitehall reminder, 1962: the pursuit of perpetual security.

3. Sir William Strath: planning for ultimate catastrophe and the survival of the state.

4. If the bomb had dropped: official government poster.

5. Air Chief Marshal Sir Kenneth Cross: to him
could have fallen the decision to bomb Russia.

6. Air Vice-Marshal Bobby Robson (*left*): hands over his squadron to John Willis, a future Vice Chief of the Defence Staff. 'We would have done it unhesitatingly', said Robson.

7. Practising the last 'scramble': aircrews race towards Vulcan bombers at RAF Scampton, August 1960.

8. Sir Michael Cary: contemplating the 'nightmarish gavotte' of a transition to nuclear war.

9. The Cary memorandum of May 1962.

10. Gervase Cowell: MI6 man in Moscow
running Penkovsky who did not believe the
fake attack-imminent signal.

11. A first draft of the 1965 doomsday drill
— By Royal Appointment.

4

'Beyond the Imagination': The Spectre of Ever-Greater Annihilation

It was . . . essential to avoid a situation in which the Government would be driven to devote resources to civil defence on a scale which would cripple the national economy, detract from our power of offence and alienate our allies in Europe . . . the Government were not prepared to devote resources to passive defence at the expense of weakening our striking force or impeding our economic recovery.

Clement Attlee addressing GEN 253, the Cabinet Committee on Civil Defence, 1 October 1948[1]

To render the UK useless as a base for any form of military operations the simplest and most effective form of attack would be by surface bursts effected in suitable meteorological conditions. These, besides causing local damage, would cause very considerable areas of the country to be affected by fall-out. We are advised that something like ten 'H' Bombs, each of a yield of about 10 megatons, delivered on the western half of the UK or in the waters close in off the Western seaboard, with the normal prevailing winds, would effectively disrupt the life of the country and make normal activity completely impossible.

Joint Intelligence Committee report on 'The "H" Bomb Threat to the UK in the Event of a General War', January 1955[2]

. . . however successful the educative process might be, it would still be impossible to forecast how the nation would react to nuclear assault. The effect of this on dense populations would remain beyond the imagination until it happened. Whether

this country could withstand an all-out attack and still be in
any state to carry on hostilities must be very doubtful.
'The Defence Implications of Fall-out from a Hydrogen
Bomb', 8 March 1955[3]

I still believe that what we've got to hang on to as administra-
tors is the paramount need to keep in existence a machine of
central control which can take hold of the situation as soon
as that initial period of agony is passed in order to provide,
as smoothly as may be, for a period of recovery thereafter.
Sir Norman Brook, Secretary of the Cabinet, on
'The Cabinet System in War', June 1959[4]

Norman Brook was the last man in Whitehall to have any illusions of
what a nuclear attack on the UK might mean. Throughout the high
Cold War, he briefed his four premiers – Attlee, Churchill, Eden and
Macmillan – on the catastrophe that awaited the UK if global war
came. As we have seen, he was the human fulcrum around which the
1954–5 rethinks took place in the shadow of the H-bomb. He drove
through the plans for pre- and post-attack always bearing in mind, as
he told his private audience of Home Office civil servants in 1959, that
'[e]ven taking the most extreme forecast or appreciation of the nature
of a future global war, we would have to hold on to political control
[by which he meant Cabinet government] for as long as possible and
aim to recover it as soon as possible thereafter.'[5] Elaborating on his
theme, Brook explained to his fellow insiders:

We plan to maintain central direction . . . even in the most rudimentary form,
for as long as possible in the intensive period of nuclear attack and – and this
is the point I want to stress – the capacity to re-assert civil control, and, as
soon as possible, central political control, for the period of recovery after the
initial nuclear phase.[6]

In a moment, we will examine the elaborate plans, which, by the turn
of the 1950s–1960s, gave a kind of flesh to the Brook philosophy.

But for anyone involved in the actual business of UK war planning
in those decades – as for any of the scholars (myself and my students

included) attempting to reconstruct this grim enterprise whereby the British state looked into the abyss – reality, ghastliness and *un*reality mix constantly. This appears to have been true at all levels and must have been so for Brook in his more anxious, private moments when contemplating that 'period of agony'[7] (where he might have spent it and with whom is the subject of Chapter 6). In my own generation, one did not have to wait until Peter Watkins's 1965 film *The War Game* (which Brook, by this time Lord Normanbrook and Chairman of the BBC, had much to do with keeping off the television screen in the 1960s[8]), to brood on one's last moments or think what one might do if the old World War II air-raid sirens whined into action telling us we had but four minutes to go.

Philip Allen, the Home Office under secretary responsible for home defence, was the Home Office representative on the 1955 Strath Committee, which was instructed to convert the JIC's appraisal of what but a few Soviet H-bombs could do to the UK, and the scientific forecasts of Bill Penney's people on the details of the practical effects of blast, heat and thermonuclear destruction, into advice for ministers on home and civil defence and how the government somehow might be carried on from the ruins. Many years later he recalled for me the ambiguities this aroused in his mind:

I can remember sitting on a committee working out the horrors of the H-bomb as distinct from the much more modest A-bomb. And, although it seemed like Never-Never Land at the time, we did work out these theoretical methods of keeping on the government – setting up organizations. One had a feeling that, if it came to it, nothing would quite work out the way one was planning. But, nevertheless, one simply had to plan.[9]

At around the time Norman Brook was lecturing the Home Office about the post-attack plans for 'a maximum degree of devolution to regions; a very small nucleus at the centre . . .' to maintain 'contacts with allies and liaison between civil and military power – and the maintenance for as long as possible of the civil power'[10] (Brook clearly thought the military could well be dominant for a period), a young military figure, Bobby Robson, was beginning his navigator training for the RAF's V-Force. As his career in the cockpit of the deterrent progressed, he acquired similar views to Philip Allen's and to Harold Macmillan's private thinking along the lines that 'any real war *must* escalate into nuclear war'.[11] Though confident that his Vulcan would have got airborne, 'I wonder if it would really have all worked. I'm pretty sure that if you got to the last resort, the whole thing has gone anyway. We all were cynical about it.'[12]

But the most vividly effective antidote against becoming over-elaborate and distracted by the detail of the transition to World War III I have encountered was provided in the spring of 1962, between the Berlin and Cuba crises, by Norman Brook's deputy, Michael Cary. It leaps out at the reader in the Cabinet Office's working file on nuclear retaliation procedures.[13] Cary was responding to a minute from Nigel Abercrombie, the Cabinet Office under secretary responsible for transition-to-war planning, about the efforts then under way to simplify the communication procedures for consultation between the US President and the British Prime Minister right up 'to the last possible moment' and the taking of 'a final decision to launch a nuclear attack'.[14] After much toing and froing between the Foreign Office, the Ministry of Defence and the Cabinet Office, a draft was prepared to be put before Macmillan and Kennedy which, Abercrombie briefed Cary, the Cabinet Office should leave in the hands of the two other Whitehall departments until the Americans had had their say.[15]

Cary's reply is a classic. Suddenly, humanity and reality trump bureaucratic fine-tuning.

Mr Abercrombie

I agree that this should go ahead as you propose, and that we should look at it again on the next round.

2. But is it really conceivable that the President & the Prime Minister, on the brink of Armageddon, will solemnly go through this nightmarish gavotte? Will they not simply ask themselves whether to use nuclears <u>at all</u> and leave the rest to the experts? In any case, if the answer is yes, we should worry.

21/5   M.C.[16]

This surely would have been close to the dreadful reality if the moment of the last resort had had to be faced.

By the time Cary, son of the novelist Joyce Cary, old Etonian and classical scholar whose private passion was the building and restoration of harpsichords,[17] pondered Armageddon, the secret state had been engaged in dancing one or other version of a 'nightmarish gavotte' for nearly fourteen years – ever since the severing of the land and water routes to Berlin in 1948. It may have taken Stalin's first direct action against the Western allies to pep up civil defence and transition-to-war planning in Whitehall, but the Prime Minister, Attlee, had been acutely aware from the moment he wrote his think piece on the atomic bomb at the end of August 1945 that much of the recent history of his country's domestic mobilization for war had, at a stroke, passed into near irrelevance. The dispersal of industry and airfields, World War II bomb shelters and air-raid precautions would henceforth be 'just futile waste'.[18]

The big planning paper prepared for the Cabinet's Ministerial Committee on Civil Defence during the first weeks of the Berlin crisis reached the same conclusion the Prime Minister had almost three years before:

There is no single solution to the problem of Civil Defence. The provision of atom bomb proof shelters for the whole nation would not in itself solve the problem; nor would the dispersion of the population and industry at an even density all over the country. In any event neither solution would be an economic or practical possibility. The solution lies in making the maximum use of a large number of expedients for minimising the effects of damage.[19]

A solution was never found. Expediency prevailed. In the trade-off between active and passive defence, the former won each time at the A-bomb and the H-bomb stages. On every occasion that the policy was reviewed until, following the 1965 rethink, substantial cost savings were made by the reduction of what limited cover there was[20] with the scaling down of the Civil Defence Corps (which had been established by the Civil Defence Act 1948) and a concentration on 'only those measures which are likely to make a contribution to national survival'.[21] In other words, from the days of Attlee's GEN 163 to Wilson PN committee, the bomb was always put before shelters.

Exactly what was meant by civil defence and home defence was a problem from the start, not least because Cabinet committees so labelled ran in parallel for much of the high Cold War. As late as October 1968, the UK Commanders-in-Chief Committee was so fretful about the lack of official definitions of the two that it produced its own:

a. <u>Home Defence</u>
The measures necessary to defend the United Kingdom against internal or external threat. In the case of a nuclear, biological or chemical attack, where no adequate defence may be possible, the measures necessary within the United Kingdom to minimise the effects of such an attack and to enable the nation to survive.
b. <u>Civil Defence</u>
That element of home defence involving the actions of Civil Government and Local Authorities in the control and administration of the nation in the setting of general war.[22]

The C-in-Cs' version reflects very much the military angle on the two concepts. A fuller, better definition which brings out the distinctions between the two has been produced by my student Nicola Bliss:

Civil defence was concerned with the protection of the British people during and after an attack on the UK. Measures . . . included: evacuation, shelter, food provision and emergency hospitals.

Home defence covered a much wider area of both civil and military preparations which aimed to ensure national survival during and after air attack. Areas . . . included: the machinery of government in war, strategic location of industry, town planning and stockpiling.[23]

In the Berlin summer of 1948, when 'Ministers agreed that paper plans for war should be brought to a high state of readiness but ruled that any steps taken should be kept within official circles since any overt action taken . . . might . . . aggravate international tension',[24] the planning process was conducted in such a rush that such niceties of definition and distinction appear (and probably were) surplus to requirements. That summer, the priorities of the civil defence and war planners were the production of 'paper plans . . . for a crash emergency' (in the case of civil defence)[25] and a new 'Government War Book designed to meet essential needs in the event of a possible emergency in the near future' for the Defence Transition Committee.[26]

The archives for both areas, the DTC especially, are far from fully declassified even now. But it is possible to reconstruct the chief anxiety of the summer and autumn of 1948 as it was simple and obvious. The civil defence planners, influenced no doubt, by the unlikelihood of the Soviet Union being capable of sustaining a major war 'before 1957', as the big July 1948 JIC assessment put it,[27] took January 1957 as the target date for 'all our preparations for Civil Defence' to be completed.[28] War, however, might come 'from some unforeseen incident or from a miscalculation of the enemy situation and intentions'. An emergency plan, therefore, had to be prepared for implementation at short notice. But, '[a]t the present time it will probably be found that the measures which could be taken in an emergency would be quite inadequate.'[29]

There was no 'probably' about it. As we have seen, the planners in 1948 'assumed that our enemy will be in possession of the atom bomb in limited numbers by 1957'. Ministers were briefed in a special appendix on the damage a Nagasaki-type plutonium bomb bursting between 500 and 1,000 feet up would do:

It is estimated that in London a crater 450 yards in diameter and 40 to 50 yards deep would be produced. Damage to underground services will be severe . . . Total collapse of all buildings including multi-storey framed structures is to be expected up to a distance of about 600 yards from ground-zero . . . and heavy internal damage, probably resulting in fires, up to at least 1,500 yards . . . Suburban houses of the type common in England . . . would be destroyed or would require demolition . . . to a distance of about 1,400 yards from ground-zero and would be rendered uninhabitable . . . to about 2,000 . . . Severe flash burns will occur on the unprotected parts of the bodies of people in the open at distance up to 2,000 or 3,000 yards from ground-zero . . . Gamma radiation from an airburst will cause death to people caught in the open to a distance of about 1,400 yards from ground-zero.[30]

The civil defence planners reckoned 'the enemy's primary objective is the immediate elimination of this country. It is believed that, to achieve this end, the enemy will adopt all-out air attacks with all the power at his command and for as long as he can maintain them. It will be assumed for planning purposes that these attacks will coincide with the outbreak of hostilities and will last for not less than four months.'[31]

The emergency plan drawn up on the basis of this analysis did not convince ministers. The Home Secretary, Chuter Ede, admitted to Attlee that it contained 'a large element of improvisation'.[32] In essence, it amounted to World War II-style provision plus evacuation from areas deemed most vulnerable, with shelters built, if the steel could be found, in such areas.[33] (Ministers agreed to halt all demolition of surviving World War II ones.[34]) The RAF would provide fifteen minutes' warning of attack if the Russian planes were coming in above 20,000 feet; less than five minutes if they flew below 3,000 feet.[35] Casualties were expressed in terms of the still vivid Great War folk-memory: '(cf., Somme, 1916, where 55,000 casualties were evacuated in the first three days). No system designed for peace purposes can cope with the evacuation, treatment and reception problems that this involves . . .'[36]

Nye Bevan, the Minister of Health (whose responsibilities at that time also included local government), was hugely sceptical when this first substantial report reached the Cabinet Committee on Civil Defence. He did not believe that the 'potential enemy' had the capability to launch attacks on this scale, but if the Russians did, 'this emergency plan was, in his view, quite inadequate'.[37] And Bevan carried his scepticism into the Cabinet Room the following month when Attlee himself convened an ad hoc Cabinet committee on the subject, adding, for good measure, that even if the Chiefs of Staff (i.e. the JIC) were to produce a new assessment indicating a lower level of threat, it 'would probably show a scale of attack against which any civil defence preparations that were possible at the present time would be ineffective'.[38] Attlee, as we have seen, shared his scepticism about the degree to which civil defence could provide serious protection at an affordable cost. Nevertheless, the committee authorized Ede to make a public statement about the 'emergency civil defence measures', such as they were.[39]

By the time Attlee left office in the autumn of 1951, the British secret state – its pace and preparations quickened by the outbreak of the Korean War in June 1950 – had made considerable strides in other, non-civil defence areas. For example, Berlin had stimulated the Prime Minister and the Cabinet Secretary to draw up plans for a World War III War Cabinet should all the JIC's reassurances suddenly have been exposed as misplaced.[40] Attlee agreed with Brook's suggestion that a War Cabinet Secretariat, fusing the Cabinet Secretariat with the Chiefs of Staff Secretariat, should be created if hostilities broke out.[41] In the spring of 1951 Attlee approved a plan whereby in a third world war, he or one of his successors would merge the job of Prime Minister and Minister of Defence as the conduct of 'strategy is indivisible'.[42]

The Chiefs themselves had had ready since May 1950 (just before Korea) an elaborate plan for their part in the transition to World War III. Broken down into three phases,

(a) Stage I – When there is a Threat of War
(b) Stage II – Precautionary Stage
(c) Stage III – War Stage,

it covered not just general strategy and allied 'Higher Direction of War' plus strategic deception plans but subversive operations, psychological warfare, biological and chemical warfare, strategic air offensive and (though the fruits of GEN 163 were not to reach the RAF in the form of a bomb for another three and a half years), 'Initiation of atomic warfare.'[43]

Once one has acquired a sense of the destructive power of a 'true' H-bomb, it is perhaps somewhat easy to forget just how dreadful the earlier atomic bombs were as the potential 'destroyer of worlds', in the phrase of Robert Oppenheimer, the physicist who led the scientific side of the Manhattan Project, borrowed from the Bhagavad Gita on witnessing the first atomic test in the New Mexico desert on 16 July 1945.[44] As the UK readied itself for the coronation of the young Queen in the spring of 1953 (amid a great deal of nonsense being spoken and written about a new Elizabethan Age[45]), the home defence planners, as they must henceforth be described, were circulating to ministers and officials within their world a picture of the kind of kingdom Her Majesty might have left if the Soviet Union, by then in its fourth year as a nuclear-weapons power, dropped 132 atomic bombs 'of the Nagasaki type' on the major population centres of her realm.

Allowing for the evacuation policy having worked[46] (5.2 million women, children and elderly plus 4 million who might evacuate themselves[47]), a body count of 1,378,000 dead and 785,000 seriously injured was compiled (see table).

Casualties and house damage from 132 atomic bombs

Area	Bomb ref Nos.	Casualties		House damage. No. of people whose houses are:-	
		Killed	Seriously injured	Destroyed or irreparably damaged	Temporarily uninhabitable by last war standards[1]
Greater London	1–35	422,000	241,000	663,000	3,273,000
Birmingham conurbation	36–47	127,000	72,000	199,000	927,000
Merseyside	48–58	106,000	59,000	165,000	723,000
Clyde	59–68	98,000	57,000	155,000	824,000
Manchester conurbation	69–76	98,000	57,000	155,000	742,000
Tyneside	77–82	45,000	26,000	71,000	394,000
Sheffield	83–87	53,000	30,000	83,000	304,000
Teesside	88–91	20,000	11,000	31,000	166,000
Bristol	92–94	25,000	14,000	39,000	203,000
Coventry	95–97	9,000	6,000	15,000	134,000
Hull	98–100	21,000	11,000	32,000	121,000
Belfast	101–102	14,000	7,000	21,000	149,000
Edinburgh	103–104	52,000	30,000	82,000	248,000
Southampton	105–106	3,000	2,000	5,000	48,000
Swansea	107–108	4,000	2,000	6,000	43,000
Aberdeen	109	9,000	5,000	14,000	98,000
Barrow	110	11,000	7,000	18,000	50,000
Bolton	111	16,000	9,000	25,000	79,000
Bradford	112	11,000	7,000	18,000	94,000
Cardiff	113	6,000	3,000	9,000	57,000
Chatham	114	8,000	4,000	12,000	56,000
Derby	115	18,000	11,000	29,000	80,000
Dundee	116	17,000	10,000	27,000	101,000
Grangemouth	117	1,000	1,000	2,000	12,000
Huddersfield	118	15,000	8,000	23,000	88,000
Leeds	119	11,000	7,000	18,000	143,000
Leicester	120	21,000	12,000	33,000	102,000
Luton	121	6,000	3,000	9,000	66,000
Nottingham	122	18,000	11,000	29,000	112,000
Newport	123	16,000	3,000	24,000	60,000
Plymouth	124	2,000	1,000	3,000	20,000
Portsmouth	125	9,000	5,000	14,000	97,000
Preston	126	17,000	10,000	27,000	100,000
St. Helens	127	11,000	7,000	18,000	90,000
Stoke	128	16,000	9,000	25,000	116,000
Sunderland	129	11,000	6,000	17,000	88,000
Warrington	130	6,000	3,000	9,000	60,000
Carlisle	131	14,000	7,000	21,000	54,000
Londonderry	132	11,000	6,000	17,000	41,000
Total		1,378,000	785,000	2,163,000	10,163,000

1 The figures given in this column are inclusive of the destroyed and irreparably damaged houses.[48]

Of course, the home defence planners did not know how many bombs the Soviet Union had in 1953 or what their targeting plans were (though they had to make assumptions about both for planning purposes). But the awesomeness of those figures to early-1950s eyes can be compared to the body counts incorporated in their own still-recent memories of World War II. Over the six years of that conflict the tally was as follows:

Deaths (military and Merchant Navy) 380,000
Deaths (civilian) 60,000
Houses destroyed 500,000
Houses severely damaged 250,000.[49]

Yet less than a year after the home defence planners more than tripled, in their minds, the combined military and civilian death toll of World War II, Norman Brook was convening his meeting of nuclear insiders as the hydrogen bomb created possibilities of a magnitude and a grimness that surpassed by far the threat to country, society and state posed by the atom bomb.

The first result during what might be called Britain's thermonuclear year from the spring of 1954 (when Brook's inner group met) to the spring of 1955 (when the Strath Committee reported on the home defence implications of the H-bomb) was, revealingly enough, the decision to upgrade the UK nuclear weapons programme from fission to fusion. Brook, however, had established a Central War Plans Secretariat in the Cabinet Office to pull all the aspects together, reporting directly to him. Its head, William Strath, was chosen in the last days of 1954 to lead a small interdepartmental group charged with examining the impact of not only the huge and immediate destructive force of an H-bomb attack on the UK but also the lethal and protracted effects of 'fall-out' on all aspects of life, not just governmental activity. The Strath Committee, quite simply, had to ponder the survivability of the nation.

In December 1954 Brook minuted the new Minister of Defence, Harold Macmillan, on the purposes of Strath;[50] in turn, Macmillan briefed Churchill.[51] Brook attached his minute to a brief from Strath covering what the Cabinet Office's chief war planner regarded as the essentials, much of which, unsurprisingly, reflected the thinking of both the JIC and the 'atomic knights':

1. The grim effects of 'fall-out', added to the destructive power of the thermonuclear weapon, make global war less likely. The possibility of mutual annihilation is too great.
2. In the next three or four years it is even less likely that Russia will provoke war, while she is unable to strike decisively against the USA.
3. But in a war the United Kingdom – the nerve centre of European resistance – would be extremely vulnerable to nuclear attack. There is not in sight any air defence system which could protect us effectively.
4. In short, possession by the West of the nuclear weapon is at present a real deterrent. Overwhelming and immediate retaliation with it is our only reliable defence.[52]

Nowhere in the files is the importance of being nuclear – the bias that trumps all other considerations, including civil defence – more graphically and directly expressed.

Strath then reprised for Macmillan and other inner-group ministers (Brook talked in his minute of a meeting in the Foreign Secretary's room on 9 December 1954 the minutes of which have yet to reach the Public Record Office[53]) the danger that, as 'major adventures became more imponderable' for the Soviet Union, other Cold War activities such as 'limited and local aggressions' may become a greater temptation. Part of countering the communist bloc was the need to demonstrate the economic superiority of the Western nations.

Severe strain could be put on resources by this combination of purposes, Strath warned. But he was convinced before his committee's three-month inquiry had fully begun that it was 'evident that civil defence in the broadest sense of the term must command a higher priority in defence planning than it has so far received'.[54] The paragraphs in which Strath explains his reasons for this resound to the sound of existing plans from the 1948–53 period being torn up:

Under nuclear bombardment we can no longer count on the United Kingdom being able to function as a main supply base . . . The widespread damage and immobilisation caused by 'fall-out' call for a radical reshaping of our plans for the defence of the home front. New problems of an unprecedented kind are created for the protection of the population – for shelter and evacuation plans. The role and organisation of the Civil Defence Services need radical overhaul. How far should they be geared to their normal tasks of fire fighting and rescue and how far to relief and decontamination measures? The part which the military forces may have to play in support of the Civil Authorities needs to be determined. The effects of radioactive contamination create vast and novel problems for the medical services and for agriculture. And finally there are the problems of the survival period.[55]

Within days Strath had been given Churchill's go-ahead for his study, the Prime Minister minuting on 14 December 1954: 'Keep me informed please.'[56]

Strath had begun his official life in the Inland Revenue, but he had spent the bulk of his career in military or military-related ministries before joining the Central Economic Planning Staff in 1947. He was seconded from the Treasury by Brook to set up the new War Plans Secretariat. His liaison with the Chiefs of Staff was General Sir Nevil Brownjohn. Sir Richard Powell and Sir Frederick Brundrett represented the administrative and the scientific sides, respectively, of the Ministry of Defence. Philip Allen and General Sir Sidney Kirkman, the Home Office Director General of Civil Defence, completed the team.

Within a month, at the Strath Committee's request, the JIC had produced a special report for them on 'The "H" Bomb Threat to the UK in the Event of a General War'.[57] The JIC gave the Strath group its planning period of five years as the JIC thought it inconceivable that the Soviet Union would launch a nuclear attack against the UK until they could deliver a devastating one on North America, which, the British intelligence world believed, would be unlikely before 1960.

Sir Patrick Dean and his JIC colleagues felt able to be precise in their attempt to penetrate what the 'Soviet objectives' for the UK would be in the event of war if ever and whenever it should break out:

(a) to knock out as quickly as possible those airfields from which nuclear attacks could be launched against the Soviet Union.

(b) to destroy the organisation of government and control.

(c) to render the UK useless as a base for any form of military operations.[58]

The JIC rounded off this grim picture of ultimate possibility with a bone-chilling addendum:

We believe that the Russians will regard the UK as such a threat that they will aim to render it unusable for a long period, and will not hesitate to destroy great parts of the UK to achieve this aim.[59]

If this assessment had leaked, it is very possible, to put it no higher, that CND would have sprung into vibrant and vociferous existence three years sooner than it did.

Intriguingly, the JIC in those first days of 1955 did not think the Soviet Union would be in a position to attack the UK with H-bombs 'before 1958', given the difficulty of producing them in a size and weight that an aircraft could carry – though reductions here were anticipated. Russian submarines could do it sooner; and ballistic missiles would be in a position to do it during the 1960s.

Where the Russians needed military results immediately in World War III, they would burst their H-bombs at 20,000 feet over London, for example, to achieve maximum blast effect. Atomic bombs, the JIC thought, 'should be adequate for airfield targets'. The effects of fall-out, however, would be 'somewhat delayed'.[60] Then came their terrifying passage, quoted at the head of this chapter, about a mere ten 10-megaton H-bombs dropped on the western side of the UK having sufficient capacity to effectively wreck the Queen's realm.

How soon would she, her ministers and her subjects know this was about to happen?

Assuming that we shall be able at least to maintain the present state of our intelligence, and in view of the intense Russian security awareness, this is by no means certain . . .[61]

Here lay an implicit admission of the lack of human agents inside the inner core of the Soviet state apparatus – the indispensable requirement for serious intelligence on intentions as opposed to capabilities. But, the JIC continued,

we (a) expect to be able to say when the Soviet leaders are making preparations for war;

and (b) should be able to estimate when those preparations are reaching various stages of readiness and the weight of attack which could be launched at each stage.[62]

Full mobilization of the Soviet Union should be detectable at least a month ahead unless it were done gradually over a very long period. Only with 'the detection of enemy aircraft on Allied radar screens' could a warning of 'actual attack' be given. As we have seen, a Russian bomber targeted for a 20,000-foot air burst could be detected 200 miles from the radars, giving a warning-time 'of the order of twenty minutes'. 'If we can use radars based in Northern Europe, the total time of warning from the UK may be as much as sixty minutes. But if the Russians are prepared to risk low level approach and delivery, we may get as little as three minutes warning of crossing the coast, but this technique is unlikely.'[63]

In a perverse way, the slim warning times became a sort of comfort to some at the centre of the British nuclear capacity in the Cold War years. It was unlike anything else they ever had to do as senior civil servants. One who had a variety of jobs on the economic and industrial side as well as the bomb once told me how 'policy failure' was knowable in those former areas. By contrast, 'I would have only known for four minutes if all the advice I had given on deterrence turned out to be wrong!'[64]

Strath and his committee worked very quickly. They reported in March 1955 and their findings were discussed by the Home Defence and Defence committees of the Cabinet.[65] Several scholars – including myself and my 'Secret State' students – spent a good part of turn-of-the-century Britain attempting to get Strath declassified. A great many interested departments had to reach agreement on it. It was finally released at the Public Record Office on 25 April 2002. Prior to this, we were able to reconstruct its essence from the briefings which surrounded it and from the minutes (which were declassified) of the ad hoc Cabinet committee Macmillan chaired on it, GEN 491, on 24 March 1955.[66] And it is interesting to see as an example of how (rather like intelligence work itself) an account of an important but carefully guarded piece of information can be reconstructed from fragments of material related to it before assessing what in the document itself added to our knowledge when, at last, we could read it in full.

On Macmillan's recommendation, a copy of the Strath Report was sent to all Cabinet ministers 'for their personal information' by the end of March.[67] Brook prepared a brief on Strath for the new Prime Minister, Sir Anthony Eden, who had succeeded Churchill on 6 April 1955. (Eden had sent Macmillan to the Foreign Office and put Selwyn Lloyd at Defence in his place.) In the third week of his premiership, Eden was invited by his Cabinet Secretary to contemplate the Strath Committee's 'broad conclusion . . . that although a determined hydrogen bomb attack against this country would cause human and material destruction on an appalling scale, it would be possible to contain its effects and enable the nation to survive if adequate preparations had been made in advance.'[68] Strath, however, had done no more than outline possible solutions to the problems posed by the H-Bomb; 'much more work must be done before it can be firmly decided how far these are practicable and financially acceptable'.[69]

Strath had, the new PM was told, ruptured important strategic assumptions of the atomic age. Because the Chiefs of Staff reckoned any future war in which the UK suffered attack would involve the H-bomb, 'we should discontinue any home defence preparations which are relevant only to war fought with nothing but conventional or atomic weapons'. Following on from this Strath, as reported by Brook, had concluded that

Because of the widespread devastation which would inevitably be caused by a hydrogen bomb attack on this country, we should discontinue any plans (e.g. for the building up of industrial war potential) which rest on the assumption that the United Kingdom would be available as a main supply base after the attack.[70]

Macmillan and his colleagues on GEN 491 had heard at their meeting on 24 March 1955 that: 'The earlier conception of a period of broken-backed warfare following the initial attack, in which this country would take part had been abandoned.' After a thermonuclear exchange, '[f]ighting would go on in other parts of the world but the main supply areas would be outside this country, possibly Australia, South Africa or even the United States.'[71] GEN 491 also faced the reality that preparations against an H-bomb attack 'were at present virtually non-existent'.[72]

Brook warned Eden:

The two most difficult and politically sensitive questions of policy are those concerning evacuation and shelter. Dispersal of the population would inevitably cause social and economic dislocation and the report rejects anything like total abandonment of the highly vulnerable areas on that account; it concludes nevertheless that some measure of evacuation would have to be undertaken if casualties on a disastrous scale were to be avoided. The proposal is that priority classes, such as mothers and young children, should be removed to safer areas but that other people should remain at work on a shift system in the high risk areas, moving out at other times to the periphery of the large towns.[73]

There was an air of unreality about some of the Strath elements which later planners did not share (as we shall see). But one hard reality, money, was a constant attender in the councils of those who pondered the cindering of the realm. As Brook reminded Eden: 'War planning is in itself an exercise in choosing between various risks: as the resources available for home defence are so limited.'[74]

Within a few years, another of the post-Strath assumptions would come to look hugely optimistic. Even before the Cuban missile crisis erupted with startling suddenness, the intelligence and war planning committees had become more and more preoccupied by what the 1952 Ministry of Defence War Book called the '"Bolt From the Blue" Emergency'.[75] GEN 491, however, carried on stressing post-Strath that 'for planning purposes, Departments should continue to proceed on the assumption that the Government would be able to detect a deterioration in the international situation some six months before war came and would know, say, seven days in advance that an attack on this country was to be expected'. For good measure GEN 491 added a Pollyanna-like statement of the obvious: 'The importance of a period of warning for the carrying out of home defence plans, for example on evacuation, emphasised the high value of good intelligence work in discovering the enemy's intentions.'[76]

The shadow of Strath reached through the 1950s and into the mid-1960s (and beyond, in the sense that the geographically small and densely populated UK will forever remain vulnerable as long as thermonuclear weapons exist). It reached into the War Cabinet's bunker when it first came into existence under the codename STOCKWELL, then BURLINGTON and later TURNSTILE from about 1960, five years after the committee reported.[77] For, after Strath, 'Ministers . . . accept[ed] the view that it would be extremely unlikely that central control would continue to operate from London after attack and that the government of the United Kingdom would be conducted by a central nucleus in protected accommodation in the country.'[78]

Bunkerdom for ministers was one thing and easily agreed; shelter for the rest of the Queen's subjects quite another. And Strath stimulated what Alban Webb has called the mid-1950s 'battle for Home Defence Policy',[79] which, at root, reflected not just the limited resources to which Brook referred but also the arguments for the primacy of active (i.e. nuclear) over passive (i.e. civil) defence. The tussle took place in a new Ministerial Committee on Home Defence which Eden set up in August 1955 under the chairmanship of the Minister of Defence.

Building on the grim picture most of the ministers round the table had absorbed when it had been presented to them by the Chiefs of Staff a year before, Strath warned that 'Hydrogen bomb war would be total war in a sense not hitherto conceived. The entire nation would be in the front line. Life and property would be obliterated by blast and fire on a vast scale. An attack of the size assumed [10 H-bombs] would unleash an explosive force equivalent to 100 million tons of TNT. This is forty-five times as great as the total tonnage of bombs delivered by all the Allies over Germany, Italy and occupied France throughout the whole of the last war . . . A single 10-megaton bomb could destroy any of our cities (except Greater London) and all, or nearly all, its inhabitants.'[80]

The essence of the Strath recommendations was that the government could seek to mitigate the consequences of a thermonuclear attack by evacuation from target areas; local dispersal of those remaining from the places at greatest risk; and the construction of shelters: 'These are not alternatives. In practice a combination of all three would be required.'[81]

When I knew that a copy of the full Strath report was on its way to the PRO's reading rooms in Kew, I wrote to the sole survivor of the group of officials who had sat with Sir William in 1955, Lord Allen of Abbeydale, asking if he would like to see it again. He would not. 'It was a terrible committee on a terrible subject', he replied. '. . . I suppose it had to be done but I don't think I want to be reminded too much by having a copy of the report.'[82] Philip Allen's 47-year-old memory caught exactly my reaction when I had finished reading the thirty-two pages plus appendices of Strath.

The most significant item it added to existing knowledge was the explicit recognition that in several parts of the shattered kingdom, civilian government would for a time have to give way to military rule. Paragraph 135, part of Section XII of the report on 'Machinery of Control' (which immediately follows the admission that the true condition of post-attack UK 'would remain beyond the imagination until it happened'), acknowledged that:

[i]n some parts of the country, particularly if several bombs fell in the same area, there might be complete chaos for a time and civil control would collapse. In such circumstances the local military commander would have to be prepared to take over from the civil authority responsibility for the maintenance of law and order and for the administration of Government. He would, if called upon, exercise his existing common-law powers to take whatever steps, however drastic, he considered necessary to restore order. He would have to direct the operations of various civil agencies, including the police, the civil defence services and the fire service. In areas less badly hit the civil authorities might still be able to retain control but only with the support of the armed services.[83]

This confirms the plan – in extreme circumstances – to reconvert Britain to a Cromwellian state ruled by major-generals with, in this case, literally *absolute* powers. When absorbed whole, it is quite plain to see why the Strath Report is (and will remain) one of the most important documents of the 1950s. Quite plainly Strath and his colleagues realized this as, paragraph by paragraph, they slogged across their terrifying terrain, for they abandoned the cautious understatement that invariably accompanies the official mind when it expresses itself on a page. Their tone is genuinely millenarian. In their opening 'Preamble', the Strath group do not spare their readers:

Fall-out, combined with the vast explosive power of the hydrogen bomb, presents problems of a revolutionary character for the defence of this country and a threat of the utmost gravity to our survival as a nation.[84]

The report then proceeds to explain why, before warning ministers of the consequences of doing nothing by way of evacuation and shelter arrangements:

If no preparations of any kind had been made in advance, a successful night attack on the main centres of population in this country with ten hydrogen bombs would, we estimate, kill about 12 million people and seriously injure or disable 4 million others – a total of about 16 million. Casualties on such a scale would be intolerable; they would mean the loss of nearly one third of the population; they would moreover include a disproportionate share of the skilled man-power on which our future would depend.[85]

In making these extrapolations, the Strath Committee was, as we have seen, heavily reliant on American data as Britain had yet to test a thermonuclear weapon of its own. Strath carefully guided his readers from the bomb bursting either in the air or on the ground, its terrible heat and blast wreaking instant havoc, to the awful fate of those away from the ground zeros doomed to slow death by fall-out:

Air Burst
The maximum area of destruction by blast and heat is attained by exploding the bomb at a certain optimum height above the ground (this may well be of the order of 10–20,000 feet). For this type of burst the fireball formed by the explosion does not touch the ground and very little debris from the ground is drawn into it. As a consequence, the radioactive fission products are not carried down to the ground by the debris but rise to a very great altitude and are distributed around the world by winds in the stratosphere. They drift to the ground very slowly over some years and, since much of their radioactivity decays, they become harmless. With this type of burst, therefore, the residual radioactivity has negligible consequences.

Ground Burst
The blast and heat effects from a ground burst would be somewhat less than

those from an air burst. But a 10-megaton ground-burst would form a crater about 1 mile across and up to 300 feet deep at its centre: and over 10 million tons of pulverised debris would be lifted to a great height and become highly contaminated with the enormous radioactivity produced by the explosion. Much of this debris (the fall-out) would drift rapidly down to the ground over a distance of one to two hundred miles, creating a region of great danger for human life due to radioactivity. In view of the very serious consequences of this feature of the explosion, the subject of fall-out will be considered in detail below. Should the bomb burst in shallow water, i.e., off the shore or in rivers, the effects would be much the same as for a ground-burst, although the problem of local decontamination might be more difficult.

<u>Destruction by Blast and Heat</u>

The following table illustrates the extent of damage by blast and heat from the explosion of a 10-megaton bomb in the air and on the ground:

		Air Burst	Ground Burst
(a) Blast:	(i) Complete devastation	12–28 square miles	
		(2–3 mile radius)	
	(ii) Houses uninhabitable,	110 square miles	80 square miles
	at least in the short term, by	(6-mile radius)	(5-mile radius)
	last war standards. Roofs of	800 square miles	450 square miles
	factories severely damaged.	(16-mile radius)	(12-mile radius)
(b) Heat:	Normal houses set on	300–700 square miles	
	fire (extent of this type of	(10–15 mile radius)	
	damage depends greatly	(average conditions of cloud and haze).	
	on weather conditions).		

For comparison the area of the Metropolitan Police District is 736 square miles.

Though the zone of major damage by blast and heat would not extend more than some 12–16 miles from the point of burst, widespread minor damage would be done to roofs, windows and light structures at much greater distances.

All Strath's readers would have had a still-vivid memory of the blitzes of World War II. The sheer impossibility of fighting the post-H-bomb fire hazard would have been instantly apparent on being told that the 'heat flash from the hydrogen bomb would start in a built-up area anything up to 100,000 fires, with a circumference of between 60 to 100 miles'.[86]

Effects on Human Life

The radioactivity of fall-out debris would affect human beings in three ways:

(a) *Gamma radiation*. Moderate doses of the penetrating gamma radiation from the fission products would cause incapacitating sickness, starting within a few hours and lasting a few weeks; heavier doses would cause death within one to six weeks.

(b) *Skin burns*. Persons who failed to cleanse themselves of any direct contamination by debris dust would suffer skin burns. Local irritation and blistering would occur around individual particles of the dust which lodged in nasal passages, ears, eyes or finger nails.

(c) *Injury from ingested radioactivity*. Leukaemia, serious thyroid injury and long-term bone disease and cancer might result from drinking highly contaminated water or milk from cows which had grazed on contaminated pasture, or from eating vegetables or crops grown on contaminated ground or which had been contaminated directly by fall-out.

The gamma radiation hazard at (a) would be of paramount importance initially, but the dangers from ingestion of radioactivity ((c) above) would continue to be important long after the gamma radiation had subsided. The skin burn hazard is unlikely to be lethal.

Effects of Gamma Radiation on Human Beings

The roentgen is the commonly accepted unit for the measurement of radiation dosage from gamma-rays. A dose of about 25 roentgens received over a brief period of time might produce temporary changes in the blood but no incapacity. A dose of about 100 roentgens received over a few hours would produce nausea and other symptoms of radiation sickness. A dose of 450 roentgens received in a few hours would be fatal to approximately half the people who suffered it and is known as the median lethal dose. The total dose accumulated within a few hours would largely determine the severity of the symptoms; a dose incurred uniformly over a period of several days would have to be about twice as great as a dose incurred in a few hours in order to produce the same severity of symptoms. The typical sequence of clinical symptoms caused by a median lethal dose would be:

First day: Sickness and vomiting.
Second week: Loss of hair begins. Loss of appetite and general depression.
Third week: Fever.
Fourth week: Severe inflammation of mouth and throat.
> Pallor.
> Blood spots under the skin.
> Diarrhoea and nose-bleeding.
> Rapid emaciation.
> Death in one case out of two, on average.

If double the median lethal dose were incurred, this sequence of symptoms would occur much more rapidly, culminating nearly always in death within about two weeks. If the dose were about one-third of the median lethal dose, the sequence of symptoms would be greatly protracted and perhaps only one half to three-quarters of the recipients would be affected; after initial sickness on the first day, the symptoms would develop mainly over the third to fifth week, and almost all persons exposed at this level would ultimately recover.

Once the symptoms of radiation sickness had developed, the chances of recovery would be greatly reduced by exposure to cold, and resistance to any form of infection would be lowered. Many radiation casualties might die because they could not be given adequate shelter or nursing.

Widespread radiation sickness from fall-out would obviously undermine morale and make it extremely difficult to establish the disciplined behaviour essential to survival.

<u>Long-term and Genetic Effects</u>

Persons who survived radiation exposures of the order of half the median lethal dose or more would be subnormal in health for perhaps a year, and might be sterile for two years or more; statistically they would also show a slightly shortened life span. Exposure to radiation would also have a genetic effect on the germ cells which transmit inherited characteristics from one generation to another. Its consequences over a large number of generations would depend upon the average dose per head of the whole population. There is a rather wide range of opinion among experts on this subject but it seems possible that genetic effects in highly civilised populations of an attack of the intensity considered in this study would hazard long-term survival, particularly if subsequent generations were also exposed to this kind of warfare.[87]

After making its strong pitch for a shelter and evacuation policy, Strath also depicted the ghastly effects of megaton warfare on animals and agriculture before turning to 'machinery of control'. This is not only intriguing in itself, it is of particular importance as the resultant Working Party on the Machinery of Government in War was the only post-Strath group whose papers were not released along with the report itself in the spring of 2002. Brook told the first meeting of the Home Defence Committee (which he chaired), convened to consider Strath on 17 March 1955, that the working party was proceeding on the 'hypothesis' that '[p]lans must . . . be made to restore central government at the earliest possible moment' post-attack and that '[p]roposals covering the central nucleus were already before ministers'.[88]

Essentially, the idea was for the 'central nucleus' to be established in secret and protected accommodation well away from London supported by a set of regional governments from which, as we have seen, military and, where possible, civilian plus military rule would be conducted in the initial aftermath of World War III. Strath urged ministers to get on with it and to recognize that far cruder and arbitrary methods would be needed than anything contemplated during the previous wars:

Certain preliminary steps are in our view essential if the regional organisation of Government is to work effectively under the stress of attack and if the civil and military authorities are to co-operate closely and efficiently as they would have to do.

(*a*). A person of sufficient standing and authority should be appointed now at each regional headquarters to exercise responsibility, under the Home Secretary, for the co-ordination of all civil defence planning at the regional level.

(*b*). Large-scale exercises should be held, in conjunction with the military, to test and train the regional organisation and the local authority civil defence organisation.

(c). Senior officers who in the event of war would be sent to the regions by the various Departments to carry on those functions of the central Government which would be devolved to the regions should be designated now. They should be informed of their designation and should be required to familiarise themselves with their regions and to take part in the exercises referred to in (b) above.

(d). Plans should be made for bringing the regional staffs up to full strength very shortly after a decision to do so was taken.

We understand that consideration is already being given to the resiting of regional headquarters and army district headquarters to remove them from the target areas and to bring them together.

To maintain control under nuclear attack would require the use of drastic emergency powers. A complicated series of Defence Regulations, providing for detailed controls, as was used in the last war would be quite unsuitable. Much more rough and ready methods would be needed to cover the period when the nation would be struggling to survive.[89]

Strath may have emphasized that its – and ministers' – tasks were 'beyond the imagination', but it came up with sixty-two specific recommendations. The Strath assumptions and proposals came to be regarded as over-optimistic within five years when new studies of 'breakdown' were undertaken in Whitehall, as we shall see in the next chapter. Yet the shadow of Strath loomed large both in secret ministerial debates which followed quickly upon its circulation and in the planning for government by bunkerdom which continued until the regional seats of government were finally stood down in 1992.[90]

During the summer of 2002, one of my students, Catherine Haddon, came across a Foreign Office file that shed a bizarre light on the Strath-related question of how many H-bombs it would take to effectively wreck the United Kingdom. It related to an encounter in July 1961, at the height of the Berlin crisis, between Nikita Khrushchev and the British Ambassador to Moscow, Sir Frank Roberts, who found themselves in each other's company at the ballet and engaged in a grim banter.

Later there was some dispute about precisely what Khrushchev had said. The Soviet leader gave his version shortly afterwards to a visiting

US diplomat, whose account was telegraphed back to London in August 1961 by the British Embassy in Washington. Khrushchev, according to this account, had claimed that, in a global nuclear war, the vast USA and USSR would survive whereas West Germany, France and the UK would 'perish' on 'the first day'. He had asked Roberts 'how many bombs would be needed to put the UK out of commission'?

'Six,' Roberts replied.

It is doubtful that Sir Frank carried the Strath assumptions in his head. If he did, it was a noble attempt to talk down the nuclear armoury the Soviet Union might target on the UK. But, according to the US account, Khrushchev would have none of it:

. . . he told the Ambassador that he had heard an anecdote about pessimists and optimists in Berlin; the pessimists thought that six bombs would be required to put the UK out of commission while the optimists felt that nine would be needed. Thus the UK Ambassador belonged to the category of pessimists. The Soviet General Staff, however, had earmarked several scores of bombs for use against the UK so that the Soviet Union had a higher opinion of the UK's resistance capacity that [sic] the UK itself.[91]

The Roberts/Khrushchev exchange was a strange and almost certainly unknowing echo of a great debate that raged among the Whitehall war planners in the early 1960s.

5

'Breakdown': Preparing for the Worst

> *. . . breakdown might be defined as occurring 'when the government of a country is no longer able to ensure that its orders are carried out'. This state of affairs could come about through breakdown of the machinery of control . . . or through the mass of people becoming preoccupied with their own survival rather than the country's war effort and prepared to run the risk of being shot rather than to obey orders which would seem to them to involve unreasonable personal risk, in a word, through the breakdown of morale.*
>
> Dr Edgar Anstey of JIGSAW on 'Note on the Concept and Definitions of Breakdown', June 1960[1]

> *I am all against installing additional equipment if it is not strictly necessary . . . It is however desirable that the Prime Minister, and we, should be told promptly if missiles are on the way, preferably before they land.*
>
> Denys Laskey, Head of the Cabinet Office's Overseas and Defence Secretariat, May 1966[2]

> *It was inescapable, it was necessary and it was lunatic.*
>
> Sir Rodric Braithwaite, former Chairman of the Joint Intelligence Committee, 2002, recalling the need to fight the Cold War and prepare for the worst[3]

The full Strath programme had one unequivocal champion in the Cabinet's Ministerial Committee on Home Defence when it began work in earnest during autumn 1955 – the Home Secretary, Gwilym Lloyd

George.* His memo to the committee of 25 October 1955 showed him to be both high-minded and humane as well as a vigorous pursuer of a policy, civil defence, for which his ministry was lead department. 'It is in my view the duty of the Government, by planning evacuation and the gradual provision of shelter, to reduce the possibilities of casualties on this scale,' he told his colleagues, adding, 'It is no use keeping any forces for the "hot war" if the morale of this country is to collapse and we lose the will to fight. I suggest that with no shelter, morale would collapse.'[4]

Lloyd George's paper contained a self-collapsing element – costings. Finance trumped humanity. Morale cannot be measured nor, therefore, priced. Buildings can. A 6-foot by 6-foot by 5-foot shelter beneath a living room would cost £100 if constructed as part of each new house (i.e. £30 million a year at then current building rates). The price would double for existing housing stock, which would come out at £1.25 billion.[5]

As soon as the committee met, the Home Secretary's paper was savaged. General Brownjohn noted that the sum involved was comparable to that required to sustain the nuclear deterrent, adding that the 'Chiefs of Staff would be seriously alarmed at a proposal that £1,250 million should be spent on what was purely a "passive measure"'.[6] From the chair, the Minister of Defence, by this time Selwyn Lloyd, backed the Chiefs, arguing that 'the primary objective was to prevent war and a sum of this order could be spent on medium bombers [i.e. the V-force] and would be more likely to influence the decision of an aggressor than the same sum spent on shelter.'[7] Lloyd George lost again when the question rose a notch in the hierarchy of decision-taking on reaching the Cabinet's Defence Committee on 7 December 1955. Research on shelters could go ahead. Surveys of existing housing stock could proceed. But the committee 'agreed that the financial and economic situation precluded a programme for the construction of domestic shelter at public expense'.[8]

---

* Son of the Great War leader, who deserves to be remembered for more than his wonderful aphorism, delivered a year before at an undergraduate meeting in Cambridge, that: 'Politicians are like monkeys. The higher they climb up the tree, the more revolting are the parts they expose' (Private information).

Despite Berlin 1961, Cuba 1962 and a host of other lesser alarms, it always did. And Britain was not unique here. As David Miller has shown:

In most countries, policies seemed to follow a seven- to ten-year cycle, varying from, at worst, almost total uninterest to, at best, a grudging and lukewarm enthusiasm. The figures speak for themselves: as a proportion of the defence budget, the USSR spent just under 1 per cent on civil defence, while the USA spent approximately 0.1 per cent, and the figure in most other countries was even less.[9]

Miller noted that the 'difficulty was that, if it was to be taken seriously, the scale of the problem was huge and the costs were enormous . . . Very few countries proved willing to undertake such measures on the necessary scale, particularly if they were achievable only at the expense of cuts in the more active part of the national defence budget'.[10]

West Germany passed a law requiring all new housing to include a cellar built to state requirements. But only Norway (62 per cent cover for the population), Sweden (70 per cent) and Switzerland (90 per cent)[11] ran really serious shelter programmes, suggesting that a country had to be both financially rich and demographically small to be adequately civilly defended. Britain did keep a substantial Civil Defence Corps costing £10 million a year[12] in being until the mid-1960s, when it fell victim to Labour's 1965 Home Defence Review. And successive economic crises saw the Wilson government putting HD on a 'care and maintenance' basis by the end of its term, spending falling from £22 million a year to between £7 million and £8 million.[13]

Yet, despite the no-shelter policy, home defence spending did rise as part of post-Strath decision-taking from £69.6 million in 1955–6 to a projected £150 million by 1960–61.[14] So on which activities were resources concentrated? In essence, four:

1: Pre-attack evacuation (priority classes being schoolchildren; mothers; expectant mothers; the aged; the infirm – just over 11 million people in all).[15]
2: Stockpiling for post-attack needs (food, oil, medical supplies).[16]
3: Public utilities (fire services, gas, electricity, water, ports, railways, communications, BBC Wartime Broadcasting Service).[17]

4: Post-attack government (TURNSTILE, regional seats of government, integration of military and civil authorities).[18]

In effect, there were twin biases at work: the deterrent and, should it fail, command and control of the survivors and supply of the basic rudiments of continued survival.

After Strath, the secret state thought in three phases:

A 'Precautionary Stage'[19] of about seven days between a period of international tension reaching a point which indicated it could trigger 'global war'.[20]
A 'Destructive Phase' in which 'the devastation caused by the nuclear attack on the United Kingdom would be very great' during a 'period which might last from 48 hours to 7 days'.[21]
A 'Survival Phase'.[22] Planning for it would be aimed 'solely at tackling the problems of survival' with a high degree of devolution, initially at least, to Civil Defence Regions, each with its own mini-government (as we have seen) of ministers, officials, police and military.[23]

As we have seen, the 'machinery of control' had been a priority from the moment Strath reported, with Macmillan's group, GEN 491, picking up strongly on Strath's recommendation 'that the regional organisation of government should be strengthened now'.[24]

The Commanders in Chief Committee swiftly did the spadework for the Chiefs of Staff on the integration of the civil and military branches of government under a Cabinet minister outside the War Cabinet, based in one of the twelve regional seats of government. Reporting to the Chiefs of Staff in June 1956, the Commanders explained that:

Because of the tremendous dislocation which nuclear attack will cause, and the complexity of the problem arising from the possibility [odd word to use given the state of knowledge following the US H-bomb tests in the Pacific] of fall-out, plans are being made for the maximum decentralisation of Government. For this purpose, joint Civil and Military Headquarters are being planned at which the Army District Commander and Regional Director of Civil Defence together with representatives of the other Services and of the Civil departments will be available to support the Regional Commissioner [the Cabinet minister] . . .

The degree to which Regional Commissioners will have to assume control within their Regions will depend upon the nature of the attack. Broadly, the functions of the Regional Commissioners will be: –

(a) Co-ordinating the Civil Defence measures of the various local authorities, Government departments and the Services within the Region.
(b) Taking control of the civil administration in the Region in the event of a breakdown of communications with the Central Government.[25]

Which minister would have gone to what bunker at various stages in the 1960s will be divulged in Chapter 7.

'Breakdown' is a word that lives in many a text of the Cold War secret state. As some of the post-Strath policies worked their way through into practical form in the late 1950s and early 1960s, the word came to acquire a very wide meaning as that special JIGSAW group we have already briefly encountered of military, scientists and civilians were brought together in great secrecy in a couple of rooms in the Old Admiralty Building on Horse Guards Parade right next to the Citadel that Penney had used in 1954 as the focus of his pictures of the destruction a 'hybrid' and a 'true' H-bomb could bring. The Joint Inter-Services Group for the Study of All-Out War for six years of the high Cold War between 1958 and 1964 were the secret state's 'what if' team. Set up by the Chief of the Defence Staff, Lord Mountbatten, in 1958, their brief was to ponder the nature, duration and likely outcome of a global war around the turn of the 1960s and 1970s. They were to range widely and report to Mountbatten and the MoD's Chief Scientific Adviser, Sir Solly Zuckerman.[26] In January 2001, a shoal of their papers (on which a forty-year retention had been imposed) reached the Public Record Office.[27]

Some of JIGSAW's output does strike an early twenty-first-century reader as being in the realms of Strangelovian fantasy. In May 1960, just as the Paris Summit fell apart after the Russians shot down the CIA's reconnaissance/spy plane carrying Gary Powers over the Urals,[28] E. A. (Ted) Lovell, a scientist seconded from the Air Ministry, placed a scenario before his JIGSAW colleagues as part of 'Some Thoughts on Deterrence or the Lack of It', which, he admitted, 'perhaps sounds fantastic and unreal' but needed contemplating nonetheless. In brief, the Russians 'put into effect their threat to shoot at any bases from which a reconnaissance flight originates and the Americans retaliate with the weight of attack which they have calculated will cause "break-down" and this consumes all their nuclear weapons'.

Khrushchev and the Soviet leadership 'have prepared for this eventuality by retiring to a deep shelter in the Urals where they have radio transmitters capable of communicating with the West and of talking to the survivors of the Russian people who have their radio sets intact'.[29] The Russians now fire missiles at heavily populated and industrial areas and ports in America, but hold back about half of their nuclear armoury. Khrushchev and the 'Russian leaders now instruct the West to pay tribute in the form of a massive aid to them and threaten any nation which offers aid to the USA'. The Soviet Union will, therefore, recover and the United States will not.[30]

JIGSAW seems to have been a wonderfully disputatious group. As Dr Ian Shaw, who was one of the pioneers of using computers to model fall-out[31] and was the War Office's scientist in the group, expressed it: 'One would need to be an incurable optimist to hope that any general statement would receive unanimous agreement in this group.'[32] Nevertheless, JIGSAW does eventually seems to have reached agreement both on the notion of 'breakdown' (the point at which survivors turn inwards, and cease to be assets to a state which has lost the capacity to govern and the means of waging war, leading both industry and society helplessly slowing down of their own accord[33]) *and* the number of thermonuclear warheads required for this (the figures cited by Shaw were 300 cities in Russia; 200 in the West, twenty of which were in the UK).[34]

It is plain from Shaw's paper that in the last months of 1960 the group were still at odds on the criteria and the numbers, but Dr Edgar Anstey, the Home Office's man on JIGSAW and a psychologist by profession, says that eventually the group did agree on three hypotheses (the last of which took care of Lovell's 'Russia wins' scenario):

1: About 30% destruction of a city renders the <u>whole</u> city population 'ineffective' – i.e. wholly preoccupied with their own survival. The survivors would become a liability rather than an asset to the country.[35]
2: A megaton delivery on a city such as Birmingham would also render 'ineffective' 50% of the population within a radius of about 20 miles, including

e.g. Coventry, where the people would see, hear and smell what happened to Birmingham, and would either take to their cellars or get into their cars and drive to where they think they might be safe.[36]

3: Our third hypothesis, confirmed by studies of the effect of intensive bombing of Germany during the last months of WW 2,[37] was that a general collapse of the national structure of a country, which we call 'Breakdown occurs when about 50% of the population have been rendered ineffective.'[38]

Dr Anstey, who with Dr Alan McDonald, a fellow Principal Scientific Officer from the Home Office, did a good deal of the work which read across the experiences of destruction of German and Japanese cities (and of Clydebank in Scotland) into post-nuclear attack possibilities, felt able to brief me on the JIGSAW 'breakdown' notions once the files arrived at the PRO:[39]

Combining these hypotheses, we calculated that the number of megaton deliveries required to cause breakdown was about 25 for the UK, and about 450 for the USA or Soviet Union. Moreover, and this was the really important finding, this scale of delivery was well within the capacity of either the USA or the Soviet Union, even <u>after</u> it had been subjected to a pre-emptive attack by its major adversary.[40]

Intriguingly enough, the eight senior members of the JIGSAW team were in Washington pooling analysis with their American counterparts in the first week of October 1962, the month of the Cuban missile crisis. In his May 1963 'Summary of JIGSAW "Breakdown Studies"', Anstey noted the impact of their conversations with the US Weapons Supply Evaluation Group in their Washington discussions in April 1960 and October 1962:

. . . WSEG and other US organisations still tend to use number of (immediate) deaths as almost the sole criterion of the effects of attack. In 1960 and again in 1962 JIGSAW maintained that deaths greatly underestimated the effects of nuclear attack and that there is little point in saving people from immediate death without securing the means of keeping them, and the nation, alive during the following months. These arguments made some impression.

The US agencies have not yet fully accepted the doctrine that breakdown could occur in the USA (this doctrine is highly objectionable for political reasons), but the exchange of views with JIGSAW has resulted in their devoting some attention to the likely consequences of deliveries of some hundreds of megaton weapons, whereas previously their studies had been confined solely to the effects of many thousands of deliveries.[41]

The effect of JIGSAW thinking can be detected (along with many other factors) in the acquisition of an invulnerable, second-strike nuclear capability in Polaris (remember Group Captain Shelfoon's elegy in praise of a 'secure' and 'quietly unobtrusive' system which is 'in every way compatible with the British character'[42]).

Many of their arguments found an echo in the justifications for the runing down of home defence following the 1965 review, much of which was based on the acceptance that the risk of nuclear war was 'very greatly reduced' as 'a consequence of the development of a second strike capability on each side, and of each side's awareness of this . . . In view of this there is stability since an aggressor who struck first would nevertheless suffer unacceptable damage in return.'[43] There are touches of JIGSAW, too, in the emphasis on concentrating resources on 'survival measures, including the control system' (by which the Home Office meant the post-attack civil administration of the UK), rather than rescue (i.e. saving the lives of those trapped in the ruins).[44] The decision to 'emphasise survival measures rather than life-saving operations' had been part of the 1960 Home Defence Review, which had led to a fall in the Civil Defence Corps from 360,000 in 1960 to about 140,000 by 1965.[45]

No shelters. Slimline Civil Defence Corps tasked to concentrate on survival and recovery rather than rescue. Increasing role of deterrence – the power to retaliate in time and with sufficient force to wreak unacceptable damage. The ministers, the military and the civil servants JIGSAW briefed at, for example, their session in the Admiralty Cinema on 16 November 1961 (Harold Watkinson, the Minister of Defence, Mountbatten and Brook leading their respective professions)[46] on what an H-bomb would do to Birmingham, as well as a general nuclear exchange between the Soviet Union and the United States, can have been left in no doubt that, in Dr Anstey's words: 'There would be complete breakdown in both of the great powers. Neither the USA nor the Soviet Union stood the slightest chance of "winning" a global nuclear war in any meaningful sense.'[47] This conviction set alongside that of the British calculations of eight million dead and eight million injured at the hands of the Royal Air Force,[48] should retaliation be ordered, would be enough to deter any likely Soviet leadership in most foreseeable circumstances from seeking a British version of 'breakdown'.

But the restless Mountbatten, at the turn of 1960–61, became anxious about the speed and reliability of exactly those retaliation drills available to Harold Macmillan.[49] As he put it to Norman Brook in February 1961, he was not convinced that Whitehall was making full use of the 'speed, capacity and presentation facilities afforded by new techniques' should the brink be reached.[50]

Mountbatten was right. Given the cost, infrastructure and regular exercising required to keep the V-bombers on their Lincolnshire airfields and capable of getting airborne within one and a half minutes of the order to scramble – not to mention the scientific effort and finance required to design and produce the nuclear weapons for their bomb bays – it is amazing to discover from the files just how rudimentary, almost casual, were the arrangements as late as 1960–61 for the Prime Minister to authorize the ultimate retaliation.

As he later made plain to Brook, Mountbatten was well aware that the President of the United States had with him at all times an officer bearing the codes that would unleash his B-52 bombers and the US's intercontinental ballistic missiles against Russian and Soviet bloc targets.[51] What, by comparison, was available to Macmillan? The Cabinet Office, prodded by the CDS's concern, produced a brief on present practices for a meeting between Mountbatten and Brook on 5 February 1961.

The JIC's view was that a pre-emptive strike by the Russians was 'unlikely' unless they felt 'unacceptably threatened', as a paper by Freddie Bishop (at that time Brook's deputy) for the Cabinet Secretary and the Chief of Defence Staff put it. This had been so fully taken to heart that no prime ministerial drill was deemed necessary to cope with such a contingency. Should it happen, Bishop explained:

Radar might give about ninety minutes' warning of the moment of a Soviet attack on this country by manned bombers, but there would be no warning of a ballistic missile attack until the completion of the Ballistic Missile Early Warning System [on Fylingdales Moor in North Yorkshire] in 1963. This system when operational, would give only a few minutes' warning of attack by ballistic missiles.

In the event, therefore, of a 'bolt out of the blue' attack . . . there might be only short radar warning, or even virtually no warning. It is hardly practicable to provide means whereby instant contact can be made with the Prime Minister, and in these circumstances it must be accepted that it may not be possible to establish contact with him before the impact of the attack.[52]

Bishop gave no reason for the impossibility of arranging constant contact or why it simply had to be accepted as given. His next sentence, on first reading, is even more alarming:

But in these circumstances, authority exists for the despatch of our nuclear bombers under 'positive control' procedures designed to prevent the launching of an attack except with specific authority from this country. It is contemplated that, if after a massive nuclear attack had been received here, it had proved impossible to establish contact with the Prime Minister, authority for our nuclear retaliatory forces to complete their mission would be provided by somebody else.[53]

Bishop did not specify who that 'somebody' would be, presumably because he was aware that Brook and Mountbatten already knew.

In fact, that 'somebody' was Air Marshal Sir Kenneth Cross, Commander-in-Chief of Bomber Command. In a letter to Cross on his appointment to the post in 1959, the Vice Chief of the Air Staff, Air Chief Marshal Sir Edmund Hudleston, had informed him in the penultimate sentence of a letter (in the grandly casual tradition) that: 'It is also appreciated that circumstances could exist, such as a total breakdown in communications, under which you would have to assume responsibility for launching the attack.'[54] It was plain from Hudleston's letter that an attempt at greater precision was underway as the 'Air Ministry now have under urgent consideration the steps which are required to bring the political machinery into line with the readiness of the weapon.'[55]

Cross had the power to order his bombers airborne as the tolerances were so fine. The planes had one and half minutes from the order being given to get off the airfields before Soviet missiles would start to fall on the runways[56] and a further one and a half minutes 'for the aircraft to be certain of getting clear of the danger area from bursts of nuclear bombs aimed at their airfields'.[57] 'Positive control' was the procedure whereby the V-force 'would take off but would not complete their mission unless they received orders to do so. Without such orders they would return to base after being airborne for a given period.'[58]

Deep within the retaliatory loop, not everyone was at ease with these arrangements whereby in a few fraught minutes, with the Prime Minister already killed by a pre-emptive strike on London or out of reach, the chief of Bomber Command, from his bunker under the Chilterns at High Wycombe, could get his planes aloft and, if Soviet bombs had burst over the UK, give them the order to fly on to their targets in Russia. Not for nothing did some civil servants privately refer to this as the 'decapitation' or 'headless chickens' scenario.[59]

In 1961, as part of the rethink of nuclear retaliation procedures, Frank Mottershead, the MOD Deputy Secretary responsible for nuclear and War Book matters, drafted an amazingly candid brief for his Permanent Secretary, Sir Eddie Playfair. It was intriguing for a number of reasons, not least because it indicated that Macmillan was not pushing for the officer-with-the-briefcase solution.

Mottershead reminded Playfair that the existing, 'relatively simple' procedures for launching nuclear retaliation had been 'exercised in skeleton form' in 1959:

the thing the exercise did throw up, which was perhaps clear to most of us before, was that we are not organised to cope with a 'bolt from the blue' attack. This is perhaps in accord with out [our] belief that there will be no such thing.[60]

To cope with such a cataclysm, Mottershead contended, 'the Prime Minister must . . . always be accompanied by a mobile secure communications set and an operator day or night' or be prepared to hand over the responsibility to a deputy whenever he is away from his desk.

Even if we do not really believe that a 'bolt from the blue' is possible, it may well be advisable to take the small insurance step of attaching to the Downing Street Secretariat and telephone system a Ministerial Deputy for nuclear retaliation purposes. There are really three possibilities, to do nothing, to lay on a full 'operational' system or to set upon an easy going insurance system. Previous forms [form?] suggest that the present Prime Minister [Macmillan] would refuse a full blown system.[61]

The section of Mottershead's brief for Playfair dealing with the powers of the C-in-C of RAF Bomber Command to authorize retaliation contains a strong echo. It was written in March 1961 – the year Neville Shute in *On the Beach* had chosen for the nuclear war that was eventually to kill every human being on the planet thanks to 'the Russo-Chinese war that had flared up out of the Russo-NATO war, that had been born of the Israeli–Arab war, initiated by Albania'.[62] Mottershead expressed concern to Playfair, in a Shute-like way, about

the classical 'destruction of Russia by mistake' situation: e.g. Egypt acquires a nuclear bomb somehow drops it on London and C. in C. Bomber Command then ensures that Russia, the United Kingdom and the USA are all destroyed by bombing Russia.[63]

Quite apart from this little gloss on Colonel Nasser, it is intriguing to note how a top civilian in the MOD had his worries about the men in uniform:

There is a lot to be said for internal consumption only for being very careful to tie down C in C Bomber Command and give him very precise instructions e.g. About getting in touch with the Americans and doing his best, by contact with any surviving authorities e.g. in NATO, to discover whether Russia launched the nuclear bomb that destroyed Whitehall, before he has a go at Russia.[64]

How CND would have loved to get their hands on the Mottershead memorandum as they prepared for the 1961 Aldermaston march the following month!

Only in 2009, when chasing up Cabinet Office nuclear retaliation material at the National Archives that had not been available when earlier editions of *The Secret State* were published, did I discover that Norman Brook had chaired a special ad hoc Cabinet committee on 'Nuclear Retaliation', GEN 735, which met over the spring and summer of 1961 to consider Mountbatten's proposals and what Freddie Bishop, at the first meeting of the committee, called 'certain gaps in the procedure for ordering nuclear retaliation which must be closed if the deterrent was to be effectively maintained'.[65] Mountbatten then made his pitch for Macmillan to adopt Eisenhower's system and had helpfully provided the members of GEN 735 with a summary of the US President's communications capabilities sent him by the White House Army Signal Agency.[66] The minutes, however, show that Mountbatten failed to persuade the meeting:

THE CHIEF OF THE DEFENCE STAFF said that in the United States a special agency . . . was able to provide instantaneous communications for the President wherever he was and at any time and he considered that we should aim at providing the same facilities for the Prime Minister. It was, however, generally agreed that this standard of communications was only necessary as provision against a 'bolt from the blue' and it was not practical for us to insure against this except by making certain that retaliation would be ordered by the most competent available authority.

Out of this came the recommendation that the Prime Minister should appoint two ministers as his nuclear deputies (more on this in Chapter 7) as well as the Commander-in-Chief, RAF Bomber Command, being empowered 'in the last resort [to] authorise retaliation on his own responsibility'.[67] This exercise also produced almost a parody of the alleged British genius for improvisation, as expressed in Freddie Bishop's memorandum:

The arrangements for recalling the Prime Minister when he is travelling out of London depend at present on communicating with known points on his route. It has been suggested that these arrangements might be supplemented in this country by installing a radio in the Prime Minister's car which would permit messages to be relayed in plain language through the Automobile Association's radio network.[68]

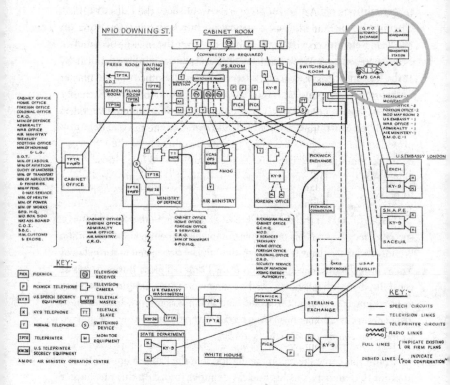

The file contains a diagram of immense complexity describing the various communication links that would be needed in a transition to war, including in its top-right corner a little graphical gem (circled).[69] And reliance was placed on the AA for some years to come. In the late 1960s, Harold Wilson's official car was in north London on its way back to Downing Street when an actual AA message crackled over about a lady whose Ford Zodiac was in need of assistance. The private secretary accompanying the PM was Michael Palliser (who went on to become head of the Diplomatic Service), who recognized his own number plate. After he had arrived home, his wife credited him with supernatural powers when he asked her why she had called out the AA.[70]

Later another truly Ealing Comedy addition to the AA's planned role in the British bit of Armageddon was declassified by the Cabinet Office. The file reveals that the new system was ready to go in May 1962 (in good time for the coming but unanticipated Cuban missile crisis); Tim Bligh, Macmillan's Principal Private Secretary, was informed of it by Bryan Saunders, his opposite number in the private office of the Minister of Works (then responsible for the Government Car Pool). In an exchange of letters that even P. G. Wodehouse could not have dreamt up, Saunders tells Bligh that the 'radios have now been fitted in the three cars':

I understand that these radios are to be maintained by Pye's [then an electronics company based in Cambridge] and it will presumably be necessary for someone to make a daily or weekly call to the AA Control Station as a check that they are in working order . . .

I understand that if an emergency arose while the Prime Minister was on the road, the proposal is to use the radio to get him to a telephone. Perhaps we should see that our drivers are provided with four pennies [in the early 1960s it was necessary to insert four old pennies and press 'Button A' before a call from a GPO call-box could be connected] – I should hate to think of you trying to get change for a sixpence from a bus conductor while those four minutes are ticking by!

Bligh, it turned out, was on top of the problem. Replying to Saunders, he wrote:

The first sentence of your last paragraph is correct. But a shortage of pennies should not present quite the difficulties which you envisage. Whilst it may be desirable, when motoring, to carry a few pennies in one's pocket, occasions do arise when by some misfortune or miscalculation they have been expended and one is penniless. In such cases, however, it is a simple matter to have the cost of any telephone call transferred by dialling 100 and requesting reversal of the charge, and this does not take any appreciable extra time. This system works in both normal and S.T.D. [Subscriber Trunk Dialling] telephone kiosks, and our drivers are aware of it.

This being Whitehall, there was a fall-back plan forming in Bligh's mind: 'We are considering the possibility of this Office taking up membership of the AA – which would give our drivers keys to AA and RAC boxes throughout the country.'[71] For those sensitive to questions of national identity, only the Brits – of all the existing nuclear powers and those to come – could have dreamt up a system whereby the Prime Minister is envisaged making a reverse-charge call from a phone box to authorize nuclear retaliation. If the file containing the Saunders–Bligh correspondence had somehow fallen into the hands of the KGB they simply would not have believed it.

In fact, out of the Mountbatten–Brook correspondence and the meetings of GEN 735, a full-blown review of nuclear retaliation procedures emerged conducted by an official Cabinet committee, GEN 743, chaired first by William Geraghty and, after he returned to the MoD from the Cabinet Office, by Nigel Abercrombie (Bishop in the meantime having in his watching role been succeeded by Cary). Macmillan approved the establishment of the 'Working Group on Nuclear Retaliation Procedures', as GEN 743 was known, in July 1961 and it reported in February 1962. As with its begetter, GEN 735, the full record of GEN 743 meetings and papers only reached the National Archives in 2008.

Out of the work of GEN 735 and GEN 743 emerged a fascinating 'family tree' of the 'Planning for War – Cabinet Committee Structure'[72] — see opposite.

Before commissioning Geraghty and his team to 'undertake a comprehensive review' of

(i) the procedure best adapted to meet the operational requirements involved in the decision to authorise nuclear retaliation; and
(ii) the communications which the Prime Minister will need for this and other purposes in a period of tension,[73]

Brook wrote one of his mind-clearing papers on 'alternative means' for authorizing 'the release of nuclear forces from this country'.[74] It should be remembered that all this work was initially carried out against the backdrop of the Berlin crisis of 1958–61 in its most acute phase. In October 1961 Macmillan actually reached the point of designating which ministers, if the crisis tipped into war, would have gone with him to the alternative seat of government and which would become Regional Commissioners in the twelve Civil Defence regions (It has now. See pages 281–3).[75]

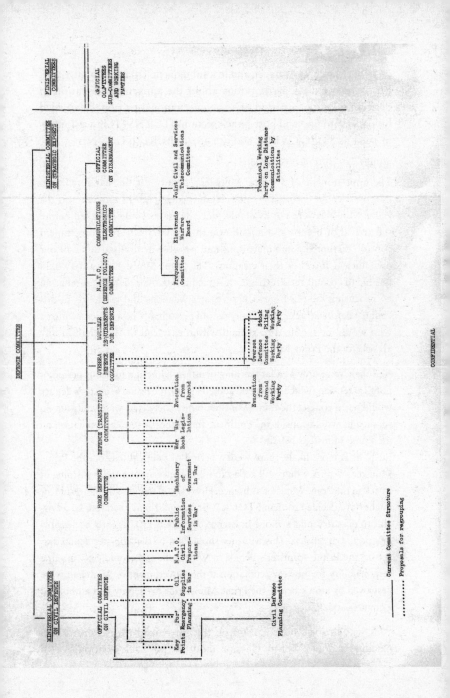

DEFENCE COMMITTEE

MINISTERIAL COMMITTEE ON CIVIL DEFENCE

MINISTERIAL COMMITTEE ON STRATEGIC EXPORTS

MINISTERIAL COMMITTEES

OFFICIAL COMMITTEES SUB-COMMITTEES AND WORKING PARTIES

OFFICIAL COMMITTEE ON CIVIL DEFENCE

HOME DEFENCE COMMITTEE

DEFENCE (TRANSITION) COMMITTEE

OVERSEA DEFENCE COMMITTEE

NUCLEAR RETIREMENTS FOR DEFENCE

N.A.T.O. (DEFENCE POLICY) COMMITTEE

COMMUNICATIONS ELECTRONICS COMMITTEE

OFFICIAL COMMITTEE ON DISARMAMENT

Key Points Emergency Planning

Oil Supplies in War

N.A.T.O. Civil Preparations

Public Information Services in War

Machinery of Government in War

War Book Legis-lation

Evacuation from Abroad

Evacuation from Abroad Working Party

Oversea Defence Committee Working Party

Stock Piling Working Party

Frequency Committee

Electronic Warfare Board

Joint Civil and Services Telecommunications Committee

Technical Working Party on Long Distance Communications by Satellites

Civil Defence Planning Committee

—————— Current Committee Structure

·········· Proposals for regrouping

CONFIDENTIAL

In his March 1961 paper, and in a subsequent letter to Mountbatten, Brook revealed his assumptions about the pattern and location of decision-taking in a period of acute international tension. He divided his paper into pre- and post-attack sections (TURNSTILE was known in 1961 as STOCKWELL and in 1962 as BURLINGTON);

(a) <u>Before Attack</u>
The appointment of a Prime Minister's deputy for nuclear retaliation purposes would ensure a greater certainty and speed of retaliation if the Prime Minister were not available, since decisions could be taken before the arrival of bombs and missiles on this country affected Government control, disrupted communications and possibly neutralised some of our own nuclear forces or their weapons. The Prime Minister's deputy would be able to consult the President, thus facilitating the process of retaliation by procuring the release of United States weapons and warheads in this country before attack. The deputy would presumably be a senior Minister, who would be required to remain within easy call of Whitehall in any absence of the Prime Minister.

(i) if there were only a radar warning of attack without a previous period of political tension (which is not considered likely), the Prime Minister's deputy would try to contact the Prime Minister immediately. If he were unable to do so, then he would consult the President and authorise nuclear retaliation on the Prime Minister's behalf.
(ii) If, as is more likely, there were a period of political tension, the Prime Minister's deputy would still act as above in the event of a radar warning of attack in the Prime Minister's absence. However, in this case the Government might have decided to man STOCKWELL, and it may therefore be advisable to plan to send a senior Minister to STOCKWELL as early as possible in a period of tension. This Minister should not be the Minister deputed to act on the Prime Minister's behalf in Whitehall, and would only assume responsibility for nuclear retaliation if the Government in Whitehall were destroyed by attack before the Prime Minister or his deputy had authorised a counter-attack.[76]

It was Brook's next paragraph that provoked Mottershead into placing his doubts before Playfair about the fall-back position:

(b) <u>After Attack</u>

If this country were hit by nuclear weapons before Bomber Command had received instructions to retaliate, it is envisaged that the Commander-in-Chief should have discretion to despatch his bomber forces under 'positive control,' and should try to seek instructions from the Government, either in Whitehall or elsewhere. If his efforts to communicate with the Government by all reasonable means should fail, then he should assume responsibility for releasing nuclear retaliatory forces on offensive missions.[77]

Brook was not convinced of the need to have a nuclear command-and-control capacity by the Prime Minister at all times. As he told Mountbatten (who disagreed[78]), it was 'hardly practicable to make communications plans which would ensure immediate contact with the Prime Minister at all times . . . If there were to be a "bolt from the blue", we must accept that it may not be possible to contact the Prime Minister before the impact of the attack.'[79]

Brook's letter is revealing, too, of his reasons for wishing the seat of government to remain in London for as long as possible at a time of acute and rising international tension; even though

STOCKWELL might have been manned and although some Ministers might have been directed there, the Prime Minister, with some of his principal colleagues and his main advisers, would remain in Whitehall until a warning of nuclear attack on this country had been received and nuclear retaliation had been authorised – but that planning for the Prime Minister's survival of attack should be confined to the arrangements already made for his speedy removal from London in an emergency.[80]

In 2001–2 I wondered what these could be. An RAF helicopter waiting on Horse Guards Parade? Evacuation by road? Or even rail? We now know the answer to this thanks to the declassification of the Operation VISITATION file – it was to be helicopters from Horse Guards Parade (see p. xxxviii). In January 2002 the Cabinet Office declassified the 1970 version of 'Essential Service Routes' that were somehow 'to be kept open after nuclear attack . . .'[81] (see map for the London section of this on p. 199), which, naturally enough, includes the route to TURNSTILE from London (see Chapter 7).

Brook went on to tell Mountbatten why he wanted to leave the resort to the last redoubt in STOCKWELL until the last minute. The Cabinet Secretary believed that:

in a period of developing international tension it would be best for the Prime Minister, and indeed his colleagues and advisers, to continue to use their normal methods and machinery of work as far as possible. The period in question might be quite protracted, and the Prime Minister's main preoccupation would be to assess the intentions of the enemy from political at least as much as military intelligence, and to supervise the conduct of political negotiations. We are more likely to secure the best setting and atmosphere for this by maintaining normal arrangements as far as possible.[82]

Brook recognized, however, that in this pre-bunker phase, 'arrangements would need to be streamlined, accelerated and supplemented . . .'[83]

Five months later, anxiety over Berlin led him to draw up in detail just such a plan to 'be prepared for a lengthy period of fluctuating political tension' to 'allow vital decisions to be taken in an orderly and speedy way'.[84] Ministers and their advisers would 'not go underground [i.e. to the bunker] . . . [b]ut the normal methods must be accelerated'.[85] For this purpose he suggested a 'Ministerial Committee on Berlin which would consist of the PM, the Home Secretary, the Chancellor of the Exchequer, the Foreign Secretary, the Commonwealth Secretary and the Minister of Defence.'[86]

Meanwhile the Geraghty/Abercrombie group worked on. Macmillan accepted their report and recommendations when Brook presented them to him in early March 1962[87] and it reflected the Cabinet Secretary's thinking rather than that of the Chief of the Defence Staff. No nuclear officer would be with the Prime Minister night and day. Should he need to be rushed back to London,

Normal communications would suffice in most circumstances except for periods when the Prime Minister is travelling by car or rail. In either case it should be possible to intercept him through police or railway channels, but the Working Group recommend that consideration should be given to providing a radio link in the Prime Minister's car.[88]

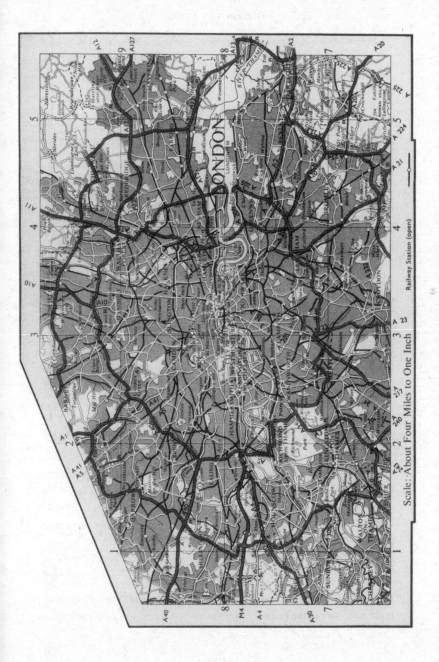

Scale: About Four Miles to One Inch

Railway Station (open)

Brook's thinking on staying put until the last minute was there, too, as was the appointment of two ministerial deputies, one of whom 'would be available to act as the Prime Minister's deputy for purposes of nuclear retaliation during any period, however short, when the Prime Minister was not immediately available.'[89]

Annex B to the Geraghty/Abercrombie report dealt with the powers of Air Marshal Cross and his successors (though not in a way that addressed the Mottershead anxiety):

The Prime Minister has agreed, as a basis for future planning, certain powers for C-in-C Bomber Command to cover the following situations.

(i) A 'bolt from the blue' – that is, a tactical warning, with no preceding period of strategic warning, that a nuclear attack is imminent;
(ii) A nuclear attack actually having been received (i.e. nuclear bombs having burst) in this country before any authority has been given to a nuclear force to retaliate.

2. These powers are as follows –

(a) To order all his bombers airborne under positive control;
(b) To seek contact with the Prime Minister or his deputy in London or at BURLINGTON, and if possible the United States authority responsible for launching United States strategic nuclear weapons from this country.[90]
(c) In the last resort, when he has confirmed that a nuclear attack has actually landed on this country, to order on his own responsibility nuclear retaliation by all means at his disposal.[91]

This annex was reflected fully in the Directive to Cross from the Chief of the Air Staff, Sir Thomas Pike, in September 1962, a few days before the Cuban missile crisis began.[92]

I have reconstructed the secret state and states of readiness aspects of the Cuban crisis in my volume on *The Prime Minister*.[93] On the instructions of Macmillan, Pike, through Cross, put the V-force on Alert Condition 3 at 1:00 p.m. on Saturday 27 October 1962.[94] This meant that

[t]he maximum number of aircraft are to be made Combat Ready. At Main Bases, aircraft planned to operate from those bases are to be prepared for

operational take-off; the remainder are to be armed and prepared for dispersal.[95]

In Exercise MICKY FINN II the month before, Cross had 112 V-bombers at his disposal as they moved through all five of the alert stages until being stood down on 22 September 1962.[96] They held the for-real Alert Condition 3 from 27 October to 5 November 1962.[97]

Norman Brook was ill and unable to be at Macmillan's side during the Cuban crisis. His place was taken by Michael Cary, who had had that memorable outburst about the 'nightmarish gavotte' on the 'brink of Armageddon' as he and Abercrombie wrestled with simplifying the nuclear release consultation procedures between Macmillan and Kennedy as part of the unfinished business of GEN 743.[98] Macmillan's group of ministers stayed in London as Brook would have wished. BURLINGTON was not manned. Nor was a half-way house committee formally established along the lines Brook had sketched the previous September for Berlin purposes. But an informal Cuba group did exist, with Macmillan and his Foreign Secretary, Lord Home, at its heart.[99]

Macmillan and his ministers had come close to authorizing a move to the 'precautionary stage' at the Cabinet meeting which would have taken place on the afternoon of Sunday 28 October 1962, had Khrushchev not backed down that lunchtime.[100] At this point the Transition to War Committee would have swung into action and the World War III drills been set in motion.[101] On Monday 29 October 1962, a letter was drafted by the Cabinet Secretariat for the Deputy Cabinet Secretary, Sir Burke Trend, to send to permanent secretaries. 'Fortunately', its opening paragraph began, 'we did not need to disturb you over the weekend, but if the Cuban situation had taken a sharp turn for the worse (as seemed likely at one time) we might well have had to call a snap meeting of the Transition to War Committee'.[102] The idea was that the Cuban near-miss should inspire a hard look at the flexibility of the war-planning machinery.[103]

It did. Cuba stimulated the secret state to devise new refinements of the drills for the 'brink of Armageddon'. The October 1962 crisis was no 'bolt from the blue' involving a sudden indication of danger on the radar screens with but a few minutes to decide what to do. Nor, as we have seen, was it the endgame of a long, slow, carefully monitored build-up of international political tension. As a result, the secret state looked afresh at its procedures and plans.

There were two significant outcomes of the 'Post-Cuba Review of War Book Planning' which Macmillan ordered from the Ministerial Committee on Home Defence 'in order to ensure', as the new Cabinet Secretary from January 1963, Sir Burke Trend, put it, 'that it was sufficiently flexible to enable us to react quickly and appropriately to a sudden emergency, in which we might have no more than two or three days' warning of the outbreak of war'.[104] On 19 November 1962 the Home Office prepared a note for the Home Defence Committee on 'Home Defence Preparedness' which was very direct about the lack of activity during the Cuban crisis and the chaos it implied would have ensued had the Cabinet met on the afternoon of 28 October and authorized the crash implementation of the Precautionary Stage:

During the Cuba crisis (23rd–28th October) no general directions were given by Ministers and no start was made on any general transition measures. If the situation had worsened and Ministers had decided that home defence steps should be taken, it is unlikely that Departments would have had seven, or even five days, in which to implement their present plans. If the situation had deteriorated very rapidly, the chances of anything effective being done in the home defence field would have been slight.[105]

Thereafter the home defence planners laboured mightily for two and a half months trying to find ways of telescoping as many home defence measures as they could from seven- to two-to-three-days implementation.[106] And by the spring of 1963, a number of changes had been agreed by ministers. For example, the Prime Minister henceforth could institute a Precautionary Stage without recourse to the Cabinet.[107]

The other result was the drafting of a ferocious Emergency Powers (Defence) Bill to be rushed through Lords and Commons in the last days of peace, granting to the Regional Commissioners such huge powers over life, property, food and finance 'as to amount to a voluntary abdication by Parliament of the whole of their functions for the period of the emergency'.[108]

Not only did this draft measure reflect the planners' belief that 'the powers now required are more extensive than those which were envisaged' as recently as 1959,[109] but the defence regulations contained in the proposed Bill 'would have to be more drastic than the Regulations in the Second World War . . .'.[110] A mere glance at clause one of the Emergency Powers (Defence) Bill for World War III makes it difficult to think of *any* powers left over life, liberty and property with which the Regional Commissioners could have been invested:

1 – (i) Her Majesty may by Order in Council make such regulations (to be known as 'Defence Regulations') as appear to Her Majesty to be necessary or expedient for any of the following purposes . . . that is to say –

(a) the public safety;

(b) the defence of the realm;

(c) the maintenance of public order;

(d) the meeting of special circumstances arising or likely to arise out of any war in which Her Majesty may be engaged or out of the threat of such a war;

(e) the efficient prosecution of any such war;

(f) the maintenance of supplies and services essential to the life of the community.[111]

The 'special circumstances' catch-all sub-section (d) would mean anything the Regional Commissioners wished it to mean once the Bill had been converted into an Act by Parliament in the last days of peace.* Until then, the country's military and/or civilian rulers in waiting had only those common-law powers in place to which the Strath Committee had alluded nearly a decade earlier.[112]

What might the civil libertarians in Parliament, had they seen the Emergency Powers (Defence) Bill, have made of its section 4, for example? This

---

* The Bill was deemed too fierce to put to Parliament in peacetime proper. Instead it would go before both Houses 'early in the Precautionary Stage . . . The point that Parliament is likely to raise fewer objections to such legislation under threat of war than it would do in peacetime is a formidable one . . .' (TNA, PRO, DEFE 4/232, 'Government War Book Planning, Brief for the Minister of Defence', 30 July 1963.) For these reasons no one outside the war-planning community had a sight of the measure until it appeared in an MOD file at the Public Record Office in the late 1990s.

covered the 'administration of justice', whereby courts delivering, under its Defence Regulations, 'a sentence of death ... (whether for an offence against Defence Regulations or for any other offence) shall provide that any proceedings in which such a sentence is so imposed shall be reviewed by not less than three persons who hold or have held high judicial office within the meaning of the Appellate Jurisdiction Act 1876'.[113]

The armed forces were, as we have seen, central to the planning. The Defence Policy Staff in the autumn of 1968 spelt out in some detail for the Chiefs of Staff just how involved those under their command would be with the police and the civil authorities generally during the transition to war and after – what they called 'the total Threat'.[114] It is an especially intriguing portrait, for not only did it draw on JIC and MI5 material,[115] its production coincided with the INVALUABLE war game.

This was a period of some anxiety for the Chiefs, not because they feared Brezhnev was about to do something rash, but because the Labour government's post-devaluation 1967–8 defence review was eating into those troops that would be needed to assist the civil authorities and protect 'key points' and military installations generally as well as fulfil the 'special tasks' laid upon them by the Government War Book. These last were very interesting in themselves, including as they did:

a. Special duties toward Royal Family	–	One Infantry Battalion [i.e. about 400 men]
b. Special duties for Central Government	–	One Infantry Battalion
c. The security of gold reserves and art treasures	–	One Infantry Battalion
d. Aid to HM Customs and to the Police in the seizing of potentially hostile ships and aircraft; possibly manned by armed crews	–	Difficult to assess but probably one Infantry Battalion.[116]

From the military perspective, this was the late-1960s image of a Britain engulfed by a third world war:

a. <u>Period of Serious International Tension</u>. The threat within the United Kingdom during this period might be limited to individual acts of sabotage against military installations particularly those with a connection with NBC [nuclear, biological, chemical] warfare. At the same time subversive groups might endeavour to create disturbances in large urban areas in order to stretch the police forces and to weaken the resolution of the Government.

b. <u>Period of Mobilisation and Initial Deployment of Armed Forces</u>. During this period the now much increased earmarked forces . . . would move from the United Kingdom to their NATO tasks, and a greater sense of the proximity of nuclear war would spread through the civil population. The enormous potential of mass media debate would leave nobody in any doubt of the possible outcome. In that atmosphere a more widespread public antagonism to military moves could develop. The previously small-scale demonstrations inspired by anarchist and communist groups could be increased by the co-operation, perhaps unwittingly given, of ordinary citizens. The attitude of the trades unions would be crucial to the quickening tempo of our military preparations. The possibility of widespread strikes including a breakdown in our public transport and shipping systems could seriously affect our delicately programmed mobilisation and movement plans. Military installations, ports and airfields, essential to our military movements, could become targets of action by anti-war groups. If only, say, 5% of our working population became actively anti-war minded, this would present a very serious security problem.[117]

We see here once more the military analysts being noticeably less sanguine than their MI5 counterparts about the possibility of countering the possible threats to military efficiency or law and order. True pessimism – or realism, as it strikes me – afflicted them at the next stage on the road to breakdown:

c. <u>Period of Direct Defence</u>. Once our forces were engaged, even in limited conflict, either in Europe or on the flanks of NATO, the importance of the United Kingdom as a military base could be crucial to our ability to support them. The public would by now be even more aware that the nation was possibly on the threshold of nuclear attack. Evacuation of likely target areas might already have started spontaneously if not officially. Anti-war action might spread and involve considerable numbers of normally stable and law-abiding people. [Huge value judgements were about (a) what would be 'normal' or rational in such circumstances, and (b) a lack of discrimination between protest and law-breaking, though there is a touch of this in what follows.] The Soviet bloc could bring to bear the full weight of their subversive activities, sabotage and psychological warfare. Key points, military headquarters, logistic installations, movement facilities and training depots could now become targets for more widespread protest action and action aimed at paralysing our military ability. The civil problems of maintaining law and order, of protecting VIPs and centres of Government, of keeping open essential routes and services, the distribution of supplies, all these would present very serious problems for the police and other agencies of government.[118]

A Vietnam factor intrudes at this point. The war in Indochina was at its height as the defence planners were drafting, and the impact of its GI body counts and the direct depiction of the effects of napalm on Vietnamese villages and villagers on television screens was a nightly influencer of US domestic opinion to a degree not experienced in any previous conflict.

d. Period of Deliberate Escalation. Once tactical nuclear weapons were used on the battle front, the horror of nuclear war would be seen in practically every home. Truly democratic countries with very limited news censorship, would be at a disadvantage over their tightly controlled enemies. All the possible reactions which might already have started in the period of direct defence would now become greatly increased. The will of the free nations would be under its greatest test and the Soviet bloc would be likely to exploit every opportunity to break it and gain a victory short of a general nuclear response.[119]

One of the paradoxes of the Cold War once both sides had acquired a thermonuclear capability was what – if anything – would be left worth having that once belonged to the vanquished, even if a 'victor', in any sense, was conceivable? The British planners side-stepped this in 1968 (though their sketch of post-attack Britain bore the imprint of the JIGSAW assumptions on 'breakdown'):

e. Period of Nuclear Exchange and its Immediate Aftermath. We do not envisage any Soviet or other externally inspired military threat in the short term. We believe the threat facing those endeavouring to save lives and restore some vestage [sic] of control would derive from basic law and order problems.

Millions of homeless, bewildered people would need rudimentary shelter and sustenance. Looting of food stocks and other essential supplies, the blocking of essential routes by refugees, the seizing of property, all these problems on a mammoth scale could overwhelm the surviving police resources.[120]

Intriguingly, the Chiefs of Staff's thinkers reckoned the threat in the protracted post-attack phase would be the enemy within rather than what might be left of the enemy without – which itself implies doubts about the efficacy of 'smashing' the CPGB or any wider round-up of those individuals MI5 thought it desirable to place within the internment camps on the Isle of Man:

f. The Long Term Post-Attack Period. As the long term battle for survival progresses, crucial struggles are likely to arise over securing sources of food and other essential commodities together with the means of transporting them by sea and air. We foresee the possibility of new threats developing affecting both our overseas activities and our home base. Subversive organisations are likely to survive and the general chaos of the post-attack struggle could provide a better opportunity for them to succeed than anything which obtained pre-attack.[121]

The planners reached the obvious conclusion that the government's post-nuclear attack plans 'to enable those who remain to survive would be largely dependant [sic] on the presence of organised and disciplined manpower'.[122] They reckoned the police would need and would ask for 36,000 members of the armed forces to assist them during the 'escalation to general war', rising to 196,000 post-attack.[123]

I must admit that when I came across the entry for the military required for the security of art treasures I jibbed somewhat in a philistine fashion. And my philistinism was not assuaged when Martin Bailey of the Art Newspaper found at the PRO the Treasury's file on 'Museums and Galleries: Disposal of Works of Art in a War Emergency'.[124] Under Operation METHODICAL, gems of national culture from the British Museum, the Guildhall and City of London Collections, the Public Record Office, the National Gallery, the Tate Gallery, the Victoria and Albert Museum, the Royal Collections and the Wallace Collection were to be moved out of London to go underground.[125]

Two quarry sites were earmarked: Manod, near Blaenau Festiniog in North Wales, and Westwood, near Bradford-on-Avon in Wiltshire. Not only were the military involved as escorts, but the 'eleven pantech-nicons' needed would, so the Ministry of Transport complained, deprive the Ministry of Health of some of the lorries they needed to evacuate medical equipment to safe areas.[126] The brief prepared for ministers in October 1963 by Sir Robert Harris, the Treasury Third Secretary responsible for museums and galleries, has, for me, an utterly surreal and superfluous air about it:

This scheme [Operation METHODICAL] . . . is based on the assumption that it would be undesirable for reasons of morale to remove the national art treasures from public exhibition until overt precautionary measures were being taken, and that at that stage it would be useless to attempt more than a severely limited operation. The proposal is, therefore, that eleven pantech-nicons should be sent, with military escort, to the major national collections in London (including the Royal Collections at Buckingham Palace and Wind-sor) where they would be loaded with as much as possible in the time and space available, and would be driven to specially prepared underground quarries in North Wales and Wiltshire or, if this proved impossible, to half-way houses in the country which have been earmarked for this purpose.[127] [Elmore Court in Gloucestershire for the Manod vans and Stonor House near Henley-on-Thames for the Westwood material.][128]

Rather weightier matters than the possible seepage of morale if much-loved pictures started disappearing from the London galleries preoccupied those more centrally involved in the doomsday sections of the secret state.

Like all else to do with nuclear war, the degradation of the United Kingdom into eleven shrivelled irradiated little fiefdoms filled with wretched and desperate survivors theoretically governed by men in bunkers and probably ruled, in reality, by armed soldiers and policemen with ultimate powers over life and death (give or take the occasional surviving judge to interpose himself or herself) is too ghastly to contem-plate. But contemplate it, in secret, the planners were regularly required to do. At every level, one finds scepticism tinged with irony on the part of those involved. Some years ago, when the first declassifications began on planning for the survival period, a former Treasury official told me that it would have been his job to advise the regional commissioner when to issue the post-attack currency from the bunker to which he had been assigned.[129] Not long after the first edition of this volume was published, one of the same official's colleagues, Russell Barratt, wrote to tell me that he had been the Treasury man assigned to the North-West Regional Commissioner near Preston as his financial adviser.

He recalled the awkwardness when the North-West's 'bunker party' met periodically in the mid-1960s to discuss their individual and collective roles:

During the later meetings it became all too evident that nobody was able to say in any convincing way what they could do effectively. But rather than confess to this impotence some people, at the last meeting, turned their attention to the unlucky Financial Adviser and began to discuss the comparatively peripheral (but to me embarrassing) question whether money would be in use after the bombs had dropped.[130]

Mr Barratt explained that the ever-methodical Treasury had prepared a brief for all its bunker people which 'was as sound in theory as it was in the circumstances unrealistic, that in the aftermath of a nuclear attack money would be of great importance as a medium of exchange; general use of money would be highly desirable to stimulate the revival of some kind of economic activity. To this end, notes and coin would have to be made available for the survivors to use.'

The Treasury brief was not precise on how the money would get to the survivors. His fellow bunker people were sceptical. Mr Barratt had to defend his department's position while feeling sympathetic towards his critics:

It was hard not to agree with them that the immediate survivors, terrified and desperate, would seek to acquire what they needed by any means available to them – barter, looting, violence or whatever. Notes and coin would be regarded by the survivors as more or less irrelevant. Who would prefer some pieces of paper to a bag of coal or a tin of meat?[131]

Such was the 'need to know' demarcation of functions, almost all the bunker people would have had no knowledge of the retaliation drills. Yet even here confusion remained at much the same time that Mr Barratt was worrying about the nuclear pound. An extraordinary file released in January 2002 showed that as late as the spring of 1966, Denys Laskey and Commander Stephens (who produced the 1965 royal drill for the end of the Queen's kingdom) were still unsure how a bolt-from-the-blue warning would reach them in the Cabinet Office and the Prime Minister next door. (Hence Laskey's minute of 5 May 1966 quoted at the head of this chapter.)

It appeared that the warning would be flashed from the Ballistic Missile Early Warning System site on Fylingdales Moor in Yorkshire to the Air Force Operations Room (AFOR) in the Ministry of Defence. But at such a moment '[n]o such arrangement exists to warn the Cabinet Office and it is thought that this could not be done direct from the A.F.O.R. without detriment to other vital tasks imposed on the Duty Officer at such a time'.[132] Eventually it was established that the Ministry of Defence's Defence Operations Centre, which 'receives the television display from the Ballistic Missile Early Warning System', would transmit to the Cabinet Office 'information of an impending missile attack within a few seconds of the warning reaching the Air Force Operations Room'.[133] Once the attack had come, how long would it take for an ancient, settled kingdom like the UK to become an irreversibly broken and perpetually indefensible realm? No one could say.

Yet if global war and general nuclear release *had* come for real in the late 1960s, the JIC had its views on where the missiles would land in the UK. This list (pp. 211–15) is full of intriguing pointers. 'Government–Central' is described as 'London' (i.e. Whitehall) and Cheltenham (i.e. GCHQ). There is no mention of the alternative seat of government under any of its codenames. Note how the Regional Seats of Government have now become 'former' (i.e. stood down, part of the care and maintenance home defence policy). The Russians are thought, however, to know where they are, which is not surprising given that the 'Spies for Peace' distributed the list during the 1963 Aldermaston march. Among the military targets, as one would expect, were the very-low-frequency signals installations at Rugby and Criggion whose purpose was (and is) to relay the Prime Minister's instructions to the commanders of

PROBABLE NUCLEAR TARGETS IN THE UNITED KINGDOM: ASSUMPTIONS FOR PLANNING

Notes: (i) Figures in brackets denote total targets in each category; (ii) (A) denotes Air Burst; (iii) (S) denotes Surface Burst

TARGETS RELATED TO ALLIED NUCLEAR STRIKE CAPABILITY (65)

CENTRES OF CONTROL ETC. (22)		Missile Weapon yield per target	Aircraft Weapon yield per target
(i) Government – Central (2)	London	8 × 1 MT(A)	2 × 500 KT(A)
	Cheltenham	2 × ½–1 MT(A)	2 × 500 KT(A)
– ex-Regional (12)	Catterick	2 × ½–3 MT(S)	2 × 1 MT(S)
	York	"	"
	Preston	"	"
	Cambridge		"
	Dover		"
	Reading	} former RSG sites	"
	Salcombe		"
	Brecon		"
	Kidderminster		"
	Armagh		"
	Edinburgh		"
	Nottingham		"

These are considered to be possible, rather than probable targets

See also paragraph 2

(ii) Military – Maritime (4)	Northwood (HQ, CINCHAN/CINCEASTLANT)	2 × ½–1 MT(A)	2 × 1 MT(S)
	Plymouth (HQ, COMCENTLANT)	"	"
	Pitreavie (HQ, COMNOPLANT)	"	"
	Fort Southwick (HQ, C-IN-C, UK Home Station)		

	2 × ½–3 MT(S)	2 × 1 MT(S)
High Wycombe (HQ, Bomber Command)	2 × ½–3 MT(S)	2 × 1 MT(S)
Ruislip (HQ, 3rd US Air Force)	"	"
Bawtry (HQ, 1 Gp. Bomber Command)	"	"

BOMBER BASES (including dispersal recovery and flight-refuelling bases) (32)

(i) RAF (26)

	2 × 500 KT(A)	2 × 1 MT(S)
Scampton	2 × 500 KT(A)	2 × 1 MT(S)
Wittering	"	"
Waddington,,	"	"
Honington	"	"
Cottesmore	"	"
Marham	"	"
Coningsby	"	"
St. Mawgan	"	"
Lossiemouth	"	"
Macrihanish	"	"
Leeming	"	"
Gaydon	"	"
Finningley	"	"
Valley	"	"
Bedford	"	"
Brawdy	"	"
Yeovilton	"	"
Lyneham	"	"
Wyton	"	"
Pershore	"	"
Boscombe Down	"	"
Kinloss	"	"
Manston	"	"
Ballykelly	"	"
Filton	"	"
Leconfield	"	"

TARGETS RELATED TO ALLIED NUCLEAR STRIKE CAPABILITY (65)
CENTRES OF CONTROL ETC. (32) (Cont'd)

	Missile Weapon yield per target	Aircraft Weapon yield per target
(ii) USAF (6)		
Alconbury	2 × 500 KT(A)	2 × 1 MT(S)
Bentwaters	"	"
Woodbridge	"	"
Wethersfield	"	"
Lakenheath	"	"
Upper Heyford	"	"

BASES ETC. FOR SEABORNE NUCLEAR STRIKE FORCES (12)

	Missile Weapon yield per target	Aircraft Weapon yield per target
(i) Bases (5)		
Garelock [i.e. Gareloch] (Clyde) } Polaris	2 × 500 KT(A)	2 × 1 MT(S)
Holy Loch } Polaris	"	"
Rosyth (SSBN Refitting Base)	1 × ½–1 MT(A)	2 × 1 MT(S)
Portsmouth } Carrier	2 × 1 MT(S)	
Devonport } Carrier	"	"
(ii) Communication Installations (7)		
VLF { Rugby, Criggion, Anthorn (NATO)	1 × 500 KT(A)	2 × 500 KT(A)
LF { Inskip, New Waltham, Londonderry } US Navy, Thurso	"	"

213

MAJOR CITIES (20)*

		4 ×	1 MT(A)	2 × 500 KT(A)
Glasgow				2 × 500 KT(A)
Birmingham			"	"
Liverpool	2 ×	1 MT(A)		"
Cardiff			"	"
Manchester			"	"
Southampton			"	"
Leeds			"	"
Newcastle			"	"
Bristol			"	"
Sheffield			"	"
Swansea			"	"
Hull			"	"
Middlesbrough			"	"
Coventry			"	"
Wolverhampton			"	"
Leicester			"	"
Stoke-on-Trent			"	"
Belfast			"	"
Edinburgh			"	"
Nottingham			"	"

TARGETS RELATING TO AID DEFENCES (18)

		Missile Weapon yield per target
CONTROL CENTRES (2)	Bentley Priory (HQ Fighter Command – after 1.3.68, Headquarters	2 × 1 MT(A) 2 × 1–3 MT(A)
	No 11 Group RAF)	
	West Drayton (Southern Joint Control Centre)	"
FIGHTER BASES (4)	Coltishall	2 × 500 KT(A)
	Leuchars	"
	Wattisham	"
	Binbrook	"

* In an earlier 1964 version of this assessment, these were headlined 'Will to Fight Targets' perhaps an example of the impact of JIGSAW's 'breakdown studies'. I am grateful to my former student, David Frank, for bringing this to my attention in PRO, CAB 158/50, JIC (63) 99 (Final), 'Form of Nuclear Attack on the United Kingdom 1970 to 1975', 6 February 1964.

	Missile Weapon yield per target	Aircraft Weapon yield per target

TARGETS RELATED TO ALLIED NUCLEAR STRIKE
CAPABILITY (65)
CENTRES OF CONTROL ETC. (32) (Cont'd)

SURFACE-TO-AIR   Woodhall Spa (a)   2 × 500 KT(A)
MISSILE SITES (3)
                    North Coates   "
                    West Raynham   "

BMEW'S (1)   Fylingdales   2 × 500 KT(A)

RADAR STATIONS (8) Boulmer (Master)   2 × 500 KT(A)
(See also footnotes Patrington (Master)   "
(c) and (d) below). Bawdsey (Master) (b)   "
                    Neatishead (Master, being rebuilt)   "
                    Buchan (Master) (Phases out 1970)   "
                    Saxa Vord (Satellite)   "
                    Staxton Wold (Radar site for Patrington) "
                    Feltwell (Over-the-horizon radar)   "

(a) Delete when Woodhall Spa phases out as a SAM site end 1967.
(b) Delete when Bawdsey phases out as a radar station in 1970.
(c) Add Orford Ness when equipped with over-the-horizon radar about 1970.
(d) Add Oakhanger DCN Satellite Commuication station when it becomes fully operational early in 1969.[134]

215

the deterrent-bearing submarines. Seventeen major cities were thought to have two 1-megaton missile air bursts awaiting them plus two 2,500-kiloton ones delivered by aircraft; Glasgow, Birmingham and Liverpool four and two; London eight and two, respectively. That is, I reckon, 'breakdown' and more.

The major V-force bases and their dispersal fields (twenty-six in all) were likely to disappear beneath two 500-kiloton missile air bursts and two 1-megaton surface bursts delivered by Soviet bombers. Many of those on the list here had an all too vivid idea of what this would mean for the ground staff and their families as their V-bombers roared up and away flat out eastwards.

If the Soviet bombs had fallen, whether in the configuration assessed by the JIC or not, the planners had no real idea of what they would be facing in the aftermath. As Sir David Omand put it (adapting Clausewitz), 'no plan survives the shock of contact with reality'.[135] But plan, simulate and exercise Whitehall and the military had to, as we shall see in the next chapter.

6

Endgames: The Transition to World War III

It is very hard to predict what the Soviet Politburo might do if really angry.

Lord Bridges, Foreign Affairs Private Secretary, to Harold Wilson, 25 June 1974[1]

It was quite extraordinary how those exercises took over people. We took it very seriously. Many hours without sleep . . . It was uncanny because you got totally caught up in the play – so you got very upset with the scale of nuclear release the exercise designers were contemplating.

Sir Kevin Tebbit, former Permanent Secretary, Ministry of Defence, 2009[2]

Some of them [ministers] quite liked talking so . . . you'd get behind time and there would be a fear that if they showed, as it were, reluctance to do what the military believed was necessary that this would weaken deterrence. So we didn't, to be honest, go around really encouraging them to do other than observe. We didn't want them playing, to be honest.

David Young, former senior Ministry of Defence official, 2009[3]

It all seemed horribly possible.

Lord Janvrin of Chalford Hill, former Private Secretary to the Queen, on taking part in late-1970s and early-1980s transition-to-war exercises as a Foreign Office official, 2009[4]

Mrs Beryl Grimble, an executive officer in the Cabinet Office who joined the Civil Service as a typist in 1936, doesn't feature in the standard accounts of the *dramatis personae* of post-war Whitehall. But she should – and will – now that a fair swathe of the paper trail covering the innermost of Britain's Cold War secrets has reached the National Archives. She was known as 'The Queen of the War Book'[5]. From 1958 to 1973, Mrs Grimble was the keeper of the 'Government War Book', which drew all the individual departmental war books together and laid out in sixteen chapters the 200 decisions required (eighty of them Cabinet ones) that paved the road from a peacetime UK to a country on the brink of Armageddon.[6] Not until the first complete 'Government War Book', the 1970 version, was declassified by the Cabinet Office for use in the Pimlott Lecture I delivered on 23 June 2009[7] could the scope and reach of Mrs Grimble's world be fully appreciated.

As she sat in her second-floor office in the Cabinet Office overlooking the garden of No. 10 Downing Street, bits of the current 'War Book' strewn across her desk (ready to be posted back incorporating the latest amendments) and old ones resting on her shelves, Beryl Grimble cannot have imagined the day they would be released to the public. 'She knew the "War Book" inside out', said Richard Ponman her clerical support.

She did make a good fist of it. She was attractive, colourful and had a fiery temper but she was kind to her juniors. They called her Aunty Beryl. You wouldn't forget her.[8]

Richard Ponman's colleague, Dennis Morris, who also worked with Mrs Grimble, remembered her as 'largish; twinset and pearls. She regarded the "War Book" as her baby and we were her nephews.'[9]

The best way to bring Mrs Grimble's Cold War world alive is to link her 'Government War Book' with the transition-to-war exercises Whitehall played every two years. Thanks to the complete 1970 volume we now have, it is possible to decode in substantial, if incomplete, detail the sequence of decisions laid out in transition-to-war drills that had been released a decade earlier. Veterans of these exercises find it chilling and absorbing to see those old files again, especially the final, nuclear-release stages. David Young, who played the Secretary of State for Defence in early 1970s war games, 'can still remember the sort of hairs on the back . . . you know, it's not an easy decision to participate in even when you know, of course, it's an exercise. But it makes you think'.[10]

The exercise for which we now have probably the fullest documentation took place in the autumn of 1968, at which time East–West relations were still tense and raw after the Soviet suppression of the 'Prague Spring' in Czechoslovakia but a few weeks before. It was codenamed INVALUABLE.

The R-hour (R stood for nuclear release) paper in the Cabinet Office's INVALUABLE file chills the blood. It was to happen over the night of 23–24 October 1968 and the simulated Ministry of Defence Chiefs of Staff Committee would have to meet through the small hours ready for the request for a nuclear release to come in from the Supreme Allied Commander Europe (SACEUR) at NATO headquarters in Brussels.[11] Its utter grimness is relieved by some eternal bureaucratic and human factors, for INVALUABLE, Britain's home-grown exercise, was running alongside NATO's FALLEX 68, codenamed GOLDEN ROD, and the two did not entirely mesh. To make matters worse, the officials simulating both the full Cabinet and its Transition to War Committee were making a fuss about lost sleep.

The Cabinet Office man impersonating the Prime Minister, Harry Lawrence-Wilson, ex-Indian Army and an old Colonial Office hand, rather tartly informed the Ministry of Defence that their players simulating the Chiefs of Staff Committee might be willing to stay up all night waiting for SACEUR's call but his people were not:

I am sure you will appreciate that civil departmental representatives on the simulated TWC/Cabinet are not expecting to be available at this time, and would not be willing to attend during the night after normal working hours: as you know, we had great difficulty in persuading departmental representatives to attend meetings during the week-end of 19th–20th October! I think that the most we can hope for is a simulated TWC/Cabinet meeting at, say, 5 p.m. on 23 October to anticipate the events which will happen during the night.[12]

It may be the end of the world they were dealing with, but the chaps could not be pushed too far, particularly if they had already sacrificed a weekend to contemplating doomsday. The World War III timetable was one thing, but the timetables of Victoria and Waterloo stations trumped it.

The bureaucratic problem vexing Harry Lawrence-Wilson and his team was that NATO's planned 'R-hour' preceded that of ORANGE (code for the Soviet Union) by fifteen minutes:

This is an accepted exercise artificiality which is contrary to current policy in that our mandatory nuclear release procedures for the V force [still the prime carrier of the UK's nuclear deterrent in autumn 1968] are based firmly on retaliation. Accordingly, this creates difficulties in realistically exercising UK nuclear release procedures.[13]

But a cunning plan was devised to reconcile the two:

The preparation of [RAF] Strike Command forces for the BLUE [NATO] R Hour phase will be in accord with normal Air Force Alert Procedures whereby States of Readiness are declared appropriate to SACEUR's Alert States. The time stated by SACEUR to be R Hour, irrespective of a positive warning of all out nuclear attack being received e.g. via BMEWS [the Ballistic Missile Early Warning System at RAF Fylingdales on the North Yorkshire Moors] will be interpreted as the time to launch the Medium Bomber Force [the RAF's V-bombers]. The time taken for the aircraft to fly from their airfields to the GO/NO GO Line [see Chapter 8], during which they remain under positive control, will permit the Release Message to be given after ORANGE R hour. In this way we will be able to comply with the exercise scenario whilst not infringing the principles of HMG's [Her Majesty's Government's] strategy or varying the mandatory RAF nuclear release procedures.[14]

Very Whitehall – due process even unto Apocalypse. Yet how else could Whitehall tackle such dreadful contingencies but by resorting to its soothing procedural automatic pilot?

There was, of course, an overall artificiality about these transition-to-war exercises as they were designed to simulate and test as many aspects as possible of the central 'Government War Book'. There were also some bits too sensitive for all members of the simulated Cabinet and Transition to War Committee to be admitted into their secrets.

These were contained in a special annex to the 'War Book' and dealt with the dispersal of ministers, key officials, military and intelligence figures to both the Central Government Wartime Headquarters at Corsham (still codenamed TURNSTILE in 1968) and the various alternative bunkers (known as the PYTHON groups), which 'are on a very limited distribution and cannot be discussed in Committee for security reasons'[15] (see Chapter 7). Allowing for these artificial elements, the Joint Intelligence Committee's Assessments Staff and the Home Office Civil Defence division had to construct scenarios which tipped the world to the brink and beyond. They always began with a change to a bunch of adventurous and aggressive nasties in the Kremlin, and so it was for INVALUABLE 1968. What follows is an anatomy of the World War III that never was in the autumn of 1968. The daily scenarios, domestic and international, are reproduced exactly as written except for the codenames of the countries involved, which I have changed to the real thing. In a strange way, these stories prepared in the Cabinet Office and the Home Office in 1968 are the secret Whitehall equivalent of Tom Clancy's novel *Red Storm Rising*, written nearly twenty years later.[16] I have reconstructed the flow of simulated events by using the 1970 'Government War Book' as a decoder of the measures Exercise INVALUABLE implemented. In the INVALUABLE files these appear only as combinations of letters and numbers or just numbers. The fit is usually, but not invariably, exact.

The INVALUABLE narrative begins menacingly, but slowly, at the end of September 1968 with the triumph of the hawkish faction in the Kremlin and the first flurry of activity at NATO headquarters and in Whitehall. Events gather menace and pace in mid-October and finish towards the end of the month when a serious East–West conventional war has broken out in Europe and is on the rim of going nuclear. Some of the individuals mentioned are – or were – definitely non-fictional, as in the case of the two journalists Harry Chapman Pincher[17] and Victor Zorza[18] in the first report produced by a special Assessments Staff Current Intelligence Group.

THE TRANSITION TO WORLD WAR III, AUTUMN 1968

Friday 27 September 1968
Joint Intelligence Committee Special Assessment
Situation report as at 0800 hours ZULU,* 27 September, 1968

Newspapers have been giving prominence to recent events in the Soviet Union, Berlin and the Middle East. The 'Sunday Telegraph' on 22nd September reported the visit of the NATO Military Committee to Greece and Turkey to discuss defensive arrangements for the area and the 'Daily Express' on 25th September carried an article by Chapman Pincher on the 'disturbing' build-up of Soviet naval units in the Mediterranean. The 'Times' on 25th September carried a report from an 'informed' source that the British Government had asked the United States and Canada to call a halt to troop withdrawals from Europe on account of the Berlin situation.

The 'Morning Star' [daily newspaper published by the Communist Party of Great Britain] has added its support to Soviet proposals that the Baltic be declared a 'Sea of Peace' and posters have been appearing calling for the withdrawal of United Kingdom from NATO and for the removal of United States bases from the United Kingdom. A new organisation calling itself War Resisters' International has been distributing leaflets calling for a total ban on nuclear weapons and for the abolition of power blocs.

In an article in the 'Guardian', Victor Zorza said it was clear that the struggle between the 'hawks' and the 'doves' in the Soviet Union had resulted in a victory for the 'hawks' and that the immediate prospect was for a return to the coldest of Cold War conditions. In a leading article, the 'Daily Telegraph' warned that the greatest danger in the world today was that of miscalculation by the new Soviet leaders. It was difficult to believe that they wanted war but there was a very real risk that they would set off a train of events that they could not control. The article concluded by saying that now more than ever before it was necessary for NATO to stand firm and to maintain its guard.

A number of letters have appeared in the newspapers expressing fears

* Military-speak for Greenwich Mean Time.

that, unlike previous crises, there was a very real danger that the present tension would lead to hostilities, and calling for the reactivation of the civil defence services [as we have seen, these had by this time been placed on a 'care-and-maintenance' basis].[19]

[At 11:30 a.m. the Cabinet's Transition to War Committee (TWC) – consisting of civil servants, military and intelligence officers – meets to prepare recommendations for the full Cabinet meeting that will follow.]

Transition to War Committee

[The TWC agrees to recommend that ministers authorize the following 'Government War Book Measures':]

1: A1 (Covert)
To Prepare for Activation of Government Headquarters in the Regions (Except Alerting of Staff).
Time required 4 weeks.

2: 4.1 (Overt)
Instructions for Police, Fire, Medical and Local Authorities.

These require the Home Office and the Scottish Home and Health Department to review Police War Instructions and the Police War Duties Manual. The Home Office and its Edinburgh equivalent are also required to draft instructions to local authorities

(A) on appointment of controllers and staff to act under directions of Regional Commissioners;
(B) on selection and improvisation of local authority controls;
(C) in consultation with the POST OFFICE, on improvising such radio and other communications as possible with available resources;
(D) on improvising fall-out refuge for the public, requisitioning land and suitable premises for this purpose.

2: 4.2 (Overt)
Bringing Medical and Dental Services to a State of Readiness.
The Department of Health and Social Security, the Scottish Home and Health

Department and the Welsh Office are to 'review state of war preparedness'.

3: 9.1 (Covert)
Review of Emergency Plans.

[Ministry of Technology to review plans for instructing industries on transition-to-war measures; for emergency legislative powers; arrangements with the Post Office for communications facilities and for the delivery of gas into the Central European Pipeline System for the British Army of the Rhine (BAOR).[20]

The TWC also agrees to recommend to ministers 'that the Ministry of Defence should be authorised to take all covert measures to bring 6 Brigade, 36 Heavy Air Defence Regiment, and 18 (Helicopter) Squadron to twenty-four hours readiness to deploy to BAOR . . .'[21]]

Cabinet

[The Cabinet invites (Cabinet Office-speak for authorizes or decides) the Defence Secretary to take the recommended covert measures involving military personnel and equipment and agrees the implementation of 'Government War Book' (GWB) measures placed before it by the TWC.

The Cabinet also takes note 'that the Foreign Secretary and the Defence Secretary would report within the next twenty-four hours what action our NATO allies were taking to meet the threat from the Soviet Union. They would also tell our NATO allies what action we had taken, and were prepared to take'.[22]]

Saturday 28 September 1968
Cabinet

[The simulated full Cabinet meets to take note that NATO's Supreme Allied Commander Europe (SACEUR) 'had requested the return [to West Germany] of 6 Brigade, 36 Heavy Air Defence Regiment and 18 (Helicopter) Squadron and that this request was strongly supported by the Governments of the United States, the Federal German Republic, Italy and Greece'.[23]]

The Cabinet also authorizes the following GWB measures:

1: A7 (Overt)
To Return Those Forces Located in the United Kingdom Which Are Under
the Operational Command of Commander-in-Chief, BAOR.
The time needed to implement this is 14 days and it assumes that the forces
concerned are at 7-days' notice and that powers will be taken to use British Rail Ferries to transport them across the Channel.

2: A16 (Overt)
To Repatriate Service Dependants from Germany.
Time needed 7 days +.[24]

[Just over a fortnight later, the pace of events picks up as Whitehall's
secret state simulates seven desperate days in October as the cold truce
between East and West that had held for twenty-three and a half years
since the fall of Hitler comes to a dreadful and brutal end. The JIC's
special assessment at noon on 16 October 1968 depicts the magnitude
of crisis and menace in central Europe, Scandinavia and the Balkans.*]

Wednesday 16 October 1968
Joint Intelligence Committee
Special assessment as at 1200 ZULU, 16 October 1968

Political
1. The Soviet Union has coupled threats with its call for a revision of the
status of the Baltic. Bulgaria has raised tension on her border with Turkey.
Turkey has protested at 'excessive' Soviet military supplies to Syria.
2. Increased Chinese hostility to its policies [is] putting the Soviet Union on
the political defensive.

---

* My own diary indicates that at six p.m. that very autumn day I climbed the stairs of
the Shrewsbury Tower in St John's College, Cambridge for a supervision with the incomparable Harry Hinsley on Bismarck. I can remember Harry, pipe in mouth, surrounded
by shaky looking towers of books suddenly producing the ethnic map of the Balkans
in the late nineteenth century, putting it on the floor, striking it with his fist and crying,
'Look at it. The scrag end of Europe!' before explaining why the great Prussian did not
believe the said Balkans were worth 'the bones of a single Pomeranian Grenadier'.

Counter-Intelligence

3. There have been no mass demonstrations in the United Kingdom but anti-NATO demonstrations continue in Europe. 'Anti-war' strikes are planned in Dutch shipyards. On 14th–15th October petrol bomb incidents damaged a total of four aircraft at five RAF bomber stations. Further sabotage in NATO countries included fuel depots and communications.

Military

4. Northern Region

(a) Soviet forces have deployed along the Russian–Norwegian border and are in positions from which an attack could be launched at any time. Several violations of the Norwegian border by Soviet aircraft have occurred.

(b) A large concentration of Soviet Bloc shipping including landing craft is building up in the Baltic. Although there is good evidence of an impending amphibious exercise in the Gulf of Danzig, this does not adequately account for the number of ships reported.

5. Central Region.

Mobilisation of East German and Czechoslovak ground forces is taking place, and intensive troops movement is reported in Bohemia. Troop movement on a large scale is also reported from Western Russia, Poland and East Germany, predominantly in a westward direction.

6. Southern Region

(a) Heavy troop movements are reported through Bulgaria towards Thrace. A clash occurred yesterday between Bulgarian and Turkish frontier units.

(b) There are reliable reports of an offer to the Soviet Union by the new Syrian government of naval and air bases.

7. Atlantic

(a) Soviet naval and merchant shipping is deploying as if for war. Merchant shipping appears to be withdrawing to neutral or friendly ports.

(b) Intense air surveillance of the Strike Fleet is being maintained.

Assessment

8. The internal pressures which are behind the Soviet Union's diplomatic, military and subversive activity have not abated. The Soviet Union still claims that her troop movements are connected only with Warsaw Pact exercises.

But this may be to give herself a pretext for retracting should she achieve her political objectives without war. Nevertheless, the high state of readiness in Central Europe is being maintained and certain military indicators are consistent with readiness to attack. The situation will need careful watching here, in Northern Norway and the sea approaches to Denmark, on Bulgaria's NATO frontiers, and on the Syrian/Turkish Frontier.[25]

[A domestic equivalent of the JIC's international assessment produced simultaneously by the Home Office fills in the story between the TWC's and the Cabinet's initial decision-taking and the unfolding fast track to the brink.]

Situation report as at 1200 hours ZULU, 16 October 1968

An initial wave of anxiety followed the announcement of the Government's decision to take Emergency Powers on 28th September. There was some absenteeism from work and some movement of families away from London and other large towns. But as the days passed without any significant deterioration in the situation – and following the Prime Minister's television broadcast on 1st October assuring the public that, although the Government had decided to take certain precautionary measures to counter the increasing belligerence of the Soviet Union, they should not regard war as inevitable and should continue their normal way of life – there was a gradual return to work and movement back to the cities. The announcement of the decision to take emergency powers was also followed by a large-scale demand for food and petrol. The demand now seems to have abated, but tinned foodstuffs are reported to be in short supply particularly in suburban areas.

A large-scale student demonstration took place in Oxford on 2nd October calling for a complete and immediate break with NATO and the dismantling of all nuclear bases in this country. The students attempted to enter various public buildings and the police had some difficulty in ejecting them. The students also succeeded in halting a convoy of six Infantry Brigade vehicles bound for Brize Norton and Lyneham [RAF stations used for the despatch of troops and equipment]. After some hours, order was restored by the police and the convoy was able to proceed. Many arrests were made and a number of people were treated in hospital for injuries.

No further large-scale demonstrations have been reported since then, although there have been isolated incidents at RAF and USAF [United States Air Force] bases and at Southampton where students held up an army convoy before they were dispersed by the police. At a dockers' rally addressed by Jack Dash [real-life militant communist shop steward in the London Docks[26]] on 10th October, a resolution was carried calling for a ban on the handling of arms and other cargo bound for BAOR. This resolution appears to have been largely ignored, but some incidents have been reported of dockers refusing to handle cargoes.

A pirate radio station calling itself the 'Voice of Peace' has been heard in the London area calling for the neutrality of the United Kingdom, and the War Registers' International Organisation has continued its poster and pamphlet campaign.

Outwardly, the people seem to be calm and life is as normal as can be expected in the circumstances. It is generally felt, however, that any further deterioration in the situation is likely to result in a return to the conditions prevailing immediately following the Government's decision to take emergency powers.[27]

Transition to War Committee

[The Transition to War Committee meets at 2:30 on Wednesday 16 October to evaluate those reports and prepare advice for a meeting of the simulated full Cabinet due to gather an hour later.

The TWC recommends that the Cabinet implement a set of measures the 'Government War Book' deems essential to be in place before warning is received of an imminent attack, all of which require the emergency powers granted to the government by Parliament and the Defence Regulations laid down in the Act, many of which would be highly visible both to the UK population and to Soviet Intelligence:[28]]

1: A12 (Overt)
Issue of billeting instructions.
Requisitioning of ships; vehicles, aircraft, petrol stations, buildings and land.
Application of restrictions on access to Protected Places.
Arrangements for the control of manpower under the Defence Regulations.
Requisitioning and distribution of certain bulk stocks of food.

Informing the Nationalised Industries that Defence Regulations are effective.

Action under the Defence Regulations affecting Regional Transport Controllers, British Railways Board, London Transport Board and British Waterways Board.

Control of use of shipbuilding facilities in the United Kingdom.

Preparation of accommodation and provision of communications for the Regional Port and Shipping Organisation and for Seamens' Pools.

Implementation of these measures will take between 3 and 21 days.

2: B5 (Covert)

To Make Necessary Approaches to States with which the United Kingdom has Mutual Treaty Obligations.

Time needed to implement between 3 and 8 days.

3: 12.22 (Overt)

Alerting of Staff Required to Specific War Stations in the Regions and Those Responsible for the Manning of Ships.

4: 2.1 (Covert)

Ministry of Defence to Bring Operations Rooms to full strength . . .

Post Office to implement pre-arranged scheme of line communications . . . [including] a system of precedence . . . to enable priority to be given to important and urgent telephone calls.

5: 3.46 (Overt)

Bringing of HM Ships and Supply Ships to Immediate Operational Readiness.

6: 6.2 (Overt)

Suspension of the National Dock Labour Scheme (to allow the Ministry of Transport to take control of ports and dock labour).

[The next measure is a detailed and elaborate plan for, in effect, voluntary self-censorship by the print and electronic media guided by a special Standing Committee on Information Policy (SCIP) chaired by the Prime Minister's Press Secretary. Beneath this will be a Press Working Party (PWP) chaired by the No. 10 Deputy Press Secretary with representatives of BBC News and Independent Television News sitting in as observers.]

7: 7.1 (Covert)

Control over the dissemination of information before the outbreak of war must rest on the voluntary co-operation of the press and broadcasting authorities and a system of intensive and continuous guidance operated by both Ministers and by the Government's press relations machinery.

[The Press Association news agency will be used to receive tele-printed messages from the government and will retransmit them to newspaper and television news offices. 'Guidance messages and requests' from the government are to be delivered personally to editors.

A huge range of notices and official announcements are prepared and ready to go. They are divided into four types.]

ADVICE TO HOUSEHOLDERS
Protection against nuclear attack and advice on first aid

MOBILISATION AND MANPOWER CONTROL NOTICES
(i) General Mobilisation of Armed Forces
(ii) Mobilisation of Fire Service Reserve
(iii) Recall of Merchant Seamen
(iv) Manning of the Merchant Navy
(v) Electricity Workers
(vi) Trained nurses and midwives – appeal for volunteers

ADVICE TO SPECIALIST SECTIONS
(i) Protection of farms and livestock
(ii) Protection of food supplies
(iii) Extended opening of food shops
(iv) Operation of commercial vehicles
(v) Employment of foreign workers
(vi) War Pensions, National Insurance Benefits and Family Allowances
(vii) Appeal to blood donors
(viii) Advice to patients
(ix) Use of fuel and power
(x) Port and shipping controls
(xi) Travel by Air

EMERGENCY ANNOUNCEMENTS
  (i) Air attack warning system
  (ii) Regional Government
  (iii) Closing of places of entertainment
  (iv) Post Office services
  (v) Mail for merchant seamen
  (vi) Amateur radio apparatus
  (vii) Restrictions on civil flying
(viii) Financial restrictions
  (ix) Limitation of cash withdrawals
  (x) Requisitioning powers
  (xi) Billeting powers

8: 7.2. (Overt)

Implementation of NATO and National Plans for the Control of Meteorological Information.

The purpose of controlling meteorological information is to deprive the enemy
of information which would be of assistance to him in planning and timing
his attack.

. . . the British Ambassador in Dublin . . . [is] . . . to approach the Government
of the Irish Republic with a view to implementing the mutual arrangements
for the control and exchange of meteorological information.[29]

Cabinet

[At 3:30 on Wednesday 16 October the full Cabinet implements the war
book measures suggested by the Transition to War Committee. It also
authorizes the deployment of the UK's contribution to NATO's European Mobile Force 'if a firm request should materialise from SACEUR'.[30]

The world scene deteriorates rapidly and visibly on Wednesday–
Thursday 16–17 October. I cannot decide if the opening sentence of
the JIC's Special Assessment distributed at noon on 17 October is an
example of the war planners attempting to cheer themselves up with a
sliver of *comédie noire* or if they really thought it was a possible and
significant contingency (point 8 of the assessment suggests it *was* a
serious element of the scenario, as we shall see shortly).]

Thursday 17 October 1968
Joint Intelligence Committee Special Assessment
Special assessment as at 1200 ZULU, 17 October 1968

Political

1. Soviet astronauts have landed on the moon. Pro-Soviet trends in Finland have alarmed Sweden. There has been a sharp rise in diplomatic tensions between the Soviet Union and NATO. As well as intensifying its Baltic propaganda the Soviet Union has now asked for salvage bases in Norway. Pressure also being applied to Denmark and Belgium. Bonn has been accused of preparing to attack East Germany.

2. Austria has appealed to the UN about military activity on her northern frontiers: The Secretary-General will appeal for relaxations of tension pm 17th October. Bulgaria, the Soviet Union and Albania are bringing pressure to bear on Greece and Turkey. Syria has offered bases to the Soviet Union.

3. China is bringing pressure to bear on Taiwan.

Counter-Intelligence

4. Communist inspired propaganda and strikes are on the increase. Half of the London docks are out and Liverpool, Hull and Bristol are affected. One-day strike tactics have brought chaos on road and rail. Extensive fire damage, possible sabotage, has been done to an SSN [Royal Navy Hunter-Killer nuclear submarine] at Birkenhead [Cammell Laird shipyard]. Further widespread sabotage targets in other NATO countries have included railways, bridges, radar and other military installations.

Military

5. Northern Region

(a) Soviet military units and Tactical Air Force aircraft have occupied a number of airfields in Finland.

(b) The expected amphibious exercise in Danzig Bay started yesterday. It is confirmed that at least ten Soviet submarines have left the Baltic during the past five days.

6. Central Region

(a) Aircraft from Western Soviet Union have deployed to airfields in Soviet Zone Germany, Poland and Czechoslovakia.

(b) Movement control offices have been established on the Soviet–Polish border. At least two Soviet tank divisions are reported moving from the Carpathian Military District into Poland.

(c) Soviet fighters have been harassing civil aircraft in the Berlin Corridors. One PANAM aircraft crashed yesterday as a result of Soviet interference.

(d) Czechoslovakia and Hungary ground forces appear to be deploying in strength in the Austrian frontier area.

7. Southern Region

(a) The construction of temporary ferries and bridges across the Danube between Rumania and Bulgaria indicates the probability of Soviet or Rumanian troops moving into Bulgaria in the immediate future.

(b) Southward troop movement is reported from Transcaucasus and Turkestan Military Districts.

Assessment

8. The deployment of Soviet Bloc forces continues in all regions, accompanied by intense air reconnaissance of border areas. Although much of the above evidence is consistent with a Soviet Bloc intention to launch conventional attacks on NATO in all regions, internal political pressures for an increasingly militant line by the Soviet Union persist. We expect these to lead to further intensification of the Soviet Union's military, diplomatic and psychological pressure on the West. Soviet moon landings have created a political euphoria in its leaders which could heighten the chances of miscalculation.

The Home Office also briefs the Transition to War Committee and the Cabinet at Noon on Thursday 17 October 1968:

Situation report as at 1200 hours ZULU

Newspapers and news bulletins have given prominence to the decision to send reservists to BAOR; only the 'Morning Star' has criticised the Government's action as 'provocative and totally unnecessary'. 'The Times' and 'The Daily Telegraph' have called upon the Government to stand firm and not to lose its nerve in the face of increased pressure from the Soviet Union.

No mass demonstrations have been reported, but numbers of individuals are carrying placards or attempting to speak at street corners. The poster campaign for the withdrawal of the United Kingdom from NATO continues unabated.

Unofficial union leaders have called for strike action by train and lorry drivers in support of the dockers' resolution calling for the refusal to handle military cargoes. There are reports that some dockers in Liverpool, Hull and Bristol have stopped work in support of the London dockers, though no widespread disruption has been caused so far.

The demand for petrol seems to be on the increase again and many garages are without supplies. The oil companies say that it may not be possible to replenish them if tanker drivers respond to the call to strike action.

The mood of the country remains generally calm, but letters are beginning to appear in newspapers asking when advice is going to be given to house-holders about protecting their homes.[31]

Transition to War Committee

The Transition to War Committee meets at 2:30 on the Thursday afternoon. It recommends the following steps to be taken by the Cabinet.

1: A6 (Overt)

Time needed to implement 9 days.

Instructions regarding evacuation of patients from military hospitals in Germany.

Manning of National/NATO military war headquarters.

Preparations for the deployment of naval forces and support units to war stations.*

Bringing HM ships and supply ships to immediate operational readiness.

Redeployment of stores to war locations, ships and establishments.

Bringing forward reserve ships and naval aircraft.

Implementation of plans for maintaining two ocean weather ships permanently on station.

Cancellation of exercises and recall of aircraft engaged on international operations, displays and visits.*

* The 1970 'Government War Book' indicates that these three 'measures would contribute directly to the mounting of the nuclear deterrent' *after* June 1969 (i.e. nine months later than the running of INVALUABLE) once the Royal Navy's Polaris submarines had taken over the primary UK deterrent role from the RAF's V-bombers'.

Recall and re-allocation of support command aircraft not devoted to RAF tasks.

Recall of BAOR personnel from leave and courses in the United Kingdom and retention in service of men serving overseas.

2: A26 (Overt)

To put the Police on a War Footing.

3: A27 (Overt)

To Put Civil Defence and Fire Services on a War Footing and to Control Road Transport.

Emergency powers needed.

4: A36 (Overt)

To Evacuate Shipping and to Transfer Ancillary Resources from Some or All of the Major Ports Scheduled for Evacuation.

Time needed up to 33 days.

5: B6 (Covert)

To Activate the Post Office Emergency Manual Switching System.

6: C6 (Covert)

To Alert Fuel and Power Industries Staff for War Duties in the Regions.

Cabinet

[At 3:30 the simulated full Cabinet meets and implements all the measures recommended by the TWC. It also declines to agree with the request from the NATO Council in Brussels for a declaration of 'Simple Alert' without knowledge of SACEUR's views and decides that both the Foreign Secretary and the Defence Secretary will need to be present at any NATO Council meeting that discusses such a declaration.[32]]

Friday 18 October 1968

[This is the day the crisis goes truly global, with serious trouble breaking out from the Middle East to the Far East, and a worsening scene from the tip of Norway to the Black Sea. It was as if the Transition to

War Committee and the Cabinet met to the sounds of 'Why do the Nations so furiously rage together?' from Handel's *Messiah*.]

Joint Intelligence Committee Special Assessment

<u>Special assessment as at 1200 ZULU, 18 October, 1968</u>

<u>Political</u>

1. In the UN the Soviet Union rejected calls for moderation and has renewed charges that NATO is preparing aggression. These charges are widely reflected in Soviet propaganda. West Germany has been accused of preparing to attack East Germany and occupy Denmark. The Soviet Union has said that allegations of traffic interference between West and East Germany must be addressed to the latter. Norway and Denmark have been accused of adopting an aggressive posture.

2. The Soviet Union has requested right to overfly Sweden. Soviet Bloc countries are evidently trying to provoke Turkey and Austria into hostile action. Belgium has been subjected to alternate threats and blandishments. In face of determined Soviet attempts to split NATO, United States has reaffirmed its support.

3. Syria has called for formation of Arab bloc against 'imperialists'. The Arabs have agreed to deny oil to Western countries involved in present European tensions.

4. China is moving against Indian frontier and activating MRBMs [Medium Range Ballistic Missiles] targeted on Tokyo.

<u>Counter-Intelligence</u>

5. Strikes and demonstrations in NATO countries have escalated to a new degree of significance. Incidents in Norway (Allied Forces North) and at army depots in West Germany involved threats to civilian workers in military establishments. Control of a demonstration in Oslo required the assistance of the army. The Forward Scatter [radar] station at Cold Blow Lane in the UK has been damaged, but there is no proof that the few sabotage incidents in this country were centrally directed. This is also true of sabotage incidents in Italy.

Military

7. Northern Region.

The amphibious force which carried out exercises in the Danzig Bay area during the past two days is now moving Westwards with troops still embarked. Its landing capacity is estimated at three regiments, and it should retain its operational capability for up to five days without refuelling.

8. Central Region

(a) Soviet and Polish airborne forces are reported moving from home locations, probably to airfields.

(b) 11 Guards Army, from Baltic Military District, is reported entering East Germany.

(c) Soviet Tactical Air Force aircraft have been identified on bases in Hungary for the first time.

(d) Abnormal air reconnaissance continues. Border violations by aircraft have been reported in several areas.

9. Southern Region

(a) The movement of Rumanian ground forces into Bulgaria has been confirmed. Soviet tactical aircraft have also been sighted on Bulgarian airfields.

(b) Soviet aircraft have been observed at bases in Syria.

Assessment

10. Intelligence indicators, though still not pointing unequivocally to imminent Soviet Bloc aggression, are now consistent with an intention to attack in all three NATO regions and against Austria. Bloc military preparations are advanced and the need to counter growing unrest in the Warsaw Pact, especially East Germany, may precipitate an early Soviet decision to launch a major offensive. Arab states and China seem bent on exploiting European tension to further their own ends.[33]

[As usual, the Home Office's A1 Division supplemented the JIC's world picture with a portrait of the UK domestic scene.]

Situation report as at 1200 hours ZULU, 18 October 1968

All newspapers give prominence to yesterday's appeal by the Secretary General of the United Nations to the leaders of the great powers to exercise restraint in their dealings with each other 'at this grave time'. The 'Morning Star' says that it is the responsibility of NATO to reduce tension by 'putting a stop to its provocative actions'.

In an article in the 'Daily Express' dealing with the Soviet landing on the Moon, Chapman Pincher suggests that this may be the first step in a Soviet plan to set up missile bases in space.

Headlines in this morning's papers refer to Soviet troop movements in Eastern Europe and report the crash of an American airliner as a result of 'buzzing' by Soviet fighters in the Berlin Air corridors; leading articles refer to the need for action but offer no concrete suggestions.

No mass demonstrations have been reported, but parties of students from the University of Kent demonstrated outside Shorncliff transit camp, and marched to Dover where they attempted to occupy the Dover Ferry terminal building in an apparent effort to delay the departure of reservists bound for BAOR. They were eventually dispersed by the police and a number of arrests were made.

The increased activity in Whitehall has attracted notice and is reported briefly – and without comment – in the 'Guardian', 'Times' and 'Daily Telegraph'. Small crowds have gathered in Downing Street and outside the Houses of Parliament, but no incidents have been reported.[34]

Transition to War Committee and Cabinet

[The Transition to War Committee meets at 2:30 p.m., the Cabinet an hour later. They recommend the Cabinet authorizes all remaining measures needed for a general mobilization[35] and the taking of control of all UK civil aviation resources over the coming three days.[36] The full Cabinet concurs. It also authorizes the Foreign and Defence Secretaries to agree to a North Atlantic Council request for a Simple Alert to be declared.

The Queen's Proclamation 'announcing general mobilisation' is to be made that evening in time for the national press to cover it the following morning. The Home Secretary is to make a television broadcast straight after the announcement of the Queen's Proclamation.[37]]

Saturday 19 October 1968
Joint Intelligence Committee Special Assessment
Special assessment as at 0800 ZULU, 19 October 1968

Political

1. Brusque protests and counter-protests have been exchanged between United States and the Soviet Union over the latter's harassment of fishing vessels. Sweden has accepted Soviet demand for conference on status of Baltic. The Soviet Union has protested at government level against Bonn's 'war preparations' against East Germany and has reiterated support of the latter. Civil unrest is increasing in East Germany. There have been further Hungarian attempts to provoke Austria. Communist-inspired riots have taken place in Tehran.

2. Chinese activity against Northern India continues.

Counter-Intelligence

3. There have been two sabotage incidents at RAF and USAF stations in United Kingdom. In other NATO countries sabotage has been widespread. As in UK and Italy, however, West Germany has been unable to ascertain whether or not these incidents are centrally controlled.

Military

4. Northern Region – Possible use of BW [biological warfare] Agents. BW aerosol containers have been found at a Norwegian air base, apparently smuggled in by an unidentified agent.

5. Central Region

(a) There has been a wave of sabotage incidents against NATO logistic installations in Germany during the last 48 hours.

(b) The Soviet Union has announced that the Berlin air corridors will be closed to all aircraft from 242100Z [sic] October, for the duration of unspecified exercises.

(c) A general decrease in flying activity throughout the Region has been noted.

(d) Czechoslovak and Hungarian forces are still deploying in the area of the Austrian frontier, and a number of border incidents are reported.

6. <u>Southern Region</u>

(a) Yugoslav forces are reported to be concentrating in the area of the Italian frontier.

(b) Elements of four Soviet divisions, including two tank divisions, have been reported entering Yugoslavia.

(c) Soviet divisions are reliably reported to be moving up to the Iranian border. Anti-government communist-inspired rioting is reported from Tehran and elsewhere in the country.

<u>Assessment</u>

7. Soviet Bloc pressure is being intensified in all regions, and there has been no relaxation in the general situation. Sweden's attempt to defuse the situation in the North is unlikely to succeed. A new dimension of gravity has been added with increasing involvement of the United States, entry of Soviet troops into Yugoslavia, and latter's move against Italy. A potential threat to Iran has emerged for the first time and that to Austria has intensified. Pressure against the NATO Southern Region has increased with Albania's build up against Greece and entry of Rumanian troops into Bulgaria. Bloc preparations continue against all regions: while absolute pointers to attack are still lacking, it could come at any time.[38]

[Like the JIC, the Home Office briefed at eight that morning for the simulated Cabinet meeting at 11:00 (no doubt Harry Lawrence-Wilson didn't want to deprive his fellow simulators of their Saturday afternoons).]

<u>Situation report as at 0800 hours ZULU, 19 October 1968</u>

Today's newspapers refer to general anxiety about the increasing international tension, and urge the Government to increase its efforts to try to arrive at an understanding with the new Soviet regime. The 'Sun' suggests that the Prime Minister should arrange a meeting with Soviet leaders in an effort to reduce tension.

Prominence is given in all newspapers to the appeal by the Archbishop of Canterbury, Cardinal Heenan and other church leaders to observe tomorrow as a national day of prayer for peace. The Chief Rabbi has asked for special prayers to be said at Jewish services today.

Apart from minor incidents at one or two RAF stations, no demonstrations have been reported during the past twenty-four hours. Anti-war rallies have been called tomorrow in London, Liverpool and Manchester. Police leave has been stopped and arrangements are being made to deal with any disorder that may occur.

Dockers at Felixstowe, engaged on loading military stores for BAOR, have struck in support of a demand for extra pay for shift work. There has been some response by train and lorry drivers to the call for unofficial strike action. Some passenger trains have had to be cancelled and the oil companies report that deliveries to garages are being hampered by the fact that only about 80 per cent of tanker drivers are at work. There has, however, been little interference with the movement of essential food and other supplies.

There have been long queues at foodshops – particularly in suburban areas. In a leading article, the 'Daily Mirror' has urged the Government to issue the 'Householders Handbook' to all householders 'before it is too late'.[39]

Cabinet

The Cabinet authorizes another spate of measures from the 'Government War Book'. (The Transition to War Committee had ceased to meet).

1: A23 (Overt)
To Impose an Embargo on Issues from Certain Designated Petroleum Filling
   Stations in Order to Ensure Post-Attack Stocks.
Emergency powers needed.
Time to complete 3 days.[40]

2: A42 (Overt)
To Take Anti-Sabotage Action against Prospective Enemy Ships and to Impede
   their Departure.[41]

4: C7 (Overt)
To Repatriate Allied Non-Combatants from Berlin.
Time required 3 to 4 days.

5: C17 (Overt)
To Divert Shipping.
Time needed 3 to 4 days.

6: C18 (Overt)
To Impose Restriction on Civil Flying.
Time needed up to 5 days.

7: C24 (Overt)
To Deploy D-Day Forces and Support Units to Their War Stations.
Time required 2 days.

[The Cabinet also agrees to bring home the ships and aircraft operating the patrols off Beira to prevent illegal oil supplies reaching the Smith regime in rebellious Southern Rhodesia. The meeting also authorizes the Prime Minister, the Foreign Secretary and the Defence Secretary to agree to any NATO requests for a Reinforced Alert or the withdrawal of Royal Navy vessels from east of Suez.[42]]

Sunday 20 October 1968

[This is the day that the 1968 World War broke out.]

Joint Intelligence Committee Special Assessment

Special assessment as at 0800 ZULU, 20 October 1968

Political
1. Czechoslovakian and Hungarian forces this morning invaded Austria. Soviet ground forces entered Finland last night.
2. US is now more closely committed after her rejection of the Soviet demand that she deal direct with East Germany over traffic interference. There are further Soviet assaults on cohesion of NATO, including general calls for its dissolution and mounting threats against Denmark, Belgium and Turkey. East Germany has charged West Germany with attempts to assassinate East German leaders. Yugoslavia's build up against Italy continues. Charges and counter-charges have been made over Hungarian and Czechoslovak incursions into Austria. With sharp intensification of crisis over the Straits Cyprus has declared she will stay out of an eastern Mediterranean anti-NATO bloc if formed.
3. China has cut off Hong Kong's water, and delivered ultimatum to Sikkim.

Counter-Intelligence

4. Labour unrest in the Ruhr is reported to be reaching crisis stage. In the UK there has been one sabotage incident against USAF Upper Heyford, but no other developments of significance. Reported plans to kidnap the UK Prime Minister are probably not inspired by the Soviet Union. There has been attempted sabotage of water installations in Bahrain and anti-NATO riots there.

5. Covert action has been taken by the Soviet Union to introduce BW agents into south Norway. Outbreaks of sickness can be expected within few days. There are no reports of similar action in the UK.

Military

6. Northern Region

(a) Further reliable reports have been received of the covert introduction of BW agents into southern Norway. Source believes that the agents concerned will become effective by 24th October.

(b) Soviet ground forces entered Finland last evening at Raja Joseppi in divisional strength. No fighting is reported and the move appears to be by agreement with the Finnish Government.

(c) The amphibious forces in the Baltic are being reinforced by additional Soviet amphibious units which were yesterday reported moving South off Memel, possibly from the Leningrad area.

7. Central Region

(a) Three Czechoslovak divisions entered Austria in the area north and north-east of Linz early this morning. Austrian forces are reported to be resisting fiercely, but their ability to fight for more than a very few days is questionable.

(b) The situation opposite NORTHAG [Northern Army Group in West Germany] is unchanged.

8. Southern Region

(a) The build-up of forces opposite the Italian/Jugoslav frontier continues. Soviet forces are now reported in the area in strength.

(b) Syrian forces are reported to be concentrated in the area north of Aleppo, and an attack against Turkey may be imminent.

(c) A force of six SUN LAMP [country unknown] FPBs [Fast Patrol Boats] made a foray into Gibraltar Bay yesterday morning. No weapons were fired, but some small boats were swamped.

Assessment

9. More widespread anti-Soviet resistance throughout Eastern Europe has complicated the Soviets' situation and increased chances of miscalculation. Further escalation of political tension against the West has brought the Soviet Union to a point from which withdrawal would be difficult. East German accusations against West Germany could be used as a pretext for an attack by the Soviet Bloc. We now assess major aggression as virtually certain. The Czechoslovak incursion into Austria is not yet assessed as invasion but the situation here is confused. Granting of bases to the Soviet Union by Syria marks a new step in pressure on Turkey and, with granting of Albanian bases, alters maritime situation in the Eastern Mediterranean. Introduction of BW agents into south Norway strongly suggests Soviet attack in that area by 24th October at latest.[43]

[The Home Office report portrays a remarkably calm UK, given the pace and menace of world events.]

Situation report as at 0800 hours ZULU, 20 October 1968

The invasion of Austria was reported in BBC news broadcasts and in special late editions of this morning's newspapers. Radio programmes are to be interrupted for news reports at hourly intervals throughout the day and the Prime Minister is to make a radio and television broadcast this evening.

The 'News of the World' asks the Prime Minister to fly immediately to seek a meeting with Soviet leaders; the 'Sunday Express' calls for an immediate military response by NATO to the invasion; and the 'Observer' urges the Government and people to remain calm.

The demand for petrol has increased and shortages have been reported in some areas as a result of the continued absence from work of a number of tanker drivers. Traffic on the roads yesterday, however, appears to have been no higher than normal. There has again been a heavy demand for foodstuffs – particularly canned goods – and shortages have been reported in some areas.

The dockers at Felixstowe have returned to work following agreement by the employers to provide 'productivity' payments. It seems likely that this settlement will encourage similar industrial action elsewhere.

It is too early to judge the reaction of the population to the events of the past twelve hours, but crowds are beginning to form in Downing Street and Whitehall. They are mostly silent, but there are isolated calls for the neutrality of the United Kingdom. So far there have been no disturbances and the crowds are well under control.[44]

[The minutes of the simulated Sunday morning Cabinet meeting are not preserved in the file. But, as they met, both the UK and the wider world were in the process of inflammation while the Cold War turned hot as the eight o'clock reports conveyed on the following morning.]

Monday 21 October 1968
Joint Intelligence Committee Special Assessment
Special assessment as at 0800 ZULU, 21 October 1968

Political

1. After yesterday's invasion by Czechoslovak and Hungarian forces Austria has now requested military assistance from NATO. Early this morning Bulgarian forces launched strong attacks on Greece and Turkey; later Albania attacked Greece. Syrian forces have attacked southern Turkey. Syria has also demanded immediate talks with Kuwait to discuss their territorial claims.

2. Bonn has protested to the Soviet Union about the closing of the Demarcation Line [between West and East Germany?], repeated border incidents, violation of her airspace and interference with Baltic shipping. The Soviet attitude to all Scandinavian countries is highly threatening. A Soviet anti-NATO resolution in the UN has been widely supported by Afro-Asian countries.

3. Public opinion in some NATO countries is divided and alarmed over the apparent imminence of war.

Counter-Intelligence

4. Widespread and systematic sabotage throughout NATO indicates that a co-ordinated effort is being made to disrupt communications, shipping, radar sites and public utilities. There are indications that 'dormant agents' [Soviet bloc 'illegal' intelligence operatives without the diplomatic cover of embassy staff] have been activated.

Military

5. There are indications that Soviet air defences are being brought to a higher alert status.

6. Northern Region Soviet ground forces are building up in the KILPISJAE-VRI area in northern Finland and an attack against Norway is considered imminent. Air reconnaissance and violations of Danish waters and Norwegian territory is being further intensified.

7. Central Region The Soviet forces in East Germany are being substantially reinforced by further Soviet formations moving through Poland. Jamming of air radio facilities may have caused the loss in East Germany of a British transport aircraft.

8. Southern Region Apparently co-ordinated attacks by Bulgaria against Greece and Turkey and Syrian incursions into Southern Turkey have been reinforced by an assault by Albania on the Epirus front in Greece. Soviet aircraft have been violating the Iranian borders and a heavy air build-up in the Trans-Caucasus Military District has been reported.

Assessment

9. The Soviet Union's attitude to all NATO and neutral countries in Europe is uniformly aggressive. There is no sign of any willingness by the Soviet Union to enter into genuine discussions of any of their demands or threats.

10. The Soviet Union's intention in attacking Austria, Greece and Turkey, and in threatening Norway and Denmark is, by concentrating first on the smaller countries, to weaken NATO's cohesion and will to fight. The Soviet Union may also aim to draw off NATO forces from the centre in the hope of creating favourable conditions for attack there. Such attack could come at any time.

11. There appears to be a grave risk that NATO countries may be politically isolated through the Soviet propaganda campaign being conducted among the non-aligned countries. Because of the success of this campaign and the threat to Iran there is a real danger of a complete cut-off of oil supplies from the Gulf.[45]

United Kingdom background situation report as at 0800 ZULU, 21 October 1968

In his television and radio broadcast last night the Prime Minister said it was quite wrong to think war was inevitable and appealed to the people to remain calm.

This morning's papers devote most of their space to the events of the last twenty-four hours. The 'Daily Mirror' has criticised the Government for not issuing advice to the public and has issued on its own initiative a supplement based on the 'Householders Handbook'. The 'Daily Telegraph' argue that the Government should introduce some form of rationing to ensure a fair distribution of food supplies to householders.

The Home Office also briefs at 8.00 a.m. in time for the morning Cabinet.

First impressions this morning suggest that the number of people entering London this morning is less than usual – particularly amongst those travelling by car. It cannot yet be said whether this is because of growing absenteeism from work. Public utilities are still functioning normally.

Church services of all denominations yesterday attracted exceptionally large congregations in response to Church leaders' appeal for a national day of prayer. Small demonstrations took place outside Westminster Abbey, Westminster Cathedral and a number of churches in University towns. No arrests were made.

Large crowds attended the anti-war rallies in London, Liverpool and Manchester yesterday. The addresses, which were given by well-known unilateralists and pacifists, were all on the theme of the warlike intentions of the United States of America and demanded a complete and immediate break with NATO and the neutrality of the United Kingdom. This was not received favourably by the large anti-Soviet elements in the crowds and fighting broke out. These developed to large proportions and it was some hours before the police were able to restore order in the areas where the meetings were held. In London, attempts were made to storm both the American and the Soviet Embassies, but the police managed to hold the crowds in check, though they had considerable trouble at the Soviet Embassy. In Liverpool and Manchester there was a 'sit-down' of students to attempt to block troop movements and train services were interrupted to some extent in consequence.

An unofficial strike of ground staff in support of demands for a 'productivity' bonus has delayed the departure of aircraft from London Airport.[46]

Cabinet

[At 10:30 on the morning of Monday 21 October 1968 the Cabinet takes the gravest step any Cabinet could ever contemplate, recorded, as always, in that dry way Cabinet note-takers have.]

The Cabinet –

. . . Took note with approval that the Prime Minister, in consultation with the Foreign Secretary and Defence Secretary, if available, would examine and if necessary authorise any requests from NATO for the use of nuclear weapons without further reference to the Cabinet.[47]

It also authorises implementation of the following 'Government War Book' measures:

1: A33 (Overt)
To Institute Naval Control of Shipping.
Emergency powers needed and 2–7 days to complete essential preparations.

2: A34 (Overt)
To Take Port and Coastal Defence Measures (Short of Laying Minefields).
7 days needed for implementation.

3: A39 (Overt)
To Lay Defensive Minefields.
14 days required for essential preparations.

4: C5 (Overt)
To Appoint Regional Commissioners and Deputy Regional Commissioners
    [see Chapter 7 for which ministers would have gone where].
2 days needed to complete essential preparatory action.
Emergency powers required.

5: C9 (Overt)
To Give Maximum Publicity to Precautionary Measures that can be Taken
    by the General Public.
2 days needed for essential preparatory actions.

6: C10 (Overt)
To Make Arrangements for the Care of the Homeless.

1 day needed for essential preparatory action.

Emergency powers required.

7: C20 (Overt)

To Instruct the Oil Industry, the Three Nationalised Fuel Industries [Coal, Gas and Electricity] and the Coal Distribution Trade to Assume Emergency Operational Control.

2 to 3 days needed for essential preparatory action.

8: C22 (Overt)

To Impede Departure of Prospective Enemy Aircraft.

Essential preparatory actions to be taken the same day.[48]

Tuesday 22 October 1968
Joint Intelligence Committee Special Assessment

Special assessment as at 1200 ZULU, 22 October 1968

Political

1. A general offensive by Soviet Bloc forces against West Germany is now in progress. There is a run on food and fuel by West European civilian populations. The Soviet Union has told Belgium that any use of nuclear weapons would entail violent reprisals. The Soviet Union is also widely publicising its nuclear retaliatory potential and appealing to Western workers to over-throw governments. Intimidation of Belgium and Denmark continues in effort to reduce NATO cohesion. Denmark has defied Soviet threats.

2. The Soviet Union has joined attacks on Greece, Turkey and Italy. Turkey has appealed to NATO and the UN.

3. There is increasing concern among [Eastern bloc] Satellites at Soviet escalation.

4. Increased North to South infiltration in Korea. China has crossed Bhutan's borders and entered certain Indian-claimed areas near Sikkim, South of the MacMahan Line.

Counter-Intelligence

5. A United Kingdom communist, after visiting the Soviet Embassy, has remarked 'We shall be engaged in nuclear war before we know where we are.'

6. Captured documents reveal existence of a Chinese plan for a major terrorist

campaign in Hong Kong. There have been no reports of sabotage in the United Kingdom in the last 24 hours. Widespread sabotage continues in NATO countries, especially against communications and railways. Demonstrations of students and others also continue in NATO countries.

7. There is evidence that BW agents have been covertly introduced into NATO countries.

Military

8. Northern Region

The Soviet Bloc amphibious forces in the Baltic are now concentrated in the area of Bornholm-Reugen, and operations to open the Straits to Soviet shipping could start at any time. Soviet airborne forces landed at TANA in Northern Norway this morning.

9. Central Region

(a) Attacks by both Soviet and Soviet Bloc forces have taken place since 1630Z yesterday against NATO forces, in what amounts to a general offensive against Central Region.

(b) Both chemical and biological weapons, but not nuclear weapons have been used.

(c) Reports so far indicate that at least eight Soviet divisions have been committed in addition to East German and Czechoslovak forces. The total number of Soviet divisions now available to the Soviet forces in East Germany is estimated to be twenty-eight.

(d) Soviet tactical air forces in East Germany and Czechoslovakia have been reinforced by almost 1,000 aircraft in the past ten days.

10. Southern Region

(a) Soviet amphibious and airborne forces have launched major assaults in the areas astride the Turkish Straits at first light this morning.

(b) The expected Soviet offensive against eastern Turkey was also launched at first light this morning. And least nine Soviet divisions are reported to be involved.

(c) Yugoslav and Soviet forces attacked Italy in the Gorizia-Trieste area this morning. And Soviet divisions have also been identified in Greek and Turkish Thrace.

(d) Chemical weapons are being used on most, if not all, these fronts.

Assessment

11. By reinforcing attacks in all regions the Soviet Union is trying to achieve political objectives before nuclear weapons are used. Her threats of nuclear war are aimed at breaking West's political will and inhibiting West from initiating nuclear attack. We assess that invasion of Denmark is imminent.[49]

[The Home Office also briefs at noon in time for the afternoon Cabinet.]

Situation report as at 1200 hours ZULU, 22 October 1968

Today's newspapers do not report the attack on West Germany, but there are reports of the fighting in Greece and Turkey, though few details seem to be known. The attack on West Germany was reported in this morning's 8.00 a.m. news bulletin, and radio programmes have been interrupted subsequently with reports of heavy fighting.

It now appears that a noticeable number of people stayed away from work yesterday – estimates range from 10 per cent [to] 15 per cent. In addition, many employers allowed their workers to return home earlier than usual and many children appeared to have stayed away from school.

It is not yet known what proportion of householders are attempting to protect their homes; but the effect of the special publicity should become apparent later today. First reports indicate that a substantial number of people have stayed away from work today and that there is heavy demand at builders' yards and hardware shops for bricks, wood, sand and other materials needed for constructing household refuge rooms.

Demand for petrol has been intense and traffic on the roads yesterday was much heavier than usual although it is too soon to say whether this is an indication of a general movement away from cities and large towns. There have again been long queues at foodshops and shoplifting is reported to be on the increase. Withdrawals from banks were slightly greater than usual.

The strike at London Airport ended when the employers agreed to the workers' demands for 'productivity' payments; similar 'settlements' have been reported from other parts of the country.

No mass demonstrations have been reported, but further student 'sit-down' demonstrations aimed at preventing the movement of troops took place in

Edinburgh and Salisbury yesterday. The students were dispersed without too much difficulty by the police, and no significant delays in the movement of troops were reported.[50]

Cabinet

[The Cabinet meets at 2:30 and takes 'note that the [NATO] Defence Planning Council had authorised the declaration of a General Alert throughout the NATO area'. It also authorizes the following GWB measures:]

1: A3 (Overt)
To Remove Major Art Treasures from London and Edinburgh.
A minimum of three days needed for essential preparatory action.

2: A29 (Overt)
To Discharge All but Acutely Ill Patients from Hospital.
3–7 days required for essential preparatory action.

3: A4 (Overt)
To Exercise Additional Control over Landing and Embarkation of People
    Subject to Immigration Control.
2 days needed for essential preparatory action.

4: A22 (Overt)
To Set Up Machinery of Justice in Wartime.
Emergency powers needed.
7 days required for essential preparatory action.

5: B1 (Covert)
To Change Premiums for Government Re-Insurance Against War Risks.
1 day needed for implementation.

6: C25 (Overt)
To Authorise the Introduction of Category One Telephone Preference Working.
12 hours needed for implementation.[51]

On the morning of Wednesday 23 October, as the Current Intelligence Group completes its final exercise report for the JIC and the

Cabinet at noon, it is plain that the crisis has escalated beyond recall and that the nuclear threshold is very close.

Wednesday 23 October 1968

Joint Intelligence Committee Special Assessment

1. Certain of the smaller Soviet Bloc countries are strongly resisting what they term the Soviet Union's 'obvious intention' to risk world-wide war. The Soviet Union has rejected Sweden's proposal for an immediate conference with NATO. Bulgarian sources indicate that any NATO use of nuclear weapons against the Soviet Union will result in retaliation with all available nuclear weapons. The Soviet Union has invaded Iran.

2. There is increased Chinese air activity on Indian frontier. Guatemala is reported to have mobilised against British Honduras.

Counter-Intelligence

3. A UK trade union leader, known to be a communist, has told the Foreign Secretary that the US plans to start nuclear war in Europe.

4. Sabotage of a naval radar station in the UK is similar to incidents in other NATO countries. A co-ordinated sabotage campaign is therefore to be presumed. Further covert use of BW is reported.

Military

5. Northern Region: The expected amphibious attack against the Danish Islands was launched early this morning in the area of FAKSE BAY. Soviet operations to seize northern Norway are also making rapid progress.

6. Central Region: Soviet-Bloc forces are advancing rapidly in Central Region. Against Northern Army Group they have captured Soltau and are approaching the River Weser south of Bremen. Further South, they have crossed the River Weser at Kassel and are reported to have reached Paderborn. NATO forces have suffered casualties from BW and CW [chemical warfare] weapons.

7. Southern Region: Intense fighting continues in Thrace and Eastern Turkey, when Soviet Bloc forces continue their advance. Soviet forces entered Iran early this morning.

Assessment

8. The Soviet Union, by a combination of military and psychological pressure, is trying to achieve its political objective quickly, presumably before the West can resolve to resort to nuclear war. We believe the Soviet Union hoped to defeat the Allies without using nuclear weapons and is probably still relying on its much publicised nuclear retaliatory capability to deter the West from resorting to nuclear war.[52]

[The final Home Office Report indicates the increasing pace of self-evacuation from urban areas.]

Situation report as at 1200 hours ZULU, 23 October 1968

Today's newspapers give particular prominence to Soviet advances into West Germany and of the fighting in Northern Norway and on the Jugoslav/Italian border. Radio programmes were interrupted this morning to report the amphibious attack against the Danish Islands. In leading articles, the 'Times' and the 'Guardian' urge that the West should not initiate a tactical nuclear exchange.

It is now clear that substantial numbers stayed away from work yesterday and others left early. Some trains have had to be cancelled because crews did not report for duty; telephone calls have been delayed; and Post Office sorting offices are undermanned and arrears of mail are building up.

Movement of families away from London and other large towns is becoming noticeable; road and rail traffic has been heavy and delays of up to two hours have been common on roads into the West Country. A substantial increase in the number of road accidents has been reported. There is so far no evidence of families sleeping 'rough' and hotels and boarding houses report only a slight increase in the number of guests; those travelling seem to have arranged to stay with relatives or friends.

Large crowds have built up at airports and cross-Channel seaports of people who have cut short visits to the United Kingdom in an effort to return home. Ships and aircraft still operating have been filled to capacity. There are reports that large numbers of Britons on the Continent are finding it difficult to return to the United Kingdom because of shortage of space on ships and aircraft.

Only one act of sabotage has been reported. Crowds in Downing Street and Parliament Square have for the most part been silent; they began to thin last night and only a few remain this morning.[53]

Cabinet

The simulated Cabinet meets at 2:30. In the slightly ornate setting of Conference Room B on the first floor of the Cabinet Office overlooking the garden of No. 10 Downing Street they agree the GWB measure controlling marine navigational lighting and note that the Irish government in Dublin has agreed to co-operate on the lights around the shores of the Republic. Finally, they agree 'To Introduce the BBC Wartime Broadcasting Service at a Specified Time', which can be done in '2–4 hours (providing all necessary preliminary action has been taken)'.[54] The record ends at this point. The meeting to consider SACEUR's request for nuclear release is not part of the paper trail released so far.*

After a wrap-up meeting of the INVALUABLE Committee in Conference Room B on the morning of 4 November 1968 which, among other things, suggested the exercise 'had shown it would be unrealistic to expect that the Cabinet would in practice be able to take the full range of decisions required by the Government War Book within the short time likely to be available',[55] the documentation of INVALUA-BLE and the notes taken by Mrs Grimble and her colleagues at the TWC and Cabinet meetings were filed away and did not emerge into the light of the National Archives Reading Rooms until January 1999.

The real-life Cabinet Office moved back from the fictional brink and to its normal coping mode not just with the Soviet Union and its

---

*Back in Cambridge, naturally oblivious to Harry Lawrence-Wilson and his team metaphorically steering the country to the brink fifty miles to the south in the Cabinet Office, I went for a morning supervision with Harry Hinsley in the College and rowed on the Cam in the afternoon. The following Sunday a real-life whiff of Cold War-related civil disorder could be detected in Mayfair when some 5,000 demonstrators turned up to protest against the Vietnam War outside the American Embassy and the demonstration teetered on the verge of a riot. (Kenneth O. Morgan, *James Callaghan, A Life*, Oxford University Press, 1997, pp. 315–16; Arthur Marwick, *The Sixties*, Oxford University Press, 1998, pp. 639–40).

allies but other seeming perpetual problems such as the weakness of the pound sterling, industrial unrest, Southern Rhodesia and the reviving 'Troubles' in Northern Ireland.

Regular transition-to-war exercises continued right up to the end of the Cold War. That they were never run for real, and that the protracted East–West struggle ended without general war and nuclear exchange, is by far the greatest shared boon of my lifetime. Beryl Grimble's War Books stayed closed except during the exercise season. And there they sit to this day, some now on the shelves at the National Archives in Kew, others still in the strongroom in the Cabinet Office's records review section in Admiralty Arch overlooking the Mall, just a few yards both from where Mrs Grimble kept them up-to-date and from Horse Guards Parade, which we can assume the Russians targeted as ground-zero for their first strike on London to decapitate British central government. In their own strange way, those old War Books are a particular kind of national monument to Britain and the Cold War, and to the dreadful might-have-been if the nuclear taboo that had held since August 1945 had finally been finally broken.

The people who compiled and exercised them had some of the grimmest jobs in post-war Whitehall. Occasionally there were attempts to lighten the gloom. David Young had a go when playing the Defence Secretary in the early 1970s. He and his fellow exercisers had 'been up most of the night' and nuclear release hour had come and gone in the small hours of a Thursday morning. Closed-circuit television had been fitted for the first time and the Cabinet Office was linked with the departments involved. David Young finished his contribution to the post-exercise briefing with the words 'Sic transit Gloria Thursday'.* Unbeknown to Mr Young the Foreign Secretary, Sir Alec Douglas-Home, was watching on CCTV. 'Who is that very foolish young man?' he enquired.[56] At the end of the 1970s, Commander Howard Mann, a former Polaris submariner then working in the Cabinet Office, brightened up a transition-to-war exercise by standing in front of the big map portraying the positions of the BLUE (NATO) and ORANGE (Soviet

---

* A Monsignor is deputed to walk in front of the Pope on ceremonial occasions metaphorically flicking dust into his eye while intoning 'Sic transit Gloria mundi' ('so passeth the glories of this world').

bloc) armies, suddenly placing a tin helmet on his head and slapping a large arrow declaring 'This Way to Walmington-on-Sea' on to the board.[57] Maybe there was a touch of *Dad's Army* about some aspects of these drills.

In the 1970s a story – for which there is not yet a corresponding declassified file – spread among Whitehall's World War III endgamers that somehow a telex had actually been sent during a transition-to-war exercise to the head of the Civil Service Catering Organization in Basingstoke instructing him to lay on three months' worth of provisions at a secure location (perhaps TURNSTILE or the regional seat of government near Reading). He dutifully rushed out and raided the local cash-and-carries and supermarkets. The cost, it was said, was carefully salted away over five or so years in various departmental budgets. It lived on in legend as the 'Government War Book' instruction that got away, until the summer of 2009, when confirmation of the story materialized from Brian Gilmore, the Civil Service Department Assistant Secretary who had played the Prime Minister in one of the mid-1970s transition-to-war exercises: 'I do . . . have an enduring memory of being briefed: Should I discover that I had received a message which required me to communicate with the Chief Executive of the Civil Service Catering Organization . . . I was on no account to do so.' Instead Mr Gilmore had to play the role himself. In the previous exercise, he recalled, the message had winged its way to the chief caterer in Basingstoke and, 'scarcely pausing to reply "Wilco", he whipped round to the local Tesco and bought them out of tinned peas!'[58]

7

'London Might Be Silenced': The Last Redoubt

It is fundamental to all TURNSTILE planning that if its location and purpose were known to the Russians it would almost certainly be destroyed.
United Kingdom Commanders-in-Chief Committee memorandum, March 1963[1]

The Chiefs of Staff never liked the idea of rushing to a bloody quarry . . . people disappearing to the West Country.
Sir Frank Cooper, former Permanent Secretary, Ministry of Defence, recalling the 1960s in 1998[2]

Dust. I couldn't believe that such a scruffy place would be the last seat of what government would be left.
Peter Hudson, former senior Cabinet Office official, recalling his first visit in the early 1970s to the Corsham Bunker in 2007[3]

STUCK HERE 4 ETERNITY.
Undated graffito by unknown hand, TURNSTILE[4]

As all good secrets should, the Prime Minister's World War III bunker has yielded its mysteries gradually and in parts. I first went there in April 2001, before its Cold War purpose was officially admitted, and saw only a bit of it. The first impression, however, was seriously powerful so I shall present it as originally written for *The Secret State* before adding on subsequent revelations and reactions as I was allowed deeper into its innermost recesses and rooms and more TURNSTILE-related documents were declassified.

Where exactly was this ultra-sensitive bunker, this 'bloody quarry' in the West Country, whose location had to be kept from Soviet Intelligence at all costs? It was a hundred feet *below* the top of Box Hill and fifty feet *above* Brunel's celebrated Box Tunnel (towards its eastern entrance), along which he drew his Great Western Railway through the Cotswolds on the last stage of its run from Paddington to Bath and Bristol (*not* to be confused with Box Hill in Surrey). According to Sir Frank Cooper, 'the very few people who were in on [the TURNSTILE secret] . . . always referred to it as "The Quarry"'.[5] Others in the inner circle knew it as 'Corsham'.[6] The military called it QOC (for 'Quarry Operations Centre').[7] Locals simply referred to the old workings (for years the quarry had been the place where that incomparable building material, Bath stone, had been cut) as 'The Deep'.[8]

As far as is known, no Prime Minister has ever paid a visit, either for real or out of curiosity (Jim Callaghan told me, 'I never visited the place . . . I practised a simulation of the occasion in a Whitehall office'[9]), to what in the event of an East–West war would have been the last redoubt of the British War Cabinet. It was ready by 1962, when Harold Macmillan laid down a prime ministerial directive that TURNSTILE was

(a) to act as the seat of Government in the period of survival and reconstruction.

(b) to be an alternative centre to London for authorising nuclear retaliation.[10]

Knowing that from the late 1970s, if not earlier, Russian intelligence had almost certainly located TURNSTILE (as a Soviet surveillance satellite was programmed to pass over it on each of its circumnavigations of the earth),[11]* and knowing, too, that by the turn of the twentieth century the bunker codenamed PINDAR, the Crisis Management Centre beneath the Ministry of Defence in Whitehall, was the place from which, heaven forbid, nuclear retaliation would henceforth be authorized by the Prime Minister, I sought permission from the

* We now know Russian Intelligence had rumbled Corsham much earlier, as we shall see shortly.

Cabinet Secretary, Sir Richard Wilson, early in 2001 to visit what remained of TURNSTILE.[12]

A member of the Cabinet Secretary's Private Office informed me that 'Box Hill, Corsham', as he called it, was now looked after by the Ministry of Defence, who would be in touch.[13] The MOD duly was. Guy Lester, Private Secretary to the Permanent Secretary, Kevin Tebbit, said 'we would be pleased to arrange for you to visit some of the site's more interesting historical areas. These include the Quarry Operations Area, the No. 10 Group wartime operations room, communications and stores areas, and the railway station . . .'[14] The site is now occupied by the ministry's Joint Support Unit, a communications installation administered by the Royal Air Force.

So, on a misty spring morning, three of us presented ourselves at the security gate of the JSU, Corsham – myself, my research assistant (my daughter, Polly) and a photographer (Jason Orton). There are, as it turns out, some sixty miles of tunnels beneath the JSU's patch. The quarry had been used during World War II as a huge ammunition depot in one section, an RAF operations centre in another and as a sizeable underground factory for making Bristol aero engines in a third.

Over the next few hours it was possible to reconstruct some of the elements which went into the making of TURNSTILE. Some (as Guy Lester had indicated), not all, because the files containing the plans, the layout and the operational drills have not been declassified, apart from a few, albeit very revealing, exceptions. And I am sure – I shall explain why in a moment – that not every bit of what once comprised TURN-STILE was laid open for our inspection. The reasons for this I can only guess at. Could it be that the facility, despite all the dereliction surrounding it, has not necessarily been pensioned off for ever? Whatever the remaining mystery, there is certainly a degree of sensitivity remaining about the early twenty-first-century 'Quarry'.

Since the RAF took it over in 1979 (they used it until 1990 as a Station Operations Room, part of RAF Rudloe Manor), new breeze-block walls and other adaptations have altered the site. In 1999 it ceased to be used at all for the last of its peacetime functions, the staff of the Service Communications Centre moving to the surface. So by the spring of 2001 TURNSTILE was a ghostly, dusty and slightly damp place, in striking contrast to the spick-and-span PINDAR with its hi-tech equipment, bright furniture and clean, filtered air.

Some 210 people were earmarked to go underground at TURN-STILE during the last phase of a transition to nuclear war[15] (precisely who we shall see shortly).* Very few would have been there before that. What would they have encountered first if the imminent catastrophe had propelled them west in the early to mid-1960s? Once inside the perimeter, they would have entered a short, tower-like building and into a pair of lifts with only two buttons – 'G' for Ground and 'Q' for Quarry. A few seconds later they would have left the lifts to pass along a corridor of offices built in the standard Ministry of Works style. Very quickly they would have emerged into a quarry gallery, oolitic limestone all around, the walls scratched with graffiti of many years' accumulation. One had an especially grim relevance – 'STUCK HERE 4 ETERNITY' – though it looks relatively fresh and could be post-1960s.

Beyond here there is no cosy, Ministry of Works, Whitehall-by-another-means feel. TURNSTILE was plainly improvised inside the eerie interlocking limestone chambers that once housed the aero engine workers. The murals left from those days add an air of utter surreality. There are sporting scenes of all kinds, with cricket and horse racing strongly represented. Bizarrely, an Anglican missionary being boiled in a pot by cannibals adorns one room. Nearby is the first-aid room. Stretchers on trolleys covered by long-since frayed blankets give a Dickensian, Miss Havisham feel. A rusty, red-cross-emblazoned tin helmet rests next to two white tea cups – enduring symbols of Britishness.

Some of the smaller rooms are crammed with army beds. Skeletal, uncomfortable-looking bunks are strewn around the larger gallery areas of the old quarry. The atmosphere here is part-pothole, part-dormitory. The cooking section is striking. Banks of huge ovens, an area of hotplates, a standard oblong canteen container for serving tureens. This might have struck those newly arriving at TURNSTILE, had it ever been activated, as it struck me, as the last-supper area.

* We now know there were many more. The figure of 210 comprised the inner group serving the Prime Minister and the World War III War Cabinet.

As a reminder of precisely what might be about to befall, an NBC (nuclear, biological, chemical) Room was nearby as were small, triangular metal discs with 'ATOM' and 'BIO' and 'GAS' stencilled on them for insertion into some unseen slot to signify conditions on Box Hill, a hundred feet above. These little triangles would have been ghastly indications of what had happened to wives and children, the world they had lost. TURNSTILE was a no-families zone.

The former RAF operations room I was shown on my first visit to Corsham (no doubt it was the one mentioned in Guy Lester's letter) was surprisingly small. It could be that the area which would have been used by the War Cabinet and the Chiefs of Staff was bigger and close by and not shown to us* – that we were, in a manner of speaking, not taken through the final 'turnstile' to the last arena of British Central Government.† In fact, on subsequent visits I discovered that the RAF operations room was within the TURNSTILE perimeter.

What of the room my team and I were admitted to that afternoon? Two things, above all, caught one's eye. The once-illuminated board beneath the ceiling listing the various alert states and the two murals on the wall, one of a tiny boxer knocking out a grinning and much larger opponent, the other of wrestlers in action. Just through the door was a large and very striking depiction of cricket on a village green. On the table lay a guide to radiation protection and some old maps. Like the furniture (standard Ministry of Works chairs), they were damp, dirty and mildewy. A train in Box Tunnel could just be heard beneath.

Somewhere nearby, towards the end of the transition (as outlined in the Stephens memo for the Queen) from MACMORRIS to VISITATION, it was planned that a human machine of 210 crown servants would swing into action. Who were they and what do their ranks and functions tell us about the overall purpose of TURNSTILE? The Queen herself was not to be with her Prime Minister and War Cabinet. She would not have had to wait for Stephens's brief in 1965 to know that.

---

* This turned out to be true.

† I suspected this was what is referred to as the 'Prime Minister's Map Room' in the list of those earmarked to go to TURNSTILE on page 266. This also turned out to be correct.

Planning for her evacuation to a safe place began in the time of her first Private Secretary, Sir Alan 'Tommy' Lascelles.[16] Once the royal yacht *Britannia* was commissioned in 1954, the plan was to get her aboard and out of danger during a period of international tension.[17] *Britannia* possessed good communications equipment (by the standards of the day), capable of reaching anywhere on the globe.[18]

The war planners realized that, as one insider put it, 'It made no sense to have the Queen with the War Cabinet in case the whole lot were wiped out together.' With an enduring sense of the personal royal prerogatives, it was appreciated that the Queen would need to appoint a new Prime Minister and senior ministers to replace the old set, if other politicians had survived, once it was safe for *Britannia* to sail back to her shattered kingdom.[19]

So who *was* earmarked for TURNSTILE? Very few would have known, including 'Turnstilers' themselves, until shortly before the cars and the train set off west. Chapter III of the 1963 MOD War Book, entitled 'Alternative War Headquarters', is the best guide we have of the run-up period before the manning of TURNSTILE. It is worth reproducing in full, even though the sections of the Government War Book referred to remain classified. At the time of my visit, we did not know where the designated departure point in London was.* We shall never know how many of those instructed to prepare for TURNSTILE would have obeyed rather than slipping out of Whitehall and back to their homes and families ('Turnstilers', after all, would include some of the people best and most graphically informed of what hydrogen bombs do).

Since the first edition of this volume was published in March 2002, I have had a number of conversations covering this very point. A retired official, who at the time of the Cuban missile crisis was private secretary to one of the senior ministers who would have accompanied Macmillan to TURNSTILE had the crisis continued and triggered the 'last redoubt' contingency, told me he would have asked his boss if the instruction to accompany him was 'an order'. If the answer had been 'yes', he would have gone. If the answer had been 'no', he would have joined his wife and family at home in Kent.[20]

* We do now (see page 275).

At the time of the missile crisis, Geoffrey Harris was Private Secretary to Sir Robert Scott, Permanent Secretary at the Ministry of Defence. He recalled a conversation with Derek Ansell, Private Secretary to Frank Mottershead, the MOD Deputy Secretary responsible for nuclear retaliation procedures:

He said that he and Mottershead had a conversation in which they speculated on the possible location of TURNSTILE. They concluded that probably it was somewhere in the Mendips. Now it could be that Mottershead knew the location, but for reasons of good security, pretended that he did not know. But there was not a great deal of point in fooling his private secretary in this way. We also discussed how likely it was that, if it looked like a nuclear strike was imminent, and that the headquarters should be manned, all those who were told to go would actually do so, leaving their families to face oblitera-tion. We thought that some would refuse to go. I do not know whether those who were on the list to go knew of their designation much in advance.[21]

Certainly Sir Derek Mitchell, who, as Principal Private Secretary to both Sir Alec Douglas-Home and Harold Wilson, would have been one of the two No. 10 private secretaries earmarked to travel west with the Prime Minister to TURNSTILE, did not know he had been so desig-nated until he read the first edition of this book. 'I was never directly involved', he said, 'but knew many of the UK participants as colleagues.'[22]

Very few people indeed would have known those intended for TURNSTILE until Appendix D to the 1963 MOD War Book was declassified in late 2000 with its depiction of the World War III War Cabinet organization – the list given here.[23]

		Total numbers required
(1) *Prime Minister and War Cabinet*		
(a) *Prime Minister*	1	
Private Secretaries	2	
Executive Officers	2	
Clerical Officers/Shorthand Typists	4	9
(b) *Other Ministers of War Cabinet rank*	5	
Personal Staff	10	15

		Total numbers required
(2) *Chief of the Defence Staff and Staff*		
Chief of the Defence Staff	1	
Personal Staff	2	
D.C.D.S. or A.C.D.S.	1	
Staff Officers	4	
Clerical Officers	2	
Shorthand Typists	2	12
(3) *Civil Secretariat*		
(staffed by Cabinet Office)		
Secretary to Cabinet	1	
Private Secretary	1	
Deputy Secretary/Under Secretary	1	
(4) *Military Secretariat (Chiefs of Staff Secretariat)*		
Secretary	1	
Deputy Secretary	1	
G.S.O.1.	3	
G.S.O.2	3	
Clerical Officers	2	
Shorthand Typists	3	13
(5) *Ministry of Defence*		
(a) Deputy Secretary	1	
Under/Assistant Secretary	1	
H.E.O./E.O.	1	
P.A.	1	
Clerk	1	5
(b) *Directorate of Forward Plans*	2	2
(c) *Chief Scientific Adviser*	2	2
(d) *Co-ordinator, Communications-Electronics Policy*	2	2
(e) *British Communications-Electronics Board*		
Deputy Director	1	
Serving Officers	4	
Experimental Officers etc.	3	
Higher Clerical Officer	1	
P.A.	1	
Typist	1	11
(f) *London Communications Security Agency*	2	2
(6) *Joint Planning Staff*		
Deputy or Assistant Secretary	1	
Clerical Officer	1	

			Total numbers required
Team {	G.S.O.1	1	
{	G.S.O.2 – F section	3	
Copy Typists		3	9
(7) *Joint Intelligence Committee*			
(a) Secretariat			
	Secretary	1	
	G.S.O.1.	1	
	Principal	1	
	Clerical Officers	3	6
(b) *Senior Representative*			
(Service Ministries.)			
J.I.B. (2), M.I.5			
M.I.6., G.C.H.Q.			8
(c) *Intelligence Staffs*			
	Admiralty	2	
	War Office	5	
	Air Ministry	7	
	M.I.6.	3	
	G.C.H.Q.	2	
	J.I.B.	5	
	Security Service	1	
	C.I.A. Representatives	2	
	Canadian Liaison Offr.	1	
	G.C.H.Q. Communications Staff	4	
	F.O. Monitors	3	
	M.I.6. Communications Staff	4	39

(8) *Combined Registry and Committee and Distribution Sections*

	From Cabinet Office	From Ministry of Defence	
H.E.O.	1		
E.O.'s	2		
C.O.'s	3	3	
Messengers	3	3	15

(9) *War Cabinet Signal Registry*
(staffed by Ministry of Defence)

H.C.O.'s		1	
C.O's		4	5

	From Cabinet Office	From Ministry of Defence	Total numbers required
(10) *Typing Pools*			
Chief Super-intendent	1		
Supervisors		2	
Typists	4	5	
Duplicator Operators	1	2	15
(11) *Prime Minister's Map Room*			
(a) Captain R.N., Colonel, or Group Captain	1		
(b) *Admiralty Component*			
Senior watchkeeper (Cdr.)	1		
Watchkeepers (Lt. Cdrs.)	3		
Chief Clerk (FO)	1		
Clerks (typists)	2		
Orderlies	3		
(c) *War Office Component*			
Senior Watchkeeper (Lt. Col.)	1		
Watchkeepers (Majors)	3		
Supervising Clerk (WO1)	1		
Chief Clerk (Sgt.)	1		
Clerks (Typists)	2		
Draughtsmen	3		
(d) *Air Ministry Office Component*			
Senior Watchkeeper (Wg. Cdr)	1		
Watchkeepers (Sqn. Ldrs.)	3		
Chief Clerk (Sgt.)	1		
Clerks (Typists)	2		
Orderlies	3	32	
GRAND TOTALS		210	

This tally neatly describes the innermost circle of the Cold War secret state, those 'special areas of Whitehall', as Sir Frank Cooper, former permanent secretary at the Ministry of Defence, described them, 'which really concentrated on the immense problems that the rise of the Soviet state and its scientific and technological progress created' and those 'special mechanisms, limited to a small number of people who were there essentially to deal with this kind of problem. And, obviously, as it potentially involved war or peace, the Prime Minister was always the epicentre of it.'[24] There was, however, 'no one from the Treasury . . . on the TURNSTILE passenger list'.[25]

That war-or-peace decision, in the era when the British deterrent was carried by a manned V-bomber aircraft, had to be made in a matter of minutes to get the planes airborne, and slightly longer to authorize their flying beyond the start-line – the point of no return. No time here for Treasury caveats about the use of expensive resources. These were the kind of decisions a Prime Minister and a War Cabinet might have had to take very shortly after passing through Door 48 at TURNSTILE. Philip Allen of the Home Office, himself earmarked to go under Box Hill with the Home Secretary, pondered after his time on the Strath Committee just how the plans would work in practice if it came to a transition to war.[26] Like Allen, Sir Frank Cooper, too, had his doubts when we talked about it for BBC Radio 4's *The Top Job* programme in the summer of 2000:

HENNESSY: Can I ask you . . . about the planning for the dispersal of government if it really had looked that World War III was imminent and the management of the residual state – what would have been left, heaven knows, after the attack – from the dispersed governments in these bunkers around the country and, above all, the one that the Prime Minister and the inner group would have gone to in Wiltshire . . . ? Could you tell me about the exercising of that? I know you were involved in it. Did British Prime Ministers ever go and sit in it [TURNSTILE] and play out their role?

COOPER: I'm a bit of a heretic about this dispersed government working smoothly under nuclear attack. I never really believed in it primarily because it was going to be such a shambles if anything like that did happen. And a picture of chaps sitting underground thinking calmly and clearly in the depths of some country shire just doesn't seem to me a likely picture . . . It was right to plan for this because it might have been possible – a big 'might' – over time to recover some degree of order through the country as a whole. And it was certainly right to have places all over the country from which you could hope to restore some kind of government and make all kinds of arrangements from medical to food. So that *did* make sense, but their sort of fingertip control over nuclear warfare seemed to me a contradiction in terms, quite frankly. I think some people certainly did practise . . . But the ministers practised in London as far as I know. I never knew a minister to go down.

HENNESSY: When you took ministers through this . . . how did it affect them?

COOPER: It was very confusing, I think, to most of them. It was very difficult to follow . . . They were awed with the responsibility of it and whether they'd get it right if it ever did happen . . . I certainly had doubts as to what would happen if it was for real and whether people would have the courage to do this, or the courage *not* to do it just as importantly – in fact, probably more importantly . . . It's the most horrifically awful decision you could possibly contemplate.[27]

It is worth examining carefully the mix of advisers a 1960s or 1970s Prime Minister compelled to contemplate such awfulness would have had at his disposal to help him 'get it right' in TURNSTILE had the whole set reached Box Hill in time.

I reckon one has to start with a cluster in the middle of the list in the MOD War Book. Under 'Intelligence Staffs' one finds space for two 'senior representatives of MI6', presumably 'C', the Chief of the Secret Intelligence Service, and a senior colleague, together with three MI6 staffers and an 'MI6 Communications Staff' of four. There were those among the war-planning community who thought that once the first nuclear weapon had been launched, by whichever side, irreversible escalation would take place until, the arsenals spent, the world would succumb to the Neville Shute *On the Beach* scenario. Writing in the mid-1950s, Shute predicted the consequence of 'The short, bewildering war [in the second half of 1961] . . . the war of which no history had ever been written or ever would be written now, that had flared all round the northern hemisphere and had died away with the last seismic record of explosion on the thirty-seventh day'.[28]

Others, however, thought the process would be neither as rapid nor as teleological – that there would be time for hotlines to buzz between the bunkers containing the heads of government of the thermonuclear powers. As we have seen, the 1968 INVALUABLE exercise was built around just such an assumption. In the first edition of this book, I recalled one insider speculating that the British Prime Minister, using MI6's separate and secure means of communication, could have instructed the MI6 Station Chief in Moscow to break cover, make contact with the Soviet leadership, announce plainly who he really was and convey the PM's message to Khrushchev or, later, Brezhnev.[29] An intelligence figure extremely well placed to know subsequently told me that such a role had never been planned for the head of the SIS contingent in the British Embassy.[30] Yet the growing preoccupation about war-through-inadvertence made thinking about possible last-minute procedures to prevent the first, limited nuclear exchange spiralling into the Neville Shute nightmare make sense in that world of desperate possibility.

One UK planner, whose experience spanned the 1960s and the 1970s, said of his craft:

In the end you had to do it because the other side might be irrational and one mustn't forget either the notorious flock of geese appearing on the radar as incoming missiles. What if, late at night with several vodkas inside them, Brezhnev and co. were approached by the Russian military saying 'you have but minutes to decide what to do'?

The same applied to both sides. In the UK there was a difference between the V-force days, when you did only have minutes to decide [to get the bombers airborne], and Polaris when you could wait.[31]

As we have seen, the Royal Navy's Polaris submarines took over the deterrent role from the RAF's V-bombers in June 1969.[32]

Had TURNSTILE ever gone operational and the Prime Minister been faced with the ultimate decision, who would have comprised his War Cabinet? The plan allowed for five 'Other Ministers of War Cabinet rank' with two 'personal staff' apiece.[33] From Chiefs of Staff planning papers for 1959, when the possible future use of TURNSTILE was very much in mind (by the last months of that year 'Structural Work for [the government's World War III] headquarters [was] almost complete, and the installation of communications [had] begun'[34]), we have precise information about which groups of ministers the very senior military would brief at the last pre-attack stage. On receipt of a 'tactical warning, i.e., when attack is imminent and the Allies have received definite information of an enemy attack having been launched, probably by the identification of enemy aircraft or missiles on the radar screen',[35] the Chiefs would proceed to a meeting with the Prime Minister and '(a) the Home Secretary, (b) the Foreign Secretary, (c) the Minister of Defence, (d) the Secretary of the Cabinet'.[36]

So, TURNSTILE planning allowed for two more *ad hominem* appointments to the War Cabinet by the Prime Minister. If the War Book drill had been followed, he would do this 'on the institution of a Precautionary Stage'.[37] At which point:

(a) Secretary of the Cabinet invites Prime Minister to select team of Ministers to proceed to TURNSTILE when order to man is given.
(b) Cabinet considers if staff designated for TURNSTILE should be warned.[38]

Three further Cabinet decisions were required before the microcosm of central government moved west to the Cotswold Station:

Cabinet decision to warn staff selected for TURNSTILE.
Cabinet decision to man TURNSTILE.
Cabinet decision to transfer control to TURNSTILE.[39]

The niceties of Cabinet government were to be preserved almost to the end.

I say 'almost' because it was a prime ministerial decision to author-ize the launch of the 'Yellow Sun' or 'Blue Steel' H-bombs or, later, the Polaris missiles, as both Jim Callaghan and Alec Home have made plain to me.[40] Following the 1961 rethink, the Cabinet Office group on retaliation procedures listed among its assumptions that

(a) The Centre of Government, including the Prime Minister, would remain in the Whitehall area during a precautionary period, though the alterna-tive seat of Government and the Regions would be manned by selected Ministers and officials . . .
(b) Two Deputies to the Prime Minister would be appointed in peacetime and one of them would be available to act as the Prime Minister's deputy for purposes of nuclear retaliation during any period, however short, when the Prime Minister was not immediately available.[41]

It is, I think, very likely (though not certain) that the Cabinet meeting Harold Macmillan planned for the afternoon of Sunday 28 October

1962 would have authorized a move to a Precautionary Stage had Khrushchev not backed down over Cuba that lunchtime. Indeed, at what was originally meant to be his pre-Cabinet meeting with the Chiefs of Staff, Peter Thorneycroft, the Minister of Defence, told his military professionals that in the changed circumstances he 'did not . . . consider that any immediate precautionary measures were necessary'.[42]

Had the crisis not eased and had the Cabinet agreed to the institution of the Precautionary Stage, who would have comprised the inner core of Macmillan's War Cabinet? His Foreign Secretary, Alec Home; his Home Secretary, Henry Brooke; plus Thorneycroft. It is likely that the First Secretary of State and Deputy Prime Minister, Rab Butler, would have filled the fourth slot. It was not known which of these was the number one designated deputy after Selwyn Lloyd had been sacked as Chancellor of the Exchequer the previous July as the most prominent victim of the 'Night of the Long Knives', when Macmillan purged a third of his Cabinet.[43]*

Within a couple of years Home was Prime Minister himself. Deep into his retirement (though not a word passed between us about TURN-STILE, a codename I did not know of at that stage), Alec Home talked to me about what one might call the last contingency of retaliation. The former premier told me the Soviet leaders could not bank on a British Prime Minister *not* pressing the button if there were 'great hordes marching right across Europe and demolishing European civilization as we know it'. I said this implied that retaliation might have been authorized before the Red Army's 'hordes' reached the Channel ports in Holland, Belgium and France. Lord Home acknowledged the possibility:

Terrible isn't it, the thought; but reason, cold reason doesn't operate in those circumstances, quite often. And I'm not sure what cold reason would tell you either, if they were on the march.[44]

So, deep in 'The Quarry' – had they reached it in time – with the PM and a small inner group of ministers primed by the Cabinet Secretary on the sequence of decisions to be taken in a matter of minutes, and with the military and the intelligence channels rapidly feeding information (perhaps into the bespoke 'Prime Minister's Map Room' for which

*It is now (see page 283).

TURNSTILE allowed[45]), the Prime Minister would seek the final counsel of his political colleagues, his number one military adviser, the Chief of the Defence Staff, and, perhaps, his Chief Scientific Adviser. If the decision to authorize retaliation were taken, what would that have meant in respect of the nuclear weaponry at the Prime Minister's sole personal disposal (as distinct from the forces assigned to NATO's Supreme Allied Commander Europe or operated under the dual-key with the United States, as were the Thor missiles at the time of Cuba)?

The sheer horror of the decision can never be properly reconstructed (and not just, mercifully, because the retaliation decision was never reached). And we cannot know how much of the thermonuclear force would have got through to their targets. But this is what the plans envisaged. When the V-force was coming into full operation, the RAF converted its planned nuclear strike capacity to a '30–40 cities' policy[46] (though by the time Macmillan left office in October 1963, improved Soviet air defences had required this to be reduced to sixteen cities[47]). In more detail, the scale of the estimated destruction was

(a) Thirty-five bombs on fifteen cities with populations in excess of 600,000.
(b) Twenty-five bombs on twenty-five cities mostly with a population in excess of 400,000.

It is estimated that when the force is armed with megaton [hydrogen] bombs the casualties per bomb dropped would be of the order of:

(a) killed about 135,000 – total about 8,000,000;
(b) injured about 135,000 – total about 8,000,000.[48]

The successor system to the V-force was intended to enable a British Prime Minister to wreak havoc on a comparable scale. 'Polaris deterrent', the small group of ministers on Harold Wilson's Ministerial Committee on Nuclear Policy (PN) were told at the end of 1967,

has been planned to have a capacity, with three submarines on station, to threaten simultaneous destruction to thirty major cities in Western Russia, and we have hitherto considered that to constitute a deterrent credible in political and military terms.[49]

These are roughly the statistics that all premiers in post during what might be called the TURNSTILE years (that is from Macmillan to Thatcher) would have carried in their heads. The figures of eight million dead plus eight million wounded are what would have stuck in my mind if I had received that briefing during the first days of my premiership, and they would have been unbearably vivid had I found myself in TURNSTILE with but minutes in which to make the decision.

That was the extent of my knowledge of the last redoubt in 2001–3 when *The Secret State* was written and published. What extra is known in 2009–10? The Ministry of Defence and the Cabinet Office declassified the 'secret' of Corsham in 2004. As a result, in June 2006 I was able to take a party of my research students to inspect those parts I had been unable to reach five years earlier.[50] With us was Sir Kevin Tebbit, who, as Permanent Secretary to the Ministry of Defence, had been instrumental in the declassification of TURNSTILE. We were able to see the substantial 1960s-style telephone exchange; the BBC studio from where the Prime Minister might have spoken to the country and the world; and the little room in which the Caversham monitoring team would have listened to Radio Moscow or the broadcasts from the Soviet equivalent of the TURNSTILE BBC cell.

What would have been Harold Macmillan's lair in 1962, had Cuba triggered World War III, was identifiable both from the TURNSTILE telephone directory[51] and from the fact that it is the only room with its own bath and loo *en suite*. It is the most austere room imaginable, carved out of the limestone, with a cold concrete floor and separated from his private office by breeze-block walls. As I had imagined in 2001, the Prime Minister's Map Room was *the* place of decision[52] and, for that reason, for me the most chilling part of the entire bunker.

It is about 50 feet long and 30 feet wide, lit with fluorescent lights and with a large whiteboard at one end (a small-scale, austerity version of Dr Strangelove's 'Big Board' in the classic 1964 Stanley Kubrick/ Peter Sellers film of that name[53]). Overlooking it is a viewing area behind a pane of glass – a decision-takers' gallery – which old Cabinet Office hands believe is where a Prime Minister, advised by the Chief of the Defence Staff, would have made the awesome judgement to authorize nuclear release.[54] As far as can be ascertained, only one official Cabinet Office meeting has been held in the Corsham Map Room – a gathering of its Advisory Group on Security and Intelligence Records chaired by Tessa Stirling, then head of the Cabinet Office's History, Records and Openness Unit, on 10 September 2008.[55]

TURNSTILE is a huge installation linked by a network of underground roads (with their own street names) along which visitors sweep on one of the mine manager Andy Quinn's trucks en route for the area where the inner core of 210 would cluster round the Prime Minister and the War Cabinet. We now know that during a Precautionary Stage a mini-Whitehall would have arrived too and been placed in a satellite system of offices, canteens and dormitories around the inner citadel. The plan embraced 4,000 of them from a swathe of government departments.[56] (By a statistical coincidence the British Forces' Post Office number for TURNSTILE, which families were to be given as farewells were made, was BFPO 4000.)[57]

The 'Check Point' for Turnstilers was to be Addison Road Station (now renamed Olympia), next to the Olympia exhibition centre. Special trains would carry them west to Warminster and buses would take them to the nearby army base at the School of Infantry on the edge of Salisbury Plain. After being fed and watered, the Turnstilers were to travel inconspicuously in army lorries up the country roads through Westbury, Trowbridge and Bradford on Avon, turning off the B-road a few miles short of Corsham.[58] Miniature versions of the TURNSTILE plans governed those ministers and officials destined for the regional seats of government. The whole enterprise was codenamed Operation REED (see diagram on page 276).

At least one family was given a hint of what would happen to Dad if Armageddon loomed. Sir Walter Marshall was Chief Scientific Adviser to the Department of Energy in the late 1970s and, as his son Jonathan recalled after reading the first edition of this book, his father (later Lord Marshall of Goring)

never told us where the bunker was but always described that he would pass 'very near to us' on the way there . . . We lived in Goring-on-Thames . . . and our house backed onto the railway line that runs from Paddington to Box Hill. The close proximity of our house and the railway line on the route of the 'final journey' clearly played on his mind. He told us that he often contemplated jumping off the train and literally landing in the back garden – a very interesting insight into the mindset of the chosen few who would

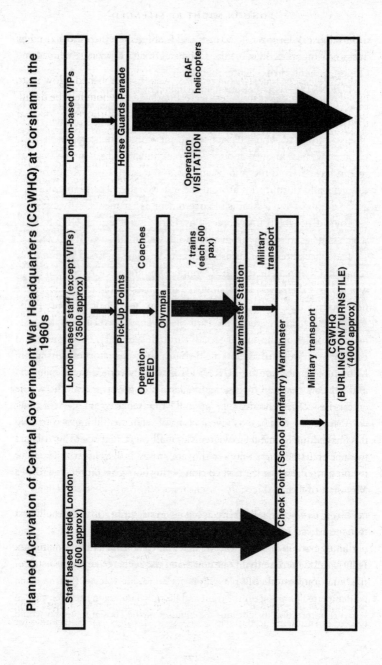

Planned Activation of Central Government War Headquarters (CGWHQ) at Corsham in the 1960s

make this trip. Remember, he was passionate about the non-destructive use of nuclear energy and for him bombs were the 'dark side' of what he believed in.[59]

Files released since *The Secret State* was first published allow us to know who the bunker ministers were and those to whom fell the dreadful duty of being alternative decision-takers for authorizing nuclear release if the Prime Minister was dead or out of reach. The first selections were made by Harold Macmillan in early October 1961 as the Berlin crisis passed through one of its particularly fraught phases (the end of the month was to see a stand-off, as telegenic as it was frightening, between Soviet and US tanks at Checkpoint Charlie between the eastern and western zones of Berlin[60]). As the Cabinet Secretary, Sir Norman Brook, was on leave, it fell to his deputy, Freddie Bishop, to brief Macmillan on the next steps, which he did on 5 October 1961 (the Corsham bunker was codenamed BURLINGTON at this stage).

Brook had drafted a brief for Macmillan on 13 September 1961 which suggests this was the first time the Cold War secret state had got as far as designating who went where to do what should World War III loom. 'I undertook', Brook reminded Macmillan,

to prepare lists of the Ministers who, in such an emergency, would (i) stay in London, (ii) proceed to Regional Headquarters and (iii) go to Burlington.

. . . I now attach a list showing a possible distribution of senior Ministers on this basis. The appendix gives a list of junior ministers who would either remain in London or be available, if necessary, for other duties. In compiling this I have assumed that the Leader of the House must remain in Whitehall and that one of the Ministers who would be nominated as one of your deputies for the purpose of authorising nuclear retaliation would go to Burlington. I have also assumed that the Secretary of State for Scotland would be in Scotland.[61]

The great Whitehall technician was coolly preparing for the worst in its most secret and starkest form.

Let us examine the nuclear deputies first. In his brief for Macmillan, Bishop said, 'I realise that these are matters which are not only distasteful but complicated', but

in seeking your approval for these lists for planning purposes I must bring to your attention the need to select two senior Ministers as your Deputies for the purposes of authorising nuclear retaliation, in the event that you yourself might not be immediately available. The proposal previously made to you [by Norman Brook] was that, when the precautionary stage had to be instituted, you would appoint a First Deputy who would act in this respect for you in London, and a Second Deputy who would be available in BURLINGTON, if communications with London failed.

The selection of the two senior Ministers must therefore be made with an eye on the lists of Ministers attached to Sir Norman Brook's minute of 13th September. It would, for example, be satisfactory if you were to select as your Deputies the Home Secretary [Rab Butler] (who it is proposed would remain in London), and the Chancellor of the Exchequer [Selwyn Lloyd] (who is to go to BURLINGTON). At some point the two ministers should be told and informed of their responsibilities.[62]

There was no question, said Bishop, of telling the substantial number of other ministers involved 'until an emergency is imminent'.[63]

The following day, in his scrawly handwriting, Macmillan, striking a macabre and Shakespearian note, wrote on Bishop's minute:

I agree the following –

First Gravedigger	Mr Butler
Second Gravedigger	Mr Lloyd
HM	
6/10/61.[64]	

Macmillan sent his letters to Butler and Lloyd on 18 October 1961. They were both sombre and explicit (the file suggests the draft had been prepared by a combination of Norman Brook and William Geraghty, the Cabinet Office's expert on nuclear retaliation procedures[65]). 'I have been considering', Macmillan wrote,

what arrangements should be made to ensure that in a time of grave international tension political authority, on behalf of the government, will always be immediately available for the purposes of nuclear retaliation if this should be required.
. . . the decision to launch nuclear weapons is one of such gravity that it should clearly be taken by Ministers, or by the Prime Minister on behalf of the Government, if it is humanly possible to arrange this. But it is the essence

of the strategic deterrent that it will be launched without fail if an enemy should attack us first with nuclear weapons, and modern developments have made it possible that the first warning of attack may be received only a few minutes before missiles land.

. . . current arrangements provide that if a nuclear attack is delivered, or is known to have been launched, I am to be consulted immediately: but if this proves impossible, the competent military authority [Commander-in-Chief RAF Bomber Command], if he is certain that an attack has in fact been made, has authority to order nuclear retaliation in the last resort without ministerial authority. This is the only practicable arrangement in the event of a nuclear attack on this country in what would otherwise be normal conditions of peace – in other words, 'a bolt from the blue'.

But, Macmillan added, 'a "bolt from the blue", which implies the failure of the deterrent policy, and which would clearly require immediate retaliation, is unlikely'.

So here is where the nuclear deputies came in.

A more likely situation would arise from an increase in international tension to the point where the Government would decide to institute the Precautionary Stage. At that stage it would be my duty . . . [that] . . . I should arrange to be immediately accessible myself at all times, as far as this is physically possible; and I should be in close touch with the President of the United States, with our other allies and with the military commanders of NATO and of our own Services. Nevertheless, there would almost certainly be some occasions when I could not be reached for immediate consultation, for instance if I were moving by car from one place to another; and I propose to nominate a Minister to act as my First Deputy, in London, for this purpose at such times.'

At this point, Geraghty (a classical scholar who had served in the Royal Horse Artillery in the war before returning to the War Office, which he had joined after Oxford in 1939) or Brook drafted one of the silkiest lines in which utter disaster has ever been couched.

There is also the possibility that London might be silenced before the necessary consultations could take place. I propose therefore to nominate another Minister as my Second Deputy from among those who would go to the alternative headquarters of the central government [BURLINGTON].

. . . It will be necessary for the First Deputy to be available to assume responsibility during any period, however short, when I am necessarily out of touch with my main communications . . . The Second Deputy will be housed at the alternative headquarters of the central government, and will have no Parliamentary or other duties which will require him to move away from his communications there. He will be in continuous touch with developments in London and will know immediately if contact is broken that he has assumed responsibility.

Macmillan's letter then informed Butler and Lloyd about each other's appointment as a nuclear deputy, adding that 'I do not propose, until the Precautionary Stage is declared to decide which will be First and which Second Deputy (that is, which of you will remain in London and which will go to the alternative headquarters of the central government').

Macmillan concluded by attaching two notes: one on the arrangements for deputizing for him, the other on the joint nuclear decision-taking procedures with the US President and the conversations needed with NATO's Supreme Allied Commander Europe before R-hour for nuclear release is declared.[66] 'I should be glad to know', he added, 'that these arrangements are acceptable to you', telling them that, in due course, they would be invited to exercise the retaliation procedures.[67]

Lloyd replied the same day, saying, 'I am of course ready to help in any way I can, and the arrangements you outline are entirely acceptable to me.'[68] Butler replied the following day, informing Macmillan that the 'arrangements you have set out in your letter are fully acceptable to me and I will of course be equally ready to take on the duty in London or in the alternative headquarters'.[69]

Thanks to Macmillan's nuclear retaliation file we also know which ministers would have gone where if bunkerdom befell Britain in the final hours of peace before a third world war. Apart from Butler and Lloyd, the ministers concerned will have gone to their graves knowing nothing about their wartime destinations. As a veteran Cabinet Office transition-to-war planner put it, 'They definitely didn't know.'[70] The list was tweaked a bit, and, naturally, it changed every time there was a reshuffle or a general election in which the government changed (we shall examine Harold Wilson's dispositions shortly).

Here is the end-of-the-world cut as attached to Brook's memo to Macmillan of 13 September 1961:

1. LONDON

Prime Minister [Harold Macmillan]
Home Secretary [R. A. Butler]
Foreign Secretary [Lord Home]
Commonwealth Secretary [Duncan Sandys]
Minister of Defence [Harold Watkinson]
Chancellor of the Duchy of Lancaster [Iain Macleod (from 9 October 1961)]
Secretary of State for Air [Julian Amery]
Chief Secretary to the Treasury [Henry Brooke (from 9 October 1961)]
Minister of State, Board of Trade [Sir Keith Joseph (from 9 October 1961)]
Lord Chancellor [Lord Kilmuir]
Attorney-General [Sir Reginald Manningham-Buller]
Minister of Works [Lord John Hope]
Minister without Portfolio [Lord Mills (from 9 October 1961)]
Minister of State for Colonial Affairs [Lord Perth]
Secretary, Department of Technical Co-operation [Dennis Vosper]

Plus at least one Junior Minister from all Departments whose Ministers go to Regions or to Burlington [I have not listed these] and the Government Whips.

2. BURLINGTON

Chancellor of the Exchequer [Selwyn Lloyd]
Colonial Secretary [Reginald Maudling (from 9 October 1961)]
President of the Board of Trade [Frederick Erroll]
Lord Privy Seal [Edward Heath]
Minister of Agriculture [Christopher Soames]
First Lord of the Admiralty [Lord Carrington]
Secretary of State for War [John Profumo]
Minister of Health [Enoch Powell]
Minister of State, Home Office [David Renton]
Minister of State, Scottish Office [Lord Craigton]
Solicitor-General [Sir Jocelyn Simon]

3. REGIONS

	Senior Ministers	Supporting Ministers
Wales	Minister of Housing [Charles Hill [from 9 October 1961)]	Lord Brecon, Minister of State for Welsh Affairs
Northern	Minister of Transport [Ernest Marples]	Mr Vane, Joint Parliamentary Secretary, Ministry of Agriculture
North-Eastern	Minister of Power [Richard Wood]	Mr Taylor, Parliamentary Under Secretary, Air Ministry
North-Midland	Minister of Aviation [Peter Thorneycroft]	Mr Godber, Minister of State, Foreign Office
Eastern	Minister of Labour [John Hare]	Mr Braine, Joint Parliamentary Under Secretary Commonwealth Relations Office
Southern	Lord President [Lord Hailsham]	Mr Sharples, Joint Parliamentary Secretary, Ministry of Pensions
South-Western	Minister of Education [Sir David Eccles]	Mr Hay, Joint Parliamentary Secretary, Ministry of Transport
Midland	Paymaster-General [Henry Brooke (from 9 October 1961)]*	Mr Fraser, Parliamentary Under Secretary, Colonial Office
North-Western	Postmaster-General [Reginald Bevins]	Mr Fletcher-Cooke, Joint Parliamentary Under Secretary, Home Office
South-Eastern	Minister of Pensions [John Boyd-Carpenter]	Mr Thompson, Parliamentary Under Secretary, Ministry of Works

Scotland

The Secretary of State for Scotland [John Maclay] supported by the Scottish Law Officers and Parliamentary Under-Secretaries of State (except that one would be in London).

---

* A problem here. Henry Brooke combined the posts of Chief Secretary to the Treasury and Paymaster-General. So, according to this list, he had to split himself in two – one half to remain in London; the other to the Midlands bunker near Kidderminster.

AVAILABLE FOR OTHER WORK

Economic Secretary, <u>Treasury</u> – Mr Barber
Joint Parliamentary Under-Secretaries
<u>Commonwealth Relations Office</u> – Duke of Devonshire
<u>Foreign Office</u> – Lord Lansdowne and Mr Thomas
<u>Home Office</u> – Lord Bathurst
Joint Parliamentary Secretaries
<u>Housing</u> – Lord Jellicoe
<u>Trade</u> – Mr Macpherson
<u>Transport</u> – Lord Chesham.[71]

The paper trail of the September–October 1961 who-does-what-and-where review also reveals the plan for who would be helicoptered with the Prime Minister at the last minute from Horse Guards Parade to Box Hill:

Prime Minister and two personal staff officers	3
Ministers	12*
Secretary of the Cabinet	1
Chiefs of Staff	4
Secretary of the Chiefs of Staff Committee	1

This leaves a reserve of 4 which could be added to the list at the last moment.[72]

There were changes to the nuclear deputies after Selwyn Lloyd was purged by Macmillan during his infamous 'Night of the Long Knives' reshuffle in July 1962. On 26 September 1962, a few days before the Cuban missile crisis erupted, Macmillan appointed the Foreign Secretary, Alec Home, as Lloyd's replacement[73] and informed Butler the same day.[74]

Home was keen to know if he would be the deputy chosen to remain in Whitehall with the Prime Minister. He minuted: 'Yes. I agree. I take it I would be the one to stay in London in charge of the Foreign Office.'[75]

His private secretary, Ian Samuel, forwarded it to Tim Bligh, Macmillan's Principal Private Secretary. Bligh tactfully replied:

---

* The twelve senior ministers on the current list of those recommended to remain in London.

You will perhaps have seen that page 4 of the Prime Minister's letter to the Foreign Secretary of September 26 said that the question of which Deputy would go where would not be settled until the Precautionary Stage. So let us hope that this issue is never solved.[76]

That was on 6 October 1962. In the next few days and weeks that issue came closer than ever before or since to being resolved as the Cuban missile crisis took the world to the nuclear rim.

How might bunker government have functioned beneath Box Hill had the nuclear threshold been crossed and World War III raged? When the GEN 735 papers were released to the National Archives they contained a Norman Brook paper from May 1961, 'STOCKWELL: COMMITTEE STRUCTURE', prepared for Harold Macmillan, which gives us an idea. Brook divided the system into four parts:

1: The War Cabinet Organisation.
2: A Home Defence *bloc.*
3: Representatives of the Service Departments and overseas Departments.
4: 'Due functioning' home Departments.

With monumental understatement, Brook told Macmillan that:

It is difficult to forecast precisely how the higher direction of the headquarters would be exercised in practice, since the organisation and conditions of work will be unprecedented and, apart from some limited home defence exercises, untried . . . The Ministers at STOCKWELL will have no Parliamentary or constituency duties to perform, and much of the normal peacetime work of Departments will probably have to be abandoned, at least for a time. Ministers may, therefore, be able and may wish to play a greater part than usual in matters of detailed administration, and the distinction between Ministerial and official functions may become blurred.

What Brook called 'the battle for survival' would also mean 'greater integration of military and civil effort than ever before'.

At the apex of the structure Brook placed the War Cabinet, consisting of 'the Prime Minister and five other Ministers, with the Chiefs of Staff and others in attendance as necessary. The War Cabinet Organisation would include the Secretary of the War Cabinet and the Chief of the Defence Staff, and would provide a combined military/civil secretariat for the War Cabinet and the Chiefs of Staff. Beneath the War Cabinet would be the Chiefs of Staff Committee, 'dealing with purely military matters'.

The 'Home Defence *bloc*' would be supervised by a Home Defence (Official) Committee chaired by the Permanent Secretary of the Home Office. Its job would be

(a) to co-ordinate the work of the civil and military organs of Government and of the State corporations, private industry, etc. on the home front;

(b) to give decisions on such work in accordance with delegated authority or within the framework of approved policy;

(c) to submit other questions for decision by the War Cabinet.

Brook urged Macmillan to commission a committee under his, Brook's, chairmanship to sort out competing priorities, such as 'over the allocation of resources to the restoration of, say, a port on the one hand or a V-bomber station on the other, or in the allocation of shipping to civil or military cargoes'. Other than that, other committees that 'are found to be necessary can very rapidly be set up at the time', but thought should be given to 'the establishment of an Information Committee to deal with day-to-day guidance to the public, and a Communications Committee to deal with the highly specialised business of maintaining communications from STOCKWELL and elsewhere'.[77]

For all the care Brook put into his 1961 planning, during the Cuban crisis – and for a time afterwards – the speed of events left the planners scrambling to catch up, as we have already seen in the post-Cuba review of 1963–4. The No. 10 retaliation file released since I wrote *The Secret State* adds another, bunker-related fragment to the post-Cuba mosaic. It had to do with the 'nuclear retaliation cell' in TURNSTILE which consisted of 'about six communications personnel from the Air Ministry'[78] whose job it was to relay the Prime Minister's instructions from Corsham to the Commander-in-Chief RAF Bomber Command in his bunker under the Chilterns near High Wycombe for onward transmission (as we shall see in the next chapter) by the Bomber Controller to the V- bomber bases and directly into the aircraft's cockpits.

The plan now was 'to man the nuclear retaliation cell at TURNSTILE

. . . some forty-eight hours ahead of the general order to man TURN-STILE, provided that this could be achieved without endangering the security of TURNSTILE as a whole. This measure is considered essential to ensure that the necessary nuclear retaliation communications at TURNSTILE are fully effective by R Hour.'[79]

By this time Sir Alec Douglas-Home (as he had become on renouncing his earldom) was Prime Minister and it fell to him to choose his own nuclear deputies. On Christmas Eve 1963 Sir Burke Trend, who had replaced Sir Norman Brook as Cabinet Secretary the previous January, gently reminded Alec Douglas-Home that the time had come to decide:

> You may remember that I mentioned to you a short time ago that it would be desirable that you should approve the appointment of two Ministerial Deputies to yourself, who would be empowered to authorise nuclear retaliation if, at the critical moment, you were not available. You said that you would like to reflect further about this; and if you have the opportunity to do so during the holiday, we could then arrange for the necessary instructions to be sent to the selected Ministers early in the New Year.

Trend, like Brook and Bishop before him, was not shy about suggesting names.

> You will recall that Mr Macmillan, when Prime Minister, appointed yourself and Mr Butler as his Deputies for this purpose. I am not sure, however, that the choice need necessarily be determined by seniority; and you may think it would now be appropriate to appoint Mr Butler and either Mr Heath or Mr Selwyn Lloyd or Mr Thorneycroft.

Butler was now Foreign Secretary, Heath President of the Board of Trade, Lloyd back as Lord Privy Seal and Leader of the House of Commons, Thorneycroft Minister of Defence.

> On present plans one of the two Deputies would remain with you in London, while the other would proceed to a separate location from which nuclear retaliation could be authorised even if London were destroyed. It would be convenient if, when you have selected the two Deputies, you would indicate the role which you would like each of them to fill.[80]

The Prime Minister *did* decide over the Christmas period, and commented on the Trend minute.

Butler and Thorneycroft. A word please about the roles. Do we want a third Deputy if Thorneycroft is tied to Defence H.Q. and occupied with its problems? A.D.-H

On New Year's Eve Tim Bligh minuted Burke Trend with the result (which was soon changed, as we shall see in a moment): 'If, as I understand, both the Foreign Secretary and the Minister of Defence are determined to stay in London it might seem appropriate to consider another senior Minister as the distant Deputy, and you might like to put this to the Prime Minister when you talk to him.'[81]

Trend and Douglas-Home had their conversation on 13 January 1964.[82] For reasons unknown, matters moved at a snail's pace thereafter. Not until 14 April 1964 did Trend report to his Cabinet Office people that Douglas-Home had chosen Selwyn Lloyd instead of Peter Thorneycroft as, following his discussion with the Cabinet Secretary, the Prime Minister believed 'that Mr Thorneycroft would be liable to be too preoccupied with other operational questions to be an appropriate deputy for the purpose in question'. The decision was 'that Mr Butler would remain with the Prime Minister in London and Mr Selwyn Lloyd would proceed to the other destination'.[83]

Perhaps it was a rethink about 'the other destination' that had caused the delay. For the draft letters for Butler and Lloyd, prepared by Colonel J. T. Paget (the Coldstream Guardsman who was Commander Stephens's predecessor on the Cabinet Office's nuclear retaliation desk), 'take into account the fact that the Second Deputy will now go to High Wycombe [the RAF Bomber Command bunker], instead of TURN-STILE'. 'I have', Paget informed Trend's deputy, Philip Rogers, 'spoken to Air Chief Marshal Sir Wallace Kyle (Vice Chief of the Air Staff), who confirmed that he does not wish to issue any further instructions for the Second Deputy, but will arrange for him to be fully briefed [a comforting thought!] on arrival at High Wycombe.'[84]

Before the Prime Minister's letters were sent to Butler and Lloyd, Douglas-Home and Trend had a further conversation as Trend recorded in a minute on 27 April 1964:

Authorisation of Nuclear Retaliation

When I mentioned this matter to you a short time ago, you decided that your two 'Deputies' in an emergency which might entail nuclear retaliation should be the Foreign Secretary and the Lord Privy Seal – the former remaining with you in London, the latter proceeding to the Headquarters of Bomber Command. If London remained intact but you were temporarily unavailable, the responsibility for authorising nuclear retaliation would be exercised by Mr Butler. If London itself were wiped out, the responsibility would devolve upon Mr Selwyn Lloyd.

Trend added another refinement to the process of appointing nuclear deputies.

In accordance with precedent, you should now send your Deputies letters on the lines of the attached drafts. It might be convenient if I delivered these personally to the recipients, with a word of explanation.[85]

Douglas-Home signed the letters on 30 April, but a note by the Foreign Secretary's Assistant Private Secretary, Tom Bridges, suggests Trend did not pay his call on Butler till the 10 June.[86]

The brink-of-the-button drill for Butler is spelt out in some detail:

TOP SECRET
ANNEX 1

NOTE OF PROPOSED ARRANGEMENTS FOR THE FUNCTIONING OF THE PRIME MINISTER'S FIRST DEPUTY FOR PURPOSES OF NUCLEAR RETALIATION

(To operate on the introduction of the Precautionary Stage).

1. It will be necessary for the First Deputy to be at all times, unless on occasion exempted by special arrangement with the Prime Minister,

(a) able to reach either No.10 Downing Street or the Prime Minister's Office at the House of Commons within thirty minutes; or such lesser period as may be advised from time to time; and

(b) in immediate telephone communication with both the above places.

2. When for any reason the Prime Minister will, for however short a period, be neither at No. 10 Downing Street nor his office at the House of Commons, his Private Secretary will warn the First Deputy who will go immediately to

No. 10 Downing Street or to the Prime Minister's Office at the House of Commons (as notified at the time) and, on arrival, will confirm with the Prime Minister that he is ready to take over.

3. The Prime Minister will await this confirmation before leaving and, on receiving it, will formally hand over responsibility to the First Deputy.

4. The First Deputy will remain at his post until, on his return to No. 10 Downing Street or to his Office at the House of Commons, the Prime Minister informs him that he has resumed responsibility.[87]

On 10 May Bridges also noted that:

The S of S [Butler] has said that he was asked by Sir B. Trend not to reply to this letter, in spite of its last paragraph. [There is no reason given for this in the file.] I have therefore told Mr [Oliver] Wright [Foreign Affairs Private Secretary in No. 10] at No. 10 that no reply will be sent.

The S of S agrees with the letter.[88]

Lloyd was much quicker off the mark. He replied to Douglas-Home on 8 May that 'I will certainly undertake the task you have assigned me'.[89]

In his letter to Lloyd, Douglas-Home takes him through the drill when, following 'an increase in international tension to the point where the Government would decide to institute the Precautionary Stage', it becomes his [the Prime Minister's]

duty (except for exceptional purposes such as international negotiations) to remain in London and to be immediately accessible myself at all times, as far as this is physically possible; and I should be in close touch with the President of the United States, with other allies and with the military commanders of NATO and of our own Services . . .

At this point Douglas-Home explains the role of the First Deputy in much the same terms as Macmillan had when appointing Lloyd a nuclear deputy in October 1961. Once more the possibility that 'London might be silenced' is put to Lloyd, but this time, the distant deputy will have less far to travel (about 30 miles as opposed to 100):

The Second Deputy will move on my instructions during the Precautionary Stage to Headquarters Bomber Command at High Wycombe. There he will be physically by the side of the A.O.C-in-C [Air Officer Commanding-in-

Chief] of Bomber Command and will be empowered to authorise nuclear retaliation were the A.O.C-in-C for any reason to lose contact with me, or with the First Deputy.[90]

The Douglas-Home/Butler/Lloyd nuclear retaliation triumvirate was in place for but a few months until the Conservative government was narrowly defeated in the general election of 15 October 1964, Harold Wilson becoming Prime Minister on the following afternoon. The doomsday drill had to start all over again and Colonel Paget, with the help of Clive Rose in the Foreign Office,[91] began what turned out to be a protracted process of redrafting the nuclear deputy letters to fit Labour's (eventually futile) pursuit of an Atlantic Nuclear Force and the degree to which it was playing down UK nuclear independence in public (as it had during the election campaign).

Not until 8 January 1965 did Trend discuss the nuclear deputies' drills with Wilson, who decided that Bert Bowden, Lord President of the Council, should be his First Deputy in London with Denis Healey, Secretary of State for Defence, going to the Bomber Command bunker as the Second.[92] (It is noticeable, but far from surprising, that Wilson did not choose his volatile no. 2 in the government, George Brown, First Secretary and Secretary of State for Economic Affairs, to be a nuclear retaliator. Brown's location in a 1960s World War III will be evident in a moment.) Getting the letters off was pressing because Exercise ARABIAN NIGHT, designed to test the UK's nuclear release procedures, was due to take place in mid-March and there were indications that Wilson wanted to take part himself.[93]

A particularly preachy (though in no way inaccurate) version of the letters was circulating among those inside the small circle of officials indoctrinated about nuclear retaliation drills about this time, reflecting the conclusion of a meeting on 20 January 1965 involving Trend, Rogers and Paget that 'the letters . . . should bring out more clearly the present Administration's attitude towards the control and use of nuclear weapons'.[94] The draft read like this:

Despite the abhorrence with which we contemplate the possibility that our nuclear weapons might ever have to be used, and the appalling consequences of a nuclear exchange in general war, we must, however reluctantly, provide against circumstances, however remote we believe them to be, in which the very existence of our country as a free nation may be threatened. In such circumstances, it is of even greater importance that strong, continuous political control should be exercised over the use of our nuclear weapons and that adequate political machinery should exist for consultation with the President of the United States of America, with NATO authorities and with our own military commanders . . .[95]

This opening paragraph did not survive.

When the letters were finally signed by Wilson on 16 July 1965 (and were delivered by hand by Trend to Healey on 19 July and to Bowden on 21 July,[96] Bowden and Healey both writing to Wilson to signify their agreement on 5 August[97]), they opened like this:

Our policy as regards the independent nuclear deterrent is based, of course, on our A.N.F. [Atlantic Nuclear Force] proposals which reflect our readiness to contribute our nuclear forces to a genuinely interdependent Atlantic organisation. But, even if the other countries concerned prove to be willing to enter into this new partnership, it will still be necessary for us to give our formal consent to the use of nuclear weapons by NATO. Moreover, we shall remain directly responsible for any British nuclear forces, e.g. in the Far East, which may remain under national command. I have therefore been giving some thought to the procedures which should govern the decision to use British nuclear weapons, if the risk of nuclear war, which fortunately seems to be coming [sic] more remote, ever became real again.[98]

What had led to the delay?

Fortunately a memo from Sir Burke Trend to Derek Mitchell, Wilson's Principal Private Secretary, of 13 July 1965 (which the Prime Minister read and ticked) explains why:

first, because as you know we are now thinking in terms of an alternative seat of Central Government in war which will not be concentrated in one place but will, in effect, be distributed over several sites;* second, because we are now having to plan for circumstances in which nuclear retaliation, if it

---

* This new contingency planning was so sensitive, and the circle who knew about it so small, that it had its own codeword security classification, TOP SECRET – ACID, which is what Trend's brief to Mitchell carried.

were ever ordered, would be effected not only by the V-bomber force but also by the Polaris submarines. These are new factors, which considerably complicate the earlier drill . . .

The solutions adopted over the next few years (and which are still operational) will be described in the next chapter. But from his memo to Mitchell, it was plain that Trend and his Cabinet Office retaliation team were still some way off thinking them through in the summer of 1965, especially

the very complicated problems of communications which are involved in the concept of conferring authority from several alternative places in the United Kingdom on a submerged nuclear force several thousand miles away! (For example, it is relatively simple to prescribe – as existing instructions prescribe – that, if the competent military authority, i.e. the A.O.C-in-C, Bomber Command, is certain that a nuclear attack has been made on this country but cannot establish contact with any member of the Government, he may, in the last resort, authorise nuclear retaliation himself. It is much more difficult to decide whether a submarine commander should – or, indeed, could – be given a corresponding authority if he were cut off from communication with this country and could not be certain, although he might suspect, that it had been subjected to nuclear attack.)

Nonetheless, it was time for the deputies' letters to be signed, 'and I will then deliver them to the recipients personally in order to explain that they are not necessarily the last word on the subject but should suffice for the time being'.[99] And so they did.

After Bowden's move to become Commonwealth Secretary in August 1966, Michael Stewart, then Secretary of State for Economic Affairs, was appointed his replacement as First Deputy, his letter being handed to him on 28 September 1966.[100] When Stewart replaced George Brown as Foreign Secretary in March 1968, Wilson agreed that he should continue as First Deputy.[101] So he and Denis Healey filled the retaliation slots until the end of the Labour government in June 1970. There was one final change of bunkers in the spring of 1969, a month before Polaris took over the primary deterrent role from the V-force. On Trend's recommendation,[102] Wilson wrote to Healey on 5 May 1969 that

Now the Polaris force is on the point of taking over the United Kingdom deterrent I have decided that, as the Second Nuclear Deputy, you should move, at the appropriate time, to the Headquarters of the C-in-C Western Fleet at Northwood [in Middlesex] instead of to High Wycombe. The other arrangements outlined in my letter of July 16, 1965, remain unchanged.[103]

Michael Stewart was similarly informed.[104]

In October 1965, Wilson agreed 'that the Home Secretary* would be the appropriate minister to accompany the Queen to her war loca-tion'[105] (the Royal Yacht *Britannia*). But not for another year was the wartime dispersal of ministers to the regional seats of government decided and, once again, the two nuclear deputies apart, none of them was to be told. Trend explained to Wilson that the list had been drawn up 'having regard to the form in which the situation (if it ever arose) would be most likely to develop – i.e. mounting tension, culminating in a last-minute political solution – the distribution proposed . . . is right insofar as it concentrates the main weight of Ministerial author-ity and experience where this would be most necessary, namely in London and in the regions, whilst still making adequate allowance for the formation of an alternative Government at TURNSTILE if need be'.[106]

Here is the Precautionary Stage list for June 1966:

REQUIRED IN LONDON
SENIOR MINISTERS

Prime Minister [Harold Wilson]
Lord President of the Council (1st Deputy) [Herbert Bowden]
Lord Chancellor [Lord Gardiner]
Chancellor of the Exchequer [Jim Callaghan]
Secretary of State for Foreign Affairs [Michael Stewart]
Secretary of State for Commonwealth Relations [Arthur Bottomley]
Minister of State, Department of Economic Affairs [Austin Albu]
Ministers of State for Foreign Affairs [Walter Padley and Eirene White]
Minister of Defence for the Royal Navy [Joseph Mallalieu]

---

* The Wilson governments of 1964–70 saw three Home Secretaries, Sir Frank Soskice, Roy Jenkins and Jim Callaghan. In June 1966 Jenkins held the office.

Minister of Defence for the Royal Air Force [Lord Shackleton]
Minister of Defence for the Army [Gerry Reynolds]
Minister of State, Home Office [Alice Bacon]
Minister of State, Scottish Office [George Willis]
Ministers of State, Board of Trade [George Darling and Roy Mason]
Minister of State, Department of Education and Science, [Edward Redhead]
Minister of State, Welsh Office, [George Thomas]
Solicitor-General, [Sir Dingle Foot]

The London team was backed up by 19 junior ministers plus the government whips in the House of Commons and the House of Lords.

ALTERNATIVE SEAT OF GOVERNMENT
TURNSTILE

First Secretary of State and Secretary of State for Economic Affairs [George Brown]
Minister of Housing and Local Government [Dick Crossman]
Lord Privy Seal [Lord Longford]
Minister of Agriculture, Fisheries and Food [Fred Peart]
Minister of Transport [Barbara Castle]
Secretary of State for the Colonies [Fred Lee]
Minister of Power [Richard Marsh]
Minister of Health [Kenneth Robinson]
Minister of Pensions and National Insurance [Margaret Herbison]
Minister of Land and Natural Resources [Fred Willey]
Chancellor of the Duchy of Lancaster [George Thomson]
Minister of Public Building and Works [Reg Prentice]
Minister without Portfolio [Lord Champion]
Chief Secretary, Treasury [John Diamond]
Minister of State for Foreign Affairs [Lord Chalfont]
Minister of State, Commonwealth Relations Office [Judith Hart]
Minister of State, Board of Trade [Lord Brown]
Minster of State, Department of Education and Science [Goronwy Roberts]

HQ BOMBER COMMAND
Secretary of State for Defence (2nd Deputy) [Denis Healey]

ATTENDING THE QUEEN
Secretary of State for the Home Department [Roy Jenkins]*

UN HQ NEW YORK
Minister of State for Foreign Affairs [Lord Caradon]

REGIONS

No. 1 Region (Northern)	Minister without Portfolio [Douglas Houghton] Joint Parliamentary Secretary, Ministry of Pensions [Norman Pentland]
No. 2 Region (North Eastern)	Minister of Aviation [Fred Mulley] Parliamentary Secretary, Board of Trade [Lord Rhodes]
No. 3 Region (North Midland)	Secretary of State for Education and Science [Anthony Crosland] Joint Parliamentary Secretary, Ministry of Agriculture, Fisheries and Food [John Mackie]
No. 4 Region (Eastern)	Minister of Technology [Frank Cousins] Joint Parliamentary Secretary, Ministry of Transport [John Morris]
No. 5 Region (South Eastern)	President of the Board of Trade [Douglas Jay] Joint Parliamentary Secretary, Ministry of Technology [Edmund Dell]
No. 6 Region (Southern)	Minister of Labour [Ray Gunter] Parliamentary Secretary, Ministry of Land and Natural Resources [not known]
No. 7 Region (South Western)	Postmaster General [Tony Benn] Joint Parliamentary Secretary, Home Office [Maurice Foley]
No. 8 Region (Wales)	Secretary of State for Wales [Cledwyn Hughes] Parliamentary Secretary for Wales [Ifor Davies]
No. 9 Region	Paymaster-General [George Wigg]

* I discovered many years later from a Buckingham Palace official that with the Home Secretary in attendance, the Queen would be able to find a quorum to enable her to convene a meeting of the Privy Council (the other two privy councillors with Her Majesty being the Duke of Edinburgh and her Private Secretary). A quorate Privy Council would enable the Queen, for example, to appoint surviving politicians to ministerial posts. The Home Secretary would board the Royal Yacht *Britannia* to join the royal party.

(Midlands)	Joint Parliamentary Secretary, Department of Education and Science [Dennis Howell]
No. 10 Region (North Western)	Minister of Overseas Development [Anthony Greenwood]
	Joint Parliamentary Secretary, Ministry of Housing [James MacColl]
Scotland	Secretary of State for Scotland [Willie Ross]
	Lord Advocate [George Scott]
	Solicitor General for Scotland [James Leechman]
	Parliamentary Secretaries for Scotland [Dickson Mabon and Lord Hughes]

Harold Wilson approved those dispositions on 6 June 1966.[107]

Within a couple of years, as we shall see, they would change significantly because of the question-mark over TURNSTILE in the mid-1960s. Worries about it had in fact begun to swirl even earlier and were put to Harold Macmillan in the spring of 1963. Trend, as part of the wider post-Cuba review, had commissioned an examination of 'the present state of our physical plans for maintaining central Government control during and after a nuclear attack on this country . . .' The 'recent activities of the Committee of 100' (the direct-action offshoot of CND) had added to his worries.[108] Worse still, MI5 had just reported 'the movements of a Soviet Naval Attaché in the neighbourhood of TURN-STILE in the last few days . . .' and the Cabinet Office had long known that the 'location of the headquarters of the central Government in time of war is information which the Russians must be presumed to treat as a major intelligence objective' and that 'the espionage agents of the Soviet Bloc in the United Kingdom will make a serious and continuous effort to obtain this information'.[109]

On first reading Burke Trend's report I thought I had made a connection with the Profumo Affair, which, just a few days later, was about to engulf Macmillan and his government, for the Assistant Russian Naval Attaché at the Soviet Embassy in London in the early 1960s was Captain Eugene Ivanov, who shared the favours of Christine Keeler with Jack Profumo, the Secretary of State for War. But I was wrong. Ivanov had left rapidly for Moscow on 29 January 1963 after Stephen Ward, the

12. (*left*) TURNSTILE calling: untouched underground telephone exchange 1960 vintage.

13. (*below*) 'STUCK HERE 4 ETERNITY': morbid greeting as you enter the TURNSTILE bunker.

14. (*top*) Peter Hudson, the author and David Young in the Prime Minister's Map Room in TURNSTILE: from here nuclear retaliation would have been authorized.

15. (*bottom*) The author in the Prime Minister's room in TURNSTILE.

16. (*top*) TURNSTILE teacups symbolize post-armageddon continuity
of the state.

17. (*bottom*) TURNSTILE canteen: Hamsters optional.

18. (*top*) The alert board for World War III.

19. (*bottom*) 'ATOM': if this had been inserted
into the bunker's slots, the world above
would have been devastated by nuclear attack.

20. The last flying Vulcan, XH558, goes climbing
in the Lake District, Windermere Air Show,
25 July 2009: Red Screes, above the Kirkstone
Pass, near Ambleside, in the background. The
photographer is Ian Finch.

21. (*above*) Sir Michael Quinlan (*far left*) visits former Warsaw Pact adversaries in Hungary, 1992.

22. (*left*) Sir Frank Cooper: the Prime Minister can only authorize nuclear retaliation, not order it.

23. (*top*) Task Force 345: the Northwood bunker under the Chilterns exercises the arrival of the Prime Minister's National Firing Directive.

24. (*middle*) Lieutenant-Commander Peter Noblett, Executive Officer of H.M.S *Vanguard*, carries the firing directive from the Wireless Office to the Control Room accompanied by Lieutenant-Commander, Mitch Puxley, Weapons Engineering Officer.

25. (*bottom*) The Captain of H.M.S *Vanguard*, Commander Richard Lindsey, watches while his officers decode the firing instruction on top of the safe containing codebooks and the Prime Ministers 'last resort' letters.

26. H.M.S *Victorious* about to dive for the launch that never was, 18 May 2009.

27. The launch in the dark: H.M.S *Victorious* fires its D5 Trident missile towards the South Atlantic at 1 a.m. on 25 May 2009. The telemetry instrumentation mast is just visible in the smoke to the right.

osteopath and close friend of Keeler's, warned him the story might be about to break.[110] So the Soviet attaché (a post which the Security Service knew was usually filled by a Russian military intelligence officer[111]) trailed from West London to Wiltshire in May 1963 was probably Ivanov's successor.

Trend reminded Macmillan of the sensitivity of TURNSTILE and its centrality to war planning from the institution of the Precautionary Stage and

from this one place, after nuclear attack, would be controlled all measures necessary for

(i) the prosecution of the war;
(ii) the conduct of Commonwealth and foreign affairs [the bunker had earmarked rooms for several members of the London Diplomatic Corps]
(iii) the maintenance, as far as possible, of the life of the country by means of a system of Regional Seats of Government, where the Commissioners [the ministers allocated to them] would have been told in advance on which matters they should act on their own initiative and on which they should (if possible) obtain direction from TURNSTILE.[112]

Macmillan had taken a close interest in the creation and progress of TURNSTILE,[113] but Trend saw a need to bring him up to date:

It is planned to move approximately 3,750 staff to TURNSTILE of whom about half will be senior civil servants and military officers.

The structural work at the site is virtually complete (except for some refinements of communications). Office equipment, essential working records, rations and other stores are already in position. The capital cost so far has been rather more than £2½ million; and maintenance costs are running at about £150,000 a year. In addition nearly £½ million a year has to be paid to the Post Office as rental for communications.

Here Trend penned his own version of 'STUCK HERE 4 ETERNITY':

The site itself is in a former quarry; and the overhead protection would not only be completely inadequate against a direct hit but would be most unlikely to survive a nuclear weapon of even ten megatons if it fell within a mile and a half radius. If the Russians made TURNSTILE itself a direct target, the accuracy of their missiles would virtually ensure a hit within a half mile radius. Moreover, if they knew the true significance of TURNSTILE, they will probably use a much larger weapon.[114]

When Trend's May 1963 brief for Macmillan was declassified, we learned that, in fact, as early as August 1962 (i.e. pre-Cuba), because of 'doubts about the degree to which the secrecy of TURNSTILE might already have been compromised; and . . . the possibility that, even without its true significance being known, it was none the less included in the list of Russian targets',[115] the Prime Minister had 'authorised . . . the development of LINSTOCK as a reserve seat of central Government in war' to be built as another underground bunker alongside the Midlands Regional Seat of Government near Kidderminster. Though work had not yet started on LINSTOCK, which was to be 'self-supporting and physically separate' from the West Midlands RSG.[116] (Work on LINSTOCK was postponed in March 1964[117] and was never completed.)

At the same time as authorizing LINSTOCK, Macmillan approved TACK – 'the provision of a number of "third reserve" seats of central Government, any one of which could assume at least nominal control if neither TURNSTILE nor LINSTOCK survived. There are four of these, situated at the Regional Seats of Government near Dover, Reading, Salcombe and Shipton. To each would be sent an additional thirty to fifty staff, including one senior Minister of the Crown.'[118]

The probable 'blowing' of TURNSTILE – 'and', as Trend put it, 'we can have no assurance to the contrary'[119] – had, by the spring of 1963, forced Trend's tiny team of TACK-indoctrinated planners[120] to come up with

Alternative Plans

We have consequently concluded that:

. . . The security of TURNSTILE has already been seriously eroded and may now be completely compromised. If not, it will only be a matter of time before it is so. Meanwhile, it may be scheduled for attack in any event. If attacked, its chances of survival are negligible. A successful attack would effectively destroy all the functions of central Government at the same time.[121]

So, dispersal was the only answer as a 'decision to build another TURNSTILE in another place would only start the process all over again' and the same argument would apply to LINSTOCK.

Trend wanted Macmillan to authorize him to pursue alternatives and listed a few:

(i) The construction of a genuinely nuclear bomb proof redoubt (possibly in addition to a dispersal plan).
(ii) Flying the central Government abroad – to (say) Canada.
(iii) Putting the central Government to sea – either above or below water.
(iv) Putting the central Government into a mobile column or columns of specially protected vehicles.
(v) Dividing the central Government control into its different functions, to produce a number of administrative and political units, self-contained and as far as possible mobile, that would be distributed over the country.[122]

A clearly vexed Trend admitted to his Prime Minister that: 'Some of these courses appear, at first sight, fantastic. But we should not dismiss them on that account: the circumstances would be fantastic.'[123]

Tim Bligh, his Principal Private Secretary, advised Macmillan to agree to Trend's request: 'The short point is that the hole in the ground near Bath must be regarded as known to Russia, and the alternative arrangements are based on locations near Regional Seats of Government. And these themselves must be presumed to be amongst Soviet targets for the first wave of nuclear attack.'[124]

All this produced a little spurt of gloomy fatalism from Harold Macmillan as he scrawled on Bligh's minute:

Yes. But whatever hole is chosen will become known.
    H.M.

This reply was transmitted verbatim by Bligh to Trend on 30 May 1963.[125]

So Trend got his review, which was codenamed ACID. As a Cabinet Office briefing paper, released along with the 1970 'Government War Book' in June 2009, explained, the concept that emerged from the ACID studies 'involved pre-strike dispersal of a small number of executive groups (each including a senior minister) and the post-strike accretion of the surviving groups at any suitable location'.[126] A special set of instructions for ACID-indoctrinated officials was circulated on 16 July 1963 which involved a lifelong 'obligation not to disclose ACID information'.[127]

By March 1964, a fifteen-page report on the ACID studies was ready for Alec Douglas-Home. The clock was ticking for the Corsham bunker:

TURNSTILE in any event possesses the great disadvantage that, once manned, it can never be used again, because its security would have been destroyed. There would therefore be a tendency to delay its manning until the last possible moment – thus adding to the risk that it would not work.[128]

The ACID review ruled out sending the government abroad. As for

constructing a genuinely nuclear-bomb proof redoubt in this country. The geological structure of the United Kingdom is such that only a pressure vessel at a depth of 2,000 to 3,000 feet under the ground would be likely to withstand the rock displacement that would result even at that depth from a direct hit by a nuclear weapon. Such a pressure vessel might ensure the survival of a handful of people, given its own air conditioning, food supplies, etc. But the result of the displacement would be to cut off both exits and communications; and, even were these capable of restoration, the value of any such solution must be open to question in the first few vital days after attack, when the need would be for an immediate rallying point for the nation.[129]

So the answer was 'that the alternative to concentration (on the lines of TURNSTILE) must be a scheme of dispersal and subsequent accretion'.

At this point there are several pages withheld as the ACID/ PYTHON/ PEBBLE/RUBBER/RUBY system (as it was successively codenamed) is too close to current arrangements for it to be fully revealed.[130]

There is enough information available, however, in the March 1964 document to give a good idea of what the dispersal plan involved.

Under such a scheme of dispersal we envisage the formation of a number of Groups – which we refer to as ACID Groups – each with the power to take over the functions of central Government in war, self-sufficient and in a pre-arranged order of priority which would be determined by the seniority of the Minister in charge of each Group. The success of an alternative plan of this nature depends upon the assessment of the chance that at least one of the Groups would survive a nuclear onslaught on this country, whatever form that onslaught might take.

These ACID Groups will possess two great advantages over TACK sites. First, they will be completely detached from Regional Seats of Government and sub-Regional headquarters and we will thus be able to select areas for their location that would give them the greatest possible chance of survival – not only from a direct hit but from heavy fallout. Secondly we might be able to have a number of alternative sites for each ACID Group – and these alternatives could themselves be changed from time to time.[131]

Would TURNSTILE have a place in the new scheme of things?

It is difficult to see an alternative role of any importance that might be given to TURNSTILE under the ACID concept. TURNSTILE itself, however, is too valuable an asset to discard entirely. In some respects it would be an ideal location for one of the ACID Groups; but its vulnerability *qua* TURNSTILE is such that we could hardly use it for so important a purpose.

In their list of recommendations (not all of which we have) the ACID team urged the 'abandonment of the LINSTOCK and TACK concepts, and the maintenance of TURNSTILE for other purposes to be determined'.

The main conclusions included the 'formation of [deleted] ACID Groups' which would

(a) Contain the potential supreme political authority; with vestigial administrative staffs; and retain control of the conduct of the war, negotiations with other Powers, and overriding authority for the Regions as far as possible.

(b) [all deleted]

(c) Be dispersed . . . [2 lines deleted] . . . in different areas of the United Kingdom either in static locations or in protected mobile columns.

(d) Have been allocated a prearranged order of priority in which to assume control.[132]

It took another four years for what was by now PYTHON to be implemented on 1 May 1968. Trend briefed Wilson on 18 April 1968 that: 'At present the arrangements for the maintenance of central Government in war are in a transitional stage when the TURNSTILE plans, which have previously been the main feature of these arrangements, have ceased to be realistic and the PYTHON plans are not yet in force.' PYTHON planning was sufficiently well advanced for it to be implemented. Wilson agreed.[133]

PYTHON, like TURNSTILE, is yielding its secrets gradually and there is still a long way to go. But historians had something of a breakthrough in the spring of 2009. After the Cabinet Office meeting on 15 May which finally cleared the 1970 Government War Book for release in time for the Pimlott Lecture the following month, an official with long experience in what used to be called the Overseas and Defence Secretariat mentioned the existence of a cupboard which for many years had stood on their floor of No. 70 Whitehall containing only the most sensitive material and to which access had been extremely restricted. It had been moved to the Cabinet Office's storeroom. Perhaps there might be more archive of interest in there? Indeed there was, including a run of War Books from 1935 to 1979.[134]

The special cupboard also contained more PYTHON material, some of which was declassifiable, including a top-secret 'Confidential Annex' dealing with 'Machinery of Government in War' kept separately from the normal minutes of the 15 February 1965 meeting of the Cabinet's Home Defence Committee.

The PYTHON concept had plainly been developed not just in response to the attentions of Soviet intelligence in the Corsham area but as a product of the post-Cuba review and the need for a '2–3 day Precautionary Stage' instead of the week which had been the norm. Philip Rogers, the Cabinet Office chairman of the HDC's Machinery of Government in War Sub-Committee, reported that:

Current planning was on the basis of a 7 day Precautionary Stage and it was clear that, in the much reduced period, it would not be possible to man TURNSTILE with the large number of those at present earmarked for it. Furthermore, in view of the scale of nuclear attack expected on the United

Kingdom, it was now thought to be prudent to plan on a policy of dispersal of central government in war ['this new PYTHON concept', Rogers called it] rather than on initial concentration at TURNSTILE.

The record of the ensuing discussion casts still more light on PYTHON thinking and the post-attack utility of TURNSTILE:

. . . Under this new concept, a series of elaborate underground headquarters for PYTHON groups was not envisaged. The facilities at TURNSTILE, even for a small PYTHON group, were much better than would be possible at other locations.

. . . The object of the PYTHON groups would be to provide a series of foci of political authority. The groups would be small numerically (perhaps 150 strong) with, inevitably, very limited capabilities. The extent of effective control that an individual PYTHON group would be able to exercise was doubtful but it was intended that surviving PYTHON groups would accrete to TURNSTILE. When in due course Departments were invited to select staff for PYTHON groups, they would be able to draw on their current TURNSTILE nominations.

. . . As the location of the Regional Seats of Government had been disclosed [by the 'Spies for Peace' in the spring of 1963], they were considered likely to be nuclear targets and were therefore unsuitable locations for PYTHON groups.[135]

The Cabinet Office's special cupboard also disgorged copies of ready-printed Royal Warrants appointing ministers Regional Commissioners and the 1968 post-PYTHON directive outlining their duties. Having these placed in their hands would have been the first ministers knew of the tasks that were to fall upon them and the locations from which they would be exercised. The constitutional documents associated with Armageddon are interesting. The room in TURNSTILE where books and manuals are stored also contains a stock of Royal Pardons to be used, presumably, if looters and others charged under the Defence Regulations were deemed wrongly convicted by a member of the judiciary in the bunker.

The October 1968 Royal Warrant reads like this:

ELIZABETH THE SECOND, by the Grace of God of the United Kingdom of Great Britain and Northern Ireland and of Our other Realms and Territories,

QUEEN, Head of the Commonwealth, Defender of the Faith, to Our

_____

Greeting!

In pursuance of Regulation 4 (2) of the Defence (Machinery of Government) Regulations We hereby appoint you the said

_____

to be a Regional Commissioner for the purposes of those Regulations.

> Given at Our Court at Saint
> **James's**
> the day of 19
> In the year of Our Reign.
>
> By Her Majesty's Command.[136]

The same file contains the 'Directive to Regional Commissioners' telling them where their 'wartime station' will be and pointing out that

. . . For the purposes of central Government under the PYTHON concept, senior Ministers of PYTHON Groups are deemed senior to all others irrespective of their peacetime seniorities.[137]

In addition, had conflict been imminent, each Regional Commissioner was to be given two pages of top-secret 'Notes of Guidance for Regional Commissioners', which would have been their first detailed immersion and indoctrination into the fate the Prime Minister's World War III appointments list was thrusting at them.

Just imagine opening the sealed envelope from the Cabinet Office and reading this:

NOTES OF GUIDANCE FOR REGIONAL COMMISSIONERS

1. You have been appointed as Regional Commissioner and assigned to one of the 10 Defence Regions in England and Wales. You should be ready to take up your appointment at short notice (if you have not already been notified by telephone of your appointment and asked to proceed to your emergency station before these notes reach you).

2. The division of England and Wales into Defence Regions is a feature of a control system planned to operate between central and local Government in a war emergency. In war each Region will be further divided into two, or in some instances three, Sub-Regions and each Sub-Region will have its own Sub-Regional Commissioner who may himself be a Minister. The names of the Sub-Regional Commissioners assigned to your Region will be given to you separately; but will remain responsible to you unless they are cut off from you and unable to make contact.

3. Each Sub-Region, of which there are 23 in England and Wales, will have its own headquarters, prepared in peacetime, known as the Sub-Regional Control (SRC). No similar headquarters have been prepared in advance for Regions as a whole, and you are therefore asked to station yourself initially at one of the SRCs in your Region, the location of which will be given to you separately. Subsequently, however, when movement and control over longer distances have again become possible after the attack, you will no doubt wish to establish your own Regional Seat of Government (RSG) in premises chosen in the light of circumstances as they become known at the time. The reason for this arrangement is that the Sub-Regional level would, in the Government's opinion, be the most appropriate level in the control system at which to deal with the problems expected to arise during and immediately after a nuclear attack. Broader questions, such as food rationing, and industrial policy, which are more appropriate to the Regional level but will not require consideration until later, will have to be left until the establishment of the RSG becomes possible.

4. If it should not prove possible to appoint a Sub-Regional Commissioner for each Sub-Region within your Region, you may be asked to take direct control of one of them until a suitable moment after the attack, perhaps when the RSG is established.

5. The Principal Officer for the Region, who will be your chief adviser, together with a small number of other senior advisers, will be available at the SRC and will be able to tell you about the emergency organisation of Government Departments and Services in the Region, and to provide you with any detailed information you may require about the resources of the Region. The remaining members of the RSG staff complement will be formed on a representative basis into three or four 'RSG Groups' and will travel when the controls are manned to separate premises in different parts of the Region which have been earmarked in peacetime, and which possess adequate fall-out protection and

modest communications. You will be informed separately of their locations. The staff will remain in these locations until you decide, in the light of the circumstances prevailing after the attack, the time and place at which it would be practicable to establish the RSG.

6. It is intended that the central Government should continue to function from London until the attack. Parliament has been, or will be, asked to confer emergency powers on the Government, in an Emergency Powers (Defence) Bill, and Defence Regulations have been, or will be, made to confer the necessary powers on appropriate authorities. These powers will probably be available at or shortly after the time when you take up your emergency station.

7. So long as Parliament is sitting and the central Government is in London, the ordinary forms of Government will be maintained. The emergency powers conferred by the Defence Regulations will be vested in the appropriate Ministers, and in exercising them, as in exercising ordinary powers, these Ministers will remain responsible to Parliament. But Ministers may delegate specific powers to you in order that you may ensure proper co-ordination of activities that could not suitably be ordered from the centre. On such matters any action which you take would be taken on behalf of the appropriate Minister, and not in your own right as a Regional Commissioner.

8. When a Proclamation is made under the Defence Act, or the attack takes place, extensive powers will devolve on you in your own right as Regional Commissioner. You will then exercise all the existing powers and emergency powers of Government within your Region, except those reserved to the central Government but including control of the Armed Forces and you may, if the situation requires it, make new laws by Ordinance. You will however take account of any directions which you may receive from the central Government: in particular, these will specify those matters which will be reserved to the central Government and on which you should not act unless specifically authorised to do so. They will include Foreign and Commonwealth relations, the offensive prosecution of the war, control of shipping and the procurement and allocation of overseas supplies. Authority may also be reserved to the central Government on other matters, such as the use of strategic stocks of food, fuel and medical supplies which may be located in your Region, and the regional ports and shipping organisation will also be responsible primarily to the central Government.

9. Further details of the arrangements made for the maintenance of Government during the emergency are contained in Volume 3 of the Government

War Book, a copy of which will be given to you with these notes. Chapter 1, describing plans for the continuation of central Government from dispersed headquarters after the attack, Chapter 4, describing the control system at Regional and Sub-Regional level, and Chapter 6, which elaborates the control system below Sub-Regional level, will be of particular interest. Other chapters deal with emergency powers, broadcasting and monitoring arrangements, communications, the administration of justice, etc.

10. The Defence Regulations will apply in Scotland and Northern Ireland as well as in England and Wales. For purposes of government in a war emergency Scotland will be divided, under the overall control of a Commissioner for Scotland into three Zones, each under a Zone Commissioner. Scottish Central Control, the headquarters of the Commissioner for Scotland, equates broadly to a Regional Seat of Government, and Zones to Sub-Regions in England and Wales. Northern Ireland will have a single separate control.[138]

I'm sure that with the exception of the two nuclear deputies, who were, as we have seen, explicitly informed of their World War III function by being briefed when they were nominated, other ministers did privately wonder what might befall them if global war came. But none of them would have known their destination or their duties until the last days of peace and, unless they are still alive and are reading this book or have trawled the files at Kew, they would have gone to their graves not knowing the answer (though in Heath's time, as we shall see in a moment, a few more of them received a little private briefing if they were PYTHON-cleared).

After the change of government in June 1970, Trend briefed Ted Heath on 29 July 1970 'on wartime plans and nuclear retaliation procedures'.

The first part of that brief (which has not been declassified) described plans for maintaining some form of government in war and included a resume of the PEBBLE plan – i.e. the plan for dispersed nuclei of Government at relatively safe sites.

Here Trend's minute reveals Heath's choice of nuclear deputies – three of them:

Subsequently you authorised me to brief the Home Secretary [Reginald Maudling], the Foreign Secretary [Sir Alec Douglas-Home – who must have been word perfect by now] and the Secretary of State for Defence [Lord Carrington] about nuclear retaliation procedures; and this briefing included an outline of the plan.

Now, in February 1971, Trend sought Heath's permission to allow certain permanent secretaries, using 'codeword indoctrination' but without exposing the planned whereabouts of the PYTHON (by now renamed PEBBLE) groups, to brief their ministers.[139] Heath agreed that six more of his ministers should be in the know. They were Anthony Barber, Chancellor of the Exchequer; Gordon Campbell, Secretary of State for Scotland; Peter Walker, Secretary of State for the Environment; Jim Prior, Secretary of State for Agriculture; John Davies, Secretary of State for Trade and Industry, and Christopher Chataway, Minister of Posts and Telecommunications.[140]

The Corsham site, however, had not quite fallen into the nuclear ashcan of Britain's most secret history. Despite PYTHON, TURNSTILE carried on. As the Cabinet Office briefing note of June 2009 explained:

Under the PYTHON concept (and its subsequent refinements) the site at Corsham (TURNSTILE from 1963 until 1970; CHANTICLEER from 1970; PERIPHERAL from 1987; EYEGLASS from 1992) ceased to have a CGWHQ [Central Government Wartime Headquarters] role other than as a possible accretion site for surviving PYTHON etc. groups post-strike or for support to PYTHON etc. groups accreted elsewhere post-strike.

TURNSTILE, was also intended to deceive Soviet satellites passing over Bath and the surrounding district. It was also an *intra*-Whitehall deception.

Knowledge of the PYTHON etc. concept was limited to a small circle of ministers and officials; a wider circle of individuals with limited access to machinery of government in war plans remained under the impression that the plan to activate the CGWHQ at Corsham during transition to war was still current. This reflected a deliberate policy to provide cover for the PYTHON etc. concept. Maintenance of communications and administrative facilities at Corsham continued. From 1979 the codeword FLEX was allocated to protect those aspects of the arrangements at Corsham that might reveal that Corsham no longer hosted the CGWHQ.[141]

Of the PYTHON locations we know of only two, both ships. One was the Royal Yacht *Britannia* for the Queen and the Home Secretary; the other the Royal Fleet Auxiliary *Engadine* (possibly for the Prime Minister's Group).[142]

When it comes to British Cold War bunkerdom, for all that its World War III War Cabinet life only lasted from 1960 to 1968, TURNSTILE, thanks to its widespread coverage in the early twenty-first century on radio and television, has captured the public's imagination as *the* last redoubt. And, each time I have gone down in the 'Q' for 'Quarry' lift with Andy Quinn into the old mine workings, I understand afresh why this is – and almost certainly will remain – so.

Now that the who-was-to-go-where-and-do-what files are released from the bondage of Whitehall's most secret cupboards, I'm more and more struck by the rich paper seam that is now available for mining and refining into a new *genre* of Cold War novel which, if it's done really well, could stand alongside John le Carré and Len Deighton on the bookshelves. The only author who came anywhere near, to my knowledge, during the Cold War was Gavin Lyall in 1985 in his *The Crocus List*.[143] Its opening section shows a touch of familiarity with Whitehall's dispersal procedures in the last hours of peace. In the novel's opening pages, Lyall's hero, Major Harry Maxim, who is indoctrinated into the, in this case fictional, version of PYTHON and VISITATION, gets into a terrific row over Sunday lunch at his parents with his CND-inclined sister, Brenda.[144]

Much remains to be discovered about the story of the last redoubts. The detailed paper trail goes cold after the Heath years, though we know that the PYTHON concept, under a variety of codenames, ran on right until the end of the Cold War and beyond (as we shall see in the next chapter). It remains in place today (minus the Royal Yacht, which is now a floating exhibition in the Port of Leith) as part of contingency planning not just for a nuclear attack but also in case a terrorist attack involving chemical, biological or radiological materials should render Whitehall incapable for a time of exercising central control of the state.[145] But none of them, I suspect, can match dusty, chilly, eerie TURNSTILE for atmospherics or for preserving an era of special moment and menace as if in aspic.

8

The Human Button:
Deciders and Deliverers

We would have done it unhesitatingly. I really mean unhesitatingly.

> Air Vice-Marshal Bobby Robson, on receiving the 'go'
> signal to guide his Vulcan bomber to its target in the
> Soviet Union, recalling the 1960s in 2001[1]

*The bolt-from-the-blue which takes out the seat of govern-
ment and its communications – this became a real topic when
the deterrent moved from the V-force to the Polaris submarines. The subs were invulnerable, but not the command and
control. The worry was, could you get the PM or an authenticated deputy into a hole-in-the-ground? The submarines
could listen in to broadcasts but not broadcast back.*

> Senor civil servant recalling the early 1970s in 2001[2]

*When you become Prime Minister the first thing they do –
after telling you how to launch the nuclear bomb – is to take
your passport away from you, and then the rest of the time
trying to get you to travel round the world.*

> Tony Blair to the 1998 Labour Party Conference[3]

*He was quite quiet when he actually heard what was at the
country's disposal.*

> General Lord Guthrie of Craigiebank, Chief of the
> Defence Staff 1997–2001, recalling Tony Blair's reaction
> on first being briefed on the Royal Navy's Trident force
> and its capability, 2008[4]

Without question.
Commander Richard Lindsey, Captain of HMS *Vanguard*,
when asked whether he would obey a prime ministerial
directive to fire a Trident missile, 2008[5]

*The thing that struck me was the colossal seriousness with
which they all took it. I think they were all aware, behind the
high theory stuff, that this was, in the end, about would you,
if you had to, press buttons? What do you write in the letter?*
Sir Michael Quinlan, former Permanent Secretary
at the Ministry of Defence, on briefing Jim Callaghan,
Margaret Thatcher and John Major on nuclear
deterrence, 2008[6]

'The letter'? This was the solution to the problem of nuclear authorization from beyond the grave in the early 1970s and the 'last resort letters', as they are known, remain the solution today. As you read this, there is a Royal Navy Trident submarine moving at a fast walking pace, several hundred feet down somewhere in the North Atlantic – huge, silent and undetectable – with more destructive power on board than all the explosives used everywhere in World War II from beginning to end. In a safe bolted to the floor of its control room are the launch codes. Inside an inner safe is the Prime Minister's 'last resort letter', written in his own hand, conveying his posthumous instructions to the captain and his executive officer.

Shortly after taking office, a new premier has to write four of these; one for each Trident submarine. The Cabinet Secretary briefs on the choices. There are four of them:

1: Retaliate
2: Don't retaliate
3: If 2, put yourself under the command of the United States, if it's still there; or sail to Australia, if it's still there; or put in at a neutral port.
4: Captain of the boat to use his own judgement.[7]

Option 4 would, I suspect, be regarded as a real abrogation of responsibility on a PM's part by most ex-Polaris or Trident commanders.

The grim briefings by the Chief of the Defence Staff and the Cabinet Secretary are the moments when a new PM really appreciates what being Prime Minister really means. The nuclear aspect of the premiership is the starkest example of a continuity running from the perilous years of the Cold War right through to today. And the human elements of the nuclear button do the same from the crews of the RAF Vulcans, Valiants and Victors and the Polaris submarines to the four Trident boats that comprise today's deterrent, which is why I have devoted a special chapter to them.

A few of the novice premiers will have been one of the two 'nuclear deputies' before becoming Prime Minister, as Alec Home was, as Foreign Secretary, in 1962–3, as we have seen in Chapter 7.[8] Jim Callaghan was one of Harold Wilson's alternative decision-takers when holding the same office in 1974–6. They are probably the only two premiers, so far, who had such a nuclear apprenticeship before entering No. 10 Downing Street.

As Charles Guthrie noted during a conversation I had with him in the autumn of 2008, 'I think, quite honestly, like most prime ministers, he [Blair] hadn't given a huge amount of thought to what this really meant . . . He could, if the circumstances demanded it, create devastation on a huge scale.'* I suggested to Lord Guthrie that whatever confronted Prime Ministers during their remaining tenure of office, the decision they made when they drafted their letters was the most awesome they would have to take.

'I'm sure that's right,' he replied. 'I'm sure people are apt to forget what huge responsibilities they have in this field.'[9]

We will never know what judgements successive premiers have placed in their beyond-the-grave letters unless they choose to tell us in retirement. For when a PM resigns, 'last resort' instructions are retrieved from the Clyde Submarine Base at Faslane by the senior military officer in the Cabinet Office's Overseas and Defence Secretariat (now the

---

* As Leader of the Opposition, David Cameron visited the Royal Navy's Devonport Dockyard in June 2008 and, as part of his tour, spent over two hours on the Trident submarine HMS *Victorious*, shortly before it sailed for the first time after its mid-life refit. The firing system was explained to him, including the safe and the purposes of its contents in the boat's control room (Private information).

Foreign and Defence Policy Secretariat), brought back to Whitehall and destroyed unread. In the spring of 1997, Tony Blair was quite exercised by the fact that a Trident submarine had put to sea just before the government changed and that John Major's 'last resort' instructions would be the ones in the safe for nearly three months. The boats' patrol cycles do not harmonize with the political one.[10]

Only one premier and one nuclear deputy have spoken publicly about the decision they made (or would have made) in response to a nuclear assault on the United Kingdom. In 1988 I asked Jim Callaghan if, in the direst circumstances, he would have authorized the launch of a Polaris missile. He told me he had, as Prime Minister, practised the launch procedures, adding:

> If that had become necessary and vital, it would have meant that the deterrent had failed, because the value of a nuclear weapon is, frankly, only as a deterrent. Because if we had got to that point, where I felt it was necessary to do it, then I would have done it. I've had terrible doubts, of course, about this. And if I had lived after having pressed that button, I could never, never have forgiven myself.[11]

Callaghan is the only Prime Minister, so far, to have made his nuclear decision public.

In these matters Mrs Thatcher is an intriguing puzzle. The nuclear question played strongly during the 1983 general election for a number of reasons: the Thatcher administration had already committed itself to replacing Polaris with Trident,[12] but the Labour manifesto had pledged a Foot government to cancel it and to place 'Britain's Polaris force . . . in the nuclear disarmament negotiations in which Britain must take part'.[13]

Shortly after the Conservatives were returned with a majority of 144,[14] the question arose once more during a House of Commons debate on Foreign Affairs and Defence when Enoch Powell, never a believer in a British deterrent,[15] devoted his formidable word power to Mrs Thatcher's declared position on the question of 'last resort' and nuclear retaliation. Powell cited what Mrs Thatcher had said 'on the day before the poll':

'Yes, of course if you have got a nuclear deterrent you have to be prepared to press the button because that deters anyone from using nuclear and also from crossing the Nato line on conventional.'[16]

Powell, who was at this stage of his career Ulster Unionist MP for Down, South, spoke of his

privilege – a privilege that I shall never forget – to be able to observe rather closely how the Prime Minister sustained the responsibility that she carried for the conduct of the [Falklands] war in which this country was engaged last year. Having done so, I do not believe that the Prime Minister would take a decision that would consign a whole generation to destruction in any conceivable circumstances whatsoever.[17]

And many years later, we learned that, in a very human aside, she had told one of her Foreign Office experts on the Soviet Union, Sir Rodric Braithwaite, quite early in her premiership, 'that she was not at all sure that, in the event, she could press the button: "I want grandchildren too . . .", she explained.[18]

When the 1979 papers were released to the National Archives in January 2010 we learned from the files a little of Mrs Thatcher's first induction into the world of nuclear release drills (as Education Secretary in the Heath government she would have been a stranger to such things), though, naturally, the files contained no hint of her decision on the retaliate/don't retaliate question.

As part of the Cabinet Office's preparation for a possible Conservative government coming into office on Friday 4 May 1979 following the election of the previous day, Sir Clive Rose, head of its Overseas and Defence Secretariat, drew up a brief on 'Nuclear Procedures' for the Cabinet Secretary, Sir John Hunt, to show Mrs Thatcher if the electorate put her into No. 10. 'A brief will be needed', he wrote on 4 April, 'on *nuclear release procedures*. I believe the right way to tackle this would be to produce a short trailer with a proposal for a presentation in the COBR [Cabinet Office Briefing Room at one end of which, in 1979, was sited the Nuclear Release Room] at a convenient time.'

Rose reckoned:

There are a number of details which it is difficult to put across in a written brief and which can best be explained orally. The trailer brief would cover the question of [Nuclear] Deputies and mention 'last resort' instructions [i.e. the four letters for the control room safes on the Polaris boats].[19]

Rose reminded Hunt that Mrs Thatcher would also need to be briefed on the nuclear consultation procedures with the US President and the West German Federal Chancellor: 'We shall also need to say something about *FILCH planning* [the codeword used to protect the PYTHON/PEBBLE plans 1970–79 – which had replaced ACID[20] in 1970].'[21]

Mrs Thatcher, when briefed during the first few days of her premiership by the Chief of the Defence Staff, Marshal of the Royal Air Force Sir Neil Cameron, about where the Polaris boat on patrol was and what the Polaris force could do, took it immensely seriously, as her Foreign Affairs Private Secretary Sir Bryan Cartledge recalls:

She was fascinated – so was I incidentally – and she took it extremely seriously and absorbed every syllable and it is, I think it must be for a new Prime Minister, a very daunting moment to realize that enormous responsibility is going to be yours from now on. I don't think she was daunted, but she certainly took it extremely seriously.[22]

During the same BBC Radio 4 programme, *Day One in No. 10*, Robin Butler, a former Cabinet Secretary, recalled (the first Cabinet Secretary ever to do so) what it was like having to brief incoming Prime Ministers on the system of 'last resort' letters (which he did for John Major in 1990 and Tony Blair in 1997):

BUTLER: Well, of course, there are desperately grave decisions which the Prime Minister may have to make in certain circumstances. For example, they may have to decide to press the nuclear button if a world war was beginning. And these must be the most desperate decisions that anybody has to make . . . But there has to be provision for what happens if the government has been destroyed by a nuclear strike and somebody has then got to say, 'Well, we have our missiles on submarines out under the seas, and what should the commanders of those submarines do?' And so there has to be a plan for what would happen in that situation, and the person to make that plan – and it has to be made in advance because the home government may have been destroyed – should be the person who has been elected as head of government. So that falls on the Prime Minister to make, and, as you say, it falls on the Prime Minister to send those instructions. Now these are desperately secret . . . they're clearly really secret because the whole point of a nuclear deterrent is that your enemy doesn't know what he may incur if he attacks you. So these are highly secret things. And only one person, who is the initiator of them, knows what the orders are – and that is the Prime Minister. Now in that case, as you say, they're likely to be handwritten – they don't have to be handwritten because if the Prime Minister can type he can type them – but the Prime Minister has to do that personally . . . it's a very sobering decision for anybody to have to make because it has to be made at a time of peace and it faces a Prime Minister immediately they come to power.

HENNESSY: You brief on the options, I think there are roughly four of them, and you don't know what goes into it?

BUTLER: Yes, yes. You leave that . . . for the Prime Minister to do privately, wrestling with their own beliefs and conscience.

HENNESSY: And they seal the letters and give them to you and they're transmitted to the boats?

BUTLER: Correct.

HENNESSY: Without giving away secrets that you can't give away (I don't mean in terms of the content, of course) but how did they react, your two Prime Ministers, when you took them through that drill?

BUTLER: They reacted as you'd expect any human being to react – soberly; shocked if they hadn't realized before that this was one of the things that they would have to do at the start of their administration. So I would say it was a shock and a sobering one.

HENNESSY: For both of them?

BUTLER: For anybody.[23]

In 1979, the nuclear weapons question played strongly in a variety of guises during Mrs Thatcher's first weeks as Prime Minister. In one of those constitutional quirks that the secret state can sometimes throw up, Jim Callaghan, the outgoing Prime Minister, decided to break the usually resilient Whitehall convention that new governments do not see the policy papers of the outgoing administration on the question of replacing Polaris with a new generation of nuclear weapons. (The standard practice is for Whitehall to prepare special briefs for an incoming government that give no trace of the private discussions of the outgoing administration.) Though the Labour Party manifesto for the October 1974 general election had stated, 'We have renounced any intention of moving towards a new generation of strategic nuclear weapons,'[24] Callaghan's highly secret Nuclear Defence Policy Group (it was not a Cabinet committee and its existence was kept from the full Cabinet) consisting of himself, the Foreign Secretary David Owen, the Defence Secretary Fred Mulley and the Chancellor of the Exchequer Denis Healey, had commissioned two studies from officials on politico-military and technical aspects of Polaris replacement which went to the small, inner group of nuclear ministers in late December 1978.[25]

During the Guadeloupe G7 summit in January 1979, Callaghan had secured a pledge from President Jimmy Carter that the US would provide the Trident C4 missile* if either Callaghan or his successor asked for it following the forthcoming general election.[26] On a note from Hunt to Cartledge about the state of play with the Carter Administration on Trident as a possible successor system to Polaris, Jim Callaghan wrote on Friday 4 May 1979, during his very last morning as Prime Minister, when he knew the election was lost and the end of his premiership but hours away:

The incoming Prime Minister should be briefed on the need for replacing Polaris (or otherwise – as she thinks!) and should decide whether to make her own approaches to President Carter.[27]

Nine years later I asked Jim Callaghan why he had wished to break the usual convention about the continuing confidentiality of a previous government's papers. 'Because', he replied, 'it was a matter of national importance. I think it is very important that succeeding ministers and

---

* In 1981 the Thatcher Cabinet decided to go for the improved D5 Trident missile – and a quiver of D5s are out deep under the Atlantic, in the care of the Royal Navy, as you read these words.

succeeding governments and administrations should not know about the political decisions of their predecessors – that is a principle I adhere to. But if one administration, or the Prime Minister, wishes to leave a note for his successor about a matter of the greatest national importance, then I think he is entitled to do so.'[28]

Mrs Thatcher wasted little time in picking up the nuclear question. It was the subject of the first ministerial ad hoc Cabinet committee she set up – MISC 7 – which met initially on 24 May 1979 and began to consider the options for Polaris replacement. She tacked on to its agenda the question of nuclear release procedures and the appointment of nuclear deputies. She decided to go for three of them – the trio of ministers who sat with her at that first meeting of MISC 7 (Willie Whitelaw, Home Secretary; Lord Carrington, Foreign Secretary; Francis Pym, Defence Secretary. Geoffrey Howe, Chancellor of the Exchequer, attended later meetings of MISC 7 but Mrs Thatcher, surprisingly, never appointed him one of her nuclear deputies even when he was Foreign Secretary between 1983 and 1989[29]).

The minute Hunt and Rose wrote after MISC 7 met on 24 May read:

4. NUCLEAR RELEASE PROCEDURES

The meeting had before them a letter of 18 May from the Secretary of the Cabinet to the Home Secretary enclosing a note on nuclear release procedures.

THE PRIME MINISTER, summing up a short discussion, said that the circumstances might arise in which one or other of the Ministers present might have to assume her personal responsibilities in the field of nuclear release. The Secretary of the Cabinet would arrange a briefing for them to explain what was involved. It was important that Ministers themselves took part in exercises to practise nuclear release procedures so that they became familiar with them . . .

The Meeting –

. . . Instructed the Secretary of the Cabinet to arrange a briefing on nuclear release procedures for the Ministers concerned and subsequently an exercise in which the procedures were practised.[30]

Mrs Thatcher did not alter the convention that ministers did not

envelope responsibility for six and a half years, acted in an unusual but
intriguing way when first faced with it in the last weeks of 1990. When
briefed by the Cabinet Secretary, Sir Robin Butler, on the need to issue
his instructions for the Polaris submarines (the first Trident boat, HMS
Vanguard, did not begin its initial operational patrol until December
1994[36]), he cancelled a planned weekend at Chequers and returned to
the Finings, his home in Huntingdon. He was said to have done so in
order to consider the letters he would draft away from the apparatus
of government. He wrote them out by hand, sealed them and returned
them to the Cabinet Secretary. It was, he once admitted privately, a
most chilling introduction to the responsibilities of the premiership.[37]
The same applied, albeit to a slightly lesser degree than the potential
button-pushers, to those indoctrinated into the most secret annex of
the Government War Book – 'Appendix Z', covering 'Nuclear Release'.
A run of Appendices Z were found in the Cabinet Office's rediscovered
cupboard in 2009 and released in December of that year with but a
couple of tiny, intelligence-related redactions.[38] They ranged from the
1961 version to the 1975 edition, on which I shall draw here.[39] In 1975,
Whitehall's 'Z' team was quite small: one copy of Appendix Z was kept
by the Foreign Affairs and Defence Private Secretary to the Prime Minister; one in the safe of the Foreign and Commonwealth Office's Defence
Department; one by the Private Secretary to the Defence Secretary; two
in the MOD's Defence Secretariat 12 (which dealt with nuclear retaliation); one by the Military Assistant to the Chief of the Defence Staff;
one in the Defence Operations Centre; one by the Secretary of the Chiefs
of Staff Committee; one by the Secretary to the Chief of the Naval Staff;
one by the nuclear side of the staff of the Commander-in-Chief, Fleet;
one by the Military Assistant to the Chief of the General Staff; one by
the Private Secretary to the Chief of the Air Staff; two more in the
relevant sections of the Air Staff (Defence Secretariat 8b and the Air Force
Operations Room). Inside the Cabinet Office, the institutional guardian
of the GWB, seven copies of Appendix Z were kept (by the Secretary of
the Cabinet; the head of its Overseas and Defence Secretariat; the Chairman of its Nuclear Release Procedures Committee (NRP); the head of
its Telecommunications Secretariat; the Secretary of the Joint Intelligence Committee the Secretaries of the NRP Committee, plus one

master copy.[40] This handful of men and women privy to the nuclear release exercises and the briefings for new Prime Ministers – plus the Prime Minister and his two nuclear deputies – were the initiates of the nuclear side of the UK Cold War secret state.

From the early 1970s, when the Cabinet Office Briefing Room was first opened, Appendix Z matters were explained to the new premier in the small Nuclear Release Room (through the door at the left-hand end of the main Cabinet Office Briefing Room) with its safe containing the codes needed for authentication of the Prime Minister's authorization to fire and the matching one held by the Chief of the Defence Staff. (In the now much-modernized COBR you can still see where the Nuclear Release Room was before it moved over the road – Whitehall – and underground into PINDAR, the Government Emergency Room in the bunker beneath the Ministry of Defence[41].) Essentially, Appendix Z 'outlines the timing of actions that are to be taken when certain Government War Book codewords are declared' by the Cabinet.

In 1975, had World War III come, the second GWB codeword (these varied between versions of the War Book) was MANUSCRIPT. It would have triggered the following:

i. SECRETARY OF THE CABINET signs letters to –
    a. Chiefs of Staff
    b. Commander-in-Chief, Fleet
    c. Air Officer Commanding-in-Chief, Strike Command
notifying them of the identities of the First and Second Nuclear Deputies.

ii. CABINET OFFICE despatches the above letters in sealed envelopes by hand to the DEFENCE OPERATIONS CENTRE, MINISTRY OF DEFENCE

iii. MINISTRY OF DEFENCE
    a. Arranges immediate delivery of envelopes to the CHIEFS OF STAFF, C-in-C FLEET and AO C-in-C STRIKE COMMAND.* Envelopes are to remain sealed until further instructions are received.
    b. Man Duty Captain and Duty Group Captain in Cabinet Office Briefing Rooms.

---

* The RAF remained a carrier of nuclear weapons until the 1998 Strategic Defence Review left the Royal Navy's Trident submarines the sole delivery system.

c. Initiates control of access to Whitehall Tunnel [which, to this day, runs between the MOD and the Cabinet Office] with Cabinet Office.[42]

In 1975, the third GWB codeword was FENCER. If issued, it would have stimulated the following actions:

i. CHIEFS OF STAFF

a. Order all unobtrusive measures –

to bring the RAF strike force to a state of operational readiness;

to bring stand-by Polaris submarines [i.e. the available ones not on patrol] to a higher state of readiness.

b. Review the need for military advice to the Cabinet Office under the arrangements for the Duty Chief of Staff.[43]

At this point, between GWB codewords three and four, the doomsday clock really begins to tick with 'Action to be taken on receipt of a positive indication that the Soviet Union or another Warsaw Pact country is about to or may be likely to start or engage in hostilities against the United Kingdom or its NATO Allies'.

On receipt of such a grave indication, the JIC declares 'Intelligence Alert – Stage 3' and its secretary informs a range of individuals and institutions, starting with the Cabinet Secretary. Thereupon the Cabinet Secretary

a. Arranges for the Cabinet to be reminded that unobtrusive measures to improve the state of readiness of the RAF strike force and the Polaris force have been initiated.

b. In consultation with the PRIVATE SECRETARY TO THE PRIME MINISTER and the HEAD OF THE TELECOMMUNICATIONS SECRETARIAT, arranges for the Prime Minister to speak to the President of the United States, as necessary, to –

1. consider the use of forces stationed in this country in respect of which a joint decision of the United Kingdom and the United States Government is required;

2. discuss the co-ordination of United Kingdom and United States policy in respect of the initiation of emergency measures and the declaration of formal Alerts by NATO Supreme Commanders.

On receipt of the fourth GWB codeword from the Cabinet –

JIGGER – the road to nuclear release approaches its final corner:

i. SECRETARY OF THE CABINET arranges for the Prime Minister to send the Minister selected as his Second Nuclear Deputy to Headquarters, C-in-C, Fleet [in the Northwood Bunker under the Chilterns], to be available for authorising nuclear release. But if both the Prime Minister and the First Nuclear Deputy are unable to be present at No. 10/Cabinet Office the Second Nuclear Deputy will remain in London.

ii. CHIEFS OF STAFF open the sealed envelopes notifying them of the identities of the First and Second Nuclear Deputies.

iii. MINISTRY OF DEFENCE authorises C-in-C Fleet and AO C-in-C STRIKE COMMAND to open the sealed envelopes notifying them of the identities of the First and Second Nuclear Deputies.

iv. SECRETARY OF THE CABINET, in consultation with the PRIVATE SECRETARY TO THE PRIME MINISTER and the HEAD OF TELE-COMMUNICATIONS SECRETARIAT, makes arrangements as required for further Cabinet or Ministerial meetings and international consultations by telephone and teleprinter in the Cabinet Office . . .[44]

The final section of Appendix Z covers the doomsday contingency:

Should the United Kingdom be attacked with nuclear weapons before Strike Command and/or Fleet have received release instructions –

i. AO C-in-C STRIKE COMMAND

    a. Has the authority to launch Strike Command Air Strike Force under positive control [i.e. he can recall them and, without a command to continue, the V-force will turn back before the Start Line is crossed].

    b. Seeks instructions from the Prime Minister or the First Nuclear Deputy on the release of air delivered nuclear weapons.

    c. If unable to contact the Prime Minister or the First Nuclear Deputy, seeks such instruction from the Second Nuclear Deputy.

    d. If b. and c. above prove impossible, attempts to obtain instructions from SACEUR [NATO's Supreme Allied Commander Europe] and to ascertain what instructions he has received for the release of air delivered nuclear weapons under joint [US/UK] control.

    e. In the last resort has delegated authority to release the Strike Command Air Strike Force onto their targets.

ii. C-in-C FLEET

    a. Seeks instructions from the Prime Minister or the First Nuclear Deputy on the release of Polaris missiles.

    b. If unable to contact the Prime Minister or the First Nuclear Deputy seeks such instructions from the Second Nuclear Deputy.

    c. If a. and b. prove impossible, special communication arrangements apply.[45]

The careful wording of C-in-C Fleet's contingency 'c' suggests that in 1975 the 'last resort' system of prime ministerial letters on the four Polaris submarines was too secret and sensitive even for the eyes of some Appendix Z initiates – the secret inside the secret, as it were.

The human button, however, that a nuclear nation needs to create and sustain in a permanent condition of readiness involves many more of the Queen's crown servants, besides the 'Z' people – some of whom devote the bulk of their working lives to it. Quite apart from the scientists, technologists and engineers working at the Atomic Weapons Establishment at Aldermaston in Berkshire or at the nearby warhead factory at Burghfield, a small but significant number of civil servants in the Cabinet Office and the Ministry of Defence are involved (plus pockets in the Treasury and the Foreign and Commonwealth Office) and a very substantial number of service personnel (so far they have all been men at the front-end on the V-bombers or in the submarines).

A recently released Cabinet Office file from 1964 illustrates vividly the number of nuclear delivery systems in being or planned in the years shortly following the Cuban missile crisis, at the height of the Cold War. There is no indication in the file why the Cabinet Office has asked the Ministry of Defence for this detailed breakdown, but its date, 22 October 1964, makes it highly likely that the brief was needed as part of the preparatory work for the meeting of Harold Wilson's MISC 16 Cabinet committee on 11 November which decided to continue with the procurement of Polaris.[46] (Wilson had become Prime Minister on 16 October.)

The document reproduced here demonstrates just how substantial and varied a nuclear capability the UK possessed in the mid-1960s and how sizeable were the plans to sustain it into the 1970s (though the Labour government cancelled the TSR.2 strike aircraft project and cut back the planned Polaris submarines from five to four[47]).

THE BRITISH NUCLEAR FORCES

1. A detailed tabular statement of our forces is at Appendix. Except where shown, sufficient warheads are available and planned for the weapon systems quoted.

STRATEGIC DETERRENT

Present Forces

2. Our existing long range forces comprise four squadrons of Victor bombers (32 aircraft) and nine squadrons of Vulcans (72 aircraft) armed with British warheads. Of these, two squadrons of Victors and three squadrons of Vulcans will be armed with Blue Steel, a stand off missile.

Future

3. To replace the V-bomber force there is a programme to build in Britain five nuclear powered submarines. Each submarine on patrol will be armed with 16 Polaris A3 missiles. The missile carcases will be provided by the United States and the warheads will be British. Arrangements have been made to buy and maintain sufficient spares to allow the maintenance of the missiles and their associated equipment to be carried out in this country.

4. The keels of the first two boats have been laid. Two more are planned to be laid in 1965 and one in 1966. The first boat is planned to be operational in June 1968 and the remainder to follow at six monthly intervals. The total of five will enable two boats to be on station and ready to fire at all times and a third at a maximum period of notice of four days.

5. The provision of the Polaris missiles is governed by a sales agreement giving effect to the Nassau Agreement. This sales agreement was signed on the 6th April 1963. It provides for continuing support of the Polaris weapons system.

6. Two of the squadrons of TSR. 2s to be assigned to SACEUR, although

primarily tactical aircraft, will be available if required, with British high yield weapons, to supplement the strategic nuclear forces.

9. The P1154, which is due to begin replacing the Hunter in 1970, will be capable of nuclear delivery. There will be two squadrons each in the United Kingdom, the Middle East and the Far East – a total of 72 aircraft. No extra nuclear weapons are, however, being provided for these aircraft.

NAVAL FORCES

Present
10. Of a possible total embarked strike force of 79 aircraft 50% of Sea Vixen and Scimitar and all Buccaneers (a total of 53 aircraft) could deliver British free falling nuclear weapons. 28 Red Beard weapons have been allocated for naval aircraft. However, all Red Beard weapons are interchangeable between RN and RAF aircraft.

Future
11. Under present plans the total number of Buccaneer and Phantoms embarked will remain at 79 and about half of these will be Buccaneers all capable of carrying a British nuclear weapon. The Phantom which will begin to replace the Sea Vixen in 1968 could be equipped for nuclear delivery. 63 lay-down low yield weapons are earmarked for the RN. These weapons will also be interchangeable between RN and RAF aircraft.

Anti-Submarine Warfare
12. The Wessex Mark 3 Helicopter due to enter service in 1967 will be able to carry the British multi-purpose nuclear weapon for use as a depth charge. The Wasp helicopter, now in Service, could also be modified to carry this weapon. It is planned that the ship-borne anti-submarine weapon IKARA, due to enter service in 1970, should be capable of carrying the same nuclear weapon as an alternative pay load. Weapons used in the anti-submarine role would be found from the total of 63 in paragraph 11 above.

TACTICAL STRIKE FORCE (NATO)

Present

13. We have four squadrons (48 aircraft) of Canberras in Germany and three squadrons of Valiants (24 aircraft), stationed in England. All are assigned to NATO, and are equipped with American warheads.

Future

14. Four squadrons (48 aircraft) of TSR 2s will replace the three squadrons of Valiants and four squadrons of Canberras, and will also be armed with American warheads. There will also be in Germany two squadrons (24 aircraft) of P1154s. They will be capable of nuclear delivery but no extra weapons are being provided for them.

BAOR

Present

15. British Army of the Rhine includes two regiments armed with Corporal missiles, and three composite regiments armed with Honest John rockets and 8-inch howitzers, all of American manufacture with American warheads.

16. No British weapons or warheads are being developed to succeed these and no final decision has been taken to acquire foreign successors. The Corporal missiles become obsolete in 1966, and the Honest John rockets and 8-inch howitzers during the period 1970–73.

MARITIME AIR FORCES

17. There are 9 Shackleton maritime reconnaissance squadrons (54 aircraft) earmarked for assignment to NATO (including the squadron based in Malta). All these squadrons are being modified so that they can carry American nuclear depth charges, which are planned to be provided from stocks allocated to NATO.

COMMAND AND CONTROL

18. The thirteen squadrons of the V-bomber force that are armed with British warheads are assigned to SACEUR on the understanding that the force has certain non-NATO, normally non-nuclear, roles for which varying numbers of aircraft may be required from time to time. Any substantial number of aircraft despatched on such roles are notified to SACEUR. This assignment to SACEUR is also subject to a general provison that they are available to him except where HMG may decide that supreme national interests are at stake.

19. An unspecified number of V-bombers with a nuclear capability are declared to SEATO [South-East Asia Treaty] in the event of major Chinese aggression.

20. The four squadrons of Canberras in Germany and three squadrons of Valiants in England that are armed with American weapons are also assigned to SACEUR. The Canberra squadrons are assigned on the understanding that up to two squadrons may be temporarily withdrawn for other tasks. (There is no proviso of this sort in the case of the Valiants).

21. All these forces in peacetime remain under national Command. In war SACEUR requires the prior sanction of 'the political authorities' before he can use nuclear weapons. He also requires the specific agreement of HMG before he can order the use of British nuclear forces that are assigned to him. There is a general understanding whereby the Prime Minister and the President of the United States would consult one another if time allowed before any United States or United Kingdom nuclear forces were released for use. In addition, they are specifically committed to taking a joint decision on the launching of a nuclear strike by American aircraft based in the United Kingdom or by the Valiant squadrons armed with American nuclear weapons.

22. Aircraft carriers remain under national command until assigned to SACLANT [Supreme Allied Commander Atlantic] which would probably not be before the declaration of the Reinforced Alert. Standing

instructions forbid the despatch of nuclear-armed aircraft except on the Government. Hence authority to act on SACLANT nuclear strike instructions would have to be signalled at the time.

23. Our carrier-borne aircraft form part of the nuclear strike capability declared to SEATO.

24. The Polaris submarines are planned to be assigned to a NATO commander with the proviso, as with the V-force at present, that they are available to him except when HMG may decide that supreme national interests are at stake.

25. The 48 TSR. 2s will be assigned to SACEUR. It will be necessary to consider what special provisos should be included in the terms of assignment (for example, to provide for the temporary withdrawal of at least part of the force for national purposes).

26. Orders for nuclear strike operations for the V-bomber aircraft would come through Bomber Command and be relayed through the British communications system. A national Command and communications system will also be available to pass orders to the British Polaris submarines. In practice therefore a British Government could, if it so wished, order the use of its major nuclear weapons or prevent them being fired on the orders of any other authority.

VULNERABILITY

27. In addition to 13 V-bombers armed with British warheads 4 Valiants and 8 Canberras armed with American weapons are constantly at 15 minutes readiness. In periods of tension when the V-force would be dispersed over 36 airfields in the United Kingdom, the force could be airborne within two minutes of the order to go. (The minimum warning time of a nuclear attack on the UK is estimated at 3½ minutes).

28. So far as can be foreseen at present, Polaris submarines at sea will be as nearly invulnerable to pre-emptive attack as anything can be.

CAPABILITIES

29. Taking into account Russian defensive capabilities, in the light of our latest intelligence, and the low flying ability of the V-bombers, it has been estimated that the V-force could destroy some 20 major Russian cities. The Polaris force will have a comparable capability.

30. The Joint Intelligence Committee believes that the destruction of 20 major cities would be an unacceptable blow at Soviet long-term economy and would seriously weaken the immediate Soviet military potential, and as such would be a sufficient deterrent.

It was this same paper on 'The British Nuclear Forces' which revealed that we would have had *less* than four minutes if the warning sirens had sounded:

VULNERABILITY

. . . In addition to 13 V-bombers [on Quick Reaction Alert] armed with British warheads 4 Valiants and 8 Canberras armed with American weapons are constantly at 15 minutes readiness. In periods of tension when the V-force would be dispersed over 36 airfields in the United Kingdom, the force could be airborne within two minutes of the order to go. (The minimum warning time of a nuclear attack on the UK is estimated at 3½ minutes.)[48]

There is no precise way to calculate the number of people who went into the making of the British human button at the policy, the manufacturing or the operational levels. But it was very considerable, especially during the years of that substantial portfolio of nuclear delivery systems on land, sea and air.

When the V-force crews look back forty-plus years, some of them, like (later Air Vice-Marshal) Nigel Baldwin, who was assigned to Vulcan squadrons between 1963 and 1968, are amazed at the nuclear burden that fell upon them:

I held, particularly as a young Vulcan captain, huge responsibilities. When I look back on it I tremble at the responsibility I had. I signed for my first nuclear weapon when I was 23 years old. When I think about it, it staggers me now. In a way I suppose we were automatons. We weren't encouraged to do much philosophical thinking about it. No, the philosophy was – this deterrent thing, if we do it properly, we won't have to do it. And we took great comfort from that.[49]

Robin Woolven, whose job it was as navigator plotter in the mid-to-late sixties to guide his Vulcan Mark 2 from RAF Scampton just north of Lincoln to thirty-five miles short of Murmansk before it released its Blue Steel missile to destroy the headquarters of the Soviet Northern Fleet, used to draw a similar comfort from deterrence theory as the Standard Vanguard cars took him and his fellow crewmen to the Quick Reaction Alert Vulcans on their operational readiness platforms past the married quarters and the primary school, knowing that no shelter existed for wives and children if world war came. 'They would die if the deterrent failed and our job was to make sure that our bit of the deterrent didn't fail.'[50]

Some V-force crew talked about 'if the worst happens . . .' to their wives and made plans. Teresa Brooks's husband Andrew, another Vulcan pilot, told her not to hang around but to grab the children and some food and blankets and 'just head for the Pennines, it's your best chance'. Both Teresa and Andrew Brooks knew his aircraft would have insufficient fuel to get back. His captain had told him 'just keep flying east, young man, and hope to settle down with a nice, warm Mongolian woman'.[51]

As he clambered into the cramped cockpit of the last still-flying Vulcan early one bright autumn morning at RAF Brize Norton in Oxfordshire in October 2008, all the years of intense training and exercising came back to Robin Woolven. He sat in his old place behind the pilots at the back between the navigator radar's seat and the chair of the air electronics officer. It was 'like sitting in a darkened cupboard flying backwards', he said.[52] The special Vulcan smell got him, too – 'a homely and familiar blend of oil, paraffin, hydraulic fluid, brake fluid, elderly electronic boxes and chaps!'[53]

For Squadron Leader Roy Brocklebank, hearing the sound of the Bomber Controller ordering the 'scramble', which Richard Knight and

I reproduced on *The Human Button*, transports him back to the sixties in an instant (at the time, he was in charge of the vault at RAF Scampton in which the super-secret targets were stored to be placed in a 'go-bag'; one for each aircraft). 'Whenever I hear the cadence of the Bomber Controller's messages, it still gives goose pimples and makes the hair on the back of my hands and legs stand up.'[54] If nuclear retaliation had been ordered in the 1960s, this is what Roy Brocklebank and his colleagues would have heard on their bases or in their cockpits:

Attention! Attention! This is the Bomber Controller for Bomb List Delta. SCRAMBLE. Authentication WHISKEY NINE JULIET. E-Hour One Zero Zero Zero Zulu.[55]

The readiness state of the V-force was exercised regularly and, every autumn, as part of Exercise MICKY FINN, the aircraft would roar off to their thirty-six dispersal fields.

Robin Woolven described MICKY FINN as the time

when the world stopped and, with no warning, aircrew and ground crew were deployed and worked from their . . . dispersal base (Royal Naval Air Station Lossiemouth and Royal Aeronautical Establishment Bedford for my 617 Squadron crew). The exercise would always involve a scramble take-off of all the aircraft from the main and dispersal bases when we, after a simultaneous four-engine start, were always airborne within less than two minutes of the scramble message if we were positioned on the operational readiness platforms at the airfield – if parked elsewhere on the airfield there followed an exciting taxi at speed in a heavily loaded aircraft. The scramble was followed by a training profile flight (with low-level Blue Steel attack) and recovery to base.[56]

Roy Brocklebank, himself a navigator radar on Vulcans, has produced a vivid cartography for the mid-sixties V-force. It illustrates their flight paths from their main and dispersed airfields for the first sixty minutes of flight 43,000 feet above the North Sea, from Bomber Controller's scramble order at E-hour up to the start-line in southern Norway (beyond which they would not fly unless they received a positive instruction to do so).

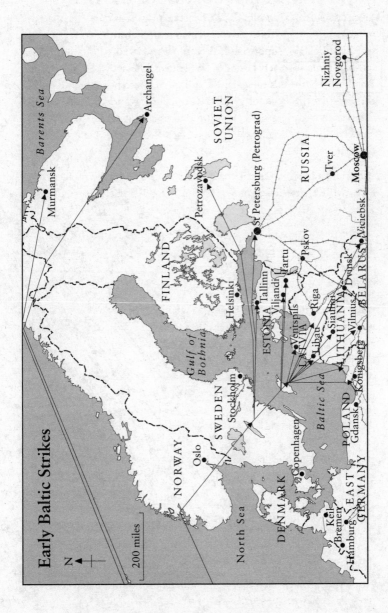

Early Baltic Strikes

N

200 miles

Barents Sea

Murmansk

Archangel

SOVIET
UNION

Nizhniy
Novgorod

Petrozavodsk

St Petersburg (Petrograd)

RUSSIA

Tver

Moscow

FINLAND

Helsinki

Pskov

Wiciebsk

Tallinn

Tartu

Viljandi

ESTONIA

Ventspils

Riga

LATVIA

Siauliai

Drujsk

BELARUS

Gulf of
Bothnia

Libau

LITHUANIA

Vilnius

SWEDEN

Stockholm

Königsberg

Baltic Sea

POLAND

NORWAY

Oslo

Copenhagen

Gdansk

North Sea

DENMARK

Kiel

Bremen

EAST
GERMANY

Hamburg

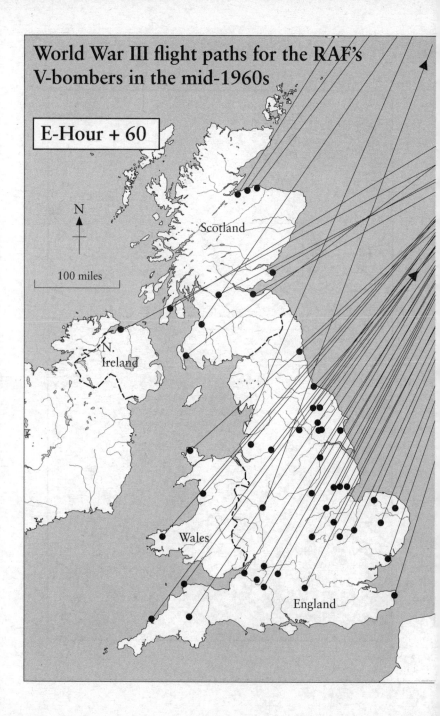

World War III flight paths for the RAF's V-bombers in the mid-1960s

E-Hour + 60

N

100 miles

Scotland

N. Ireland

Wales

England

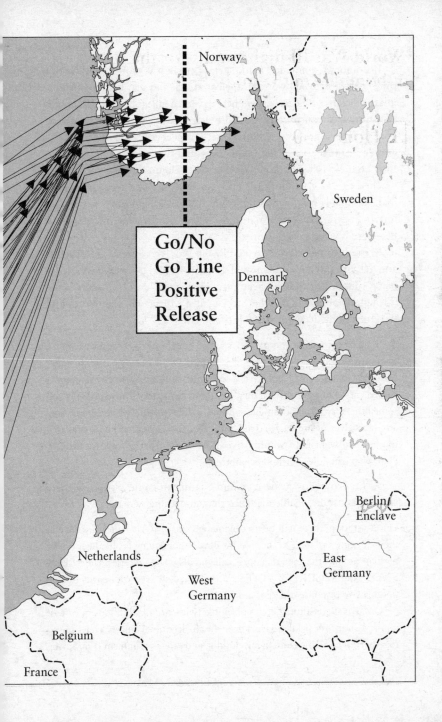

If Bomber Command Headquarters at High Wycombe had by this time been destroyed by Soviet nuclear attack and was unable to transmit the 'Positive Release' order, there existed a fall-back. The BBC Light Programme's transmitters at Droitwich in Worcestershire 'would be used to relay a pre-recorded message – simple, effective, powerful and very long range' – and the bombers would fly across the 'Go/No Go Line' to their assigned targets in the Soviet Union.[57] The V-force never reached the 'Go/No Go Line' even on exercise. The crews, however, had examined every inch of their World War III flight paths to the 'Go' line and beyond and, quite naturally, had imagined what it would have been like if it happened for real.

In the autumn of 2008 I asked Robin Woolven to reimagine the life and activities of a Vulcan crew if global war had come in 1966, from being summoned to RAF Scampton during an 'Increased Alert State' through to launching the Blue Steel against Murmansk and the attempt to return home to what was left of the UK.

. . . if out of normal duty hours, crews would be called in by cascade telephone to ensure all crews not on leave were informed. Coaches may be sent to larger Married Quarters [MQ] sites to collect airmen. Officers (aircrew) sometimes shared cars if driving in from off-base accommodation. Those in MQs and some others left cars for families who were often privately briefed to evacuate themselves to family or friends in Wales, the Lake District or similar if the balloon went up. I would drive in from my married quarter at RAF Hemswell (six miles north of Scampton . . .)[58]

As he drove down the A15 and Scampton came into view there would be instant, visible evidence that something was up:

On the station, there will be an obvious increased RAF Police presence at the main gate and the entrance to Ops Block – something is obviously amiss, perhaps not like the annual major recall and dispersal exercises. The ALERT STATE and SECURITY STATE . . . will be displayed on boards (unless unobtrusive response ordered) . . .

On arrival constituted crews assemble (with *ad hoc* additions in case of non-appearance or sickness [apart from the air electronics officers, crews stayed together]) then change into flying clothing and safety equipment (Life Saving

Jacket, Air Vent suits, protective clothing [e.g. parkas for those overflying Arctic tundra]) and await instructions from Air Plans through the Ops centre.

The 'Battle Order' will be displayed in the Briefing Room with captain's name, squadron, call signs etc. and aircraft number allocated. Routes should be shown as tapes on the wall maps as the Briefing Room is a secure area – but not as secure as the (locked) target study rooms . . .

Briefing material (target, route, met forecast etc.) issued to crews. Navigator plots the briefed route with briefed times, low level routes etc. [the Vulcans would descend rapidly about 250 miles from their targets to between 200 and 500 feet above ground level – this took about 30 miles to effect[59]]. With the flight plan information, the co-pilot plots fuel graph for the whole sortie. The AEO [air electronics off] briefs on signals policy, briefed frequencies and Bomber Command and Group broadcasts, electronic countermeasures briefing . . . Captain (the first pilot of the crew) checks as much as he can and, generally being the most experienced pilot, asks the questions to ensure his crew know what is required of them and how they are to achieve the task . . . If this is an atomic, chemical or biological war we are collecting NBC [nuclear/biological/chemical] gear, respirator and personal weapon (.38 revolver in 1966) . . . The ammunition was encased in a small plastic envelope . . .[60]

V-force crews tended to be very familiar, thanks to hours of target study, with the destination of their weapon and the route to reach it:

If we are attacking one of the previously planned Russian targets, the crews will be issued with their 'go-bags' and this will be for an 'Allocated Line Number' (ALN) the real target. If so the Navigator Radar will have his 'overlays' prepared which he will compare with his actual radar picture at the particular high or low level of the route. Crew with ALNs will have low level large scale topographical maps in plasticised folders with the briefed route drawn in together with the [Soviet] defence installations (latest Surface to Air Missile sites etc.) provided by JARIC [the Joint Air Reconnaissance Intelligence Centre at Nuneham Park near Huntingdon]. If new targets are introduced the crew will need to use all available intelligence to draw up their radar overlays, high and low level routes on large scale topographical maps etc.

V-force veterans are also subject to the most frequent question put to Everest mountaineers:

Crews will be topped up with food and drink in the aircrew restaurant until called to their aircraft . . . the sole toilet facility once in the cockpit was a number of long black rubber 'pee tubes' with their chrome snap lid tops – the tubes were fitted into a retaining clip and one hoped they were held in place securely . . .

The crews 'will probably appear calm and professional but will really be quite tense as it really looks and feels as if we are going to war'.

If the alert state moves to five minutes' readiness the crews will be driven rapidly by coach or lorry to their aircraft, which are guarded by RAF police with dogs. Then the crew check their weapons:

Depending on the weapon loaded, safety pins may have to be withdrawn, pipes disconnected and Bomb Release Safety Locks set . . .

Quickly up the entrance ladder, the last man in pulling the ladder up behind him . . . As soon as the crew enter the aircraft the rear-crew compartment curtains will be drawn so the only natural light, regardless of the time of day, will be entering through the pilot's canopy and the lights in the rear-crew compartment will be adjusted to a low level so that displays . . . will be the main source of light . . . and the Nav Plotter will have his white 'Anglepoise' light adjusted to illuminate his charts . . .

Crew rapidly settle into their seats, attaching emergency oxygen . . . Intercom plugged in helmets . . . The microphones will be switched on and off depending on the situation as many actions require frequent transmissions, particularly running through the many checklists . . .

The voice of the Bomber Controller is continually (every half minute or so) coming into the aircraft via the teletalk line. The aircraft power is on and, depending on the readiness state, the door shut, the bomb doors shut, engine start if called for . . . the checklists crisply and intelligently . . . almost chanted by respective crew members, the captain calling the shots and setting the pace as the four engines rapidly burst into life. Dials and flashing lights everywhere . . . The need to properly authenticate any significant instruction, 'scramble' for instance, will come with authentication which several crew members will record (captain on his knee pad) . . . i.e. that it is that word or phrase as in the sealed envelope in the 'Go Bag'.

With but two minutes to go, how might the crew feel?

This will be a very familiar routine but the fact that this is all for real will add greatly to the urgency and gravity of the well-rehearsed routines . . . no short cuts and no humour . . . even on training sorties as we were dealing with tens of tons of aviation fuel, dangerous chemicals such as hydrogen peroxide [the Blue Steel was filled with hydrogen peroxide and oxygen] and our own lives (most of us husbands and fathers) as well as the lives of the near ground crews.

The order to 'scramble' coming over the teletalk

will have an 'E' hour ['E' stood for 'Execution'[61]] quoted, and on this time are all the route and target timings based . . . there will be no scope for any 'moralising' about families left in their homes and children in schools, the time will be fully taken up with rapidly and safely responding to achieve what is required and what they have practised many times before . . . *I honestly never heard any doubts ever being expressed about what we were training for, where and how we were going, what we were going to deliver or any doubt at all that we would not get the job done on the day.*[62]

It's happened. The 'scramble' order is given and the crew have authenticated it:

the aircraft on the ORPs [operational readiness platforms] will be the first airborne and well within two minutes and almost in formation with aircraft staggered by taking left and right hand sides of the runway . . . the aircraft then climb on their briefed tracks, all one assumes in total radio silence – but there will be much intercom as the crew go through their procedures.

The Vulcan, too, will be tuned to RAF radio frequencies and the BBC Light Programme. Other V-bombers may be visible as they converge from the main and the thirty-six dispersal airfields.[63] As Roy Brocklebank put it: 'Flying up the North Sea they would hope to avoid any enemy bombers crossing their tracks below them and avoid East German early warning radars.'[64]

Navigator plotters like Robin Woolven will at this stage 'be intent on obtaining one or two radar fixes transiting the North Sea . . . All the while the crews will be listening intently to the . . . radio frequencies for any messages either recalling the force (suitably authenticated) or the "Go" or "Release" message (again authenticated) before the aircraft reach the line, normally (if such a word is appropriate here) Longitude 8 East.'[65]

Now the V-force is approaching truly unknown territory in every sense:

Assuming the 'Release' message, suitably authenticated, is received by the time we reach the Release Line, the atmosphere will be even more intense as we have never got to this stage or have flown over this area before. Every effort will be made to adhere to the briefed heights, remaining on briefed track (for safety as there will be no aircraft lights on any of the aircraft) and, with the benefit of a further fix, the descent point will be reached.[66]

From 1964, the V-force, facing an ever greater threat from Soviet surface-to-air missiles (SAMs), adopted a low-level approach (between 200 and 500 feet, depending on the terrain[67]) from about 250 miles away from their targets, as we have seen.[68] By the time of their final approach they were nearer to 200 feet.[69] As part of the shift from high- to low-level attack, the V-bombers changed the paint on their airframes, 'the overall anti-flash white livery was replaced by matt grey/green camouflage . . .'[70] As Roy Brocklebank's map shows, the Murmansk and Archangel Vulcans would turn inland only when they reached northern Norway (to avoid overflying neutral Sweden). Once inside what Robin Woolven called 'the missile belt',[71] the concentration level is intense and the ride bumpy (the crews had practised flying low over the Arctic tundra in northern Canada[72]).

The Nav Plotter will now be using his marked large scale topographical map giving a running commentary to the crew of what they should be seeing ahead and to the side . . . The Nav Rad will have his low level overlays to match with the radar screen . . . All the while the AEO will have his tail-warning gear on, looking for enemy fighters/SAMs and his ECM [electronic counter-measure] gear will be listening for SAM radars searching for us or locking on. In case of the latter he will operate his jammers and dispense 'window' deception material (radar reflecting metallic strips) from the launchers.

The final stage of the attack has been reached:

On the low level run-in to the missile release point . . . the crew will be much stressed but grimly working 'just like training', with the pilots confirming track is keeping with the Plotter's narrative description of hills, lakes, habitation and other landscape features. Meanwhile the Blue Steel missile's health will have been constantly monitored, the inertial navigation platform alignment refined by radar fixes . . . As they approach the briefed weapon release point the checklists are again run through, the missile power unit being started (it has been running on aircraft power to this point) and, at the correct point (probably about 35 miles short of the target), the missile is fired and the aircraft goes into an escape manoeuvre.[73]

Two crewmen were the button-pressers in a Vulcan – the captain and the navigator plotter. 'Button', in fact, is the wrong word. On the Blue Steel-carrying Vulcan, it took the form of switches. The captain threw his first, leaving the navigator plotter to use his at the precise moment required. As it shed its Blue Steel, the Vulcan would leap a bit, but not as much as if it were dropping a Yellow Sun H-bomb. If the Vulcan was delivering a hydrogen bomb, it would be a combination of the captain and the navigator radar who would launch it, pressing buttons rather than throwing switches.[74] The escape manoeuvre required a very tight turn at very low altitude and, as in the case of the Murmansk Vulcan, trying to get back to what was left of the UK if the target was in western Russia and fuel allowed, with 'any relief about a successful sortie . . . far outweighed by . . . concern for the post nuclear-exchange world and for families in particular'.[75]

The Blue Steel-carrying Vulcans would have relatively easily avoided being wrecked by the blast of their weapons. The crews dropping the H-bombs, as opposed to launching the Blue Steel missiles, had the toughest task. They would let the weapon go somewhere between 10,000 and 11,000 feet (to which they would climb in their final approach) five or six miles from the target. Immediately they would turn through 140 degrees while still climbing and be far enough away to survive the blast, which would hit them inside a minute, though the aircraft would shudder vigorously.[76]

The Vulcan was and remains a highly attention-seeking deterrence machine. I shall never forget witnessing one take off into a bright

Oxfordshire sky on 16 October 2008. While the crew were briefing for a flight to an air display at Farnborough, I asked the captain of XH558, Squadron Leader Martin Withers, to make the noisiest possible take-off so that we could record the sound for *The Human Button* BBC Radio 4 documentary. He obliged. Once airborne, the huge aircraft climbed steeply and noisily, its four Olympus engines deafening and shaking us (particularly my producer, Richard Knight, who had his earphones on).

A few days later, recording at the Royal Navy's Northwood bunker and the Trident submarine base at Faslane, the contrast was very marked. Silence and unobtrusiveness reigned. The Trident boats when operational at sea are controlled by the commander of Task Force 345 from Northwood. To reach him you have to descend into the heavily protected installation known as 'The Hole'. You go through a final air lock and past the armed Royal Marines who guard the underground cell and finally into a very ordinary looking office with a small computer at one end and two cupboards containing codes at the other with a table in between. So prosaic is it that CTF345 Commander Mark Honorarty, the former captain of the Trident submarine HMS *Vengeance*, apologizes for the lack of a sinister man sitting in the corner and stroking a grey cat (though he's known as 'H', which adds a faint whiff of Bondery to the scene).

Task Force 345 is the third stage of the firing chain. The first is the Prime Minister and the Chief of the Defence Staff (more on that in a moment). The second is the two Cabinet Office authenticators operating from PINDAR beneath the Ministry of Defence: the military officer assigned to the Cabinet Office's Foreign Policy and Defence Secretariat and his civilian equivalent, a Grade 7 (or Principal rank) civil servant usually on secondment from the Ministry of Defence.

The Northwood cell is manned twenty-four hours a day by a pair of naval officers. When they exercise the firing drill, it runs like this:

First the computer emits three blasts on its klaxon; the fourth is a quick double blast; the fifth like the first three. There follows a ping as the computer prints out the message. A naval rating tears it off and hands it to one of the officer authenticators.

Officer A: 'Prime Minister's Directive received. Standby to authenticate. Ready. Alpha Nine Four Zero Charlie' [for illustrative purposes only].

Officer B: 'Prime Minister's Directive authenticates. Your reply is Alpha X-Ray Five Bravo Delta' [ditto].

Officer A: 'Concur. Prime Minister's Directive authenticates. Stand by to submit the National Fire Control Message.'

The signal is then encoded and transmitted to the Trident submarine on patrol via the very-low-frequency aerials located near Welshpool and just south of the Solway Firth. The submarine keeps in touch with Northwood by trailing a 'wire' just below the surface several hundred feet above its patrolling depth.

This is what it sounded like in October 2008 when HMS *Vanguard* simulated part of the firing chain for *The Human Button* programme. First of all, the Tannoy sounded throughout the boat (we were finishing lunch in the ward room, to be precise): 'EXO [executive officer]. WEO [weapons engineering officer]. Wireless office.'

Lieutenant Commander Peter Noblett, the EXO (no. 2 on the boat) and, Lieutenant Commander Mitch Puxley, the WEO, go straight to the wireless room. The message comes in and a teleprinter reproduces it. The radio crew begin the chain of oral exchanges and confirmations.

WEO: 'Groups complete. Keys 35.'

'13:20:31.'

WEO: 'Time of handover.'

'13:20:34.'

EXO: 'Okay. Good copy received.'

The EXO raises his right hand, holding the message aloft (so that all can see he is not substituting a counterfeit) as he and the WEO walk to the submarine's control room where the captain of the *Vanguard*, Commander Richard Lindsey, is waiting. With the strategic missile officer (SMO), they move to the safe fixed to the floor. An armed rating pulls a curtain around them. The captain and the EXO open the outer safe and retrieve the codes:

EXO: 'My half authenticates, sir.'

WEO: 'My half authenticates, sir.'

Captain: 'Message authenticates correctly. EXO, bring the submarine to ACTION STATIONS.'

EXO: 'Ship control to ACTION STATIONS. Missile for strategic launch.'

At this point a klaxon-like horn (technically known as a 'general alarm') sounds three times. A message is 'piped' throughout the submarine: 'ACTION STATIONS. ACTION STATIONS. ACTION STATIONS. Missile for strategic launch.'

EXO: 'Full rise on the foreplanes. Two up. Stop engine.'

'Two up. Stop engine.'

'Level bubble.'

EXO: 'Very good. Slow start. Revolution two zero.'

'Revolution two zero.'

EXO: 'Hover command. Commence hovering.'

'Commence hovering.'

EXO: 'Stop engine.'

'Stop engine.'

The submarine comes up to the 'hover depth' (which is classified) and halts:

EXO: 'Ship control. In condition one SQ.'

'Condition one SQ. Roger.'

The sound now transfers to the 'Missile Control Centre'.

WEO: 'WEO in the Missile Control Centre. Clocks.'

'Check.'

SMO: 'Ready for handover. Target package has been activated. Missile spinning up.'

WEO: 'Roger. I have the system. WEO, fire control. Fire control in condition one SQ.'

WEO: 'Weapons system in condition one SQ for strategic launch.'

From the control room the captain says: 'The WEO has my permission to fire.'

The WEO has the firing trigger in his hand. It is a Colt .45 pistol with a wire running from its butt. (The practice one is black; the for-real one is red.)

WEO: 'Supervisor. WEO. Initiate five one.'

The Colt trigger clicks.

WEO: 'One away.'[77]

Were it for real, that would be the sound of the end of the world.

The nearest the Royal Navy's submariners have come to the real thing are the test firings the Polaris and Trident submarines undertake off Cape Canaveral, Florida, at the end of their so-called Long Overhaul Period – the DASO (demonstration and shakedown operation, pronounced 'day-so'). Toby Elliott, who was captain of HMS *Resolution* during the Cold War,[78] recalled it as a particularly sobering moment when interviewed for *The Human Button*:

> You have on board the American Shakedown people who help with the train-ing . . . And . . . when you hear the launch has been successful and the warhead has arrived spot on down the range they all go round with cigars and clapping everyone on the back . . . And I remember to this day . . . we all sat there and we were rather stunned. We didn't feel elated about the whole thing at all. We were actually all thinking, 'Gosh. This is what it would feel like for real.'
>
> The only thing you feel as each missile goes is the submarine shudders. It's rather like how I imagine an earthquake . . . We were thinking, all of us . . . this is probably the only time we get that sense of what it would be like.[79]

Every few years, as part of the refit cycle of the Royal Navy's Trident boats, another set of submariners acquires that sobering experience of a missile surging out of the vessel and tons of seawater rushing in to fill the space.

In the spring of 2009 HMS *Victorious*, the second boat in the Vanguard class, completed its mid-life refit at Devonport and set out on its DASO before returning to Faslane to resume its patrols. Early on the morning of Friday 15 May, I joined *Victorious* at Port Canaveral in Florida, a few miles south of Cape Canaveral, as the submarine prepared for the dress-rehearsal of its test launch of the D5 missile. That Friday and during the days that followed I compiled a 'Diary of a Launch', or, as it turned out, a 'Diary of the Launch-That-Never-Was' as will be explained shortly.

FRIDAY 15 MAY 2009

The boat is berthed at a remote jetty some distance beyond the dock where the huge cruise liners (including a Disney one for Disneyland just beyond Orlando) put in. The US Navy bus drops the Anglo-American contingent in bright, early morning sunshine beside the nearest thing I have ever encountered to a 'special nuclear relationship' hut run by the US Naval Ordnance Test Unit. Inside are jolly ladies distributing bagels, jam and coffee. The walls are strewn with pictures, documents and memorabilia starting right back in the early days post-Nassau 1962 and the Polaris Sales Agreement 1963. It's plain from the outset that the two navies are fused and will remain so for the duration of this operation. The boat, once we board, is full of Royal Navy and US Navy personnel and civilian technicians who together will be auditing every move of *Victorious*'s crew and validating the Royal Navy's Trident procedures. The reverse is true when US Navy Ohio Class Trident boats go through their DASOs.

Individual touches are carefully asserted, however. Suitably bagelled and caffeined, the visiting party climb the gangway while on *Victorious*'s casing, a Highlander sailor in a kilt pipes us on board. It's not clear if every Royal Navy Trident boat is required to have a piper on board, but it's a nice touch.

The US admirals start and sustain a running commentary on the Brits and their underwater habits as we clamber down ladders and make our way through the boat's passageways into the ward room.

US Admiral One: 'That's a nice laundry. Ours are crap.'

US Admiral Two: 'We don't have carpets like this in our ward rooms.'

UK Admiral (with a touch of pride): 'Wilton.'

The two US admirals are very tall men. Like several of the Brits on board, they are veterans of patrols 'Up North' in the hunter-killer submarines that watched and listened to the doings of the Soviet Northern Fleet off Murmansk during the Cold War. They are used to somewhat taller US boats and keep catching their heads. 'It's all that protein you consume when you're young,' I explain. They are ace comparators of submarine decor, fixtures and fittings.

Between them, the combined UK/US admiralty aboard have been inside all the world's ballistic missile-carrying nuclear submarines except for the Chinese boats. US/UK style is to keep their ward rooms havens of Formica (less of a fire hazard).

'The Russians' are all spartan and stainless steel. But they have a sauna and a plunge pool.'

'The French have *wood-panelled* ward rooms *and* a fish tank!'

More coffee, then the briefing begins from the UK rear admiral in charge of the DASO, Steve Lloyd. He states its purpose plainly ('This is a very visible demonstration that the UK has a deterrent') and then weaves in the historical context. 'It's fifteen years since the Royal Navy first fired a Trident missile. It's fifteen years before "Successor" [the project name for the planned, new upgraded system] will do the same. Last month we celebrated the fortieth anniversary of continuous at-sea deterrence [when the first Polaris boats took over the primary deterrent role from the RAF V-force].' He runs through the entire US–UK collaboration from Nassau to now.

The three-and-a-half-year refit includes a new core for *Victorious*'s pressurized water reactor, which will last to the end of its operational life; the boat's sound 'signature' will be even quieter and harder to detect deep in the Atlantic thanks to noise improvements. It's absorbed 2.7 million man-hours of work; 2,600 new items have been manufactured; 6,500 welds have been, well, welded; 8,000 acoustic tiles fitted to the casing; and 32,000 litres of paint applied generally since *Victorious* came out of service to start her refit in January 2005.

The boat is gently rocking from side to side now, which indicates we are out in the Atlantic and on the way to the test launch area about sixty miles east of Cape Canaveral. One's nose, lungs and metabolism are already adjusting to the typical nuclear submarine cocktail of smells – oil, cooking, the monoethanolamine used to 'scrub' carbon dioxide out of the air plus about 160 blokes. This concoction, which doesn't exactly cry out to be bottled and sold like some kind of underwater 'Brut', lingers in your lungs and clings to your clothes for quite a time after going ashore.

The whole experience has a whiff of a secret 'special op'. In fact, the world's other nuclear powers represented on the United Nations

Security Council (Russia, France and China) have already been told, under the terms of an international agreement, that a test will take place in the next few days along the range that stretches from the patch of sea to which we are headed to way down in the South Atlantic beyond Ascension Island.

Victorious's crew are remarkably forbearing. Their concentration levels are necessarily high and the crew seem especially highly tuned as the pre-launch drills unfold. Yet their boat, where space is always at a premium, is even more packed today with US/UK navy monitors and assessors – and now a bunch of VIPs as well. The captain, Commander David Pollock (who, I am told, does 'iron man' marathons), reassuringly appears as cool as ice and snatches conversations with us when he can. Later, with minutes to go to the simulated launch, one of the American admirals, Willy Hilarides, talks me through what is happening in the control room where the captain is sitting in his high chair giving the orders. We are watching close by just the other side of his indicator panel. 'Look at him,' says the admiral. 'He's at the top of his game. All his years in the navy have been a preparation for this.'

In a way, I feel wholly unprepared for this even though it's the fourth time I've been on a Trident submarine and, last time, Commander Richard Lindsey simulated much of the last fifteen minutes of the launch drill for *The Human Button*. This time, I've had the fullest initiation of them all. Entering the huge white forest of a Royal Navy Trident submarine's missile compartment (the American Trident tubes are orange) always has a quietening effect on me. But never before have I peered into the front end of a D5 missile and seen its innards.

Rather prosaically it's called the 'equipment section' and it's the machinery from which, with all the booster sections of the missile discarded, the conical re-entry vehicles (hydrogen bombs, in plain language) are launched before their return to the earth's atmosphere. There is room for two technicians to crawl inside for checking and maintenance purposes (the two-man rule holds here as it does all the way down the firing chain from the Prime Minister and the Chief of the Defence Staff). The technicians must shed anything droppable, such as rings on their fingers, before climbing up the short ladder through the missile tube hatch and into the front end. Once inside they can only use certain handholds, which are painted yellow. The rest of the equipment section they cannot touch. The warheads, inert ones in this case, are two to three feet above you.

Awesome is an inadequate word to describe such close proximity to these unimaginably powerful weapons. But if awe was not the reaction there would be something amiss. And as one of the US admirals put it, every time a US Ohio or a UK Vanguard class boat goes out on patrol, it represents, in itself, in terms of its destructive power, probably the fifth or sixth 'most powerful nuclear entity in the world'.

As the clock ticks towards T- (for test) hour, what one might call the food and power side of keeping a Trident submarine going is borne in upon us. These, too, albeit in lesser terms, are awesome enterprises. The 'Manoeuvring Room' where the reactor control is located, is required to propel the boat at 14 knots (as *Victorious*, still on the surface, sails towards the test area) and 4 knots when the boat is on its long, slow, near silent and undetectable patrol. Gazing down through heavily protected glass to the tops of the Rolls-Royce pressurized water reactor's control rods, it seems that this power plant could produce sufficient electricity to keep my London borough, Waltham Forest, going.

As for the provision of human energy, *Victorious*'s young supply officer, on whom the morale of the boat depends for over ninety days, explains his 17.5-ton, 22,000 item, £45,000 worth of inventory. It comes out at 280lb per person per patrol. 'We just eat our way in,' he says, through 75,000 eggs, half a ton of bacon, 3 tons of potatoes and 14,000 sausages, and drink through 45,000 tea bags. It's food – not reactor power – that determines how long the Royal Navy's Trident boats can patrol. If the freezer breaks down or the patrol is extended, the supply officer operates a system of rationing.

Other human needs are harder to satisfy on the boat – not least contact with families. Once a week each member of the crew receives a 'family gram' of forty words in length via the 'Wireless Telegraphy Room'. Once a day they get a rather staccato news summary of what is happening in the rest of the world.

But the strategic purpose of the 3,000-foot 'wire' *Victorious* trails from its patrol depth to just beneath the surface, as we have seen, is to maintain continuous contact with CTF345 at Northwood in case the firing message is transmitted. There are, in fact, eight different ways of getting that signal to the boat. Very-low-frequency transmission is the primary method as such signals are immensely difficult to jam.

T-hour is now close. They are going to simulate it twice. Missile 3 will go first. Missile 10 is the fall-back in case of a technical problem with 3. The plan is to stand beside 3 when it goes and to be in the control room when it's 10's turn. The Missile Control Centre has already simulated for us its final seconds down to T-hour. Once the weapons engineer officer has declared '3 away' for real, he will have joined perhaps the most exclusive club in the UK. There are seven Royal Navy sailors who have pulled the Red Colt .45 trigger and launched a Trident D5 (there have been eight shots; one officer did it twice). *Victorious*'s WEO will be the eighth individual member once number 3 is on its way to the South Atlantic.

We are now dived and in the hover. There is barely a perception of movement. The dive was scarcely perceptible too after 'DIVING STATIONS' has been 'piped' throughout the boat, followed by three blasts on what sounds like a horn.

Concentration in the control room is pretty fierce for the dive and the adjustments to the boat's trim that follow. *Victorious* is checked for leaks. There are none. Mild feeling of relief (this is my first ever dive).

Beside '3' in the missile compartment we hear the control room say, 'T minus ten and counting.'

There are two Royal Navy technicians, closely watched by a US Navy monitor, by tube no. 3, checking the missile's condition. We reach T minus four and the count is halted. The controllers at Cape Canaveral have decided to simulate a low-flying aircraft in the test area to keep everyone on his toes. We repair to the ward room for coffee and muffins until the count is restarted.

'T minus one and counting.'

There is a rush of air and a rumble as the hydraulics open hatch number 3.

'Ten seconds.'

'Three away.'

Another rush of air and you can feel the hatch closing. It's as if one has gone over a speed-bump. The sensation, we are told, will be somewhat greater on the day as 60 tons of missile swoop to the surface and 56 tons of sea water pour in.

The simulated launch of '10' is delayed by cloud cover (this may well be real rather than simulated). Eventually all is ready. You could bottle the concentration in the control room. Commander Pollock says, 'WEO has my permission to fire.' Sixteen thousand tons of Barrow-welded submarine is barely moving at its secret hover depth.

'T minus one minute.'

No. 10 hatch opens.

'Thirty seconds.'

'Missile away.'

Relief in the control room. The boat can now surface and head back to Port Canaveral.

'Stand by to surface.'

This, too, is barely perceptible. There is a slight change of air pressure as in an aircraft coming in to land.

Post-launch, the executive officer, Lieutenant Commander Graham Holmes (a Cold War and Falklands veteran of impressive size and possessor, therefore, of the inevitable nickname 'Tiny') hosts an agreeable dinner in whose preparation the galley has spared no effort. There are toasts. (For 'The Queen', sitting down, as is naval tradition; for 'The President of the United States', standing up).

It's 11 p.m. now. We're going to be much later back to Port Canaveral than anticipated thanks to that simulated light aircraft and that possibly real cumulus cloud.

Paul Cornish of Chatham House and I clamber up seemingly endless vertical ladders to the top of the conning tower, 'the Fin'. Surprisingly, there's only room for four. The young officer-of-the-watch; his look-out sweeping the horizon with his binoculars; Paul and myself. 'It's one of the great moments, saying "I have the submarine" and taking the watch up here,' explains the young officer, and extraordinary it is.

Driving through the Atlantic at 14 knots on a starlight tropical night with a warm breeze above you, the winking lights of the boat behind you, *Victorious*'s pennant and the White Ensign flying inches from your head and Port Canaveral twenty miles ahead, you feel entirely apart not just from the vast sea monster beneath you but from the world. All you can hear is the sound of the huge wave crashing over the bow in front of you.

There is an immense contrast between that easy tropical night, the equally easy chat between the four of us on the cramped bridge and the bulk and purpose of that enormous machine below. For once on a Trident submarine you feel strangely detached from the problems and paradoxes of nuclear weapons policy and deterrence. And it is hard to remember just how politically charged these boats, their purpose and their planned successors are back home.

It's midnight now and time for a change of crew atop the Fin to guide us towards the Florida shore and harbour. Back into the ward room for coffee and a pair of episodes of *Gavin and Stacey* on the screen the sailors lash-up for their DVDs. I apologize vaguely to the American admirals for this, to my mind, particularly ghastly version of British culture being imposed upon them so late at night after a long day on and under the sea. 'Don't worry,' they courteously reply, 'you should see some of the programmes *we* show.' I'm not sure if they mean on the Ohio boats or in the USA generally. The senior Ministry of Defence official next to me on the ward room bench is fast asleep. Lucky man.

Sometime after 1 a.m. we are alongside. We have been on the boat for about sixteen hours. Stylish to the end, the Royal Navy has lined the casing with small lights to guide our way to the gangway; rows of sailors standing to attention either side. Everything disciplined and choreographed in stark contrast to those elected crown servants in Parliament back home who are reeling from daily expenses revelations in the *Telegraph*. News of this reaches us in bits – as, a little later, do the last hours of Speaker Martin. The sailors can scarcely comprehend it. One fiddled rail fare to Plymouth or Helensburgh and they would be out of the Naval Service. Quite right too, they say.

SUNDAY 17 MAY 2009

The *big* VIPs have arrived, including John Hutton, Secretary of State for Defence (humanly and visibly relieved to be away from the Westminster political storm for a few days), and the affable and intelligent First Sea Lord-elect, Rear Admiral Sir Mark Stanhope (everyone is terribly pleased about his new appointment). Before the pre-launch dinner, our dress-rehearsal on Friday stopping short of releasing a missile from its tube, in the Cocoa Beach Oceanfront Hilton Royal Marines beat retreat, stunning in their tropical whites. In the dining room four more Royal Marines are playing string quartets.

John Hutton makes a good speech. He's plainly immensely proud of the workforce in his Barrow constituency who have made the Vanguard class and will do the same for what are still called the 'Successor' boats. Rear Admiral Lloyd tells some rather good Churchill jokes, which always go down well with an American audience. Admiral Steve Johnson replies for the United States. He says he is 'amazed and astounded' at how the UK has maintained continuous sea deterrence for forty years with just four boats in its Polaris and Trident squadrons. It is, he adds, a source of 'constant envy' for the US Navy. This goes down terribly well with the Brits.

MONDAY 18 MAY 2009

Launch day. Up immensely early to board the USNS *Waters*, a huge vessel brimming with electronics and telemetry, which is to carry us out to the launch area. American hospitality is wonderfully ruinous for the complexion – it's cakes and coffee hour-upon-hour topped off by the most lavish of barbecues in the evening. But there are many hours to kill before the launch.

The time is partly filled by a Brits-only 'Chatham House Rules' seminar on the British nuclear weapons programme – past, present and future, chaired by Rear Admiral Simon Lister, Director, Submarines. Present is quite a slice of crown service in uniform and out – army, navy, air force, Civil Service, Diplomatic Service. The three academics go first (myself, John Simpson and Paul Cornish). We start with a scattering of key declassified documents from the pioneering 1940s.

With scrupulous naval attention to detail, someone has written 'downgraded' next to 'Top Secret' on the minutes of Attlee's Cabinet committee which took the decision to manufacture the first British bomb in January 1947. This was declassified in 1983 and sent to the Public Record Office, but, as is patiently explained to me, the guards on the gate at Port Canaveral would not have known this had they searched our bags on the way in.

I relate the story of Ernie Bevin, late and after a good lunch, turning round the ministerial discussion in September 1946 and insisting there must be 'a bloody Union Jack' on top of the bomb. But for Ernie, I say, very probably we wouldn't be here waiting to see that D5 burst out of the ocean. The 'Successor' boats have yet to be named. Why not the 'B' class (to follow the 'R's and the 'V's) with HMS *Ernest Bevin* as the flagship? The chances, I suspect, are nil, given the Royal Navy's tradition of reviving old names. (Queen Elizabeth II and the Prince of Wales excepted in the case of the pair of planned aircraft carriers.)

Michael Quinlan, though he had died in February, is a very real presence at the seminar – constantly referred to in the discussion and the eight interlocking factors he detected in the UK debate, as outlined in his Foreword to *Cabinets and the Bomb*,[80] have been given to all participants in their document pack.

The seminar intermits so that we can view HMS *Victorious*, which has caught us up (the USNS *Waters* is rather slow) and is now about 500 yards away with its tall telemetry instrumentation mast rising high from its casing. The sky is darkening ominously behind the big boat. If there is lightning within a fifty-mile radius the launch will be off as the telemetry will be seriously affected (the missile, if fired, would still reach its precise destination but the supporting measurements would be distorted).

The seminar resumes. News that *Victorious* is about to dive is piped over the Tannoy. Back to the deck.

2:45 p.m. *Victorious* starts to dive.

2:50 p.m. Only its Fin and its rudder and the telemetry mast are visible.

2:51 p.m. There is a flash of lightning in the blackening sky beyond the submarine.

2:56 p.m. Another flash of lightning.

A senior military man next to me quips: 'That's God saying *I* do thunderbolts!' The seminar resumes. The countdown has been suspended because of the storm. We fear we won't see a launch. We're right. The storm has prevailed. *Victorious* has a few days, 'window' to come out and try again. But the crew will have to do it without the benefit of VIPs on board as tight schedules are taking them to Texas and Washington or back to London and Abbey Wood (near Bristol, where the UK's Strategic Systems Executive is located) tomorrow.

The USNS *Waters* plods back to Port Canaveral. Once again we have been at sea for about sixteen hours. As we wait to disembark, the skies open and a tropical downpour descends. White uniforms and linen suits are soaked in the time it takes to run the few yards down the gangway to the buses. The heavens are telling.

TUESDAY 19 MAY 2009

News reaches me (via Jon Snow of Channel 4 News on the telephone from London) that the House of Commons Speaker will announce his resignation that afternoon (I am too remote for Jon's people to get a camera crew to me for an interview – a bit of a relief as I'm a tad short of sleep).

As the bus arrives to take we observers back to Orlando airport, I ask the senior Treasury man who was on board *Victorious* with John Hutton the day before what he makes of the Royal Navy's Trident submariners now he has spent a good deal of time with them. 'They're monastic. A priesthood,' he replies. We disembark at the airport. 'I've got it,' I say. 'We'll call them "The Tridentines".' The Treasury man laughs.

HMS *Victorious* finally got its missile away on Monday 25 May in the dark at about one o'clock in the morning – a week late – and the warheads landed exactly where they were intended to. It was the longest flight ever for a Royal Navy D5. It's distance? Classified information for a good while yet. End of diary. Back to the wider picture.

The human button is an extended one and it embraces the 'Quinlan Paradox'. As Sir Michael himself explained it in the final months of his life, at RAF Brize Norton in October 2008, waiting to witness the last airworthy Vulcan take off:

On the one hand, you make it as likely as possible that if they drive you to it, you will really do it. But precisely by doing that you are trying to maxim-ise the unlikelihood that you will ever be driven to it – that the other side will ever dare to provoke you enough. And, on the whole, the ops [operations] people were on the first part of that paradox – that is, making it entirely credible that we had thought through it and we would really do it if we were driven to it. And, on the other hand, the policy people were in the deterrence business, trying to maximize the likelihood that we would never be so driven.[81]

Quinlan assumed rationality on the part of the nuclear regimes, however authoritarian and brutish, who might threaten the UK with nuclear weapons. A change to a Politburo of truly nasty chancers in Moscow was, as we have seen, one of the Cold War anxieties of JIC analysts and the compilers of transition-to-war exercise scenarios. But what if rationality flies out of the window in No. 10 or one of the prime ministerial redoubts intended to shelter him or her in a period of severe international tension?

In the summer of 2000 I put such a scenario to Sir Frank Cooper:

HENNESSY: Can I ask you a question which tends to lurk in people's minds about this? What if a Prime Minister went bananas . . . at a period of high international tension and authorized the release of the British nuclear weapon and the military advisers concerned, and those small groups of civil servants who were involved as well, realized that the Prime Minister was crackers – what would happen?

COOPER: Well, the key word is 'authorized'. The Prime Minister can only authorize the use of force or the use of nuclear weapons or anything of that kind; he cannot give an order. The only legitimate orders can be given by commissioned officers of Her Majesty's Forces. And this is a fine distinc-tion but not unimportant.

HENNESSY: So, what would happen if I was Prime Minister and you were my Chief of the Defence Staff and I said: 'Frank, I authorize the use of the British nuclear weapon', and you thought I was bananas? What would you do?

COOPER: Well, I'd argue with the Prime Minister for some time. You might not have a lot of time but I'd certainly argue with him and, in the last analysis, say: 'Well, I'm not going to do that' – which would probably mean you'd get court-martialled if you survived. But it may be totally against your military judgement. Now the Prime Minister's response to that would be to fire me straightaway and get a more pliant officer.[82]

Sir Frank went on to explain that 'this distinction between authorization and the power to give orders is a very important one . . . this is where you are into the royal prerogative basically. And, you know, there are many, many cases where the royal prerogative actually plays a very useful part in life and if you didn't have it you *would* need a written constitution.'[83] As we have seen, the Northwood bunker receives a 'Prime Minister's Directive', but Cooper's point is based on the fact that a PM cannot issue such a directive unless the Chief of the Defence Staff concurs and places his codes alongside those of the Prime Minister.

This careful delineation of powers, which Sir Frank took great pains to make sure I understood, puzzled a number of those privy to nuclear retaliation procedures when the 'Cooper axiom' appeared in the first edition of this volume in 2002 shortly after his death. His peers were reluctant to dissent, partly because he had been so close to the subject for so long and partly because, as Michael Quinlan put it, Frank Cooper was plainly 'the best' Permanent Secretary the Ministry of Defence has ever had – 'every other holder of the post would unhesitatingly say the same'.[84]

The consensus among them was that Cooper was *technically* right to distinguish between *authorization* of a nuclear release and the *order* to use the weapons. But in real-time decision-making, it would not arise.[85] It could be, others suggested, that Frank Cooper thought there *should* be a genuine – as opposed to a technical – distinction between a Prime Minister and his or her chief military adviser and had made this point powerfully and publicly in the hope that it *would* become a convention of Britain's famously *un*written constitution.[86]

I asked Sir Michael Quinlan about the 'Cooper axiom' in October 2008:

QUINLAN: I think, with due respect to Frank, that's over elaborate. I think the reality is that the Queen is indeed the ultimate authority. In all practical terms the Prime Minister is. And if the Prime Minister did something which . . . was plainly lunatic, plainly unjustifiable militarily . . . I think that the Chief of the Defence Staff, or anyone else in the command chain like the Commander-in-Chief of Naval Forces which ultimately would deliver it, would have to take their own personal responsibility.

HENNESSY: And stop it? Not do it?

QUINLAN: Not do it. But I don't think they would found themselves on some elaborate theory of the constitution . . .

I asked Sir Michael what he would do if he found himself in a bunker in such circumstances and his opinion was sought (the Permanent Secretary to the Ministry of Defence was not – is not – part of the firing chain).

QUINLAN: Colossally hypothetical, but if I thought that what the Prime Minister was minded was plainly barmy, I would have consulted with others around me like the Chief of the Defence Staff . . . Again one would have to take one's own personal responsibility to influence things in this extraordinary situation for whatever one thought was the right thing to do . . .[87]

The key figure, in real-time political terms, should a Prime Minister lose it in such nuclear circumstances, would be the Chief of the Defence Staff, who with the premier makes up the first of the pairs that comprise the firing chain from the prime ministerial bunker to the Royal Navy Trident submarine on patrol. No serving or retired CDS had talked about this publicly until Lord Guthrie did so for *The Human Button* documentary (first broadcast on BBC Radion 4 on 2 December 2008):

I think the Chief of Defence Staff, if he really did think the Prime Minister had gone mad, would make quite sure that that order was not obeyed. And I think that you have to remember that actually Prime Ministers, they give direction – they tell the Chief of the Defence Staff what they want – but it's not Prime Ministers who actually tell a sailor to press a button in the middle of the Atlantic . . . The Prime Minister could not directly deal with a boat which was at sea . . . But if I thought the Prime Minister was mad, of course I wouldn't [pass on his directive].

This, I suggested, would give time for men in white coats to be summoned as only the Queen can appoint a new CDS:

You could say that. The Prime Minister can certainly sack the Chief of Defence Staff. He might find a more pliable one, I suppose. But these things can't happen terribly quickly. And I suspect that during the time when he was hunting around for a new Chief of Defence Staff common sense would prevail.[88]

The British constitution abhors writing things down. But with the transcripts of the Cooper, Quinlan and Guthrie testimony, do we now have just that for the Prime Minister-going-barmy contingency? I think we do. I certainly hope we do. For the prime duty of this part of the human button is to be *the* ultimate human safeguard should circumstances require.

9

The Safety of the Realm Since 2001

*. . . what I find troubling today is that whilst the direction
of the nuclear threat has now changed, the danger to our
civilisation from other methods of mass destruction is now
probably greater than it was then.*

Lord Callaghan of Cardiff, 2002, recalling his own
initiation into nuclear retaliation procedures on becoming
Prime Minister in 1976[1]

*The Soviet Union, in its ponderous, bureaucratic way, was
predictable. But intelligence in this new world disorder is the
world's most difficult jigsaw.*

Sir Christopher Mallaby, former head of the Cabinet
Office's Overseas and Defence Secretariat, 2002[2]

*We did assume rationality with the Sovs. Now in Al-Qaeda
you have a bunch of people who just want to kill you . . . and
it doesn't matter what the target is and who gets in the way.*

Senior Whitehall contingency planner, 2002[3]

*The [intelligence and security] community has come together
because abroad has come home.*

Senior Secret Intelligence Service officer, 2005[4]

I wish life were like Spooks, *where everything is knowable,
and solvable by six people. But those whose plans we wish
to detect in advance are determined to conceal from us
what they intend to do. And every day they learn – from
the mistakes of others, from what they discover of our*

capabilities, from evidence presented in court and from leaks to the media.

Dame Eliza Manningham-Buller, Director-General of the
Security Service, MI5, addressing the Mile End Group,
9 November 2006[5]

. . . we must ensure that terrorists never acquire a nuclear weapon. This is the most immediate and extreme threat to global security. One terrorist with a nuclear weapon could unleash massive destruction.

President Barack Obama, Prague Speech, 5 April 2009[6]

The bureaucratic spoor of the secret state can be very revealing. In the mid-1970s, the Cabinet's Ministerial Committee on Terrorism commissioned a report on the international – as distinct from the Northern Ireland-related – variant of the threat. It was signed off on 4 March 1975 by the chairman of the Official Committee on Terrorism, Sir Arthur Petersen, Permanent Secretary at the Home Office, an affable man who kept a pub in Lincolnshire in retirement. It was classified 'Secret', and no hint of it reached the public; the Wilson government would not have conceived of releasing even a part of it (even those sections that did not contain operational detail). It was a mere thirteen pages long and it concentrated almost exclusively on the handling of aircraft hijacking after a spate of such incidents involving British aircraft at home and abroad and the results of a command-and-control exercise, codenamed WEST RIDING, mounted in June 1974.[7] Among the improvements suggested for command-and-control procedures during such crises and discussion of the difficulties surrounding the despatch of the Special Air Service PAGODA troop to incidents abroad, some attention was given to the psychology of Middle-East related terrorism. But this was limited to the handling of crises, not the mentalities and motivations that generated the action in the first place.

Fast forward thirty-four years to March 2009 and the Brown government issued 'Pursue Prevent Protect Prepare: The United Kingdom's Strategy for Countering International Terrorism'.[8] It was 174 pages long and contained a remarkable range of detail on the history of terrorist threats to the UK, including an assessment of possible future manifestations; details of the titular 'four Ps' strategy, including a section on chemical, biological, radiological and nuclear weapons and explosives; and rounding off with a communications strategy, for countering the growth of extremism which might spawn terrorist operations or lead to sections of the British Muslim community opting out of UK democratic procedures on the grounds that Western democracy, in contrast to their theocentric beliefs, puts man at the centre of the system rather than God, or, as the document put it, 'to challenge views which fall short of supporting violence and are within the law, but which reject and undermine our shared values and jeopardise community cohesion'.[9]

The contrast between the secrecy and the scope of the Petersen Report and 'Pursue Prevent Protect Prepare' was as remarkable as it was vivid. The 2009 document was accompanied, in my case, by a letter addressed 'Dear Stakeholder' (a term which would have baffled Arthur Petersen and, to be candid, repels me) from the official who oversaw its presentation, Charles Farr, Director-General of the Office for Security and Counter Terrorism in the Home Office.[10]

If in the spring of 1975 some inspired horizon-scanner (another term which the Petersen generation would find strange) in Whitehall had circulated a memo around the Intelligence and Security Committee forecasting that thirty years on the number one priority for the UK's secret services would be international terrorism, that MI5 and SIS had doubled in size over the first decade of the twenty-first century to cope with it and that a proportion of that threat came from young jihadists living in British towns and cities who had passed through British schools and universities, they would simply not have been believed. Nor would they have been believed if they had predicted the demise of the Soviet Union without a whiff of global war or threatened nuclear exchange by 1991.

Yet there is a kind of continuity between the mid-1970s and now. Sir Richard Mottram, who joined the Cabinet Office's Overseas and Defence Secretariat shortly after Petersen reported and retired from the Cabinet Office as Permanent Secretary, Intelligence, Security and Resilience and Chairman of the Joint Intelligence Committee in 2007, noticed that 'the interesting thing about the Petersen document is that

one of the issues – Palestine – is still with us, but it's a different mani-
festation. You've moved from a situation where hijacking was the
chosen means to suicide bombing.'[11]

For those who lived their secret lives operating against the Soviet
Union, its allies and its clandestine agents, the changes remain breath-
taking even after a decade of countering Al-Qaeda and its associates.
And few doubt which is the tougher target. As one Cold War veteran
put it in the days after 'Pursue Prevent Protect and Prepare' was issued:

With the Soviet Union we were dealing with a formed state you could put
pressure on. What we're dealing with now is inchoate and so emotional. This
threat is much harder to deal with. Where is the core of this terrorism? It
feeds on local problems. And while Palestine goes on, there is a kind of toxic
debt swilling round the system.

Penetrating Al-Qaeda is very difficult indeed. In the Cold War, if you could
recruit a Penkovsky or a Gordievsky, you could get pretty close to the centre.
But if you recruit someone in say Iraq, you get nowhere near the centre. And
we won't know how much of a centre there is until Osama bin Laden is
clobbered. Al-Qaeda probably doesn't need much of a centre anyway.

So far, he reckoned, 'all we are doing is stopping terrorist attacks.
It's a bit like shooting down V-1's in World War II as they were flying
over rather than stopping their production. That is what Charlie Farr
(Head of the Home Office's Office for Security and Counter-Terrorism)
is trying to do something about.'[12] That indeed was the thrust of
'CONTEST 2' (CONTEST = Counter Terrorism Strategy), as the
March 2009 document is called in Whitehall shorthand, as we shall
see in a moment.

In a public lecture to the Policy Exchange think tank a couple of
days after 'Pursue Prevent Protect and Prepare' was issued, Charles
Farr traced the history of Whitehall and international terrorism from
the early 1970s to the early 2000s and acknowledged the degree to
which for Western states in the 1980s 'the significance' of the shift from
solely Palestine-related terrorism to what we face today 'was unclear
for much longer than now seems possible'.[13]

'Pursue Prevent Protect and Prepare' analysed 'how the terrorist
threat has changed' and stressed the Mottram point:

International terrorism in the UK and against UK interests overseas during the 1970s and 1980s was usually associated with the single issue of Palestine. Targets attacked or threatened in the UK were very often Israeli and/or Jewish. The groups responsible were predominantly secular and did not espouse Islamist rhetoric or objectives. They claimed no religious justification for their actions. They did not aim to cause mass casualties, which they judged would not assist in achieving their political goals. The use of chemical, biological, radiological or nuclear weapons was neither considered nor a practical option. Those responsible for attacks here very often came into the country from outside for that purpose and made little or no attempt to appeal directly to or recruit British nationals or people living here.[14]

That single paragraph captures the history, the changes and the magnitude of the current threat and the degree to which we did not, as a country, realize we were living in a different world until the attacks on the Twin Towers in New York and the Pentagon in Washington on 11 September 2001 (even though 'the first Al-Qaeda-related plot against the UK' was the one MI5 'discovered and disrupted in November 2000 in Birmingham', as the then Director-General of the Security Service, Dame Eliza Manningham-Buller, explained to the Mile End Group during a lecture at Queen Mary College, University of London, in November 2006[15]). This new world, as Richard Mottram put it, resulted in a 'new calculus of threat', ushering in an era 'of terrorists with the goal of causing casualties on a massive scale, undeterred by the fear of alienating the public or their own supporters – that is, a scale of terrorist challenge and, importantly, of consequence going well beyond that which the UK had experienced in thirty years of Irish terrorism'.[16]

The attacks on the London Underground and upon a bus near Euston Station in London on 7 July 2005 added a dimension of shock and immediacy to the UK's growing awareness of the perils of jihadi-inspired terrorism and, once the bombers were identified, to a realization of the degree of radicalization and the violent expression of it that existed among some of our fellow citizens. It felt, with these first home-grown suicide bombers, as if British society has passed through a valve through which it could never wholly return. And, indeed, it had.

How long it seemed since the hopeful, early post-Cold War days when even those quite free of 'end of history'[17] delusions could none-theless anticipate a sustained easement in terms of the spectrum of threats facing the UK. As Professor Sir Michael Howard put it, when recalling the mood of 1989–90 in 2007 in his *Liberation or Cata-strophe*:

My own world had survived intact and me with it, though at times it had seemed a very close-run thing. A little mild triumphalism did not seem out of order.

This understandable euphoria did not make me believe, as it did some of my friends across the Atlantic, that we had reached 'The End of History'. In my earlier writings I had admitted to a Hegelian belief in the historical dialec-tic, whereby the solution to every problem produces in its turn further challenges; together with a more controversial Kantian conviction that in overcoming and facing fresh challenges mankind has at least the opportunity for moral improvement.

Sir Michael now entered a *mea culpa*:

So I should not have been surprised to find that the liberal capitalism that seemed so triumphant in the West [was] regarded with so much smouldering resentment in the regions suffering from the social upheavals it had caused; and that such resentment should find expression not in traditional inter-state conflict, but in horrific acts of terrorism directed against the most secure and prosperous regions of the developed world. Clearly history was not dead; it may have taken a brief holiday, but was now back on the job.[18]

But there were some in early 1990s Whitehall who behaved as if history *had* ended with the demise of the Soviet Union, at least in terms of the money needed to finance the UK's secret agencies. The attack on their budgets went beyond the traditional Treasury belief that, in public expenditure terms, as one senior figure put it, 'the agencies get away with murder (I don't mean that literally!)'.[19] Sir Colin McColl, whose term as SIS chief, 1988–94, spanned the great transition, recalls being greeted at early-1990s meetings in Whitehall with the words 'Are you still here?', to which he would reply by pointing out that never more than fifty per cent of his service's work was directed at the Soviet Union and its allies.[20] We have already seen how it took Michael Quinlan's mid-1990s efforts to help fend off still deeper Treasury-driven cuts in the budgets of the secret agencies.

Yet there was one observer, writing at the very time the East–West tectonic plates were readjusting themselves and mesmerizing us, who did foresee what was to come that would so change the 'battle rhythms' (to use the argot of today) of the secret state. He was not a spy or an intelligence analyst but a social anthropologist – the polymathic Ernest Gellner. In 1991 he published an essay titled 'An Anthropological View of War and Violence', in which he wrote:

. . . the destabilizing and hence conflict-engendering consequences of developing technology . . . [means] . . . aggression will continue to trump defence, but the means of aggression will become increasingly cheap, widely available and so to speak portable; this diffusion will almost inevitably in the end lead to these means coming into the possession of someone inclined, through fanaticism or folly, to deploy them.[21]

Gellner was particularly attuned to this theme and to capturing the hidden significances of the shifting, early post-Cold War scene, for he was as steeped in both the politics and the societies of the Soviet Union and eastern Europe as he was in the politics of the Middle East and the anthropology of Muslim societies in general.[22]

Looking back at the recently ended Cold War and the nuclear dimension which had made it so utterly different from previous great power rivalries and confrontations, Gellner observed that:

The powerful and destructive weapons were so complex that they could only be acquired in any large quantity by a very small number of superpowers. These tend to be endowed with at least relatively pacific populations: the new weapons could only be produced by industrial machines, whose members are not literally warriors in any old sense, but instead are highly trained technical personnel, whose work and education incline them to lead inherently pacific lives.[23]

Gellner had no illusions about the Soviet Union and its leaderships. Quite the reverse. Nor, I suspect, did he see perfection in the White House during the Cold War years. But, he reckoned: 'The authorities in the superpowers in question were also at least relatively rational and moderate: they were not, by temperament or ethos, committed to either a cult of wild risk-taking as inherently admirable and noble, nor were they, whatever their formal pronouncements, fanatical enough to fight for their belief system irrespective of risk.'[24]

In the early 1990s Gellner sensed that 'All these assumptions may in due course cease to hold', and that 'hugely destructive weapons may no longer be so difficult to manufacture to the point where 'they may become increasingly available by purchase, or even by local production, even to societies whose members are not pervaded by a relatively pacific, productive ethos'. He also foresaw the terrifying combination of weapons of mass destruction and the suicide bomber:

. . . while a large armoury may be needed if there is to be any prospect of victory and survival, a much smaller one will do for a determined blackmailer. He knows that his success will depend on the credibility of his threat. He will realise that his threat will only carry conviction if *he really does mean it*, whatever the cost to *him* if his bluff is called. He may be willing to pay that price, even though he knows that, if his bluff is indeed called, he will himself perish together with his enemies.[25]

Gellner concluded prophetically that as 'the proliferation of high-tech weapons proceeds, the probability of some of them being acquired by groups endowed with such a state of mind eventually becomes very great. The present [i.e. early-1990s] increase in international terrorism offers a small but frightening foretaste, as yet on only a moderate scale, of such a situation.'[26] Gellner died in November 1995. He did not live to witness the jihadist attacks on New York and Washington in September 2001 or those in London in July 2005. But he had foreseen with astonishing prescience the combination of social, political and technological factors that are now making the weather for the guardians of national security in early twenty-first-century Whitehall.

Since 2001 Whitehall's secret state has remade itself to a remarkable degree, which is not fully appreciated by the public (though the debates about the length of time a terrorism suspect can be detained without charge, and what UK intelligence officers should and should not do in their relations with allies whose views on interrogation techniques and torture are not those of Her Majesty's government, are vibrant and real

– as they should be). It was a former Cabinet Secretary, Lord Wilson of Dinton, who made a remark to my students that captures this.[27] The British, Richard Wilson said, have the habit of going into their big changes 'as if under anaesthetic'. (He had in mind the UK's accession to the European Community in 1973 and the devolution plus human rights legislation in the late 1990s). Only much later, he explained, do people realize the significance of these huge constitutional changes and ask, 'Is that what we really meant?'

The construction of what I have called 'the new protective state'[28] generally falls, I think, into this 'under anaesthetic' category. Though there is one significant difference. The state that was pieced together at some speed after the Berlin blockade began in June 1948 and was refined over the ensuing forty years was, to adapt General de Gaulle (who liked, as we have seen, to describe the state as 'the coldest of cold monsters'), cold, monstrous *and* secretive. The post-2001 UK protective state may deserve the first two adjectives, but the third, relatively, does not apply.

The degree of openness about much of it (the sources and methods of intelligence-gathering, and certain protective measures and plans justifiably excepted) has been remarkable by previous UK standards. For example, it would have been inconceivable when the Security Service, MI5, was compiling its lists of CPGB members during the Cold War for its director-general to have come down the Mile End Road to deliver a public assessment of the threat to a university seminar as Eliza Manningham-Buller did on 'The International Terrorist Threat to the United Kingdom' for the Mile End Group on 9 November 2006; a practice continued by her successor, Jonathan Evans.[29]

The same judgement applies to what one might call core policy statements on threats and remedies. This is vividly illustrated by comparing the statement we have already examined in the 1957 Defence White Paper on the need for it to 'be frankly recognised that there is at present no means of providing adequate protection for the people of this country against the consequences of an attack with nuclear weapons',[30] which was as candid as it was rare in the Cold War, with the 2006 White Paper 'Countering International Terrorism':

The Government assesses that the current threat in the UK from Islamist terrorism is serious and sustained. British citizens also face the threat of terrorist attacks when abroad. Overall, we judge that the scale of the threat is potentially still increasing and is not likely to diminish significantly for some years.

The UK has achieved some significant successes in dealing with potential attacks by Islamist terrorists since before 2001.* A number of credible plans to cause loss of life have been disrupted . . . However, as the tragic attacks of 7 July 2005 have shown, it is not possible to eliminate completely the threat of terrorist attacks in this country.[31]

The level of candour about the limits to what can be done may have been comparable in the 1957 and 2006 White Papers, but the detail and openness of the portrait in the 2006 document of the state's apparatus for counter-attacking the leading threat of the day would have left the generation which drafted the 1957 assessment in surprised disbelief.

There is, of course, another huge difference. Nothing in the worst possibilities contemplated by the Cabinet Office's Civil Contingencies Secretariat since its creation in July 2001[32] comes anywhere near the desperate and irreversible destruction considered by the Strath Committee or the JIGSAW group. But, as the 2006 White Paper acknowledges:

Given the vast range of potential terrorist attack scenarios, with a wide range of potential consequences, it is neither practicable nor prudent to plan for every scenario. Instead, planning seeks to build generic capabilities and plans, able to be drawn on flexibly in the response to a wide range of terrorist (and other) events.[33]

The bunker planning still bears a marked resemblance to the PYTHON arrangements (though the Royal Yacht is no more, the Queen, as one would expect, will be well taken care of[34]). And, in the first days

---

* We know from Christopher Andrew's authorized history of MI5 'that a year before 9/11, thanks to its counter-proliferation operations, the Security Service – without realizing it at the time – succeeded in disrupting an attempt by Al-Qaida to develop biological weapons' involving the Pakistani microbiologist Rauf Ahmad (Christopher Andrew, *The Defence of the Realm: The Authorized History of MI5*, Allen Lane, 2009, p. 807).

following the 11 September 2001 attacks, the Cabinet Office dusted off the old 'nuclear deputies' files and Tony Blair resumed the practice of appointing two alternative retaliator ministers lest he should be wiped out by an atomic bolt-from-the-blue (the practice had lapsed at some point between the end of the Cold War and his assumption of the premiership in 1997).[35] But there is a profound difference between Cold War post-attack capabilities and today's capacities in proportion to the threats faced. At no time between 1948, when the Civil Defence Bill was rushed through Parliament during the Berlin airlift, and the fall of the Berlin Wall forty-one years later did the UK possess a home defence capacity anywhere near capable of coping with a nuclear attack.[36] By the end of the first decade of the twenty-first century Britain has a civil defence system that approaches reality in terms of likely emergencies (though, naturally, some, like the contingency of an asteroid striking the earth – which was the subject of a contingency exercise in the United States in December 2008 – still retain a Strath-like capacity to chill and numb[37]).

Whitehall's early twenty-first-century review, which fed into the making of the Civil Contingencies Act 2004, looked not just at the impact of terrorist attacks but at a range of possible emergencies. These include what we called before global warming 'acts of God' (such as floods); epidemics affecting humans or animals; the impact of small groups threatening parts of the so-called 'critical national infrastructure' (such as the fuel protestors in 2000); or industrial disputes that jeopardize the supply of the essentials of life (food, fuel, water, transport). The 2004 Act swept up the old Emergency Powers Act 1920 and the Civil Defence Act 1948 and fused the updated powers into a single statute giving legal cover to the generic capabilities needed to deal with the consequences of terrorist attacks or other factors that might seriously and harmfully affect people, infrastructure, essential services and systems.

Examples cited in the subsequent 2006 White Paper (the first to spell out the government's counter-terrorist strategy at length) included the 7,000-plus police officers trained to deal with threats arising from chemical, biological, radiological or nuclear attack; investment in mass decontamination equipment; search-and-rescue and emergency water-pumping capabilities and the ability to deploy them at national, regional and local levels.[38] The Civil Contingencies Act 2004 also placed great, if temporary, powers in the hands of the state to regain control of the formerly nationalized, now privatized and fragmented, public utilities such as gas, water and electricity, should catastrophe strike. In FALLEX and WINTEX days (until the mid-1980s at least) it was relatively simple to exert command and control over the public corporations. Now only the National Health Service and the Post Office, of all the Cold War nationalized or state service partners, remain in the hands of the state.

Another profound change between the Cold War secret state and the new protective state is in the intelligence aspect, which was and is central to both (though old Cold War hands will see much that is familiar in the 'intelligence flows' diagrams on pages 380 and 388). Two differences in particular stand out.

Firstly, the Cold War intelligence contest was state to state. Today's counter-terrorism attack has a swathe of targets, some of which are states, but the most worrying single player of the early twenty-first century so far is Al-Qaeda. Al-Qaeda does not possess a state. It is in some ways equally dangerous, being a source of inspiration and guidance through individuals and the internet with followers and imitators across a large part of the globe in the form of loose networks or clusters of people.

The second great difference is intelligence 'secrets and mysteries'. The ingredients have been reversed. During the Cold War, 'secrets' were the knowledge that could, albeit often with difficulty, be acquired from open and clandestine sources, human or technical means, for much of the time. Examples included the size and capabilities and delivery systems of the Soviet Union's nuclear forces (always the number one priority for collectors) and the order of battle plans of the Warsaw Pact. The 'mysteries' were the intentions of the Soviet leadership – hence the change to a Politburo of risk-taking aggressive types in the Kremlin as the first JIC-crafted scenario for all those transition-to-war exercises.

Today's 'secrets and mysteries' calculations are very different. The intentions of Al-Qaeda and its imitators are murderously plain. It's where its operatives are – in which hotel room; which British back street; which instrument have they picked, rucksack or car, for their bombs and what ingredients have gone into the making of their devices – *those* are the early twenty-first-century mysteries. It's like dealing all the time with the Soviet 'illegals' who never went near the Soviet bloc embassies or trade missions in London and had no diplomatic cover like the KGB or GRU professionals tasked to filch the Queen's secrets. Added to this, the internet gives the inspirers, briefers and trainers of jihadists on UK soil a swift, real-time communications capability that neither side enjoyed at any stage in the Cold War. Surveillance techniques have developed powerfully, too, since the end of the Cold War, so, albeit in a different way, the sense of being involved in a technology race has persisted from the great East–West confrontation into this one, which may, like its predecessor, determine much of the 'battle rhythms' of the UK secret state for another forty years. There exists, too, an important difference on a human level. A senior SIS officer, whose service spanned the Cold War, the curious limbo of the 1990s and the post-9/11 world, found himself in conversation with a retired KGB opposite number. 'In the Cold War,' the Russian said, 'there was respect. We respected each other's professionalism. Not now with the people we are dealing with.'[39]

As with all threats, there has been an element of catching up in Whitehall, after both 11 September 2001 and 7 July 2005. Christopher Andrew's judgement, as the authorized historian of MI5, was that 'the Security Service was slow to see the coming menace of Islamist terrorism'.[40] The wording of the 2006 White Paper suggests this was true also of the home-grown threat. After noting that '[a]s we saw in the tragic events of 7 July 2005, terrorists inspired by Islamist extremism may come from within British communities – the bombers were British citizens brought up in this country', and, after listing Libya, Algeria, Jordan, Saudi Arabia, Iraq and Somalia as the territorial sources of 'terrorist suspects investigated in the UK', the document deals in a quiet way with the surprise and anxiety felt inside the British intelligence community at the magnitude of the domestic as well as the global problem by recognizing 'that the scale of the threat is potentially still increasing'.[41]

At the time the White Paper was published in July 2006, it was estimated that inside the UK 1,200 people were actively involved in jihadist terrorist or terrorism-supporting activities. There were about twenty investigations running into overlapping groups amounting to some 200 individuals. A month after the White Paper was published, MI5 blunted a planned attack on seven flights from Heathrow to cities in North America by suicide bombers trained to detonate while on board explosives concealed in soft-drink bottles. The Security Service, according to its authorized historian, reckoned this plot to be 'potentially the most dangerous terrorist conspiracy in British history'.[42] Operation OVERT eventually led to successful prosecutions. By the time Dame Eliza Manningham-Buller delivered her threat assessment to the Mile End Group in November 2007, the figures were about thirty plots, which 'often have links back to al-Qaeda in Pakistan and through those links al-Qaeda gives guidance and training to its largely British foot soldiers here on an extensive and growing scale'.[43] How many 'foot soldiers' did she have in mind?

What I can say is that today, my officers and the police are working to contend with some 200 groupings or networks, totalling over 1,600 identified individuals (and there will be many we don't know of) who are actively engaged in plotting, or facilitating, terrorist acts here and overseas.

The extremists are motivated by a sense of grievance and injustice driven by their interpretation of the history between the West and the Muslim world. This view is shared, in some degree, by a far wider constituency. If the opinion polls conducted in the UK since July 2005 are only broadly accurate, over 100,000 of our citizens consider that the July 2005 attacks in London were justified.[44]

Distinguishing between helpers and operators – periphery and core – was plainly vexing. By contrast, at the height of the Provisional IRA activities in the early 1980s, British intelligence estimated that the organization had about 10,000 sympathizers in Northern Ireland, 1,200 of whom were prepared to give support to around 600 active terrorists.[45] By the late 2000s, two-thirds of MI5's effort was devoted to countering Islamist terrorism and this in a service that was well on the way to doubling its size since 9/11.[46] In fact, probably unprecedented levels of co-operation between all three secret agencies and the police had led to eighty-six people being convicted in UK courts of Islamist terrorism between January 2007 and January 2009, with half of them pleading guilty.[47]

In the first decade of the twenty-first century, budgets grew, and ever greater numbers of the state's secret servants increasingly operated to the new 'battle rhythms' determined by the percussive effect of jihadist terrorism. By the end of 2009 a very senior figure in the British intelligence community was sure that all 'the extra money for MI5, MI6 and GCHQ means that many more undesirables are being kept tabs on'.[48] The structure of the secret state progressively adapted, too, to the new protective duties that fell to it. The most significant addition to the inherited institutional armoury was the creation, at the suggestion of Eliza Manningham-Buller, of a cross-agency, inter-departmental, multi-disciplinary Joint Terrorism Analysis Centre (JTAC) in June 2003 accountable to the Director-General of MI5 'as well as to an oversight board of senior customers across Whitehall. The DG reported on it to the JIC. During its first nine months JTAC processed more than 25,000 items of intelligence and issued over 3,000 reports.'[49] It now handles about a thousand intelligence items a week. It's numbers have settled down at around 130 staff, ten of whom work there on a visiting basis from one or other of its sixteen partner organizations, which include several Whitehall departments and agencies, the military and the police (all lodged inside the MI5 headquarters, Thames House). The head of JTAC can notify the Cabinet Office that he/she (JTAC has had two male chiefs and one female head so far[50]) intends to raise the UK threat level. The Cabinet Office then decides whether or not to activate COBR[51] (the Cabinet Office's emergency system, which has two locations within easy reach of all the Whitehall players. COBR stands for Cabinet Office Briefing Room and is popularly known as 'COBRA').

There are five threat levels:

Low: an attack is unlikely
Moderate: an attack is possible, but not likely
Substantial: an attack is a strong possibility
Severe: an attack is highly likely
Critical: an attack is expected imminently.[52]

JTAC emerged, as an intelligence officer closely involved in its foundation put it, as a 'story of pragmatic British improvisation'.[53] It is squarely inside the classic UK intelligence tradition in that JTAC only does assessment and analysis, not policy advice – apart from the requirement laid on its head of deciding threat levels.

In the 1980s and 1990s, MI5 deployed about half a dozen officers on international counter-terrorism (i.e. terrorism not related to Northern Ireland). Their job was to keep an eye on the threat posed by an

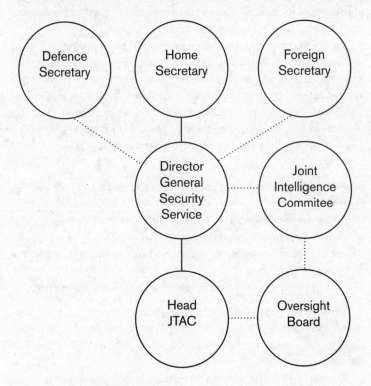

Joint Terrorism Analysis Centre accountabilities

array of groups in the Middle East especially, and to react to SIS and GCHQ reports on them.[54] Post-9/11, it was instantly appreciated, as one MI5 insider expressed it, that 'our job was not going to be the same again'. The Security Service set up CTAC, its Counter Terrorism Analysis Centre, and the Ministry of Defence's Defence Intelligence Staff created DITAC, the Defence International Terrorism Analysis Centre. Both CTAC and DITAC went into the fusion from which JTAC emerged in June 2003 after a presentation to the Joint Intelligence Committee in January 2003 which then approved its creation.[55]

JTAC has its own internal accountability structure (see figure on p. 375). Its director reports twice yearly to the JTAC Oversight Board, consisting of its main Whitehall customers and chaired by the head of the Cabinet Office's Assessments Staff.

The JTAC product represents a substantial and continuous flow of intelligence across Whitehall, the military and the police. These reports reflect JTAC's work on thematic problems (such as the roots of the radicalization of young Muslims living in the UK) and local, regional and country variations of the threat posed chiefly by Islamist terrorism (Northern Ireland-related terrorism is handled separately by MI5). JTAC reports, all emblazoned with its purple rose logo, take a variety of forms:

Terrorism threat alerts: swift assessments of intelligence about possible attacks.

Terrorism reports: all other aspects, including regional assessments and changes in terrorist methodology and strategy.

Threat level advice: assessments of threats to specific events, e.g. the 2012 Olympics in London.

Country assessments: covering terrorist threats to UK interests abroad.

JTAC also feeds analyses and assessments into a range of law-enforcement and other agencies and provides reports to allied intelligence services or those with whom the UK has other kinds of liaison arrangements.[56]

Essentially, JTAC brings together existing counter-international terrorism expertise across the crown and public services into what amounts to a thinking vacuum cleaner for all the particles thrown up by the range of threats it faces, with a set of attachments for the rapid appraisal and dissemination of the threats, patterns and contingencies those particles represent. At the turn of 2009/10, it gives every appearance of being a permanent fixture in the architecture of the UK secret state, and it has spawned a number of imitators across the developed world.

But it has not simply been the arrangements for gathering and assessing intelligence on threats which have changed; the decision-taking structures up to Cabinet committee level mutated, too, as the decade deepened, and changed substantially between CONTEST 1 and CONTEST 2, as we shall now see.

In 2006 I attempted an 'overflight' of the decision-taking, operational and intelligence aspects of the 'new protective state'. The picture below reflected the four Ps (pursuit, prevention, protection and preparation)

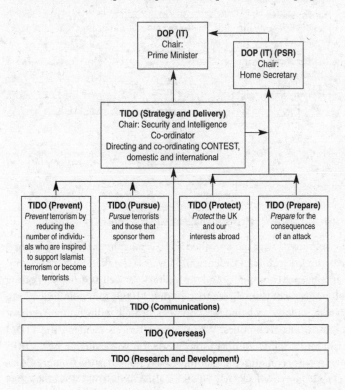

which were and remain at the heart of the government's counter-terrorist strategy[57] (though, later, the Director-General of MI5, Jonathan Evans, added an informal fifth P – 'perseverance' – in an address to his staff in 2009).[58]

Under CONTEST 1, the system was overseen by a sub-committee of the Cabinet's Defence and Overseas Policy Committee known as DOP(IT), i.e. Defence and Overseas Policy (International Terrorism), which the Prime Minister, Tony Blair, chaired.[59] Much of the detailed work was undertaken by DOP(IT) (PSR – Protection, Security and Resilience), chaired by the Home Secretary. Beneath the two ministerially

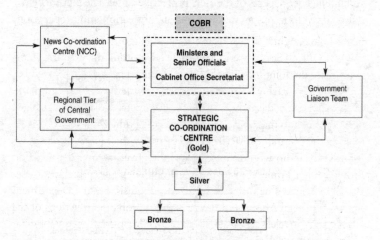

Crisis management structure

led committees was the so-called TIDO machine (TIDO indicating Terrorism International Defence and Overseas) staffed by civil servants, the intelligence community and the military. As well as groups reflecting the four Ps, there were three cross-cutting TIDOs for communications, overseas, and research and development, dealing with counter-terrorist equipment and techniques. When, after a serious incident, the TIDO system mutates into an operations mode,[60] it was overseen by COBR, the emergency committee at that time solely housed in the Cabinet Office Briefing Room (itself an early 1970s creation of the Cold War co-located with the Prime Minister's 'Nuclear Release Room').[61] The composition of COBR depends on the nature of the crisis and, when ministers are present, it is chaired by either the Prime Minister or the Home Secretary. As the Crisis Management structure (2006) diagram above indicates, it is linked televisually and electronically with comparable emergency rooms in the regions, and, if necessary, in the UK's military districts. The conduct of operations reflects the standard cascade of command from 'gold' through 'silver' to 'bronze' used by the police in major operations linking top commanders with the officer in charge on the spot.

The intelligence flows diagram (page 380) is largely self-explanatory. It incorporates one of the changes recommended by the Butler inquiry into intelligence relating to the Iraq War of 2003, most notably the creation of a Head of Intelligence Analysis, the first holder of the post being Jane Knight.[62] It also reflects the fusing of the functions of the Cabinet Office's Security and Intelligence Co-ordinator with the chairmanship of the Joint Intelligence Committee that occurred in November 2005 when Sir Richard Mottram replaced Bill Jeffrey as Co-ordinator.

In March 2007, the architecture of the new protective state was changed again largely into the design pressed upon the Prime Minister Tony Blair (then in the last months of his premiership) by the Home Secretary, Dr John Reid[63] (who would himself leave the government when Gordon Brown became Prime Minister the following June). The spring 2007 redesign also created a Ministry of Justice from a fusion of the Department of Constitutional Affairs and the prison and probation functions of the Home Office to release ministerial time and departmental energy for what Blair called 'a step change in our approach to managing the terrorist threat to the UK and winning the battle for hearts and minds'.[64]

Blair explained that what he called 'the continuing and growing threat from terrorism' meant he was 'strengthening the role of the Home Secretary and the capabilities of his Department' in facing it. A new Office for Security and Counter-Terrorism inside the Home Office would take overall responsibility for CONTEST from the Cabinet Office. As part of it, a Research, Information and Communications Unit would be created (this had conscious echoes of the Foreign Office's Cold War Information and Research Department, which operated between 1948 and 1977[65]) to work, as Blair put it, 'in support of the struggle for ideas and values'.[66]

On top of this, Blair also announced on 29 March 2007 a new Cabinet committee structure:

A new Ministerial Committee on Security and Terrorism will be established subsuming the current Defence and Overseas Policy (International Terrorism)

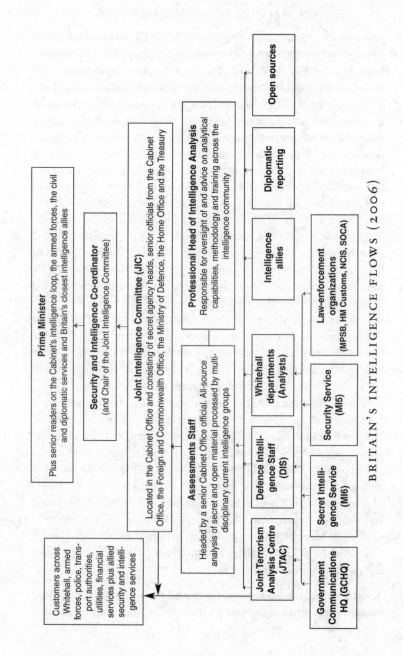

BRITAIN'S INTELLIGENCE FLOWS (2006)

Prime Minister
Plus senior readers on the Cabinet's intelligence loop, the armed forces, the civil and diplomatic services and Britain's closest intelligence allies

Security and Intelligence Co-ordinator
(and Chair of the Joint Intelligence Committee)

Joint Intelligence Committee (JIC)
Located in the Cabinet Office and consisting of secret agency heads, senior officials from the Cabinet Office, the Foreign and Commonwealth Office, the Ministry of Defence, the Home Office and the Treasury

Professional Head of Intelligence Analysis
Responsible for oversight of and advice on analytical capabilities, methodology and training across the intelligence community

Assessments Staff
Headed by a senior Cabinet Office official. All-source analysis of secret and open material processed by multi-disciplinary current intelligence groups

Customers across Whitehall, armed forces, police, transport authorities, utilities, financial services plus allied security and intelligence services

Open sources

Diplomatic reporting

Intelligence allies

Law-enforcement organizations
(MPSB, HM Customs, NCIS, SOCA)

Whitehall departments
(Analysts)

Defence Intelligence Staff (DIS)

Security Service (MI5)

Joint Terrorism Analysis Centre (JTAC)

Secret Intelligence Service (MI6)

Government Communications HQ (GCHQ)

Committee and the counter-radicalisation aspects of the Domestic Affairs Committee's work. The Prime Minister will chair the Committee, with the Home Secretary normally acting as deputy chair, although other Ministers such as the Foreign Secretary, and the Secretary of State for Communities and Local Government, will deputise as appropriate. It will be supported by a sub-committee focusing on counter-radicalisation which will be chaired by the Secretary of State for Communities and Local Government. The committee will meet regularly, and will be supported by a more frequent meeting focusing on the threat to the UK, which will be chaired by the Home Secretary.[67]

The new protective architecture lasted for only three months in this configuration (though the new Office for Security and Counter-Terrorism did endure, and very much makes the running as I write in late 2009), for Gordon Brown moved from the Treasury to No. 10 in June 2007 with a desire to create a British version of a national security council in the shape of his Cabinet Committee on National Security, International Relations and Development (NSID), which, with its sub-committees (as we shall see in a moment), replaced Blair's brief spring 2007 structure. There were also changes in the arrangements at the centre with the splitting of the chairmanship of the Joint Intelligence Committee (which passed to Alex Allan) and the job of Co-ordinator of Security and Intelligence (which went to Robert Hannigan) on Sir Richard Mottram's retirement.

Another Blair innovation that survived the change of premiership was the Prime Minister's 'Daily Highlights' intelligence briefing prepared by the head of the Assessments Staff in the Cabinet Office. But the JIC's weekly intelligence summary, the 'Red Book', having continuously irrigated the minds of the inner loop of ministers since 1951, ceased to be in the spring of 2008, the argument being that it was read with insufficient attention by some of its customers. This I found unconvincing. The world had not noticeably become a more benign place – quite the reverse. The problem, surely, lay with the drafters of the 'Red Book' and the attention spans of some of its readers.[68]

The following year in 2009 Alex Allan reviewed the processes the JIC and the Joint Intelligence Organization used to commission work and the quality of its product. There was a fear on the inside that it was becoming an adjunct of what Walter Bagehot called the 'dignified' part of the constitution, rather than the 'efficient'.[69] From March to October 2009 the JIC went over to meeting fortnightly for the first time since its creation in 1936. The argument for this was that too often its regular members were sending their deputies rather than turning up themselves. In my judgement, the same arguments applied here as they did in the abandonment of the 'Red Book'. The world had not turned more malleable. The problem lay with JIC collegiality. Happily, the weekly meeting was restored after the JIC's annual 'away-day' in September 2009 when it was agreed they had been missing collective discussion on Assessments Staff papers that really merited it.[70]

Out of the Allan Review, and the cumulative experiences since 9/11, including the banking and related crises of 2007–8, on top of his earlier assumption of the job of Professional Head of Intelligence Analysis, came newly minted terms of reference for the JIC:

- To assess events and situations relating to external affairs, defence, terrorism, major international criminal activity, scientific, technical and international economic matters and other transnational issues, drawing on secret intelligence, diplomatic reporting and open source materials.
- To monitor and give early warning of the development of direct and indirect threats and opportunities in those fields to British interests or policies and to the international community as a whole.
- To keep under review threats to security at home and overseas and to deal with such security problems as may be referred to it.
- To contribute to the formulation of statements of the requirements and priorities for intelligence gathering and other tasks to be conducted by the Intelligence Agencies.
- To maintain oversight of the intelligence community's analytical capability through the Professional Head of Intelligence Analysis.
- To maintain liaison with Commonwealth and foreign intelligence organisations as appropriate, and to consider the extent to which its product can be made available to them.*

* In 2009, it retained the long-standing practice of having intelligence liaison officials from the US Embassy and the Canadian and Australian High Commissions in London during the first part of the weekly JIC meeting (private information).

In addition to these six functions, the new JIC terms of reference stated that: 'Members of the Committee are to bring to the attention of their Ministers and Departments, as appropriate, assessments that appear to require operational, planning or policy action. The chairman is specifically charged with ensuring that the committee's monitoring and warning role is discharged effectively.'[71]

In addition to Alex Allan's review, the Cabinet Secretary, Sir Gus O'Donnell (who had restored the practice of the Cabinet Secretary holding responsibility as accounting officer for the budgets of the secret agencies – known as the Single Intelligence Account – when Richard Mottram retired in 2007), commissioned his former private secretary Ciaran Martin in 2008 to conduct another review and to produce a paper on 'Improving the Central Intelligence Machinery'. He reported in July 2009 and a copy was provided to the House of Lords Select Committee on the Constitution as part of its inquiry into the structure and functions of the Cabinet Office.

The Martin Review recommended a new sub-committee of NSID to cover intelligence policy as well as resourcing (on which the long-standing and now superseded Permanent Secretaries' Intelligence and Security Committee (PSIS) had concentrated), including ethical, operational and legal questions of the kind raised by cases before the courts alleging UK connivance in torture practised on detainees held by non-British jurisdictions. This gap was the major weakness it identified. It also recommended an enhanced Cabinet Office intelligence policy capability to run alongside its secret budgeting functions. The overall aim of the Martin Review was to clarify and sharpen up the relationship between the secret agencies and the Cabinet Office, which '[o]f necessity . . . will involve some degree of *challenge*, both to the Agencies and on their behalf. But it is equally important that the Cabinet Office is able to provide some mechanism for *coherence* among the Agencies: indeed it can be argued that part of the central role is to promote the reality of an intelligence community whilst respecting the strong identity and culture of individual services.'[72]

Out of the Blair/Reid changes, the Brown innovations and the Allan and Martin reviews, it is now possible to depict the new protective state architecture Mark II, as I did with the help of the Cabinet Office in

October–November 2009, albeit with all of us knowing that Conservative plans for a National Security Council would change the design yet again if David Cameron and his party won the general election of 2010.[*]

But here is the architecture as it stood in late 2009.

First the Cabinet committee structure (see opposite), which reflects the entire width of NSID's reach (although it is noticeable how many of its sub-groups have a protective state/security and intelligence element within them). There is no 'War Cabinet' for Afghanistan as such, but NSID (A and P) might be seen as one by another means.

In place of the operational diagram of 2006, Whitehall's counter-terrorism architecture in late 2009 (see page 386) embraces both the Home Secretary Alan Johnson's Weekly Security Meeting *and* the Counter Terrorism Strategy (or CONTEST) Board chaired by the Home Office Permanent Secretary Sir David Normington, or the Director of the Office for Security and Counter-Terrorism Charles Farr.

---

[*] When the Conservative blueprint eventually appeared in January 2010, embedded in 'A Resilient Nation: National Security – The Conservative Approach', its centrepiece, as expected, was a new National Security Council, which would 'operate, while fighting [in Afghanistan] continues, as a de facto War Cabinet', to which 'the leaders of the main opposition parties' would be invited to attend 'on a regular basis'. The Cameron approach also involved a streamlining of the Brown Cabinet committee structure and a clear intention of ensuring a 'separation of accountability between intelligence assessment on the one hand, and national security policy/policy-making on the other'. The proposed NSC would be chaired by the Prime Minister (in his absence by the Foreign Secretary, whose Foreign Office would be restored to a more central place in the governing firmament). The NSC would replace Brown's NSID and the Ministerial Civil Contingencies Committee. It would be serviced by a National Security Secretariat in the Cabinet Office headed by a National Security Adviser (who would be an official, not a minister). The NSC would consist of, in addition to the Prime Minister and the Foreign Secretary, the Chancellor of the Exchequer, the Home Secretary, the Defence Secretary, the Secretary of State for International Development and a new Security Minister. Under the full Cabinet, the NSC would take responsibility 'for all national security policy decisions' and the formulation of a 'long-term National Security Strategy' which would not be an annual production, but a document to be updated 'once in the course of every Parliament'. It would also oversee the conducting of a Strategic Defence and Security Review ('A Resilient Nation', pp. 3–67). David Cameron became Prime Minister as this book went to press and his National Security Council was the first of his cabinet Sub-groups to meet.

Cabinet Committee Structure (autumn/winter, 2009–10)

National Security, International Relations
and Development Committee (NSID)
Chair: The Prime Minister

NSID (official)
Chair: Security & Intelligence Co-ordinator

NSID (OD) Overseas and Defence Chair: The Prime Minister

NSID (E) Tackling Extremism Chair: The Prime Minister

NSID (PSR) Protective Security & Resilience Chair: Home Secretary

NSID (PSR) (O) Protective Security & Resilience (official) Chair: Head of Cabinet Office Contingencies Secretariat

NSID (I) Intelligence Chair: The Prime Minister

NSID (I) (O) Intelligence (official, Chair: The Cabinet Secretary

NSID (A+P) Afghanistan & Pakistan Chair: The Prime Minister

NSID (NS) Nuclear Security Chair: The Prime Minister

NSID (NS) (O) Nuclear Security (official) Chair: Security & Intelligence Co-ordinator

NSID (CP) (O) Counter Proliferation (official) Chair: Head of Cabinet Office Foreign Policy & Defence Secretariat

NSID (OA) (A) Africa Chair: International Development Secretary

NSID (OD) (T) Trade Chair: International Development Secretary

NSID (EU) Europe Chair: Foreign Secretary

Whitehall's Counter-Terrorism Architecture (autumn/winter, 2009–10)

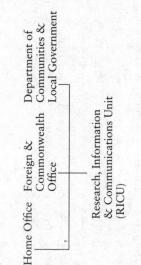

Home Secretary's weekly security meeting participants include: MI5; JTAC; SIS; GCHQ; Ministry of Defence; Foreign & Commonwealth Office; Office for Security & Counter-Terrorism; Department of Communities & Local Government; Departments of Children & Schools; Department of Transport; Treasury; Cabinet Office; Office of the Government Chief Scientist; Association of Chief Police Officers; Research & Communications Unit

Home Office   Foreign & Commonwealth Office   Department of Communities & Local Government

Research, Information & Communications Unit (RICU)

Counter-Terrorism Strategy (Contest) Board
Chairman Permanent Secretary, Home Office: Director, Office for Security & Counter-Terrorism

Prevent Sub-Board   Protect Sub-Board   Prepare Sub-Board   Pursue Sub-Board

Office for Security & Counter-Terrorism (Home Office)

The UK intelligence flows diagram of 2006 has been amended (for example to include the Strategic Horizons Unit) and extended to include the flow of advice based upon it (see page 388).

Organograms have their uses; they are a bone structure which gives shape to the institutional expression of Whitehall and national anxieties in a particular period, but, in terms of drawing out those anxieties, they only go so far. What are the flesh-and-blood anxieties of those who inhabit these structures?

At the top of everyone's anxiety list is, of course, the strategic level threat that would suddenly occur if a terrorist group acquired WMD capacity in the form of chemical, biological, radiological or nuclear weapons. Other strategic anxieties accumulate, such as climate change, and, to some extent, additions to the list of failed states or the factors that go into the 'swarming stage' that can suddenly trigger a mass migration.[73] Michael Howard was right. History has failed to end – with a vengeance.

The 'abroad coming home' factor, as the SIS officer put it in 2005, has had an effect on the UK way beyond the state apparatus, which, through Parliament, has strewn the law with a string of statutes from the Anti-Terrorism, Crime and Security Act 2001 onwards, that have curtailed domestic liberties to a degree experienced neither during the Cold War nor the forty-plus years of Irish-related terrorism. Jihadist terrorism has stretched the open society in the UK in ways it has never been tested before and we may well be but nine or ten years into another forty-year struggle. The liberty/coercion equation has been and will remain at the heart of every element of the counter-terrorism strategies that have dominated the defence of the realm since September 2001, especially in the days after an atrocity.

Philip Bobbitt in his *Terror and Consent* describes as 'the most difficult intelligence challenge of all' the question of 'how to develop rules that will effectively empower the secret state that protects us without compromising our commitment to the rule of law'.[74] The problem existed during the Cold War in terms of how best to deal with the Communist Party of Great Britain or with those crown servants about whom the positive vetting system raised doubts. But current anxieties raise it on a much greater scale, as Bobbitt recognized in 2008:

UK Intelligence Reporting and Policy Advice Flows (autumn/winter, 2009–10)

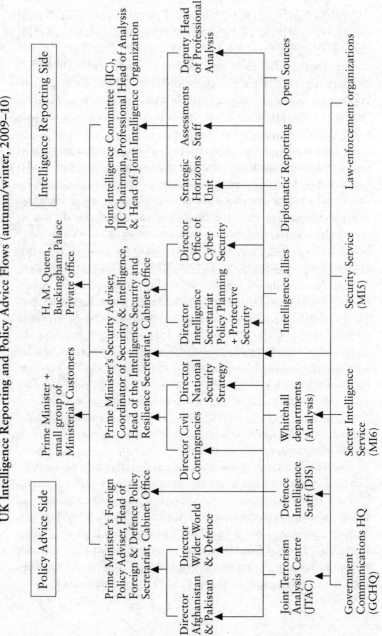

The end of the Cold War was brought about in part because of technologies that empowered the individual and whetted people's appetites for more control over their lives. These same developments also empower networks of terrorists, and the war they will soon be capable of waging has little in common with the industrial warfare of the twentieth century.[75]

One gets the sense that, as with the Soviet Union's penetration of Whitehall in the 1930s and 1940s, the secret state is once more engaged in a continuous process of catch-up. And so am I. For all the growth in general awareness at the possibility of cyber attack (with China generally thought inside the UK intelligence community to be the most adept of the great powers[76]), I was, for example, taken aback in February 2010 to hear a scientist at the heart of the secret state describing the real possibility of a handful of young men with laptops, not a state, 'being in a position to bring down a state'.[77]

Such a contingency would have been beyond the imagination of that scientist's equivalents sixty years earlier, which is not to diminish the very real sense of threat in the late 1940s and early 1950s. For though the requirements of preparing a country for the worst change dramatically and unforeseeably as they have in my lifetime, there are some striking continuities. For example, for all the shifts in geopolitics and the threats the UK has faced over the past sixty years, there is a chilling symmetry between 1950 and 2010 in certain respects. This book begins (see p. xxxii) with the top-secret work of the euphemistically titled Imports Research Committee on the possibility of a '"suicide" aircraft' flying unannounced and incommunicado into British airspace with a 'key point' as its target. The contingency planners of 2010 and the small number of ministers (who include the Prime Minister and the Home Secretary) who have to contemplate and exercise the contingency of a potential 'suicide' aircraft flying into UK airspace from the Middle East or North Africa, refusing to answer calls from air-traffic control, losing height and soon to pass over the M25, have the same decision to face and the same feelings to feel as their equivalents in the early 1950s as the Typhoons on quick-reaction alert at RAF Coningsby are in the air and ready to fire. The threats may change, but the 'cold rules for national safety' have their own dreadful imperatives, generation upon generation.

We didn't need to do that when we were top nation. We need to nowadays.

Senior member of the UK intelligence community on
writing national security strategies, 2009[4]

I would love it if we could become like Norway, where you can pick and choose. You can kind of do good round the world if you feel you've got the money and if you run out of money, you don't need to do anything as it were. Nobody expects anything of you. But it's going to be a very very long time before people stop expecting something extra of us. We are now paying the price in these terms for our history – for having ruled a quarter of the world's population right up to 1945. And it's a very short time ago and you cannot simply wish that away in a matter of half-a-century.

Sir Anthony Parsons, former Ambassador
to the United Nations, 1992[5]

All the evidence suggests that those in power as I write – and those who would like to replace them – have not the slightest desire to abandon the wish for the United Kingdom to bring 'something extra' to the world. And even if, as a country, Britain decided to slim and tone itself down into a medium-sized advanced country inside a huge regional grouping called 'Europe' and to let its former great powerdom rest peacefully in the history seminar rooms of its universities, there is not the slimmest reason to think the world and its problems would cease to bother these islands. Parsons' Law of 1992, as quoted above, holds good in 2010.

What, therefore, might be the ingredients of an early twenty-first-century national security strategy? The first ever attempt by a UK government to answer that question was published on 19 March 2008. Of itself, this was a moment of some historical significance. We had managed as a country without such a piece of paper when we staggered into territorial empire in the eighteenth and nineteenth centuries and when we tottered out, with as much dignity as we could muster (quite a lot, as it happens), in the twentieth. We survived two total wars and a cold one between 1914 and 1990 without feeling compelled to write down what we were for and how we related to the rest of the world. So the contents of what is intended henceforth to be an annual exercise will be a valuable, if shorthand, source for future historians wishing to reconstruct the hierarchy of anxieties bothering successive sets of guardians of the UK's 'cold rules for national safety'.

The shadows cast over Whitehall's serenity in the spring of 2008 were as follows:

Terrorism.

Nuclear weapons and other weapons of mass destruction.

Transnational organized crime.

Global instability and conflict and frail and fragile states.

Civil emergencies (e.g. infectious disease, extreme weather).

State-led threats to the United Kingdom (e.g. covert action by foreign intelligence services, state-sponsored terrorism, cyber attack).

Challenges to the rules-based international system.

Climate change.

Competition for energy.

Poverty, inequality and poor governance (other people's poor governance, not ours).

Global trends (the technological and other vulnerabilities that come with globalization).

The 2008 prototype ranged from strengthening international organizations (NATO, the European Union and the UN Security Council), to offering a 'new bargain' to non-nuclear powers to enable them to develop civil nuclear power without creating the risk of weapons proliferation, and bilateral agreements with countries on counter-terrorism. It covered, too, domestic arrangements such as expanding the Joint Terrorism Analysis Centre and a more integrated approach to the 'underlying drivers of insecurity', including 'tackling the violent extremism which drives terrorism; conflict mediation; post-conflict stabilisation; and the effects on security of the long-term challenges of climate change and global poverty'.[6]

The second 'National Security Strategy', published in June 2009, swept up a similar spectrum of anxieties, plus the unanticipated economic storm that had engulfed the world since the publication of the first strategy document fifteen months earlier:

Over the past year, the banking crisis and the ensuing synchronised global economic downturn has shaken confidence in the rapid process of globalisation and increasing interdependence seen over the past twenty years. Economic downturns inevitably lead to a cyclical slowdown in cross-border economic activities such as trade and direct foreign investment. But the magnitude of the current crisis and its rapid transformation across borders raises the risk that there will be a change in attitudes towards globalisation, and a less permissive environment may result going forwards [these last two words being obligatory linguistic litter in early twenty-first century Whitehall]. Regrettably, protectionist measures have already been taken in some countries.[7]

With the crunch-panic-recession of 2007–9 in mind, what, had I drafted it, would I have added to the original 2008 'National Security Strategy' (for I would have subtracted nothing)? With hindsight, it would have been much improved – and its foresight enhanced – had it contained a passage along the lines of this one delivered by Mervyn King, Governor of the Bank of England, in March 2009 to the Worshipful Company of International Bankers:

Banks are dangerous institutions. They borrow short and lend long. They create liabilities which promise to be liquid and hold few liquid assets themselves . . . Banks have changed. They have encouraged the expansion of proprietary trading, the funding of long-term assets in short-term wholesale markets, a rapid expansion of balance sheets and a marked rise in leverage . . . And the complexity of the products being created made it hard to evaluate the underlying risks.[8]

The 2008 'National Security Strategy' was a stranger to this terrain, even though the summer of 2007 had seen the collapse of Northern Rock and the autumn of 2008 was to see the most extraordinary financial and economic jolt to the peacetime economic well-being of the UK in the lifetime of anyone under the age of seventy-five.

Governor King's speech in the spring of 2009 contained a huge lesson for the compilers of national security strategies. 'Why', he asked, 'did banks change so much and take risks which eventually led to some spectacular downfalls? Ultimately, the main factor was an inability to perceive the true nature of the risks involved. In this they were not alone'.[9]

He then turned to the Keynes of nearly eighty years earlier who had, if only we'd read him, warned of what was to become of us in the early twenty-first century. 'John Maynard Keynes,' said Mervyn King,

took pains to distinguish between risk, where probabilities or frequencies could be calculated, and uncertainty, where there is no scientific basis on which to form any probability estimates. Keynes went on, in an article published in 1937, to spell out exactly how we tend to behave in the face of such ignorance. It explains a great deal of recent behaviour in financial markets. Keynes argued that uncertainty affects our behaviour in three ways:

(1) We assume that the present is a much more serviceable guide to the future than a candid examination of past experience would show it to have been hitherto. In other words we largely ignore the prospect of future changes about the actual character of which we know nothing.

(2) We assume that the *existing* state of opinion as expressed in prices and the character of existing output is based on a *correct* summing-up of future prospects, so that we can accept it as such until something new and relevant comes into the picture.

(3) Knowing that our own individual judgement is worthless, we endeavour to fall back on the judgement of the rest of the world which is perhaps better informed. That is, we endeavour to conform to the behaviour of the majority or the average. The psychology of a society of individuals each of whom is endeavouring to copy the others leads to what we may strictly term a *conventional* judgement.[10]

So the Keynes-derived lessons Governor King was urging upon those still (like me) struggling to fathom what had just struck the UK and why were all applicable to the guardians of national security and the drafters of strategies to help sustain it: Beware conventional wisdoms; search for the lessons of history where you can find them.

In 2005, for example, the fifth edition was published of a rich primer on *Manias, Panics and Crashes* in Charles Kindleberger and Robert Aliber's *A History of Financial Crises*. In their concluding section they declared both prophetically as well as historically that the monetary history of the last four hundred years has been replete with financial crises. The pattern was that investor optimism increased as economies expanded, the rate of growth of credit increased and economic growth accelerated, and an increasing number of individuals began to invest for short-term capital gains rather than for the returns associated with the productivity of the assets they were acquiring. The increase in the supply of credit and more buoyant economic outlook often led to economic booms as investment spending increased in response to the more optimistic outlook and the greater availability of credit, and household spending increased as personal wealth surged.[11]

So far, over 400 years, such epochs had always ended in tears. In 2007–8 another one turned lachrymose as gravity reasserted itself. History helps the framers of nostrums of national security – especially if it is tempered by a sense of humility. And, as a former SIS officer puts it, we need to realize that the *first* people we have to defend ourselves against are ourselves – our self-delusions, distortions and the language in which we express them – before we turn to those wretched people, their isms and, in the case of nasty nations, their hostile intelligence services, who threaten our safety, our prospects and our well-being.

On the question of humility, just think how many significant events in post-war Britain turned out to lie beyond the range of prediction, horizon-scanning and the national security givens of the day. If, for example, in April 1949 when Ernie Bevin signed the NATO Treaty (of which he had been a leading architect) for Britain you had told him that its key clause, Article 5 (binding all its signatories to aid each other in the case of attack on any one of them[12]), would be invoked in the by now non-communist Balkans in the 1990s and in Afghanistan in the early 2000s, he simply would not have believed you. Similarly, had some bright spark in the Ministry of Defence in 1966, when the proposed new aircraft carrier for the seventies and eighties, the CVA01, was cancelled,[13] suggested that one day we might need a carrier-led task force to sail 8,000 miles to the South Atlantic to recapture the Falkland Islands, he would have been sectioned or, at the very least, retired early. In one of the last papers he drafted, entitled 'Shaping the Defence Programme: Some Platitudes', Michael Quinlan (who was himself involved in the CVA01 decision) developed:

A theorem: *In matters of military contingency, the expected, precisely because it is expected, is not to be expected.* Rationale: What we expect, we plan and provide for; what we plan and provide for, we thereby deter; what we deter does not happen. What does happen is what we did not deter, because we did not plan and provide for it, because we did not expect it.[14]

Quinlan's Law, therefore, must be added to our tales of the unexpected.

To the two Hs of history and humility we need to add three more in compiling any national security strategy. Firstly, it has to be holistic. Threats do not conveniently pigeonhole themselves into those which can go to the Treasury or the Bank of England, to the Joint Intelligence Committee or the Civil Contingencies Secretariat, the Foreign and Commonwealth Office or the Ministry of Defence, the Department for Energy and Climate Change or the Office of the Government Chief Scientist. Neither can threats be divided between 'other side' and 'own side'.

The fourth H is honesty. Government must be as frank with its public as is compatible with the genuine requirements of security. And here we touch again on the indispensability of language whose clarity and candour treats citizens as grown-ups to be talked with rather than voters to be manipulated. We start as a country from a very low base here. As I write, the mistrust of ministers (and politicians generally) is palpable. The politics of recession are always scratchy. And when this collides and fuses with the politics of an approaching election, a truly malign political ecology results which coarsens political exchange still further and the vortex of mistrust grows worse. When it comes to threats and resilience, we really do need a new deal between the state and the citizen and a substantial leap in the quality and honesty of political language is central to it.

The final H is hangover (avoidance of). Though we cannot shrug off the hand that our history has dealt us, with the concomitant expectations/obligations referred to by Sir Anthony Parsons, we must always subject future foreign, defence, intelligence and military procurement policies to the question posed by a senior SIS figure in those strange limbo years between the fall of the Berlin Wall and the attacks on New York and Washington almost twelve years later. Are we, he asked during a lunchtime discussion at SIS headquarters in Vauxhall Cross, suffering from 'the itch after the amputation?'[15] This can be a stretching requirement for a country, a people and a polity always and everywhere highly reluctant to contemplate a future as a humdrum, mediocre figure in the world playing at or just below its weight. There remain, too, those expectations that other countries have of the UK in terms of international presence.

One does not require a deep immersion in the world of the Whitehall horizon-scanners to know that, as Fred Astaire used to sing, 'There May Be Trouble Ahead'. This is certainly not a moment to contemplate a benign cycle of increasing easement at home or abroad. Game-raising is required all round. And to increase the chances that both government and governed might 'rise to the level of events' (to borrow a phrase beloved of Roy Jenkins), the remedies are both human and organizational. On the human side we need no law, no extra parcel of public expenditure. As Tony Wright, Labour MP for Cannock and Chairman of the House of Commons Public Administration Select Committee put it in his *Political Quarterly* Lecture in March 2009, to improve 'the emaciated quality of our civic life',

. . . politicians could play it straight. Journalists could play it fair. Parties could resist the rise of a political class. Ministers could make sure that Cabinet government works. MPs could decide that Parliament matters (and clean up their expenses!). Interest groups could say who should have less if they are to have more. Civil Servants could tell truth to power. Governments could promise less and perform more. Intellectuals could abandon their 'mechanical snigger' as Orwell called it. Social scientists could start writing in good plain English. The blogosphere could exchange rant for reason. Electors could decide to become critical citizens.

Quite a manifesto. But, as Tony Wright points out: 'None of this requires a written constitution, a bill of rights, proportional representation, or an elected House of Lords however desirable these might or might not be. But it does require a change of culture'[16] and a rediscovery of the better aspects of our crown service tradition, speaking truth unto power especially.

If the Wright prescriptions *were* lived up to, they would go a long way to meeting the need to first defend ourselves against ourselves and would, in my view, be a major contribution to the non-physical resilience of the UK. Such improvements are entirely possible whatever the rest of the world is doing. So are changes in our machinery of government and our deployment of our one, fixed national capital asset – our brain power (provided our schools and universities keep this in good repair). How might Whitehall arrange itself so that (a) its own human capacities add up to more than the sum of their parts, and (b) government makes proper use of those clusters of grey cells that don't happen to be on its payroll?

The first requirement is for a Prime Minister so to organize his colleagues that collectively they think and act as intelligent customers for the huge array of departments, agencies, secretariats and units that feed – or should feed – information, analysis and advice into their decision-making processes. Gordon Brown's creation in 2007 of his Ministerial Committee on National Security, International Relations and Development (NSID) was a good idea. But its terms of reference were huge – 'To consider issues relating to national security, and the Government's European and international development policies'[17] – embracing the whole spectrum of hard and soft power, diplomacy, politico-military matters, trade, aid, intelligence and security.

To work properly, NSID (or an equivalent) would need to meet regularly (which it does not – the bulk of its work is delegated to sub-committees). Careful thought, integration of questions that cannot and should not be sliced up, serious attempts at foresight and regular discussion must be the ingredients of any British version of a national security council. Similarly, the Cabinet Secretary should commission a capability review of how existing departments, agencies, secretariats and units feed into the work of NSID or its equivalent. So far, there has only been an examination of the relationship between the Cabinet Office and the secret agencies.[18] Three of the four Cabinet secretariats under the Brown-shaped architecture seriously overlapped – International Economic Affairs and Europe; Foreign and Defence Policy; and Security, Intelligence and Resilience. This was not a sustainable division of labour.

On intelligence, resilience and foresight there were a clutch of promising developments in 2008–9. The new Cabinet Office Strategic

Horizons Unit to co-ordinate horizon-scanning and the creation of a National Security Forum of knowledgeable outsiders are good moves towards harnessing a wider swathe of experience and intelligence. Institution building has its perils. In no way should the sustained value of, for example, the JIC's Assessments Staff or the Joint Terrorism Analysis Centre be jeopardized by creating yet another overarching body into which they would feed, And yet, the multiplicity of little platoons beneath NSID would, in my judgement, not have matched requirements had NSID operated in an enhanced fashion. And given the nature of the threats the UK faces, it is harmful as well as impossible to separate out 'home' and 'abroad' in the way that the Cabinet Office has traditionally done in peacetime. And the country really does need Whitehall, the Bank of England and the Financial Services Authority to create the equivalent of the JIC's Assessments Staff to concentrate continuously on that blurred, yet menacing, financial and economic horizon.

One possible solution would be to appoint a very seasoned senior politician, close to the Prime Minister of the day and with no burning desire to usurp and succeed him (probably, though not necessarily, on grounds of age), to be Secretary of State for National Security and no. 2 on NSID. The new minister would need to be Cabinet Office based and serviced by all the Cabinet secretariats. The model here could be successive Lord Presidents of the Council (Sir John Anderson and Clem Attlee), whom Churchill appointed to oversee the home front while he got on with running the war with the Chiefs of Staff between 1940 and 1945.

The choice of individual would be crucial and just as critical to success as any tweaking of the machinery of government. Above all others, for example, the Secretary of State for National Security would possess the duty of speaking truth unto power to the Prime Minister and the Cabinet, especially when it appeared to his or her colleagues that he or she was trespassing on *their* policy terrain. If they wished for a job description there is one that shines through from the past. It's the reply given to Jim Callaghan by the Chief of the Secret Intelligence Service, Sir Maurice Oldfield, in the spring of 1974 when he met the just-appointed Foreign Secretary for their first briefing.

CALLAGHAN: What is your job, Sir Maurice?

OLDFIELD: My job, Secretary of State, is to bring you unwelcome news.[19]

Such a requirement needs not just the right appointee but a Prime Minister self-confident enough and sufficiently determined to make this national security duo work through thick and thin. Such human factors would play powerfully down the national security food chain in terms of making full use of outsiders who, as Bletchley Park people recall only too well, can be as gifted as they are unhouse-trained in Whitehall's ways.

The ingredients of annual national security strategies will fluctuate. Some, I suspect, will be as good as permanent, at least in my lifetime. For example, without the UK's intelligence collaboration with the USA, based on a range of secret agreements that date from 1946, Britain would instantly cease to be one of the three powers with global intelligence reach. Similarly, were a future US President to tear up the 1958 agreement whereby the US and the UK pool nuclear weapons knowledge and designs and suspend the 1963 Polaris Sales Agreement, Britain would cease to be a nuclear weapons power in about a year to eighteen months. Do not expect, however, future national security strategies to express it in quite that way.

But whatever the shifting, moving parts of these productions, each Whitehall and Cabinet Room generation needs to treat as a first-order requirement the question of how best to organize its processes, mechanics and *mentalités*. Thought is needed, too, about how best to organize a national conversation about facing up to the realities of what confronts us and how best to increase our chances of coping with, containing or, where possible, averting the threats that will or might face us.

We have over a hundred years of usable experience here. Much of it takes the form of frozen history – in the National Archives at Kew. With a bit of effort and imagination historians can get those documents to warm up, twitch a little, finally to breathe and to talk. And, like the National Health Service, it is free at the point of delivery. We also, thanks to our tradition of crown service, enjoy the great benefit of a strategic reserve of retired officials, diplomats, scientists, military and intelligence officers who grew up in the shadow of World War II, were recruited and shaped during a perilous Cold War and who, in many cases, had to deal with jihadist terrorism and its consequences before they retired. If, as a country, we don't make use of these human, paper and historical reserves to sustain and enhance our national security thinking and capabilities, we really will need defending against ourselves. For, as a country and a people we can be avoidably undone with nobody to blame but ourselves.

Each generation, when it is minded to refashion past 'cold rules for national safety' into a current 'national security strategy' finds itself faced with a flurry of competing sounds, emotions and impulses. First, there is the ticking clock – the feeling that probably some awful cataclysm awaits, a peculiarly malign mix of circumstances whose combination cannot be foreseen. There follows from that an impulse to prepare. If one is of a certain age, the desire for a half-decent world for one's children and grandchildren comes into play, too.

Yet, in government, these most admirable of human impulses can be trumped by the 'it's all too difficult' and 'it probably won't happen; certainly not on my watch' get-out clauses that are so often deployed to provide aid and succour to tired and overworked minds grown jaded with constant struggle against difficult colleagues, a stroppy Parliament and a relentlessly brutal, trivializing and uncomprehending media.

By the turn of the twentieth and twenty-first centuries, too, the internal relationships of Whitehall – its psychological hidden wiring – were adding still further human barriers for those who wished, in Douglas Hurd's phrase, 'to rub ministers' noses in the future'.[20] As a senior official put it privately to me during the summer of 2009: 'I fear that today horizon-scanning work is more difficult because we face a deficit of trust between officials and politicians of whatever party, which makes speaking truth unto power – or even speaking unto power about potentially difficult trade-offs which may arise in certain circumstances – risky in terms of a continuing relationship.'[21] A few weeks later I put the same speaking-truth-unto-power point to another senior Whitehall figure crucial to the well-being of the state. 'It's tricky,' he said simply and with an air of resignation.[22]

Hearing those two crown servants reflecting on the *mentalités* of their political chiefs left me wondering if Tomasi di Lampedusa's Prince of Salina was right, in Sicily in 1860 (as portrayed in the pages of *The Leopard*), when he tells the emissary from Piedmont: 'I am without illusions; what would the senate do with me, an inexperienced legislator who lacks the faculty of self-deception, an essential requisite for any one wanting to guide others?'[23] And yet if the Prince of Salina's depiction of the self-deluding nature of much of the political class already holds good in twenty-first-century Whitehall, the prospects are worrying. To have a better chance of facing the world as it is, with perhaps a chance of improving it here and there, barriers of attitude in government, especially in its secret state configurations, need attention even more than institutional ones in our ministerial, official and military ranks; we need more crown servants prepared to speak truth unto power and fewer of those who, as Nassim Taleb put it, think 'that it's better to be wrong rather than alone'.[24]

Epilogue: Living on the Dark Side

This was the hard world of shocks and accidents, threats and crises, the raw material of international life, before the policy-makers could impose their patterns on it. Here the news was usually bad, more about the errors, less about the achievements. It was the dark side of the moon, history pre-eminently as the record of the crimes and follies of mankind.

Sir Percy Cradock on chairing the Joint
Intelligence Committee[1]

My predecessor said: 'To begin with, you'll not really under-stand what this is about, and, when you do, you'll be terrified.'

David Young recalling taking over the nuclear release
procedures desk in the Ministry of Defence in 1970[2]

A high proportion of the crown servants whose secret lives are covered by one or other aspect of this book lived – or live – on 'the dark side'. Most would have expected never to be able to talk about it at any stage of their subsequent lives, given the unlikelihood of the Cold War ending (or terminating benignly)* and the ferocity of their indoctrinations into their bit of the secret state and the lifelong obligations of confidentiality that went with such initiations. Only with the declassifications of the 1990s and 2000s inspired by the 'Waldegrave Initiative' were such obligations lifted – partly though, never wholly.

---

* As I write these words a 1979 JIC assessment of 'Soviet External Policies' has just been declassified which ends with the words '. . . they will not give up' (TNA, PRO, CAB 186/28, JIC (79) 5, 'Soviet External Policies', 14 May 1979).[3]

The 'dark-siders' in this study tend to cluster round the worlds of intelligence and nuclear weapons – the first and last lines of the country's defence, respectively. In my experience, most of them, in different ways, remain permanently touched by their own particular brand of secret crown service. In numerical terms, relative to other state activities, they represent a pretty thin first line and an even thinner last line.

Those who worked on the dark side of the secret state during the Cold War lived their professional lives in what social anthropologists might have regarded as special 'enclaves'[3] in which peer considerations, particular kinds of socialization and exceptional pressures operate, whether they be submariners on a Polaris boat or SIS officers in a small but vulnerable station in a Soviet bloc capital or 'nuclear release' Appendix Z people. They were, and are, worlds apart unto themselves, even if part of a common enterprise – the defence of the realm in the round. A cluster of priesthoods, to borrow the phrase spoken by the Treasury official of the Royal Navy's Trident submariners in May 2009.

Counter-intelligence and security considerations during the Cold War contributed powerfully to this apartness through the strict need-to-know principle. This was designed to limit the damage of a successful recruitment of a penetration agent-in-place by the KGB or GRU. It meant many individual secret servants of the Queen knowing a very great deal of the functional secrets of their particular Cold War craft but very little detail about the bigger picture unless their career path took them unusually wide or they found themselves Secretary of the Cabinet with an exceptionally broad overview of the secret state. This last is a point scholars, especially younger ones, must always bear in mind now that we can pursue our shared goal of catch-up history and wander across a range of files which, when created, need-to-know would have confined to very few pairs of eyes.

What was it actually like to have to live on 'the dark side'? How do you cope with the potential immensity of what you do if you are part of the nuclear planning world or the deterrent business? Or the dangers involved to yourself and others if you are a case officer running agents against tyrannies. What is it like if you can talk to nobody outside those with whom you work most closely about what you do? How do you cope if your profession requires you to live like this year on year?

There were few jobs darker in the British Cold War secret state than to be a scientist in the Home Office dealing with civil defence and the 'what ifs' should the bombs drop and the missiles fly. As part of her doctoral research, Melissa Smith uncovered a secret, in-house publication which, from 1961 on, helped them live with the enormities they contemplated every day – they wrote and circulated a journal among themselves called *Fission Fragments*. They found space amid the grim stories and assessments which made up the bulk of the magazine for a bit of light relief.

There was a popular practice in many local newspapers of the time to have a weekly 'Spot the ball' competition; an action photo of the local football team minus the ball. If your cross marked the spot, you won a prize. In 1965 *Fission Fragments* found a way to do the same for its own ghostly and esoteric world. It printed the fall-out plumes from an imagined attack by 2-megaton hydrogen bombs and invited its readers to work out where ground zero was. It called it 'Spot the Bomb'.[4] So did the Home Office Armageddon lifers cope.

It is bad enough even if your exposure to the extreme version of such pressures is relatively short lived, as Peter Hudson recalled of his time in the Cabinet Office's Overseas and Defence Secretariat in the late sixties and early seventies when we talked deep below the Cotswolds in TURNSTILE for *The Human Button*. I asked him what he had thought about the prospect of leaving his family for the prime ministerial bunker as World War III neared.

'I remember having retrospective black thoughts of what I would do if it really happened,' he said. He consoled himself by thinking that his tour of duty in the Cabinet Office was 'nearly finished . . . What would you do, leaving your family like that? I really wasn't at all sure that I didn't rather the balloon had gone up before I got to that stage. I resolutely refused to think of parting from my family . . .'

He couldn't talk to his wife about it, could he?

'No, I didn't. Just bottled it. Not agreeable. I tried to think of it very much as an academic problem affecting some other person.'[5]

David Young's time as an Appendix Z-man overlapped with Peter Hudson's spell in the Cabinet Office. He may well have been the one and only ex-CND marcher ever who was on the Appendix Z circulation list ('I presented the positive vetters with a bit of a challenge!'[6]). 'The abiding feeling amongst us,' he recalled, 'was that this is not war games; that this is pretty serious stuff. At the time of the Cuban missile crisis I did feel nuclear war was imminent . . . I entered the Air Ministry in 1963 with a real fear that there would be a nuclear war.'

Had this feeling dissipated by the time he moved into Defence Secretariat 12 in 1970?

'By no means . . . The bolt-from-the-blue seemed wholly improbable; but never impossible. You could just imagine someone in the Kremlin having a go.'

His job involved 'not just nuclear release but contingency plans, the future of the deterrent, NATO's Nuclear Planning Group . . . It was a pretty extraordinary job to be given at the age of thirty . . . There weren't that many people to talk to. The whole atmosphere of the Ministry of Defence was need-to-know. It was pretty tight . . . Literally, only a handful in the MOD knew.'

How did he cope?

'In the end, I'm an incurable optimist. I could get worried about this, but I could shake it off. I'm a great compartmentalizer. I wouldn't take my work home.'[7]

Submariners on Polaris or Trident boats became weapons engineering officers as lieutenant commanders at much the same age that David Young moved to the MOD's nuclear release desk. One Royal Navy officer who was twenty-nine when first 'his finger was on the button' (the Colt .45 trigger on a Trident) took comfort from 'the nuclear safety rules written in our books', with two people in the loop at every stage:

When you read those rules it's all about preventing inadvertent launch except when fully authorized by the Prime Minister. Irrespective of whether you are committed to nuclear weapons or not, by being in the loop you can ensure that proper control is maintained.

I rationalized it in my mind that the primary purpose is to maintain peace. Most people I talk to rationalize it like that. It's all about the care and preservation of the system and making sure no one can tamper with it.

He regarded his fellow submariners on the deterrent boats as 'a unique bunch of individuals'. Like David Young, he tried not to think about it when not on duty. 'It's a bit like being married. I've been married longer than I have not. And I've been involved in this business longer than I've not.'[8]

Unlike the civil servants or diplomats who serve relatively short spells close to the last line of national defence, the Royal Navy's submariners on the nuclear weapons side can spend a high proportion of their careers involved with the boats, their missiles and their command-and-control systems. The same applies to many of the crown servants at or close to the first line. Both locations are places for people who really believe in what they do. The submarines and the SIS stations are not for the tepid. As one former station chief in a Soviet bloc capital put it:

Once you'd been living in an eastern European country for more than a couple of weeks, you understood why there was a constant current of dissidents and why some dissidents were prepared to risk their lives and oppose in secret and to spy for the West. I was also strengthened in my belief that what I was doing was just and justified. I was also very conscious of how very difficult it was to do our job and to keep our agents safe.[9]

The risk was far greater for the agent than the officer running him:

For us, the case officers, there was no physical danger. We had diplomatic cover and the worst that could happen was embarrassment, publicity, to be sent home *persona non grata*. It is true, however, that on the rare occasions that one of us was caught with an agent, the effect was traumatic – the shock of the event itself, the secret police at the door, rough handling, searching, the noise was frightening. Worst, I think, was the knowledge that we had been discovered or fooled in the sense of the agent being a plant, or taken one risk too many. And, worst of all, our agent, not us, would be tried and shot. For in all of the work of [the Secret Intelligence] Service then, and I guess, now our overriding responsibility was the safety and well-being of our agents.

Of course, the retired officer continued,

they were all sorts; not all idealists, though almost all had a strong streak of idealism. But all were brave and all were putting their trust in us. Their welfare came first and secrets second. Morality and practicality went hand-in-hand. It was right to put their safety first. It was also good sense because good agents were rare. Their best defence was to avoid suspicion that anything clandestine was happening.[10]

As another SIS officer explained, those posted to eastern Europe during the Cold War were always married, preferably with children: 'We didn't want heroes or fanatics. We wanted people who were grounded . . . rooted.'[11]

Rather like the submariners on Polaris or Trident boats on patrol being on the *qui vive* all the time in case the signal should come in from CTF345 at Northwood, the SIS officer behind the Iron Curtain was never really off duty. As the first veteran explained:

In an eastern European country working undercover in an Embassy, all our professional and family lives, our office routines and picnics from the day of our arrival were arranged undetectably to weave in clandestine meetings even though secret meetings were infrequent and brief. Our official lives were busy; our real purpose was always present to keep our agents safe and to get their intelligence to where it would serve their purpose and ours.[12]

Recruiting and running agents to work for the Queen behind the Iron Curtain, or in a Soviet Embassy in another capital (including your own in the case of Oleg Gordievsky), was very different from attempting to penetrate a terrorist organization. This aspect of the dark side, however, has a common thread, as a former SIS Soviet bloc officer with later experience of Middle East-related terrorism explained, 'because if they're important, they're likely to be threatening'.[13]

Agents recruited from inside terrorist organizations, however, are different from the between sixty and eighty agents SIS ran in the Soviet bloc between 1956 (when a new system was put in place for handling agents separately rather than as part of an always vulnerable network[14]) and the end of the Cold War.[15] As the officer who spanned Soviet bloc operations and after put it: 'The first thing, when you're trying to make friends with them and recruit them, is that they had their reasons for getting involved in terrorism. You have to try and get access to those reasons. (Some of the people are very impressive; one man I knew had been in solitary confinement for years.)' But, he added, in terms of self-motivation and learning to live on the dark side, 'one never gives up on people'.[16]

Some shades of the dark side are relatively recent, however. As a senior and veteran intelligence officer put it when talking about 'the dark side of dealing with Al-Qaeda', those within the UK intelligence community both have to counter AQ darkness and to deal with states that are themselves pretty dark. Dealing with countries that do not sign up to the international human rights norms supported by the UK is everyday business for us now. These states do not have the equivalent of the Police and Criminal Evidence Act . . . The fundamental cross the UK has to bear is that if we're going to occupy a position as one of the countries that seems to be most at risk from AQ and if we're going to counter it – which we must – there is no option but to conduct such intelligence relationships (including with the previous United States administration which had a different notion of international law). So we are always going to have to make judgements that, in retrospect, will be contentious within our own courts and jurisdiction.[17]

At the time of writing a number of cases are before the courts in just that area, including one relating to a former detainee in Guantanamo, which the Whitehall secret state has regarded as 'an eccentric legal entity'[18] from its foundation. Currently, too, the guidelines for UK intelligence officers dealing with liaison services in countries that use torture are being revised and the intention is that the new ones (but not the earlier post-9/11 versions) will be published.[19]

The dilemma posed in this area by tackling what the current Director-General of MI5, Jonathan Evans, called 'the most immediate and acute peacetime threat in the . . . history of my service',[20] was described publicly by his predecessor, Dame Eliza Manningham-Buller, in a witness statement to the Law Lords on 20 September 2005. 'Al-Qaida and its affiliates', she said, 'pose a uniquely transnational threat which requires an international response. This has led to increased co-operation between governments, including on security/intelligence channels.'[21]

She explained to the Law Lords how difficult it was for MI5 and SIS to judge the way in which such transmitted intelligence has been acquired:

. . . its provenance is often obscured by the foreign service in order to protect sensitive sources or to comply with local legislation. Where circumstances permit, the Agencies will of course seek to acquire as much context as possible, particularly if the intelligence is threat-related. However, our ability to do this effectively is often limited. Even if the foreign intelligence service is not prevented from disclosing such information by local legislation, it will usually decline to provide it to protect its source. In such circumstances the Agencies will generally not press to be told the source, as to do so would be likely to damage co-operation and the future flow of intelligence from the originating source.[22]

The need to act swiftly and pre-emptively was plainly paramount in Dame Eliza's statement to the Law Lords:

Where more context can be obtained it may assist the Agencies in assessing the reliability of the reporting. However, where the reporting is threat-related, the desire for context will usually be subservient to the need to take action to establish the facts, in order to protect life. Most credible threat-reporting received by the Agencies requires immediate action. Often there is no specific timescale attached to the reporting, but public safety concerns dictate that the Agencies work from a position of possible imminence. The need to react swiftly to safeguard life precludes the possibility of spending days or weeks probing the precise sourcing of the intelligence before taking action upon it, especially when such probing is in any event unlikely to be productive.[23]

She also touched upon intelligence acquired from interrogations of detainees in other countries' jurisdictions – a question which was to acquire greater salience and publicity as the decade deepened:

In some cases, it may be apparent to the Agencies that the intelligence has been obtained from individuals in detention ('detainee reporting'), though, even then, the Agencies will often not know the location or details of detention. We treat such intelligence with great care, for two main reasons: detainees can seek to mislead their questioners, and, where the Agencies are not aware of the circumstances in which the intelligence was obtained it is likely to be more difficult to assess its reliability. However, experience proves that detainee reporting can be accurate and may enable lives to be saved.[24]

There is external evidence, too, of internal anxiety about some of the dark side – or potentially dark side – activities of the current secret state in the *Annual Report 2007–2008* from the Intelligence and Security Committee comprised of parliamentarians from both the House of Commons and the House of Lords. It refers to the Intelligence Services' Staff Counsellor, who has existed in the Cabinet Office since 1987[25] (the job is currently held by Desmond Bowen, a former senior civil servant in the Ministry of Defence and the Cabinet Office). The ISC report also mentioned – and welcomed – the creation inside MI5 of a bespoke Security Service Ethical Counsellor, in the person of a former deputy director-general of MI5 and surveyed the range of concerns brought before him:

whether the Service had adequate mechanisms to evaluate the mental and physical health risks to ICT [International Counter Terrorism] agents; whether the Service should be involved in PREVENT work given the pressure it faces to tackle the terrorist threat directly; whether it was ethical for the Government to seek to alter the ideological views of its citizens (as part of its counter-radicalisation strategy); and whether there are sufficient controls for sharing information with countries that do not comply with international standards for the treatment of those in detention and whether guidance for staff on these matters was sufficiently accessible and understood.[26]

The Director-General of MI5, Jonathan Evans, has stated publicly 'that the Security Service does not torture people, nor do we collude in torture or solicit others to torture people on our behalf'.[27] His former opposite number at SIS, Sir John Scarlett, said the same in the *MI6: A Century in the Shadows* series on BBC Radio 4 in August 2009 (adding: 'We are not in the business of going out and shooting people in dark alleys . . . We do not have a licence to kill'[28]). But Evans has also acknowledged that there was a great deal to be learned 'in the period immediately after 9/11', and not just about the nature of Al-Qaeda but also about US practices after the atrocities of that day:

I do not defend the abuses that have recently come to light within the US system since 9/11. Nor would I dispute the judgement of the Intelligence and Security Committee in its 2005 Report on the Handling of Detainees and its 2007 Report on Rendition, that the [Security] Service, among others, was slow to detect the emerging pattern of US practice in the period after 9/11. But it is important to recognise that we do not control what other countries do, that operational decisions have to be taken within the knowledge available, even if it is incomplete, and when the emerging pattern of US policy was detected necessary improvements were made. And we should recall that notwithstanding these serious issues, the UK has gained huge intelligence benefits from our co-operation with the US agencies in recent years, and the US agencies have been generous in sharing intelligence with us.[29]

He had no doubt, however, that 'we would have been derelict in our duty if we had not worked, circumspectly, with overseas liaisons who were in a position to provide intelligence that could safeguard this country from attack'[30] (a view I share).

The problem arises in another especially acute and not widely appreciated context – the degree to which British intelligence passes on information about individuals to intelligence services in countries with a seriously dark side, knowing the danger of swift arrest and torture that might bring. And the revised guidelines when published will cover, as one insider put it, 'how we transact business with countries that have a dark side and don't observe UK norms'.[31]

There exists a wider, post-9/11 difficulty for those whom the Queen pays to live the bulk of their working lives in these shadows made more sombre still by ethical and moral ambiguities. And the problem is more acute than when dealing either with the Soviet bloc or the Provisional IRA. It is a question of relative consensus – the degree of agreement about the nature and magnitude of the threat posed to the UK by jihadi-inspired terrorism from without and within and from a combination of the two.

For all the capabilities/intentions problem posed by the Soviet Union and its allies during the Cold War, there was, as a veteran intelligence officer put it, 'a feeling of a given . . . that there was a vital strategic threat from a powerful bloc with a scenario available to the other side that could put the country's lights out militarily. This broadly commanded a political consensus that the UK was facing a threat that was not very readable and potentially menacing.' During the forty-year threat from Irish terrorism, there was also a general consensus about curbing it – 'the givens of the dark menaces we confronted' – though that consensus did not extend 'to the Falls Road or in South Armagh'.[32]

But with Al-Qaeda, the intelligence veteran argued,

there are differences which make our lives more ambiguous and troubled . . . and there is not the same national consensus on how much this threatens us because it's much more complicated. AQ is not a state (though the Americans treat it as an entity that wages war in the way a state would). There are enduringly ambiguous questions about, is Islam hostile to the West? (It isn't.) Is the UK's counter-terrorism strategy well judged? AQ aren't going to turn out our lights in the way the Russians might have . . . It's hard to predict its trajectory. And then there is the need to deal with states that are themselves pretty dark . . . And also today there's much more debate in the country about aspects of counter-terrorism and our staff have the same questions in their heads as members of the public. So it's got to be a more troubled, ambiguous era, though none of that is to say there is any diminution on the part of the staff in their desire to counter threats.[33]

In making those judgements, this veteran was reflecting a generation of intelligence officers the variety of whose experience, because it embraces operations against the Soviet-bloc, the Provisional IRA and Al-Qaeda, will never be replicated. Another member of the Cold War generation that 'ran through' explained that some aspects of living on the dark sire span intelligence work whatever the threat currently being faced. Usually (certainly if they are SIS officers) the Queen's secret servants are assigned an orthodox-sounding cover job in the Foreign and Commonwealth Office which is straightforward enough. But creating an alternative cover-person can be more testing. It's not just a matter of using a different working-name, it's a question of designing and sustaining a plausible fire-proof alias in terms of passport, driving licence, bank account. And it can be difficult to prevent your professional deceptions from seeping into your private life. Deceiving for the Queen can come with a stress-laden price tag.[34]

Another factor not lost on those intelligence and security veterans living on the current dark side is the degree to which the earlier shades have not gone away. MI5 in Northern Ireland retains the lead in operating against so-called dissident republicans, whose collective threat does not match that of the Provisional IRA at the height of its campaign, but it's serious enough to have absorbed 15 per cent of MI5's resources in 2007–8.[35] (Coping with Islamist terrorism in its various forms takes two thirds of the total.[36])

In another area of counter-intelligence, the old battle rhythms are not entirely stilled either. As MI5's Director-General, Jonathan Evans, told the Society of Editors in November 2007,

Since the end of the Cold War we have seen no decrease in the number of undeclared Russian intelligence officers in the UK – at the Russian Embassy and associated organisations conducting covert activity in this country. So despite the Cold War ending nearly two decades ago, my Service is still expending resources to defend the UK against unreconstructed attempts by Russia, China and others, to spy on us.

Evans expressed 'some disappointment' at having 'to devote significant amounts of equipment, money and staff to countering this threat. They are resources which I *would far rather* devote to countering the threat from international terrorism – a threat to the whole international community, not just the UK.'[37] This problem plainly is not just a Cold-War hangover and is another example of continuity between the secret state of the 1940s, 50s, 60s, 70s, 80s and now.

The early twenty-first-century secret state puts quite a bit of effort into transmitting its past history to the considerable number of younger staff recruited into the rapidly expanding secret services since 9/11. Christopher Andrew's authorized history of MI5, which was published in 2009, was the most public example of this. Another will be Keith Jeffery's official history of the Secret Intelligence Service 1909–49.[38]

Like the armed forces, the secret services place a good deal of importance on institutional memory and the sense of specialness this can bring. Since the late eighties and early nineties, the intelligence and security agencies have become creatures of statute and contain within their walls posses of lawyers.* As a result, much of their constitutional DNA is captured in statute, the Security Service Act, 1989 and the Intelligence Services Act, 1994 in particular. But, as is the way of UK crown service, a good deal of what is thought to matter is passed down orally and learnt by the new recruits watching the more seasoned at work. In fact, much of the British intelligence tradition – those 'deals' I mentioned in 'The Cold Rules for National Safety' chapter – is passed down by the secret world's equivalent of Aboriginal 'Songlines' (the Australian Aborigines survived thanks to the songs sung by elders to the next generation about how to cross unforgiving desert and

---

* In my days on *The Times* in the 1970s they possessed only one, whom MI5 and MI6 shared; occasionally he would pop in to see the editor; we called him 'The Ghost'.

bush without maps to find life-preserving waterholes and shelter[39]).

Until very recently, the songs were sung very much in private. For example, Admiral John Godfrey, head of the Naval Intelligence Department in World War II (for whom Ian Fleming worked and on whom he modelled 'M' in the Bond novels),[40] liked to say the two most ruinous flaws in a spy were 'wishfulness' and 'yesmanship'.[41]

Nowadays, intelligence chiefs can pass on their most cherished songlines in public – most easily if they have retired – as Eliza Manningham-Buller did in her 'Reflections on Intelligence' Lord Speaker's Mile End Group Lecture at the House of Lords in March 2010 when she warned against what she called the 'seduction of intelligence':

It rarely offers completeness or certainty. And it needs context from other material, such as diplomatic reporting and open sources. Above all those who read it must not be seduced by its attractions or attach too great a significance to it. The excitement which is sometimes engendered about how it was obtained risks colouring its importance.

With a general election but a few weeks away, she said: 'Whether or not there is a change of government, I would advise new Ministers to approach intelligence material with healthy scepticism and questioning.'[42]

Such internal generational transmission now, more than ever, given the avowal of SIS in 1994 (the first time its peacetime existence was publicly acknowledged) plus the statutes and the oversight, is matched by an external, public phenomenon – the need for the renewal of consent for the existence and the activities of the intelligence and security sections of the secret state in each generation. And here, the bit of the deal that most matters – whatever the configuration of threats the country faces – was captured as long ago as 1945 by Karl Popper in his *The Open Society and Its Enemies*:

We must plan for freedom and not only for security, if for no other reason than that only freedom can make security secure.[43]

It has never been better put. And, generation upon generation, Popper's wisdom should stand as the balancing nostrum that justifies the work and sustenance of a secret state within an open society.

Notes

PROLOGUE TO THE NEW EDITION:
THE COLD RULES FOR NATIONAL SAFETY

1. Ronald Robinson and John Gallagher with Alice Denny, *Africa and the Victorians: The Official Mind of Imperialism* (Papermac edn, 1965), p. 463.
2. Conversation with Sir Richard Dearlove, 24 February 2009.
3. Conversation with Sir Richard Mottram, 23 February 2009.
4. Private information.
5. In fact, he was quoting Nietzsche. On 18 June 1949, de Gaulle said to General Leclerc: '. . .[D]ressant devant nous les intérêts des Etats qui sont, comme le dit Nietzsche "les monstres plus froids des monstres froids."' Conversation with Professor Julian Jackson, 17 September 2007.
6. Sir David Omand, Whitehall and Industry Group Masterclass on 'Security, Resilience and Intelligence', 24 February 2009.
7. Private information.
8. See Philip Bobbitt, *Terror and Consent: The Wars for the Twenty-First Century* (Penguin, 2008).
9. *Review of Intelligence on Weapons of Mass Destruction*, HC, 898 (Stationery Office, 2004), pp. 7–16; Lady Manningham-Buller, 'Reflections on Intelligence', Lord Speaker's Mile End Group Lecture, House of Lords, 9 March 2010.
10. *Review of Intelligence Requirements and Resources. Part I: Processes for Handling. Report by Sir Michael Quinlan, Cabinet Office, 31 March 1994*. The document was declassified on 23 August 2006. Sir Richard Mottram to Peter Hennessy.
11. Sir Michael Quinlan, 'The Future of Covert Intelligence', in Harold Shukman (ed.), *Intelligence Services in the 21st Century: Agents for Change* (St Ermin's Press, 2000), pp. 61–70.
12. Private information.

13. Quinlan, 'The Future of Covert Intelligence', p. 64.
14. Private information.
15. Quinlan, 'The Future of Covert Intelligence', p. 70.
16. Ibid., pp. 65–6.
17. Mary Douglas, 'Dealing with Uncertainty'. The Multatuli Lecture, Leuven, 2001. I am grateful to Sir Mark Allen for drawing this lecture to my attention.
18. *Review of Intelligence on Weapons of Mass Destruction*, p. 14.
19. Ibid.
20. Ibid.
21. Ibid., pp. 14–15.
22. Ibid., p. 15.
23. Private information.
24. *Review of Intelligence on Weapons of Mass Destruction*, pp. 99–102.
25. Private information.
26. Richard H. Rovere, *Arrivals and Departures: A Journalist's Memoirs* (Macmillan, 1976), p. 115. I am grateful to Andrew Arends for bringing this to my attention.
27. Peter Hennessy, *Muddling Through: Power, Politics and the Quality of Government in Post-war Britain* (Gollancz, 1996), p. 146.
28. Private information.
29. J. Kenneth McDonald, 'How Much Did Intelligence Matter in the Cold War?' in *Did Intelligence Matter in the Cold War?* (Norwegian Institute for Defence Studies, 2006), pp. 46–9.
30. Michael Herman, 'Intelligence Effects on the Cold War: Some Reflections', ibid., pp. 9–41.
31. Ibid.
32. See pp. 7–12.
33. Private information.
34. Private information.

INTRODUCTION:
FROM TOTAL WAR TO ABSOLUTE WAR?

1. Sir Michael Quinlan, 'Remarks at Launch of *The Secret State*', London, 4 March 2002.
2. Reproduced in Arthur Koestler, *The Yogi and the Commissar and Other Essays* (Cape, 1945), p. 256.
3. Churchill spurned suggestions that even the three service ministers, let alone the War Cabinet or its Defence Committee, should be brought into the

secret. Churchill alone took the decision to give the UK's consent (required under the secret Quebec Agreement of 1943) for the first atomic weapons to be dropped on Japan. Martin Gilbert, *Winston S. Churchill: Road to Victory. 1941–1945* (Heinemann, 1986), p. 715; The National Archives (TNA), Public Record Office (PRO), PREM 11/565, 'Record of Events Leading to Dropping of Bombs on Hiroshima and Nagasaki', Cherwell to Churchill, 28 January 1953.

4. For the contribution of the Soviet Union's atomic spies to the construction of the first Russian weapon see David Holloway, *Stalin and the Bomb: The Soviet Union and Atomic Energy, 1939–1956* (Yale, 1994), pp. 222–3.

5. George Steiner, *Grammars of Creation* (Faber, 2001), p. 2.

6. Macmillan quoted Kennedy to this effect during a Cabinet meeting in the early days of the Cuban missile crisis. TNA, PRO, CAB 128/36, CC (62) 61st Conclusions, 23 October 1962.

7. Peter Hennessy, *The Prime Minister: The Office and Its Holders Since 1945* (Penguin, 2000), p. 451.

8. Chairman of the Joint Intelligence Committee, 1984–92.

9. Permanent Secretary at the Ministry of Defence, 1988–92. Sir Michael conducted in 1994 a still partially classified review of the purposes and organization of the UK intelligence and security services in the post-Cold War period for the Major government. Sir Michael Quinlan, 'The Future of Covert Intelligence', in Harold Shukman (ed.), *Agents for Change: Intelligence Services in the 21st Century* (St Ermin's Press, 2000), pp. 61–71.

10. Richard J. Aldrich, *The Hidden Hand: Britain, America and Cold War Secret Intelligence* (John Murray, 2001). See also W. Scott Lucas and C. J. Morris, 'A Very British Crusade: The Information Research Department and the Beginning of the Cold War', in Richard J. Aldrich (ed.), *British Intelligence, Strategy and the Cold War* (Routledge, 1992), pp. 85–110.

11. Percy Cradock, *Know Your Enemy: How the Joint Intelligence Committee Saw the World* (John Murray, 2002).

12. Michael Quinlan, *Thinking about Nuclear Weapons* (RUSI, 1997).

13. Michael Herman, *Intelligence Power in Peace and War* (Cambridge University Press, 1996); Michael Herman, *Intelligence Services in the Information Age: Theory and Practice* (Frank Cass, 2001).

14. Conversation with Bob Salem, 25 May 2002.

15. Conversation with Giles Dolphin, 19 September 2002.

16. Patrick Wintour, 'Blair: The Daily Threat of Terror', *Guardian*, 12 November 2002.

17. TNA, PRO, AVIA 65/2055, 'Clandestine Introduction of Weapons into the UK: Import Research Committee, 1950–1954'; IR (50) 7, 'Ministry of

Defence. Imports Research Committee. Examination of Problem in Period of Tension', Note by the Chairman, 29 November 1950.

18. Ibid., IR (50) 5 Final, 'Ministry of Defence. Imports Research Committee. Report to the Chiefs of Staff', 2 November 1950. I am grateful to Dr Stephen Twigge of the National Archive for bringing this file to my attention.

PRELUDE: 'THE QUEEN MUST BE TOLD'

1. The National Archives (TNA), Public Record Office (PRO), CAB 21/5655, 'Government War Book, 1964–1968'.
2. *The Times*, 1 October 1938.
3. Mrs Tessa Stirling to Peter Hennessy, 26 January 2001.
4. TNA, PRO, CAB 21/5655, Grimble to Paget and Fraser, 2 November 1964; Paget to Hill, 3 November 1964.
5. Ibid., Grimble to Paget, 13 November 1964.
6. Conversation with Sir Derek Mitchell, 9 April 2001.
7. TNA, PRO, CAB 21/5655.
8. Ibid., Stephens to Laskey, 23 February 1965.
9. Ibid., Stephens to Laskey, 5 March 1965.
10. Ibid.
11. Ibid., McIndoe to Mitchell, 9 March 1965.
12. Ibid.
13. TNA, PRO, DEFE 2/225, 'Ministry of Defence War Book 1963', 15 August 1963.
14. Conversation with W. T. McIndoe, 9 April 2001.
15. Conversation with Sir Derek Mitchell, 9 April 2001.
16. TNA, PRO, DEFE 2/225, 'Ministry of Defence War Book', Appendix A, 'NATO Alert System'.
17. Ibid.
18. Ibid.
19. Ibid.
20. TNA, PRO, DEFE 2/225, 'Ministry of Defence War Book', Appendix F – Part 1, 'Handling of Government War Book Messages within the Ministry of Defence'.
21. Ibid.
22. *The Works of William Shakespeare Gathered into One Volume* (Shakespeare Head Press/Blackwell, 1938), pp. 496–7.
23. Michael Howard, 'Military Experience in Literature', Tredegar Memorial

Lecture to the Royal Society of Literature, October 1976, reproduced in Michael Howard, *The Lessons of History* (Oxford University Press, 1991), p. 180.

24. TNA, PRO, DEFE 2/225, 'Ministry of Defence War Book', Chapter IV, 'Mobilisation'.

25. TNA, PRO, CAB 21/5655.

26. Private information.

27. TNA, PRO, PREM 11/5222. Orme to Bligh, 18 August 1959, plus the attachment on Operation VISITATION. I am grateful to James Waller for alerting me to the release of this file. Waller to Hennessy, 14 June 2007.

28. Eric Hobsbawm (in conversation with Antonio Polito), *The New Century* (Abacus, 2000), p. 51.

1 'SECRETS AND MYSTERIES': THE INTELLIGENCE PICTURE

1. The National Archives (TNA), Public Record Office (PRO), CAB 81/132, JIC (46) 1 (o).

2. TNA, PRO, CAB 158/1, JIC (47) 7/2.

3. Private information.

4. Bruce Chatwin, *The Songlines* (Vintage edn, 1998).

5. Private information.

6. *MI6: A Century in the Shadows*, Part One, 'Gadgets and Green Ink', first broadcast on BBC Radio 4, 27 July 2009.

7. Gordon Barrass, *The Great Cold War: A Journey Through the Hall of Mirrors* (Stanford University Press, 2009), p. 389.

8. Anthony King (ed.), Robert J. Wybrow (compiler), *British Political Opinion 1937–2000: The Gallup Polls* (Politico's, 2000), p. 322. This poll was taken in October 1950.

9. House of Commons *Official Report*, Session 1952–3, Vol. 518, cols. 221–2.

10. David Butler and Gareth Butler, *Twentieth-Century British Political Facts 1900–2000* (Macmillan, 2000), p. 520.

11. Ibid.

12. Denis Healey, *My Secret Planet* (Michael Joseph, 1992), p. 83.

13. Michael Howard, 'Empires, Nations and Wars', the Yigal Allon Memorial Lecture, 1982, reproduced in Michael Howard, *The Lessons of History* (OUP, 1991), p. 47.

14. Private information.

15. See his 'Up from the Country: Cabinet Office Impressions 1972–75', in

Michael Herman, *Intelligence Services in the Information Age* (Frank Cass, 2001), pp. 164–79

16. Michael Herman, 'The Role of Military Intelligence since 1945'. Paper delivered to the Twentieth Century British Politics and Administration Seminar at the Institute of Historical Research, University of London, 24 May 1989.

17. Jeremy Black, *The Politics of James Bond: From Fleming's Novels to the Big Screen* (Praeger, 2002), p. xiii.

18. John le Carré, *Tinker, Tailor, Soldier, Spy* (Hodder, 1974) p. 28.

19. Ibid. p. 125.

20. TNA, PRO, CAB 161/4, 'Cabinet Committee Organisation', 1949.

21. TNA, PRO, CAB 161/13, 'Cabinet Committee Organisation', 1962.

22. Percy Cradock, *In Pursuit of British Interests: Reflections of Foreign Policy under Margaret Thatcher and John Major* (John Murray, 1997), p. 40.

23. Ibid., pp. 39–41.

24. In conversation with Peter Hennessy on 29 August 2000 for the BBC Radio 4 programme *The Top Job*.

25. Private information.

26. Cradock, *In Pursuit of British Interests*, p. 121.

27. Richard J. Aldrich, *The Hidden Hand: Britain, America and Cold War Secret Intelligence* (John Murray, 2001), p. 43.

28. Alex Danchev and Daniel Todman (eds.), *Field Marshal Lord Alanbrooke: War Diaries 1939–45* (Weidenfeld and Nicolson, 2001), p. 575. Diary entry for 27 July 1944.

29. Michael Herman, 'The Cold War: Did Intelligence Make a Difference?' Paper produced for the Royal International Affairs/BBC conference, Cold War: Heroes, Villains and Spies, 10 September 1998, and reproduced in Herman, *Intelligence Services in the Information Age*, pp. 159–63. For the distinction between 'secrets' and 'mysteries', I am grateful to Sir Michael Quinlan, 'The Future of Covert Intelligence', in Harold Shukman (ed.), *Agents for Change: Intelligence Services in the 21st Century* (St Ermin's Press, 2000), p. 65.

30. TNA, PRO, PREM 13/1343, 'Correspondence with Cabinet Office on Joint Intelligence Committee Current Assessments', anonymous JIC official to Michael Palliser, 31 October 1966.

31. TNA, PRO, CAB 158/45 Part I, JIC (62) 21, 'Indications of Sino-Soviet Bloc Preparations for Early War', 26 February 1962.

32. Ibid.

33. Ibid.

34. Ibid.

35. Private information.

36. TNA, PRO, CAB 158/45 Part I, JIC (62) 21.

37. Ibid.

38. Private Information.

39. TNA, PRO, CAB 158/45 Part I, JIC (62) 21.

40. Ibid.

41. Herman, 'The Cold War: Did Intelligence Make a Difference?'

42. Ibid.

43. I have taken an example at random. See TNA, PRO, CAB 158/23, 'Weekly Summary of Current Intelligence as at 5 January 1956'.

44. Herman, 'The Cold War: Did Intelligence Make a Difference?'

45. TNA, PRO, CAB 81/132, JIC (46) 1 (o).

46. Ibid., JIC (44) 466 (o).

47. Danchev and Todman (eds.), *Alanbrooke: War Diaries 1939–1945*, p. 697. Diary entry for 11 June 1945.

48. TNA, PRO, PREM 11/2418, 'Middle East 1957–58', Brook to Macmillan, 6 December 1967.

49. Michael Howard, 'Every Club in the Bag', *London Review of Books*, 10 September 1992, p. 3.

50. Michael Dockrill, *British Defence since 1945* (Blackwell, 1988), Appendix IV, pp. 151–2.

51. TNA, PRO, PREM 13/2688, 'Reorganisation of Central Machinery for Politico-military Planning and Intelligence, 1967–1968', Trend to Wilson, 13 March 1967.

52. TNA, PRO, CAB 81/132, JIC (46) 1 (o).

53. Ibid.

54. Ibid.

55. Bradley F. Smith, *Sharing Secrets with Stalin: How the Allies Traded Intelligence, 1941–1945* (University Press of Kansas, 1996), p. 254.

56. TNA, PRO, CAB 81/132, JIC (46) 1 (o).

57. Smith, *Sharing Secrets with Stalin*, p. 254. Smith discovered the evidence for this in TNA, PRO, WO 208/4566.

58. TNA, PRO, CAB 81/132, JIC (46) 1 (o).

59. Oleg Tsarev, 'Intelligence in the Cold War', in Shukman (ed.), *Agents For Change*, p. 22.

60. Ibid., p. 41.

61. Ibid., p. 44.

62. Ibid., p. 32.

63. TNA, PRO, CAB 81/132, JIC (46) 1 (o).

64. Christopher Andrew and Vasili Mitrokhin, *The Mitrokhin Archive: The KGB in Europe and the West* (Penguin, 1999), p. 156.

65. TNA, PRO, CAB 81/132, JIC (46) 1 (o).

66. Ibid.

67. Ibid.

68. Private information.

69. Andrew and Mitrokhin, *The Mitrokhin Archive*, pp. 180–81.

70. Christopher Andrew, 'The Venona Secret', in Robertson (ed.), *War, Resistance and Intelligence*, pp. 203–26.

71. Ibid., p. 213.

72. Ibid., p. 209.

73. TNA, PRO, CAB 130/17, JIC (46) 70 (0), 'The Spread of Communism Throughout the World and the Extent of Its Direction from Moscow', 23 September 1946.

74. TNA, PRO, CAB 130/20, GEN 183/1st Meeting, 16 June 1947.

75. TNA, PRO, PREM 8/1365, 'Proposed Activities Behind the Iron Curtain', Brook to Attlee, 30 November 1950; TNA, PRO, PREM 11/174, 'Request by Prime Minister for List of All Committees in Whitehall', Brook to Churchill, 20 November 1951. The minutes of these two official committees remain classified.

76. TNA, PRO, CAB 130/17, JIC (46) 70 (0).

77. Ibid.

78. Ibid.

79. Private information from one of the undergraduates who *did* become influential in public life but was certainly *never* a helper of Soviet intelligence.

80. Francis Beckett, *Enemy Within: The Rise and Fall of the British Communist Party* (John Murray, 1995), p. 221.

81. Private information.

82. TNA, PRO, CAB 158/1, 'Soviet Interests, Intentions and Capabilities – General', JIC (47) 7/2, 6 August 1947.

83. Peter Hennessy, *Never Again: Britain 1945–51* (Cape, 1992), p. 296.

84. TNA, PRO, CAB 158/1, JIC (47) 7/2.

85. Denis Healey, 'NATO, Britain and Soviet Military Policy', *Orbis*, Vol. 13, No. 1, Spring 1969, p. 48.

86. TNA, PRO, CAB 158/1, JIC (47) 7/2.

87. Richard Aldrich and Michael Coleman, 'The Cold War, the JIC and British Signals Intelligence, 1948', *Intelligence and National Security*, Vol. 4, No. 3, July 1989, Appendix 2.

88. TNA, PRO, CAB 158/1, JIC (47) 7/2.

89. Christopher Andrew, *The Defence of the Realm: The Authorized History of MI5* (Penguin, 2009), pp. 416–19. Peter Wright, *Spycatcher* (Viking, 1987), p. 364; Peter Hennessy, *The Prime Minister: The Office and Its Holders since 1945* (Penguin, 2000), pp. 372–4.

90. Dr Craig had in mind Aldrich and Coleman, 'The Cold War, the JIC and British Signals Intelligence, 1948'.

91. Alexander Craig, 'The Joint Intelligence Committee and British Intelligence Assessment, 1945–1956', unpublished PhD, Faculty of History, University of Cambridge, 1999, p. 260.

92. TNA, PRO, CAB 158/1, JIC (47) 7/2.

93. TNA, PRO, DEFE 4/14, COS (48) 97th Meeting, 12 July 1948.

94. I am grateful to Dr Craig for this information. Craig, 'The Joint Intelligence Committee and British Intelligence Assessment, 1945–1956', pp. 95–6.

95. Ibid., p. 90.

96. Ibid., p. 91, 93.

97. TNA, PRO, DEFE 6/56, JP (59) 68 Final, 27 May 1959, 'Berlin Contingency Planning. Report by the Joint Planning Staff'.

98. For the Brownell Report on US SIGINT see Craig, 'The Joint Intelligence Committee and British Intelligence Assessment, 1945–1956', pp. 109–10. For the creation of the NSA see Aldrich, *The Hidden Hand*, pp. 401–2.

99. Christopher Andrew, 'Intelligence and International Relations in the Early Cold War', *Review of International Studies*, 24 (1998), p. 329.

100. Aldrich, *The Hidden Hand*, p. 277.

101. Craig, 'The Joint Intelligence Committee and British Intelligence Assessment, 1945–1956', p. 109.

102. Aldrich, *The Hidden Hand*, p. 271.

103. Tom Dibble, 'The Missing Dimension? An Evaluation of the Intelligence Input into UK Policy Making During the Korean War in the Light of Recently Released Joint Intelligence Committee Files', unpublished MA research methods thesis, Department of History, Queen Mary, University of London, 1997.

104. TNA, PRO, CAB 158/11, Part 1, JIC (50) 77, 'The Likelihood of War with the Soviet Union and the Date by which Soviet Leaders Might Be Prepared to Risk It', 18 August 1950.

105. Ibid.

106. TNA, PRO, PREM 11/159, 'Paper by Vice-Admiral Longley-Cook entitled "Where Are We Going?" giving his views on the policies of US and Soviet Union, and UK attitude towards them', NID 7956, 6 July 1951.

107. TNA, PRO, CAB 158/11, Part 1, JIC (50) 77.

108. TNA, PRO, PREM 11/159, 'Where Are We Going?'

109. TNA, PRO, PREM 11/669, draft Cabinet Paper on 'Two-Power Meeting with Soviet Government', August 1954.

110. Neville Shute, *On the Beach* (Heinemann, 1957).

111. James Lees-Milne, *A Mingled Measure: Diaries 1953–1972* (John Murray, 1994), p. 68, diary entry for 13 September 1957.

112. Martin Gilbert, Churchill's official biographer, mentions the episode but does not record any outcome. Martin Gilbert, *Never Despair: Winston S. Churchill 1945–1965* (Heinemann, 1988), pp. 1250–5.

113. TNA, PRO, CAB 81/132, JIC (46) 1 (o).

114. Ibid.

115. Ibid.

116. Jeremy Isaacs and Taylor Downing, *Cold War* (Bantam, 1998), pp. 146–7.

117. TNA, PRO, CAB 158/1, JIC (47) 7 (2).

118. TNA, PRO, CAB 158/4, JIC (48) 26 (o).

119. Lorna Arnold, *Britain and the H-Bomb* (Palgrave, 2001), p. 9.

120. Chapman Pincher, 'Fuchs Gave Bomb to Russia', *Daily Express*, 2 March 1950.

121. Andrew and Mitrokhin, *The Mitrokhin Archive*, p. 155.

122. Arnold, *Britain and the H-Bomb*, p. 23.

123. Andrew and Mitrokhin, *The Mitrokhin Archive*, p. 153.

124. David Holloway, *Stalin and the Bomb: The Soviet Union and Atomic Energy* (Yale, 1994), p. 222.

125. Arnold, *Britain and the H-Bomb*, p. 25.

126. For recent scholarship see Holloway, *Stalin and the Bomb*, p. 123. For Fuchs's interrogation by Michael Perrin see TNA, PRO, AB1/695, 'Perrin Interviews with Dr Fuchs, January–March, 1950', 'Record of Interview with Dr K. Fuchs on 30th January 1950 by M. W. Perrin'.

127. TNA, PRO, DEFE 41/126, 'Atomic Energy Intelligence', briefing 9–19 June 1952. I am very grateful to Professor Richard Aldrich for bringing this file to my attention.

128. TNA, PRO, CAB 158/11, Part 2, JIC (50) 111, 'Likelihood of Total War with the Soviet Union up to the End of 1954', 15 February 1951.

129. Ibid.

130. Ibid.

131. Arnold, *Britain and the H-Bomb*, pp. 6–31.

132. TNA, PRO, CAB 158/21, JIC (55) 58, 'Likely Soviet Courses of Action up to 1st January 1957', 30 September 1955.

133. Ibid.

134. TNA, PRO, CAB 158/26, JIC (56) 136, 'The Extent to which the Present State of Tension Has Increased the Chances of Miscalculation which Might Lead to Global War', 13 December 1956.

135. Ibid.

136. TNA, PRO, CAB 158/29, JIC (57) 62, 'The Possibility of Hostilities Short of Global War up to 1965', 20 September 1957. Alban Webb's work is contained in 'An Analysis of the Joint Intelligence Committee's Assessment

of the Soviet Threat and Input into the Cuban Missile Crisis and its Aftermath'
unpublished undergraduate research project, Department of History, Queen
Mary, University of London, 2001.

137. Isaacs and Downing, *Cold War*, p. 182.

138. TNA, PRO, CAB 158/44, JIC (62) 10, 'The Likelihood of War with the
Soviet Union up to 1966', 9 February 1962.

139. Ibid.

140. TNA, PRO, CAB 158/47, JIC (62) 101, 'Soviet Motives in Cuba', 6
December 1962.

141. TNA, PRO, CAB 158/44, JIC (62) 10.

142. Ibid.

143. TNA, PRO, CAB 158/47, JIC (62) 101.

144. TNA, PRO, CAB 158/47, JIC (62) 93, 'The Threat Posed by Soviet
Missiles in Cuba', 26 October 1962.

145. L. V. Scott, 'Intelligence and the Cuban Missile Crisis', paper read to the
UK Study Group on Intelligence meeting at the Public Record Office, 15
September 1999. I am grateful to Dr Scott for permission to quote from it.

146. TNA, PRO, CAB 158/47, JIC (62) 101.

147. House of Commons *Official Report*, 5 December 1962, Vol. 668, cols.
1463–8. The minister speaking these words, C. M. Woodhouse, Parliamentary
Under Secretary at the Home Office, was answering a question about civil
defence and the Cuban missile crisis.

148. His grandson, Lord Stockton, quoted in Hennessy, *The Prime Minister*,
pp. 102–3.

149. Ibid., pp. 129–33.

150. Ibid., pp. 122–3.

151. TNA, PRO, CAB 158/47, JIC (62) 99, 'Possible Soviet Response to a
US Decision to Bomb or Invade Cuba', 27 October 1962.

152. Ibid.

153. Ibid.

154. Craig, 'The Joint Intelligence Committee and British Intelligence Assessment, 1945–1956', p. 261.

155. Ibid.

156. See George Kennedy Young, *Who Is My Liege?* (Gentry Books, 1972).

157. See Peter Wright, *Spycatcher* (Viking, 1987).

158. Private information.

159. Private information.

160. Private information.

161. Private information.

162. Private information.

163. Hennessy, *The Prime Minister*, p. 130.

164. Private information. See Mr Cowell's obituary in *The Times*, 8 May 2000.

2 THE IMPORTANCE OF BEING NUCLEAR: THE BOMB AND THE FEAR OF ESCALATION

1. Quoted in Peter Hennessy, *Muddling Through: Power, Politics and the Quality of Government in Post-war Britain* (Gollancz, 1996), p. 106.

2. Miles Jebb (ed.), *The Diaries of Cynthia Gladwyn* (Constable, 1995), p. 195. Diary entry for 12 December 1956.

3. The National Archives (TNA), Public Record Office (PRO), DEFE 10/402, 'Study Group', 1960. The paper's author was Group Captain Alan Shelfoon, a member of the Joint Inter-Service Group for the Study of All-Out Warfare.

4. TNA, PRO, CAB 134/3121 Part 2, 'Minority Report by Lord Rothschild', attached to the Report from the Kings Norton Working Party on Atomic Weapons Establishments, 31 July 1968.

5. Hennessy, *Muddling Through*, p. 129.

6. Peter Hennessy, *The Hidden Wiring: Unearthing the British Constitution* (Gollancz, 1995), p. 204.

7. Chiefly in Peter Hennessy, *The Prime Minister: The Office and Its Holders since 1945* (Penguin, 2000 and 2001). See also Peter Hennessy, *Cabinet* (Blackwell, 1986), Chapter 4, 'Cabinets and the Bomb', pp. 123–62.

8. Timothy Garton Ash, *We the People: The Revolution of '89 Witnessed in Warsaw, Budapest, Berlin and Prague* (Penguin, 1999), pp. 65–9.

9. Margaret Gowing, *Britain and Atomic Energy 1939–1945* (Macmillan, 1964); Margaret Gowing, *Independence and Deterrence: Britain and Atomic Energy, 1945–1952*, Vol. I: *Policy Making*, Vol. II: *Policy Execution* (Macmillan, 1974).

10. TNA, PRO, CAB 130/3, GEN 75, 'Papers 1945–47'; GEN 75/1, 'THE ATOMIC BOMB. Memorandum by the Prime Minister', 28 August 1945.

11. Brian Cathcart, *Test of Greatness: Britain's Struggle for the Atom Bomb* (John Murray, 1994), pp. 8–25.

12. Michael Howard, 'Every Club in the Bag', *London Review of Books*, 10 September 1992.

13. TNA, PRO, CAB 130/2, GEN 75/8th Meeting, 18 December 1945.

14. Ibid.

15. TNA, PRO, AIR 2/5960, 'Draft Air Staff Requirement. No. OR/230'.

16. Sir Michael Perrin speaking on BBC2's *Timewatch*, 29 September 1982.

17. TNA, PRO, CAB 130/2, GEN 75/15th Meeting, 25 October 1946.

18. Ibid.

19. *Timewatch*, 29 September 1982.

20. TNA, PRO, PREM 8/911, 'Proposals Agreed that Research and Development Work on Atomic Energy Be Undertaken', 1947–47; 'Note by the Controller of Production of Atomic Energy', 31 December 1946.

21. Hennessy, *Cabinet*, p. 127.

22. TNA, PRO, CAB 130/16, GEN 163/1st Meeting, 8 January 1947, 'Confidential Annex Minute 1. Research in Atomic Weapons'.

23. Francis Williams, *A Prime Minister Remembers* (Heinemann, 1961), pp. 118–19.

24. Ibid., p. 119.

25. Lorna Arnold, *Britain and the H-bomb* (Palgrave, 2001), p. 235.

26. TNA, PRO, CAB 134/808, DP (54) 6, 'United Kingdom Defence Policy. Memorandum by the Chiefs of Staff', 1 June 1954.

27. I am grateful to Alban Webb for finding this file when first released. TNA, PRO, CAB 130/101. The minute is simply entitled 'Note of a Meeting' but it has 'GEN 465 1st' placed on it in handwriting and it forms part of the GEN 465 archive.

28. Ibid., 'Note of a Meeting Held in Sir Norman Brook's Room', 12 March 1954.

29. TNA, PRO, CAB 134/808, DP (54) 6.

30. TNA, PRO, CAB 130/101, Note of Brook's meeting, 12 March 1954.

31. Ibid.

32. David Holloway, *Stalin and the Bomb: The Soviet Union and Atomic Energy 1939–1956* (Yale, 1994), p. 315.

33. Arnold, *Britain and the H-bomb*, p. 30.

34. He did this for me on more than one occasion in the late 1980s, especially when I was helping to prepare the BBC Radio 4 documentary *A Bloody Union Jack on Top of It*.

35. TNA, PRO, CAB 130/101, Note of Brook's meeting, 12 March 1954.

36. Ibid.

37. Ibid.

38. The Macmillan Diary, Department of Western Manuscripts, Bodleian Library, University of Oxford, File d.19, diary entry for 26 January 1955.

39. Hennessy, *Muddling Through*, pp. 105–6.

40. TNA, PRO, CAB 130/101, Note of Brook's meeting, 12 March 1954.

41. Ibid.

42. Ibid., GEN 464/1st Meeting, 'Atomic Energy Development', 13 April 1954.

43. Ibid.

44. Hennessy, *Cabinet*, p. 137.

45. TNA, PRO, CAB 128/27, CC (54) 47th Conclusions, 7 July 1954.

46. TNA, PRO, CAB 134/808, DP (54) 6, 1 June 1954.

47. Ibid., DP (54) 2nd Meeting, 19 May 1954.

48. Ibid., DP (54) 6, 1 June 1954.

49. TNA, PRO, CAB 129/69, C (54) 249, 'United Kingdom Defence Policy', 23 July 1954.

50. Compare paragraph a of DP (54) 6 with paragraph 9 of C (54) 249 where the figures are replaced with 'x' and 'y'.

51. TNA, PRO, CAB 129/69, C (54) 249.

52. Ibid.

53. TNA, PRO, CAB 134/808, DP (54) 6, 1 June 1954.

54. Ibid., DP (54) 3rd Meeting, 16 June 1954, 'Confidential Annex. Atomic Weapons Programme'.

55. Hennessy, *The Prime Minister*, p. 199; Macmillan Diary, c.16/1, entry for 10 July 1954.

56. TNA, PRO, CAB 128/27, CC (54) 47th Conclusions, 7 July 1954.

57. Ibid.

58. Ibid., CC (54) 48th Conclusions, 8 July 1954.

59. Ibid. See also Christopher Driver, *The Disarmers: A Study in Protest* (Hodder, 1964), pp. 200–201.

60. TNA, PRO, CAB 128/27, CC (54) 48th Conclusions, 8 July 1954.

61. Ibid.

62. Ibid.

63. Martin Gilbert, *Never Despair: Winston S. Churchill 1945–1965* (Heinemann, 1988), p. 1092.

64. TNA, PRO, CAB 128/27, CC (54) 48th Conclusions, 8 July 1954.

65. TNA, PRO, PREM 11/747, Churchill to the Queen, 16 July 1954.

66. TNA, PRO, CAB 128/27, CC (54) 53rd Conclusions, 26 July 1954.

67. 'Statement on Defence: 1955', Cmd 9391 (HMSO, 1955).

68. Arnold, *Britain and the H-Bomb*, p. 84.

69. Ibid., pp. 131–64; 235–6.

70. Ibid., p. 209.

71. Victor Macklen, who was present at the meeting, speaking in *A Bloody Union Jack on Top of It*; Hennessy, *Muddling Through*, p. 108.

72. Cmnd. 537 (HMSO, 1958).

73. Hennessy, *The Prime Minister*, p. 113.

74. Cathcart, *Test of Greatness*, p. 273.

75. TNA, PRO, AIR 8/2400, 'Medium Bomber Force: Size and Composition'; Defence Board, 'The V-Bomber Force and the Powered Bomb,

Memorandum by the Secretary of State for Air', DB (58) 10, 29 October 1958.

76. Professor Nailor was speaking in *A Bloody Union Jack on Top of It*. Hennessy, *Muddling Through*, p. 109.

77. For Blue Streak cancellation and Skybolt decision-making see Ian Clark, *Nuclear Diplomacy and the Special Relationship: Britain's Deterrent and America 1957–1962* (Oxford University Press, 1994), pp. 176–89, 251–64, 353–73.

78. Sir Philip de Zulueta was speaking in *A Bloody Union Jack on Top of It*. Hennessy, *Muddling Through*, p. 110.

79. Peter Hennessy and Caroline Anstey, 'Moneybags and Brains: The Anglo-American "Special Relationship" since' 1945, Strathclyde/*Analysis* papers No. 1 (Department of Government, University of Strathclyde, 1990), p. 11.

80. Lord Home speaking in *A Bloody Union Jack on Top of It*. Hennessy, *Muddling Through*, p. 111.

81. Ibid., p. 112.

82. Clark, *Nuclear Diplomacy and the Special Relationship*, pp. 409–15.

83. Hennessy, *Muddling Through*, p. 112.

84. The phrase is that of Denis Greenhill, former head of the Diplomatic Service, who saw Macmillan in action with Kennedy on several occasions. Conversation with Lord Greenhill, 4 March 1996.

85. TNA, PRO, PREM 11/3689, 'Situation in Cuba, Part 2, 1962', FO telegram No. 7396 to Washington, Macmillan to Kennedy, 22 October 1962.

86. TNA, PRO, PREM 11/2718, 'Future of Berlin and Germany: Meeting of Foreign Ministers . . .?', Brook to Macmillan, 28 July 1961; Macmillan to Brook, 29 July 1961.

87. TNA, PRO, CAB 158/47, JIC (62) 70, 'Escalation', 14 November 1962. It has emblazoned on it 'TOP SECRET – CAN/UK/US EYES ONLY.'

88. Ibid.

89. Ibid.

90. Ibid.

91. Macmillan Diary, file. d.42, entry for 25 June 1961.

92. TNA, PRO, CAB 158/47, JIC (62) 70.

93. Iverach McDonald, *A Man of the Times: Talks and Travels in a Disrupted World* (Hamish Hamilton, 1976), p. 184.

94. TNA, PRO, CAB 158/45, Part 1, JIC (61) 77, 'The United Kingdom Nuclear Deterrent', 23 January 1962.

95. TNA, PRO, CAB 128/36, CC (62) 76th Conclusions, 21 December 1962.

96. TNA, PRO, PREM 11/4147, 'Discussions on Intermediate Range Ballistic Missiles (IRBMs): Part 5, 1962–63. Nassau Agreement', Paris to the Foreign Office, 2 January 1963.

97. TNA, PRO, PREM 11/4412, 'Summary of Tasks Ahead: Prime Minister wrote to Private Secretary and Ministers'; 'Polaris', Prime Minister's Personal Minute M.343/62, 26 December 1962.

98. Hennessy, *The Prime Minister*, pp. 225–6.

99. TNA, PRO, PREM 11/4147, 'Record of a Meeting at Admiralty House at 6.00 p.m. on Monday December 31, 1962'.

100. Ibid.

101. TNA, PRO, PREM 11/4148, 'Discussions on Intermediate Range Ballistic Missiles (IRBMs): Part 6', Amery to Thorneycroft, 15 January 1963; Thorneycroft to Amery, 28 January 1963.

102. TNA, PRO, CAB 128/37, CC (63) 2nd Conclusions, 3 January 1963.

103. As Minister Resident in the Middle East he had explained to Richard Crossman that: 'We . . . are Greeks in this American empire . . . We must run the Allied Forces HQ as the Greeks ran the operations of the Emperor Claudius', *Sunday Telegraph*, 9 February 1964.

104. TNA, PRO, CAB 128/37 CC (63) 2nd Conclusions.

105. Ibid.

106. Ibid.

107. Michael Quinlan, *Thinking about Nuclear Weapons* (RUSI, 1997), p. 76.

108. TNA, PRO, PREM 11/4285, 'Development of Nuclear Disarmament: Memorandum by the Home Office; Prime Minister Asked about Views of Opposition', Michael Fraser [Conservative Research Department] to John Wyndham [Macmillan's personal assistant in No. 10], 22 April 1963.

109. Ibid. 'Defence' attachment by Fraser.

110. 'Let's Go With Labour for the New Britain' (Labour Party, September 1964), available in F. W. S.Craig, *British General Election Manifestos 1918–1966* (Political Reference Publications, 1970). The section dealing with Labour's 1964 defence policy is on pp. 245–6.

111. TNA, PRO, PREM 11/4285, Fraser to Wyndham, 22 April 1963.

112. See Hennessy, *The Prime Minister*, pp. 61–3.

113. Hennessy, *Muddling Through*, p. 114.

114. TNA, PRO, PREM 11/4733, 'Talks on Defence Policy with Members of HM Opposition', Thorneycroft to Douglas-Home, 3 February 1964.

115. Richard E. Neustadt, *Report to J.F.K.: The Skybolt Crisis in Perspective* (Cornell University Press, 1999).

116. Conversation with Professor Richard Neustadt, 16 January 1997.

117. TNA, PRO, CAB 130/212, MISC 16/1st Meeting, 11 November 1964.

118. Ibid.

119. TNA, PRO, CAB 130/213, MISC 17/4th Meeting, 22 November 1964; PRO, CAB 128/39, CC (64) 11th Conclusions, 26 November 1964.

120. TNA, PRO, CAB 148/19, ODP (65) 5th Meeting, 29 January 1965.

121. Denis Healey, *The Time of My Life* (Michael Joseph, 1989), p. 302.

122. TNA, PRO, CAB 128/39 CC (64) 11th Conclusions, 26 November 1964.

123. TNA, PRO, CAB 134/3120, PN (66) 1st Meeting, 28 September 1966.

124. TNA, PRO, CAB 164/713, Healey to Wilson, 3 August 1967.

125. Ibid.

126. Hennessy, *Muddling Through*, p. 115.

127. TNA, PRO, CAB 130/212, MISC 16/1st Meeting, 11 November 1964.

128. Hennessy, *Muddling Through*, p. 116.

129. TNA, PRO, CAB 134/3120, PN (67) 4th Meeting, 5 December 1967. See also Matthew Grant, '"Destined for the Junkyard of Steptoe and Son?" Polaris Improvement: The First Steps, 1965–70', unpublished undergraduate thesis, Queen Mary, University of London, 2001.

130. Hennessy, *Cabinet*, pp. 148–53; Peter Hennessy, *What the Papers Never Said* (Politics Association, 1985), pp. 113–39.

131. TNA, PRO, CAB 134/3120, PN (67) 6, 1 December 1967, 'British Nuclear Weapons Policy'.

132. Hennessy, *The Prime Minister*, p. 291.

133. Driver, *The Disarmers*, pp. 52–3.

134. A. J. P. Taylor, *A Personal History* (Hamish Hamilton, 1983), p. 228.

135. Sir Michael Quinlan in conversation with Sir John Willis and the author, the National Archives, Kew, 6 May 2004.

136. TNA, PRO, DEFE 19/275, 'Duff–Mason Report on Factors Relating to the Further Consideration of the Future of the UK Nuclear Deterrent', Hunt to Callaghan, 28 November 1977; Stowe to Hunt, 30 January 1978.

137. Sir Kevin was speaking at a Royal United Services Institute Seminar on 'Cabinets and the Bomb', 2 September 2009.

138. Professor Nye was speaking at a seminar in Moscow in 2006. See Gordon S. Barrass, *The Great Cold War: A Journey through the Hall of Mirrors* (Stanford University Press, 2009), pp. 373–4.

139. Private information.

3 DEFENDING THE REALM:
VETTING, FILING AND SMASHING

1. The National Archives (TNA), Public Record Office (PRO), CAB 130/37, 'The Communist Party. Its Strengths and Activities: Its Penetration of Government Organisations and of the Trade Unions', attached as an appendix to a

report prepared by a working party on 'Security Measures against Encroachments by Communists or Fascists in the United Kingdom' for ministers in GEN 226, the Cabinet Committee on European Policy, and circulated to them on 26 May 1948.

2. Christopher Andrew and Vasili Mitrokhin, *The Mitrokhin Archive: The KGB in Europe and the West* (Penguin, 1999), p. 209.

3. TNA, PRO, CAB 130/20, PV (50) 11, 'Committee on Positive Vetting: Report', 27 October 1950.

4. TNA, PRO, CAB 158/24, JIC (56) 41, 'Likely Scale and Nature of an Attack on the United Kingdom in a Global War up to 1960', 10 May 1956.

5. This is the title of the most recent history of the CPGB. Francis Beckett, *The Enemy Within: The Rise and Fall of the British Communist Party* (John Murray, 1995).

6. Ibid., pp. 1–8, 221.

7. Eric Hobsbawm, *The New Century* (Abacus, 2000), p. 159.

8. Eric Hobsbawm to Peter Hennessy, 8 March 2001.

9. TNA, PRO, CAB 130/37, 'The Communist Party'.

10. John Curry, *The Security Service 1908–1945* (Public Record Office, 1999), p. 82.

11. Ibid.

12. Ibid., pp. 350–51.

13. John Le Carré, *Tinker, Tailor, Soldier, Spy* (Hodder, 1974), pp. 97–115.

14. Curry, *The Security Service 1908–1945*, p. 351.

15. Christopher Andrew, *The Defence of the Realm: The Authorized History of MI5* (Penguin Books, 2009), p. 131.

16. TNA, PRO, CAB 130/20, 'Some Past Cases of Communist Espionage', Annex to GEN 183/1, Cabinet Committee on Subversive Activities, 'The Employment of Civil Servants etc., Exposed to Communist Influence: Report of Working Party', 29 May 1947.

17. Curry, *The Secret Service, 1908–1945*, pp. 354–5.

18. Ibid., p. 355.

19. Ibid.

20. Private information.

21. Private information.

22. Curry, *The Security Service 1908–1945*, p. 357.

23. TNA, PRO, CAB 130/17, JIC (46) 70 (o), 'The Spread of Communism Throughout the World and the Extent of Its Direction from Moscow', 23 September 1946.

24. Curry, *The Security Service 1908–1945*, p. 357.

25. TNA, PRO, CAB 130/37, 'The Communist Party'.

26. Ibid.

27. Ibid. See also Philip Deery, '"The Secret Battalion": Communism in Britain during the Cold War', *Contemporary British History*, Vol. 13, No. 4 (Winter 1999), pp. 1–28.

28. TNA, PRO, CAB 130/37, 'The Communist Party'.

29. TNA, PRO, CAB 130/17, JIC (46) 70 (0).

30. For the minutes and memoranda of GEN 183 see TNA, PRO, CAB 130/20.

31. Andrew and Mitrokhin, *The Mitrokhin Archive*, pp. 165–6, 184.

32. TNA, PRO, CAB 130/17, JIC (46) 70 (0).

33. Andrew and Mitrokhin, *The Mitrokhin Archive*, p. 180.

34. TNA, PRO, CAB 130/20, GEN 183/1, 'The Employment of Civil Servants, etc., Exposed to Communist Influence'.

35. Ibid.

36. Andrew, *The Defence of the Realm*, p. 402.

37. TNA, PRO, CAB 130/20, GEN 183/1.

38. Ibid.

39. Ibid.

40. Margaret Gowing, *Independence and Deterrence: Britain and Atomic Energy 1945–1952*, Vol. II: *Policy Execution* (Macmillan, 1974), p. 142.

41. TNA, PRO, CAB 130/20, 'The Employment of Civil Servants, etc., Exposed to Communist Influence'.

42. TNA, PRO, CAB 130/37, 'The Communist Party'.

43. Andrew and Mitrokhin, *The Mitrokhin Archive*, p. 188.

44. TNA, PRO, CAB 130/20, 'The Employment of Civil Servants, etc., Exposed to Communist Influence'.

45. Ibid.

46. Ibid.

47. Ibid.

48. Ibid.

49. TNA, PRO, CAB 130/20, GEN 183/1st Meeting, 16 June 1947.

50. Ibid.

51. Ibid.

52. Ibid., 'The Employment of Civil Servants, etc., Exposed to Communist Influence'.

53. House of Commons *Official Report*, 15 March 1948, Vol. 448, cols. 1703–8.

54. TNA, PRO, CAB 130/20, 'The Employment of Civil Servants, etc., Exposed to Communist Influence'.

55. TNA, PRO, CAB 130/37, GEN 226/1, 'Security Measures against

Encroachments by Communists or Fascists in the United Kingdom. Report by a Working Party'.

56. Ibid., 'The Communist Party'.

57. Andrew and Mitrokhin, *The Mitrokhin Archive*, p. 151.

58. Ibid., pp. 203–4.

59. TNA, PRO, CAB 120/30, PV (50) 11, 'Committee on Positive Vetting. Report', 27 October 1950. For the 5 April meeting of GEN 183, see ibid., GEN 183/5th Meeting.

60. Chapman Pincher, *Too Secret Too Long: The Great Betrayal of Britain's Crucial Secrets and the Cover-up* (Sidgwick & Jackson, 1984). See also Nigel West, *Molehunt: The Full Story of the Soviet Spy in MI5* (Coronet, 1987).

61. Richard Rovere, *Senator Joe McCarthy* (Meridian, 1960), p. 124. See also David Caute, *The Great Fear: The Anti-Communist Purge under Truman and Eisenhower* (Secker and Warburg, 1978).

62. Margaret Gowing, *Independence and Deterrence: Britain and Atomic Energy 1945–1952*, Vol. I: *Policy Making*. (Macmillan, 1974), pp. 241–72.

63. Peter Hennessy and Gail Brownfeld, 'Britain's Cold War Security Purge, The Origins of Positive Vetting', *Historical Journal*, 25, 4 (1982), p. 965.

64. TNA, PRO, CAB 120/30, PV (50) 11.

65. TNA, PRO, CAB 120/30, GEN 183/1st Meeting, 15 June 1947.

66. TNA, PRO, CAB 120/30, PV (50) 11.

67. Ibid.

68. Ibid.

69. Ibid.

70. Ibid.

71. Ibid.

72. Andrew and Mitrokhin, *The Mitrokhin Archive*, p. 188.

73. TNA, PRO, CAB 120/30, PV (50) 11.

74. Ibid.

75. Ibid.

76. Ibid.

77. Ibid. O'Donovan's *Observer* article is quoted in Kenneth Harris, *Attlee* (Weidenfeld and Nicolson, 1982), pp. 490–91.

78. TNA, PRO, CAB 130/20, GEN 183/6th Meeting, 13 November 1950.

79. Andrew, *The Defence of the Realm*, pp. 389–99.

80. 'Making Whitehall Mole-Proof', *The Economist*, 5 June 1982.

81. 'Report of the Security Commission', Cmnd. 8540 (HMSO, 1982)

82. Daniel Sherman, 'Personnel Security in the Public Service: From Positive Vetting to the Radcliffe Report', unpublished undergraduate thesis, Department of History, Queen Mary College, University of London, 2002.

83. TNA, PRO, CAB 21/452–7, 'Manual of Personnel Security Measures', 13 June 1957.

84. Sherman, 'Personnel Security in the Public Service'.

85. TNA, PRO, DEFE 4/67, Chiefs of Staff Committee Meeting, 11 December 1953.

86. TNA, PRO, PREM 11/1585, 'Extension of Positive Vetting Arrangements to Non-Civil Servants', 1954–56, Gwilym Lloyd George to Sir Anthony Eden, 24 January 1955.

87. Private information.

88. TNA, PRO, AIR 2/14582, 'Air Ministry Security Clearance of Civilian Staff: Notice to Directors and Heads of Division', 8 August 1962.

89. Ibid., 'Security Questionnaire'.

90. 'Security Procedures and Practices in the Public Service', Cmnd. 1681 (HMSO, 1962).

91. TNA, PRO, PREM 11/5087, 'Officers of Civil Service Staff Associations with Communist Sympathies', Chief Secretary to Prime Minister, August 1962–May 1963.

92. Private information.

93. Private information.

94. TNA, PRO, CAB 130/37, GEN 226/1, 'The Communist Party'.

95. Ibid.

96. Ibid.

97. TNA, PRO, PREM 11/1238, 'Communist Influence in Industry and Trade Unions', Brook to Eden, 28 April 1956.

98. TNA, PRO, CAB 158/25, JIC (56) 95, 'Discussion in Moscow between the British Communist Party and CPSU representatives, May/June 1956', 3 September 1956.

99. Beckett, *Enemy Within*, p. 191.

100. Curry, *The Security Service 1908–1945*, pp. 352–4.

101. Andrew and Mitrokhin, *The Mitrokhin Archive*, p. 167.

102. Beckett, *Enemy Within*, pp. 86–7.

103. Andrew and Mitrokhin, *The Mitrokhin Archive*, p. 167.

104. Private information.

105. Andrew, *The Defence of the Realm*, p. 402.

106. Obituary, 'Julia Pirie', *Daily Telegraph*, 29 October 2008.

107. Ibid.

108. TNA, PRO, AIR 20/11367, 'Air Ministry. Notice to Directors and Heads of Division. Routine War Planning'. Extract from the Minutes of the Defence Transition Committee Meeting, 5 January 1949. For the wartime camps see

Ronald Stent, *A Bespattered Page? The Internment of His Majesty's Most Loyal Enemy Aliens* (André Deutsch, 1980).

109. TNA, PRO, KV 4/225, 'Policy: Setting Up of Detention Camps in the UK for the Detention of British Subjects and the Internment of Aliens in the Event of an Emergency 1948–54', 'Internment Camps in War. Summary of Agreed Plans as of February 1954'.

110. Curry, *The Security Service 1908–1945*, p. 82.

111. Beckett, *Enemy Within*, pp. 9–17.

112. Ibid., p. 78.

113. House of Commons *Official Report*, 12 May 1948, Vol. 450, col. 2117.

114. Peter Hennessy, *What the Papers Never Said* (Politics Association, 1985), pp. 23–7.

115. Christopher Driver, *The Disarmers: A Study In Protest* (Hodder, 1964), p. 18.

116. Ibid.

117. TNA, PRO, PREM 11/4285, 'Development of Nuclear Disarmament Movement: Memorandum by Home Office; Prime Minister Asked about Views of Opposition'.

118. Driver, *The Disarmers*, p. 149.

119. Ibid., p. 149. See also Richard Taylor, *Against the Bomb: The British Peace Movement 1958–1965* (Oxford University Press, 1988), p. 97.

120. Ibid., p. 258.

121. Ibid., p. 259.

122. Ibid., p. 260.

123. TNA, PRO, PREM 11/4285, Cunningham to Woodfield, 17 April 1963.

124. Ibid., 'Development of Nuclear Disarmament Movement'.

125. Driver, *The Disarmers*, p. 24.

126. TNA, PRO, PREM 11/4285, 'Development of Nuclear Disarmament Movement'.

127. Lorna Arnold, *Britain and the H-Bomb* (Palgrave, 2001), p. 18.

128. Ibid., p. 19.

129. Driver, *The Disarmers*, p. 26.

130. TNA, PRO, PREM 11/4285, 'Development of Nuclear Disarmament Movement'.

131. Driver, *The Disarmers*, p. 27.

132. TNA, PRO, PREM 11/4285, 'Development of Nuclear Disarmament Movement'.

133. Ibid.

134. Driver, *The Disarmers*, p. 35.

135. Ibid.

136. Ibid., pp. 354–6.

137. TNA, PRO, PREM 11/4285, 'Development of Nuclear Disarmament Movement'.

138. Driver, *The Disarmers*, p. 36.

139. For an interesting account of the environmental and civic version of single-issue pressure grouping see Mike Robinson, *The Greening of British Party Politics* (Manchester University Press, 1992).

140. Driver, *The Disarmers*, pp. 42–53.

141. TNA, PRO, PREM 11/4285, 'The Development of the Nuclear Disarmament Movement'.

142. Driver, *The Disarmers*, p. 74.

143. 'Defence: Outline of Future Policy', Cmd. 124 (HMSO, 1957).

144. Ibid.

145. Ibid.

146. Michael Foot, *Aneurin Bevan: 1897–1960* (Gollancz, 1997), pp. 554–5.

147. Driver, *The Disarmers*, p. 99.

148. Ibid., pp. 94–5.

149. 'Sir David Spedding', *The Times*, 14 June 2001.

150. Private information.

151. Graham Payn and Sheridan Morley (eds.), *The Noël Coward Diaries* (Macmillan, 1982), p. 361. Diary entry for 4 August 1957.

152. P. G. Wodehouse, *Plum Pie* (Herbert Jenkins, 1960), pp. 119–39.

153. Beckett, *Enemy Within*, p. 148.

154. Ibid., p. 161.

155. Ibid.

156. Driver, *The Disarmers*, p. 72.

157. Ibid.

158. Ibid., pp. 65–6.

159. TNA, PRO, PREM 11/4285, 'Development of Nuclear Disarmament Movement'.

160. Anthony Hartley, *A State of England* (Hutchinson, 1963), p. 90. A. J. P. Taylor, *A Personal History* (Hamish Hamilton, 1983), p. 227.

161. Driver, *The Disarmers*, pp. 157–9.

162. Ibid., p. 35.

163. TNA, PRO, PREM 11/4285, 'Development of Nuclear Disarmament Movement'.

164. Ibid.

165. Driver, *The Disarmers*, p. 107.

166. TNA, PRO, PREM 11/4285, 'Development of Nuclear Disarmament Movement'.

167. Driver, *The Disarmers*, pp. 163–70.

168. George Blake, *No Other Choice: An Autobiography* (Cape, 1990), p. 223.

169. Ibid., pp. 222–47.

170. TNA, PRO, PREM 11/4285, 'Development of Nuclear Disarmament Movement'.

171. Ibid.

172. TNA, PRO, CAB 158/47, JIC (62) 104, 'Anti-Nuclear Demonstrations at RAF Airfields in a Period of Tension', 16 November 1962.

173. Ibid.

174. For the genesis of the quickly iconic CND symbol see Driver, *The Disarmers*, pp. 58–9.

175. Arthur Marwick, *The Sixties: Cultural Revolution in Britain, France, Italy and the United States c.1958–c.1974* (Oxford University Press, 1998), pp. 65–6.

176. Ibid., p. 635.

177. TNA, PRO, PREM 4/232, DP 32/68 (D), 'Security of the United Kingdom Base in the Pre-Attack Phase of General War. Report by the Defence Policy Staff', October 1968.

178. Ibid., Annex A. The MI5 report was numbered D/DISSEC/7/3/1 and dated 9 September 1968.

179. Ibid.

180. Ibid.

181. TNA, PRO, DEFE 4/232, 'Security of the United Kingdom Base in the Pre-Attack Phase of General War', Annex A.

182. Ibid.

183. Andrew and Mitrokhin, *The Mitrokhin Archive*, p. 488.

184. Ibid., p. 499.

185. TNA, PRO, PREM 13/2009, 'Soviet Intelligence Activities in the UK', Stewart to Wilson, 27 September 1968.

186. Andrew and Mitrokhin, *The Mitrokhin Archive*, p. 499.

187. For details of this see G. Bennett and K. A. Hamilton (eds.), *Documents On British Policy Overseas, Series III*, Vol. 1: *Britain and the Soviet Union 1968–1972* (Stationery Office, 1997), pp. 359–96.

188. George Walden, *Lucky George: Memoirs of an Anti-Politician* (Penguin, 1999), p. 146.

189. Ibid.

190. Andrew and Mitrokhin, *The Mitrokhin Archive*, p. 499.

191. Private information.

192. TNA, PRO, CAB 130/20, GEN 183/1, 29 May 1947.

193. TNA, PRO, CAB 186/8, Part 2, JIC (A) (71) 16, 'The Security of the United Kingdom Base in a Situation Leading to a Threat of General War'.

194. Ibid.

195. Ibid.

196. Ibid.

197. Ibid.

198. Ibid., 'Annex: Subversive Organisations in the United Kingdom', 23 March 1971.

199. Private information.

4 'BEYOND THE IMAGINATION': THE SPECTRE OF EVER-GREATER ANNIHILATION

1. The National Archives (TNA), Public Record Office (PRO), CAB 130/41, GEN 253/1st Meeting, 1 October 1948.

2. TNA, PRO, CAB 158/20, JIC (55) 12, 'The "H" Bomb Threat to the UK in the Event of a General War', 13 January 1955.

3. TNA, PRO, CAB 134/940, HDC (55) 3, 'The Defence Implications of Fall-out from a Hydrogen Bomb: Report by a Group of Officials', 8 March 1955.

4. TNA, PRO, CAB 21/4959, 'Sir Norman Brook: Miscellaneous Engagements and Personal Correspondence 1961–1964', 'Cabinet Government', a private lecture to Home Office officials, 26 June 1959.

5. Ibid.

6. Ibid.

7. Ibid.

8. Richard Taylor, *Against the Bomb: The British Peace Movement 1958–1965* (Oxford University Press, 1988), p. 99.

9. Lord Allen of Abbeydale interviewed for the Channel 4/Wide Vision Productions programme *What Has Become of Us?*, 31 May 1994.

10. TNA, PRO, CAB 21/4959, Brook to the Home Office, 26 June 1959.

11. TNA, PRO, PREM 11/3815, Prime Minister's Personal Minute M 243A/61, Macmillan to Brook, 29 July 1961.

12. Conversation with Air Vice-Marshal Bobby Robson, 26 July 2001.

13. I am very grateful to my daughter Polly for finding this at the Public Record Office in July 2001.

14. TNA, PRO, CAB 21/4840, 'Nuclear Retaliation Consultative Procedures.

Draft Memorandum for discussion with US Government', L. J. Sabattini's MOD redraft of 16 May 1962.

15. Ibid., Abercrombie to Cary, 17 May 1962.

16. Ibid., Cary to Abercrombie, 21 May 1962.

17. Private information.

18. TNA, PRO, CAB 130/3, GEN 75/1, 'THE ATOMIC BOMB. Memorandum by the Prime Minister', 28 August 1945.

19. TNA, PRO, CAB 134/82, CDC (48) 10 Revise, 'Background and Policy for Civil Defence Planning', 7 July 1948.

20. TNA, PRO, CAB 134/2634, CD (O) (PC) (66) 3, Civil Defence Planning Committee, 'Home Defence Review. Note by the Home Office', 4 February 1966.

21. Ibid., CD (O) (PC) (66) 7, 'The Home Defence Review. Presentation of Government Policy. Note by the Home Office', 25 May 1966.

22. TNA, PRO, DEFE 4/232, CIC 5/68, 'The Military Aspects of Home Defence of the United Kingdom. A Memorandum by the United Kingdom Commanders-in-Chief', 1 October 1968.

23. Nicola Bliss, 'The Role of Sir Norman Brook in the Construction of the Cold War State 1945–1961', unpublished MA in Contemporary British History thesis, Department of History, Queen Mary College, University of London, 2000.

24. TNA, PRO, AIR 20/11367, 'Air Ministry. Notice to Directors and Heads of Division. Routine War Planning', 16 December 1948.

25. TNA, PRO, CAB 134/80, CD (M) (48) 1st Meeting, 16 September 1948.

26. TNA, PRO, AIR 20/11367, Extract from the Conclusions of DTC (48) 4th Meeting, 4 December 1948.

27. TNA, PRO, CAB 158/4, JIC (48) 26 (o), 'Russian Interests, Intentions and Capabilities', 23 July 1948.

28. TNA, PRO, CAB 134/82, CDC (48) 10 Revise, 7 July 1948.

29. Ibid.

30. Ibid.

31. Ibid.

32. TNA, PRO, PREM 8/1355, Chuter Ede to Attlee, 29 September 1948.

33. TNA, PRO, CAB 134/82, CDC (48) 10 Revise, 7 July 1948.

34. TNA, PRO, CAB 134/80, CD (M) 48 1st Meeting, 16 September 1948.

35. TNA, PRO, CAB 134/82, CDC (48) 10 Revise, 7 July 1948.

36. Ibid.

37. TNA, PRO, CAB 134/80, CD (M) 48 1st Meeting, 16 September 1948.

38. TNA, PRO, CAB 130/41, GEN 253/1st Meeting, 10 October 1948.

39. Ibid.

40. TNA, PRO, CAB 21/1885, 'Situation in Berlin (June–July 1948)', Brook to Attlee, 29 June 1948.

41. TNA, PRO, CAB 21/1647, 'Structure of a War Cabinet, 1949–1951', 'Note for the Record', Sir Norman Brook, 14 February 1951.

42. Ibid., Attlee to Shinwell, 12 March 1951.

43. TNA, PRO, AIR 20/11367, JP (49) 157 Revised Final, 'Transition from Peace to War – Record of Decisions to Be Taken by the Chiefs of Staff. Report by the Joint Planning Staff', 4 May 1950.

44. Elizabeth Knowles (ed.), *The Oxford Dictionary of Twentieth Century Quotations* (Oxford University Press, 1998), p. 236.

45. Richard Weight, *Patriots* (Macmillan, 2002).

46. TNA, PRO, CAB 134/942, HDC (53) 5 Revise, Home Defence Committee, Working Party, 'Estimates of Casualties and House Damage. Note by the Home Office', May 1953.

47. Ibid., HDC (WP) (53) 8 Revise, 'The Distribution of the Population', 15 May 1953.

48. Ibid., 'Estimates of Casualties and House Damage'.

49. Peter Hennessy, *Never Again: Britain 1945–1951* (Cape, 1992), p. 99.

50. TNA, PRO, DEFE 13/45, Brook to Macmillan, 8 December 1954.

51. Ibid., Macmillan to Churchill, 13 December 1954.

52. Ibid., Strath's notes on 'Fall-out'.

53. Ibid., Brook to Macmillan, 8 December 1954.

54. Ibid., Strath's notes on 'Fall-out'.

55. Ibid.

56. Ibid. This is written on Macmillan's minute to him of 13 December 1954.

57. TNA, PRO, CAB 158/20, JIC (55) 12, 13 January 1955.

58. Ibid.

59. Ibid.

60. Ibid.

61. Ibid.

62. Ibid.

63. Ibid.

64. Private information.

65. TNA, PRO, DEFE 13/45, Brook to Macmillan, 7 March 1955.

66. TNA, PRO, CAB 130/109, GEN 491, 'Defence Implications of Fall-out from a Hydrogen Bomb', 1st Meeting, 24 March 1955.

67. TNA, PRO, DEFE 13/45, 'The Defence Implications of Fall-out from a Hydrogen Bomb', Brook to Eden, 21 April 1955; TNA, PRO, CAB 130/109, GEN 491, 24 March 1955.

68. TNA, PRO, DEFE 13/45, Brook to Eden, 21 April 1955.

69. Ibid.

70. Ibid.

71. TNA, PRO, CAB 130/109, GEN 491/1st Meeting.

72. Ibid.

73. TNA, PRO, DEFE 13/45, Brook to Eden, 21 April 1955.

74. Ibid.

75. TNA, PRO, DEFE 7/2056, 'Ministry of Defence War Book', August 1952.

76. TNA, PRO, CAB 130/109, GEN 491/1st Meeting.

77. TNA, PRO, DEFE 7/731, 'Home Defence Committee: Working Party on Machinery of Government in War: Minutes of Meetings and Related Papers 1958–59', Day to Wright, 18 November 1959.

78. TNA, PRO, AIR 8/2376, 'UK Command Organisation in War, 1950–1957', 'UK Command Structure in War: The Higher Military Organisation to Assist the Civil Authorities to Meet Thermo-Nuclear Attack. Report by the UK Commanders-in-Chief Committee', 6 June 1956.

79. Alban Webb, 'The Impact of the Strath Report: The Formation of Home and Civil Defence Policy in the Thermo-nuclear Age and Its Development', unpublished undergraduate thesis, Department of History, Queen Mary College, University of London, 2001.

80. TNA, PRO, CAB 134/1245, Home Defence (Ministerial) Committee, 'Shelter Policy: Memorandum by the Home Secretary', 'Appendix: Report by a Group of Officials on "The Defence Implications of 'Fall-out' from a Hydrogen Bomb"', 25 October 1955.

81. Ibid.

82. Letter from Lord Allen of Abbeydale to the author, 13 March 2002.

83. TNA, PRO, CAB 134/940, HDC (55) 3.

84. Ibid.

85. Ibid.

86. Ibid.

87. Ibid.

88. TNA, PRO, CAB 134/940, HDC (55) 3 1st Meeting, 17 March 1955.

89. TNA, PRO, CAB 134/940, HDC (55) 3.

90. Private information.

91. TNA, PRO, FO 371/160546, 'Soviet Attitudes towards Peace Treaty and Status of Berlin', Hood to Samuel, 17 August 1961.

5 'BREAKDOWN': PREPARING FOR THE WORST

1. The National Archives (TNA), Public Record Office (PRO), DEFE 10/402, 'Study Group', 1960, SG (60) 35, 'Note on the Concept and Definitions of Breakdown', 10 June 1960.

2. TNA, PRO, CAB 164/801, 'Main Issues Requiring Early Action by the Government', D. S. Laskey to J. E. Fraser, 5 May 1966.

3. Conversation with Sir Rodric Braithwaite, 18 April 2002.

4. TNA, PRO, CAB 134/1245, 'Shelter Policy: Memorandum by the Home Secretary', 25 October 1955.

5. Ibid.

6. Ibid., HD (M) (55) 2nd Meeting, 27 October 1955.

7. Ibid.

8. TNA, PRO, CAB 131/16. DC (55) 17th Meeting, 7 December 1955.

9. David Miller, *The Cold War: A Military History* (John Murray, 1998), p. 149.

10. Ibid.

11. Ibid., p. 153.

12. TNA, PRO, CAB 134/2634, CD (o) (PC) (66) 7, 25 May 1966.

13. TNA, PRO, CAB 134/2871, HDC (69) 5, 'The Care and Maintenance Decision', 17 June 1969.

14. TNA, PRO, CAB 134/1245, HD (M) (55) 12 Final, 30 November 1955.

15. TNA, PRO, CAB 134/1206, Ministerial Committee on Civil Defence, CDC (55) 3, 'Evacuation and Peripheral Dispersal: Report by the Official Committee on Civil Defence with Notes by the Home Defence Committee', 29 December 1955.

16. TNA, PRO, CAB 134/1245, HD (M) (55) 12 Final, 30 November 1955.

17. Ibid.

18. Ibid., 'Annex A: Defence Expenditure by Civil Departments: Report by the Home Defence Committee', 11 October 1955.

19. TNA, PRO, DEFE 7/731, 'Central Government in Global War: The Military Organisation', Annex to COS (59) 91, 28 April 1959.

20. TNA, PRO, CAB 21/4704, 'Plans for Censorship in Event of Emergency', Padmore to Brook, 4 January 1957.

21. TNA, PRO, DEFE 7/731, 'Central Government in Global War: The Military Organisation'.

22. Ibid.

23. TNA, PRO, CAB 21/4959, Brook, 'Cabinet Government'.

24. TNA, PRO, CAB 130/109, GEN 491/1st Meeting, 24 March 1955.

25. TNA, PRO, AIR 8/2376, 'UK Command Structure in War'.

26. I am very grateful to Dr Edgar Anstey for taking me through the origins and functions of JIGSAW. Letter from Dr Anstey (and related conversations) in August 2001.

27. TNA, PRO, DEFE 10/402, 'Study Group', 1960. For the background to JIGSAW and an appraisal of the nature of its work see Richard Moore, 'A

JIGSAW Puzzle for Operational Researchers: British Global War Studies, 1954–1962', *Journal of Strategic Studies*, Vol. 20, No. 2 (June 1997), pp. 75–91.

28. Jeremy Isaacs and Taylor Downing, *Cold War* (Bantam, 1998), p. 161.

29. TNA, PRO, DEFE 10/402, SG (60) 30, 'Some Thoughts on Deterrence or the Lack of It', E. A. Lovell, 31 May 1960.

30. Ibid.

31. Moore, 'A JIGSAW Puzzle for Operational Researchers', p. 86.

32. TNA, PRO, DEFE 10/402, SG (60) 79, 'Breakdown in JIGSAW', 29 November 1960.

33. A summary of Dr Shaw's summary, ibid.

34. Ibid.

35. Ibid., SG (63) 13, 'Likely Effects of Nuclear Weapons on the People and Economy of a Country', 'Hypothesis I', E. Anstey, 20 May 1963.

36. Ibid., SG (60) 56, 'Birmingham Study', W. G. Weeks, 6 September 1960; SG (63) 13, 'Likely Effects of Nuclear Weapons on the People and Economy of a Country', 'Hypothesis II', E. Anstey, 20 May 1963.

37. Ibid., SG (60) 36, 'Effects of Damage on a Nation', A. G. McDonald, 13 June 1960.

38. Ibid., SG (63) 13, 'Likely Effects of Nuclear Weapons on the People and Economy of a Country', 'Hypothesis III', E. Anstey, 20 May 1963.

39. Letter from Dr Edgar Anstey, 17 August 2001.

40. Ibid.

41. TNA, PRO, DEFE 10/402, SG (63) 13, 'Likely Effects of Nuclear Weapons on the People and Economy of a Country', E. Anstey, 20 May 1963.

42. Ibid., SG (60) 39, 'A New Strategic Deterrent for the UK', A. J. Shelfoon, 17 June 1960; see also ibid., SG (60) 42, 'The Requirements for a UK Nuclear Deterrent', J. A. Randall, 27 June 1960.

43. TNA, PRO, CAB 134/2634, CD (O) (PC) (66), Cabinet Civil Defence Planning Committee, 'The Home Defence Review. Presentation of Government Policy. Note by the Home Office', 25 May 1966.

44. Ibid.

45. Ibid.

46. TNA, PRO, DEFE 10/404, SG (61) 46, 'Defence Board Presentation', N. L. A. Jewell, 10 October 1961. See also ibid., 'Effects of Nuclear Weapons: Note for the Minister of Defence . . .', J. C. Kendrew, 31 May 1961. Moore, 'A JIGSAW Puzzle for Operational Researchers', pp. 86–7; letter from Dr Edgar Anstey, 17 August 2001.

47. Ibid.

48. TNA, PRO, AIR 8/2400, 'Medium Bomber Force: Size and Composition',

Defence Board, 'The V-Bomber Force and the Powered Bomb. Memorandum by the Secretary of State for Air', DB (58) 10, Annex, 'Russian Capacity to Absorb Damage', 29 October 1958.

49. TNA, PRO, DEFE 25/49, 'Nuclear Retaliation Procedures – Communications', Mountbatten of Burma, 'Note to the Government Communications Electronics Board', 1 December 1960.

50. Ibid., Mountbatten to Brook, 6 February 1961. I am grateful to Nicola Bliss for first bringing this correspondence to my attention.

51. Ibid., Mountbatten to Brook, 28 April 1961.

52. Ibid., 'Nuclear Retaliation Procedures: Communications', paper prepared by F. A. Bishop, 30 January 1961.

53. Ibid.

54. TNA, PRO, AIR 8/2238, 'Operational Readiness of Bomber Command, 1958–1961', Hudleston to Cross, 11 August 1959.

55. Ibid.

56. Ibid. See also TNA, PRO, DEFE 25/49, GEN 743/10 Revise, 'Nuclear Retaliation Procedures. Report from the Working Group', 23 January 1962.

57. Ibid.

58. Ibid.

59. Peter Hennessy, *The Prime Minister: The Office and Its Holders since 1945* (Penguin, 2000), p. 116.

60. TNA, PRO, DEFE 25/49, Mottershead to Playfair, 13 March 1961.

61. Ibid.

62. Neville Shute, *On The Beach* (Heinemann, 1957), p. 11.

63. TNA, PRO, DEFE 25/49, Mottershead to Playfair, 13 March 1961.

64. Ibid.

65. TNA, PRO, CAB 130/1281, GEN 735/1st Meeting, 3 May 1961.

66. Ibid., 'Annex'.

67. Ibid.

68. F. A. Bishop, 'Nuclear Retaliation Procedures: Communications', 30 January 1961.

69. TNA, PRO, DEFE 25/49. The diagram was originally created as part of the Geraghty Report; TNA, PRO, CAB 130/128, GEN 743/10 Revise, 23 January 1962, 'Nuclear Retaliation Procedures. Draft Report, Annex C'.

70. Sir Michael gave me permission to identify him in October 2009.

71. TNA, PRO, PREM 11/5223, 'Machinery of Government in War; Plans for the Central Nucleus (Including STOCKWELL/BURLINGTON); Nuclear Retaliation Procedures; Exercises; Part 4', Saunders to Bligh, 22 May 1962; Bligh to Saunders, 23 May 1962.

72. TNA, PRO, CAB 130/177, Nuclear Retaliation Procedures Working

Group, GEN 735/3, 'Planning for War – Cabinet Committee Structure', 28 June 1961.

73. TNA, PRO, DEFE 25/49, Brook to Mountbatten, 2 August 1961. For the full record of GEN 743 deliberations see TNA, PRO, CAB 130/128.

74. TNA, PRO, PREM 11/5233, Sir Norman Brook, 'Nuclear Retaliation: Alternative Procedures', March 1961.

75. TNA, PRO, CAB 21/4959, Bishop to Brook, October 1961.

76. TNA, PRO, DEFE 25/49, Brook, 'Nuclear Retaliation: Alternative Procedures'.

77. Ibid.

78. Ibid., Mountbatten to Brook, 28 April 1961.

79. Ibid., Brook to Mountbatten, 20 April 1961.

80. Ibid.

81. TNA, PRO, CAB 134/2888.

82. TNA, PRO, DEFE 25/49.

83. Ibid.

84. PRO, PREM 11/3815, 'Organisation of Government to Deal with a Crisis in Berlin'.

85. Ibid.

86. Ibid.

87. TNA, PRO, CAB 21/4840, 'Nuclear Retaliation Procedures', Brook to Macmillan, 6 March 1962; Bright to J. H. Robertson, 7 March 1962. On 6 March, Macmillan had initialled 'I approve' on Brook's minute.

88. TNA, PRO, DEFE 25/49, GEN 743/10 Revise, 'Nuclear Retaliation Procedures. Report'.

89. Ibid.

90. For the history and detail of this see Stephen Twigge and L. V. Scott, *Planning Armageddon: Britain and the United States and the Command of Western Nuclear Forces 1945–1964* (Harwood Academic Publishers, 2000), pp. 99–146.

91. TNA, PRO, DEFE 25/49, 'Nuclear Retaliation Procedures. Report', Annex B, 'Powers of Commander-in-Chief, Bomber Command'.

92. TNA, PRO, AIR 8/2530, 'Command Directives', 1962–1965, 'Supplementary Directive', Chief of the Air Staff to the Commander-in-Chief, RAF Bomber Command, 25 September 1962.

93. Hennessy, *The Prime Minister*, pp. 117–36.

94. TNA, PRO, DEFE 32/7, 'Chiefs of Staff Committee: Secretary's Standard Files, 1962', Annex to COS 1546/29/10/62, 'Record of a Conversation between the Chief of the Air Staff, First Sea Lord and the Chief of the Imperial General Staff held in the Ministry of Defence at 14.30, Saturday 27 October 1962'.

95. TNA, PRO, AIR 28/1657, 'Operation Record Book. RAF Waddington. January 1961–October 1962', Wing Commander O. E. Ness to RAF Waddington, 14 July 1961.

96. TNA, PRO, AIR 24/2688, 'HQ Bomber Command October 1962. Post-Exercise Report on Exercise Mickey Finn II'.

97. TNA, PRO, AIR 25/1703, 'Operational Record Book, Headquarters No. 1 Group, October 1962'.

98. TNA, PRO, CAB 21/4840, Cary to Abercrombie, 21 May 1962.

99. Hennessy, *The Prime Minister*, pp. 121–5.

100. Ibid., p. 128.

101. TNA, PRO, CAB 21/4888, 'Revised Government War Book. Revision', May–December 1962, Leavett to Trend, 29 October 1962.

102. Ibid.

103. Ibid.

104. TNA, PRO, DEFE 12/321, 'Government War Book 1963–1964', Trend to Thorneycroft, 21 May 1963. See also TNA, PRO, CAB 134/2027, HDC (63) 16, 'Cuba Review of Government War Book Planning: Note by the Chairman', 27 August 1963.

105. TNA, PRO, CAB 134/2021, HDC (62) 13, 'Home Defence Preparedness. Note by the Home Office', 19 November 1962.

106. TNA, PRO CAB 134/2035, HDC (WB) (63) 2 Final, Cabinet, Home Defence Committee, War Book Sub-Committee, 'Flexibility in Government War Book Planning. Note by the Secretaries', 31 January 1963.

107. TNA, PRO, DEFE 12/321, 'Review of Government War Book Planning in the Light of the Cuba Crisis'.

108. Ibid. The draft Bill is appended as Annex B.

109. Ibid., 'Review of Government War Book Planning in the Light of the Cuba Crisis', Cabinet Office, 20 May 1963.

110. Ibid., Emergency Powers (Defence) Bill, Annex B.

111. Ibid., Emergency Powers (Defence) Bill, Draft, 19 March 1963.

112. TNA, PRO, CAB 134/940, HDC (55) 3, 'The Defence Implications of Fall-out from a Hydrogen Bomb: Report by a Group of Officials', 8 March 1955.

113. Ibid., Emergency Powers (Defence) Bill, Draft, 19 March 1963.

114. TNA, PRO, DEFE 4/232, 'Military Aspects of the Home Defence of the United Kingdom', 1 October 1968.

115. Ibid.

116. Ibid.

117. Ibid.

118. Ibid.

119. Ibid.

120. Ibid.

121. Ibid.

122. Ibid.

123. Ibid.

124. TNA, PRO, T 227/3419, 'Museums and Galleries: Disposal of Works of Art in a War Emergency'. I am very grateful to Mr Bailey for bringing this file to my attention.

125. Ibid., 'Treasury War Planning', K. E. Couzens to Anthony Rawlinson, 9 December 1964.

126. Ibid., Brian Davies to Mary Loughnane, 1 June 1964.

127. Ibid., R. M. J. Harris to the Economic Secretary and the Chief Secretary to the Treasury, 22 October 1963.

128. Ibid., 'Operation Methodical', 1964 version.

129. Private information.

130. Letter from F. R. Barratt to the author, 25 June 2002.

131. Ibid.

132. TNA, PRO, CAB 164/801, 'Main Issues Requiring Early Action by the Government', J. L. Wright to Commander Stephens, 17 June 1966.

133. Ibid., Group Captain A. C. Blythe to Commander J. R. Stephens, 27 June 1966.

134. PRO, DEFE 4/224, 'Probable Nuclear Targets in the United Kingdom: Assumptions for Planning', COS 1929/2/11/67.

135. Sir David Omand, 'Intelligence Secrets and Media Spotlights: Balancing Illumination and Dark Corners', in *Spinning Intelligence. Why Intelligence Needs the Media. Why the Media Needs Intelligence* (Hurst, 2009), p. 414.

6 ENDGAMES: THE TRANSITION TO WORLD WAR III

1. The National Archives (TNA), Public Record Office (PRO), PREM 16/2259, 'SOVIET UNION: Joint Intelligence Committee (JIC) Assessments of Soviet Threat; Soviet Defence Policy and Strategy'. Bridges was commenting on JIC (A) (74) 17, 'Soviet Activities in the Middle East'.

2. Conversation with Sir Kevin Tebbit, 10 May 2009.

3. BBC Radio 4, *Today*, 23 June 2009.

4. Conversation with Lord Janvrin, 28 January 2009.

5. Conversation with Richard Ponman, 10 June 2009.

6. TNA, PRO, CAB 134/2880, HDC (WB) (70) (6), 'Government War Book', 'Introduction'.

7. Peter Hennessy, '"Inescapable, Necessary and Lunatic": Whitehall's

Transition-to-War Planning for World War III', in *Twentieth Century British History*, vol xxi no. 2 2010, pp. 206–224.

8. Conversation with Richard Ponman, 10 June 2009.

9. Conversation with Dennis Morris, 24 June 2009.

10. BBC Radio 4, *Today*, 23 June 2009.

11. TNA, PRO, CAB 164/375, 'Government War Book Exercises Held During 1968: INVALUABLE'.

12. Ibid., Lawrence-Wilson to Nash, Draft Letter.

13. Ibid., Draft, 'Exercise Golden Rod Nuclear Release Procedures. Selective Release of Nuclear Weapons', Annex A to XCS/3/7/11, 16 October 1968.

14. Ibid.

15. Ibid., 'General Brief for Exercise INVALUABLE', Hermitage to Lawrence-Wilson, 26 September 1968.

16. Tom Clancy, *Red Storm Rising* (Putnam's, 1986).

17. In 2009, at the age of 95, he was still producing books. See Chapman Pincher, *Treachery, Betrayals, Blunders and Cover-Ups: Espionage Against America and Great Britain* (Random House, 2009).

18. Michael Wright, *Victor Zorza: A Life Amid Loss* (Observatory Publications, 2006).

19. TNA, PRO, CAB 130/397, 'Cabinet. Invaluable Committee'; MISC 222 (68) 2, 'JIC Special Assessments as at 0800 (Z) Hours, 27 September 1968'.

20. TNA, PRO, CAB 134/2880, HDC (WB) (70) (6), 'Government War Book'.

21. TNA, PRO, CAB 130/397, MISC 222 (68) 1st Meeting (TWC), 27 September 1968.

22. Ibid., MISC 222 (68) 1st Meeting (CAB), 27 September 1968.

23. Ibid., MISC 222 (68) 2nd Meeting (CAB), 28 September 1968.

24. TNA, PRO, CAB 134/2880, HDC (WB) (70) (6) 'Government War Book'.

25. TNA, PRO, CAB 130/397, MISC 222 (68) 5, 'Joint Intelligence Committee Special Assessment as at 1200 (Z) Hours, 16 October 1968'.

26. Jack Dash had led an unofficial strike in the London docks in 1967. See Geoffrey Goodman, *The Awkward Warrior. Frank Cousins: His Life and Times* (Davis-Poynter, 1979), p. 543.

27. TNA, PRO, CAB 130/397, MISC 222 (68) 6, 'United Kingdom Background Situation Report at 1200 (Z) Hours, 16 October 1968'.

28. Ibid., MISC 222 (68) 2nd Meeting (TWC), 16 October 1968.

29. TNA, PRO, CAB 134/2880, HDC (WB) (70) (6), 'Government War Book'.

30. TNA, PRO, CAB 130/397, MISC 222 (68) 3rd Meeting (CAB), 16 October 1968.

31. Ibid., MISC 222 (68) 4th Meeting (TWC), 17 October 1968.

32. Ibid., MISC 222 (68) 5th Meeting (CAB), 17 October 1968.

33. Ibid., MISC 222 (68) 9, 18 October 1968.

34. Ibid., MISC 222 (68) 10, 18 October 1968.

35. TNA, PRO, CAB 164/375.

36. TNA, PRO, CAB 134/2880, HDC (WB) (70) (6), 'Government War Book'; CAB 130/397, MISC 222 (68) 5th Meeting (TWC), 18 October 1968.

37. Ibid., MISC 222 (68) 6th Meeting (CAB), 18 October 1968.

38. Ibid., MISC 222 (68) 12, 19 October 1968.

39. Ibid., MISC 222 (68) 11, 19 October 1968.

40. TNA, PRO, CAB 134/2880, HDC (WB) (70) (6), 'Government War Book'.

41. TNA, PRO, CAB 164/375.

42. TNA, PRO, CAB 130/397, MISC 222 (68) 7th Meeting (CAB), 19 October 1968.

43. Ibid., MISC 222 (68) 14, 20 October 1968.

44. Ibid., MISC 222 (68) 13, 20 October 1968.

45. Ibid., MISC 222 (68) 16, 21 October 1968.

46. Ibid., MISC 222 (68) 15, 21 October 1968.

47. Ibid., MISC 222 (68) 8th Meeting (CAB), 21 October 1968.

48. TNA, PRO, CAB 134/2880, HDC (WB) (70) (6), 'Government War Book'.

49. TNA, PRO, CAB 130/397, MISC 222 (68) 17, 22 October 1968.

50. Ibid., MISC 222 (68) 18, 22 October 1968.

51. Ibid., MISC 222 (68) 9th Meeting (CAB), 22 October 1968; TNA, PRO, CAB 134/2880, HDC (WB) (70) (6), 'Government War Book'.

52. TNA, PRO, CAB 130/397, MISC 222 (68) 20, 23 October 1968.

53. Ibid., MISC 222 (68) 19, 23 October 1968.

54. Ibid., MISC 222 (68) 10th Meeting (CAB), 23 October 1968.

55. Ibid., MISC 222 (68) 11th Meeting, 4 November 1968.

56. David Young speaking on BBC Radio 4, *Today*, 23 June 2009.

57. Conversation with Ron Lawrence of the Cabinet Office, 27 July 2009.

58. Brian Gilmore to Peter Hennessy, 5 August 2009.

7 'LONDON MIGHT BE SILENCED': THE LAST REDOUBT

1. The National Archives (TNA), Public Record Office (PRO), DEFE 5/136, 'Chiefs of Staff Committee Memoranda, 20 February–28 May 1963', Annex to COS 96/63, 'United Kingdom Commanders in Chief Committee. Terms of reference'.

2. Sir Frank Cooper in conversation with Tom Dibble and Peter Hennessy, 4 August 1998.

3. Conversation with Peter Hudson, 16 August 2007.

4. Seen by the author on his first visit, 27 April 2001.

5. Conversation with Sir Frank Cooper, 18 May 2001.

6. Private information.

7. Briefing by Wing Commander Steven Greenwood, RAF, Commanding Officer, Joint Support Unit, Corsham, 27 April 2001.

8. Ibid.

9. Letter from Lord Callaghan of Cardiff to Peter Hennessy, 23 April 2002.

10. TNA, PRO, DEFE 5/136, Annex to COS 96/63.

11. Private information.

12. A small group of students and I were permitted to visit the Crisis Management Centre on 15 March 2001.

13. Conversation with Richard Abel, 21 February 2001.

14. Letter from Guy Lester to the author, 28 March 2001.

15. TNA, PRO, DEFE 2/225, 'Ministry of Defence War Book, August 1963', Appendix D, 'Turnstile Staff Requirements'.

16. Private information.

17. Private information.

18. Private information.

19. Private information.

20. Private information.

21. Letter from Geoffrey Harris to Peter Hennessy, 28 April 2002.

22. Letter from Sir Derek Mitchell to Peter Hennessy, 28 June 2002.

23. TNA, PRO, DEFE 2/225, 'Ministry of Defence War Book, August 1963', Appendix D, 'Turnstile Staff Requirements'.

24. Sir Frank Cooper interviewed for the BBC Radio 4 programme *The Top Job*, 8 August 2000.

25. Letter from Sir Derek Mitchell to Peter Hennessy, 28 June 2002.

26. Lord Allen of Abbeydale interviewed for the Channel 4/Wide Vision Productions programme *What Has Become of Us?*, 31 May 1994.

27. Sir Frank Cooper, 8 August 2000.

28. Neville Shute, *On the Beach* (Heinemann, 1957), pp. 3–4.

29. Private information.

30. Private information.

31. Private information.

32. Peter Hennessy, *Muddling Through: Power, Politics and the Quality of Government in Post-war Britain* (Gollancz, 1996), p. 116.

33. TNA, PRO, DEFE 2/225, 'Ministry of Defence War Book, August 1963', Appendix D, 'Turnstile Staff Requirements'.

34. TNA, PRO, DEFE 7/731, 'Home Defence Committee: Working Party on

Machinery of Government in War: Minutes of Meetings and Related Papers, 1958–59', Day to Wright, 18 November 1959.

35. TNA, PRO, DEFE 7/737, 'Supplement to Ministry of Defence War Book', Annex to COS (59) 1.

36. TNA, PRO, DEFE 7/731, 'Action to Be Taken by the Chiefs of Staff on a Tactical Warning', Appendix II to Annex to COS (59) 12.

37. TNA, PRO, DEFE 2/225, 'Ministry of Defence War Book, August 1963, Chapter III – Alternative War Headquarters'.

38. Ibid.

39. Ibid.

40. Peter Hennessy, *The Hidden Wiring: Unearthing the British Constitution* (Gollancz, 1995), p. 90.

41. TNA, PRO, DEFE 25/49, 'Nuclear Retaliation Procedures', report from GEN 743/10 Revise, 23 January 1962.

42. TNA, PRO, DEFE 13/212, MM/COS (62) 7, 'Record of a Meeting Between the Minister of Defence and the Chiefs of Staff on Sunday 28 October 1962'.

43. D. R. Thorpe, *Selwyn Lloyd* (Cape, 1989), p. 424.

44. Hennessy, *Muddling Through*, p. 129. The conversation took place in 1989 for the BBC Radio 3 *Premiership* series.

45. TNA, PRO, DEFE 2/225, 'Ministry of Defence War Book, August 1963', Appendix D, 'Turnstile Staff Requirements'.

46. TNA, PRO, AIR 8/2400, 'Medium Range Bomber Force: Size and Composition', 'Russian Capacity to Absorb Damage', Annex to DB (58) 10.

47. TNA, PRO, AIR 8/2201, 'UK/US Co-Ordination: Offensive Bomber Operations 1957–1962', 'Strategic Strike Planning by Bomber Command'.

48. TNA, PRO, AIR 8/2400, 'Russian Capacity to Absorb Damage'.

49. TNA, PRO, CAB 134/3120, 'Ministerial Committee on Nuclear Policy' (PN) (67) 6, 'British Nuclear Policy', 1 December 1967.

50. I am very grateful to Wing Commander Steve Rover-Parkes and Andy Quinn, JSCH Mines Manager, for showing us around 'Site 3' on 19 June 2006.

51. TNA, PRO, CAB 175/26, 'Central Government War Headquarters at Corsham: Telephone Directory'.

52. Plans for the bunker's War Room/Map Room can be found in TNA, PRO, CAB 21/4191, 'Manning of BURLINGTON', 'Organizations, Functions and Layout in Central Nucleus of Government in War', Digney to Darracott, 10 May 1956.

53. *Dr Strangelove, or How I Learned to Stop Worrying and Love the Bomb* (Columbia Pictures, 1964).

54. Conversation with Peter Hudson, 16 August 2007.

55. The author was present.

56. TNA, PRO, CAB 21/4135, 'Stockwell – Chiefs of Staff Presentation', August 1960.

57. TNA, PRO, WO 32/20122, 'First Information Slip'.

58. Ibid.

59. E-mail from Dr Jonathan Marshall, 13 October 2009.

60. Jeremy Isaacs and Taylor Downing, *Cold War* (Bantam, 1998), p. 182.

61. TNA, PRO, CAB 21/6081, 'Machinery of Government in War: Burlington: Ministerial Nominations', Brook to Macmillan, 13 September 1961.

62. Ibid., Bishop to Macmillan, 5 October 1961.

63. Ibid.

64. Ibid. For the original 'gravediggers' see *The Works of William Shakespeare* (Shakespeare Head Press/Blackwell, 1938), 'Hamlet', Act V, scene i, lines 1–231.

65. TNA, PRO, CAB 21/6081, Geraghty to Bligh, 13 October 1961.

66. Ibid., Macmillan to Butler and Lloyd, 18 October 1961, Annexes 1 and 2.

67. Ibid.

68. Ibid., Lloyd to Macmillan, 18 October 1961.

69. Ibid., Butler to Macmillan, 19 October 1961.

70. Private information.

71. PRO, CAB 21/6081, appendix to Brook's memo to Macmillan, 13 September 1961.

72. Ibid., Stephenson to Butt, 4 October 1961.

73. Ibid., Macmillan to Home, 26 September 1962.

74. Ibid., Macmillan to Butler, 26 September 1962.

75. Ibid., Samuel to Bligh, 5 October 1962.

76. Ibid., Bligh to Samuel, 6 October 1962.

77. TNA, PRO, CAB 130/128, GEN 735/4, 'Stockwell: Committee Structure. Note by the Secretary of the Cabinet', 12 July 1961.

78. TNA, PRO, CAB 21/6081, Paget to de Thuillier, 23 January 1964.

79. Ibid.

80. Ibid., Trend to Douglas-Home, 24 December 1963.

81. Ibid., Bligh to Trend, 31 December 1963.

82. Ibid., Trend to Cary, 13 January 1964.

83. Ibid., Trend to Rogers, 14 April 1964.

84. Ibid., Paget to Rogers, 17 April 1964.

85. Ibid., Trend to Douglas-Home, 27 April 1964.

86. Ibid. It is written in longhand in the top right-hand corner of Douglas-Home to Butler, 30 April 1964.

87. Ibid., Annex I.

88. Ibid., 'Note for record', T. E. Bridges, 10 June 1964.

89. Ibid., Lloyd to Douglas-Home, 8 May 1964.

90. Ibid., Douglas-Home to Lloyd, 30 April 1964.

91. Ibid., Paget to MacIntosh, 3 November 1964.

92. Ibid., Fraser to McIndoe, 12 March 1965.

93. Ibid. No files for Exercise ARABIAN NIGHT have survived. Letter from Alan Glennie, Head of Records and Archives Team, Cabinet Office, to Peter Hennessy, 12 August 2009.

94. TNA, PRO, CAB 21/6081., Fraser to McIndoe, 15 March 1965.

95. Ibid., draft on 12 March 1965.

96. Ibid., McIndoe to Mitchell, 21 July 1965.

97. Ibid., Bowden to Wilson; Healey to Wilson, 5 August 1965.

98. Ibid., Wilson to Bowden and Healey, 16 July 1965.

99. TNA, PRO, PREM 13/3565, 'DEFENCE. Machinery of Government in War; Plans for the Central Nucleus; Nuclear Retaliation Procedures; Exercises; Part 4', Trend to Mitchell, 13 July 1965.

100. Ibid., note on file, 28 September 1966.

101. Ibid., Trend to Wilson, 22 March 1968.

102. Ibid., Trend to Wilson, 25 April 1969.

103. Ibid., Wilson to Healey, 5 May 1969.

104. Ibid., Wilson to Stewart, 5 May 1969.

105. Ibid., Trend to Wilson, 3 June 1966.

106. Ibid., Trend to Wilson, 3 June 1966.

107. Ibid., Halls to Trend, 6 June 1966.

108. TNA, PRO, PREM 11/5224, 'Machinery of Government in War; Part 3', Trend to Macmillan, 28 May 1963.

109. Ibid.

110. *The Denning Report: The Profumo Affair* (Pimlico, 1992), p. 86. Originally published as Cmnd. 2152 (HMSO, 1963) on 26 September 1963.

111. Ibid., p. 7.

112. TNA, PRO, PREM 11/5524, Trend to Macmillan, 28 May 1963.

113. Peter Hennessy, *Having It So Good: Britain in the Fifties* (Penguin, 2007), pp. 595–6.

114. TNA, PRO, PREM 11/5524, Trend to Macmillan, 28 May 1963.

115. Ibid.

116. Ibid.

117. Ibid., Trend to Douglas-Home, 26 March 1964 and accompanying 'Machinery of Government in War'.

118. Ibid., Trend to Macmillan, 28 May 1963.

119. Ibid.

120. Ibid. His brief was classified 'TOP SECRET – TACK'.

121. Ibid., Trend to Macmillan, 28 May 1963.

122. Ibid.

123. Ibid.

124. Ibid., Bligh to Macmillan, 29 May 1963.

125. Ibid.

126. 'Outline Details Concerning PYTHON etc.', Cabinet Office, June 2009.

127. TNA, PRO, PREM 11/5224, 'Instructions on the Handling of ACID Information', Annex A.

128. Ibid., 'Machinery of Government in War', March 1964.

129. Ibid.

130. 'Outline Details Concerning PYTHON etc.'.

131. TNA, PRO, PREM 11/5224, 'Machinery of Government in War', March 1964.

132. Ibid.

133. Ibid., Trend to Wilson, 18 April 1968.

134. TNA, PRO, CAB 175/5–24.

135. TNA, PRO, CAB, HDC (65) 1st Meeting, Item 4, 15 February 1965, CONFIDENTIAL ANNEX, . . . 'Machinery of Government in War'.

136. TNA, PRO, CAB 175/28, soon to arrive at TNA.

137. Ibid.

138. Ibid.

139. Ibid., 'Machinery of Government in War', 19 February 1971.

140. Ibid., Heath signed this off on 24 February 1971.

141. 'Outline Details Concerning PYTHON etc.'.

142. Letter from Alan Glennie to Peter Hennessy, 12 August 2009. Mr Glennie wrote: 'The names of the two ships involved – RFA Engadine and HMY Britannia – were recently disclosed in response to a FOI [Freedom of Information Act] request. The names of the ships are contained in an Official Committee on Home Defence Machinery of Government in War Sub-Committee paper (HDO (MG) (67) (28), item 5, part of CAB 134/4295), which is retained in the Cabinet Office on security grounds under Section 3 (4) of the Public Records Act'.

143. Gavin Lyall, The Crocus List (first published by Hodder, 1985). I am grateful to Gavin Lyall's widow, Katherine Whitehorn, for alerting me to The Crocus List when we were discussing the hidden history of the Cold War with our mutual friend Barbara Hosking on 14 September 2009.

144. Ibid. (Coronet edn, 1993), pp. 7–12.

145. Private information.

8 THE HUMAN BUTTON: DECIDERS AND DELIVERERS

1. Conversation with Air Vice-Marshal Bobby Robson, 26 July 2001.
2. Private information.
3. 'The Lighter Touch', *The Times*, 30 September 1998.
4. General Lord Guthrie of Craigiebank, interview for the BBC Radio 4 documentary *The Human Button* (broadcast 2 December 2008), 23 October 2008.
5. Commander Richard Lindsey RN, interview for *The Human Button*, 30 October 2008.
6. Sir Michael Quinlan, interview for *The Human Button*, 16 October 2008.
7. Private information.
8. The National Archives (TNA), Public Record Office (PRO), CAB 21/6081, 'Machinery of Government in War: Burlington: Ministerial Nominations', Macmillan to Home, 26 September 1962.
9. Conversation with Lord Guthrie, 23 October 2008.
10. Private information.
11. Lord Callaghan speaking in *A Bloody Union Jack on Top of It*, BBC Radio 4, May 1988. See also Peter Hennessy, *Muddling Through: Power, Politics and the Quality of Government in Post-war Britain* (Gollancz, 1996), p. 129.
12. Margaret Thatcher, *The Downing Street Years* (HarperCollins, 1993), pp. 246–8.
13. Iain Dale (ed.), *Labour Party General Election Manifestos, 1900–1997* (Routledge/Politico's, 2000), p. 283.
14. David Butler, *British General Elections since 1945* (Blackwell, 1989), p. 37.
15. Simon Heffer, *Like the Roman: The Life of Enoch Powell* (Weidenfeld and Nicolson, 1998), pp. 129–30.
16. House of Commons *Official Report*, 28 June 1983, Vol. 44, col. 496.
17. Ibid., col. 495.
18. Rodric Braithwaite, *Across the Moscow River: The World Turned Upside Down* (Yale, 2002), p. 52.
19. TNA, PRO, CAB 165/1082, 'Election Business Committee; Contingency Briefs and Party Manifestos', Rose to Hunt, 4 April 1979.
20. 'Codewords Association with Machinery of Government in War [MGW] etc.', Cabinet Office, 20 May 2009.
21. TNA, PRO, CAB 165/1082, Rose to Hunt, 4 April 1979.
22. Sir Bryan Cartledge speaking on *Day One in No. 10* Part Two, broadcast on BBC Radio 4 19 May 2010.
23. Lord Butler of Brockwell, speaking on *Day One in No. 10*.

24. 'Britain Will Win With Labour', in Dale (ed.), *Labour Party General Election Manifestos, 1900–1997*, p. 212.

25. TNA, PRO, PREM 16/1978, 'British Strategic Nuclear Deterrent'.

26. Ibid.

27. Ibid., 'Nuclear Matters', Hunt to Cartledge, 27 March 1979. Callaghan has hand dated his instructions to Hunt and Cartledge on this note 4 May 1979.

28. Hennessy, *Muddling Through*, pp. 126–7.

29. Private information.

30. TNA, PRO, CAB 130/1109, MISC 7 (79) 1st Meeting, 24 May 1979.

31. Private information.

32. TNA, PRO, PREM 16/1971, 'Appointment of Nuclear Deputies, 1974–79'; Prime Minister's Personal Minute, M17w/74, 1 April 1974, Prime Minister's Personal Minute, M33c/T6, 23 June 1976. Letter from Alan Glennie, 10 May 2010.

33. Ibid.

34. TNA, PRO, CAB 21/477/1, Wilson to Healey, 16 July 1965; Healey to Wilson, 5 August 1965.

35. Lord Healey of Riddlesden, interview for *The Human Button*, 28 October 2008.

36. Peter Hennessy, *Cabinets and the Bomb* (British Academy/Oxford University Press, 2007), p. 18.

37. Private information.

38. I am very grateful to Alan Glennie and Nick Weekes of the Cabinet Office for getting the 'Z' appendices to me in time for inclusion in this book.

39. TNA, PRO, CAB 175/14, HDC (WB) (61) 4, Appendix Z, 16 November 1961; HDC (WB) (64) 9, Appendix Z, 24 August 1964; CAB 175/15, HDC (WB) (66) 11, Appendix Z; CAB 175/19, GWB (69) 1, 2 July 1969; GWB (72), 24 July 1972; CAB 175/18, GWB 21 March 1975, Appendix Z, 'Nuclear Release'.

40. Ibid.

41. Private information.

42. TNA, PRO, CAB 175/18, Appendix Z.

43. Ibid.

44. Ibid.

45. Ibid.

46. TNA, PRO, CAB 130/212, MISC 16/1st Meeting, 'Atlantic Nuclear Force'.

47. For the decision to cancel TSR.2 see Denis Healey, *The Time of My Life* (Michael Joseph, 1989), p. 273; for the decision to build four Polaris sub-marines see TNA, PRO, CAB 148/18, OPD (65) 5th Meeting, 29 January 1965.

48. TNA, PRO, CAB 21/4/63/2, Bourn to McIndoe, 22 October 1964, enclosing 'British Nuclear Forces'.

49. Air Vice-Marshal Nigel Baldwin, speaking on *The Human Button*.

50. Squadron Leader Robin Woolven, speaking on *The Human Button*.

51. Teresa Brooks, speaking on *The Human Button*.

52. Robin Woolven, speaking on *The Human Button*.

53. E-mail from Robin Woolven, 21 October 2008.

54. Squadron Leader Roy Brocklebank, speaking on *The Human Button*.

55. Roy Brocklebank, 'Bomber Command 1960s: This Presentation Was Top Secret', paper presented to Charterhouse School, 28 March 2008. It was later published under the title 'World War III – The 1960's Version', in the *Journal of Navigation*, Vol. 58, No. 3, September 2005, pp. 341–7.

56. E-mail from Robin Woolven, 14 October 2008.

57. Brocklebank, 'Bomber Command 1960s'.

58. E-mail from Robin Woolven, 14 October 2008.

59. Brocklebank, 'Bomber Command 1960s'.

60. E-mail from Robin Woolven, 14 October 2008.

61. Brocklebank, 'Bomber Command 1960s'.

62. E-mail from Robin Woolven, 14 October 2008.

63. Ibid.

64. Brocklebank, 'Bomber Command 1960s'.

65. E-mail from Robin Woolven, 14 October 2008.

66. Ibid.

67. Conversation with Robin Woolven, 7 February 2010.

68. Brocklebank, 'Bomber Command 1960s'.

69. Conversation with Robin Woolven, 15 March 2009.

70. Peter R. March, *The Vulcan Story* (Sutton, 2006), p. 53.

71. Conversation with Robin Woolven, 15 March 2009.

72. E-mail from Robin Woolven, 14 October 2008.

73. Ibid.

74. E-mails from Robin Woolven, 16 and 18 March 2009. Conversation with Roy Brocklebank, 24 March 2009.

75. E-mail from Robin Woolven, 14 October 2008.

76. Conversation with Roy Brocklebank, 7 February 2010.

77. The Trident firing chain as heard on *The Human Button*.

78. For an account of his career see Jim Ring, *We Come Unseen: The Untold Story of Britain's Cold War Submariners* (John Murray, 2003), pp. 164–8, 251.

79. Toby Elliott, speaking on *The Human Button*.

80. Michael Quinlan, 'Foreword', in Hennessy, *Cabinets and the Bomb*, pp. ix–xi.

81. Sir Michael Quinlan, speaking on *The Human Button*.
82. Conversation with Sir Frank Cooper, 8 August 2001.
83. Ibid.
84. Sir Michael Quinlan, 'Remarks at launch of *The Secret State*', 4 March 2002.
85. Private information.
86. Private information.
87. Conversation with Sir Michael Quinlan, 16 October 2008.
88. Lord Guthrie, speaking on *The Human Button*.

9 THE SAFETY OF THE REALM SINCE 2001

1. Letter from Lord Callaghan of Cardiff to the author, 23 April 2002.
2. Conversation with Sir Christopher Mallaby, 25 June 2002.
3. Private information.
4. Quoted in Peter Hennessy, 'Cats' Eyes in the Dark', *The Economist*, 19 March 2005.
5. Her speech on 'The International Terrorist Threat to the United Kingdom' is reproduced in Peter Hennessy (ed.), *The New Protective State: Government, Intelligence and Terrorism* (Continuum, 2007), pp. 66–73.
6. 'Let Us Reach for a Better Future', *The Times*, 6 April 2009.
7. The National Archives (TNA), Public Record Office (PRO), CAB 134/3973, TM (75) 1, 'Counter-Terrorist Arrangements: Memorandum by the Chairman of the Official Committee', 4 March 1975.
8. 'Pursue Prevent Protect Prepare: The United Kingdom's Strategy for Countering International Terrorism', Cm. 7547 (Stationery Office, March 2009).
9. Ibid., p. 81.
10. Charles Farr's 'Dear Stakeholder' 'CONTEST' letter was dated 23 March 2009.
11. Conversation with Sir Richard Mottram, 4 April 2009.
12. Private information.
13. Charles Farr, 'Terrorism and Counter-Terrorism: What Next?' Third Annual Colin Cramphorn Memorial Lecture, Policy Exchange, 25 March 2009.
14. 'Pursue Prevent Protect Prepare', p. 35.
15. Manningham-Buller, 'The International Terrorist Threat to the United Kingdom', in Hennessy (ed.), *The New Protective State*, p. 67.
16. Richard Mottram, 'Protecting the Citizen in the Twenty-First Century: Issues and Challenges', in ibid., p. 46.
17. The phrase that will be forever associated with the ex-US State Department official Francis Fukuyama, thanks to his eponymous book, *The End of History*,

18. Michael Howard, *Liberation or Catastrophe?: Reflections on the History of the Twentieth Century* (Continuum, 2007), p. vii.

19. Private information.

20. Sir Colin McColl speaking on Part 3 of Gordon Corera's *MI6: A Century in the Shadows*, BBC Radio 4, first broadcast on 10 August 2009.

21. Ernest Gellner, *Anthropology and Politics: Revolutions in the Sacred Grove* (Blackwell, 1995), p. 171. His essay was originally published under the title I have cited in Robert A. Hinde (ed.), *The Institution of War* (Comminan, 1991), pp. 62–80.

22. Gellner's books included *Muslim Society* (Cambridge University Press, 1981); *Nations and Nationalism* (Blackwell, 1983); *Culture, Identity and Politics* (Cambridge University Press, 1987); *Plough, Sword and Book* (Collins Harvill, 1988); *Relativism and the Social Sciences* (Cambridge University Press, 1985); *Language and Solitude* (Cambridge University Press, 1998); *Conditions of Liberty: Civil Society and Its Rivals* (Hamish Hamilton, 1994).

23. Gellner, *Anthropology and Politics*, p. 170.

24. Ibid.

25. Ibid., pp. 170–71.

26. Ibid., p. 171.

27. Lord Wilson of Dinton made his remark public in 'Tomorrow's Government', Royal Society of Arts Lecture, 1 March 2006.

28. See Peter Hennessy, 'From Secret State to Protective State', in Hennessy (ed.), *The New Protective State*, pp. 1–41.

29. Manningham-Buller, 'The International Terrorist Threat to the United Kingdom', in ibid., pp. 66–73; Christopher Andrew, *The Defence of the Realm: The Authorized History of MI5* (Penguin, 2009), pp. 813–30.

30. 'Defence: Outline of Future Policy', Cmnd. 124 (HMSO, 1957).

31. 'Countering International Terrorism: The United Kingdom's Strategy', Cm. 6888 (Stationery Office, July 2006), p. 8.

32. Ibid., p. 26.

33. Ibid.

34. Private information.

35. Private information.

36. Matthew Grant, *After the Bomb: Civil Defence and Nuclear War in Cold War Britain, 1945–1968* (Palgrave, 2009).

37. David Shiga, 'It's behind you!', *New Scientist*, 26 September 2009, pp. 30–33.

38. 'Countering International Terrorism', p. 26.

39. Private information.

40. Andrew, *The Defence of the Realm*, p. 846.

41. 'Countering International Terrorism', p. 8.

42. Andrew, *The Defence of the Realm*, p. 826.

43. Manningham-Buller, 'The International Terrorist Threat to the United Kingdom', in Hennessy (ed.), *The New Protective State*, p. 68.

44. Ibid., p. 67.

45. Private information.

46. Andrew, *The Defence of the Realm*, p. 827.

47. Ibid., p. 828.

48. Private information.

49. Andrew, *The Defence of the Realm*, pp. 817–18.

50. Private information.

51. Andrew, *The Defence of the Realm*, p. 818.

52. 'Threat Levels: The System to Assess the Threat from International Terrorism' (Stationery Office, July 2006), p. 2.

53. Private information.

54. Private information.

55. Private information.

56. Private information.

57. 'Countering International Terrorism', p. 9.

58. Andrew, *The Defence of the Realm*, p. 828.

59. This and the two organograms that follow were prepared initially by the author and Sir David Omand, when Co-ordinator of Security and Intelligence, and updated in early 2006 by the Cabinet Office before Sir Richard Mottram and the author addressed a seminar at the National Liberal Club in London on 8 February 2006 organized jointly by the *Guardian* and the First Division Association of Civil Servants. The original organograms were published in *RUSI Journal*, Vol. 150, No. 3 (June 2003) to accompany papers by Omand and Hennessy. The original 'British Intelligence Flows' diagram accompanied 'Cat's Eyes in the Dark' in *The Economist*, 19–25 March 2005.

60. As it did in the small hours of 10 August 2006 as twenty-three arrests were being made of those suspected of preparing to bring down ten transatlantic airliners. (See Philip Webster, Sean O'Neill and Stewart Tendler, 'A Plan "to commit unimaginable mass murder"', *The Times*, 11 August 2006.)

61. TNA, PRO, HO 223/129, GEN 8 (71) 1 Final, 'Crisis Management Working Party. Costed Proposals for the Whitehall Situation Centre', 1 July 1971.

62. 'Review of Intelligence in Weapons of Mass Destruction: Report of a Committee of Privy Counsellors', HC 898 (Stationery Office, July 2004).

63. Conversation with Dr John Reid, 29 March 2007.

64. Prime Minister's Written Ministerial Statement on Machinery of Government, House of Commons *Official Report*, 29 March 2007, cols. 133–5WS
65. Private information.
66. Prime Minister's Written Ministerial Statement . . ., 29 March 2007.
67. Ibid.
68. Private information.
69. Private information.
70. Private information.
71. I am grateful to the Cabinet Office for providing me with a copy of these terms of reference in October 2009.
72. 'Improving the Central Intelligence Machinery' (Cabinet Office, July 2009), Annex I.
73. S. R. Eyre, 'Man the Pest: The Dim Chances of Survival', *New York Review*, 18 November 1971.
74. Philip Bobbitt, *Terror and Consent: The Wars for the Twenty-First Century* (Penguin, 2008), p. 289.
75. Ibid., p. 309.
76. Private information.
77. Private information.

10 TOWARDS A NATIONAL SECURITY STRATEGY

1. Mervyn King, Governor of the Bank of England, 'Finance: A Return from Risk', speech to the Worshipful Company of International Bankers, Mansion House, 17 March 2009.
2. J. M. Keynes, 'Economic Possibilities for Our Grandchildren (1930), in J. M. Keynes, *Essays in Persuasion* (Rupert Hart-Davis, 1952), pp. 359–60.
3. Eric Hobsbawm, 'Socialism has Failed. Now Capitalism is Bankrupt. So What Comes Next?', *Guardian*, 10 April 2009.
4. Private information.
5. Peter Hennessy and Zareer Masani, 'Out of the Midday Sun? Britain and the Great Power Impulse', Strathclyde/*Analysis* papers on Government and Politics (Department of Government, University of Strathclyde, 1992), p. 4.
6. 'The National Security Strategy of the United Kingdom: Security in an Interdependent world', Cm. 7291 (Cabinet Office, March 2008), pp. 10–24. See also the Cabinet Office press release 'Government Publishes First National Security Strategy', 19 March 2008 (CAB/033/08).
7. 'Security for the Next Generation. The National Security Strategy of the United Kingdom: Update 2009', Cm. 7590 (Cabinet Office, June 2009).

8. King, 'Finance: A Return from Risk'.

9. Ibid.

10. Ibid.

11. Charles P. Kindleberger and Robert Z. Aliber, *Manias, Panics and Crashes: A History of Financial Crises* (Palgrave/Macmillan, 2005), p. 239.

12. The full treaty can be read in Appendix B of Nicholas Henderson, *The Birth of NATO* (Weidenfeld and Nicolson, 1982), pp. 119–22.

13. Michael Dockrill, *British Defence since 1945* (Blackwell, 1988), p. 92.

14. Michael Quinlan, 'Shaping the Defence Programme: Some Platitudes', 1 December 2008. Unpublished paper in Sir Michael Quinlan's private archive. I am very grateful to Lady Quinlan for her permission to quote from it.

15. Private information.

16. Tony Wright delivered his lecture at the House of Commons on 4 March 2009. It is reproduced in *Political Quarterly*, Vol. 80, No. 4, pp. 575–88.

17. 'Ministerial Committees of the Cabinet: Composition and Terms of Reference (Cabinet Office, November 2008).

18. Private information.

19. Private information.

20. Douglas Hurd, *An End to Promises: Sketch of a Government 1970–74* (Collins, 1979), p. 39.

21. Private information.

22. Private information.

23. Tomasi di Lampedusa, *The Leopard*, first published 1958 (Vintage, 2007).

24. Nassim Taleb, the author of *The Black Swan: The Impact of the Highly Improbable* (Penguin, 2007), delivered this view in an interview in the *Wall Street Journal* on 24 April 2007.

EPILOGUE: LIVING ON THE DARK SIDE

1. Percy Cradock, *In Pursuit of British Interests: Reflections on Foreign Policy under Margaret Thatcher and John Major* (John Murray, 1997), p. 37.

2. Conversation with David Young, 10 December 2009.

3. Mary Douglas, *Natural Symbols: Explorations in Cosmology* (first published 1970; Routledge Classics edn, 2003), see Chapter 4, 'Grid and Group', pp. 55–71.

4. Melissa Smith, 'Planning for the Last Time: Government Science, Civil Defence and the Public, 1945–68', unpublished PhD thesis, Faculty of Life Sciences, University of Manchester, March 2010. For the inception of *Fission Fragments*, see The National Archive (TNA), Public Record Office (PRO),

HO 229/1, '*Fission Fragments*, March 1961'. For 'Spot the Bomb', see HO 229/5, '*Fission Fragments*, October 1963'.

5. Peter Hudson, speaking on *The Human Button*, first broadcast on BBC Radio 4, 2 December 2008.

6. Conversation with David Young, 10 December 2009.

7. Ibid.

8. Private information.

9. Private information.

10. Private information.

11. Private information.

12. Private information.

13. Private information.

14. For the role of the SIS officer Harold Shergold in designing and operating the new system see Peter Hennessy, *Having It So Good: Britain in the Fifties* (Penguin, 2007), pp. 317–18.

15. Private information.

16. Private information.

17. Private information.

18. Private information.

19. Private information.

20. Jonathan Evans, 'Intelligence, Counter-Terrorism and Trust', Society of Editors Conference, Manchester, 5 November 2007.

21. In the House of Lords on Appeal from Her Majesty's Court of Appeal (England) between *A and others* v *Secretary of State for the Home Department*, Statement of Eliza Manningham-Buller, 20 September 2005.

22. Ibid.

23. Ibid.

24. Ibid.

25. Peter Hennessy, *Whitehall* (Pimlico, 2001), pp. 475–6.

26. Intelligence and Security Committee, *Annual Report 2007–2008* (Stationery Office, 2009), p. 19, footnote 56.

27. Jonathan Evans, 'Defending the Realm', Policy and Politics Annual Lecture, University of Bristol, 15 October 2009.

28. *MI6: A Century in the Shadows*, part III, first broadcast on BBC Radio 4, 10 August 2009.

29. Evans, 'Defending the Realm'.

30. Ibid.

31. Private information.

32. Private information.

33. Private information.

34. Private information.

35. Christopher Andrew, *The Defence of the Realm: The Authorized History of MI5* (Penguin, 2009), pp. 826–7.

36. Ibid., p. 827.

37. Evans, 'Intelligence, Counter-Terrorism and Trust'.

38. To be published by Bloomsbury in 2010.

39. Bruce Chatwin, *The Songlines* (Cape, 1987).

40. Andrew Lycett, *Ian Fleming* (Phoenix, 1995), p. 222.

41. Ben Macintyre, *Operation Mincemeat* (Bloomsbury, 2010), p. 167.

42. Lady Manningham-Buller, 'Reflections on Intelligence', Lord Speaker's Mile End Road Group Lecture, House of Lords, 9 March 2010.

43. K. R. Popper, *The Open Society and Its Enemies*, Vol. 2: *The High Tide of Prophecy: Hegel, Marx and the Aftermath* (Routledge, Kegan and Paul, 1945), p. 194.

Index

Figures in italics indicate tables, documents and a diagram.

Abercrombie, Nigel 156, 194, 198, 200–201
Aboriginal 'Songlines' 414–15
ACID (codename for bunker system) 299–301, 315
Addison, Lord 51
Addison Road Station (now Olympia) 275
Admiralty Cinema 186
Admiralty House 67, 69
Afghanistan 384, 395
Agreement for Co-operation on Uses of Atomic Energy for Mutual Defence Purposes (1958) 62
air bursts (hydrogen bombs) 172
Air Force Operations Room (AFOR) 210
Al Qaeda xxiii, 363–4, 369, 371, 373, 409, 411, 413
Aldermaston see Atomic Weapons Research Establishment, Aldermaston
Aldermaston Marches 108, 111–13, 118–19, 190, 210
Aldrich, Professor Richard 6, 28–9
Alexander, Horace 110
Alexander, Lord (A. V.) 51, 56, 93, 108

Aliber, Robert 394–5
Allan, Alex 381–3
Allen, Philip, Lord Allen of Abbeydale 155–6, 165, 171, 268
Allocated Line Numbers (ALN) for the V-bombers 337
Alphand, Herve 68–9
Amalgamated Engineering and Foundry Workers' Union 140
Amber list (1962) 7–12
'An Anthropological View of War and Violence' (Gellner) 366
Anarchist Federation of Britain 135–6
Anderson, Sir John 399
Andrew, Professor Christopher 19, 27–8, 102, 106–7, 121, 369, 372, 414
Andropov, Yuri 121
Annual Report 2007–8 (Intelligence and Security Committee) 411
Ansell, Derek 264
Anstey, Dr Edgar 184–7
Appendix Z team 320
ARABIAN NIGHT (exercise) 290
Arnold, Lorna 34, 35, 61
Arrowsmith, Pat 111

Arzamas-16 secret nuclear-weapons
    city 33
asteroid contingency 370
Atlantic Nuclear Force (ANF)
    (proposed) 74–5, 290–91
atomic bomb *see* nuclear weapons
Atomic Weapons Research
    Establishment, Aldermaston
    77, 108, 112, 324
Attlee, Clement
    penetration of the nuclear
        capacities of US/UK 22
    and Russian objectives 29
    and the atomic bomb 45, 48–52,
        157, 162, 353–4
    and GEN 183 88, 91–2
    security advice 89–91
    and GEN 226 94
    procedures for positive vetting
        94–5, 101
    on the Winnifrith Report 95
    Cabinet Committee on
        Subversive Activities 100–
        101
    and the CND 108
    civil defence planning 160–61
    overseeing the home front 399
Automobile Association (AA) 191–3,
    192

Bagehot, Walter 382
Bagot, Miss Millicent 85
Bailey, Martin 207
Baker, S. J. (Joseph) 96
Baldwin, Nigel 330–31
Ballistic Missile Early Warning
        System Station, Fylingdales,
        Yorkshire 121, 188, 210, 220
Barber, Anthony 308
Barratt, Russell 209

BBC (British Broadcasting
        Corporation)
    The Human Button (Radio 4)
        xxiv, 342–3, 345, 348, 358,
        405
    *A Bloody Union Jack on Top of
        It* (Radio 4) 54, 73
    wartime broadcasting service
        255
    The Top Job (Radio 4) 268
    Day One in No. 10 (Radio 4)
        315
    use of Light Programme
        transmitters 336, 339
    MI6: A Century in the Shadows
        (Radio 4) 411
Beckett, Francis 114
Beria, Lavrenti 33
Berlin 26–7, 39–40
Berlin Crisis, First (1948–9) 27, 48,
        157–8, 160
Berlin Crisis, Second (1958–61)
        65–6, 194, 277
Berlin Wall 370
Beurton, Ursula 35
Bevan, Aneurin 160
Bevin, Ernest
    and Berlin crises 27
    and the British bomb 50–51,
        112–13, 354
    and GEN 183 93
    on the Winnifrith Report 95
    and the NATO Treaty 395
BFPO 4000 (TURNSTILE) 275
Bhagavad Gita 161
Bikini Atoll nuclear test 109
bin Laden, Osama xxii
'Bingo Bans the Bomb'
        (Wodehouse) 113
Birch, Reg 140

Bishop, Freddie 187–8, 191, *191*, 277, 286

Black Panther Movement (BPM) 151–2

Blair, Tony xvi, xviii, xxii, xxxii, 47, 312–13, 315, 370, 378–9, 381, 384

Blake, George 116–17

Bletchley Park xvi, 400

Bligh, Tim 193–4, 284, 287, 299

Bliss, Nicola 158

'Blue Danube' atomic bomb 62

Blue Steel H-bombs 271, 325, 331–2, 336, 339, 341

Blue Streak ballistic missile 63

Blunt, Anthony 18, 88, 105

Bobbitt, Philip 387, 389

'Bolt From the Blue Emergency' (MOD War Book) 169, 197, 200–201, 210, 279, 370

Bowden, Bert 290, 292

Bowen, Desmond 410–11

Braithwaite, Sir Rodric 314

'Bravo' nuclear test, Pacific 52

Brezhnev, Leonid 204, 270

Bridges, Sir Edward 93, 96

Bridges, Tom 288–9

Britannia (royal yacht) 263, 293, 295, 309

British Academy and Mile End Group 78

British Army of the Rhine (BAOR) 224, 228, 327

British Commonwealth 22

British Movement 144–5

Brittain, Vera 108

Brock, Hugh 110–111

Brocklebank, Roy 331–2, 339–40

Brockway, Fenner 109

Brook, Sir Norman (later Lord Normanbrook)

secret nuclear meeting 12/3/54 52–6

meeting with Americans 64

and Churchill 67

and the CPGB 105, 125

plans for pre-and post-nuclear attack 154–5

proposal to create War Cabinet Secretariat 160–61

Central War Plans Secretariat 163–4

brief on Strath Report 167–9

first meeting of the Home Defence Committee 176

JIGSAW brief 16/11/61 186–8

and GEN 735 (Nuclear Retaliation) 191, 194

March 1961 paper 196–8, 200

'for-real' alert condition 3 (27/10/62) 201

and BURLINGTON 277–8, 281–3

paper on STOCKWELL structure 284–5

replaced as Cabinet Secretary 286

Brooke, Henry 272

Brooke, Sir Alan 6

Brooks, Andrew 331

Brooks, Teresa 331

Brown, George (later Lord George-Brown) 290, 292

Brown, Gordon 361–2, 379, 381, 384, 398

Brown, Laurence 111

Brownjohn, General Sir Neville 165, 180

Brundrett, Sir Frederick 165

Buccaneer aircraft 326
Burgess, Guy 17, 18, 88, 102–3
BURLINGTON (central government
    bunker, Cotswalds) 170, 196,
    200–201, 277–9, 280, 281–3
Butler inquiry 379
Butler, Lord of Saffron Walden (R.
    A. 'Rab') xvii, 56, 67–8, 272,
    278, 280, 283, 286–90
Butler Report (2004) xvii–xix
Butler, Robin (Lord Butler of
    Brockwell) 315–16, 320

CAB 21/5655 xxxiii–xxxiv, xxxvi
Cabinet committees
    on Subversive Activities 22, 88,
        92, 100–101
    GEN 163 47, 49, 51, 157, 161
    GEN 75 (Atomic Energy)
        48–50, 65
    GEN 464 55–6, 61
    MISC 16 74, 76, 324
    MISC 17 75
    GEN 183 88, 90–95, 97, 101–2,
        122
    GEN 226 94–5
    GEN 772 (FELSTEAD
        committee) 118
    on Civil Defence 160
    GEN 491 167–9, 182
    GEN 735 (Nuclear Retaliation)
        191, 191, 194
    GEN 743 (Working Group on
        Nuclear Retaliation
        Procedures) 194, 201
    Transition to War (TWC) 223–4,
        227–8
    MISC 7 318
    structure of 379, 380, 385–6
    National Security, International
        Relations, Development
        (NSID) 381, 398–9
    on Security and Terrorism 381
Cabinet Office
    and the JIC 14
    group on retaliation procedures
        27
    and trade unionists 104
    Central War Plans Secretariat
        163–5
    Home Defence/Defence
        committees 167
    Briefing Room 321
    Civil Contingencies Secretariat
        369
    enhanced intelligence policy
        capability 383
    Strategic Horizons Unit 398–9
    Intelligence Services' Counsellor
        (ISC) 411
Cairncross, John 17, 18, 88
Calder, Lord Ritchie 108
Callaghan of Cardiff, James
    Callaghan, Lord 78, 259, 271,
        312–13, 316–19, 399–400
Cambridge University communist
    graduates 88
Cameron, David 312, 384
Cameron, Sir Neil 315
Campaign for Nuclear
    Disarmament (CND) 56, 78,
        82, 107–119, 166, 190
Campbell, Gordon 308
Canada
    Gouzenko revelations 89
    Nunn May's exposure 90
    Royal Commission report 90–92
Canberra bombers 327–30, *see also*
    V-bombers
Carrington, Lord 308, 318–19

Carter, Jimmy 317
Cartledge, Sir Bryan 315, 317
Cary, Joyce 156
Cary, Michael 156–7, 201
Castro, Fidel 41
Cathcart, Brian 48
Central Government Wartime HQ, Corsham 221, 258–64, 264–7, 268–9, 271–5, 276, 284–6, 297–300, 302, 308–9, see also BURLINGTON; STOCKWELL; TURNSTILE; CHANTICLEER
Chalk River establishment, Ontario 90
Chamberlain, Neville xxxiii
CHANTICLEER see Central Government Wartime HQ, Corsham
Chataway, Christopher 308
Checkpoint Charlie 40, 277
'Chevaline' programme 77, see also Polaris missiles
Chiang Kai Shek 60–61
China 60, 348, 389, 414
Christmas Island 61, 110
Churchill, Sir Winston
    and nuclear weapons xxxviii, 52, 54–9, 62, 65, 115, 417–18n.3
    review of the situation in Europe 14
    thoughts on war 32–3
    F Branch memo 85
    and positive vetting 96, 102
    and the Strath Committee 163, 165
Chuter Ede, James 93, 160
CIA (Central Intelligence Agency) 28

Civil Contingencies Act 2004 370–71
civil defence 158–9, 164–5, 170, 181–3
Civil Defence Act 1948 157, 370
Civil Defence Corps 157, 181, 186
Civil Service
    Communism in 94–5
    and unreliables 100
    positive vetting in 104
COBR (Cabinet Office Briefing Room) 315, 321, 374, 378, 378
Cockcroft, Sir John 52
Cold War
    East-West confrontation xiv–xvi
    systems xxiii
    casualties of xxviii
    professionals' contest 2–6
    British Government's assessment 18
    the 'high' 24, 29, 154, 158
    nuclear factor 48
    strategic threat on steroids 80
    state shaped by 92
    limited and local aggressions 164
    and the war books 256
    Soviet Northern Fleet 331, 346
    anxieties 356
    reflections on 366–7, 371, 389, 403, 413–14
Collins, Canon 109, 111
Comfort, Alex 110
Comintern 84
Committee of 100 108, 115–18
Committee for Direct Action against Nuclear War see Direct Action Committee (DAC)

Committee on International
Terrorism *see* DOP(IT)
Defence and Overseas Policy
(International Terrorism)
Committee on Positive Vetting (PV)
95–6
Communism (Home) Official
Committee 22
Communism (Overseas) Official
Committee 22
Communist Federation of Britain
Marxist-Leninist (CFBM)
140–41
Communist front organisations 129
Communist Party of Great Britain
(CPGB)
loyalty of the most gifted 23
history of 82–7, 89, 91–2
MI5 surveillance of 104–8,
118–20, 122, 368
long decline of 114, 118
JIC analysis 124–8, 152
and nuclear exchange 207
Communist Party of Great Britain
Marxist-Leninist (CPBML)
140
Communist Party of Ireland
149–50
CONTEST 1 xv, 378
CONTEST 2 377, 379, 384
Cooper, Sir Frank 259, 267–9,
356–7, 359
Cornish, Paul 351, 353
Counter Terrorism Analysis Centre
(CTAC) 375–6
Coward, Noël 112
Cowell, Gervase 44–5
Cradock, Sir Percy 5
Craig, Alex 26–7
Crawley, Aidan 101

Criggion very low frequency signals
installation 210, 216
Cripps, Sir Stafford 50–51
Crisis Management (2006) diagram
378
Crocus List, The (Gavin Lyall) 309
Cromby, Cecily xxxi
Crookshank, Harry 59
Cross, Air Marshal Sir Kenneth
188–9, 200–201
Cuba group (committee) 201
Cuban missile crisis
'Red List' warning indicators for
1962 7
JIC envisages possibility of
39–44
and Macmillan 42, 271–2,
418n.6
within weeks of Nassau
Conference 65–7
CND and Committee of 100
116–18
analogous to a 'Bolt From the
Blue' 169
and the JIGSAW team 185
and new radio system in PM's
cars 193
V- Bombers on alert/review of
War Book planning 200–202
and nuclear deputies 284
post-Cuba review of 1963–4
285
imminence of nuclear war 406
Cunningham, Sir Charles 109
Curry, John 84, 88, 91, 105, 107,
122
CVA01 (cancelled aircraft carrier)
395
Czechoslovakia 125, 219

'Daily Highlights' intelligence
    briefing 381
Dalton, Hugh 50–51
DASO (demonstration and
    shakedown operation, 2009)
    345–6
Davies, John 308
de Gaulle, President (Charles) xiii,
    68, 368
de Zulueta, Philip 64–5, 68
Dean, Sir Patrick 165
Dearlove, Richard xxiv
Deep, The see Central Government
    Wartime HQ, Corsham
Defence Committee 195
Defence International Terrorism
    Analysis Centre (DITAC)
    375–6
Defence Operations Centre (MOD)
    210
Defence and Overseas Policy
    (International Terrorism)
    Committee 381
Defence Policy Committee (DPC)
    56–7, 59, 61
Defence of the Realm, The
    (Andrew) 102
defence review (1967–8) 204
Defence Secretariat 12 320
Defence Transition Committee
    (DTC) 106, 158–9
Department V (KGB) 121
di Lampedusa, Tomasi 402
Dibble, Tom 28
Dickson, Air Chief Marshal Sir
    William 57
Dietrich, Marlene 113
Diplock, Lord 102
Direct Action Committee (DAC)
    110–111, 115–16

Dixon, Sir Pierson 69–70
DOP(IT) Defence and Overseas
    Policy (International
    Terrorism) 378
Douglas, Mary xix, xxi
Driver, Christopher 108–112,
    114–16
Duff, Peggy 110
Duff, Sir Antony 78
Duff-Mason Report 78–9

'E' hour 339
Eden, Sir Anthony 56, 105, 168–9
Eisenhower, Dwight D. 56, 62, 64
Elizabeth II, Queen
    and the Government War Book
        xxxiv–xxxvi, xxxix
    coronation of 161
    wrecking of her Realm 166
    planning for her evacuation
        262–3
    and the Privy Council 293
    war location 293
    bunker planning for 369
Elliott, Toby 345
Emergency Powers Act 1920 370
Emergency Powers (Defence) Bill
    202–4
Engadine (Royal Fleet Auxiliary
    vessel) 309
English Communist Movement 142
English Student Movement 142
Eniwetok nuclear test, Pacific 1952
    53
Epsom racecourse, Surrey 107
Evans, Jonathan 368, 377, 409,
    411, 413–14
Exercise MICKY FINN II 201

Falkland Islands 395

FALLEX/INVALUABLE
transition-to-war exercise
(1968) 39, 120, 126, 219,
371
Farr, Charles 362–3
Federal Bureau of Investigation
(FBI) 98, 101
FENCER (GWB code word) 321
FILCH planning *see* PEBBLE;
PYTHON groups
Fission Fragments (journal) 405
Fleming, Ian 415
Foot, Michael 313
Formosa 60–61
Fraser, Michael 73
Free Citizen (newspaper) 151
Freedom Press 135–6
Freeman, Peter xvii–xxi
Friends (periodical) 139
Fry, Ruth 110
Fuchs, Klaus 34–5, 95–6, 101–2

G7 summit (Guadeloupe January
1979) 317
Gaitskell, Hugh 72, 114
gamma radiation 174–5
Geertz, Clifford 47
Gellner, Ernest 366–7
George VI, King 87
Geraghty, William 194, 198, 200,
278–9
Germany
Nazi 1, 2, 15
centrality to the Cold War 26
Western Zones 36
Gilmore, Brian 257
'Go/No Go Line' 336, 340
Godfrey, Admiral John 415
GOLDEN ROD (exercise) 219
Gollan, John 83, 106, 114

Gorbachev, Mikhail xix, 3, 48
Gordievsky, Oleg 408
Gouzenko, Igor 21, 88–90
Government War Book (GWB)
prelude xxxiv–xxxvii
anxieties of 1948 106
anxieties of 1968 204
and NATO 205
and Mrs Beryl Grimble 218, 255
transition-to-war exercises
220–21, 223, 228, 255–7
and TURNSTILE 263, 267, 271
and ACID 300
clearance for release 302
Appendix Z 320–23, 405–6
Grant, Matthew 75–7
'Grapple' hybrid H-bomb 61, *see
also* nuclear weapons
'Grapple X' 'true' H-bomb 61
Great Britain *see* United Kingdom
Greenpeace 111
Grimble, Beryl xxxiv, 218, 255
ground bursts (hydrogen bombs)
172–3
Grovesnor Square demonstration
(March 1968) 119
GRU (Soviet military intelligence)
35–6, 88, 90, 93, 99–100,
106, 121–2, 404
Guthrie, Charles (Lord) 312, 358–9

Haddon, Catherine 177
Hamm, Jeffrey 144
Hanchanda, Abhimanyu 141
Hannigan, Robert 381
Hansman, Laurence 110
Harding, Field Marshal Sir John 57
Harris, Geoffrey 264
Harris, Sir Robert 208
Hartley, Anthony 115

Healey, Lord (Denis) 3, 24, 74–6, 290, 292, 317, 319
Heath, Sir Edward 69–70, 72, 121, 286, 307–8
Henderson, Arthur 102
Hennessy, Polly xxx
Herman, Michael 4, 6, 12–13
Hilarides, Willy 348
Hinsley, Sir Harry xxi
Hiroshima bombing (August 1945) 48
History of Financial Crises, A (Aliber) 394–5
Hitler, Adolf 15
HMS *Resolution* (Polaris submarine) 345, *see also* Polaris submarines
HMS *Vanguard* (Trident submarine) 342
HMS *Vengeance* (Trident submarine) 342
HMS *Victorious* (Trident submarine) 312, 345–51, 354–5, *see also* Trident submarines
Hobsbawm, Eric xxxviii–xxxix, 82–3
Hollis, Sir Roger 96–7, 99
Holloway Prison 107
Holmes, Graham 351
home defence *see* civil defence
Home Defence Review (1960) 186
Home Defence Review (1965) 181
Home, Lord (Alec Douglas)
    warnings xxii
    Nassau Agreement 67, 69
    and Harold Wilson 73–4
    expulsion of KGB/GRU officers 121
    and the informal Cuba group 201
    transition-to-war exercises comment 256
    and TURNSTILE 271–2
    choosing nuclear deputies 283–4, 286–90, 307–8, 312
    and ACID 300
Honecker, Erich 48
Hoover, J. Edgar 85, 98
Horner, Arthur 105
Horsburgh, Florence 60
Howard, Professor Sir Michael 3, 14, 49, 365, 387
Howe (Sir), Geoffrey (Lord) 318
Hudleston, Air Chief Marshal Sir Edmund 188–9
Hudson, Peter 405
Hungarian uprising 23, 38–9, 114, 125
Hunt, Sir John (Lord) 314, 317–19
Hunter aircraft 326
Hurd, Douglas (Lord) 401
Hutton, John 352–3, 355
hydrogen bomb
    development by UK 52–61
    and Macmillan 61–2, 156
    and A. J. P. Taylor 78
    anti-nuclear agitation in 1957 109–110, 112
    and the JIC 155
    and civil defence 157
    awesome destructive power of 161, 163
    Soviet bombs 166
    and the Strath Committee 168, 170, 172–4, 177
    Blue Steel 271, 325, 331–2, 336, 339, 341
    V-Bomber crews 341, *see also* nuclear weapons

Hydrogen Bomb National
  Campaign 109–110

Imports Research Committee (IRC)
  xxxii, 389
'Improving the Central Intelligence
  Machinery' (Martin Review)
  383–4
In Pursuit of British Interests
  (Cradock) 5–6
'Increased Alert State' 336–7
Intelligence Services Act 1994 414
international counter-terrorism 375
International Marxist Group (IMG)
  126, 132, 152
International Socialism Group (IS)
  126, 133–4
International Times (periodical)
  139
International Working Men's
  Association 136
INVALUABLE (1968 war game)
  39, 204, 219, 220–22, 255
IOC (Intelligence Operations
  Centre) xxiii
Iran 20, 239–40, 246, 253
Iraq War 2003 xx, 379
Irish Republican Army (IRA) 146–
  8, 412–13
Isaacs, George 93
Islamic terrorism 369, 371, 373
Isle of Man 106–7
Ivanov, Captain Eugene 297

Jeffery, Keith 414
Jeffrey, Sir Bill 379
Jenkins, Roy 77, 397
JIGGER (GWB code word) 321
JIGSAW group 64, 67, 183–6, 206,
  369

'Joe 19' nuclear test 53
Johnson, Admiral Steve 353
Johnson, Alan 384
Joint Air Reconnaissance
  Intelligence Centre (JARIC)
  337
Joint Intelligence Committee (JIC)
  Wednesday meetings xxiv
  at the apex of British intelligence
    4–7
  background of 4–7
  'Weekly Summary of Current
    Intelligence' 13–15
  Soviet threat assessments 16–22,
    25–6
  JIC (46) 1 (o) document 18–19,
    21, 88, 93, 105, 118
  Berlin crises 27
  'Russian preparedness for war'
    item 28–30
  nuclear weapons assessment
    33–5, 330
  war by miscalculation 36–7,
    40–41
  H-bomb assault estimate 37–41,
    155
  and FALLEX/INVALUABLE 39,
    120
  and the Cuban Missile Crisis
    42–3, 118
  on escalation 66–7
  Committee of 100 116
  possible future transition to war
    118
  archives 122
  categories of subversive
    organisations 122–7
  and NATO 123
  subversive organisations annexe
    on UK threat 127

likelihood of Soviet Union
sustaining major war before
1957 159–60
and the Strath Committee 164–5
'H-Bomb Threat to the UK in
the Event of a General War'
165–7
pre-emptive strike view 187
views on where missiles would
land in UK 210
and Intelligence Alert-Stage 3
322
Cold War anxieties 356
and Sir Richard Mottram 363
the 'Red Book' 381–2
splitting of the chairmanship
381
new Terms of Reference 382–4
Assessments Staff 399
Joint Inter-Services Group for the
Study of All-Out War *see*
JIGSAW
Joint Support Unit 260
Joint Terrorism Analysis Centre
(JTAC) 374–6, 392, 399
Jordan, Colin 145
JTAC (Joint Terrorism Analysis
Centre) xxiii

Keeler, Christine 297
Kennedy, John Fitzgerald
on intelligence cables xxii
and the Cold War xxviii–xxix
Nassau agreement 64–5, 67–71
offers Polaris to France 69
nuclear release consultations
201
Keynes, John Maynard (Lord) 394
KGB, archive 18, 36, 88, 90, 93,
105–6, 121–2, 194, 404

Khrushchev, Nikita
Cuban missile crisis xxviii–xxix,
41–2, 65, 67, 201, 272
and the Hungarian uprising 23
and Churchill 32
Berlin conference deadlines 40
Roberts/Khrushchev exchange
177–8
deep shelter in the Urals 184
war-through-inadvertence
scenario 270
Khryuchkov, Vladimir 5
Kindlebergers, Charles 394–5
King, Mervyn 393–4
King Street, London (CPGB
headquarters) 105–6, 114,
128
Kings Norton Report (1968) 77
Kirkman, General Sir Sidney 165
Klugmann, James 105–6
Knight, Jane 379
Knight, Richard 331–2, 342
Korean War 3, 14, 27–9, 101,
160
Krotenschield, Boris 105
Kubrick, Stanley 274
Kurchatov, Igor 34–5
Kyle, Air Chief Marshal Sir Wallace
287–8

Labour Party 108, 112–14
Lascelles, Sir Alan 'Tommy' 263
Laskey, Denys xxxv, 210
'last resort letters' 311–13, 315
Lawrence-Wilson, Harry 219–20,
255
le Carré, John 4
League of Empire Loyalists 143
Lees-Milne, James 32
Lenin, Vladimir Ilyich 107

Lester, Guy 260, 262
Liberation or Catastrophe
    (Howard) 365
Lindsey, Commander Richard 343,
    348
LINSTOCK (planned reserve seat
    of central Government)
    298–9, 302
Lippmann, Walter 67
Lister, Rear Admiral Simon 353
Lloyd George, Gwilym 179–80
Lloyd, Rear-Admiral Steve 353
Lloyd, Selwyn 168, 180, 272, 278,
    280, 283, 286–90
London Underground
    Soviet sabotage plans 121–2
    7/7/05 attacks 364, 367, 369
Long Overhaul Period (Polaris/
    Trident) 345
Longley-Cook, Vice Admiral
    29–32
Lovell, E. A. (Ted) 183
Lucky George (Walden) 121
Lyalin, Oleg 121–2
Lyall, Gavin 309

McCarthy, Joe 96
McColl, Sir Colin 2, 365–6
McDonald, Dr Alan 185
McDonald, Iverach 67
McGrigor, Admiral of the Fleet Sir
    Rhoderick 57
'Machinery of Government in War'
    (confidential annex) 302
McIndoe, W. I. xxxv–xxxvi
Maclean, Donald 18, 88, 102–3
McMahon Act (1946) 71, 96
Macmillan, Harold, 1st Earl of
    Stockton
    nuclear deputies xvi
    the international stalemate
        xxviii
    Cuban missile crisis 42, 271–2,
        418n.6
    and the hydrogen bomb 61–2,
        156
    and land-based ballistic missiles
        63–5, 115, 430n.84
    Nassau agreement 64–70, 72
    independent nuclear deterrent
        68, 71–3, 431n.103
    and CND 108–9, 111, 114–15,
        117
    Committee of 100 116
    transition-to-war planning 156
    and the Strath Committee 163–
        4, 167–8, 182
    nuclear retaliation 187, 189–90,
        198, 200–201, 319
    and GEN 743 194
    and TURNSTILE 259, 274, 277,
        286, 296–8
    leaves office (1963) 273
    and BURLINGTON 277–81,
        283–4
    and STOCKWELL 284–5
    dispersal proposals 299
McNamara, Robert 64
'Magnificent Five' (Soviet agents)
    88–9
Major, John xvii–xviii, 313, 315,
    319–20
Manhattan Project 49, 90, 96, 161
Manias, Panics and Crashes
    (Kindlebergers) 394–5
Mann, Commander Howard
    256
Manningham-Buller, Dame Eliza
    (later Baroness) xvii, 364,
    368, 373–4, 409–410, 415

Manod, Blaenau Festiniog, Wales 208

MANUSCRIPT (GWB code word) 321

Mao Tse-Tung 142

Marshall, Jonathan 275, 277

Marshall Plan 24

Marshall, Sir Walter (later Lord Marshall of Goring) 275

Martin, Ciaran 383

Marwick, Arthur 119

Marxism 138

Mason, Sir Ronald 78

Matsu 61

Maudling, Reginald 307

May, Alan Nunn 90

Methodist Conference, London 60

Metropolitan Police District 173

MI5 see Security Service

MI6 see Secret Intelligence Service

Miller, David 181

Milligan, Spike 110

Ministerial Committees
  Nuclear Policy (PN) 75, 77
  Civil Defence 157
  Home Defence 170, 202

Ministry of Defence 169–70

Mitchell, Graham 96–7, 99

Mitchell, Sir Derek xxxiv, xxxvi, 264, 291–2

Mitrokhin Archive 93, 121

Mitrokhin, Vasili 18–19, 105, 121

Molotov, Vyacheslav 24

Morris, Dennis 218

Morrison, Herbert 51

Mosley, Sir Oswald 144

Mottershead, Frank 189–90, 196, 200, 264

Mottram, Sir Richard xxv, 362–4, 379, 381, 383

Mountbatten, Lord 183, 186–8, 191, 194, 197

Mulley, Fred (Lord) 317

multilateral force (MLF) (proposed) 74–5

Muslim societies 366

Mutual Defence Agreement 1958 xxiv

Nagasaki bombing (August 1945) 48

Nailor, Peter 63

Nassau agreement 64–73, 325, 346

Nasser, Colonel Gamal Abdel 190

National Council for the Abolition of Nuclear Weapons Tests 110–111

National Disobedience Day 116

National Front 143

National Patriotic front (NPF) 145–6

National Security Council (NSC) (proposed) 384

National Security Forum 399

National Security Strategy (2008) (proposed) 393

National Security Strategy (June 2009) 382–3

National Union of Students 126

NATO
  US and a preventive war against Russia 30
  comparable size of Soviet navy 37
  doctrine of containment 38–9
  and Soviet armed response 43
  UK use of nuclear weapons 48, 67
  nuclear weapons inside 74–5
  JIC study 123

and the Government War Book
205
and Exercise INVALUABLE
220–22
and the Transition To War
Committee 224
and TURNSTILE 273
joint nuclear decision-taking
procedures 280, 291
Tactical Strike Force 327
Article 5 of the Treaty 395
Nuclear Planning Group 406
negative vetting 95
Neustadt, Dick 74
'New Left' Group 137–8
New Left Review 138
New Protective state 368, 377
No.10 retaliation file 285–6
Northern Ireland terrorism 376
Northern Rock Building Society
393
Northern Star (journal) 151
Northwood Bunker, the Chilterns
323, 342–3, 349–50, 357
Nuclear Defence Policy Group
(Callaghan Committee) 317
Nuclear Planning Group (NATO)
406
nuclear release procedures 313–16,
318–24, 330, 378, 406
'nuclear retaliation cell'
(TURNSTILE) 285–7
nuclear targets in UK 211–15
nuclear weapons
hydrogen bomb see hydrogen bomb
Cold War threat 25
United States monopoly of 33
Soviet accumulation of 37
atomic bomb 48–51, 62, 157,
159, 163

'hybrid' H-bomb 61, 183
'true' H-bomb 61–2, 183
nuclear weapons state (NWS) 79
Nye, Joe 80

Obama, President xvi
O'Brien, John 143
OCPs (operational clandestine
premises; safe houses) 83
O'Donnell, Sir Gus 383
O'Donovan, Patrick 101
Office for Security and Counter-
Terrorism (Home Office) 379
Official Committee on Terrorism
361
Official Secrets Act 1911 104
Oldfield, Sir Maurice 399–400
Omand, Sir David xv, 216
'Open Society and Its Enemies, The'
(Popper) 415
Operation FOOT 121
Operation HILLARY 107, 118
Operation METHODICAL 207
Operation OVERT 373
Operation REED 275, 276
Operation VISITATION xxxviii, 197
Oppenheimer, Robert 161
ORANGE (code for Soviet Union)
220, 256
Orton, Jason 260
Owen, David 317
Oz (periodical) 139

P1154 aircraft 326
Paget, Colonel J. T. 287, 290–91
Palliser, Sir Michael 5, 192
Parsons, Sir Anthony 391, 396
PEBBLE (plan for dispersed 'nuclei'
of Government) 307–8
Penkovsky, Colonel Oleg 44

Penney, Sir William 52–4, 155, 183
People's Democracy 150–51
Permanent Secretaries' Intelligence
    and Security Committee
    (PSIS) 383
Perrin, Sir Michael 50
Persia see Iran
Petersen, Sir Arthur 361–3
Phantom aircraft 326
Philby, Kim 17–19, 88
Phoenix see IOC (Intelligence
    Operations Centre)
Pike, Sir Thomas 200
Pimlott Lecture 218, 302
Pincher, Harry Chapman 34–5,
    221–2, 450n.17
PINDAR (Crisis Management
    Centre) 259, 261, 321, 342
Pirie, Julia 106
Playfair, Sir Eddie 189–90, 196
Plowden, Edwin (later Lord) 52,
    54–5, 61
plutonium 49, 53, 159
Polaris missiles
    and JIGSAW 64, 186
    supreme national interests 68–70,
    72–7
    Britain as a big player 115
    and TURNSTILE 270–71, 273
    and nuclear retaliation 292
    primary deterrent role from the
    V-force 293, 347
    replacement of 313, 317–18
    John Major instructions 320
    state of readiness 322, 324
    procurement of 324–5
    assignment of 329
    destructive capacity 330
    test firings (DASO) 345
    Sales Agreement 1963 346, 400

continuous sea deterrence 353
    nuclear safety rules 406
Polaris submarines (Resolution
    class) 312, 315, 325, 345
Pollitt, Harry 23, 83, 86
Pollock, Commander David 348
Ponman, Richard 218
Popper, Karl 415
Portal, Lord 50–51
positive vetting 94–5, 99, 101–4
    Winnifrith Committee (1950)
    95–101, 104
'Post-Cuba Review of War Book
    Planning' 202
Pottle, Pat 116–17
Powell, Enoch 313–14
Powell, Sir Richard 52, 165
Powers, Gary 183
'Prague Spring' 219
Precautionary Stage 272, 279–80,
    284, 289, 293–6, 297
Press Association 230
Prime Minister's bunker see Central
    Government Wartime
    Headquarters
Prime Minister's Directive 357
Profumo Affair 296–7
Profumo, John 297
Provisional IRA xv, 373
'Pursue Prevent Protect Prepare'
    (Strategy for International
    Terrorism) 362–4
Pym, Francis 318
PYTHON groups (alternative
    bunkers) 221, 302–4, 304,
    307–9, 369

Quarry Operations Centre (QOC)
    see Central Government
    Wartime HQ, Corsham

Quemoy 61
Quinlan, Sir Michael
the Quinlan Report xvii–xix, xxi
    defence intellectual xxv, xxx
    the nuclear taboo xxviii
    and the Nassau Agreement 72
    and the Duff-Mason Report
        78–9
    the 'Quinlan Paradox' 354–6
    and the 'Cooper Axiom' 357–9
    and Treasury cuts 365–6
    'Shaping the Defence
        Programme paper 395–6
    'Quinlan's Law' 396
    report for the Major
        government 418n.9
Quinn, Andy 275, 309

R-hour 219–20
Radcliffe Report (1962) 104
RAF
    Wittering 62
    Ruislip 116
    Bomber Command 188–91,
        197, 200, 286–8, 290, 292,
        319, 329, 336
    Strike Command 220, 323
    Rudloe Manor 260
    Brize Norton 331
    Scampton 331–2, 336
    Hemswell 336
    Coningsby 389
Randle, Michael 116–17
Red Army 3, 12, 22, 24, 31
Red Beard weapons 326
red book 27
Red Hole (journal) 132
Red/Amber list (1962) 7–12
'Reflections on Intelligence'
        (Manningham-Buller) 415

Regional Commissioners 181–2,
        194, 202–3, 209, 303–4,
        304–7
Regional Seats of Government
        (RSG) 298–9, 301, 303, 305–
        6
Reid, John 379, 384
Revolutionary Communist Party
        122
Revolutionary Marxist Leninist
        League (RMLL) 141–2
Revolutionary Socialist League
        (RSL) 134–5
Revolutionary Socialist Students
        Federation 138
Rhyl, North Wales 107
Rickett, Sir Dennis 50
Roberts, Sir Frank 44, 177–8
Robertson, General Sir Brian 27
Robson, Air Vice Marshal Bobby
        155
Rogers, Philip 287, 291, 302
Rose, Sir Clive 290, 314, 318–19
Rothschild, Victor 77
Rovere, Richard xxii
Royal Aeronautical Establishment,
        Bedford 332
Royal Naval Air Station,
        Lossiemouth 332
Royal Navy Clyde Submarine Base,
        Faslane 312
Royal Pardons 303
Royal Warrant (October 1968)
        304–7
RSG-6, Warren Row 108–9
Rugby very low frequency signals
        installation 210, 216
Russell, Earl (Bertrand) 110,
        115–16
Russia see Soviet Union

SACEUR (Supreme Allied
     Commander Europe) 75,
     219–20, 224, 255, 323, 325–7
SACLANT (Supreme Allied
     Commander Atlantic) 328–9
Salisbury, Marquess of 56, 59
Samuel, Ian 284
Sandys Defence White Paper 56
Sandys, Duncan 59, 64, 68, 112
Saor Eire 149
Saunders, Bryan 193–4
Scarlett, Sir John 411–12
Scimitar aircraft 326
Scott, Dr Len 41
Scott, Rev. Michael 116
Scott, Sir Robert 264
Sea Vixen aircraft 326
SEATO 328–9
Secret Intelligence Service (MI6)
     KGB archive 18, 105
     life in the Soviet bloc 21
     Special Political Action section
          43–4
     Philby heads Section IX 88
     war-through-inadvertence
          scenario 270
     officers/agents in 407–8
Secretary of State for National
     Security (proposal) 399
Security Commission 102
'Security Questionnaire' 103–4
Security Service Act 1989 414
Security Service (MI5)
     and Klaus Fuchs 35
     assessment of the CPGB 83–6,
          105–6, 114–15
     F Branch 84–5, 89–91
     F.2.b 85
     Young Communist League
          (YCL) 87, 89, 91
     vetting procedure 91, 96–8, 102
     World War III internment plans
          106–7
     and CND 109, 111, 116–17
     and the DAC 110
     Committee of 100 117
     'Security of UK Base in Pre-
          Attack Phase of General
          War' (1968) 119–21
Select Committees
     on Un-British Activities 96
     on the Constitution (House of
          Lords) 383
Semipalatinsk test site, Kazakhstan
     53
Semipalatinsk-21 34
7/7 bombings xxii
'Shaping the Defence Programme:
     Some Platitudes' (Quinlan)
     395–6
Shaw, Dr Ian 184
Shelfoon, Group Captain 186
Sherman, Daniel 102
Shinwell, Emmanuel, Lord 101
Shute, Neville 113, 190, 269–70
SIGINT (signals intelligence) 21,
     28, 100
Sillitoe, Sir Percy 93–5, 97
Simpson, John 353
Single Intelligence Account
     (budgets of the secret
     agencies) 383
Sinn Fein 147–8
Skybolt stand-off missile 64, 70, 72,
     74
Smith, Bradley 16
Smith, Melissa 405
Smithers, Sir Waldron 96
Socialist Labour League (SLL)
     130–31

Socialist Labour League Young
Socialists 131
Solidarity 137
Solidarity Front of Arab and
Palestine Liberation 141
Soper, Dr Donald 109
Soviet Northern Fleet 331, 346
Soviet Union (USSR)
Cold War actions xxiii
Cuban missile crisis 7, 39–43,
66–7
Red/Amber list 7–12
and the JIC 13, 127
strategic interests 14–15
JIC's pessimistic assessment
16–21, 24, 26–9
satellite states 19–20
and nuclear weapons 25, 33–40,
66, 178
Berlin crises 27
inevitability of war 28–31
United States monopoly of
atomic weapons 33
hydrogen bomb development
52–4, 58–9, 61
nuclear gap 63
on escalation 66–7
anti-ballistic missile screen 77
JIC prospect of an Anglo-Soviet
war 125
likelihood of sustaining a major
war before 1957 159, 161
likely objectives in the UK in the
event of war 165–7, 299
U2 affair 183–4
V-bomber targets 330
defence installations 337
unspectacular demise 362
and the SIS 408
Spartacus League (SL) 133

Special Operations Executive (SOE)
85
Spedding, Sir David 113
'Spies for Peace' 108, 210
'Spot the Bomb' 405
Springhall, David 85, 90
Stalin, Joseph
and the Manhattan Project
xxviii
and Soviet position in last weeks
of 1944 15
JIC's view of 16–18, 24
and British anxiety 18–19, 25
and nuclear weapons 33, 35
recruiters in British universities
86–8
and UK civil servants 86–8
Stanhope, Admiral Sir Mark 353
Steele, Harold and Sheila 110
Steiner, George xxviii
Stephens, Commander J. R. xxxv,
210, 287
Stewart, Michael (Lord) 121, 292–3
Stirling, Tessa xxxiii, 275
STOCKWELL (central government
bunker) 170, 196–8, 284–5,
see also Central Government
Wartime HQ, Corsham
Strachey, John 101–2
Strategic Defence and Security
Review (proposed) 384
Strategic Horizons Unit 387
Strath Committee (1955) 155,
163–5, 167–78, 180–82,
203, 268, 369
Strath, Sir William 163–5, 167, 170
'successor' project (Trident) 347
Suez crisis (1956) 38
'suicide' aircraft 389
surface-to-air missiles (SAMs) 340

Swinton, Lord 56
Syndicalist Workers Federation
    (SWF) 136-7

TACK ('third reserve' seats of
    central government) 298,
    301
Tactical Strike Force 327
Taleb, Nassim 402
Task Force 345 342
Taylor, A. J. P. 78, 111, 115
Tebbit, Sir Kevin 79, 260, 274
Teller, Edwin 61
Terror and Consent (Bobbitt) 387,
    389
Thatcher, Margaret (Baroness)
    313-19
Thor missiles 273
Thorneycroft, Peter 64, 68-70, 73,
    272, 286-7
TIDO (Terrorism International
    Defence and Overseas) 378
trade unions, and the CPGB 105
Transition to War Committee/
    exercises 201, 219-20, 255
Transport and General Workers
    Union 125
Trend, Sir Burke (Lord) 14, 202,
    286-8, 290-93, 296-9, 302,
    307-8
Trident missiles 47, 77, 313, 317,
    348-50, 406
Trident submarines (Vanguard
    class) 311-13, 342-53, 355,
    358, 404
Trotskyists 103, 126, 137-8
Truman, Harry 17, 28, 34
Tsarev, Oleg 17-18
TSR 2 strike aircraft 324-6
Turkey 20

TURNSTILE (central government
    bunker, Cotswalds)
    description xxxviii, 170
    home defence spending on 182
    catering provisions for 256
    functioning of 259-64
    and Macmillan 259, 274, 277,
        286, 296-8
    and the Government War Book
        (GWB) 263, 267, 271-2
    manning of 264-7
    the last redoubt 269-75, 308-9
    and Polaris 270-71, 273
    nuclear retaliation cell 285-7
    Precautionary Stage list 293,
        294-5, 296-303
    Peter Hudson recalls 405
    and Sir Norman Brook 196-7,
        see also Central Government
        Wartime HQ, Corsham

U2 reconnaissance/spy plane 183
UK Intelligence Reporting 388
Ulster Volunteer Force (UVF) 148
United Kingdom
    attitude to Soviet Union 18-19
    penetration of diplomatic/
        nuclear capacities 21-2
    first/second Berlin crisis 27
    secret intelligence agreement
        with USA 27
    nuclear programme 47-58
    independent nuclear capability
        62
    restoration of US/UK
        collaboration 63-5
    access to US technology 76
    reluctant nuclear state 79-80
    attitude to positive vetting
        102-3

United Kingdom (*cont.*)
  categories of subversive
    organisations 122–4
  war with Soviet Union scenario
    164–5
  1960's military perspective on
    World War III 204–5
  intelligence collaboration with
    USA 400
United States of America (USA)
  early Corona satellites 12
  attitude to Soviet Union 18
  penetration of diplomatic/
    nuclear capacities 21–2
  secret intelligence agreement
    with UK 27
  inevitability of war 29–31
  monopoly of atomic weapons 33
  Cuban Missile Crisis 41–3
  and the McMahon Act 1946 49
  'Bravo' nuclear test, Pacific 52
  hydrogen bomb development
    52–4, 56, 58–9, 61
  restoration of US/UK
    collaboration 63
  UK access to technology of 76
  security checks 98, 102
  Bikini Atoll nuclear test 109
  Vietnam Solidarity Campaign
    119
  U2 affair 183–4
  President's ultimate retaliation
    codes 187
  nuclear preparedness with UK
    322–3, 328
  test launching Trident missiles
    345–7
  9/11 attacks 367, 411–12
  intelligence collaboration with
    UK 400

Uren, Captain Desmond 85
US Naval Ordnance Test Unit
  346
US Navy Ohio Class Trident
  submarines 346

Waters 353, 355

V-bombers
  placed on Alert Condition
    27/10/62 42, 200–201
  planning of 49
  coming on stream/obsolescence
    62–4, 71
  proposed assignment to an
    Atlantic Nuclear Force 74–6
  on the horizon 112
  Soviet sabotage plans 121
  authorising ultimate retaliation
    187, 189
  Soviet targets 216
  and R Hour 220
  and TURNSTILE 268, 270, 273
  and nuclear retaliation 286,
    292, 323, 333–5
  primary deterrent role to Polaris
    293, 347
  strategic deterrent 325
  and SACEUR 328
  assignment of 329
  destructive capacity 330
  USSR targets 330
  readiness state of 332, 337–40
  flight paths 336
  final stage/nuclear release 340–41
  replacement by Polaris 347
Valiant bombers 63, 312, 328–30
validation, analysis, assessment xx
Vanguard class submarines 353
Vassall, John 104

VENONA traffic 21–2, 87–8, 90, 95–6, 99–100
Victor bombers 63, 312, 325
Vietnam Solidarity Campaign 119, 138
Vietnam War 115, 206
Vulcan bombers 63, 156, 312, 325, 330–32, 336, 341–2, 355

Waldegrave Initiative xxix, xxxiv, 404
Walden, George 121
Walker, Patrick Gordon 74–6
Walker, Peter 308
War Cabinet 160–61, 262–3, 268
War Game, The (Watkins) 155
Ward, Stephen 297
Warsaw Pact countries 127, 371
Wasp helicopter 326
Watkins, Peter 155
Watkinson, Harold 186
Webb, Alban 39, 170
Welsh, Eric 36
Wessex helicopter 326
West Midlands Regional Seat of Government (Kidderminster) 298
WEST RIDING (command-and-control exercise) 361
Westwood, Bradford-on-Avon, Wiltshire 208
Wethersfield demonstration 118
White House Army Signal Agency 191
White Papers
  1957 (Defence) 368
  2006 (Countering International Terrorism) 368, 370, 372–3
White, Sir Dick 44
Whitelaw, William (Lord) 318

Williams, Francis (Lord) 51–2
Wilmot, John 51
Wilson of Dinton, Lord 368
Wilson, Harold (Lord Wilson of Rievaulx) 26
nuclear policy 72–8
  and Oleg Lyalin 121
  PN committee 157, 273
  and home defence 181
  and nuclear retaliation 192
  and the nuclear deputies' 90–93, 296, 312, 319
  and the PYTHON plans 302
  handling of aircraft hijacking 361
Wilson, Sir Richard xvi
Winnifrith, John 96–7
WINTEX exercises 319, 371
Withers, Martin 342
WMD capacity 387
Wodehouse, P. G. 113
Woolven, Robin 331, 336–7, 339–40
Working Party on the Machinery of Government in War 176
World War II
  body count tally 163
  allied bombing 170
  the blitzes 173, 185
World War III
  American/Soviet views on 36, 39
  destruction of Communist Party in UK 82
  internment plans 106–7
  dialogue between President/British PM 156
  plans for a War Cabinet for 160–61
  communications in transition to war 161

World War III (*cont.*)
  regional governments 176, 203
  1960's British military
    perspective 204–5
  UK 1960's military perspective
    on 204–5
  timetables 220
  'that-never-was' (autumn 1968)
    221
  transition to 222
  planning dispersal of
    government 268
  Cuban Missile crisis 274
  and BURLINGTON 277
  and TURNSTILE 309
  and MANUSCRIPT 321
  V Bomber flight paths 336
    the ministerial bunker 405
Wormwood Scrubs prison 117
Wright, Sir Oliver 289
Wright, Peter 43
Wright, Tony 397
Wyndham, John 73

Yellow Sun Mark H-bombs 271,
    341
Young Communist League (YCL)
    87, 89, 91, 94, 128
Young, David 218–19, 256, 405–7
Young, George Kennedy 43
Yugoslav communists 105–6

Zorza, Victor 221–2
Zuckerman, Sir Solly 183